3078
AF Manual 5

survival

TRAINING EDITION

DEPARTMENT OF THE AIR FORCE

19990810 146

FOREWORD

This Manual is designed for use of students in the Air Force survival training courses. It amplifies AFM 64-5, Survival, by including training information not covered in the kit edition because of weight and size of limitations. AFM 64-3 can also be used as a source book of survival information. It includes much detailed information which would have been beyond the intended scope of the smaller publication; it tells the reader not only *what* he must do but also *why* he must do it.

Because of the global responsibilities of the United States Air Force, all Air Force personnel face the possibility of survival in a remote or desolate area of the world. It is the purpose of this Manual to prepare all personnel participating in flights on military aircraft for an intelligent approach to any possible survival situation. The reader is shown that nature and the elements are neither friendly nor hostile and that the training and attitude he carries with him will determine his success in survival.

The Manual opens with a discussion of the problems and techniques of general land survival: psychological problems, immediate action, camping and woodcraft, travel, clothing, signaling, food, and other related subjects. Then the ensuing chapters cover the special requirements for survival in the following areas: Arctic, desert, Tropics, sea, and sea ice.

Recommendations or suggestions for the improvement of this Manual are encouraged. Comments or recommendations should be forwarded through channels to the Director of Personnel Procurement and Training, Headquarters USAF, Washington 25, D. C.

By order of the Secretary of the Air Force:

N. F. Twining
Chief of Staff, United States Air Force

OFFICIAL:

E. E. Toro
Colonel, USAF
Air Adjutant General

DISTRIBUTION:

Zone of Interior and Overseas	
Headquarters USAF	150
Major air commands, except	5
Air Training Command	3,925
Continental Air Command	4,200
Air University	1,490
Subordinate air commands	5
Air divisions	3
Wings	1
2200th Test Squadron, Headquarters Continental Air Command	5

°Special

°Commanders may requisition additional copies as needed in survival courses of instruction through normal supply channels in accordance with AFR 67-1.

This Air Force Manual contains copyright material

contents

The discussion of coconuts on pp. 262-263 and the material concerning the preparation and use of breadfruit and pandanus on pp. 296-299 are reprinted from Bishop Museum Bulletin No. 200, The Material Culture of Kapingamarangi, Bernice P. Bishop Museum, Honolulu.

. . . .

All photographs on the following pages are reprinted from Vegetationsbilder, by permission of the Attorney General of the United States:
Pages 53, 55-82, 85-88, 90-92, 162-166, 205-207, 255-260, 315, and 317-320.

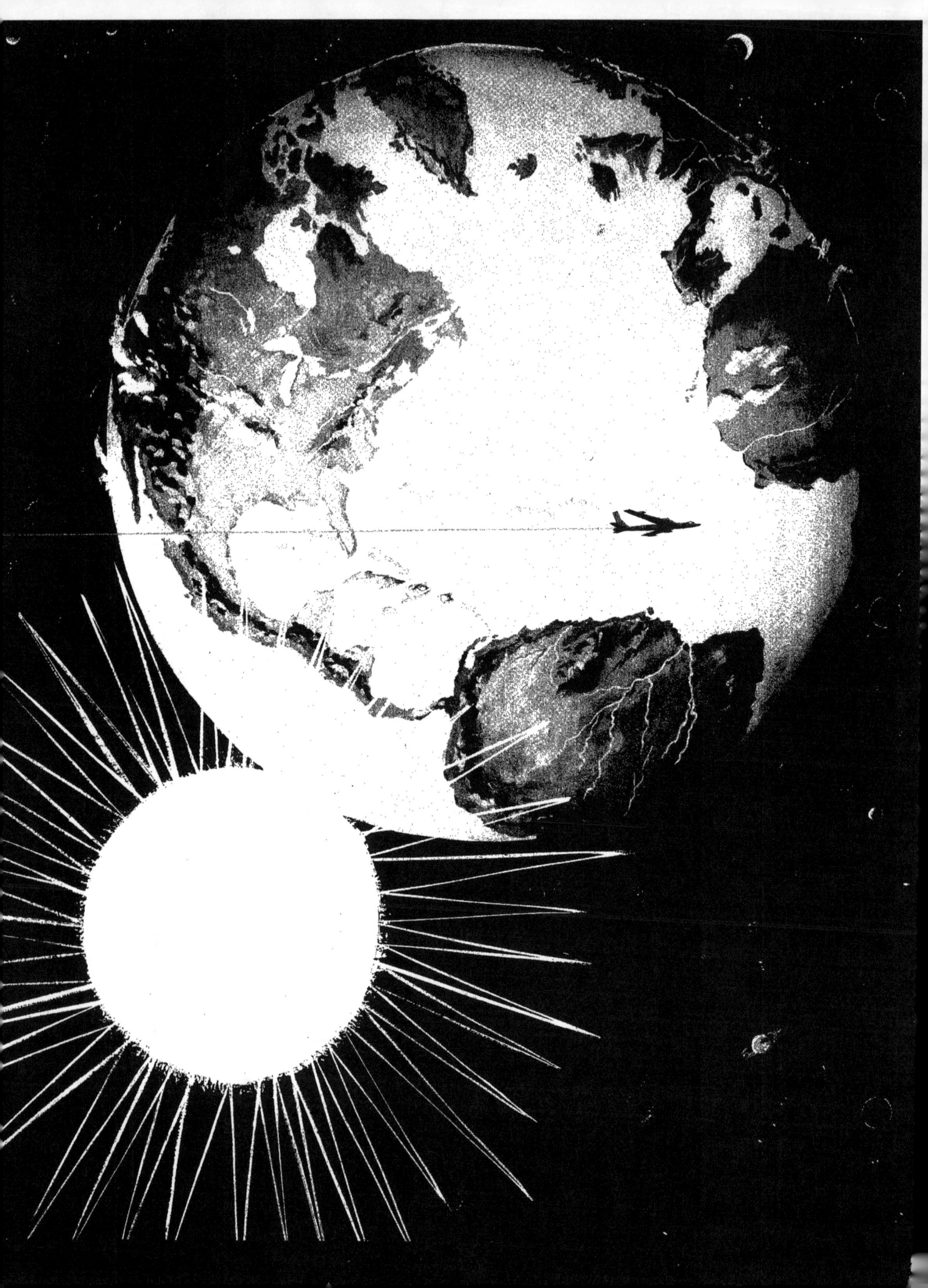

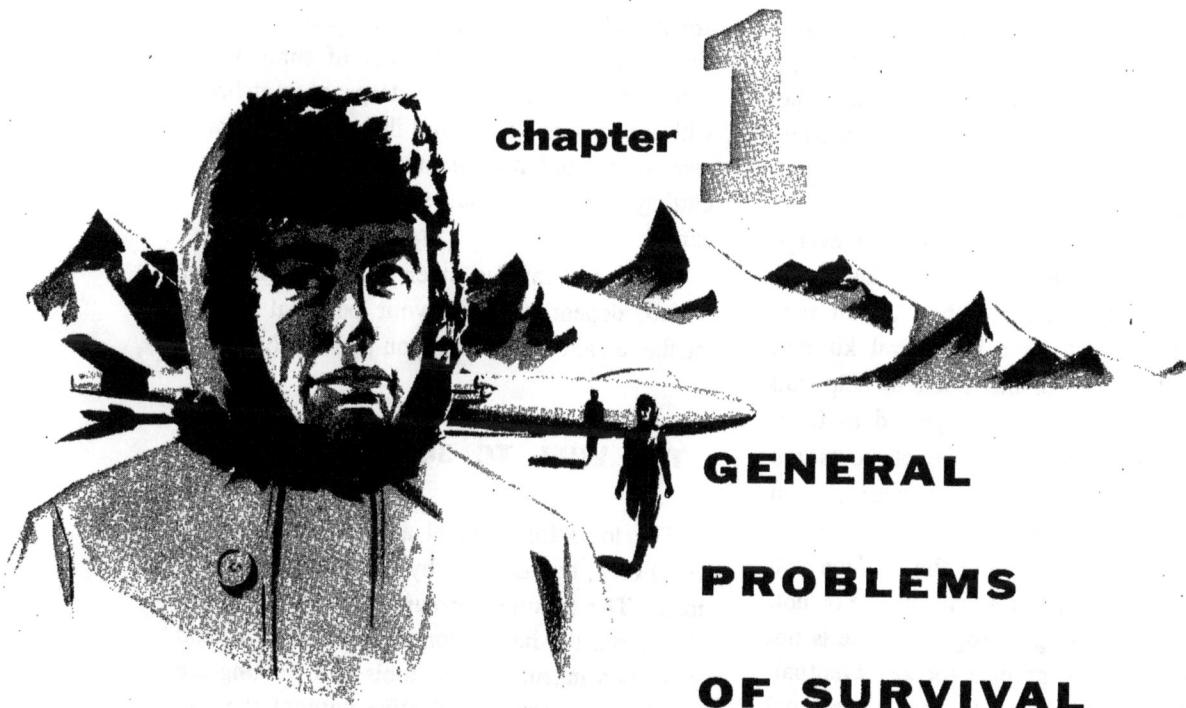

1

GENERAL

PROBLEMS

OF SURVIVAL

Survival training is like insurance; you never need it "until you need it." How convenient it would be if you could just skip your life insurance premiums until, say, the month before you die. However, that's not the way it works out.

Besides, comparing survival training with life insurance is misleading. Life insurance doesn't guarantee that you have a good chance of living longer; survival training does. Survival training is a *real* form of "life insurance," and the odds are that you'll be around to collect on the policy.

You won't require statistics to show that all Air Force personnel need such insurance these days. The air age has taken care of that for you. Aircraft of many nations can pick their own battlefields and targets. Obscure areas of the globe have suddenly assumed military and political significance. The waging of global war and the equally difficult task of maintaining global peace have wrapped the world in a net of crisscrossing aircraft vapor trails.

Because of this situation, the United States

Air Force is operating a "global airline." Sometimes the cargo is destruction, sometimes it is men, and sometimes it is supplies. Destinations of its aircraft are equally broad: across the Arctic to the North Pole; above the Sahara Desert to the Near East; over the Pacific Ocean to the Far East. It doesn't take much imagination to realize the vastness of these operations and the variety of terrains which they cover. Give your imagination a little more play and you can begin to realize what could happen to the crew of an aircraft forced to crash, land, or bail out under such unfamiliar conditions. If your imagination is further stimulated, you're probably into the next chapter of this book already, and more power to you.

Practically everyone in the Air Force is fair game to such an emergency. No matter what your assignment, whether it be administrative clerk, supply officer, radio operator, or pilot, the odds are that you will be a crew member or a passenger on a military aircraft at least once during your hitch, and probably many times. And anyone who flies should learn to expect the unexpected at any time.

But to expect is not enough; you must anticipate and prepare for the unexpected. That is the purpose of this book: to anticipate the general and some of the specific problems which you will encounter, and to prepare you to solve them.

You won't be expected to remember everything you read, or everything the instructor might tell you. Chances are that, if you prepare properly, you'll have a survival kit and a condensed version of this book to help you out. You will, however, be expected to learn one thing: that nature and the elements are neither your special friend nor your special enemy; that they are actually disinterested; and that it is up to you, and the attitude you carry with you, whether you will survive or not.

And finally, carrying a proper attitude is not enough — it pays to prepare for any eventuality by carrying on your person a personal survival kit. The standard issue kits may be packed in an unavailable liferaft or left on the aircraft during a sudden bailout. A special kit, secured in some fashion to your flight clothing, can be assembled and should include some of the essential items for survival.

A few of the items that may be included are small fishhooks, first aid equipment, 6 or 8 eightpenny nails, 8 or 10 feet of snare wire, a pair of pliers, and a waterproof matchbox with a compass on top and flint on the bottom. Use waterproof matches to fill the matchbox, cutting the sticks in half so that twice as many can be carried.

There are various other items that may be added, depending upon your personal desires or the terrain over which you plan to fly.

THE WILL TO SURVIVE

The tools for survival are furnished by the Air Force, by you, and by the natural environment. The training for survival will stem from this book, the instruction you will receive, and your own ingenuity. But tools and training are not enough; none is effective without the will to survive.

In fact, the records prove that will alone has often been the only factor in many survival case histories. While these histories are not held up as classroom examples of "how to survive," they do show that stubborn, strong will-power can conquer many obstacles.

One man, stranded without food or water on a vast stretch of Arizona desert for 8 days, traveled 150 miles in daytime temperatures as high as 120°. The lack of water caused him to lose 25% of his weight (a 10% loss is often fatal) through dehydration. He had crawled the last 8 miles completely naked, and the doctors found his blood to be so thick that the lacerations he suffered did not bleed until he had gotten considerable water into his system. He had done nothing right, had no survival training. But he *wanted* to survive and he *did* survive, through nothing but willpower and the grace of God.

You will encounter other stories of equally harrowing experiences both in this book and in your formal instruction. Don't accept them as advice. They merely show what can be done with no experience, thought, or training. Add-

ing your training and equipment to this will to survive, you will find that you can do the same thing a lot more cheaply and pleasantly should the need arise.

WHAT IT TAKES TO SURVIVE

When you find yourself in a survival situation, there are several facts which you should remember. One fact is this: the obstacles you have to overcome aren't so much natural ones as they are mental ones. Wherever you may be, remember that other people have gone there intentionally, and that some people have chosen to live there. With varying degrees of effort, these people have adjusted to the demands of terrain, climate, and environment. Your problem is a bit different, however, because you didn't expect to be there. Chances are that you'll never really expect to have a crash landing over the jungle or bail out into the ocean, for no matter how well prepared you are, you will probably never completely convince yourself that "it can happen to you."

But it can, as the records show, so before you start collecting survival facts and information, you should understand what these psychological obstacles are which you must overcome. These obstacles all fall under the general heading of that very normal and common emotion called *fear*. Fear of the unknown — fear of discomfort — fear of people — fear of your own weaknesses. You fear the terrain and the climate because they are new and strange. Because this environment is different, you fear the discomforts which might result and you may fear the people who are there. And in many cases, even though these other fears are overcome to some extent, a lack of confidence in their own fortitude and ability has broken people who could otherwise have fared much better.

Though all this is natural, it is not necessary. There are ways of alleviating the needless extra burden that these implanted fears will add.

Your *fear of the unknown* will be alleviated

by proper training and briefing. You'll learn something of the geography, topography, and climate of the areas you will cross. You'll be taught methods of getting food and water, and you'll be shown the ways to travel through the terrain.

Much of this previous information will eliminate most of your *fear of discomfort*. You'll also learn how to find natural shelter and how to give medical aid, even to yourself. Most important, you will learn that rest can be more valuable than speed. Whether you are struggling through jungle undergrowth, fighting the battle of a dwindling water supply in the desert, or making your way across Arctic ice, you will be more successful and comfortable if you make your way with careful planning instead of a blind and exhausting dash. Also, adding to your comfort will be the knowledge that the Air Force has not forgotten you and is concerned with your recovery.

Fear of the natives, like fear of the terrain, can be relieved by previous knowledge and some common sense. Unless they have been allied with the enemy, you will have little to fear and everything to gain from thoughtful contact with the natives of whatever friendly or neutral country in which you may find yourself. (Enemy territory, of course, presents a different problem.) By knowing their customs in advance, and using common decency, you'll have little trouble from natives, and possibly get a lot of assistance. (One survivor in the South Pacific during World War II taught the natives how to make better hunting bows and quickly won his way to their hearts and to safety.)

3

Fear of your own weaknesses is more difficult to overcome. If you are fortunate enough to have had considerable outdoor experience, or previous experience in environment similar to that in which you find yourself, you should have confidence in your ability to live off the land. If not, take advantage of any opportunity to go through an Air Force survival school, in which you will have a chance to test your skill and training before it really counts. Even without all this experience, the training you'll receive will be enough to give you some confidence. A few hours spent in applying what you've learned, and finding that it works and that you can accomplish things which previously seemed impossible, will remove any doubt about your personal ability and stamina.

ORGANIZATION OF THIS MANUAL

The next chapter will present the problems of survival which may confront survivors in any land area. The three subsequent chapters will expand on this information and give some detailed procedures and survival techniques for specific land areas of the globe, including Arctic, desert, and tropic regions.

Then the important problem of survival on floating sea ice is covered, followed by a detailed discussion of sea survival.

NOTE: If this manual is not to be covered in its entirety, the introductory chapter, and chapter 2, if applicable, should be read first.

chapter **2**

PROBLEMS

OF GENERAL

LAND SURVIVAL

The conditions which you find in a survival situation will often depend upon the factors which preceded it. Not all survival emergencies result from a crash landing. An unexpected crackup, a forced landing on a natural airstrip, a bailout, or even isolation from a ground party can result in your being faced with the problem of survival.

An unexpected crash usually indicates the demolition of the aircraft and severe injury or death to many of the crew and passengers. A crash landing or a ditching near shore suggests a hazardous but anticipated landing in which the aircraft is damaged but the crew is fairly intact. A forced landing due to engine trouble or fuel shortage would indicate that the aircraft and its crew were intact but that the aircraft was at least temporarily inoperative. Or, persons or a party involved in a ground operation, such as the installation or operation of a radio or weather station, might easily become separated from the rest of the group and find themselves suddenly faced with a definite survival problem. Bailout from a disabled air-

craft can also present such a problem.

Thus, previous events have a definite influence on your ability to cope with the problems of survival. An unexpected crash in which the aircraft is demolished and there are several dead and injured leaves little for the survivors to do but give first aid and make the best of what they have. After a forced or crash landing, shelter, supplies, radio equipment (in some cases), and a number of able-bodied survivors are often available. A bailout or sudden isolation would put a man on his own to a greater degree.

However, unless the contrary is specified, survival procedures outlined in this manual will assume a certain survival situation. They will assume that the aircraft is disabled but that most of the crew is in condition to travel or to forage for food, shelter, and fuel while waiting to be rescued, and that there is a survival kit available. Other situations, such as those involving severe injuries or little equipment, will require modifications in procedures, and these will be specially cited.

5

This chapter presents the general problems of land survival which will usually confront personnel to some degree in either tropical, Arctic, or desert regions. While temperate regions have not been covered as an individual subject in this manual, the hints on woodsmanship and land travel given in this chapter (and in parts of other chapters) will be directly applicable to conditions in such regions as Europe, the United States, or sections of Asia.

In starting any survival effort, remember that the intelligent discipline and organization with which the individual or group approaches the problems will determine the success of any survival procedures. The establishment of an unhurried routine will bring about the calm and confidence without which considered decisions are impossible. In a survival situation, every decision is important.

All information in this manual will be presented as if directed to the person in charge of a survivor party. Not everyone who reads this manual may have such a responsibility, but the training and ability to accept such a responsibility is invaluable to any survivor.

IMMEDIATE ACTION

Notify *any* communications facility at the first sign of inflight difficulty. Experience has proved that aircraft emergencies are usually preceded by a series of events. *Don't wait* — let the people on the ground know your situation and intentions. Give your position and time, true course, altitude, and ground speed. If the operational efficiency of your aircraft has been impaired, a rescue aircraft will be dispatched to intercept you and escort you to safety. If you are forced to ditch, crashland, or bail out before help arrives, your chances of rescue are almost assured.

Assuming that you are down, and that you are able to survey the situation and evaluate your problem, there are certain initial procedures that should be followed.

Determine whether or not you are in hostile territory.

If you have bailed out, make your way to the crashed aircraft. Rescuers can spot it easier than they can a person.

If the aircraft has been damaged on landing, stay away from the aircraft until the engines have cooled and any spilled fuel has evaporated.

Then check on the condition of the crew and passengers. If bailouts have occurred, look for isolated members of the party. Necessary medical aid should be given, either based on material in the next section of this chapter or on previous Air Force training. Make the injured men comfortable, and be careful in removing casualties from the aircraft, particularly men with injured backs and fractures.

If the weather is severe, throw up a temporary shelter, using parts of the aircraft and parachute canopy. If you need a fire, start one at once. Hot drinks, if available, will be stimulating.

If the emergency radio is operative, use it as soon as possible. If it is not operative, gather all available signaling equipment and use it as outlined in the section on signaling. Sweep the horizon with the signal mirror at frequent intervals. If you use the emergency radio or the aircraft communications system, be careful to conserve your electrical power. Use this equipment according to procedures given in your briefing.

After these basic essentials have been covered, relax and rest until you are over the shock of the crash and the excitement of the unexpected landing. It is most important to regain your equilibrium and to settle your nerves. Leave extensive preparations and planning until later.

After you have rested, organize the crew and your temporary camp. Organization and planning are as important in themselves as they are in the actions that result from them. Case histories of many previous unsuccessful survival situations show that the main pitfall of attempts at survival have been the blind and almost hysterical actions of the men. Intelligent and considered planning is absorbing and gives the mind a discipline and orderliness which are so vital in emergencies such as this.

The first step in the organization of the party will be to appoint individual members to specific jobs, based on previous knowledge of their abilities and their physical and mental capacities to handle them. Pool all food and equipment in charge of one man. Prepare a shelter in a manner indicated later in this chapter, to protect yourself from rain, sun, snow, wind, cold, or insects. Collect all possible fuel, the variety of which will be determined by your geographical location. Try always to have at least a day's supply of fuel on hand. Then look for water and for animal and plant food as prescribed in various specific discussions throughout this manual.

As another start toward organization and self-discipline, begin a log book, making brief but accurate entries including:

Date and cause of crash.
Probable location.
Roster and condition of personnel.
Inventory of supplies.
Weather conditions.
Other pertinent data.

In fact and fiction, countless survival stories have included references to patiently kept log books. The log book is valuable both in that it gives the survivors a record of their activities and the passage of time, and in that it furnishes military authorities with valuable information for future survival training planning.

Determine your position by the best means available (see section on direction and position finding), and include this position in any radio messages you may transmit. If position is based on celestial observations, transmit the observation also.

Stay with Your Aircraft, If Practicable

Your chances of being located and rescued are greatly increased if you can stay with your aircraft and await rescue. Aircraft wreckage is much easier for your rescuers to sight, and it provides many items for your survival and comfort. Have patience; rescue is on the way. Even if you are unable to notify a communications facility of your trouble, skilled rescue personnel will go into immediate action at any time you fail to make a scheduled position report or fail to arrive at your destination.

If You Must Travel

Travel from the crash site should be undertaken only under the following conditions.

If you are sure of your position, know the location of aid, and are physically capable of navigating and surviving until that location is reached, travel may be undertaken.

If you depart the crash site, leave a message giving data and hour of departure and direction of travel. Mark trail at periodic intervals.

If you are in thick forest and jungle areas where an aircraft wreckage may be very difficult to see, proceed to a body of water or open clearing, where your chances of being sighted will be greatly improved.

Emergency Signaling

Familiarize yourself with emergency signaling methods and improvise as many signaling devices as possible. Be prepared to signal at the first sound or sight of a friendly aircraft. In addition to the signaling methods contained in the Air Force Survival Manual, 64-5, the following techniques are recommended:

If down in a controlled forest area, start a green brush fire to attract forestry personnel in observation towers. Keep fire under control to prevent spreading.

Make all signal fires downwind from campsite and ground signaling devices to prevent obliterating view from the air.

If sufficient fuel is not available for continuous burning of signal fires, keep fuel dry and ready for instant use. Be sure a combustible material is used to start oil fires.

Immediately upon hearing or sighting a friendly aircraft, transmit a tone signal with your emergency transceiver for automatic homing.

Rescue by Helicopter

If in rough terrain, and landing by helicopters is not possible, proceed to a relatively level surface where the helicopter can hover and pick you up by hoist and sling. Get into the sling in the same way you would put on a coat. Be sure to face the drop cable. If you are injured and unable to get into or stay in sling, a medical technician will be lowered to assist you.

If in a liferaft, use sea anchor and paddles to prevent the liferaft from drifting away because of rotor blade downdraft. Stay in the raft.

Rescue in Hostile Area

If on land, take cover in the immediate vicinity, use escape and evasion methods, and be prepared to signal friendly forces. Do not signal until you have identified the forces as friendly. Advise rescue aircraft and supporting fighter cover of any enemy troop positions which may jeopardize a rescue pickup.

Upon instruction of the rescue aircraft, proceed to an area where a better pickup may be made because of more favorable terrain or absence of enemy troops, to a water area for rescue amphibians, and to relatively level terrain for helicopters. Use smoke signals or some other visible means to indicate wind direction.

If rescue is delayed for any reason and the rescue aircraft has to depart, follow the instructions of the rescue aircraft. Normally, you will be instructed to remain in the immediate vicinity and be prepared to signal upon the rescue aircraft's return.

The preceding instructions are, of course, based on an assumed situation, and are subject to modifications brought about by other circumstances. Specific procedures for following these instructions will be covered throughout the manual as they apply in specific geographical areas.

FIRST AID

Illness and injury are always potential survival companions. Situations may arise where *treatment* is mandatory. But, remember that unless administered by a specially trained person, medical treatment other than the simplest first aid may be dangerous. If you don't know the procedure for treatment or if you have reason to expect medical assistance soon, it is better to merely make the person as comfortable as possible than to injure him more severely by improper treatment. However, the information given in this section will cover most of the injuries that you will encounter in an aircraft accident.

The most likely injuries will be cuts and bruises, fractures, concussions, internal injuries, and burns. Keep the injured men lying down, and if they are unconscious or have head injuries, keep them face down. Handle injured men very carefully, especially if they seem to be suffering from a fracture or a back injury. If the men are suffering from head injuries, difficult breathing, flushed face, or bleeding from ears, nose or throat, keep their heads slightly elevated. Give as much treatment for shock as possible under the circumstances if such a condition is noticed.

● ● ●

The following procedures should be followed carefully.

Bleeding

Serious bleeding must be controlled as soon as possible. The following methods, in the order of presentation, are recommended.

Place sterile pad directly on wound and apply pressure by hand or by bandaging *firmly*. Do not be impatient. Stick to this method, if possible.

Finger pressure on the pressure points shown in illustrations will control arterial bleeding. Arterial bleeding may be recognized by noting any bright red blood spurting freely from a wound.

BLEEDING IN SCALP ABOVE THE EAR. Light pressure in front of the middle ear.

BLEEDING ON OUTSIDE OR INSIDE OF HEAD. Moderate pressure on neck about 3" below ear and 3" above collarbone — push artery against spine.

BLEEDING IN THE CHEEK. Very light pressure in notch on under edge of jaw ⅔ back from tip of chin.

BLEEDING IN THE LOWER ARM. Strong pressure on inside of arm halfway between shoulder and elbow.

BLEEDING IN THE ARM. Firm pressure behind the middle of collarbone — push artery against first rib.

BLEEDING ABOVE THE KNEE. Strong pressure in groin with heel of hand — push artery against pelvic bone.

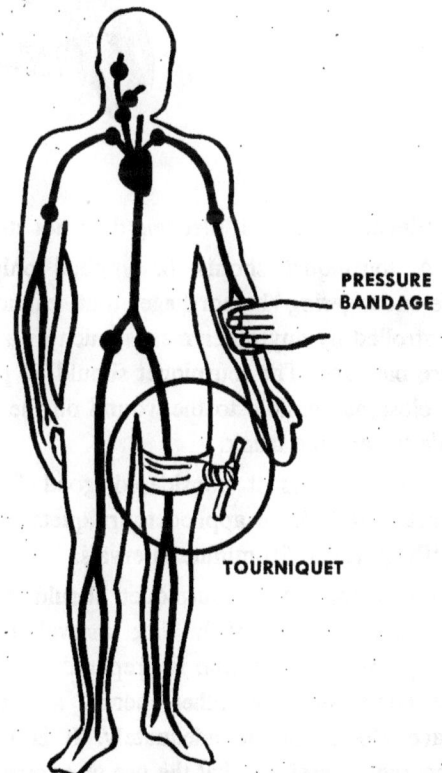

PRESSURE BANDAGE

TOURNIQUET

BLEEDING BELOW THE KNEE AND ELBOW. Use tourniquet between crotch and knee.

Armlift-shoulder blade pressure method of artificial respiration

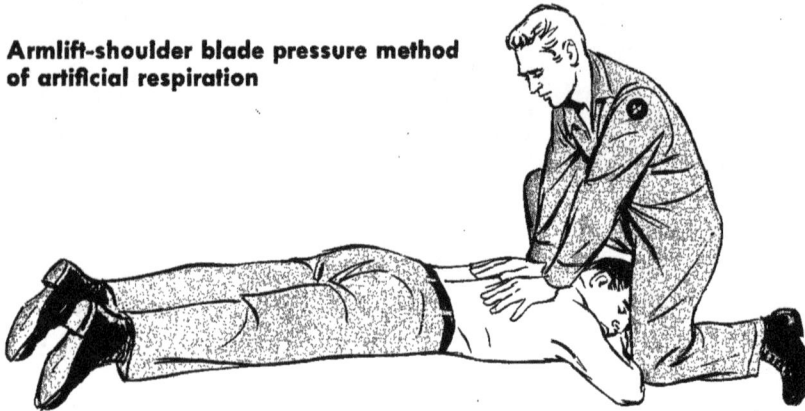

1. Place the patient face down with head resting on hands.
2. Open his mouth, remove foreign articles, including false teeth, and be sure that tongue is forward.
3. Kneel at patient's head and grasp elbows, drawing them up and forward.
4. Release elbows and push down on both shoulder blades.
5. Repeat above in rhythm 12 times per minute.

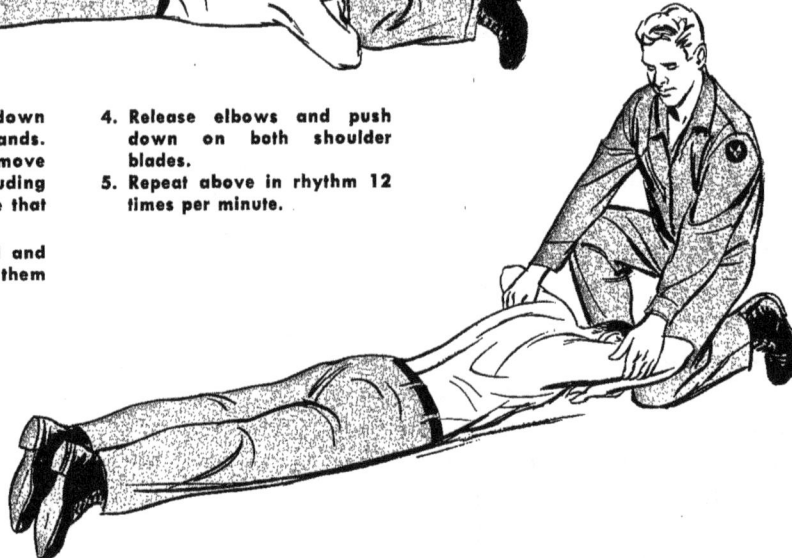

Elevate the limb if bleeding does not stop.

A tourniquet should be applied only for life-endangering hemorrhage that cannot be controlled by any other means, such as a pressure bandage. The tourniquet should be placed as close as possible to the wound on the other side toward the trunk.

No longer is it considered good first-aid practice to release applied tourniquets periodically at 15- to 30-minute intervals.

Once applied, a tourniquet should not be released regardless of the time interval elapsed, except by someone who is prepared to control the hemorrhage by other means, and to replace blood volume adequately. It is readily apparent, therefore, that the use of a tourniquet is indicated only in extremely serious cases, such as complete severance of a limb. Try whenever humanly possible to rely on the use of pressure to control bleeding.

Cessation of Breathing

If breathing has stopped, apply artificial respiration at once. Be sure that the patient's tongue is pulled forward.

SHOULDER-BLADE (BACK) PRESSURE ARM-LIFT METHOD OF ARTIFICIAL RESPIRATION.

1. Place the patient face down with his head resting on hands.

2. Open his mouth, remove foreign articles, including false teeth, and make sure that tongue is forward.

3. Kneel at patient's head. Place index fingers on lower ribs. Rock forward until your arms are vertical.

4. Roll off to the outside with a snap and grasp patient's elbows. Rock back on heels, release elbows smartly.

5. Repeat above rhythmically 12 times each minute.

Keep up artificial respiration at a normal rate until breathing is restored or patient is unquestionably dead (listen for heart beat with ear against his bare chest). Keep him quiet when breathing starts. If you have oxygen, give it in alternate 5-minute periods after breathing starts. Do not give the oxygen with the tank valve wide open.

Head Injuries

Look for head injuries or fractured skull (indicated by unequal pupils of the eye, bleeding from ears or into skin around eyes). Keep patient warm and dry, and handle gently. *Don't give morphine to men with head injuries.*

Chest Wounds

If an injured person has an open chest wound, through which air can be heard sucking, cover the wound with a large dressing. Air entering the wound will collapse the lungs; consequently, the pad should be firmly applied at the moment of maximum exhalation, just before more air is sucked in. It should be firm enough to make a seal but not tight enough to stop chest movement entirely.

Shock

All personnel will suffer some shock after an emergency landing. Men in shock may have pale, cold skin; they may sweat, breathe rapidly, and have a weak pulse; they may be confused or unconscious.

Lay the patient down flat on his back. Raise the feet, unless contraindicated (head injuries, breathing difficulties, flushed face, or bleeding from ears, nose, or mouth).

Keep him warm but not overheated. If he is conscious and not injured internally, give him warm drinks; do not give alcohol.

If oxygen is available give it to the patient.

If the patient is in severe pain from injury, give a morphine injection (syrette) according to directions on the container. (Always give the injection above the tourniquet, or on the uninjured extremity.)

Be reassuring and cheerful with men in shock.

Eye Injuries

Clean the wound and the eye by washing with sterile water. Use atrophine ointment or antibiotic ointment such as penicillin, terramycin, etc., when available. Cover the eye with sterile dressing. Give aspirin for pain.

To remove a foreign body in the eye, first irrigate with sterile water. If not successful, then wind sterile cotton on a match stick to make an applicator. Moisten with sterile water and attempt to dislodge the foreign body by several gentle swipes over the affected area. If this is unsuccessful, make no further attempt to remove it but use atrophine ointment and antibiotics.

Urine is a primitive but effective source of sterile washing solution for eye injuries.

Fractures

Handle injured men with care to avoid causing them more injury. Splint them where they lie.

Don't attempt to remove clothing from a fractured limb in the normal manner. If a wound exists, cut or tear away clothing and treat before splinting. Clothing tears best at the seams.

Improvise splints from pieces of equipment or from a tight roll of clothing; pad with soft materials. The splint should be long enough to support the joints above and below the fracture.

Give a morphine injection (syrette) for severe pain (except for head injuries.)

Keep the patient lying quiet; don't move him.

Sprains

Bandage and keep sprained part at rest. Cold localized applications may prevent swelling. When swelling has decreased (in 6 to 8 hours) localized application of heat will ease pain. Elevate the injured extremity.

If it is necessary to use the sprained limb, immobilize the injured area as much as possible with a splint or heavy wrapping. If only sprained, a limb can be used to the limit that pain will permit.

Preventing Infection

In administering to a wounded person, cut or tear away clothing necessary to get at a wound. Don't touch a wound with fingers or dirty objects. Don't suck any wounds other than snake bites. (See section on snake bite.)

Apply sterile dressing to wound with a firm pressure. Tie firmly but not too tightly.

Keep wounded part at rest.

Iodine may be used to sterilize skin areas surrounding a wound but should not be poured directly into an open wound. Let iodine dry in air before applying bandage.

Burns

Don't touch a burned part with fingers. Cover freely with *burn ointment*. Apply thick gauze pack; bandage firmly. Don't change bandage. If pain is severe, give a morphine injection. *Give large amounts of fluid.* Keep the burned part at rest. Splints may sometimes be used to good advantage. If necessary to open blisters, use sterilized needle to pierce through the skin at the base of blister. Apply a sterile bandage after draining.

Illness

The prevention of illness is a factor in survival which deserves constant attention. Personnel incapacitated by illness are just as much casualties as severely injured ones. Food must be cooked, water boiled, and waste properly disposed to maintain good health.

For colds, fevers, and intestinal disorders, rest and hot liquids are the best treatments you will probably have available. APC's and aspirin will aid in the control of fever and the relief of pain.

Improvised Medical Equipment

Bandages and dressings can be made fairly sterile by boiling or steaming (preferably) them in a covered container. Freezing or charring with heat is also advantageous.

A good substitute for burn ointment can be made by keeping pressure dressing moist with boiled water to which salt has been added (if available).

If regular medical supplies are not available, use your ingenuity and improvise substitutes. Try to keep all equipment as sterile as possible. Extreme heat is your best method of doing this.

SIGNALING

The aircraft commander or other leader should appoint some member of the party to gather natural and supplied signal materials and prepare them for immediate use.

The length of time before you are rescued will depend to a considerable extent on the effectiveness of your signals and the speed with which you can have them ready for use. Select the location of each signal carefully, and don't set off a holiday fireworks display when you are first spotted. You may need more signals to guide further rescue parties or aircraft. Take care of your signaling equipment.

One man, a group of men, or even an aircraft, is not too easy to spot from the air, especially when visibility is limited. Your emergency signaling equipment is designed to make you "bigger" and easier to find.

Radio

Your aircraft radio or emergency radio is your best rescue aid. Try to make contact at once. Try to get a fix; if the radio is serviceable, you can transmit your position. When using the aircraft radio, save the battery; try to get an engine or auxiliary generator operating and charge the battery with it. If you have a battery-operated transceiver, conserve the power supply as much as possible, and keep the battery warm.

If you are using the Gibson girl type of emergency transmitter, the effective range of your signal will be determined by your physical environment. At sea you may send a signal 500 miles; on a lake or river it will reach only 50-150 miles. On the edge of a body of water the distance will decrease to 30-50 miles, and on land, with the set grounded in moist earth, your range will probably be only 5 or 10 miles.

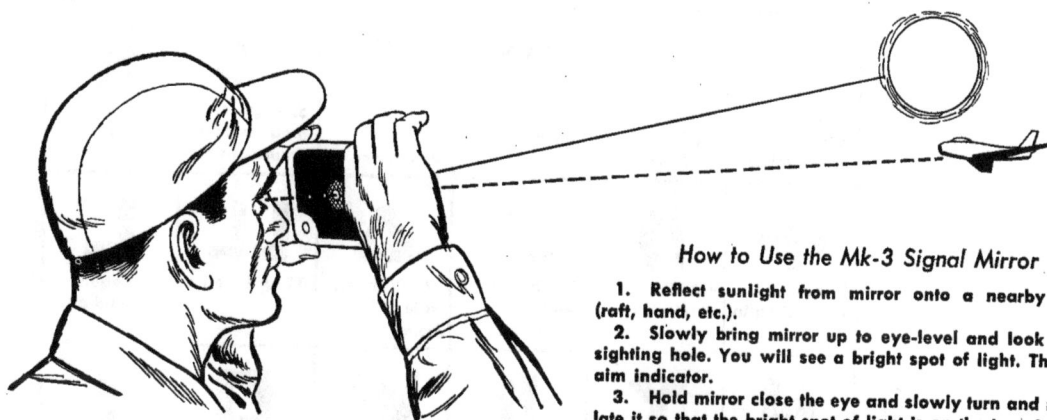

How to Use the Mk-3 Signal Mirror

1. Reflect sunlight from mirror onto a nearby surface (raft, hand, etc.).
2. Slowly bring mirror up to eye-level and look through sighting hole. You will see a bright spot of light. This is the aim indicator.
3. Hold mirror close the eye and slowly turn and manipulate it so that the bright spot of light is on the target.
4. Even though no aircraft or ships are in sight, continue sweeping the horizon, for mirror flashes may be seen for many miles, even in hazy weather.

You may have a URC-4 or URC-11 emergency transceiver in your aircraft or kit. This is housed in a vest, and is a UHF-VHF transmitter-receiver with an approximate line-of-sight signal range of 20 miles. With this set you can transmit either voice or cw signals. The receiver is usually adjusted to operate on the same frequency as the transmitter, which is preset to standard distress frequencies of 121.5 megacycles and 243 megacycles.

In all cases, do not raise or fly an antenna during electrical storms.

Smoke Flares

When signaling, use smoke by day, bright flame by night. Add engine oil, rags soaked in oil, or pieces of rubber (matting or electrical insulation) to make black smoke; add green leaves, moss, or a little water to send up billows of white smoke. Keep plenty of spare fuel on hand.

In general, smoke signals are effective only on comparatively clear and calm days. High winds, rain, or snow tend to disperse the smoke and lessen the chance of it being seen. Smoke signals should not be depended on when used in heavily wooded areas, and should, if possible, be used in open terrain.

Try to create a smoke which contrasts with its background. Against snow, dark smoke is most effective; against dark turf, white smoke is best. However, to render a sky-silhouetted column of smoke visible to a *land* rescue party, dark smoke should be used against overcast skies and light smoke against clear skies.

Signaling aids, such as flares and smoke grenades, must be kept dry. Use them only when friendly aircraft are sighted or heard.

Signal Mirror

New signal mirrors have been developed for the various survival kits. Follow the instructions on the back of the mirror in your kit. However, there are certain general instructions which hold true for the use of any signal mirror.

Don't continue to flash the mirror in the direction of the rescue aircraft after the receipt of your signal has been acknowledged, unless it appears that the rescuers have lost your exact position. If possible, try to spot the mirror under a wing on the rear of the aircraft. If spotted on the pilot's compartment, it may blind him.

Practice signaling with the mirror in kit. A mirror can be improvised from a ration tin by punching a hole in the center of the lid. An emergency signal mirror can also be made from the aluminum skin of the aircraft. A bright polish can be obtained by rubbing dirt over the surface until highly buffed and wiping it off with cloth.

Keep the mirror clean. On hazy days, aircraft can see the flash of the mirror before survivors can see the aircraft; so flash the mirror in the direction of the aircraft when you hear it, even when you cannot see it.

Ground-air emergency code

I 1. Require doctor — serious injuries	**II** 2. Require medical supplies.	**X** 3. Unable to proceed.	**F** 4. Require food and water.	**⌄** 5. Require firearms and ammunition.	**K** 6. Indicate direction to proceed.
↑ 7. Am proceeding in this direction.	**I▷** 8. Will attempt to take off.	**⌐** 9. Aircraft badly damaged.	**△** 10. Probably safe to land here.	**LL** 11. All well.	**L** 12. Require fuel and oil.
N 13. No — negative.	**Y** 14. Yes — affirmative.	**⊥** 15. Not understood.	**W** 16. Require engineer.	**□** 17. Require compass and map.	**⋮** 18. Require signal lamp.

Night Signaling

When tested away from other manmade lights, signal flares, Aldis lamps, and aircraft landing lights have been seen up to 85 miles away. At night, signal with a flashlight or the blinker signaling light of the emergency radio. If the aircraft landing lights are intact and you can get an engine going, remove the lights and extend them for signaling. But do not waste the battery — save it for the radio.

Other Signaling Methods

Make a spruce or conifer torch, selecting a tree with the densest possible foliage. Place dry tinder in the lower branches to light it.

Place or wave the yellow-and-blue cloth signal panel in the open where it can be seen. Spread-out parachutes. Make a pattern of orange-colored Mae Wests. Line up cowl panels from engine nacelles upside down on aircraft wings or ground; polish the inside surfaces — as mentioned before, they make good reflectors. Arrange your ground signals in big geometric patterns rather than at random — they will attract more attention that way. If regular panels are not available, use 3- by 12-foot strips from parachute. Rocks, sod, logs, or sticks can also be used.

If you are in a wooded area, spread the parachute canopy over the tree tops, if possible. If not, take the canopy into a stream and tie it to both banks with shroud lines. This leaves the canopy clear from overhead obstacles and in view of search aircraft.

Body signals

Panel Signals

Survivors use liferaft sails to convey signals

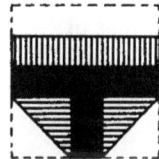

▦ YELLOW

■ BLUE

ON LAND: Need quinine or atabrine. **ON SEA:** Need sun cover.

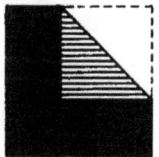

ON LAND: Need gas and oil, plane is flyable.

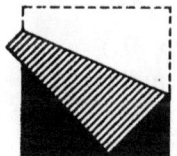

ON LAND AND AT SEA: Plane is flyable, need tools.

ON LAND AND AT SEA: Need first aid supplies.

ON LAND AND AT SEA: O.K. to land, arrow shows landing direction.

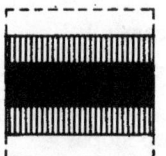

ON LAND: Indicate direction of nearest civilization. **AT SEA:** Indicate direction of rescue craft.

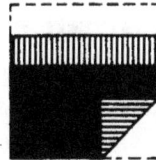

Have abandoned plane. ON LAND: Walking in this direction. **AT SEA:** Drifting.

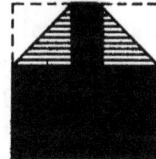

ON LAND: Need warm clothing. **AT SEA:** Need exposure suit or clothing indicated.

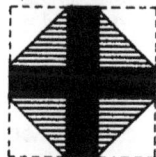

ON LAND AND AT SEA: Need medical attention.

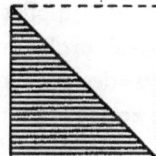

ON LAND AND AT SEA: Need food and water.

AT SEA: Need equipment as indicated. Signals follow.

LAND AND SEA: Do not attempt landing.

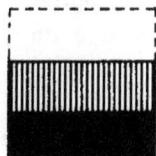

ON LAND: Should we wait for rescue plane? **AT SEA:** Notify rescue agency of my position.

Use the fluorescent dye available in the life raft or Mae West kit for signaling on water or snow. Use it carefully, for a little goes a long way; use it only downwind for the fine dye will penetrate clothing or food. On rivers, throw it out into the current for a quick spread.

Even if the Gibson Girl radio is inoperative, use the kite alone for a signal. Also, the Gibson Girl balloon can be used as a signal.

Do everything you can to disturb the "natural" look of the ground. If you are down in grass and scrub lands, cut giant markers — a circular path, 8-12 feet in width and 60-75 feet in diameter, is easily seen from the air. A trampled or burned grass pattern will show from the air.

If you can climb a tall tree, hoist a large white or colored improvised flag on a pole lashed to the top.

MESSAGE RECEIVED AND UNDERSTOOD
Aircraft will indicate that ground signals have been seen and understood by —

DAY OR MOONLIGHT: Rocking from side to side

NIGHT: Making green flashes with signal lamp

MESSAGE RECEIVED AND NOT UNDERSTOOD
Aircraft will indicate that ground signals have been seen but *not* understood by —

DAY OR MOONLIGHT: Making a complete right hand circle

NIGHT: Making red flashes with signal lamp

Standard aircraft acknowledgments

DECISION TO STAY AT THE AIRCRAFT OR LEAVE

In hostile areas, move out as briefed.

In friendly areas, the best advise is to stay with the aircraft and await rescue. Most rescues have been made when downed crews remained with the aircraft. Leave the aircraft only when:

a. You are *certain* of your position and *know* that you can reach water, shelter, food, and help with available equipment.

b. After waiting several days, you are convinced that rescue is not coming and you are equipped to travel.

Before making a decision, consider these important points:

Advantages of Staying with the Aircraft

The aircraft is easier to spot from the air than men traveling. Someone may have seen you come down and may be along to investigate.

The aircraft or parts from it will provide you with shelter, signaling aids, and other equipment (use cowling for reflector signals, tubing for shelter framework, gasoline and oil for fires, generator for radio power).

You will avoid the hazards and difficulties of travel.

Chances for Rescue

Your chances are good (1) if you have made radio contact; (2) if you have come down on course or near a traveled air route; (3) if weather and air observation conditions are good.

Knowledge of Location

You must know your location to decide intelligently whether to wait for rescue or to determine a destination and route if you undertake to travel out.

Try to locate your position by studying your maps, landmarks, and flight data, or by taking celestial observations.

Choice of Destination

Try to determine the nearest rescue point, the distance to it, the possible difficulties and hazards of travel, and the probable facilities and supplies at the destination.

Condition of Personnel

Consider your physical condition and that of the other men in the party and estimate your ability to endure travel. If there are injured men, try to get help. Send the best fitted men — two if possible. To travel alone is dangerous.

Before you make a decision, consider all the facts.

If you have decided to stay, then consider these problems:

a. Your health and body care; the sanitation of your camp. (See page 24.)

b. Your program for rest and shelter. (See page 16.)

c. Your water supplies. (See page 25.)

d. Your food problems. (See page 27.)

If you have decided to travel, then these are your problems:

a. Which direction? (See page 99.)

b. What plan are you following?

c. What to take along? (See page 117.)

SHELTER

In any area, you can improvise shelter from parts of your aircraft and emergency equipment or from natural materials in the vicinity.

The kind of shelter you make depends on whether you need protection from rain, cold, heat, sunshine, or insects, and also whether your camp is only for a night or for many days. Practical shelters for all conditions are shown in the appropriate chapters.

Pick the location for your camp carefully. Try to be near fuel and water — especially water.

Don't make camp at the base of steep slopes or in areas where you run the risk of avalanches, drifting snow, floods, rockfalls, or battering by winds.

FIRE-MAKING

You will need fire for warmth, for keeping dry, for signaling, for cooking, or for purifying water by boiling. Follow the tried and proved advice below.

Don't build your fire too big. Small fires require less fuel and are easier to control; and their heat can be concentrated. In cold weather small fires arranged in a circle around an individual are much more effective than one large fire.

Fire thong

Use a thong of dry rattan of other long, strong fiber, and rub with a steady but increasing rhythm.

Fire saw

Split bamboo or soft wood makes a good fire saw. Dry sheath of coconut flower is a good base wood.

Preparing Fireplace

Prepare the location of your fire carefully. Clear away leaves, twigs, moss, and dry grass, so that you don't start a grass or forest fire. If the ground is dry, scrape down to bare dirt. If the fire must be built on snow or ice or wet ground, build a platform of logs or flat stones.

To get the most warmth and to protect fire from wind, build it against a rock or wall of logs which will serve as a reflector to direct the heat into your shelter. Cooking fires should be walled in by logs or stones but only to provide a platform for your cooking pot. Beware of wet or porous rocks — they may explode when heated.

Kindling and Fuel

Most fuels cannot be started burning directly from a match. You will need some easily inflammable kindling to get your fire going. Good natural kindling materials are: thin sticks of dry wood, dry bark, (all birch bark and the shredded inner bark of cedar and cottonwood) wood shavings, palm leaves, twigs, ground-lying lichens, dead, upright grass straw, ferns, and down from birds or seed (such as cattails and milk weed). If sticks are used for kindling, split them and cut long thin shavings; leave the shavings attached. Crumpled paper or empty waxed ration boxes are good kindling. Charred cloth is also effective. Store kindling in shelter to keep dry. A little gasoline poured on the fuel *before* it is lighted will help it start burning. Don't pour gasoline on a fire already started, even if it is only smoldering, or in a confined shelter.

For fuel, use dry standing dead wood and dry dead branches. Dead wood is easy to split and break — pound it on a rock. The inside of fallen tree trunks and large branches may be dry even if the outside is wet; use the heart of the wood. Almost anywhere you can find green wood that can be made to burn, especially if finely split. In treeless areas, you can find other natural fuels, such as dry grass which you can twist into bunches; peat dry enough to burn (found at the top of undercut banks), dried animal dung, animal fats, and sometimes even coal, oil shale, or oil sand lying on the surface. If you have no natural fuels, but if you are with the aircraft you can burn gasoline and lubricating oil or a mixture of both (see page 20).

Fire-Making with Matches and Lighter

Prepare fireplace, getting all your materials together before you try to start the fire. Make sure your matches, kindling, and fuel are dry. Have enough fuel on hand to keep fire going. Arrange small amount of kindling in low pyramid, close enough together so flames can lick from one piece to another. Leave a small opening for lighting and air circulation.

Save matches by using a "shave stick," or make a fagot of thin, dry twigs, tied loosely. Shield match from wind, and light fagot or shave stick. Apply this to lower windward side of kindling, shielding it from wind as you do so. If you have a candle, save it for future emergency use.

Small pieces of wood or other fuel can be laid gently on kindling before lighting or can be added after kindling begins to burn. Lay on smaller pieces first, adding larger pieces of fuel as fire takes hold. (Don't smother fire by crushing down kindling with heavy wood). Don't make the fire too big. Don't waste fuel.

Fire-Making with Special Equipment

If you have a fusee signal flare in your kit and all other fire-starting methods fail, light it by striking the self-contained flint and steel. Although it may mean wasting a signal, you can light a fire from the flame.

Some emergency kits contain small fire starters, cans of special fuels, windproof matches, and other aids.

Fire-Making without Matches

First, find or prepare one of the following kinds of tinder: very dry powdered wood, finely shredded dry bark, or the shredded pith of a dead palm frond; lint from unravelled cloth, cotton, twine, rope, or first-aid gauze bandage, fuzzy or wooly material scraped from plants; fine bird feathers or birds' nests; field-mouse nests, or fine wood dust produced by insects, often under bark of dead trees. Tinder must be bone-dry. You can make it burn more easily by adding a few drops of gasoline or by mixing in with powder taken from a cartridge. Once tinder is prepared, put some in a waterproof container for future use.

Once you have the tinder, light it in a place sheltered from the wind. Try the following methods.

Flint and Steel

This is the easiest and most reliable way of making a fire without matches. Use the flint fastened to the bottom of your waterproof match case. If you have no flint, look for a piece of hard rock from which you can strike sparks. If no sparks fly when it is struck with steel, throw it away and find another. Hold your hands close over the dry tinder; strike flat with a knife blade or other small piece of steel, with a sharp, scraping, downward motion so that the sparks fall in the center of the tinder. The addition of a few drops of gasoline before striking the flint will make the tinder flame up — for safety, keep your head to one side. When tinder begins to smolder, fan or blow it gently into a flame. Then transfer blazing tinder to your kindling pile or add kindling gradually to the tinder.

Flint and steel

Burning glass

TINDER AND
WOOD DUST

Bow and drill

Hand holding drill socket is braced against left shin. Wood dust piles on tinder as drill spins.

PLOUGH
BOARD

PLOW

TINDER

Fire plough

Run plough back and forth in groove with a steady but increasing rhythm until smoke in tinder indicates a spark.

Burning Glass

A convex lens can be used in bright sunlight to concentrate the sun's rays on the tinder. A 2-inch lens will start a fire most any time the sun is shining. Smaller lenses will do the job if the sun is high and the air clear.

Friction

There are many methods of making fire by friction (bow and drill, fire plough, fire thong, etc.) but all require practice. If you are acquainted with one of these methods, use it, but remember that flint and steel will give you the same results with less work. These methods are shown in the illustration.

Electric Spark

If you are with the aircraft and have a live storage battery, direct a spark onto the tinder by scratching the ends of wires together to produce an arc.

Burning Aircraft Fuel

If you are with the aircraft, you can improvise a stove to burn fuel, lubricating oil, or a mixture of both. Place 1 or 2 inches of sand or fine gravel in the bottom of a can or other container and add gasoline. Be careful when lighting; the gas may explode at first. Make slots at the top of the can to let flame and smoke out, and punch holes just above the

Striking knife on bottom of waterproof match box

level of the sand to provide a draft. To make a fire burn longer, mix gasoline with oil. If you have no can simply dig a hole in the ground, fill it with sand, pour on gasoline, and light; take care to protect your face and hands. Do not allow the fuel to collect in puddles.

You can burn lubricating oil as fuel by using a wick arrangement. Make the wick of string, rope, rag, sphagnum moss, or even a cigarette, and rest it on the edge of a receptacle filled with oil. You can also soak rags, paper, wood, or other fuel in oil and throw them on your fire.

You can make a stove of any empty waxed ration carton by cutting off one end and punching a hole in each side near the unopened end.

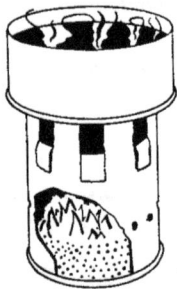

Improvised stove using aviation fuel

Improvised stove using wick to burn oil or animal fat

Stand the carton on the closed end; stuff an empty sack loosely inside the carton, leaving an end hanging over top; light this end — the stove will burn from the top down and will boil more than a pint of water.

Useful Hints

Don't waste your matches by trying to light a poorly prepared fire. Don't use matches for lighting cigarettes; get a light from your fire or use a burning lens. Don't build unnecessary fires; save your fuel. Practice primitive methods of making fires *before* all of your matches are gone.

Carry some dry tinder with you in a waterproof container. Expose it to the sun on dry days. Adding a little powdered charcoal will improve it. Collect good tinder wherever you find it. Cotton cloth is good tinder, especially if scorched or charred. Works well with burning glass or flint and steel.

Collect kindling along trail before you make camp. Keep firewood dry under shelter. Dry damp wood near fire so you can use it later. Save some of your best kindling and fuel for quick fire-making in the morning.

To split logs, whittle hardwood wedges and drive them into cracks in the log with a rock or club; split wood burns more easily. Never swing an ax toward your foot or other parts of your body.

To make a fire last overnight, place large logs over it so that the fire will burn into the heart of the logs. When a good bed of coals has been formed, cover it lightly, first with ashes and then dry earth. In the morning the fire will still be smoldering.

Fire can be carried from one place to another in the form of a lighted punk, smoldering coconut husk, or slow-burning coals. When you want a new fire, add tinder or small fuel and fan or blow the smoldering material into flame.

Don't waste fire making materials. Use only what is necessary to start a fire and to keep it going for the purpose needed. Put out the fire when you leave the camp site with water and mineral soil. Mix it well until you can insert your hand.

SURVIVAL WEAPONS

M6 over-and-under
.410-.22

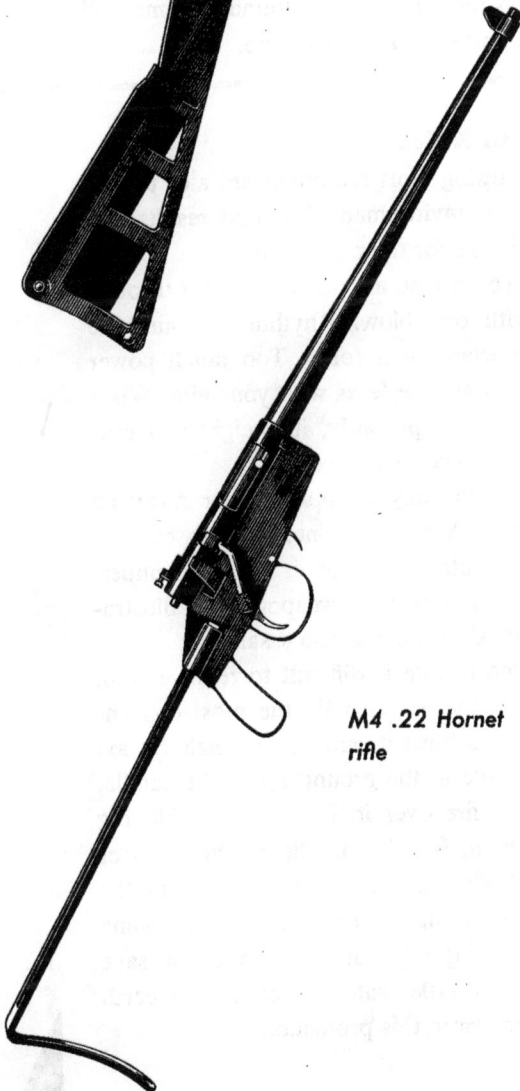

M4 .22 Hornet
rifle

Several weapons are included in various Air Force survival kits: the M4 caliber .22 Hornet rifle, the M6 over-and-under .410-.22 weapon, and the standard-issue, caliber .30 carbine.

The M4 Hornet is a caliber .22 rifle chambered to use the special Hornet cartridge, with a 4-shot clip. This cartridge has a longer and heavier slug than the .22 "plinking" load, and the cartridge case is enlarged to contain a heavier powder load. The cartridge was originally designed for varmint hunting (woodchucks, porcupines, gophers, etc.) but can be used on larger animals. It is a very accurate cartridge, with a high muzzle velocity and extremely flat trajectory. However, it should be used carefully on very small animals, such as squirrels or cottontail rabbits, because its high velocity and comparatively heavy slug will usually cause extreme damage to the meat.

The M6 .410-.22 is a weapon which combines a small-gage shotgun and a caliber .22 rifle chambered for the Hornet cartridge. The rifle is mounted above the shotgun barrel. The shotgun is used for birds, squirrel, and rabbits. The rifle is used for shots at small game which is out of range of the shotgun.

Use

The shotgun load has an effective range of 20-25 yards against birds and an effective range of 15 to 20 yards against small animals. Don't waste ammunition on long shots, especially long wing shots.

The survival rifle can kill at ranges over 200 yards, but your chances of hitting game in a vital spot at ranges over 100 yards are very slight.

Remember, most big game is actually killed at ranges under 60 yards. Unless it is impossible to secure a clean kill by closer stalking, never attempt to kill by shooting over 100 yards. Make sure of your first shot, for it may be your last one at that particular animal — and your ammunition supply is only what you are carrying with you.

Follow these rules when hunting:

1. Carry your weapon so that, if you fall, it will not be damaged.

2. Get as close as possible to the game before shooting.

3. Don't shoot rapid fire. One shot will do the job if aimed properly.

4. Fire from as steady a position as possible. Remember — survival rifles are light and any unsteadiness on your part due to exertion or excitement will set the barrel to trembling. The prone position is best for a steady shot, but sitting or kneeling positions may have to be used. Use a rest such as a log or stone for the barrel whenever you can; but put your hand between the rest and the gun barrel or the gun will shoot wild. Never fire offhand unless time prevents your taking another position.

5. Aim at a vital spot. The shoulder or chest is probably the best spot for medium and large game. Do not shoot unless a vital spot is open.

6. Do not trust your first shot even if game appears to have fallen dead. Reload immediately but keep your eye on the game.

7. Look for blood if game runs away after first shot. If blood is found, wait at least 30 minutes before following. Wounded game will lie down and stiffen if given time.

Field Maintenance

Your survival weapons are built to withstand survival conditions, but they do require intelligent care if they are to function when you need them.

Keep your weapon clean. If possible, cover it when it's not in use. Keep the action, receiver walls, bolt and assembly, and especially the barrel, clean and free from oil, dirt, snow, or mud. If the barrel is obstructed by mud, snow, or any foreign substance, clean it out before shooting. Never try to shoot out an obstruction. The barrel will burst.

Don't use your weapon as a club, hammer, or pry bar. It is a precision-made instrument on which your life may depend.

Don't over-oil your weapon. Only a few drops on moving parts are needed. In extreme cold, use no oil.

A piece of cloth on a string pulled through the barrel is a handy substitute for a ramrod and cleaning patch.

If you must give the barrel a thorough cleaning and have no powder solvent, pour boiling water through it from the breech. Mop up the excess water by pulling a cloth on a string through the barrel, and the hot barrel will dry itself.

Axes and Knives

Your cutting tools are important aids to survival in any environment. For best results, use them and care for them properly.

When you use an ax, don't try to cut through a tree with one blow. Rhythm and aim are more important than force. Too much power behind a swing interferes with your aim. When the ax is swung properly, its weight will provide all the power you need.

Before doing any chopping, clear away all obstructions. A branch, vine, or bush can deflect an ax onto your foot or leg. Remember, an ax can be a wicked weapon. The illustrations below show how to use it safely.

A broken handle is difficult to remove from the head of the ax. Usually the most convenient way is to burn it out. For a single-bit ax, bury the blade in the ground up to the handle, and build a fire over it. For a double-bit, dig a little trench, lay the middle of the ax over it, cover both bits with earth, and build the fire. The covering of earth keeps the flame from the cutting edge of the ax and will save its temper. A little water added to the earth will further insure this protection.

If you have to improvise a new handle, save time and trouble by making a straight handle instead of a curved one like the original. Use a young, straight hardwood without knots. Whittle it roughly into shape and finish it by shaving. Split the end of the handle that fits into the ax head. After it is fitted, pound a thin, dry wooden wedge into the split. Use the ax awhile, pound the wedge in again, then trim it off flush with the ax. Scrape the handle smooth to remove splinters. The new handle can also be seasoned to prevent shrinkage by "scorching" it in the fire.

Your survival kit may include a file or a whetstone. If you haven't a sharpening tool, look for a natural whetstone. You will need it to sharpen your knives and axes.

Any sandstone will sharpen tools; but a gray, somewhat clayey sandstone gives better results. Avoid using quartz. You can recognize quartz instantly by scratching your knife blade with it — quartz is the only common mineral that will bite into steel.

If you don't find sandstone, look for granite or any glittering, crystalline rock except marble. If you use granite, rub two pieces of the stone together until they are smooth before you use one as a grindstone.

Axes can be sharpened best by using both file and whetstone, but a stone alone will keep the ax usable. Use the file every few days, the whetstone after each using. Always push the file away from the blade.

Put a finer edge on your ax with the whetstone. Wet the stone and move it in a circular motion from the middle of the blade to the edge.

A snow knife can be sharpened with file alone. Other knives are sharpened with the whetstone alone. Hold the blade at a slight angle to the stone. Push the blade away from you. Sharpen the blade alternately. You can get a keener edge by gradually decreasing the pressure on the blade.

Sharpen a machete as you would a knife.

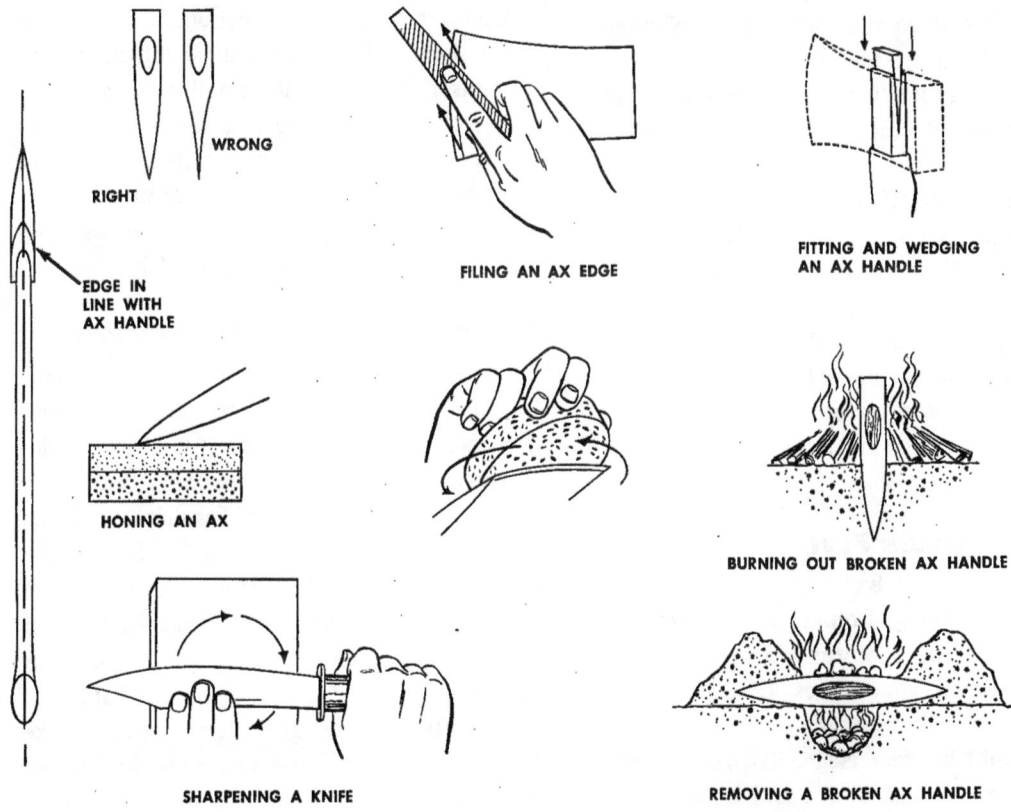

RIGHT WRONG
EDGE IN LINE WITH AX HANDLE
FILING AN AX EDGE
FITTING AND WEDGING AN AX HANDLE
HONING AN AX
BURNING OUT BROKEN AX HANDLE
SHARPENING A KNIFE
REMOVING A BROKEN AX HANDLE

Repairing an ax

CLOTHING

Never discard any clothing. Clothing used properly can keep you cool as well as warm. It also protects you against sunburn, insects, pests, and scratches. It can be used for barter.

Try to keep your clothing clean and in repair. Clean clothes are better insulators than dirty clothes and they last longer.

Try to keep your clothing and shoes dry; use a drying rack in front of a fire. Don't put your wet shoes too close to the fire or they will stiffen and crack. Drying your clothes in the smoke of the fire will help get rid of insects. Turn clothes inside out.

Select your clothing wisely, maintain it conscientiously, and protect it carefully.

HEALTH AND SANITATION

Keeping well is especially important when you are stranded on your own. Your physical condition will have a lot to do with your coming out safely. Protection against heat and cold and knowledge of how to find water and food are important to your health. But there are more rules you should follow.

Save your strength. Avoid fatigue. Get enough sleep. Even if you can't sleep at first, lie down, relax, loosen up. Stop worrying; learn to take it easy. If you are doing hard work or walking, rest for ten minutes each hour. It is usually wise to stop traveling early enough in the day to make a comfortable camp. The rest you get will pay off.

Take Care of your Feet

Take care of your feet if you anticipate doing a lot of walking. Prepare in advance. Be sure your feet and footgear are in good condition. Break in your shoes (and yourself) slowly.

Feet should be kept clean. Toenails should be cut straight across. Bathe and massage the feet daily.

Remove clots of wool from socks. Keep your socks clean and change them frequently, if possible.

Inspect the inside of your shoes and the inside and outside of socks for possible sources of friction. Improvised insoles may reduce friction inside shoes.

Air shoes at night by putting them on small stakes. This keeps inside of shoes dry and eliminates danger of scorpions, centipedes and other crawling vermin.

Examine your feet when you first stop, to see if there are any red spots or blisters. Apply adhesive smoothly on your skin where shoes rub. If you have a blister, pierce through the thick skin at its base with a flame-sterilized needle and press out the fluid. Don't remove the protective skin over the blister. Sterilize the area around the blister before puncturing. (Otherwise, the sterile needle will carry germs from the surrounding area into the blister.) Apply sterile dressing after drainage. (See First Aid, this chapter.)

Guard against skin infection. Your skin is the first line of defense against infection. Use an antiseptic on even the smallest scratch, cut, or insect bite. Keep your fingernails cut short to prevent infection from scratching. Cuts and scratches are apt to get seriously infected, especially in the tropics. A bad infection may hurt your chance of coming out safely.

Guard Against Intestinal Sickness

Diarrhea and other intestinal sicknesses may be caused by change of water and food, contaminated water or spoiled food, excess fatigue, overeating in hot weather, or using dirty dishes. Purify all water used for drinking, either by purification tablets or by boiling for 20 minutes. Cook the plants you eat, or wash them carefully with purified water. Make a habit of personal cleanliness; wash your hands with soap and water, if possible, before eating. If one member of your group gets diarrhea, take special care to enforce measures for proper disposal of human waste and to insure cleanliness in handling food and water. Make sure feces are buried. Don't let affected members handle food and cooking utensils. Field treatment of diarrhea is necessarily limited. Rest and fast — except for drinking water — for 24 hours; then take only liquid foods such as soup and tea, and avoid sugars and starches. Keep up a large intake of water, with salt tablets. Eat several meals instead of one or two large ones. Overeating of fruit, especially green fruit, may cause a temporary diarrhea. Eliminating fruit from the diet, temporarily, will relieve this condition.

Don't worry about lack of bowel movement; this will take care of itself in a few days, provided you have an adequate daily supply of water.

Keep Your Body and Clothing Clean

You will feel better and keep free from skin infections and body parasites. Examine each other for external parasites.

Keep Your Camp Clean

Dump garbage in a pit or in a spot away from camp where it will not blow about. Dig a latrine or designate a latrine area away from the camp and water supply.

Burn all garbage, cans, papers, cartons, etc., before covering your garbage pit. If this is not done, animals will uncover the pit and spread the refuse about the grounds.

WATER

Water will be one of your first and most important needs. Start looking for it immediately. You may get along for weeks without food, but you can't live long without water, especially in hot areas where you lose large quantities of water through sweating.

Even in cold areas your body needs 2 quarts of water a day to maintain efficiency. Any lower intake results in loss of efficiency. If you delay drinking, you will have to make it up later on.

Purify all water before drinking, either (1) by boiling for 1 minute; or (2) by using as directed the water purification tablets in your first aid kit, or (3) by adding 8 drops of 2% solution of iodine to a quart (canteenful) of water and letting it stand for 10 minutes before drinking. Rainwater collected directly in clean containers or in plants is generally safe to drink without purifying. Boiling is surest and best purification method.

Don't drink urine. It contains too much body waste to be healthful.

Ground Water

When no surface water is available, you may want to tap the earth's supply of ground water — rain or snow that has sunk into the earth instead of remaining on the surface; to run off in streams and rivers. It sinks deep, leaving a thickness of drier earth above.

Access to this water supply depends upon the kind of ground — whether it is rock or some loose material like clay, gravel, or sand.

ROCK. In rocky ground, look for springs and seepages. Limestones and lavas have more and larger springs than any other rocks.

Limestones are soluble; and ground water etches out caverns in them — some large enough for you to explore and many just cracks, an inch or so high, that the water has enlarged. Look in these caverns, large and small, for springs. If you go into a large one beyond sight of the entrance, be careful — don't get lost. Travel with a string or cord tied to a solid object at the entrance. Lacking a cord, mark your route every few feet on wall or floor.

Most lava rocks contain millions of bubble-holes; ground water may seep through them. Look for springs along the walls of valleys that cross the lava flow. Some flows have no bubbles but do have "organ pipe" joints — vertical cracks that part the rocks into columns a foot or more thick and 20 feet or more high. At the foot of these joints you may find water creeping out as seepage or pouring out in springs.

Look for seepage where a dry canyon cuts through a layer of porous sandstone.

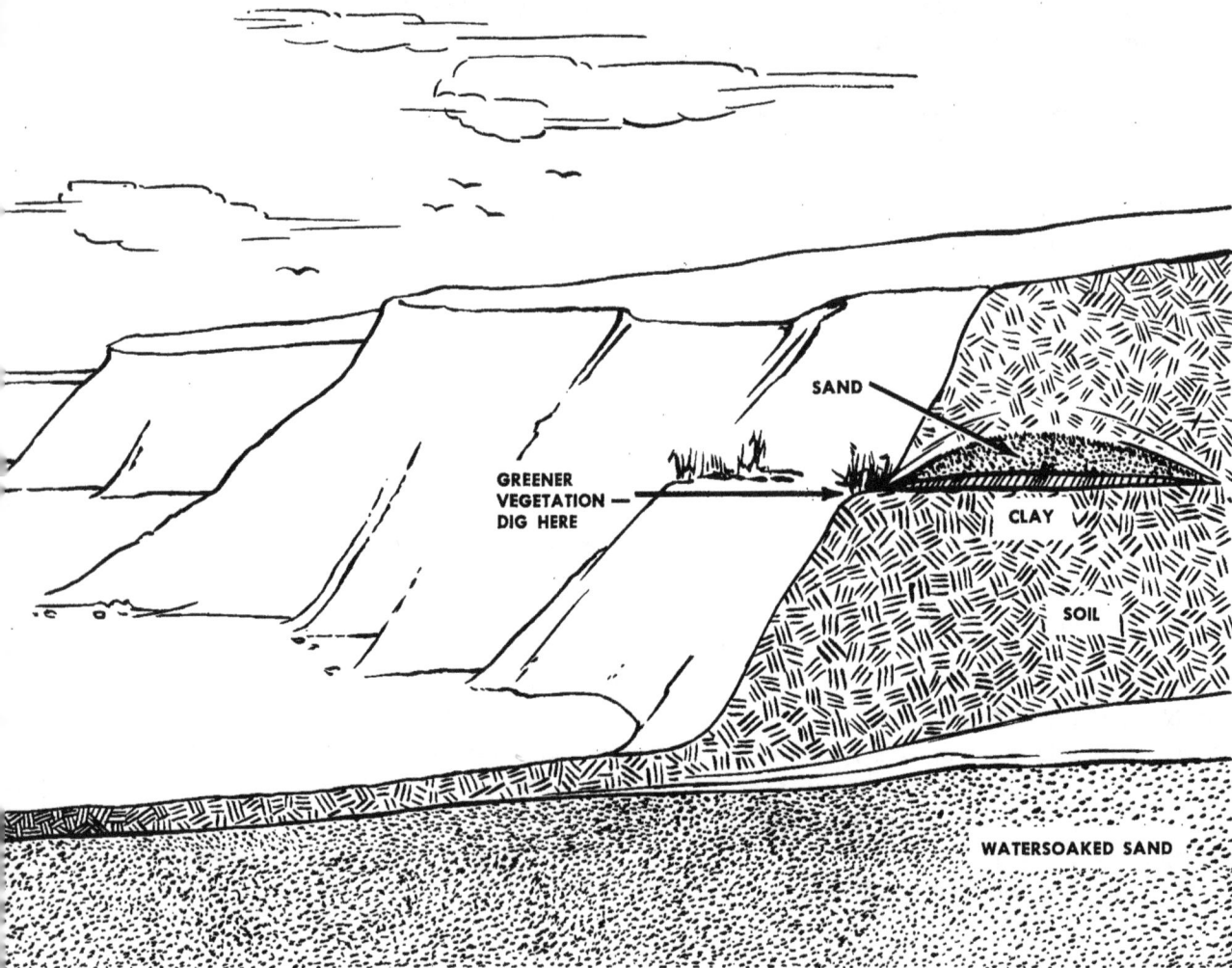

GREENER
VEGETATION —
DIG HERE

SAND

CLAY

SOIL

WATERSOAKED SAND

Perched water

Most common rocks, like granite, contain water only in irregular cracks. Look over the hillsides to see where the grass is lush and green. Then dig your ditch at the base of the green zone and wait for water to seep into it.

LOOSE GROUND. Water is more abundant and easier to find in loose sediments than in rocks. Look for springs along valley floors or down along their sloping sides. The flat benches or terraces of land above river valleys usually yield springs or seepages along their bases, even when the stream is dry.

Don't waste your time digging for water unless you have some sign that water is there.

Dig in the floor of a valley under a steep slope, especially if the bluff is cut in a terrace; or dig out a lush green spot where a spring has been during the wet season.

Water moves slowly through clay, but many clays contain strips of sand which may yield springs. Look for a wet place on the surface of a clay bluff and try digging it out. Try wet spots at the foot of the bluff.

Along coasts you may find water in the dunes above the beach or even in the beach itself, well back from the high-tide line. Look in the hollows between sand dunes for visible water — dig, if the sand seems moist.

FOOD

General Rules

a. Take stock of your available food and water. Estimate the number of days you expect to be on your own. (The pickup time may vary from a few hours to several months, depending on the environment and available rescue facilities in the area. Divide available food into thirds; allow two-thirds for the first half of your estimated time before rescue, and save the remaining one-third for the second half.

b. If you decide to divide your party, give each man traveling out for help about twice as much food as you give each man remaining with the airplane. In this way, the men resting at the aircraft and those walking out will stay in about the same physical condition for about the same length of time, and the safety and rescue prospects of all will be increased.

c. If you have less than a quart of water daily, avoid dry, starchy, and highly flavored foods and meat. Keep in mind that eating increases thirst. Best foods to eat are those with high carbohydrate content, such as hard candy and fruit bars, if available.

d. Every bit of work requires additional food and water; remember that the less you work, the less food and water you will need.

e. You can live many days without food if you have water. When water is no problem, drink more than your normal amount to keep fit.

f. Always be on the lookout for wild foods. Live off the land whenever possible. *Save your rations for emergencies.*

g. Eat regularly, if possible; don't nibble! On limited rations, plan for one good meal daily; then sit down and make a feast of it. Two meals a day are preferable, especially if one of them is hot. If you are collecting wild foods, plan a hot meal. Cooking usually makes the food safer, more digestible, and more palatable. On the other hand, some foods such as sapodilla, star apple, soursop, and memdrillos are not palatable unless eaten raw. The time you spend cooking will give you a good rest period.

h. Native food may be more appetizing if they are eaten by themselves. Mixing rations and native foods usually does not pay. In many countries, vegetables are often contaminated by the human dung which the natives use as fertilizer. Such diseases as dysentery are carried in this way. If possible, you should select and prepare your own meals when you find yourself in such a situation. If necessary to avoid offending the natives, indicate that your peculiar taboos require you to prepare your own food.

Prepared Foods

The food in your survival kit has been especially developed to provide you with proper sustenance in survival emergencies. When you eat it as directed on the package, it will keep you at maximum efficiency. Save it for emergency use if you can find enough other food at hand.

Wild Foods

Learn to overcome your prejudices. Foods that may not look good to eat are often part of the natives' regular diet. Wild foods are good foods, with high vitamin and mineral content. Fleshy-leafed plants make good salad greens and fresh fruits provide fluid when water supplies are low. Eat enough to satisfy.

With a few exceptions, all animals are edible when freshly killed. Don't eat toads. Never eat fish with slimy gills, sunken eyes, flabby flesh or skin, or an unpleasant odor. If the flesh remains dented when you press your thumb against it, the fish is probably stale and should not be eaten. For poisonous and venomous fish, see pages 237 and 239; for poisonous plants and mushrooms, see pages 48, 50, and 171.

Where to Look for Food

You should be able to find something to eat wherever you are. One of the best hunting grounds for survival food is along the sea coast, between the high and low water mark. Other likely spots are the area between the beach and a coral reef; the marshes, mud flats, or mangrove swamps where a river flows into the ocean or into a larger river; river banks, inland water holes, shores of ponds and lakes; margins of forests, natural meadows, protected mountain slopes, abandoned cultivated fields.

ANIMAL FOOD

Animal food will give you the most food value per pound. Anything that creeps, crawls, swims, or flies is a possible source of food. People eat grasshoppers, hairless caterpillars, wood-boring beetle larvae and pupae, ant eggs, spider bodies, and termites. Such insects are high in fat and should be cooked until dried. You have probably eaten insects as contaminants in flour, corn meal, rice, beans, fruits, and greens of your daily food, and in stores in general.

HUNTING HINTS

Most warm-blooded, hairy animals are wary and hard to catch. To hunt them requires skill and patience. The best method for a beginner is "still hunting." Find a place where animals pass — a trail, watering place, or feeding ground. Hide nearby, always downwind so the animal can't smell you, and wait for game to come within range. Remain absolutely motionless. You can stalk an animal upwind by moving very slowly and noiselessly, keeping under cover as much as possible. Move only when the animal is feeding or looking the other way. Freeze when he looks your way.

The best time to hunt is in the very early morning or dusk. In your travels, keep alert for animal signs such as tracks, trampled underbrush, or droppings. On narrow trails be ready for game using same pathways.

Game is most plentiful and most easily found near water, in forest clearings, or along the edge of thickets. Many animals live in holes in the ground or in hollow trees. Poke a flexible stick into the hole to determine if it is inhabited. If you use a forked stick, twist it quickly when you come in contact with the body of a small animal and you may entangle enough

fur in the small fork to pull the animal out of the hole. Use a stick to tease the animal into running out, but first close off other exits. Animals in hollow trees can be smoked out by a fire built at the base of the tree; be ready to club the animal as it comes out.

Night hunting or fishing is usually best, since most animals move at night. Use a flashlight or make a torch to shine in the animals' eyes. They will be partly blinded by the light and you can get much closer than in the daytime. If you have no gun try to kill the animals with a club or a sharpened stick used as a spear. Eyes of spiders and insects are good reflectors, so don't be surprised if you "shine up" eyes and can't find the rest of the creature. Eyes of spiny lobsters on reefs shine red. Remember that large animals, when wounded or with their young, can be dangerous. Be sure that the animal is dead, not just wounded and playing possum.

Along river and lake shores, small freshwater turtles can often be found sunning themselves. If they dash into shallow water, you can still get them. Watch out for mouth and claws. Frogs and snakes also sun and feed along streams. Use two hands to catch a frog — one to attract it and keep it busy while you grab it with the other. All snakes, except sea snakes, are good to eat; use a long forked stick to catch them.

Both marine and dry-land lizards are edible. Use a noose or small fishhook baited with a bright cloth lure, or use a slingshot or club.

Never overlook small birds and their nests. All bird eggs are edible when fresh, even with embryos. Large wading birds such as cranes and herons, often nest in mangrove swamps or in high trees near water. Ducks, geese, and swans are to be expected in tundra areas. During the moulting season, these birds can be clubbed or netted. Sea birds along low coastlines frequently nest on sand bars or low sand islands. Steep rocky coasts are favorite nesting places for gulls, auks, murres, and cormorants. Try catching birds at night when they are roosting.

SNARES, TRAPS, AND DEADFALLS

Ptarmigan or
small bird snare

Pilot
chute
release
lock

Improvised
trigger

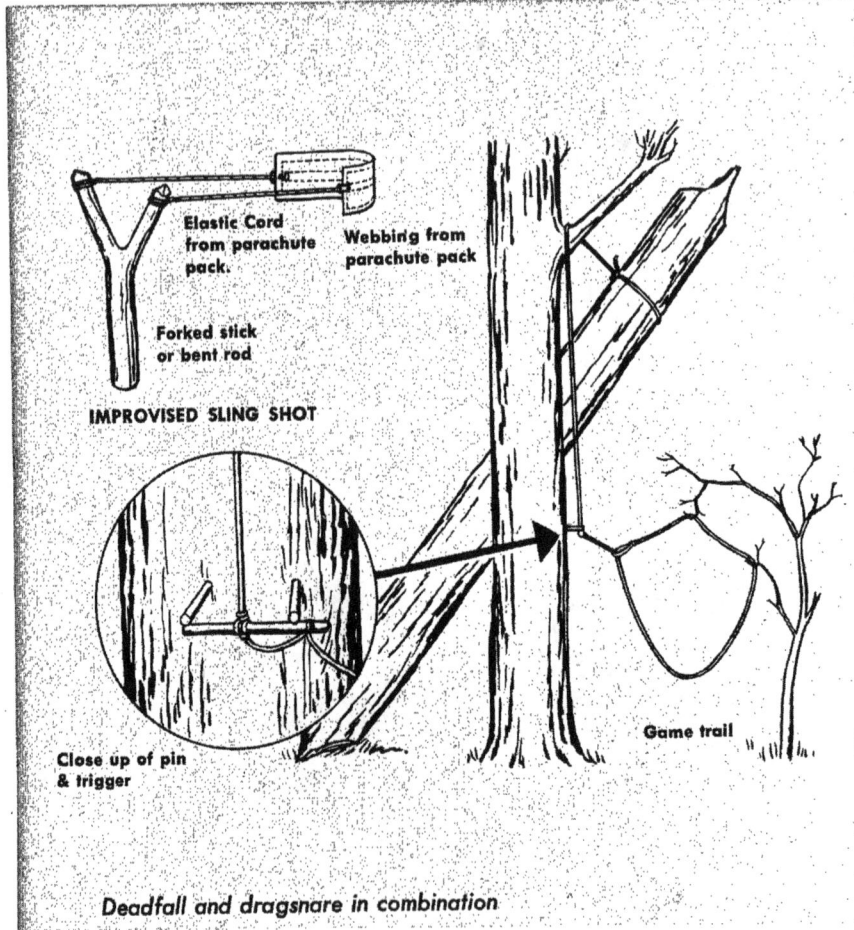

Elastic Cord
from parachute
pack.

Webbing from
parachute pack

Forked stick
or bent rod

IMPROVISED SLING SHOT

Close up of pin
& trigger

Game trail

Deadfall and dragsnare in combination

Small game
trail snare
with drag

Small game snares

Snaring of small game is useful during periods of food shortages, especially in the absence of firearms or during periods of imposed silence. Set your snares in game trails or frequently used runways, which you can recognize by fresh tracks and droppings.

All snares and traps should be simple in construction and should be set out as soon as possible and before darkness. Any spot used as a butchering place will attract other animals. It is a good place to watch for game during the next 24 hours. Use entrails for bait.

Place your traps where the trail is narrow. Arrange pickets, brush, or obstacles in such a manner as to force the animal to pass through the snare. Be sure that the loop is large enough for the head to pass through but not so large that the body will go through. Disturb natural surroundings as little as possible.

Small rodents may be snared in any area with a string noose laid around a hole or burrow. Conceal yourself or lie flat on the ground a short distance away. Jerk the noose tight when the animal pops his head out or steps into the noose.

The twitch-up snare — a noose attached to a sapling — jerks the animal up into the air and keeping his carcass out of reach of other animals. This type of snare is not recommended for very cold climates, since the bent sapling may freeze in position and will not spring up when released.

Medium to large animals can be captured in deadfalls, but this type trap is recommended only where big game exists in such quantities as to justify the time and effort spent in construction. Build your deadfall close to or across a game trail, beside a stream, or on a ridge. Take care to see that the fall log slides smoothly between the upright guide posts and that the bait is placed at a sufficient distance from the bottom log to insure time for the fall log to fall before the animal can withdraw its head. In a trip-spring deadfall, no bait is used. The log is tripped by the animal's touching a trip string set across the trail.

An untended noose or deadfall is preferred, since it leaves you free for other duties. Check traps early in the morning.

You can make a simple slingshot with the elastic from your parachute pack and a forked stick or the metal rods in your tie-down kit. With practice you can kill any small animal.

Birds can be caught with the gill net in the survival kit. At night, set up the net vertically to the ground in some natural flyway, such as an opening in dense foliage. During the day, anchor one end of the net to the ground and attach the other end to a tree limb so that you can release it from a distance. Bait the area under the net, wait for the birds to gather, and then pull down the net.

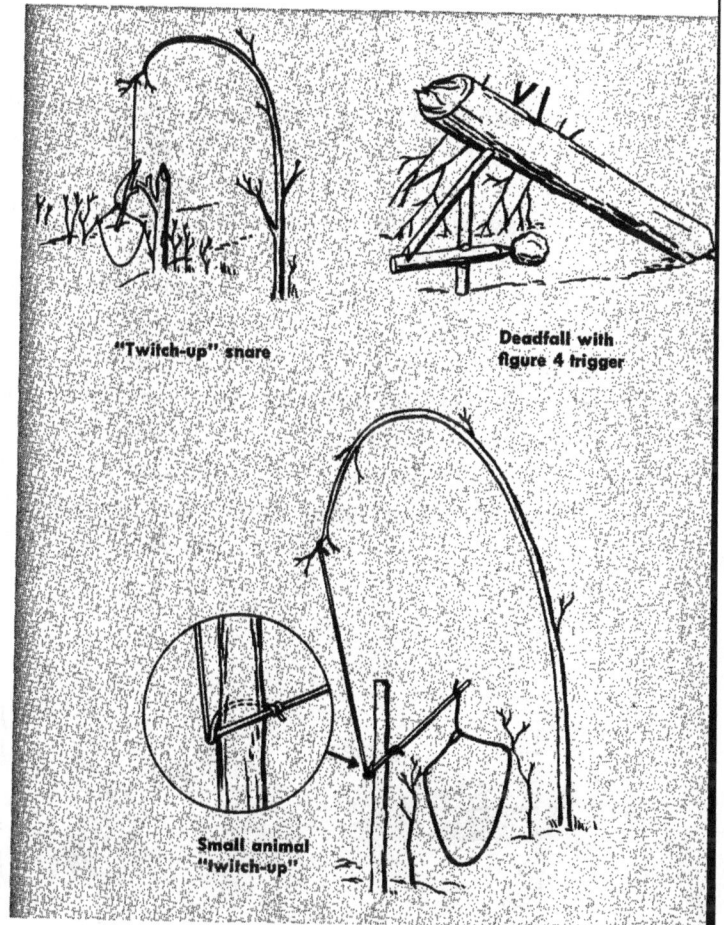

"Twitch-up" snare

Deadfall with figure 4 trigger

Small animal "twitch-up"

Small animal traps and snares

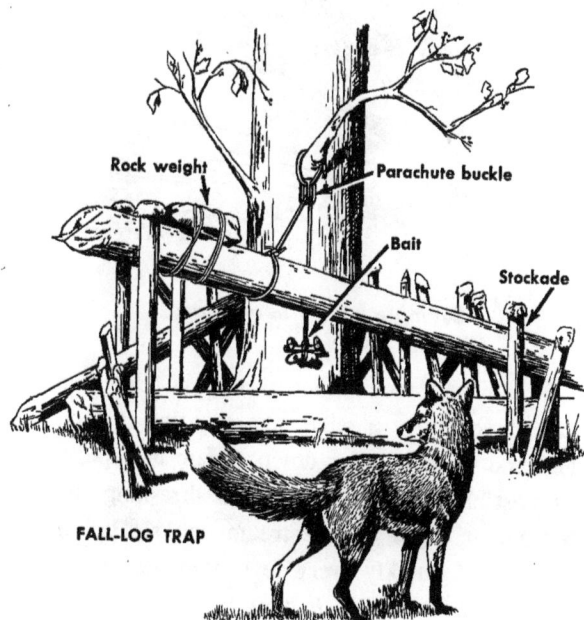

Rock weight

Parachute buckle

Bait

Stockade

FALL-LOG TRAP

FISHING HINTS

To catch fish use the hook and line in your emergency kit, trying the smaller hooks first. Use insects, shellfish, worms, or meat for bait. Try to see what the fish are eating. Artificial lures can be made from pieces of brightly colored cloth, feathers, or bits of bright metal or foil. A length of wire between the line and the hook will prevent a fish from biting the line in two. If you have no hooks, improvise them from wire or insignia pins, or carve them out of bone or hard wood. You can make a line by unraveling a parachute shroud line or by twisting threads from cloth or plant fibers. If the fish won't take bait, try to hook them in the stomach as they swim by.

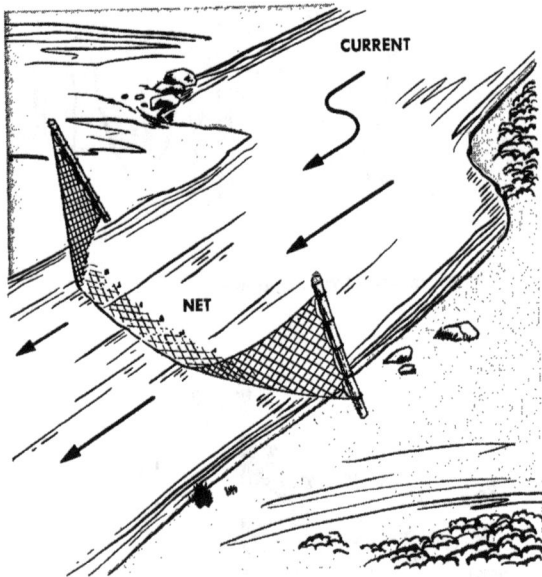

Setting a gill net in a stream

Better and more efficient than a line is a net. If you have a seine, attach poles at each end and work it up or down stream as rapidly as possible, moving stones and threshing the bottom or edges of the stream banks. Gather up the net quickly every few moments so the fish will not escape. If you have a gill net, avoid damaging it in rough water. Stones may

be used as anchors and wood for floats. A gill net set at a slight angle to the current will tend to drain clear any floating refuse that comes down the stream, making the net less visible. Absolutely quiet stream water is hard to find. The net will occasionally catch diving birds which try to rob your gill net.

In fresh water, usually the deepest water is the best place to fish. In shallow streams the best places are pools below falls, at the foot of rapids, or behind rocks. The best time to fish is usually early morning or late evening. Sometimes fishing is best at night, especially if you have a light to attract the fish. Fish can sometimes be killed with the back side of a machete; or they can be speared with a sharpened stick. Before you give up, try fishing in all kinds of water and depths, at all times, and with all types of bait. There are a few safety rules to observe. Watch out for slippery rocks; keep out of the surf particularly when the tide is changing.

Shrimp and prawns live on or near the sea bottom and may be scraped up. They may also be lured to the surface by light at night. Catch them with a hand net made from parachute cloth. Lobsters and crawfish are creeping forms found on the bottom in water 10-30 feet deep. Use lobster traps, a jig, or a baited hook, or lift your catch out of the water with a dip net. Crabs creep, climb, and burrow; they are easily caught in shallow water with a dip net or in traps baited with fish heads or animal guts.

Fish traps or weirs are very useful for catching both fresh and salt water fish, especially those that move in schools. In lakes or large streams, fish tend to approach the banks and shallows in the morning and evening. Sea fish, traveling in large schools, regularly approach the shore with the incoming tide, often moving parallel to the shore and guided by obstructions in the water.

A fish trap is basically an inclosure with a blind opening where two fencelike walls extend out, like a funnel, from the entrance. The time and effort you put into building a fish trap

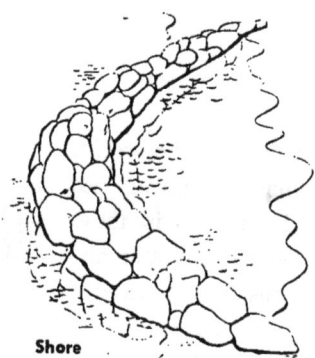

Shore

TIDAL FLAT FISH TRAP

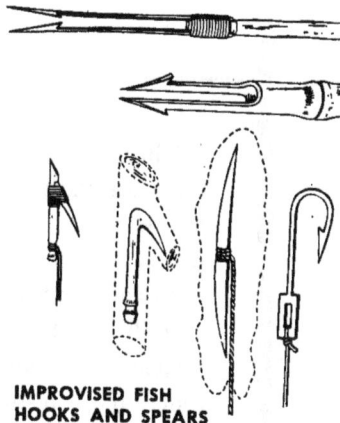

IMPROVISED FISH HOOKS AND SPEARS

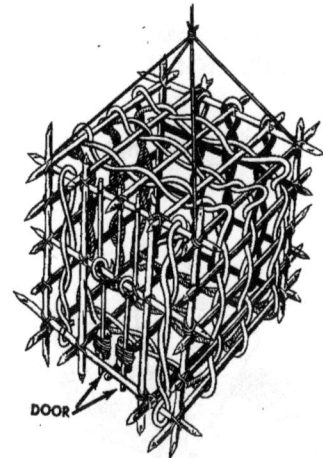

DOOR

BOX-TYPE LOBSTER TRAP
Door rods (sapling or wire) are hinged so that they swing freely and will drop behind the lobster after it enters.

Maze-type fish traps

Current

should depend on your need for food and the length of time you plan to stay in one spot.

Pick your trap location at high tide; build at low tide. One to two hours of work should do the job. Consider your location and try to adapt natural features which will reduce your labors.

On rock shores, use natural rock pools. On coral islands, use natural pools on the surface of reefs, by blocking openings as the tide recedes. On sandy shores, use sand bars and the ditches they inclose. The best fishing off sandy beaches is in the lee of offshore sand bars.

Note the swimming habits of fish. Build your simple weir as a low stone wall extending out into the water and forming an angle with the shore. If you plan a more complex brush weir, choose protected bays or inlets, using the narrowest area and extending one arm almost to the shore. Place nets across mouths of streams.

In small, shallow streams, make your fish traps with stakes or brush set into the stream bottom or weighted down with stones so that the stream is almost blocked except for a small narrow opening into a stone or brush pen or shallow water. Wade into the stream, herding

the fish into your trap. Catch or club them when they get into shallow water. Mud-bottom streams can be trampled until roiled, then seined. The fish are blinded and cannot avoid the nets.

Look for fresh water crawfish, snails, and clams under rocks, logs, overhanging bushes, or in mud bottoms.

Fish may be confined in properly built inclosures and kept for days, since the incoming water keeps them fed. In many cases it may be advantageous to keep them alive until needed and thus assure a fresh supply without danger of spoilage.

Mangrove swamps are often good fishing grounds. At low tide, clusters of oysters are exposed on the mangrove "knees," or lower branches, along with mussels. Clams can be found in the mud at the base of trees. Crabs are very active among branches or roots and over mud. Fish can be caught at high tide. Snails are found on mud or clinging to roots. Do not eat shellfish that are not covered at high tide or those from a colony containing obviously diseased members.

PLANTS USED TO STUPEFY FISH

Barringtonia

CROSS SECTION
OF SEED POD
SEED POD
X SECTION

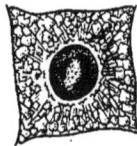

PINK FLOWERS

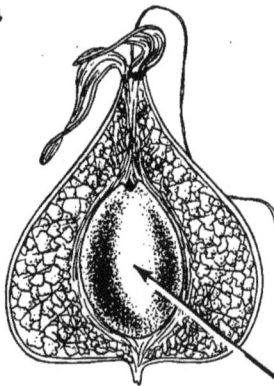

CRUSH POISONOUS
SEED

Throughout the warm regions of the world, there are various plants which the natives use for poisoning fish. The active poison in these plants is harmful only to cold blooded animals. Man can eat fish killed by this poison without any ill effects whatsoever. In the southwest Pacific, the seeds and bark from the barringtonia tree, illustrated on this page, are commonly used as a source of fish poison.

The barringtonia tree usually grows along the seashore. In southeast Asia, the derris plant is widely used as a source of fish poison. The derris plant, a large woody vine, is also used to produce a commercial fish poison called rotenone.

The most common method of using fish-poison plants is to crush the plant parts (most often the roots) and mix them in water. Drop large quantities of the crushed plants into pools or the headwaters of small streams containing fish. Within a short time, the fish will rise in a helpless state to the surface. After putting in the poison, follow slowly down stream and pick up the fish as they come to the surface, sink to the bottom, or swim crazily to the bank. A stick dam or obstruction will aid you in collecting fish as they float downstream.

Commercial rotenone can be used in much the same manner as crushed derris roots. However, rotenone has no effect if dusted over the surface of a pond. It must be mixed to a chocolate-malted consistency with a little water, and then distributed in the water. If the concentration is strong, it will take effect within 2 minutes in warm water, or it may take an hour in colder water. Fish sick enough to turn over on their backs will eventually die. An ounce of 12% rotenone will kill every fish for a half mile down a stream that is about 25 feet wide.

A few facts to remember about the use of rotenone are:

a. It is very swift-acting in warm water at 70° F. and above.

b. It works more slowly in cold water and is not practical in water below 50° or 55° F.

c. It can best be applied in small ponds, streams, or tidal pools.

d. Don't use too much or it will be wasted. However, too little will not be effective.

A small container of 12% rotenone (1-2 oz.) would be a valuable addition to any emergency kit. It should not be exposed unnecessarily to air or light. It will retain its toxicity best if kept in a dark-colored vial.

Lime thrown in a small pond or tidal pool will kill a fish in the pool. Burn coral and sea shells to obtain lime.

PLANT FOOD

The thought of having a diet of "rabbit food" thrust on him is often repugnant to the stranded airman, and such an idea is likely to be the first to occur to him when confronted with the necessity of eating wild plants in a strange area of the globe. Many people have the misconception that they will have to crawl around on all fours, chewing dry grass like a sick hound dog. Such is not the case if the survival episode is entered into with the confidence and intelligence that can only be based on knowledge or experience.

If you know what to look for in the area in which you find yourself stranded, can identify it, and know how to prepare it properly for eating, there is no reason why you can't find sustenance, at least, and perhaps some real good eating. In many isolated regions a survivor who has had some previous instruction in plant finding can enjoy dishes which the folks back home consider delicacies.

Now, harbor no illusions. You probably won't have the balanced diet during a survival experience that you'd get at the dining hall or at home. Depending on your survival area and your equipment and your ability to forage for all kinds of food, your diet will possibly be unbalanced — too much meat and fat in some cases, too much fruit and vegetables in others. But remember, if your diet tips in favor of plant foods, you'll be much better off in most cases than if you were existing mainly on a menu of meat. Of course, in the Arctic regions, the heat-producing ingredients of meat and fats are essential to the diet, but elsewhere a strictly vegetarian diet will sustain you quite well. Meat supplies the body with proteins, which build muscle, but many plant foods (especially seeds and nuts) supply enough for normal efficiency. Plants, however, provide carbohydrates, which give the body energy and supply calories. Carbohydrates keep your weight and energy up, and include such important food products as starches and sugars.

As a documented and authoritative example of the value of a strictly plant diet in survival, the case of a Chinese botanist who had been drafted into the Japanese Army during World War II can be cited. Isolated with his company in a remote section of the Philippines, this Chinese botanist kept 60 of his fellow soldiers alive for 16 months by finding wild plants and preparing them properly. He selected 6 men to assist him, and then found 25 examples of edible plants in the vicinity of their camp. He acquainted the men with these samples, showing them what parts of the plants could be used as food. Then he sent the men out to look for similar plants and had them separate the new plants according to the original examples, to avoid any poisonous plant mingling with the edible ones.

The results of this effort were impressive. Though all the men had a natural desire for ordinary food, none suffered physically from the plant food diet. The report was especially valuable because the botanist, with typical Oriental detachment, was able to keep a careful record of all the food used, the results, and the comments of the men. This case history reflects the same opinions as those found in questionnaires directed to American survivors during World War II.

Another advantage to a plant diet is availability. In many cases, you may be in a situation in which you can't forage for animal food. You may be injured, unarmed, in enemy territory, exhausted, or in an area which just has a lack of wild life.

Finally, there is one basic reason to look to plant food as your main source of sustenance. Both animal life and human life depend on it. Animals do not offer the broad food values of plants, because they, like us, depend on plants as the major basic source of sustenance.

Animals and humans are dependent on plants, because plants are independent. Given air, water, light, and enough heat, plants react with the native chemicals of the earth and convert these elements into vital food products. In fact, a plant is the most efficient food factory there is. If plants were being advertised, you would be told that they contain that "miracle ingredient," chlorophyll, which they do have, and have had long before toothpaste and dog food. Chlorophyll is one of the basic products of photosynthesis, the process in which water, air, and light unite to give the plant its green color and its rich food value.

So, you see that plants are readily available in any areas which can supply the simple requirements and that plants provide both of the basic body needs, carbohydrates and proteins. Maybe rabbits and sick hound dogs aren't so bad off, after all.

If you're convinced that you can depend on plants for your daily food needs, the next question in your mind is "where to get what, and how." A good question, for which there are some good answers.

KINDS OF PLANTS AND WHERE TO FIND THEM

Experts estimate that there are about 300,-000 classified plants growing on the surface of the earth, including many which thrive on mountain tops and on the floors of the oceans. However, you won't need to know about all these plants unless you're exceptionally reckless or exceptionally hungry. For the purpose of your study, and perhaps your later use, the brief discussions and the illustrations in this manual will touch only on plant foods which fill certain requirements.

The first consideration, of course, is that the plant be edible, and preferably palatable. It must be fairly abundant in the area or areas in which it is found, and if it includes an inedible or poisonous variety in its family, the edible plant must be distinguishable to the average eye from the inedible or poisonous one. Usually a plant has been selected because one special part is edible, such as the stalk, the fruit, or the nut.

Most of the plants, especially those illustrated in the manual, will be good general examples of food courses which are similar to many other plants of the same variety. *Familiarity with these "pilot plants" should enable you to evaluate the food possibilities of other plants with which you are not directly acquainted.* For example, the color of the juice in the stalk of one plant might lead you to try another one in which the juice seemed to be of the same color and consistency. You will never have the time or the inclination to learn all of the estimated 120,000 varieties of edible plants. As in other aspects of the survival problem, you will have to rely on a bit of training and a lot of sound judgment.

Before you learn what to look for and where to look for it, you will find it valuable to know just a bit about the edible parts of plants.

EDIBLE PARTS OF FOOD PLANTS

You will find few plants of which every component is edible, but many plants which you may encounter will have one or more identifiable parts that have considerable food or thirst-quenching value. The great variety of plant component-parts which might contain substance of food value is shown by the following list. Each of these parts will be described and illustrated, and the accompanying discussion will define the climatic or geographic zone in which plants bearing each part can be found.

  a. *Underground parts*: tubers, roots, rootstalks, and bulbs.
  b. *Stems and leaves* (potherbs): shoots, stems, leaves, pith, and bark.
  c. *Flower parts*: flowers and pollen.
  d. *Fruits*: seeds and grains, nuts, fleshy fruits (dessert and vegetables), and seed pods.
  e. *Gums and resins.*
  f. *Saps.*

Nuts

Nuts are among the most nutritious of all raw plant foods and contain an abundance of valuable protein. Plants bearing edible nuts occur in all the climatic zones of the world and in all continents, except the Arctic regions. Inhabitants of the temperate zones are familiar with walnuts, filberts, almonds, hickory nuts, acorns, hazelnuts, beechnuts, and pine nuts, to mention just a few. In the tropical zones are found coconuts and other palm nuts, brazil nuts, cashew nuts, and macadamia nuts.

The following plants with edible nuts are illustrated on the pages indicated.

  a. English walnut (p. 72).
  b. Hazelnut (p. 71).
  c. Chestnut (p. 70).
  d. Almond (p. 68).
  e. Beechnut (p. 67).
  f. Swiss stone pine (p. 66).
  g. Trapa nut (p. 65).
  h. Indian almond (p. 288).
  i. Buri palm (p. 294).
  j. Sugar palm (p. 292).
  k. Sago palm (p. 265).
  l. Acorn (p. 69).
  m. Coconut (p. 260).
  n. Pistachio nut (p. 209).
  o. Cashew nut (p. 295).

Most nuts can be eaten raw, but some kinds, such as acorns, are better cooked.

Seeds and Grains

Seeds of many plants, such as buckwheat, ragweed, amaranth, goosefoot (chenopodium), and the beans and peas from beanlike plants, contain oils and are rich in protein. The grains of all cereals and many other grasses, including millet, are also an extremely valuable source of plant protein. They may either be ground between stones, mixed with water and cooked to make porridge, or parched or roasted over hot stones. In this state they are still wholesome and may be kept for long periods without further preparation.

The following plants with edible seeds and grains are illustrated on the pages indicated.

  a. Baobab (p. 321).
  b. Sorrel (p. 217).
  c. Sea orach (p. 218).
  d. Screw pine (p. 208).
  e. Amaranth (p. 302).
  f. Luffa (p. 308).
  g. Lotus lily (p. 310).
  h. Portulaca (p. 311).
  i. Nipa palm (p. 267).
  j. Rice, perl millet, Italian millet (p. 285).
  k. Goa bean (p. 301).
  l. St. Johns bread (p. 208).
  m. Colocynth (p. 215).

Tubers

The potato is an example of an edible tuber. Many other kinds of plants produce tubers including, the tropical yam, the Eskimo potato, and tropical water lilies. All tubers are found below ground and must be dug out. Tubers are rich in starch and should be cooked by roasting in an earth oven (see p. 249) or by boiling.

The following plants with edible tubers are illustrated on the pages indicated.

  a. Yam (p. 291).
  b. East Indian arrowroot (p. 287).

c. Tropical yam (p. 277).

d. Taro (p. 313).

e. Water lily (p. 74).

Roots and Rootstalks

Edible roots are often several feet in length and usually are not swollen. Many plants produce roots which may be eaten for food.

Edible rootstalks are underground stems which have become much thickened. Some kinds are several inches thick, and in comparison to true roots, are usually relatively short and jointed.

Both true roots and rootstalks are storage organs rich in stored starch.

The following plants with edible *roots* are illustrated on the pages indicated.

a. Baobab (p. 321).

b. Horse-radish tree (p. 289).

c. Screw pine (p. 208).

The following plants with edible *rootstalks* (rhizomes) are illustrated on the pages indicated.

a. Ti plant (p. 290).

b. Water plantain (p. 60).

c. Flowering rush (p. 77).

d. Manioc, or tapioca plant (p. 309).

e. Lotus lily (p. 310).

f. Canna (p. 281).

g. Cattail (p. 58).

Bulbs

The most common edible bulb is the wild onion, which easily can be detected by its characteristic odor. In Asia Minor and central Asia, the bulb of the wild tulip may be eaten. Wild onions may be eaten uncooked, but other kinds of bulbs are more palatable if cooked. All bulbs contain a high percentage of starch. (Some bulbs are poisonous; see death camas, p. 176.)

The following plants with edible bulbs are illustrated on the pages indicated.

a. Tulip (p. 211).

b. Onion (p. 212).

Shoots and Stems

All edible shoots grow in much the same fashion as asparagus. The young shoots of ferns (fiddleheads) and especially those of bamboo and numerous kinds of palms are desirable for food. Some kinds of shoots may be eaten uncooked, but most are better if first parboiled for 5 to 10 minutes, the water drained off, and the shoots reboiled until they are sufficiently cooked for eating.

The following plants with edible shoots and stems are illustrated on the pages indicated.

a. Mescal (shoots) (p. 220).

b. Palms.

Coconut shoots (p. 260).

Rattan shoots (p. 303).

Sugar palm shoots (p. 292).

Buri palm shoots (p. 294).

Sago palm shoots (p. 265).

Nipa palm shoots (p. 267).

c. Luffa (p. 308).

d. Sugar cane (p. 280).

e. Water lily (p. 270).

f. Banana (p. 274).

g. Papaya (p. 275).

h. Cattail (p. 58).

i. Prickly pear (p. 213).

j. Colocynth (p. 215).

Leaves

The leaves of spinach-type plants (potherbs), such as wild mustard, wild lettuce, lambs quarter, and many others may be eaten either raw or cooked. Prolonged cooking, however, destroys most of the vitamins. Plants which produce edible leaves are perhaps the most numerous of all edible plants.

The young tender leaves of nearly all non-poisonous plants are edible. Testing the different kinds will be one of the joys of the survival experience.

The following plants with edible leaves are illustrated on the pages indicated.

a. Baobab (p. 321).
b. Ti plant (p. 290).
c. Water fern (p. 273).
d. Spreading wood fern (p. 83).
e. Horse-radish tree (p. 289).
f. Sorrel (p. 217).
g. Chicory (p. 61).
h. Willow (p. 167).
i. Sea orach (p. 218).
j. Ceylon spinach (p. 300).
k. Goa bean (p. 301).
l. Amaranth (p. 302).
m. Tamarind (p. 305).
n. Lotus lily (p. 310).
o. Portulaca (p. 311).
p. Poke (p. 269).
q. Papaya (p. 275).
r. Rhubarb (p. 76).
s. Prickly pear (p. 213).

Pith

Some plants have an edible pith in the center of the stem. The pith of some kinds of tropical plants is quite large. The pith of the sago palm is particularly valuable because of its high food value.

The following palms with edible pith (starch) are illustrated on the pages indicated.

a. Fishtail (p. 293).
b. Buri (p. 294).
c. Sugar (p. 292).
d. Rattan (p. 303).
e. Sago (p. 265).
f. Coconut (p. 260).

Pollen

Pollen looks like yellow dust. All pollen is high in food value, and in some plants, especially the cattail, quantities of pollen may easily be collected and eaten as a kind of gruel (see illustration on p. 58).

Flowers

Fresh flowers may be eaten as a part of a salad or to supplement a stew. The hibiscus flower is commonly eaten throughout the south-west Pacific area. In South America, the people of the Andes eat nasturtium flowers. In India it is common to eat the flowers of many kinds of plants as part of a vegetable curry. Flowers of desert plants may also be eaten.

Plants with edible flowers are illustrated on the pages indicated.

a. Abal (p. 221).
b. Horse-radish tree (p. 289).
c. Caper (p. 219).
d. Luffa (p. 308).
e. Banana (p. 274).
f. Papaya (p. 275).
g. Colocynth (p. 215).

Fruits

Edible fruits can be divided into *dessert,* or sweet kinds, and *vegetable,* or nonsweet kinds. Both are the seedbearing part of the plant.

Dessert fruits are often plentiful, in all areas of the world where plants grow. For instance, in the far North there are blueberries and crowberries; in the Temperate Zones cherries, plums, and apples; and in the American deserts fleshy cactus fruits. Tropical areas have more kinds of edible fruit than other areas, and a list would be endless. Typical examples of edible fruits are illustrated under the appropriate sections further on. Dessert fruits may be cooked or, for maximum vitamin content, left uncooked.

Common vegetable fruits include the tomato, cucumber, pepper, eggplant, and okra.

Plants with edible fruits (dessert) are illustrated on the pages indicated.

a. Rose (p. 306).
b. Blueberry (p. 169).
c. Cloud berry (p. 168).
d. Mulberry (p. 64).
e. Grape (p. 63).
f. Baobab (p. 321).
g. Crabapple (p. 62).
h. Cashew (p. 295).
i. Bignay (p. 304).

j. Rose apple (p. 306).
k. Bael fruit (p. 307).
l. Custard apple, soursop, bullock's heart, (p. 279).
m. Mango (p. 282).
n. Fig (p. 284).
o. Poke (p. 269).
p. Papaya (p. 275).
q. Banana (p. 274).
r. Jujube (p. 210).

Plants with edible fruits (vegetables) are illustrated on the pages indicated.

a. Caper (p. 219).
b. Breadfruit (p. 296).
c. Luffa (p. 308).
d. Plantain (p. 60).

Seed Pods

Seed pods are really fruits (vegetable), but it is better to list them as a separate food source, because of the large number of edible seed pods in the bean and pea family. *Young* bean pods may be boiled until tender.

Plants with edible seed pods are illustrated on the pages indicated.

a. Horse-radish tree (p. 289).
b. Mescal (p. 220).
c. Goa bean (p. 301).
d. Tamarind (p. 305).

Pulps

The pulp around the seeds of many fruits is the only part eaten, as, for example, the pomegranate. Some fruits produce sweet pulp; others have a tasteless or even bitter pulp. Plants that produce edible pulp include the custard apple, inga pod, breadfruit, and tamarind. In the case of breadfruit, the pulp must be cooked, whereas in other plants the pulp may be eaten uncooked. The edibility rules (p. 41) should be used in all cases of doubt.

Plants with edible pulp are illustrated on the pages indicated.

a. Baobab (p. 321)
b. Juniper (p. 78).
c. Screw pine (p. 208).
d. Tamarind (p. 305).

Sap and Thirst Quenchers

In desert and tropical forest areas, drinking water is often scarce. Vines or other plant parts may be tapped as a potential source of drinking water or water substitute. The sap of palms, for instance, is a thirst-quencher. The liquid is obtained by decapitating the flower stalk and letting the fluid drain into some sort of vessel (such as a bamboo joint). Furthermore, palm sap, with its high sugar content, is highly nutritious. Drinking water can be obtained from the ti plant, grape vine, rattan palm, coconut palm, cactus, and the malee plant.

The best method of procuring drinking water from vines is as follows: Make a slanting cut high on the stem, and then cut the vine off about 6 feet below this cut. Water will begin to flow at the lower end. Either drink directly from the freshly cut end or let the liquid drain into a container.

Plants with edible sap and drinking water illustrated on the pages indicated.

a. Grape (p. 63).
b. Fishtail palm (p. 293).
c. Buri palm (sap) (p. 294).
d. Sugar palm (sap) (p. 292).
e. Rattan palm (water) (p. 303).
f. Nipa palm (sap) (p. 267).
g. Sugar cane (sap) (p. 280).
h. Coconut palm (sap) (p. 260).
i. Acacia (water) (p. 214).
j. Saxaul (water) (p. 216).
k. Agave (p. 220).
l. Cactus (p. 205).

Gums and Resins

When plant sap collects on the outside of the plant and hardens as a deposit, it is called *gum,* if soft and soluble in water, and *resin,* if hard and not soluble in water. You are perhaps familiar with the gum which exudes from cherry trees and the resin which seeps from pine trees. These plant byproducts are edible and are a good source of nutritious food which should not be overlooked.

Barks

The inner bark of a tree — the layer next to the wood — may be eaten raw or cooked. Under famine conditions, it is possible in northern areas to make flour from the inner bark of such trees as the cottonwood, aspen, birch, willow, and pine. The outer bark should be avoided in all cases, because this part contains large amounts of bitter tannin. Pine bark is high in vitamin C. The outer bark of pines can be scraped away and the inner bark stripped from the trunk and eaten fresh, dried, or cooked. It may also be pulverized into flour. Bark is most palatable when newly formed in spring. As food, bark will be most useful in the Arctic regions, where plant food will often be scarce.

EDIBILITY RULES

1. Never eat large quantities of a strange plant food without first testing it.

2. When cooking facilities are available:

a. Get rid of any disagreeable taste by boiling the plant in water for 5 to 15 minutes.

b. Take a teaspoonful of the plant food, prepared in the way it will be used, hold it in your mouth for 5 minutes. If, by this time, no burning sensation occurs, swallow it. Wait 8 hours. If no ill effects such as nausea, cramps, or diarrhea come about, eat a handful and wait 8 hours. If no ill effects show up at the end of this time, the plant food may be considered edible. Remember that olives are bitter and grapefruit is sour, and that you are trying a new food, so that an unpleasant taste does not always mean the plant is poisonous or even unpalatable.

3. When cooking facilities are *not* available; follow instructions in paragraph 2b above.

In general it is considered safe to try foods that you observe being eaten by birds and mammals. Food eaten by rodents (mice, rats, rabbits, beavers, squirrels, muskrats), or by monkeys, baboons, bears, raccoons, and various other omnivorous animals (meat and plant eaters) usually will be safe for eating.

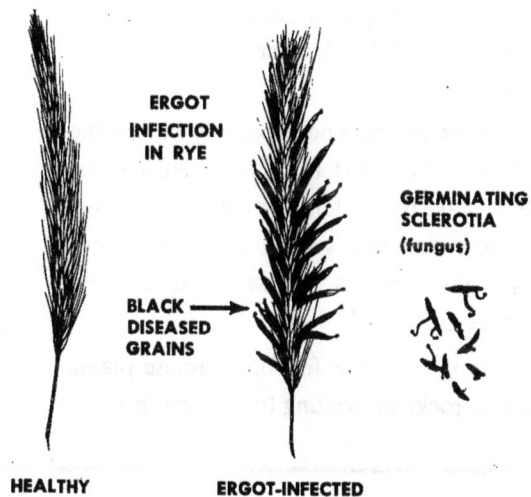

ERGOT INFECTION IN RYE

GERMINATING SCLEROTIA (fungus)

BLACK → DISEASED GRAINS

HEALTHY   ERGOT-INFECTED

CAUTION

1. Cook all plant foods when in doubt about the edibility (see *mushrooms,* page 46).

2. Small quantities of a poisonous plant will not necessarily be dangerous. A noteworthy explanation is the death angel mushroom (*Amanita phalloides*), which may prove fatal after eating a few spoonfuls.

3. Cooking will not dissipate the poisonous properties of mushrooms.

4. Avoid eating untested plants having a milky juice or letting the juice contact the skin. Exceptions to this include wild figs, breadfruit, and papaya, all of which contain milky juice but which are quite harmless and nonpoisonous, *cooked* or *uncooked.*

5. To avoid ergot poisoning from eating infected heads of cereal grains or other food grasses, discard all grain heads having black spurs in place of normal seed grains.

SEAWEEDS ─────────────────────────────────

Seaweed is a form of marine algae, and many varieties which are quite edible may be found on or near the shores of the larger ocean areas. Properly prepared seaweed can be an important part of the diet, and is for millions of people.

In large quantities, and especially before the stomach is conditioned to it, seaweed may be a violent cathartic. Eaten in moderation, however, it is a valuable source of iodine, other minerals, and vitamin C, which is a good scurvy preventive.

In selecting seaweeds for food, choose plants attached to rocks or floating free, because those stranded on the beach for any length of time may be spoiled or decayed. Thin, tender varieties can be dried over a fire or dried in the sun until crisp and then crushed and used in a soup or broth to add flavor. The thick, leathery seaweeds should be washed and then boiled for a short time to soften them, after which they may be eaten together with other foods, such as fish or vegetables. Some kinds can be eaten raw, after you have first tested them for edibility.

The following list of edible seaweeds gives a description of the plant, tells where it may be found, and in many cases suggests a method of preparation. Each variety is illustrated.

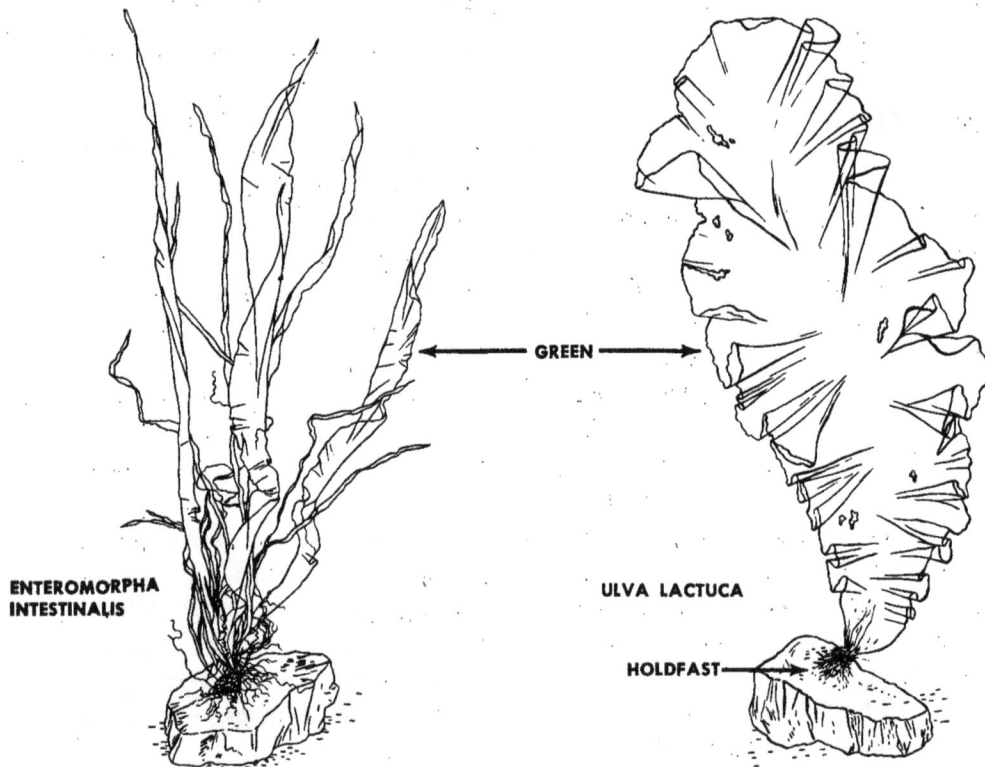

ENTEROMORPHA INTESTINALIS

GREEN

ULVA LACTUCA

HOLDFAST

Green Seaweeds

Common green seaweed, often called sea lettuce (*Ulva lactuca*), occurs abundantly on both sides of the Pacific and North Atlantic oceans. It is used in the same manner as garden lettuce, after having been washed in clean water.

STALKS 1-5 FT. LONG

OLIVE-GREEN
OR BROWN

HOLDFAST

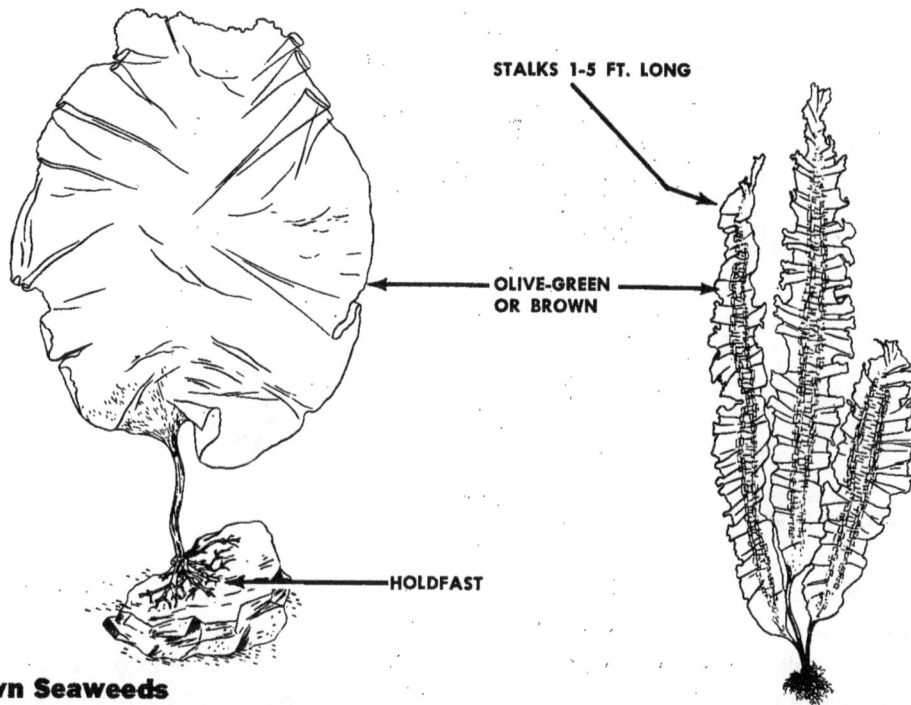

Brown Seaweeds

The most common edible brown seaweeds are the sugar wrack, kelp, and Irish moss.

SUGAR WRACK (*Laminaria saccharina*). The young stalks of the sugar wrack are sweet to the taste. It is found on both sides of the Atlantic, and on the coasts of China and Japan.

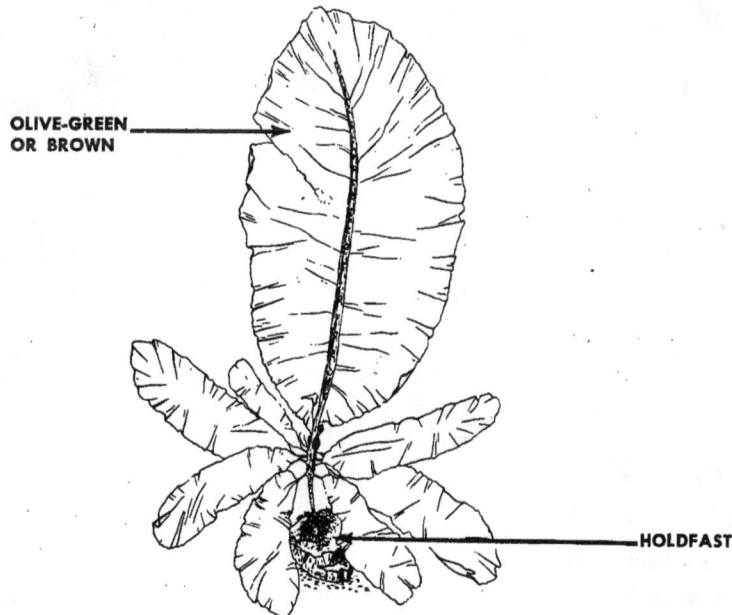

OLIVE-GREEN
OR BROWN

HOLDFAST

EDIBLE KELP (*Alaria esculenta*). Edible kelp has a short cylindrical stem and thin, wavy olive-green or brown fronds from 1 to several feet in length. It is found in both the Atlantic and Pacific Oceans, usually below the high tide line on submerged ledges and rocky bottoms. It should be boiled before eating to soften it, after which it can be mixed with vegetables or soup.

REDDISH TO WHITE

HOLDFAST ATTACHES TO ROCK

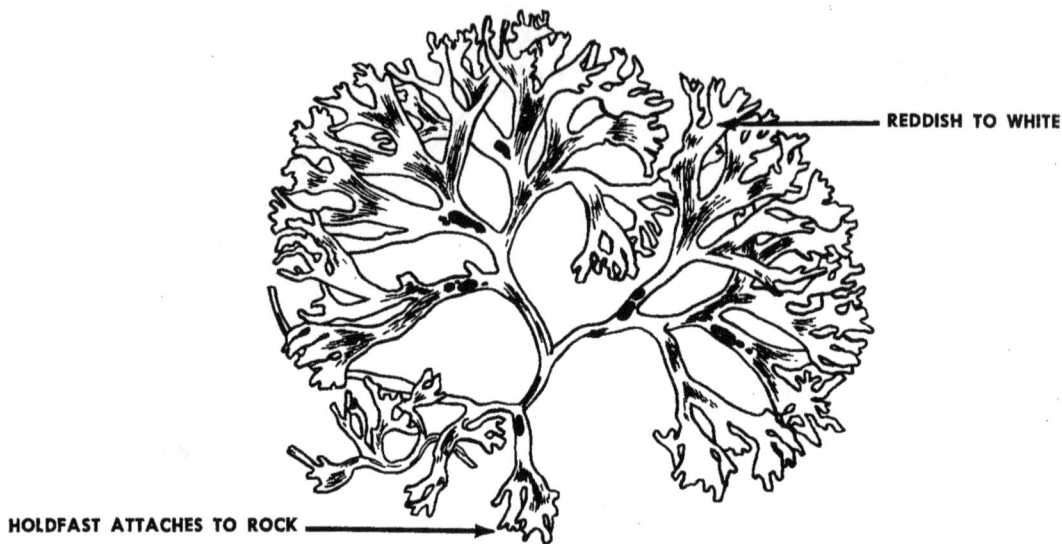

IRISH MOSS (*Chondrus crispus*). Irish moss, a variety of brown seaweed, is quite edible, and is often offered for sale in market places. It is found on both sides of the Atlantic Ocean and can be identified by its tough, elastic, and leathery texture. However, when dried it becomes crisp and shrunken; it should be boiled before eating. It can be found at or just below the high tide line, but is often cast up on the shore.

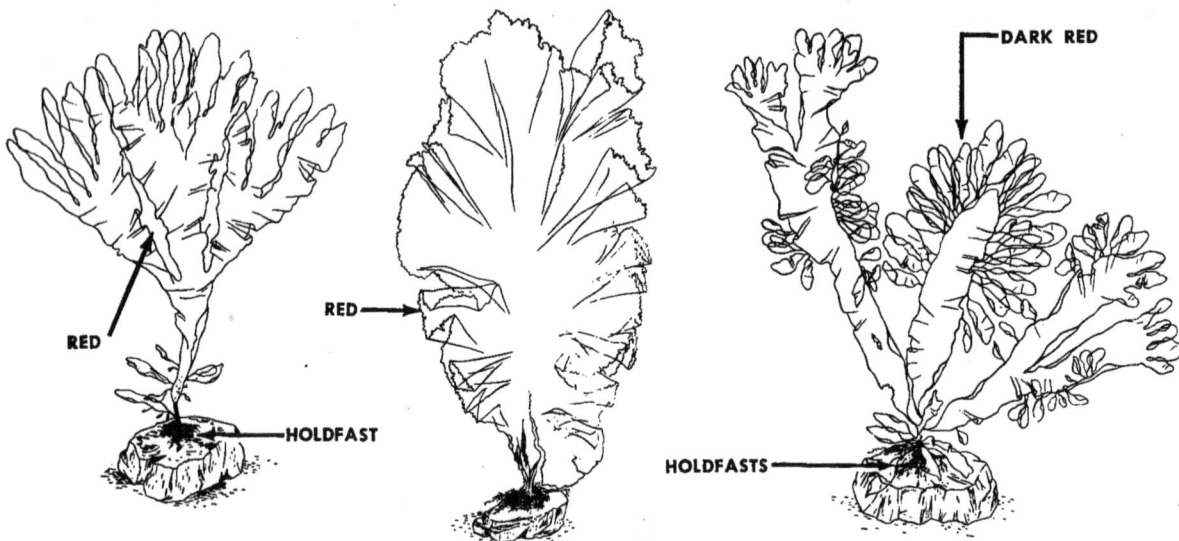

RED

HOLDFAST

RED

DARK RED

HOLDFASTS

Three forms of dulse

Red Seaweeds

Red seaweeds can usually be identified by their characteristic reddish tint, especially the edible varieties. The most common and edible red seaweeds include the dulse, laver, and many warm-water varieties.

DULSE (*Rhodymenia palmata*). Dulse has a very short stem which quickly broadens into a thin, broad, fan-shaped expanse which is dark red and divided by several clefts into short, round-tipped lobes. The entire plant is from a few inches to a foot in length. It is found attached to rocks or coarser seaweeds, usually at the low-tide level, on both sides of the Atlantic and in the Mediterranean. It is leathery in consistency but is sweet to the taste. If dried and rolled, it can be used as chewing tobacco.

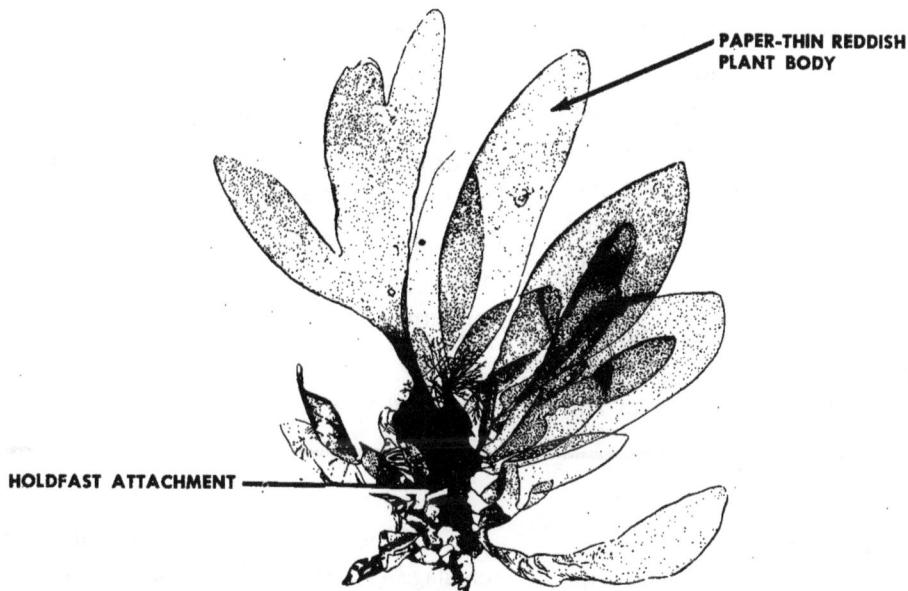

PAPER-THIN REDDISH PLANT BODY

HOLDFAST ATTACHMENT

LAVER (*Porphyra*). Laver is usually red, dark purple, or purplish-brown, and has a satiny sheen or a filmy luster. It is common to both the Atlantic and Pacific areas, where it has been used as food for centuries. It is used as a relish, or is cleaned and then boiled gently until tender. It can also be pulverized and added to crushed grains and fried in the form of flatcakes. During World War II, laver was chewed for its thirst-quenching value by New Zealand native troops. Laver is usually found on the beach at the low tide level.

RED WARM-WATER SEAWEED. A great variety of red seaweed is found in the South Pacific area. This seaweed accounts for a large portion of the native diet.

GELATINOUS

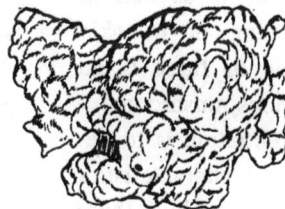

Blue-green colonies spread over ground in grassy meadows

Nostoc grows on ground

Freshwater Algae

A freshwater variety of seaweed which is common in China (and also in America and Europe) is the marine alga known as common Nostoc (*nostoc commune*), and its variety, flagellated nostoc. The latter is peculiar to northwestern China, but common Nostoc may be found in pools in the spring. It forms green, round jellylike lobules about the size of marbles. It is usually dried and used in soups.

FUNGI

At least 16,000 varieties of edible fungi are known to grow in different parts of the world. Yet, the word "fungi" has an unfortunate connotation to many people — they forget that the mushrooms they eat on their steaks and the moldy part of the blue cheese they spread on their crackers are common forms of fungi. While fungi are not an effective substitute for meat, they do compare favorably with many common leafy vegetables in food content and are often available in many areas where other kinds of edible plants are scarce.

For example, fungi are very common in the wet weather of early spring and late fall in the temperate zones of the world, especially in the pine and spruce-fir forest regions of northern Asia, Europe, and North America.

Edible mushrooms can be boiled, baked, or used in stews.

Gilled Fungi (Mushrooms)

As mentioned above, mushrooms are the most common of edible fungi, but they have been subjected to an uncommon share of myth and folklore. The term "toadstools" has been used to describe any inedible or poisonous variety of mushroom for so long that people think it is the name for another variety of fungus. Actually, "mushroom" is a more widely accepted name for these plants. The distinguishing characteristics ascribed to them by some people are present in edible as well as poisonous types. Odor, peeling of its skin bruises, livid colors — none of these is an acceptable criterion of poisonous mushrooms.

The best method of differentiation is to become familiar with the general characteristics of mushrooms which are edible and of those which are poisonous. The illustrations on the following pages indicate some of the obvious characteristics.

However, a supplementary list of hints to guide you in the selection of edible mushrooms is also included below.

● ● ●

SELECTION OF EDIBLE GILLED FUNGI.

1. Dig the gilled mushroom completely out of the ground before making a decision as to its edibility, for it is especially important to eliminate those mushrooms with a cup, or volva, at the base (see illustration on page 47).

2. Avoid all gilled mushrooms in the button stage (see illustration on page 49).

3. Avoid all ground-growing mushrooms with the underside of the cap full of minute, reddish pores (see illustration of the *Boletus*, page 48).

4. Avoid all gilled mushrooms with a membranelike cup or scaly bulbs at the base.

5. Avoid all gilled mushrooms with white or pale milky juice.

6. Avoid all gilled woodland mushrooms with a smooth, flat, reddish top and white gills radiating out from the stem like spokes.

7. Avoid yellow or yellowish-orange mushrooms growing on old stumps. If they have crowded and solid stems, convex overlapping caps, broad gills extending irregularly down the stem, or surfaces that glow phosphorescently in the dark, they are probably poisonous.

8. Avoid *any* mushrooms which seem to be too ripe, water-soaked, spoiled, or maggoty. Any food can be poisonous, or at least inedible, when it is decayed or otherwise affected.

Nongilled Fungi

Among the nongilled fungi which grow in abundance throughout the world are the puffballs, morels, coral fungi, coral hydnums, and cup fungi. These are illustrated in the drawings on page 47. None of these is poisonous when eaten fresh.

EDIBLE FUNGI

GILLS

Veil may or
may not be present

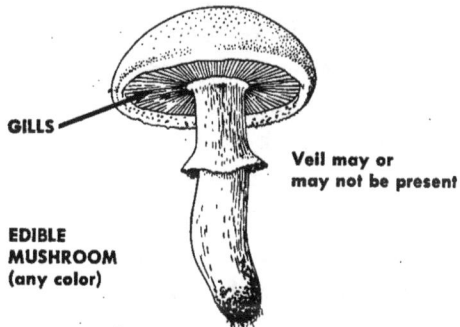

**EDIBLE
MUSHROOM
(any color)**

(Note absence
of basal cup)

Usually found
on dead wood →

**SULFURPOLYPORE
(2-4 in.)**

(Bright yellow
to salmon pink)

CUP FUNGUS
(Orange, brown
or white)

(1-3 in. high)

CORAL FUNGUS
(White, orange, yellow,
pale violet, buff)
(2-6 in. high)

MOREL
(Ashen-gray)

PUFFBALLS
(Chalk-white
inside)

(1-12 in. in
diameter)

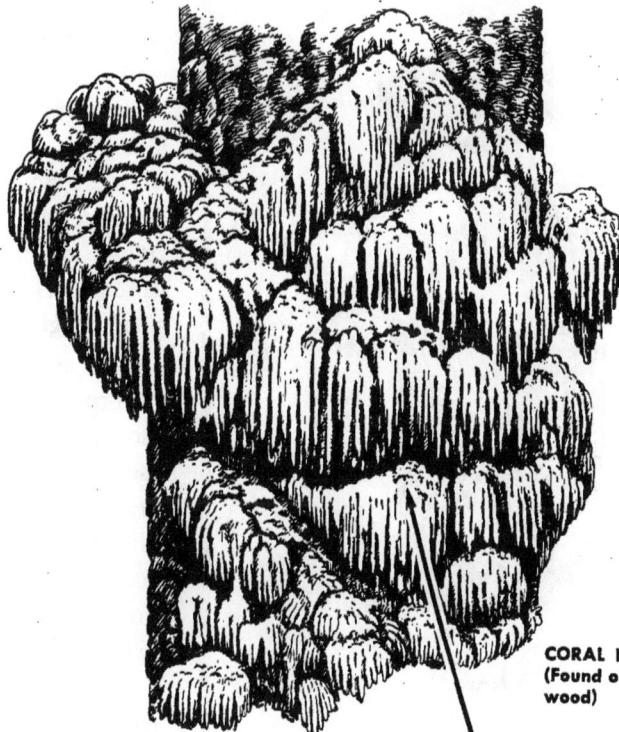

CORAL HYDNUM
(Found on dead
wood)

(waxy white)

EDIBLE FUNGI

DEAD
TREE
TRUNK

Jew's ear fungus (Auricularia)

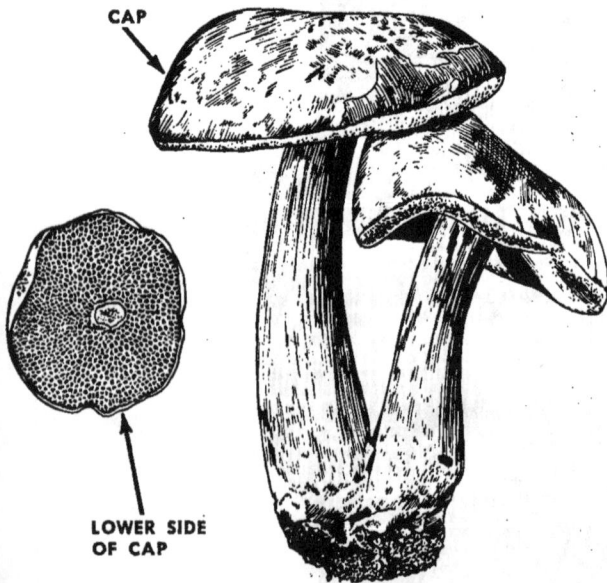

CAP

LOWER SIDE
OF CAP

Boletus

Jew's Ear Fungus (Auricularia)

WHERE FOUND. (Regions 1, 2, 5, 6, and 12 defined later in this chapter.) The Jew's ear fungus is worldwide in its occurrence. It is a common tropical fungus and is found in temperate regions as well, in both the northern and southern hemispheres. Look for the Jew's ear fungus on decaying logs on the forest floor or on dead trees.

APPEARANCE. The mature Jew's ear is a curious growth. The body of the plant is irregularly ear-shaped, flabby, brown, or sometimes slightly tinged with violet and semitransparent. It is smooth on both sides or has a few shallow folds on the under surface.

WHAT TO EAT. The Jew's ear fungus is prepared for eating in the same fashion as other kinds of edible fungi. Only young plants should be used.

• • •

Poisonous Mushrooms

The most violently poisonous mushrooms are those of the *Amanite* family, the most deadly of these being *Amanita phalloides,* or Death Angel. This mushroom is widespread in Europe, Asia, and America but seems to be more common in the north temperate regions than in the tropical and warm areas. Its characteristics are obvious, as indicated by the drawing on page 49, and there should be no difficulty in distinguishing this type from the edible varieties. This and other poisonous varieties of gilled fungi are illustrated on page 49.

If illness occurs after you have eaten some mushrooms, induce vomiting by tickling the back of the throat. Do not take water until after vomiting for it might dilute and spread the poison. However, after vomiting, drink a mixture of lukewarm water and powdered charcoal. Under survival conditions, the only remedy is continued vomiting, "charcoal soup," and rest.

Remember —— 98% of all wild mushrooms are edible.

POISONOUS MUSHROOMS

REDDISH-WHITE
CAP WITH
WHITE FLECKS

Fly agaric
(Amanita muscaria)

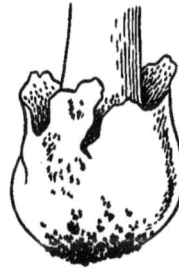

A

B

C

IDENTIFYING CUPS

D

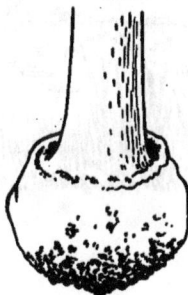

E

F

IDENTIFYING CUPS

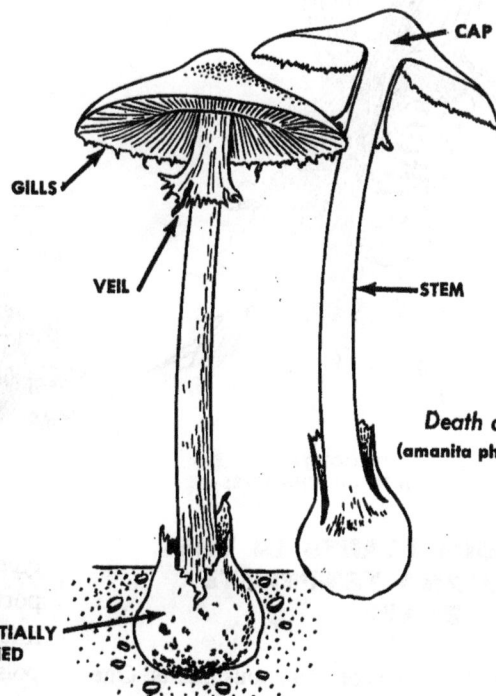

CAP

GILLS

VEIL

STEM

Death angel
(amanita phalloides)

PARTIALLY
BURIED
CUP

WATER HEMLOCK

POISONOUS

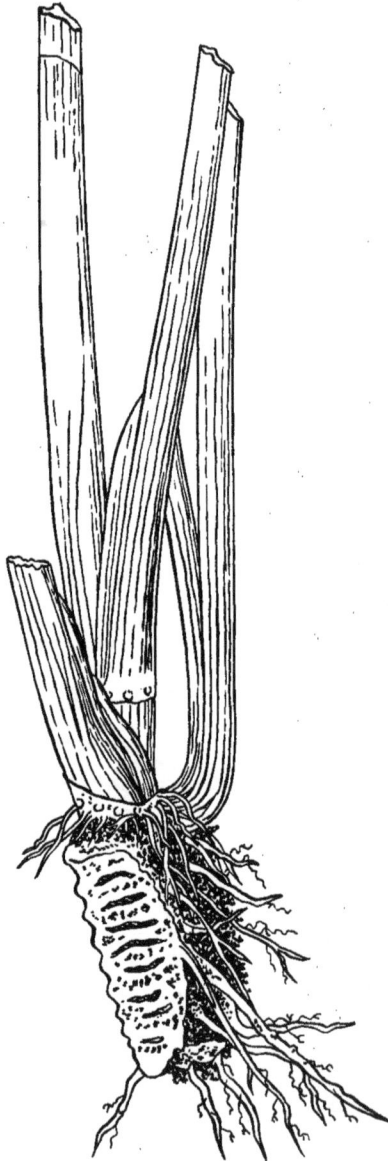

ROOTSTALK
WITH AIR CHAMBERS

POISONOUS PLANTS IN THE TROPICS AND TEMPERATE ZONES

There are two types of poisonous plants. One type poisons on contact. An example of this type is poison ivy, which affects the external portions of the body. The other type poisons internally. Poison hemlock is an example. The poisoning occurs from having eaten a portion of the plant — fruit, stem, leaf, root.

Poisonous on Contact

If you are familiar with poison ivy or poison oak in the United States and are aware of the abundance of these plants, you have already seen poisonous plants of this type in as plentiful a state as they occur anywhere in the world.

In tropical regions, many kinds of plants poison by contact. The family to which the American poison oak and poison ivy belong has tropical types which are dangerous. The plants of this family are mostly trees and shrubs. The poison is usually exuded by the bark, which is often identified by streaks of black ooze along the trunk. If you come into contact with a poisonous plant of this sort, the treatment is the same as for poison ivy and poison oak. Wash the poisonous oil away with soap and water and apply a bandage to prevent spreading.

In the moist tropics of southeast Asia, for instance, the poisonous members of the cashew family are called rengas. The leaves of the cashew nut (*Anacardium occidentale*), which is illustrated on p. 295, are poisonous to some people.

Poisonous Internally

One of the greatest concerns of the survivor will be whether a strange plant is poisonous to eat. Use the edibility rules in all cases of doubt. Try to learn what is good, and stick to those kinds. Try a nibble first, not a whole handful. Make sure that you can identify the water hemlock.

STINGING PLANTS

Nettles are the commonest kind of stinging plant in the North Temperate Zone. In the Tropics, the tree nettle and the cowhage have stinging hairs. The tree nettle carries an irritating poison which is formic acid. The action of the cowhage is merely mechanical. Recovery from the effects of these plants will occur in a relatively short time.

For discussion of poisonous Arctic plants see p. 171.

NATURAL VEGETATION REGIONS OF THE WORLD

The plant cover of the world can be described in terms of 12 natural vegetation regions. These regions, like the major climatic zones, are not as sharply defined as they may appear on a map. Transitional areas will exist between any vegetation and climatic region and its neighbor.

In this manual, the discussions of vegetation regions are limited to the more typical aspects of each region. The 12 regions are as follows:

Natural Vegetation Region	Climatic Zone
1. Rain forest.	
2. Semievergreen seasonal forest.	Tropics
3. Scrub and thorn forest.	
4. Savanna.	
5. Evergreen scrub forest.	
6. Hardwood (seasonal) and mixed hardwood-coniferous forest.	Temperate
7. Coniferous forest.	
8. Prairie.	
9. Steppe.	
10. Desert scrub and waste.	Any climatic zone.
11. Tundra.	Arctic
12. Mountainous area (undifferentiated highland).	Temperate and Tropics

The vegetation regions of the Temperate Zone, including the mountains, are described in this chapter. The vegetation regions of the Tropics, deserts, and Arctic are described in the chapters dealing with those areas.

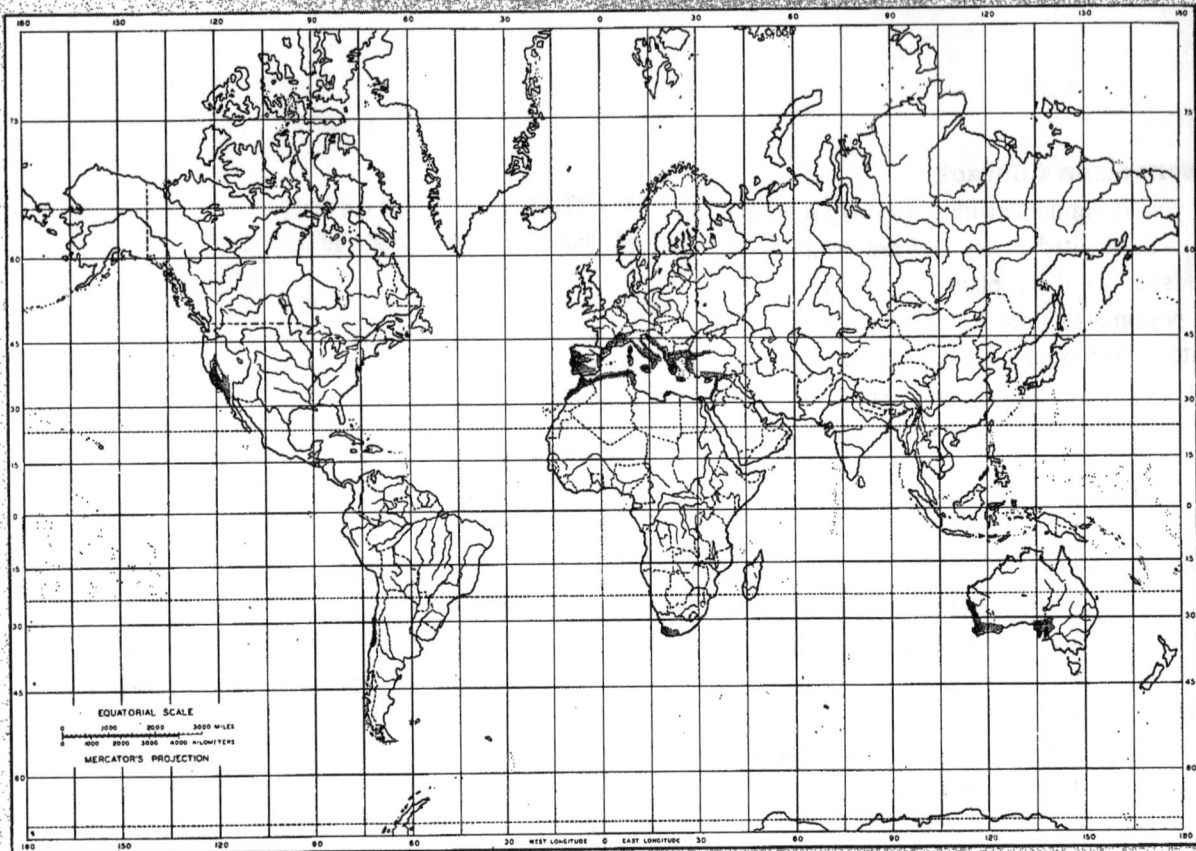

TEMPERATE EVERGREEN SCRUB FOREST

The temperature evergreen scrub forest exists in areas with mild winter temperatures, winter rain, and prolonged summer drought (winter frost is rare). The plants are mostly evergreen shrubs and small trees with hard, thick, leathery leaves.

The total land area covered by the temperate evergreen scrub forest is small in comparison to other vegetation types. The development of the evergreen scrub is mainly near coastal areas. These areas are:

a. Europe — countries bordering the Mediterranean Sea. In Turkey, especially along the Black Sea area, this type is called "machee."

b. Africa — southwestern extremity (essentially the Cape Colony).

c. South America — central Chile.

d. Australia — south and southwestern parts.

e. North America — coastal districts of California, where it is called chaparral.

The vegetation of the temperate scrub is similar in aspect wherever it occurs, although the kinds of plants are different in each geographical area.

The evergreen scrub forest consists of densely packed vegetation, an almost impenetrable growth of shrubs with small, thick, leathery evergreen leaves, measuring 2 to 4 inches. The shrubs are sometimes waist high and often head high, which makes passing through them practically impossible. The branches are tough, wiry, and difficult to bend. Trees are usually very much scattered, except where they occur in groves near a stream. Usually both trees and shrubs have undivided leaves. Grasses and brightly colored spring-flowering bulbs and other flowers may also be found.

The survivor will find relatively few kinds of edible plant foods within the evergreen scrub forest. During the growing season, usually only the spring months, the following kinds of plant foods could be expected to be available.

a. Seeds and grains (from grasses).

b. Tubers.

c. Rootstalks.

d. Bulbs.

e. Roots.

f. Shoots (potherbs).

g. Fruits (dessert) (from the flowering shrubs).

h. Seed pods.

Evergreen scrub forest, Southwest Australia

© Vegetationsbilder

Island of Crete

© Vegetationsbilder

Machee on Corsica

© Vegetationsbilder

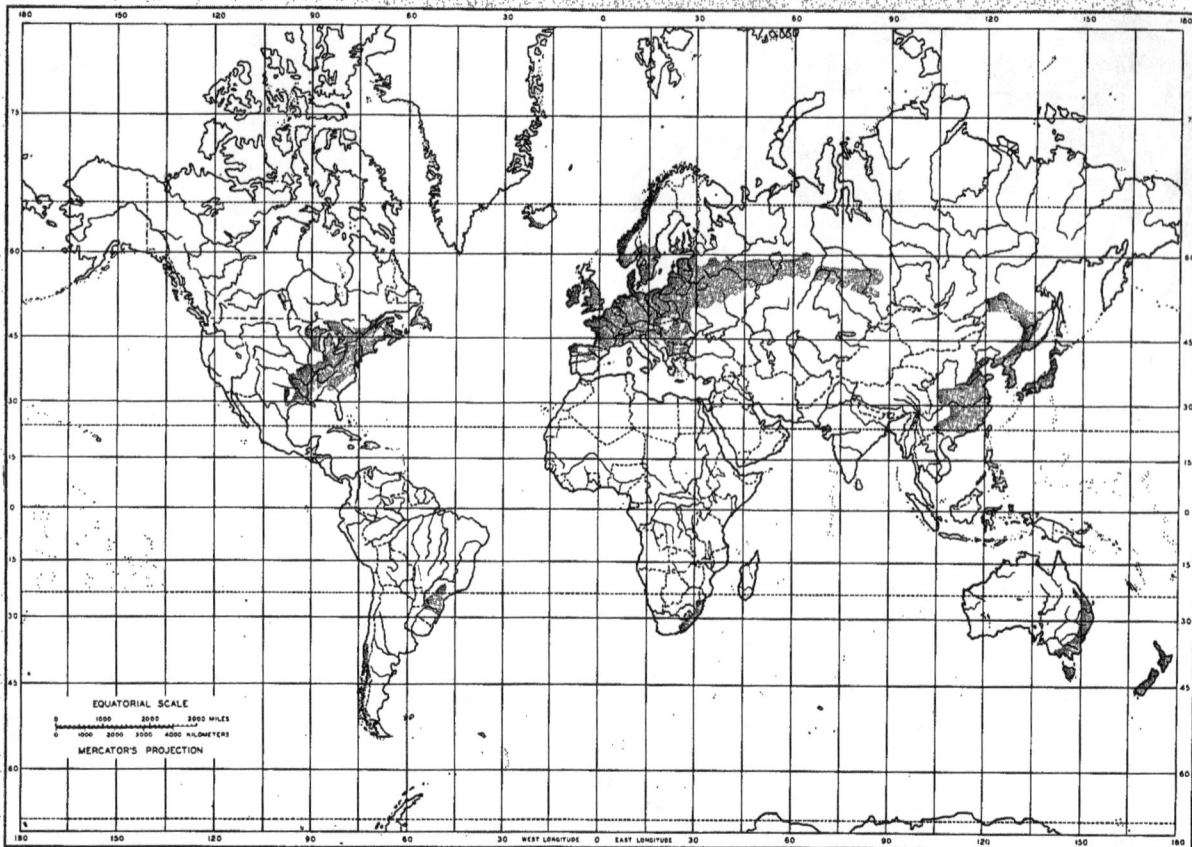

HARDWOOD (SEASONAL) AND MIXED HARDWOOD-CONIFEROUS FOREST

The hardwood (broad-leaved) and mixed hardwood-coniferous forest manifests the following characteristics.

a. Warm summer with rain, winters cold and drier. Drought periods of short duration.

b. Only three stories of vegetation (trees, shrubs, herbs).

c. Broadleaf trees without leaves in winter.

d. Mature trees uniform in height.

e. Unimpeded view into interior of forest.

f. Few herbs, ferns, mosses in summer, but abundance of edible fungi in spring and autumn on forest floor.

g. Trunks of trees covered with thick-fissured dark-colored bark.

h. Resting buds inclosed in hard scaly protecting leaves frequently covered with gum or resin.

i. For the most part, leaves are thin and delicate, rarely thick and leathery like those of tropical rain forest trees.

The hardwood and mixed hardwood-conif-erous forest that predominates over much of eastern United States is typical of this vegetation type. The hardwood forest is wholly temperate in character. Even at the height of summer, the appearance is very different from the broadleaved evergreen coniferous forest farther north. By contrast with the tropical evergreen forest with its richly shaded but chiefly dark glossy green canopy, the broad-leaved temperate forest extends in a uniformly bright green expanse. (For comparison, see discussion on tropical rain forest, p. 252).

The temperate hardwood (seasonal) and mixed hardwood-coniferous (pine-spruce-fir) forest vegetation type occupies extensive areas in several parts of the world. These areas include:

a. North America — eastern United States.

b. South America — southern Chile, southeastern Brazil.

c. Europe — western and northern Europe, southern Scandanavia, southeastern Europe (Balkans).

54

d. Asia — southcentral Siberia, southeastern Siberia and part of Manchuria, Korea (throughout), Japan (throughout), China (throughout except the extreme south and extreme north).

e. Oceania — New Zealand.

The edible food plants in this vegetation zone are numerous, and a long array of edible kinds will be available. Some of the plants are illustrated in the following paragraphs.

© Vegetationsbilder

Brazilian pine forest, Southern Brazil

Hardwood and coniferous forest, Yunnan, China

© Vegetationsbilder

© Vegetationsbilder

Kamtschatka peninsula, Angelica meadow

Kamtschatka peninsula, Birch forest

© Vegetationsbilder

© Vegetationsbilder

Asia Minor and South-
East Russia

© Vegetationsbilder

Northeastern Burma, Western
Yunnan, China, Walnut forest

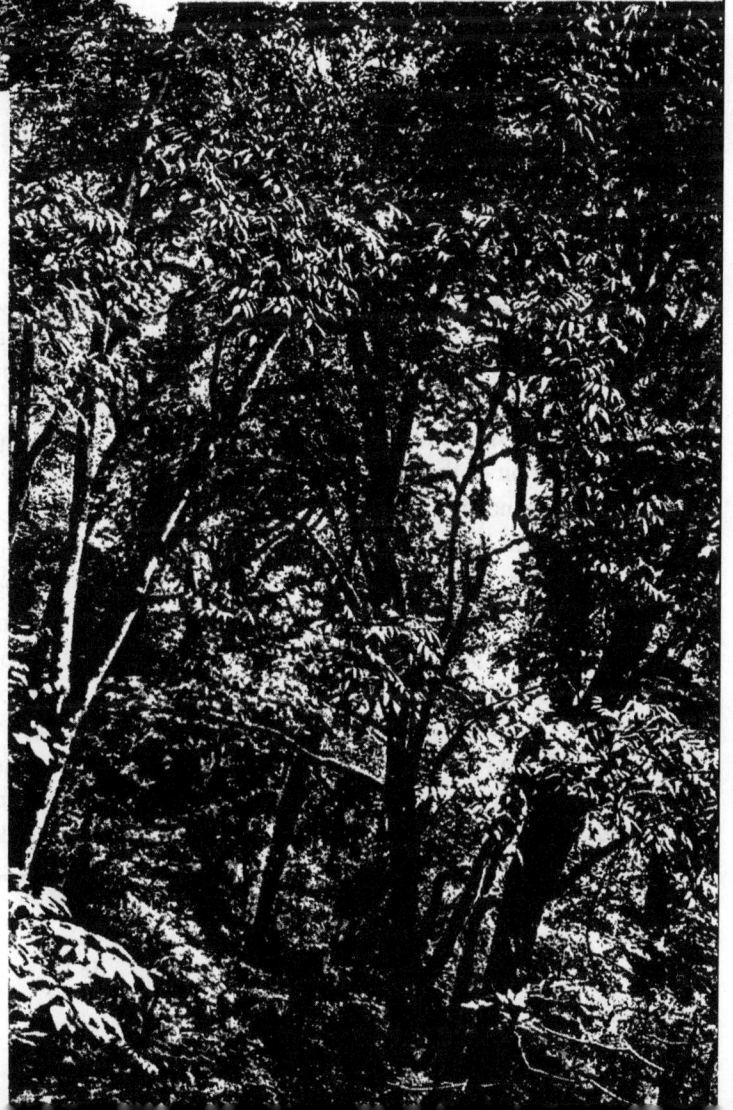

EDIBLE POLLEN

YOUNG, EDIBLE
LEAF SHOOT

Ground
level

EDIBLE ROOTSTALK

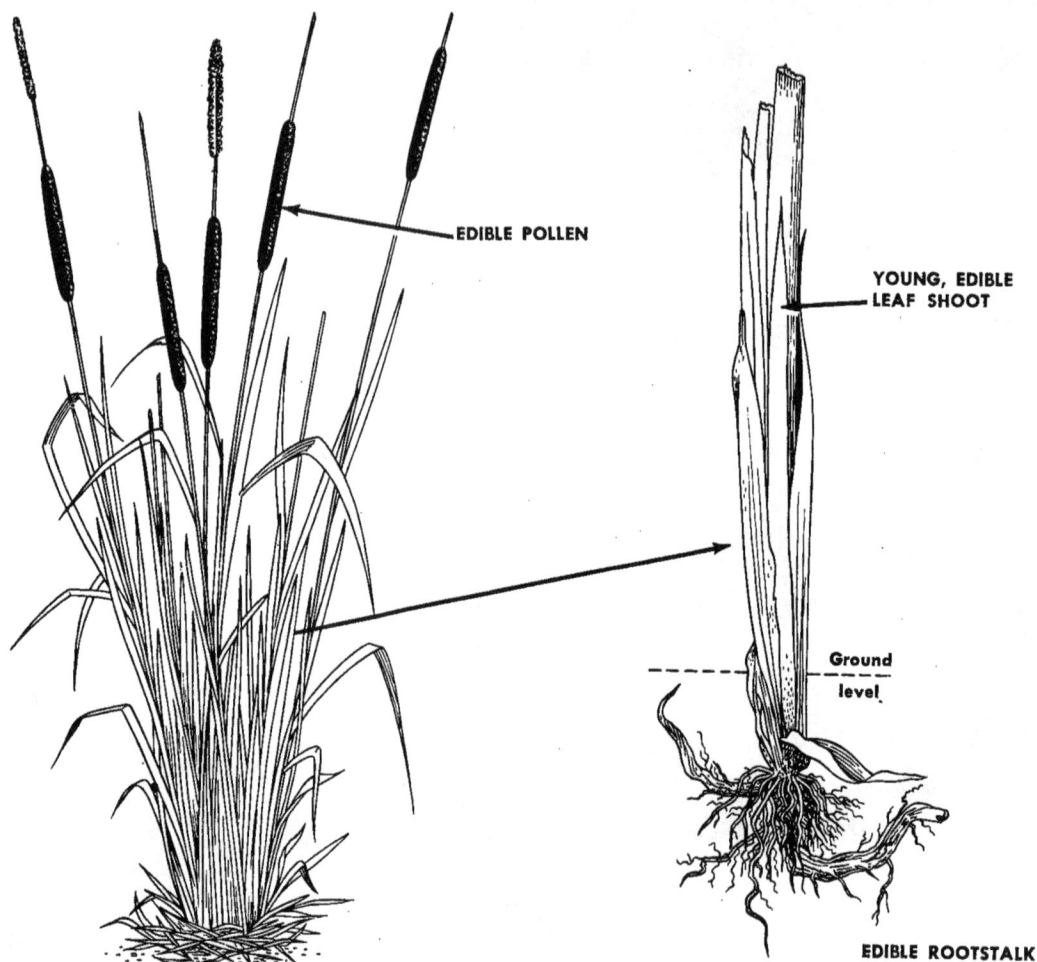

Cattail, or Elephant Grass (Typha)

WHERE FOUND. (Regions 1, 2, 6, 7, 9, 12.) The cattail is worldwide in distribution, with the exception of the tundra and forested regions of the far north. The cattail is a marshland plant which is found over large areas along lakes, ponds, and the backwaters of rivers.

APPEARANCE. Tall plants, 6-15 feet tall with erect, stiff, tapelike, pale-green leaves 1/4-1 inch broad. Rootstalk creeping and branching, 1/2 to 1-inch thick. Flowers in dense terminal spikes, the lower part of the spike at first green, finally brown and producing "cotton" (fluffy seeds); the topmost flowering spike is yellow, and sheds edible pollen.

WHAT TO EAT. The young growing shoots are succulent and nutritious when boiled like asparagus. The rootstalks produce the most nutritious part of the cattail; these contain up to 46% starch and 11% sugar. The best time for collecting these underground parts is late in the fall and through the winter to early spring. At this time the storage organs have the most food value.

To prepare the rootstalks for food, peel off the outer covering and grate the white inner part. This may be eaten boiled or raw.

The yellow pollen from the flowers can be mixed with water into small cakes and steamed as a kind of bread.

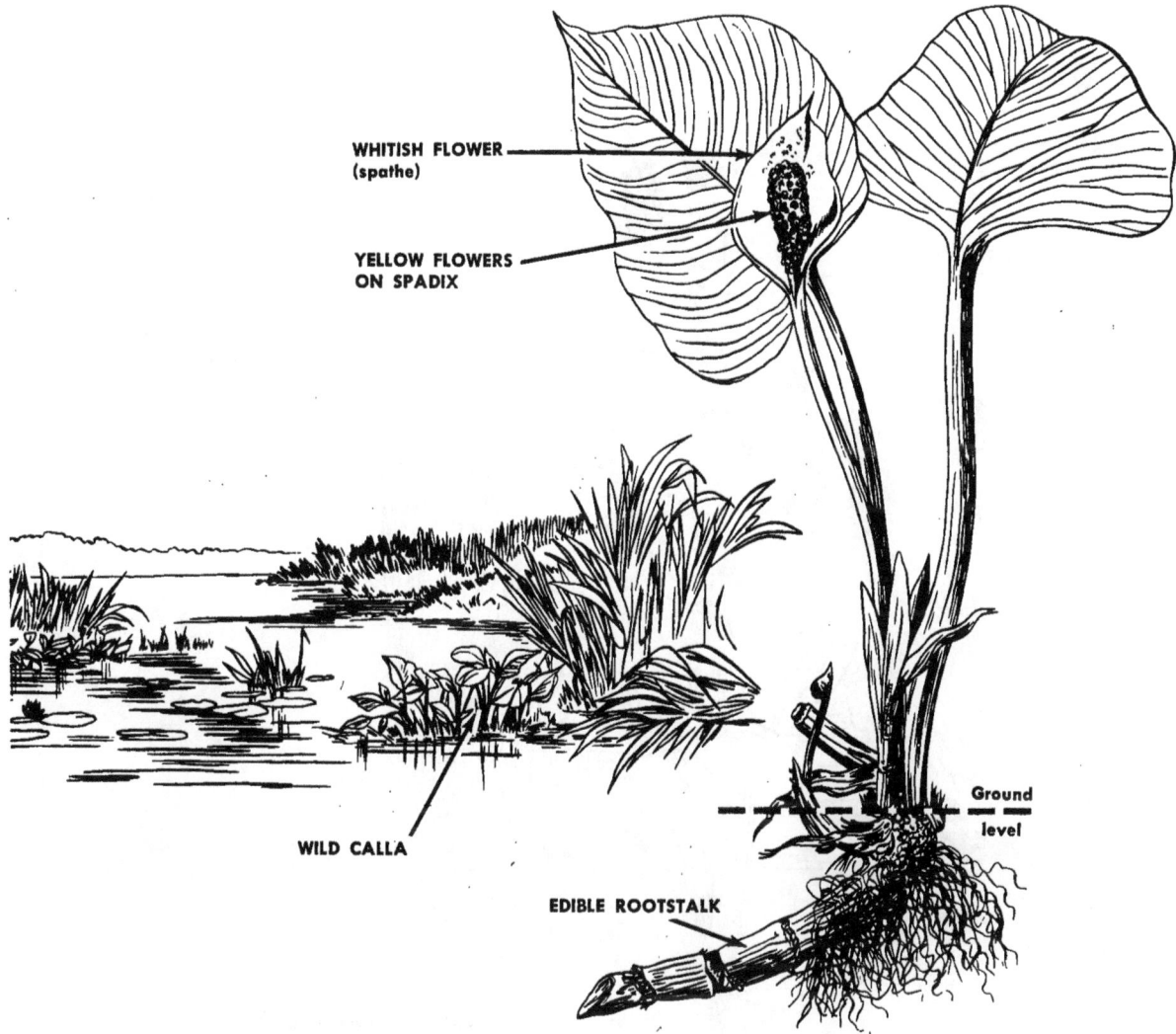

WHITISH FLOWER (spathe)

YELLOW FLOWERS ON SPADIX

WILD CALLA

EDIBLE ROOTSTALK

Ground level

Wild Calla, Water Arum (Calla palustris)

WHERE FOUND. (Regions 6, 7, 9.) The wild calla occurs most frequently around fresh water lakes, ponds, and along streams where the plants are partly submerged in a few inches of water. The wild calla is often abundant in such places in central and northern Europe and northern Asia. It also occurs in northeastern North America.

APPEARANCE. The wild calla is an herbaceous plant with heart-shaped leaves on long stalks up to a foot long. The flowers resemble somewhat the cultivated calla lily but are smaller.

WHAT TO EAT. Like most members of the calla lily family, the plant parts are filled with acrid crystals, making these parts unpalatable until the bitterness is dissipated by drying or cooking. The roots of the wild calla contain this bitter property which may be eliminated by cooking the roots. The cooked starchy roots are pulverized and dried into a crude flour or farina. This is cooked as a sort of porridge.

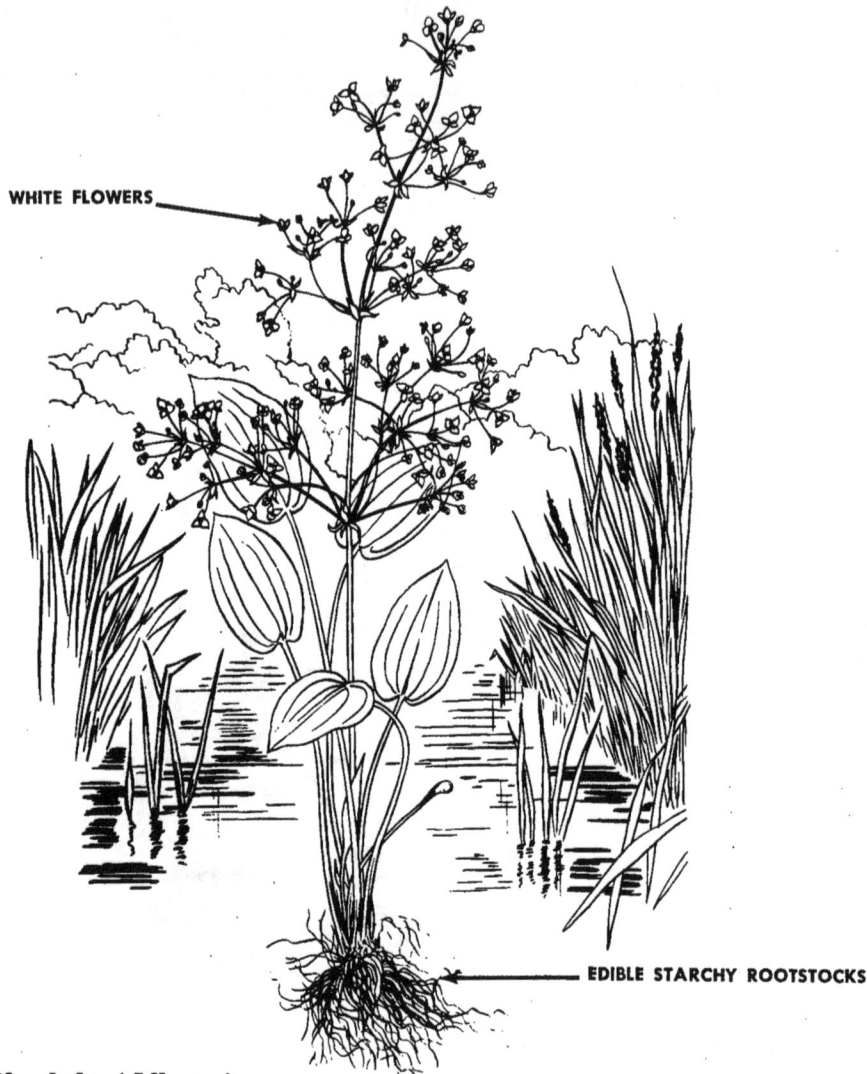

WHITE FLOWERS

EDIBLE STARCHY ROOTSTOCKS

Water Plantain (Alisma)

WHERE FOUND. (Regions 4, 6, 7, 8.) The water plantain occurs most frequently around fresh water lakes, ponds, and streams, where the plants are often partly submerged in a few inches of water. The water plantain is often abundant in marshy places throughout the North Temperate Zone, especially in the cooler parts. It is not found on the tundra nor in the subtropics or Tropics.

APPEARANCE. The water plantain produces rosettes of long-stalked and smooth leaves often heart-shaped and with 3 to 9 parallel ribs. The plants produce white flowers.

WHAT TO EAT. The solid bulblike part below ground is the part to be eaten. These thickened underground parts are acrid to the taste but after thoroughly drying, they become palatable. They are starchy and should be cooked like potatoes.

BLUE FLOWERS

PULVERIZED ROOT MAKES
COFFEE SUBSTITUTE

SALAD
GREENS

COMMON ALONG
ROADSIDES

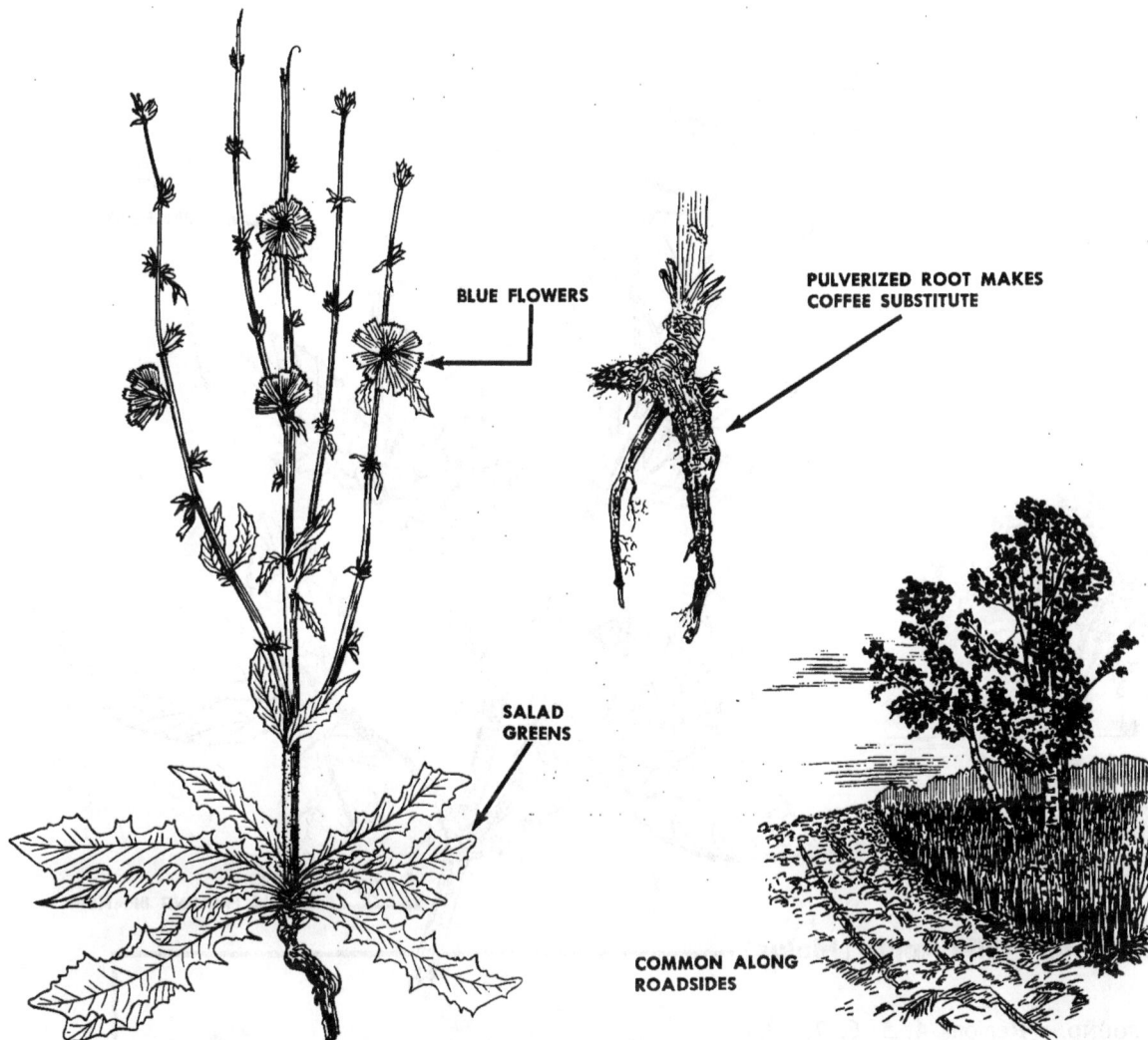

Wild Chicory (Cichorium intybus)

WHERE FOUND. (Regions 3, 4, 5, 6, 7, 8, 9, 10.) Wild chicory is a native of Europe and Asia, but it is now very generally distributed throughout the United States as a weed along roadsides and in fields. In Europe and Asia it is also a weed and is abundant in fields and pastures. It also occurs in Africa.

APPEARANCE. The leaves (which may be eaten) are clustered at ground level at the top of a strong underground carrotlike root. The leaves resemble the dandelion in shape but are thicker and rougher. The wiry stems rise 2 to 4 feet and are covered in summer with numerous bright blue heads of flowers again resembling the dandelion, except for color.

WHAT TO EAT. The chicory plant is often abundant in the areas where it occurs. The tender young leaves are eaten fresh as a salad. The roots of this plant have long been the source of chicory, which is the bitter constituent in adulterated coffee. The wild roots may be dug at any time of the year (but preferably in autumn) and pulverized. A brew of chicory root will make a somewhat bitter substitute for coffee.

MATURE FRUIT

10-30 FT. HIGH

FRUITING BRANCH

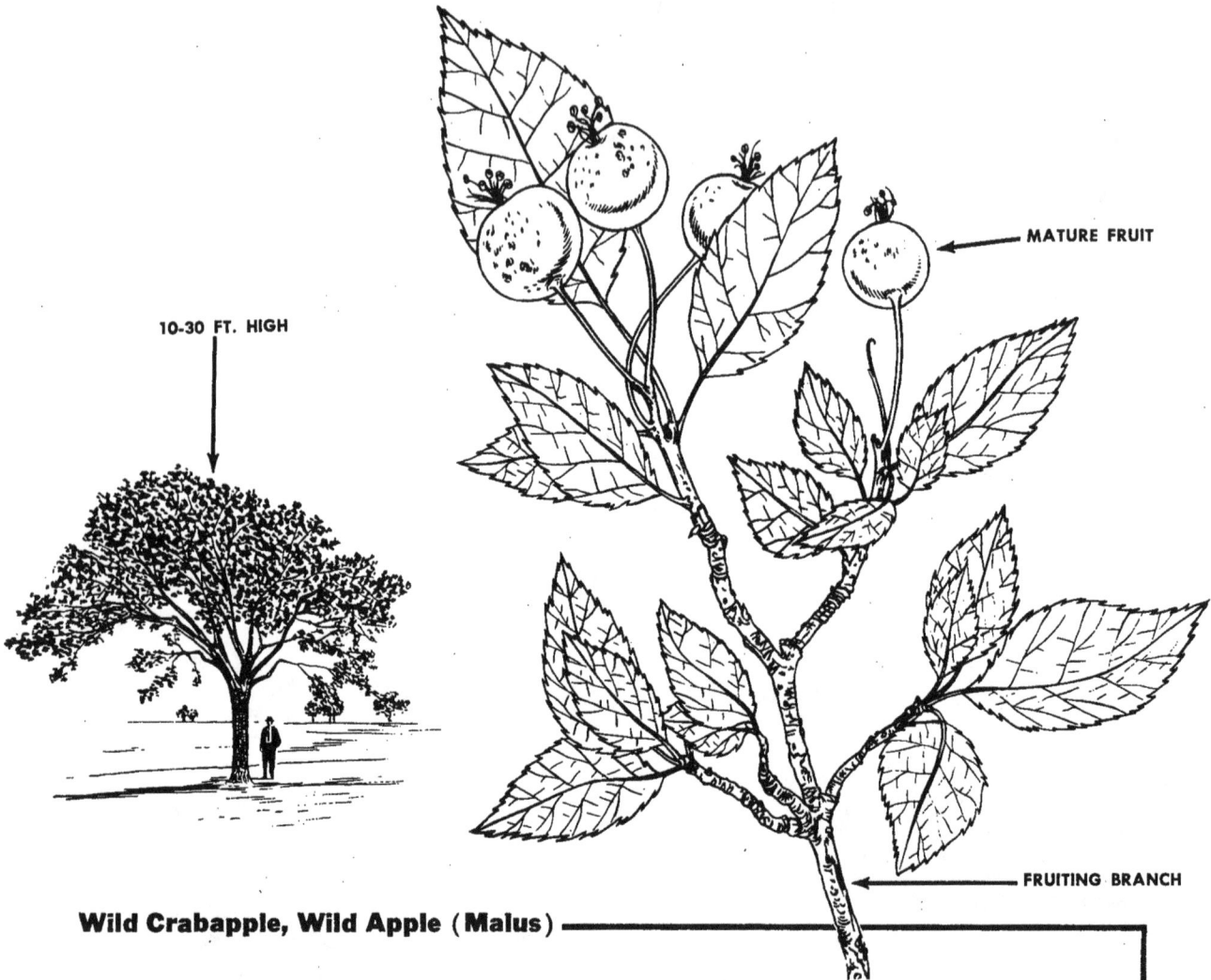

Wild Crabapple, Wild Apple (Malus)

WHERE FOUND. (Regions 4, 5, 6, 7, 12.) The common apple known in cultivation came from Europe. Many kinds of wild apples, all relatives of the common apple, occur in the United States, especially the eastern part, and a few kinds occur in western United States. Wild apples are common throughout the temperate parts of Asia and also in Europe. Wild apples are found in open woodlands, and rarely can they be found in densely forested regions. Most frequently they occur on the edge of woods or in fields.

APPEARANCE. Most wild apples look sufficiently like their tame relatives to be easily recognized by the survivor, whether it be in Turkey or in China. The size of wild apple varieties, of course, is considerably smaller than cultivated kinds. The largest kinds of wild apple usually never exceed 2 to 3 inches in diameter, and most often less.

WHAT TO EAT. Wild apples may be prepared in the same manner for eating as cultivated kinds; that is, they may be eaten fresh when ripe or else cooked. If it becomes necessary to store up food for some time, the apples can be cut into thin slices and dried.

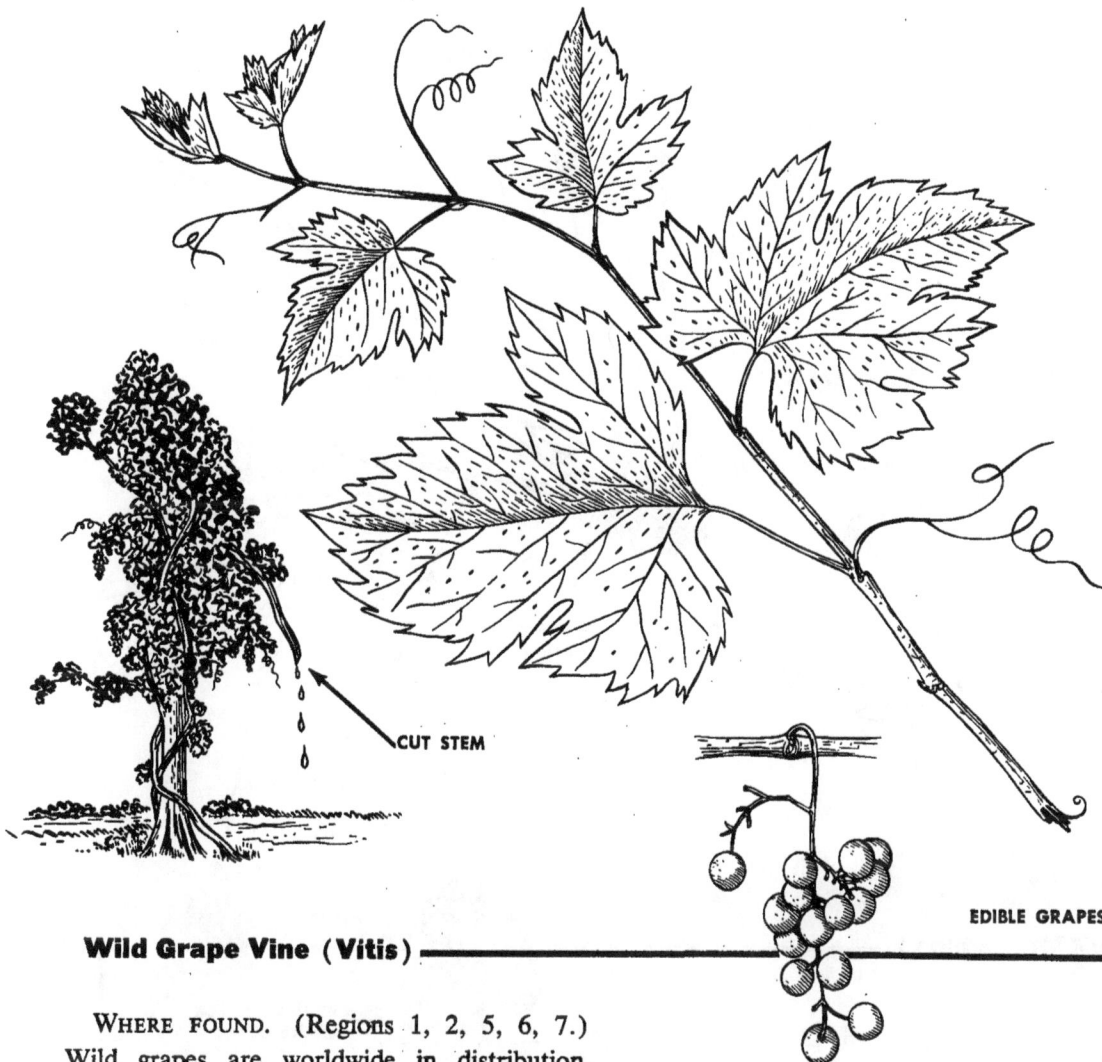

CUT STEM

EDIBLE GRAPES

Wild Grape Vine (Vitis)

WHERE FOUND. (Regions 1, 2, 5, 6, 7.) Wild grapes are worldwide in distribution, some kinds occur on deserts, others in temperate forests and others in tropical areas. Wild grapes are, of course, found commonly throughout eastern United States as well as in the southwestern desert areas. Most kinds are rampant climbers over other vegetation. The edge of forested areas would be the best site to look for wild grapes. Wild grapes also occur in Mexico. In the Old World, wild grapes occur from the Mediterranean region eastward through Asia, the East Indies, and to Australia. Africa also has several kinds of wild grape.

APPEARANCE. The grape vine climbs with the aid of tendrils. Most grape vines produce deeply lobed leaves similar to the cultivated grape. Wild grapes grow in pyramidal, hanging bunches and are black, blue to amber, or white in color when ripe.

WHAT TO EAT. The ripe grape is the portion eaten. Grapes are rich in natural sugars, and for this reason they are much sought after as a source of energy giving wild food. None are poisonous.

WATER FROM SEVERED GRAPEVINE STEMS. Cut off the vine at the bottom and place the hanging end above in a container. Make a slant-wise cut into the vine about 6 feet up on the hanging part, which allows contact with the air and a free flow of water below. As water diminishes in volume make additional slantwise cuts lower down.

LEAF VARIATION

FRUITING
BRANCH

20-40 FT. HIGH

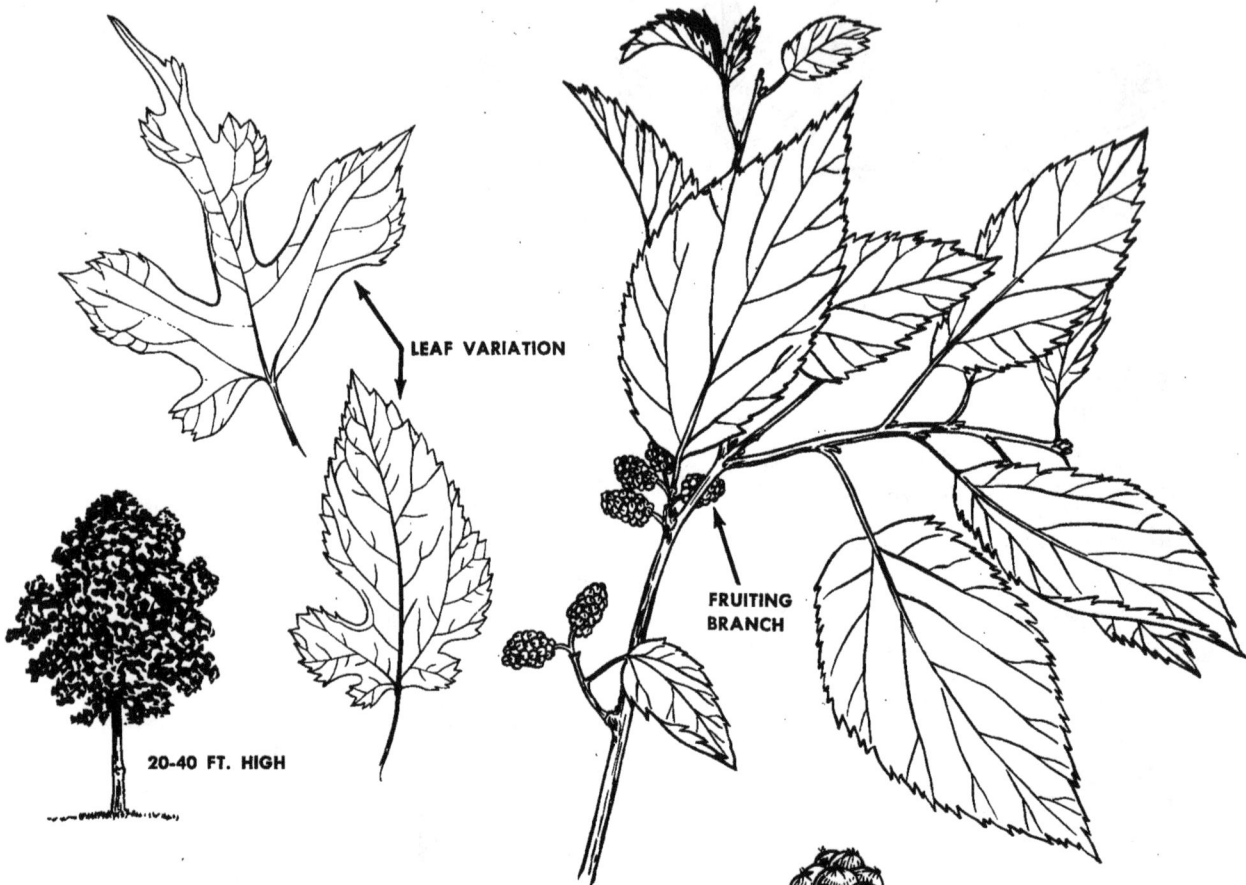

Mulberry (Morus alba)

REDDISH-BLACK
EDIBLE BERRY

WHERE FOUND. (Regions 1, 2, 6, 12.) Mulberry trees occur in North and South America, Europe, Asia and Africa. They are widely cultivated in Asia and from this course, the mulberry has spread widely. In the wild state, mulberry trees are found in forested areas, but the mulberry has weedy tendencies and as a result of this propensity mulberry trees might be found along roadsides and in abandoned fields in any of the countries in which it now occurs.

APPEARANCE. The white mulberry, as depicted in the illustration above, is typical of the most widely distributed of all the mulberries. The most characteristic feature of the mulberry is the fruit which looks like a blackberry. Mulberry trees often attain large proportions at maturity, varying from 20-60 feet tall and usually forming a wide spreading crown.

WHAT TO EAT. The edible fruits are about 1-2 inches long and of the thickness of the small finger, very sweet, and the trees are often inexhaustibly prolific. The mature fruit varies in color from red to black. A well-laden tree at fruiting time will support the appetites of several men for some days. The ripe fruit can be dried in the sun and eaten later on.

FLOATING LEAVES

UNDERWATER LEAVES

PODS UNDER WATER

EDIBLE SEED
INSIDE POD

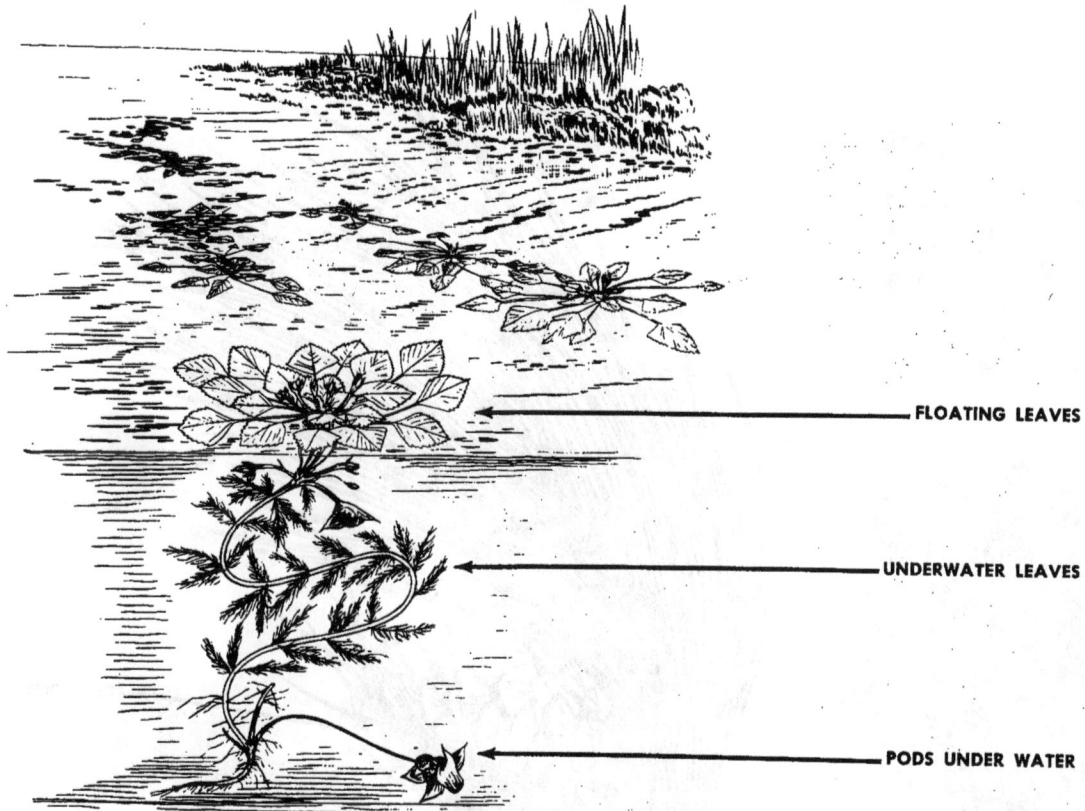

Trapa Nut, Water Chestnut (Trapa natans)

WHERE FOUND. (Regions 1, 2, 6.) The trapa nut is a native of Asia, but it has been spread very widely to many parts of the world, in both temperate and tropical areas, including North America, Africa, and Australia. It has been used in Europe for centuries as an article of food, especially in times of scarcity. The trapa nut is found as a free-floating plant which covers large areas wherever it occurs, mainly on rivers, lakes, and ponds in quiet water.

APPEARANCE. The trapa nut has two kinds of leaves. The submerged ones are root-like, long, slender, and feathery. The floating leaves form a rosette on the surface of the water, with coarsely toothed leaf blades and inflated leafstalks. The nuts borne underneath the water are an inch or two broad and usually armed with four strong spines which gives the appearance of a horned steer.

WHAT TO EAT. The seed inside the horny structure is extracted, and this is roasted, like chestnuts over hot embers of the fire, or else boiled. They are not as appetizing as some kinds of food, but they are nourishing.

PINE CONE

PINE NUTS

BRANCH

PINE CONE

EDIBLE PINE NUT

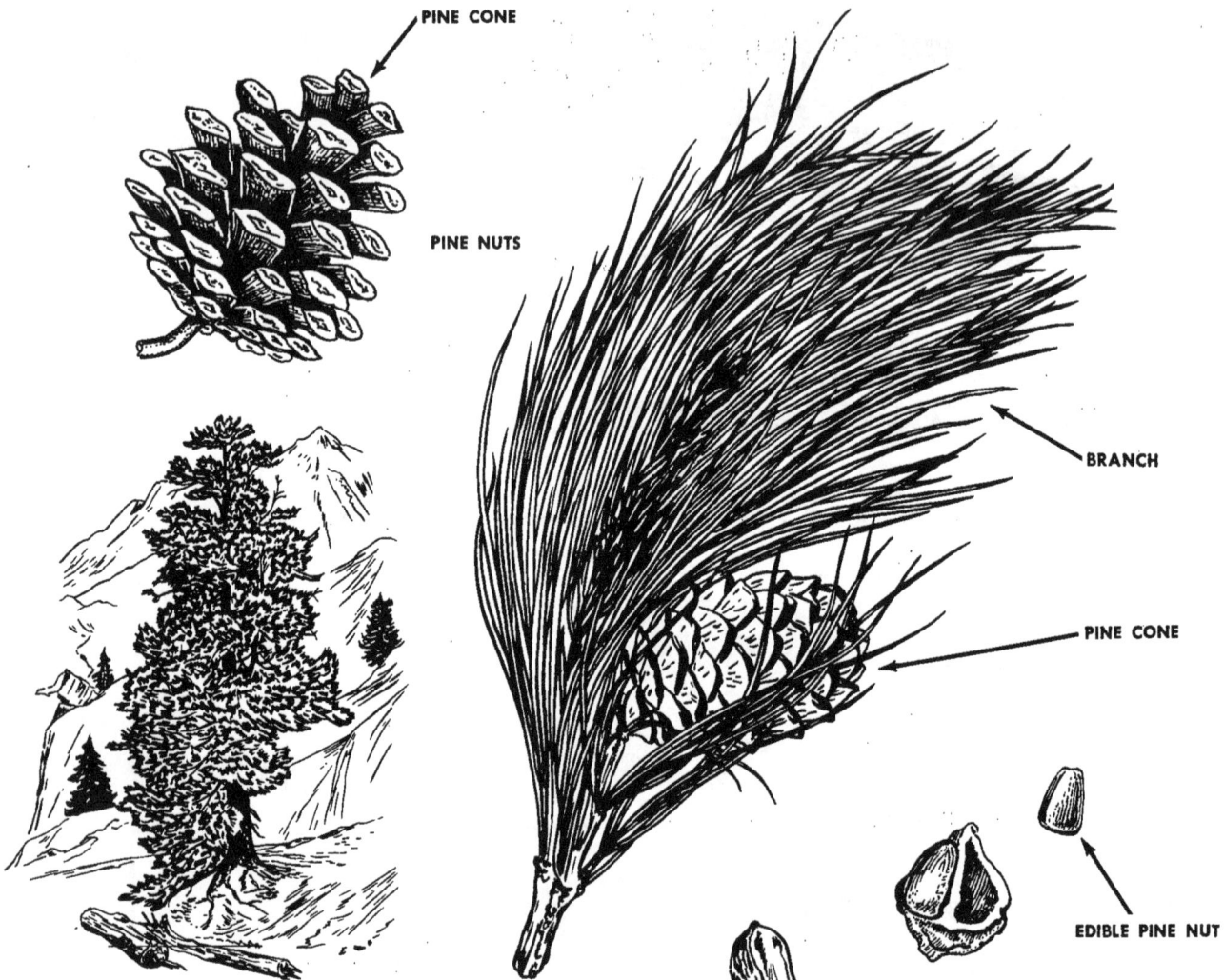

Pine Nuts (Pinus cembra)

PINE NUTS

WHERE FOUND. (Region 6, 7, 12.) Pines occur throughout the North Temperate Zone and frequently cover extensive areas in North America, Europe, Asia, and North Africa. Pines are common in the United States, both east and west. The Swiss stone pine, for example, is found widely in central Europe and across northern Siberia.

APPEARANCE. All species of pine are evergreen trees. The leaves or needles are produced in bunches or fascicles of from one to five. The edible seeds or nuts are produced in woody cones which hang either separately or in clusters, usually near the tips of the branches.

WHAT TO EAT. Edible pine nuts are found at the base of the cone scales. The nuts, when mature, will readily fall out of the ripe cone and these may be eaten as is or slightly roasted over hot embers. It is well known that the peasantry of Siberia have subsisted on pine nuts as their sole source of food in winter.

HUSK
SURROUNDING
NUT

NUT

EDIBLE NUT
(ENLARGED)

BEECHNUT

FOREST BEECHNUT
(Smooth, light bark)

LEAF

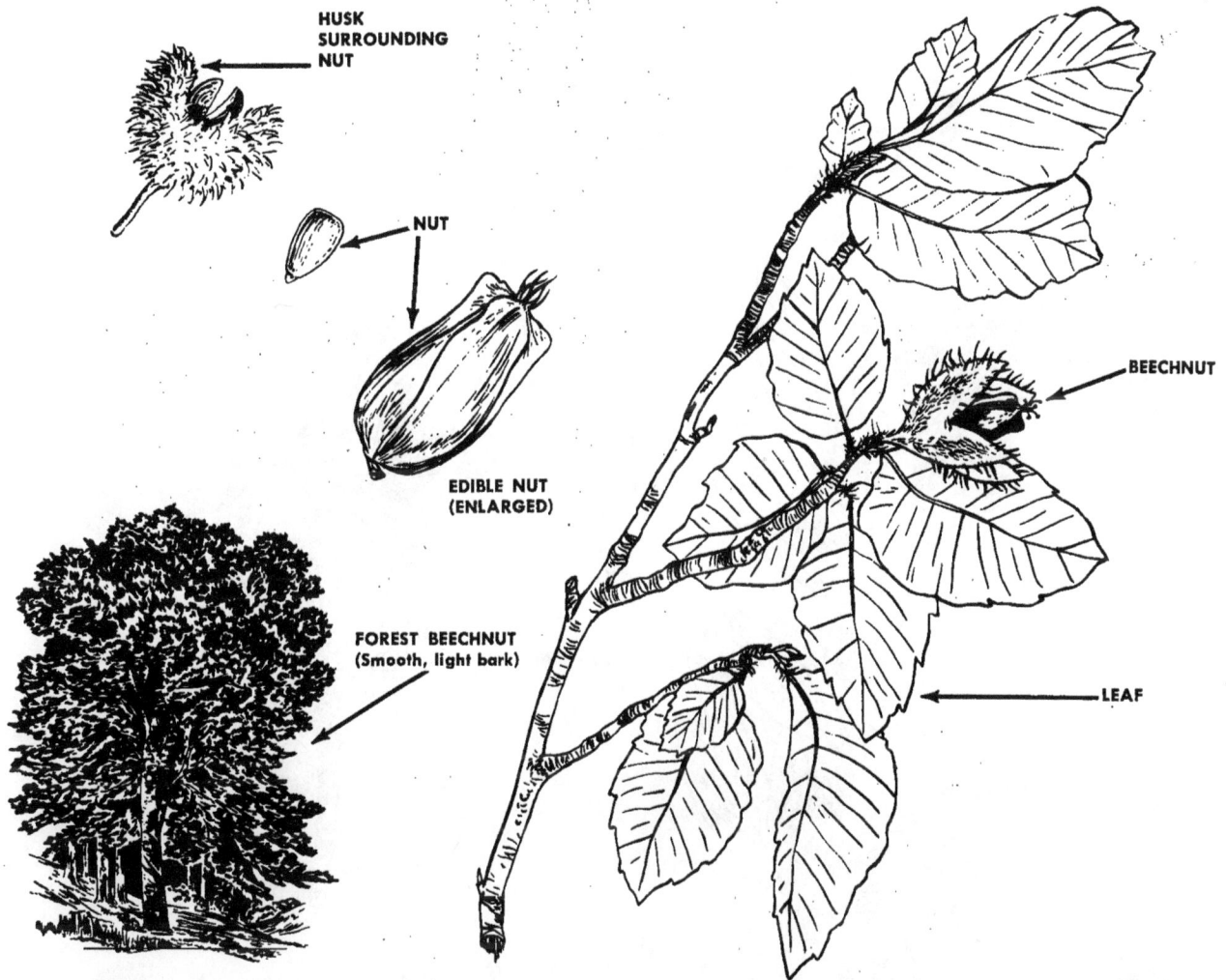

Beechnuts (Fagus)

WHERE FOUND. (Regions 6, 7, 12.) The beechnut tree is wild in eastern United States, Europe, Asia, and north Africa. The beechnut occurs in moist areas and is a tree of the forest. It is common throughout southeastern Europe and across temperate Asia. It does not occur in tropical or subarctic areas. Beech relatives occur in Chile, New Guinea, and New Zealand.

APPEARANCE. Beech trees are large (30-80 feet), forest trees of noble character, symmetrical form and have smooth, light-gray bark and clean, dark-green foliage. The character of the bark plus the clusters of prickly seed pods will clearly distinguish the beech tree in the field.

WHAT TO EAT. The mature beechnuts readily fall out of the husklike seed pods. These dark brown triangular nuts may be eaten by breaking the thin shell with the finger nail and removing the white, sweet kernel inside. Beechnuts are one of the most delicious of all wild nuts, and because of the high oil content of the kernels, they are considered a most useful survival food.

A secondary use of beechnuts is as a coffee substitute. They may be roasted so that the kernel becomes golden brown and quite hard. The kernel is then pulverized and, after boiling or steeping in hot water, a passable substitute for coffee is the result.

YOUNG ALMOND FRUIT

FLOWERING BRANCH

RIPE ALMONDS

EDIBLE NUTS

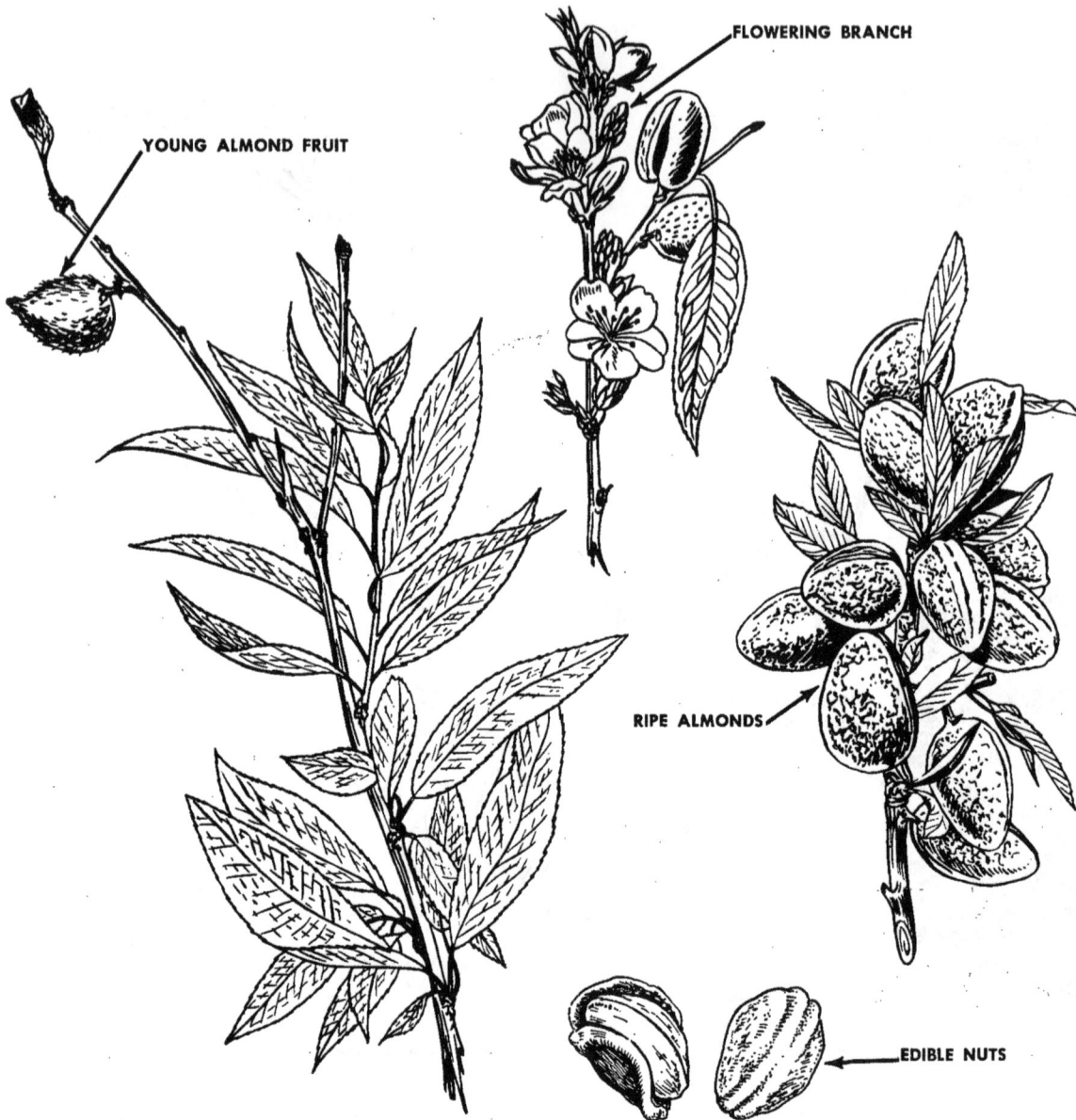

Almonds (Prunus amygdalus)

WHERE FOUND. (Regions 3, 5, 10.) The wild almond occurs in the semidesert areas of the Old World in southern Europe, the eastern Mediterranean, Iran, Arabia, China, Madeira, the Azores and the Canary Islands.

APPEARANCE. The almond is a tree sometimes growing to 40 feet. In appearance, it looks not unlike a peach tree. The fresh almond fruit resembles a gnarled unripe peach with its stone (the almond itself) covered with a thick, dry, wooly skin. The almond fruit is found in clusters over the tree.

WHAT TO EAT. The mature almond fruit splits open longitudinally down the side, exposing the ripe almond nut. The dry kernel may be easily obtained by simply cracking open the hard stone. Almond meats are rich in food value, like all nuts, and should be gathered in large quantities and shelled for further use as survival food. Subsistence for rather long periods could be maintained solely from almonds. They may be boiled, in which case the outer covering of the kernel comes off and only the white meat remains.

LARGE OAK

ACORNS

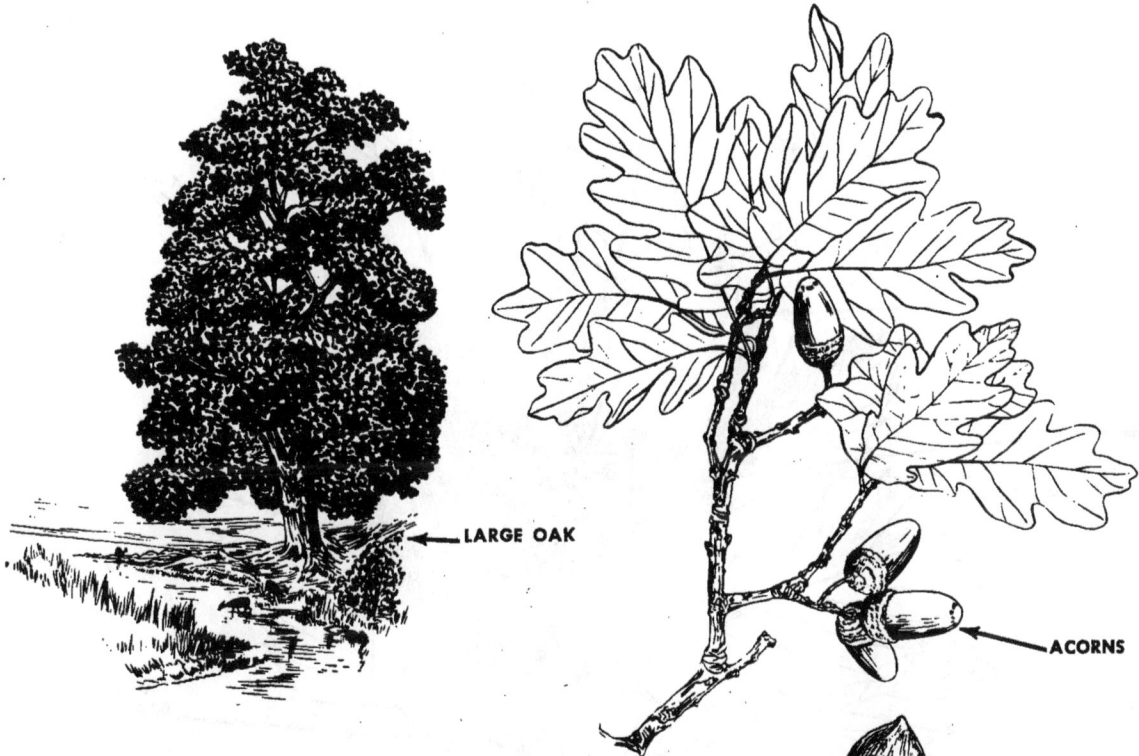

Acorns (Quercus robur)—English Oak

EDIBLE ACORNS

WHERE FOUND. (Regions 1, 2, 5, 6, 7, 12.) The example chosen represents a kind of oak that is widely distributed from the Mediterranean countries eastward well into western Asia. However, many kinds of oak are found in the North Temperate Zone. The English oak is typical of the oaks of the North Temperate Zone.

There are tropical oak species, too, but these almost always have undivided leaves, in contrast with the usually deep-lobed leaves of temperate kinds. The tropical oaks occur principally in southeastern Asia, and a few kinds occur in Central America. The oaks as a group are principally forest trees.

APPEARANCE. The English oak is a stately tree, often of rather gigantic proportions, up to 60 feet or more in height. Its acorns grow out of a cup, some being much longer than broad. However, in other kinds the mature acorn will be almost round. The leaves of most temperate zone oaks are deeply lobed like the English oak, whereas the leaves of most tropical kinds have smooth or only slightly notched margins.

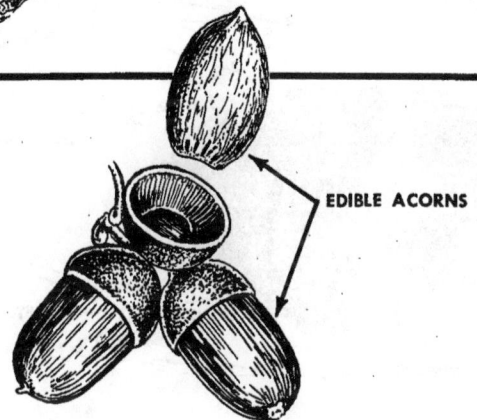

WHAT TO EAT. Acorns are unpalatable raw because of the bitter tannin properties of the kernel.

To rid the acorns of their bitter properties, boil them for 2 hours, then pour off water, and soak again in cold water with occasional changes. After about 3 to 4 days, grind the acorns into a paste. This paste may be made into a mush by mixing half and half with water and cooking it. Or, this paste may be spread out, dried, and kept for further use as flour.

MALE FLOWERS

Nuts develop here

FLOWERING
BRANCH

HUSK

60 FT. TALL

EDIBLE NUT

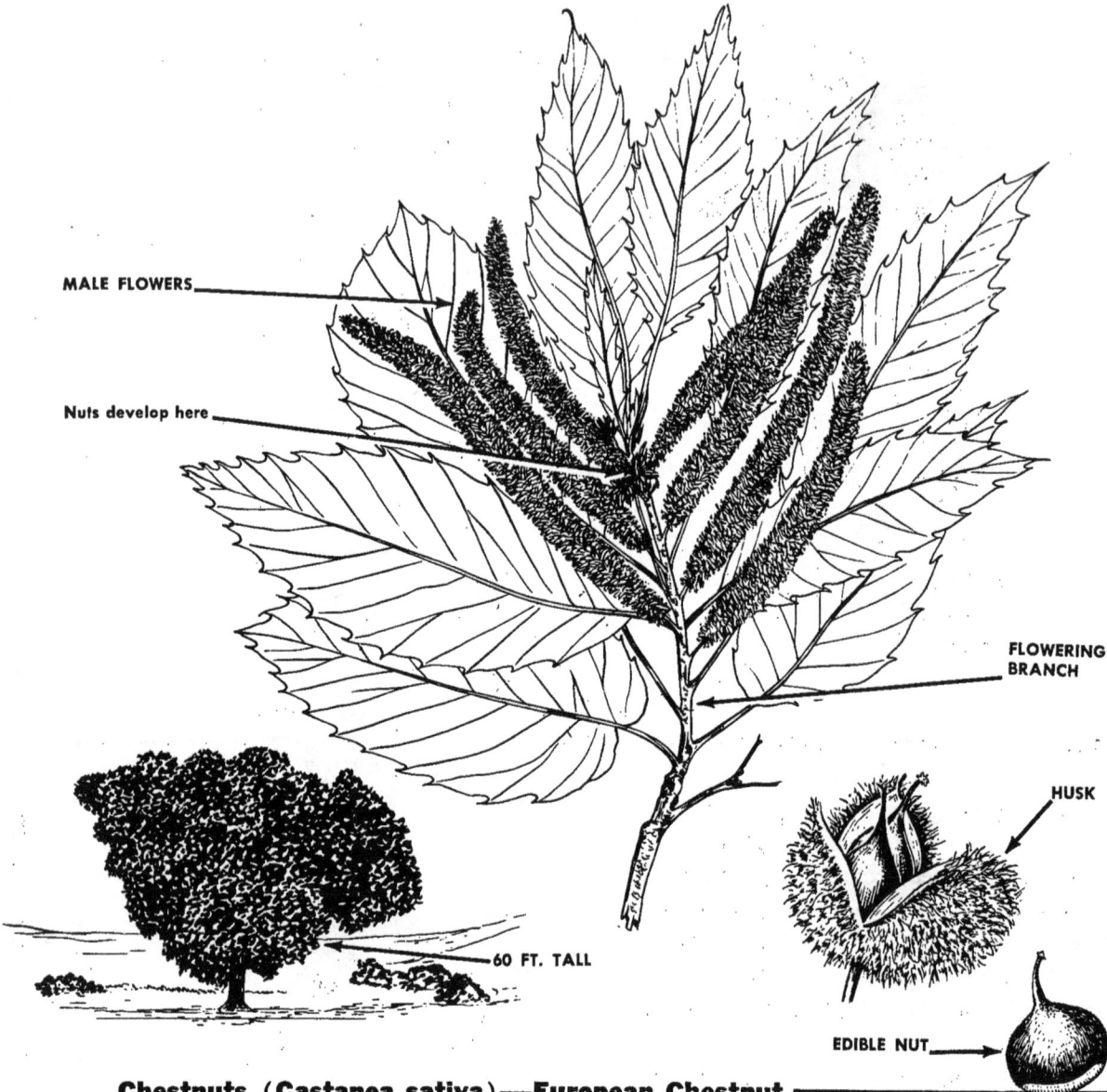

Chestnuts (Castanea sativa)—European Chestnut

WHERE FOUND. (Regions 2, 6, 7, 12.) Wild chestnuts occur over all of middle and south Europe and across middle Asia to China and Japan. They are relatively abundant along the edge of meadows and as a forest tree. The European chestnut is one of the commonest varieties and for this reason serves to illustrate this kind of nut. Wild chestnuts in Asia belong to related chestnut species, but the characteristics of the nut as depicted in the illustration above is typical of most other sorts.

APPEARANCE. The European chestnut is usually a large tree, up to 60 feet high.

WHAT TO EAT. Chestnuts are highly useful as survival food. Ripe nuts are usually picked in autumn, although unripe nuts picked while green may also be used for food. Perhaps the easiest method of preparation for the survivor is to roast the ripe nuts in embers. Cooked in this way, the roasted nuts are quite tasty, and large quantities may be eaten. Another method is to boil the kernels after removing the outside shell. After being boiled until fairly soft, the nuts may be mashed like potatoes.

HAZELNUTS

VARIETIES OF
EDIBLE NUTS

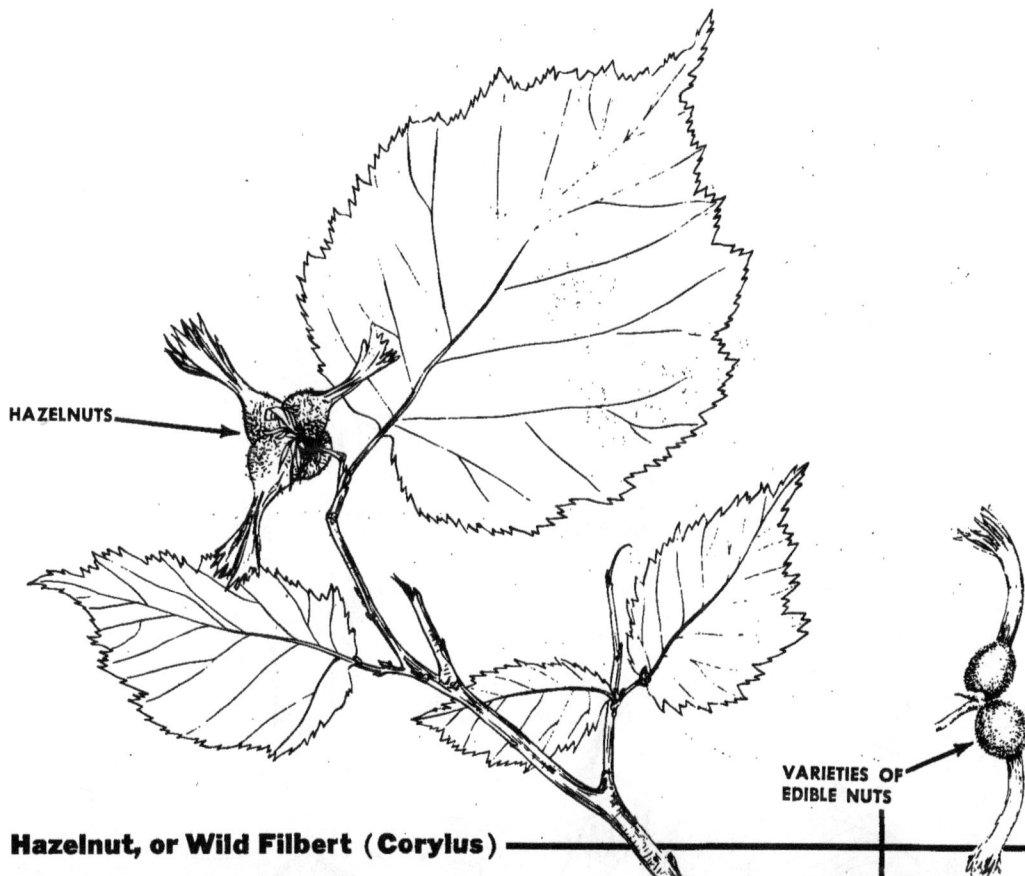

Hazelnut, or Wild Filbert (Corylus)

WHERE FOUND. (Regions 6, 7, 12.) Hazelnuts are found over wide areas in the United States, especially the eastern half of the country but also along the Pacific coast. These nuts are also found in Europe, where they are called filberts. In Asia the hazelnut is also common, especially in eastern Asia from the Himalayas to China and Japan. Hazelnuts grow mostly on bushes or large shrubs, although at least two kinds of hazelnuts grow on sizable trees, especially the varieties in Asia Minor and in China. The hazelnut usually occurs in the dense thickets along stream banks and open places. They are not plants of the dense forest.

APPEARANCE. The hazelnut is enveloped by a very bristly husk which is conspicuously contracted above the nut into a long neck. The different species vary in this respect as to size and shape. The nuts are borne on bushes 6 to 12 feet tall. One kind in Turkey and another in China are large trees.

WHAT TO EAT. Hazelnuts ripen in the autumn, at which time they can be cracked and the inside kernel eaten. The dried nut is extremely delicious, The high oil content gives this nut great value as survival food. In the unripe stage the kernel may be cracked out and eaten fresh.

WALNUTS

Walnut (Juglans regia) English Walnut

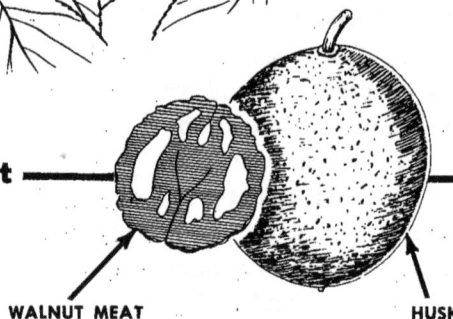

WALNUT MEAT   HUSK

WHERE FOUND. (Regions 5, 6, 12.) The English walnut in the wild state is found from southeastern Europe across Asia to China. It is abundant in the Himalayas. Several other species of walnut are found in China and Japan. The black walnut is common in the eastern United States.

APPEARANCE. Walnuts grow on trees of considerable proportions, often reaching 60 feet in height. The divided leaves are characteristic of all kinds of walnut species. The walnut itself is enclosed by a thick outer husk which must be removed to reach the hard inner shell of the nut.

WHAT TO EAT. The nut kernel ripens in the autumn and may be broken out in the ordinary way by cracking the shell. Walnut meats are highly nutritious because of the protein and oil content of the nut.

PINK, RED AND
YELLOW FLOWERS

FRUIT RIPE IN
AUTUMN

EDIBLE FRUIT
(Rose hip)

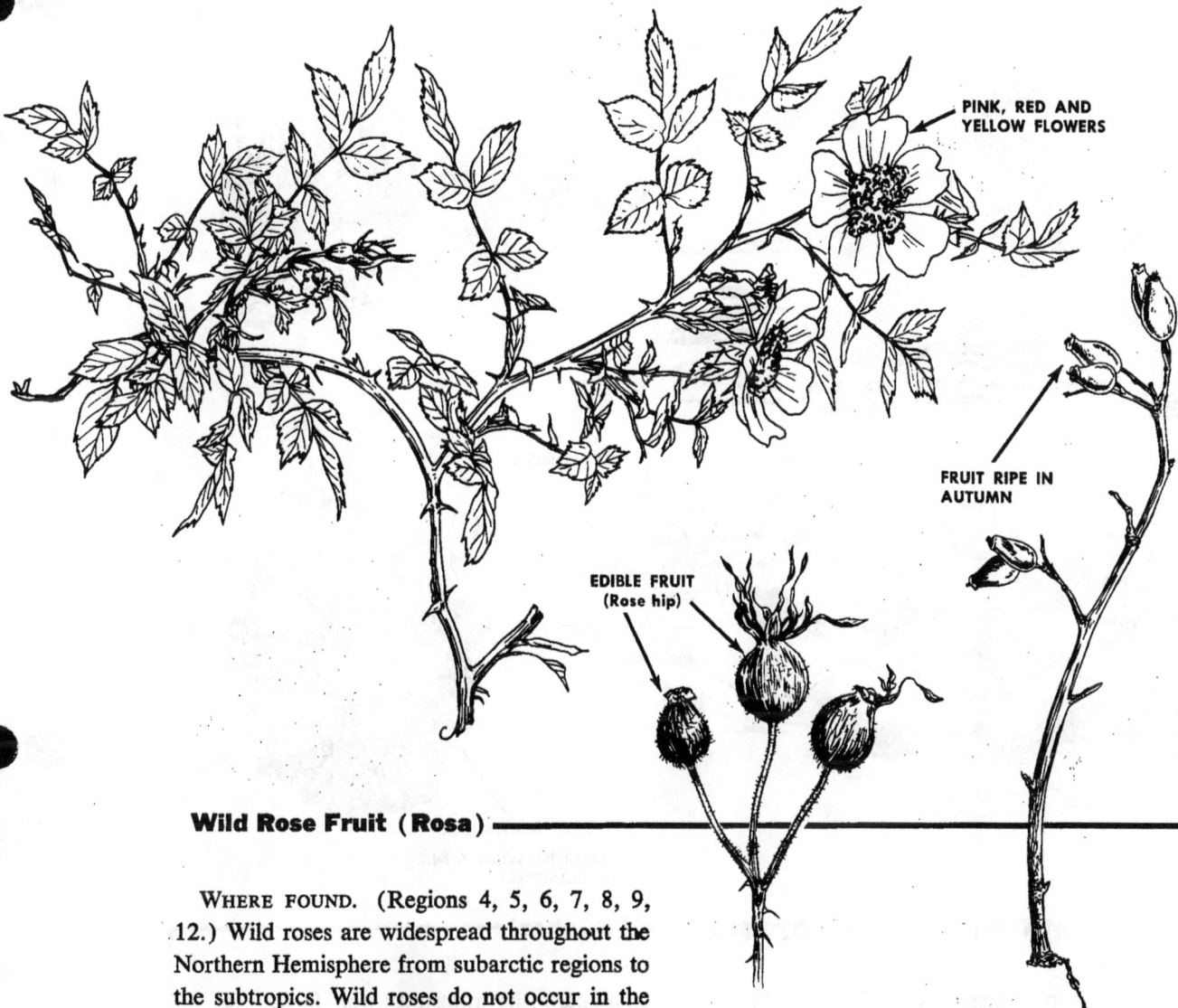

Wild Rose Fruit (Rosa)

WHERE FOUND. (Regions 4, 5, 6, 7, 8, 9, 12.) Wild roses are widespread throughout the Northern Hemisphere from subarctic regions to the subtropics. Wild roses do not occur in the wet, humid tropics, except in high mountain areas. Do not look for wild roses in the thickest patch of forest; most kinds occur on the edge of woods or in fields. Wild roses do not occur in the southern hemisphere.

APPEARANCE. Wild roses form low and arching shrubs up to 10 feet tall, or else they grow as extremely large and vigorous climbers. All wild roses have divided leaves similar to the cultivated rose. Their stems or canes are almost always thorny. The edible rose fruits are produced at the tips of branches in arching clusters. The fruit is usually red or orange, and rarely yellow, and is more or less bottle-shaped.

WHAT TO EAT. The ripe fruit is called the "rose hip." These ripen from late summer to autumn and should not be eaten until quite soft; they remain on the bush nearly all winter. Some sorts taste flat, but others will be quite sweet to the taste. The pulp only should be eaten. Rose hips are a very good source for vitamin A, and many kinds are good antiscorbutics (preventing scurvy).

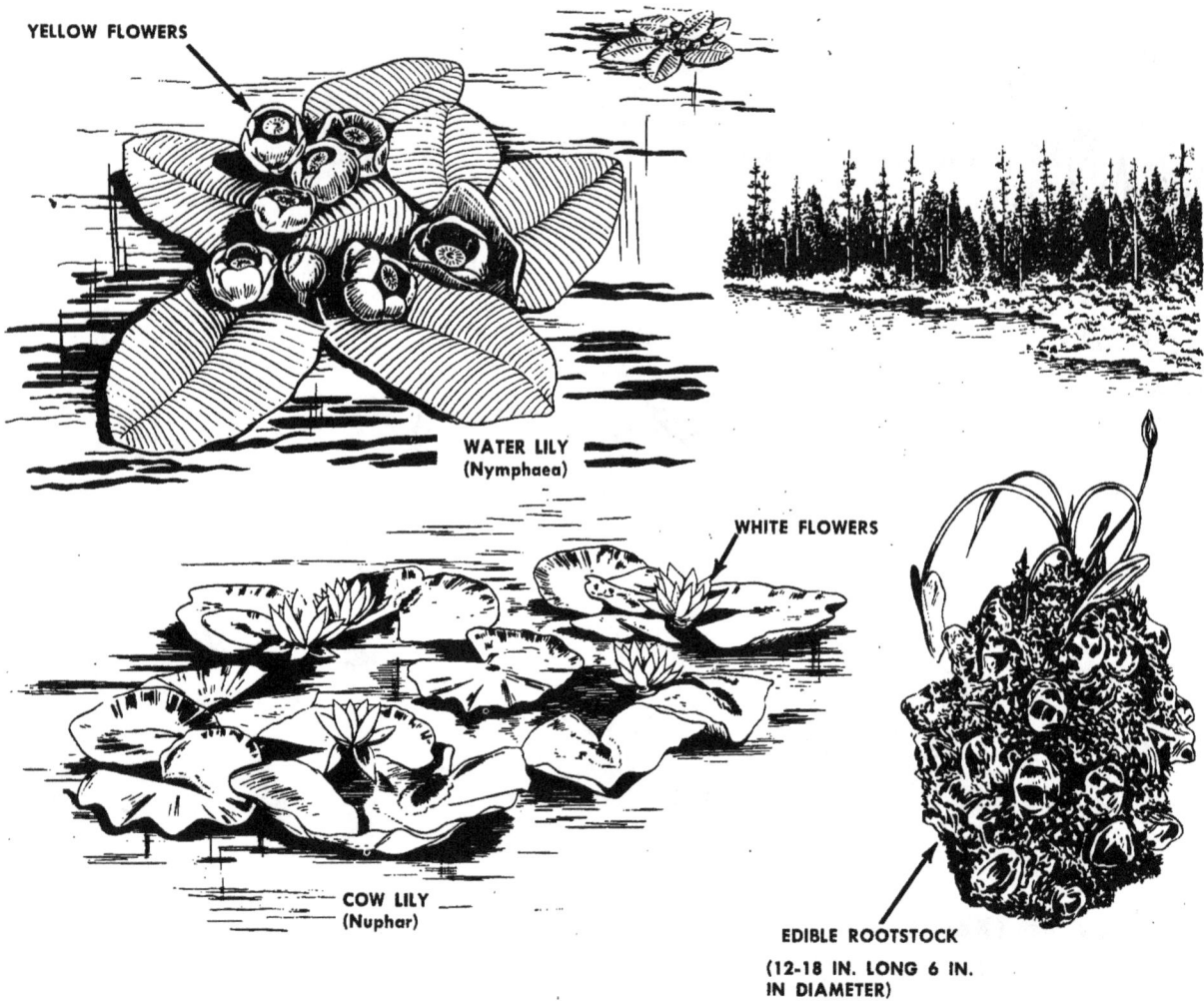

YELLOW FLOWERS

WATER LILY
(Nymphaea)

WHITE FLOWERS

COW LILY
(Nuphar)

EDIBLE ROOTSTOCK
(12-18 IN. LONG 6 IN.
IN DIAMETER)

Water Lily of Temperate Zone (Nymphaea and Nuphar)

WHERE FOUND. (Regions 6, 7, 9, 12.) The water lily is found mostly in lakes and ponds, more commonly in the moist parts of the North Temperate Zone in the United States and Canada, Europe, and middle to northern Asia, except the Arctic and subarctic parts. (See separate discussion of tropical water lilies as food plants, p. 270.)

APPEARANCE. Nymphaea has large white flowers which float *on* the surface of the water. Nuphar has smaller, cup-shaped yellow flowers which are elevated *above* the surface.

WHAT TO EAT. Water lily rootstalks are best collected in the fall for maximum food value, although they may be collected at any season the demand requires.

To prepare the rootstalks for food, peel away the brown corky rind, then slice the white inner portion thinly, dry, and then grind or pulverize. Following this, soak the meal in water, stirring from time to time, pour off the water carefully, and add new water 2 to 3 times to remove the strong taste. Dry the flour and remove the coarse pieces. A gruel may be prepared from this flour or it may be used as thickening in soups.

The seeds may also be used by letting the immense seed vessels dry in the sun, after which the seeds may be easily washed out. After being parched or browned over a fire, the seeds may later be ground into a nourishing meal.

ORANGE FLOWERS
(2-4 IN. DIAMETER)

BULBILS

BULB 4-8 IN.
BELOW GROUND

SCALY BULB
(2-3 IN. DIAMETER)

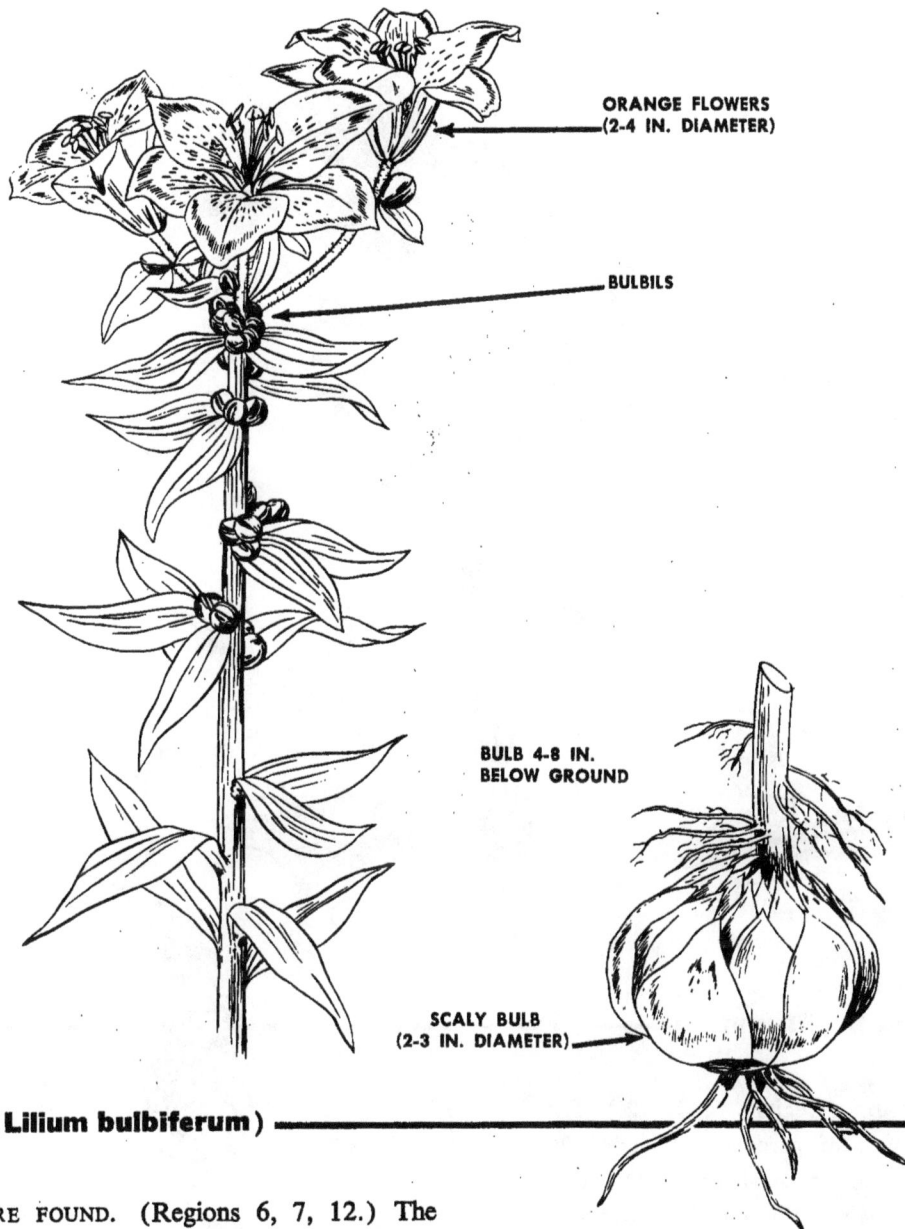

Lily (Lilium bulbiferum)

WHERE FOUND. (Regions 6, 7, 12.) The wild lily occurs over much of the northern hemisphere, particularly in the temperate parts. Lilies are usually found in wooded areas with high to moderate rainfall, from both western and eastern United States, Europe, and across Asia to China and Japan. A large number of lilies are found in Chinese-Himalayan area. The lily illustrated is a native of central Europe.

APPEARANCE. Lilies grow from scaly bulbs. The stems usually rise to several feet in height. The flowers are showy, ranging from white, red, pink to brownish.

WHAT TO EAT. The bulbs are scaly, white, and full of edible starch. They may be eaten cooked or uncooked.

EDIBLE
STEMS

WHITE TO PINKISH
FLOWERS

3-10 FT. TALL

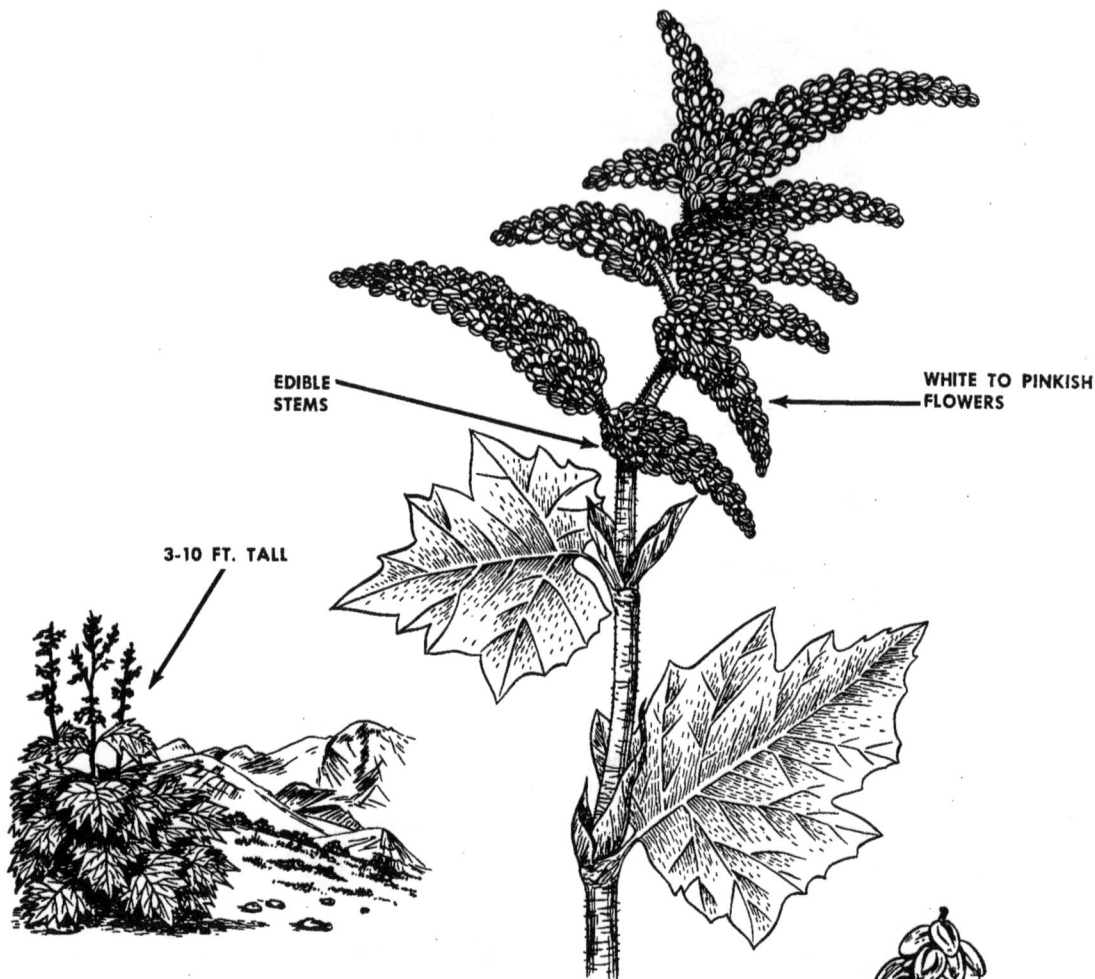

Wild Rhubarb (Rheum)

WHERE FOUND. (Regions 6, 7, 12.) The cultivated rhubarb of gardens has about 20 wild relatives which occur from southeastern Europe to Asia Minor through the mountainous regions of central Asia to China. The wild rhubarbs grow mainly in open places, borders of woods, along streams, and on mountain slopes.

APPEARANCE. The large leaves, sometimes nearly 3 feet long and as wide, arise mainly from the base on long stout stalks, most of which are edible. The plants often assume a handsome appearance because of the large leaves. The flowering stalks rise above the large leaves, and while in flower the plants seem to be covered by large white plumes.

WHAT TO EAT. Like the common cultivated rhubarb, the stems of the wild sorts may be eaten as a vegetable. Some kinds will no doubt be strong and bitter, but this condition can be alleviated by repeated boilings in water.

DEEP PINK FLOWERS

3 FT. TALL

EDIBLE ROOTSTOCKS

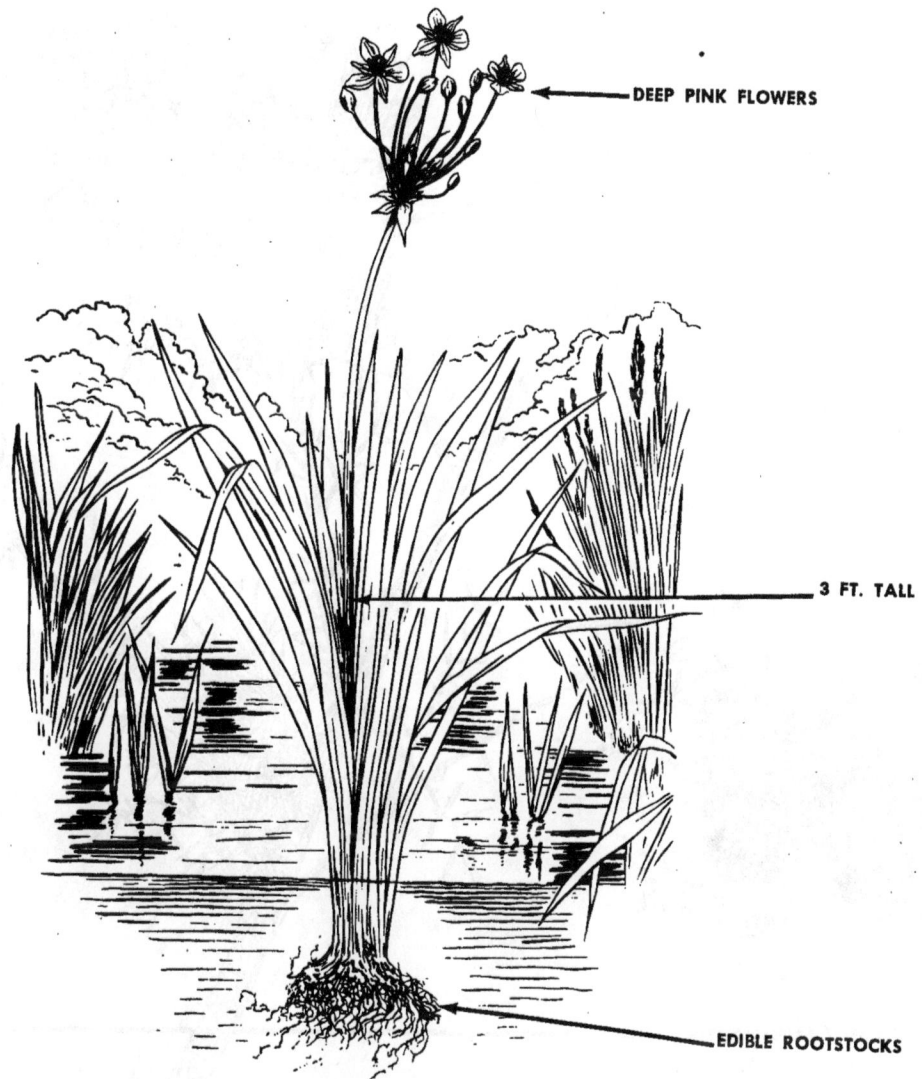

Flowering Rush (Butomus umbellatus)

WHERE FOUND. (Regions 6, 7, 12.) The flowering rush occurs along river banks, margins of lakes and ponds, and marshy meadows over much of Europe and temperate Asia. It occurs throughout much of Russia and temperate Siberia.

APPEARANCE. The plants usually grow submerged in a few inches in water. The mature plants are 3 or more feet high with loose clusters of showy rose-colored and green flowers. The edible underground rootstalk is thick and fleshy and has many grainlike and easily broken off tubers late in the fall.

WHAT TO EAT. The underground rootstalks are full of edible starch. These rootstalks should be dug, peeled, and cooked in the same way as potatoes. Another method used extensively by the people of northern Asia is to roast these rootstalks, after which the outer skin is peeled and the inner starchy part eaten.

EDIBLE PULP IN BERRIES

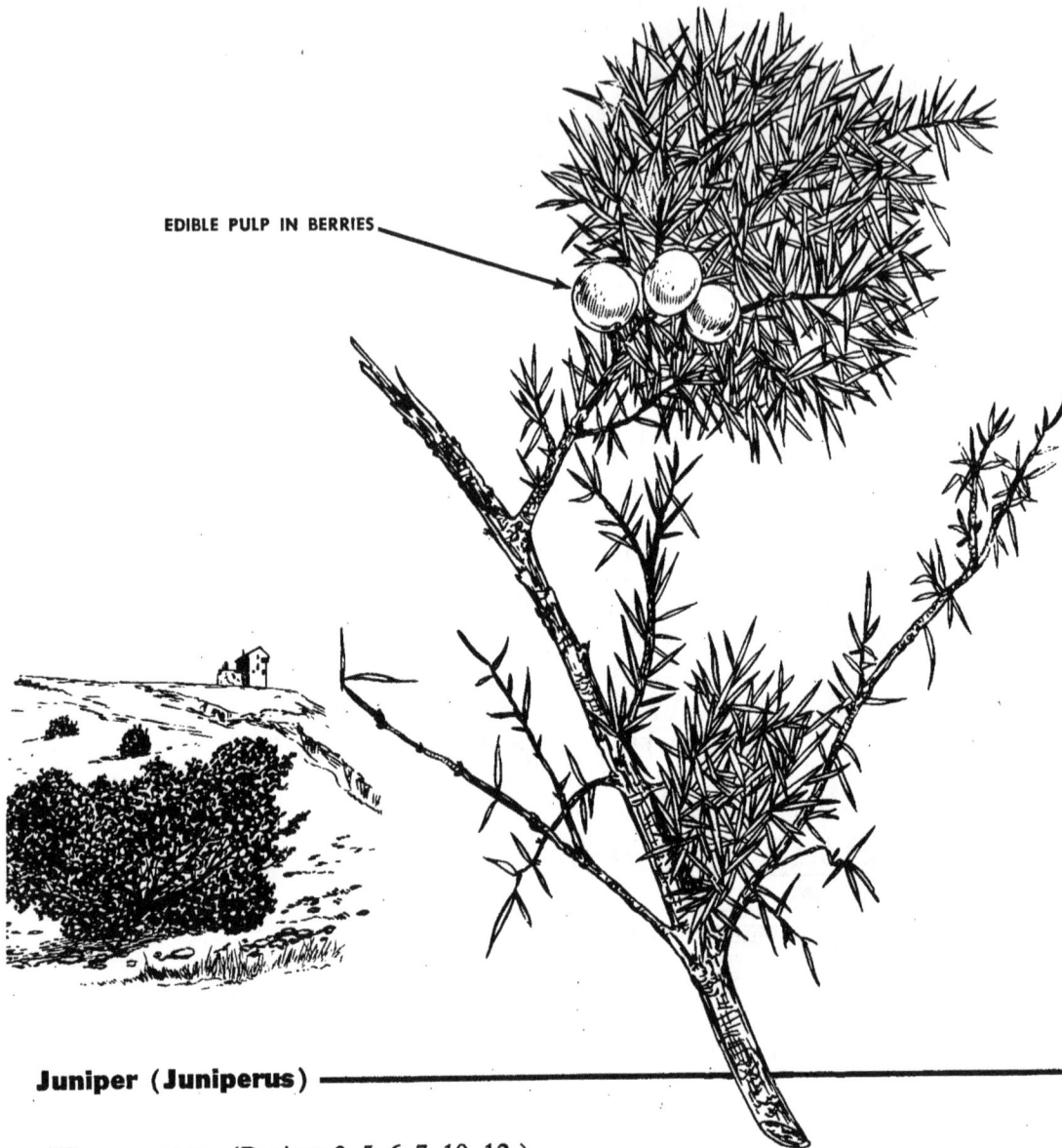

Juniper (Juniperus)

WHERE FOUND. (Regions 3, 5, 6, 7, 10, 12.) Juniper trees are found in the northern hemisphere, especially in the drier areas and in mountainous regions. In North America, junipers are common in western United States and Mexico, but certain kinds occur in mountainous regions. Other kinds occur in southeastern Europe, and across Asia to Japan. Junipers occur also in the mountains of North Africa.

APPEARANCE. Junipers are usually trees, but sometimes occur as ground shrubs. All kinds are evergreen, and the leaves are usually sharply pointed, awl-shaped, and not much larger than a needle. The edible berries are usually blue in color and are borne in clusters near the ends of the branches.

WHAT TO EAT. The principal reason for including the juniper as a survival food is because of its abundance in the regions where it is found. The berries on some, especially those kinds with berries the size of small marbles, are full of a nourishing pulp. Some kinds with small berries are not palatable.

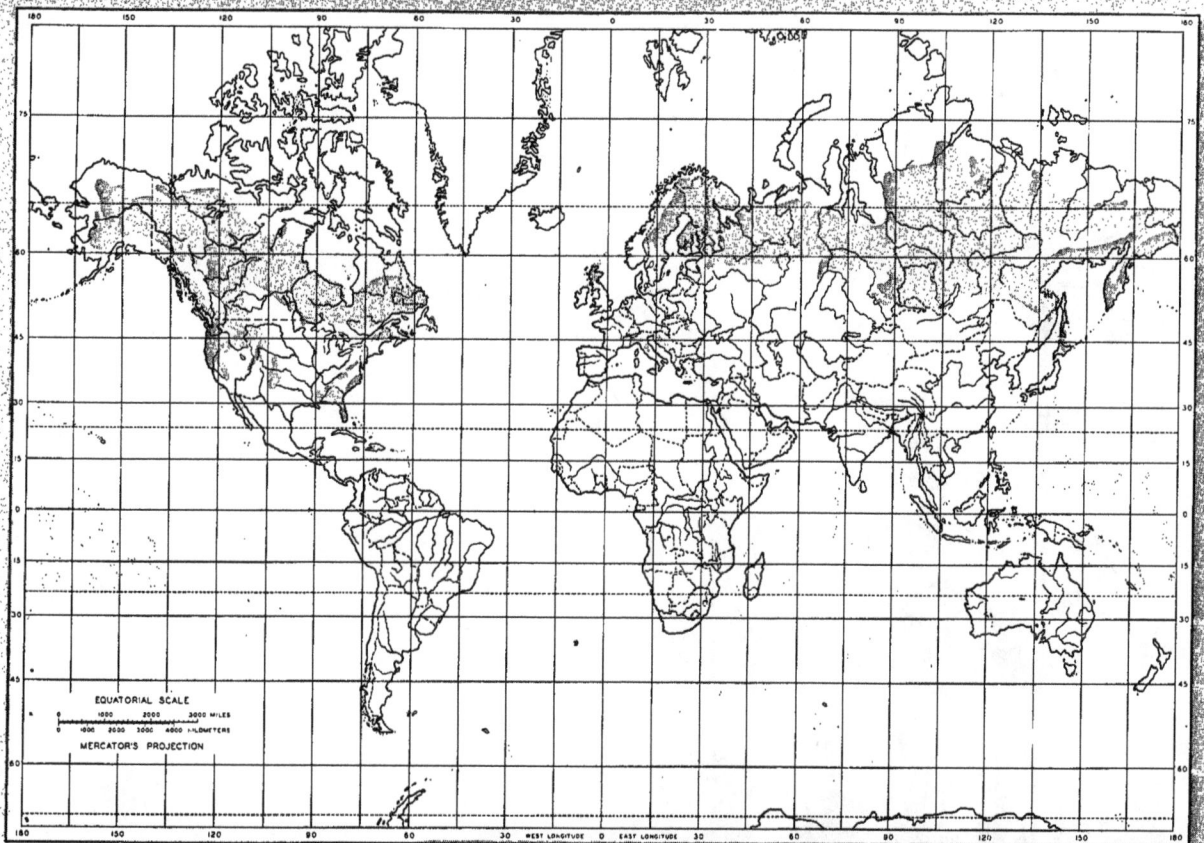

CONIFEROUS FOREST

The characteristics of the coniferous forest (spruce, pine, fir, and cedar) are as follows:

a. Rainy summer season with cold, snowy winters.

b. Three stories of vegetation (trees, large shrubs, herbs).

c. Herbs not abundant, ferns somewhat more abundant, and mosses very abundant on forest floor.

d. Trees are needle-bearing evergreen species (conifers), such as firs, pines, spruces, cedars, larches.

Vast areas in the Northern Hemisphere are covered by coniferous forests. In these areas broad-leaved hardwood trees fill a minor function and occur only as the understory of vegetation.

If forced to survive in these areas for long periods, especially in winter, the survivor will find that edible food plants are scarce. In winter the chief edible food plants available will be:

a. Rootstalks.

b. Bulbs.

c. Roots.

d. Seeds.

e. Resins (from pines).

f. Infusions (teas) from evergreen needles.

g. Bark (inner part).

During the summer months considerably more plants will be available for food, including:

a. Nuts.

b. Shoots (potherbs).

c. Leaves (potherbs).

d. Pollen (cattail).

e. Flowers.

f. Fruits (dessert).

g. Fiddleheads (ferns).

h. Mushrooms and other edible fungi.

Coniferous forest belts occur in the following parts of the world:

a. North America — western United States (Rocky Mountains and Pacific Coast States), and in much of middle Canada extending in a belt from southeastern to northwestern Canada into central Alaska.

b. Europe — southern Scandanavia, northern Russia.

c. Asia — much of central and northern Siberia.

Northern Russian forest

© Vegetationsbilder

© Vegetationsbilder

Cattail swamp

Subarctic forest

© Vegetationsbilder

Alaskan conifers

© Vegetationsbilder

FERN FROND

EDIBLE FIDDLEHEAD

Ground
level

EDIBLE
LEAFSTOCK

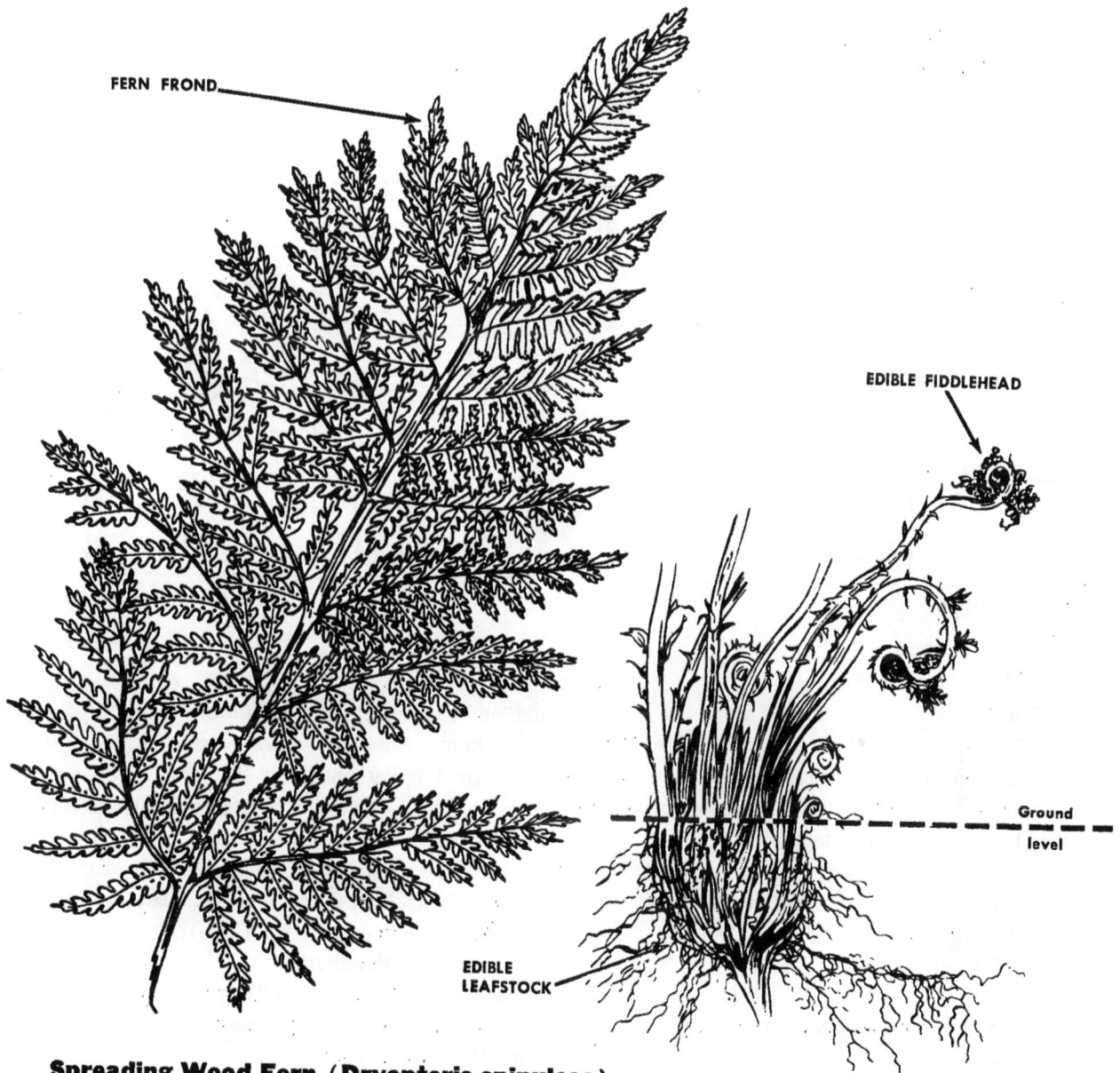

Spreading Wood Fern (Dryopteris spinulosa)

WHERE FOUND. (Regions 7, 12.) The spreading wood fern is a northern fern, especially abundant in the Alaskan and adjoining Siberian areas. It occurs in woodland areas and mountainous regions.

APPEARANCE. This fern sprouts from stout underground stems (rhizomes), which are covered with old leafstalk bases that resemble a bunch of small bananas.

USES. The old leafstalks on the underground stem, are roasted, after which the shiny brown covering is removed and the inner portion is eaten. The natives have used these ferns for centuries as a source of food.

The young fronds or fiddleheads may be collected in early spring and then boiled or steamed and eaten like asparagus.

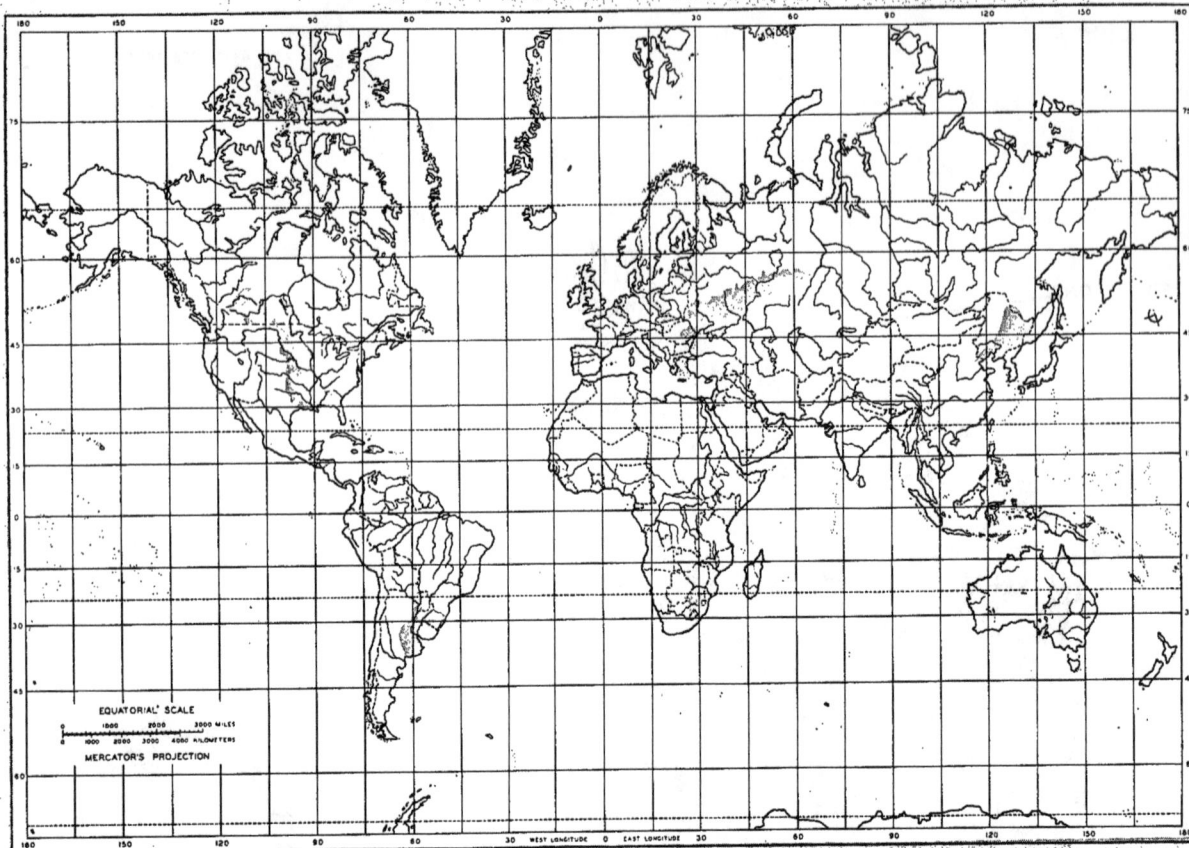

PRAIRIE

The prairie and the steppe areas are very closely related. However, the true prairie will support a somewhat different flora than the steppe, and for this reason it is important that they be discussed separately.

The chief distinction between prairie and steppe is the seasonal distribution of rainfall.

Prairie	Steppe
Rainfall 30-40 inches a year.	15-30 inches a year;
Subsoil — permanently moist.	Permanently dry.

In both, the precipitation comes during the short growing season (spring). Summers are hot with intermittent showers that are insufficient for the growth of grasses.

The chief prairie regions of the world are:

a. North America — south central Canada, and east central United States.

b. South America — northeastern Argentina, Uruguay, Paraguay, and Brazil.

c. Africa — Union of South Africa (parts of southern Transvaal and Orange Free State).

d. Europe — parts of Hungary, Rumania, and Russia (Ukraine and in a belt extending through central Russia to the Urals).

e. Asia — Manchuria.

The following food plants of prairies are illustrated on the pages indicated.

a. Water plantain (p. 60).

b. Chicory (p. 61).

c. Rose (p. 306).

d. Sorrel (p. 217).

e. Wild onion (p. 212).

f. Tulip (p. 211).

g. Lily (p. 270).

84

Mesopotamian grassland

© Vegetationsbilder

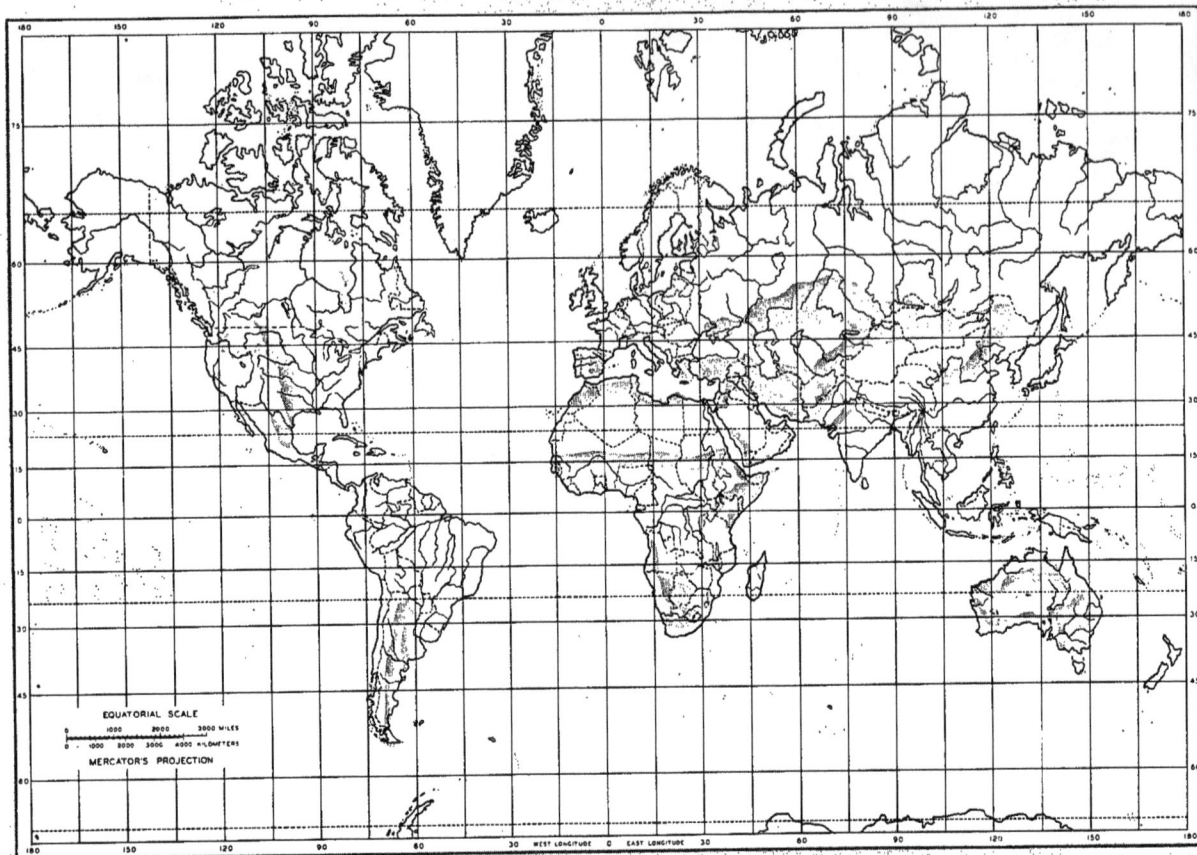

STEPPE

The part of Russia extending from the Volga River through central Asia to the Gobi Desert has been referred to as the steppes. However, as a vegetation type, the steppe grassland occurs in many other parts of the world. The rainfall in steppe areas averages 15-30 inches per year, as compared to that of prairie areas with 30-40 inches per year. The subsoil in typical steppe areas is permanently dry, and the area is treeless, except for protected river bottoms. The general aspect of the steppe, like the prairie, is a broad treeless expanse of open countryside, which may be quite rolling in places.

The principal areas of steppe are:

a. North America — western Great Plains of the United States.

b. South America — Argentina.

c. Africa — narrow belt extending across Africa on the southern rim of the Sahara, and parts of Ethiopia and Kenya.

d. Europe — southeastern Russia.

e. Asia — Asia Minor (Turkey), Iran, Baluchistan, Pakistan, Turkestan, and a broad belt through central Asia.

f. Australia — fringes of the great central desert, especially in eastern Australia.

The following food plants of steppes are illustrated on the pages indicated.

a. Sea orach (p. 218).

b. Sorrel (p. 217).

c. Baobab (p. 321).

d. Rose (p. 306).

e. Chicory(p. 61).

f. Wild calla (p. 59).

© Vegetationsbilder

Forest steppe, USSR

Kurdistan

© Vegetationsbilder

© Vegetationsbilder   Southeast Russia

Asia Minor   © Vegetationsbilder

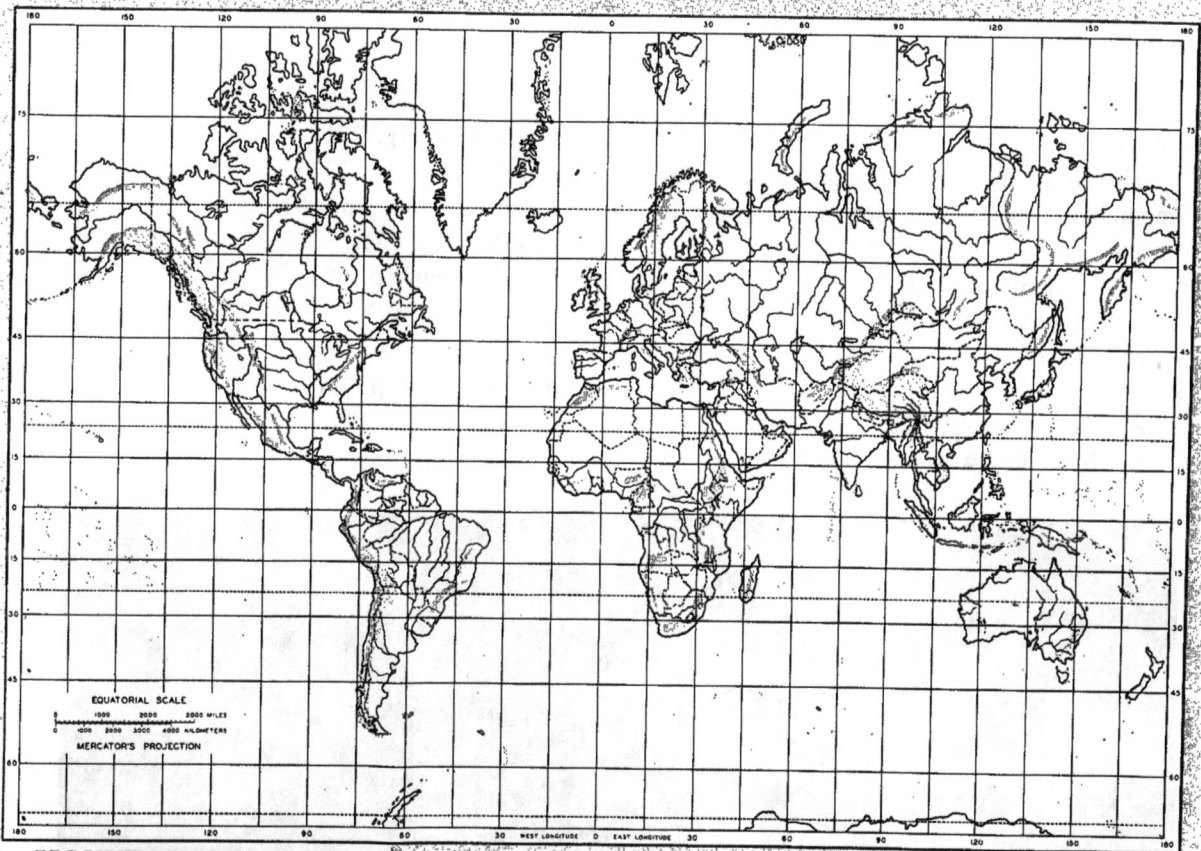

MOUNTAINOUS AREAS

The major mountainous regions of the world occur principally in the temperate and tropical zones. By comparison to the total land areas, the area covered by the mountains is relatively small. However, the great diversification in terrain and climate of mountainous regions presents a totally different problem for the survivor than, say, adjoining plateau or neighboring tropical rain forest.

In either the temperate or tropical zones, a distinct zonation in climate occurs on a mountain side. The base of the mountain may be a jungle, and the top may be snow-covered and much like a tundra in aspect. Each mountain system presents its own special problem for the survivor, and the food plants are different, for the most part, from one mountain system to the other.

The major mountain systems of the world are as follows:

a. North America — Cordilleras (including Rocky Mountains, Cascade and Sierra Nevada of western United States). Appalachian Mountains, Sierra Madre (both east and west) in Mexico, and central mountain chain through Central America.

b. South America — Andean chain extending from Colombia to Terra del Feugo.

c. Europe — Pyrennes, Alps of Central Europe, and Caucasus of southern Russia.

d. Asia — Tian Shan of central Asia, Himalayas, Tibetan Plateau, Java, and New Guinea.

e. Africa — Cameroon Mountains and mountains of East Africa (Uganda and Kenya): Ruenzori, Kenya, Aberdare, and Kilimanjaro.

Food plants of mountainous regions are as diverse as the multitudinous array of mountains themselves. Many kinds of plants are restricted to a certain mountain side, although the survivor will recognize many kinds of plants at high elevations that may also be seen on the broad valleys below. This is particularly true in temperate areas. However, in tropical areas the zonation of vegetation is very pronounced, so that the flora of the seacoast, in the Philippines, is wholly different from that of the inland mountain tops. No specific food plants of tropical mountain areas are illustrated.

The following food plants of temperate mountain regions are shown on the pages indicated.

a. Wild rhubarb (p. 76).
b. Cattail (p. 58).
c. Flowering rush (p. 77).
d. Juniper (p. 78).
e. Crabapple (p. 62).
f. Spreading wood fern (p. 83).

g. Bracken (p. 271).
h. Polypody (p. 271).
i. Mushrooms (p. 46).
j. Pine (p. 66).
k. Beechnut (p. 67).
l. Oak (p. 69).
m. Chestnut (p. 70).
n. Hazelnut (p. 71).
o. Walnut (p. 72).
p. Rose (p. 73).

Balkan mountains

© Vegetationsbilder

© Vegetationsbilder

Iranian mountains

North Iran

© Vegetationsbilder

© Vegetationsbilder

Mountains of Salween, Irrawaddy

Mountains of North Greece

© Vegetationsbilder

PREPARATION OF PLANT FOOD

Boiling, roasting, baking, and frying — in that order — are the most efficient ways of preparing foods. Pit cooking or clambake style (oven) is slower but requires less attention, protects food from flies and other pests, and reveals no flame at night (an advantage if you are in enemy territory, no advantage if you are signaling for help).

The principal areas of steppe are:

Rock Oven

The rock oven is described on page 98.

Drying Plant Food

Plant food can be dried by wind, air, sun, or fire, with or without the aid of smoke. A combination of these can be used. The main object is to get rid of the water. Plantains, bananas, breadfruit, leaves, berries and other wild fruits can be dried. Cut them into thin slices and place in the sun or dry over a fire. Mushrooms dry easily, and in the dried state keep indefinitely. Soak them in water before using.

Cooking Accessories and Utensils

Leaves can be used to wrap certain foods for consignment to the cooking oven. In the southwest Pacific the leaves of the breadfruit, for instance, and those of the banana are commonly used to wrap food before cooking. This keeps the food from getting covered with sand and soil and prevents it from being burnt to a parched ember while cooking. In other parts of the world where breadfruit and banana leaves are not obtainable, any type of thick foliage plant may be used for food wrapping. But avoid using a type that will give an unpleasant flavor. Also, in the southwest Pacific and other areas where the screw pine (*Pandanus,* see illustration p. 208), grows, the leaves of this plant are very often used for wrapping fish. Palm leaves or the limber parts of a vine or branch may be used for tying the leaves securely around the wrapped food.

Both green and mature coconut shells form natural casseroles for cooking, as do hollow gourds. Marine shells are often used for scraping, peeling, and grating. Along inland rivers and lakes, fresh water bivalve and clam shells may also be used. Whenever shells are used for scraping or cutting, crack off part of the curved edge to form a straight, sharp edge. Hold the shell with the fingers on the inner surface, with the thumb on the outer surface, and make backhand strokes away from the operator.

FOOD PREPARATION

Animal

Survivors must know how to exploit to their advantage the meat of game and fish and how to accomplish this with the least effort and physical exertion. Many men have died from starvation because they had failed to take full advantage of a game carcass. They abandoned the carcass on the mistaken theory that they could secure more game whenever needed.

Transportation of Meat After the Kill

If the animal is large, the first impulse will usually be to begin operations by packing the meat to camp. If possible, pack your camp to the animal so more of the meat can be utilized.

A procedure often advocated for transporting the kill is to use the skin as a sled for dragging the meat to camp. When the entire animal is dragged this procedure may prove satisfactory only on frozen lakes or rivers over very smooth snow-covered terrain, or, in the case of seals, on polar ice. In rough or brush-covered country, however, it is generally most difficult, if not impossible, to use this method. Mountain sheep or other large mountain animals can frequently be dragged down a snow-filled gully to the base of the mountain. Of course, where meat is the only consideration, and you do not care about the condition of the skin, mountain game can sometimes be rolled downhill for long distances. First, gut the animal and sew up the incision. Once the bottom of the hill is reached, almost invariably the method is either to back-pack your meat to camp, making several trips if no other survivors are present, or pack your camp to the animal. Under survival conditions, your home is on your back. Obviously, there is no reason to pack 100 pounds of meat to camp when you can pack your outfit to the animal.

In cases where the weight of the meat proves excessive and moving of the base camp is not practicable, eat some of the animal at the scene of the kill.

To avoid spoilage, eat the heart, liver, and kidneys as soon as possible.

All of the meaty parts of skull such as the brain, tongue, eyes, and flesh should also be eaten.

In a severe hunger emergency, the intestines, thoroughly cleaned in water, wrapped around a stick and roasted over coals, will be found palatable. The large intestine, cooked in this manner, is considered a delicacy by northern natives.

Where to make preliminary cuts
(Follow dotted lines)

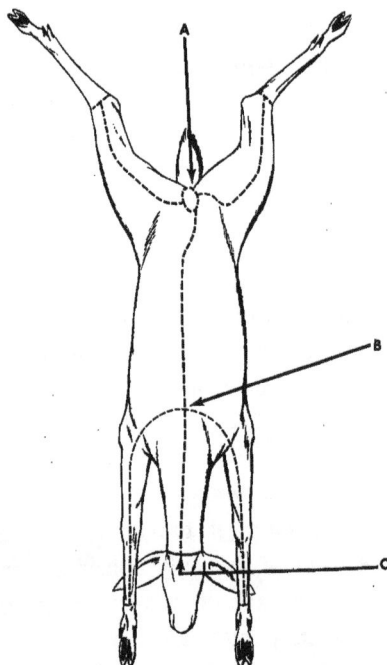

Remove the bones from the meat. Leg bones laid on a bed of coals will roast quickly and can be easily cracked with light taps of a knife or stone to expose the marrow, which is highly prized as food by all hunters.

Skinning and Butchering

Under survival conditions, skinning and butchering must be done carefully so that every edible pound of meat can be saved.

The first step in skinning is to turn the animal on its back and with a sharp knife cut through the skin on a straight line, from the end of the tail bone to a point under its neck, A-C on the diagram. In making this cut, pass around the anus and, with great care, press the skin open until you can insert the first two fingers of the left hand between the skin and the thin membrane inclosing the guts. When the fingers can be forced forward, place the blade of the knife between the fingers, blade up, with the knife held firmly in the right hand. As you force forward the fingers of the left hand, palm upward, follow it with the knife blade, cutting the skin but not cutting the membrane. If the animal is a male, cut the skin parallel to, but not touching, the penis. If the tube leading from the bladder is accidentally cut, a messy job and unclean meat will result. If the gall or urine bladders are broken, washing will help clean the tainted meat. Otherwise, however, it is best not to wash meat but to allow it to form a protective glaze.

The illustration on this page shows preliminary cuts made in skinning and butchering. On reaching the ribs, it will no longer be possible to force the fingers forward, because the skin adheres more strongly to flesh and bone. Furthermore, care is no longer necessary. The cut to point C can be quickly completed by alternately forcing the knife under the skin and lifting it. With the central cut completed, make side cuts consisting of incisions through the skin, running from central cut A-C up the back of each leg to the knee and hock joints. Then make cuts around the front legs just above the knee and around the hind legs above the hocks. Make the final cross cut at point C, and then cut completely around the neck and back of the ears. Now is the time to begin skinning.

On a small or medium-sized animal, one man can skin on each side. The easiest method is to begin at the corners where the cuts meet. When the animal is large, three men can skin at the same time. However you should remember that when it is getting dark and hands are clumsy because of the cold, a sharp skinning knife can make a deep wound. So, keep well away from the man next to you. When you have skinned down on the animal's side as far as you can, roll the carcass on its side to continue on the back. Before doing so, spread out the loose skin to prevent the meat from touching the ground and picking up sand and dirt. Follow the same procedure on the opposite side until the skin is free. If you decide before skinning that you do not want the skin, a rough job can be done. However, think well before throwing the skin away. A square of skin, long enough to reach from your head to your knees, will not weigh much when green dried, and is one of the best ground cloths to use under your sleeping bag on frozen ground or snow. Snow will not stick to the skin if you lay it hair side up.

Immediately after a kill is the best time to skin and butcher. However, if you kill an animal late in the day, you can make the preliminary cut, A-C, gut the animal, and return early next morning to do the skinning. But be sure to place the carcass so that predators cannot get to it. Then, if the site is visited, the marauder will usually eat only the guts. In opening the membrane inclosing the guts follow the same procedure you followed in cutting the skin, using the fingers of the left hand as a guard for the knife and to separate the intestines from the membrane. You can cut away this thin membrane along the ribs and sides in order to see better. Be careful to avoid cutting the intestines or bladder. The large intestine passes through an aperture in the pelvis. This tube must be separated with a knife from the bone surrounding it. Tie a knot in the bladder tube to prevent the escape of urine. With these steps accomplished, the insides can be easily disengaged from the back and removed from the carcass.

The intestines of a well-conditioned animal will be covered with a lace-like layer of fat, which can be lifted off and placed on nearby bushes to dry for later use. The kidneys are embedded in the back, forward of the pelvis, and are covered with fat. Running forward from the kidneys on each side of the backbone are two long strips of meat called tenderloin or backstrap, which can be cut out. This is eaten after the liver, heart, and kidneys. It is usually very tender. Edible meat can also be removed from the head, brisket, ribs, backbone, and pelvis. The hams of a large animal are not usually considered good eating. Northern natives frequently feed them to the dogs.

When preparing meat under survival conditions, take care not to discard edible fat. This is especially important when, as is often the case in the Arctic, diet must consist mostly entirely of meat. Fat must be eaten in order to provide a complete diet. Many men think that they are unable to eat fat. This is because with a plentiful, civilized diet, meat fat is not a necessity. Under emergency conditions, however, when sugar or vegetable oils are lacking, fat *must* be eaten. Rabbits lack fat, and the fact that a man will die on a diet consisting of rabbit *meat alone* indicates the importance of fat in a primitive diet. The same is true of birds such as the ptarmigan.

Birds should be handled in the same manner as other animals. They should be drawn after killing and protected from flies. Birds that carry no fat, such as ptarmigan, crow, and owl, may be skinned. The skins of waterfowl are usually fat and, for this reason, these birds should be plucked and cooked with the skin on. The giblets may also be eaten.

Carrion-eating birds, such as vultures, must be boiled for at least 20 minutes, to kill parasites, before further cooking or eating. Fish-eating birds have a strong, fish-oil flavor. This may be lessened by baking them in mud, or by skinning prior to cooking.

The best meat on a lizard is hind quarters and tail. Eat the legs of a frog. Turtles have flesh on legs, neck, and tail, and tucked away between their shells.

Skin all frogs and snakes. Remove and discard skin, head, and viscera.

Care of Meat

PROTECTION FROM FLIES. The greatest danger to meat comes during weather warm enough to allow flies to deposit their eggs, or "blow" the meat. Even while you are skinning an animal, flies can enter bullet holes or any small cavity and lay eggs, which turn into maggots in a few days. The *only* way of preventing fly blow is to make it impossible for a fly to touch the meat. Do this by wrapping the meat loosely in parachute material or other fabric. Wrap it loosely, so that an airspace of an inch or two is formed between the meat and the sack.

When meat is to be backpacked during the day, it should then be rolled in fabric or clothing and placed inside the pack to be carried. This soft material will act as a nonconductor in keeping the meat cool.

In sparsely settled regions, native dogs will smell meat at incredible distances and raid the meat cache at night. Be careful to guard meat from dogs and other predatory animals.

SMOKING OR DRYING MEAT. Cutting meat across the grain in thin strips and either drying it in the wind or smoke will produce "jerky." In warm or damp weather when meat deteriorates rapidly, smoking over a smoldering fire can prevent its spoiling for some time. Take care to keep the meat from getting too hot.

Willow, alders, cottonwood, birch, and dwarf birch make the best smoking woods. Pitch woods, such as fir and pine, should not be used as they will make the meat unpalatable.

A paratepee would work well for the smoking process. By tying meat to the upper ends of the poles and closing the smoke flaps, a good concentration of smoke is obtained. Efficient smoking also can be done by laying fabric over a drying rack and building the fire underneath.

Hang all drying meat high to keep it away from animals. Cover to prevent blowfly infestation. If mold forms on the outside, brush or wash off before eating. In damp weather, smoked or air-dried meat must be redried to prevent molding.

Reptile meat may be dried by placing on hot rocks or hanging in the sun.

PRESERVING COOKED MEAT. To preserve cooked animal food, recook it once each day, especially in warm weather.

Cleaning and Scaling Fish

Immediately after you land a fish, bleed it by cutting out the gills and large blood vessels that lie next to the backbone. Scale and wash the fish in clean water.

Some fish, such as members of the trout family, do not need to be scaled. Others such as catfish and sturgeon have no scales but you can skin them.

Some small salt water fish can be eaten with a minimum of cleaning. Their scales are loose and drop off or can be washed off immediately after the fish are caught. The stomach and intestines can be flipped out with the thumb. These fish are oily, highly nutritious, and good — even raw.

Preservation of Fish

The method used to preserve fish through several days of warm weather is similar to that used in preserving meat.

When there is no danger of predatory animals disturbing the fish, lay the fish on the available fabric as shown in the diagram. Allow fish to cool all night. Early the next morning, before the air gets warm, turn down the upper edge of the tarp over the top line of fish and turn up the lower edge, B, over the lower line. Then begin on the edge of the tarp, C, and roll the tarp around the fish in such a manner that each fish is completely enfolded with

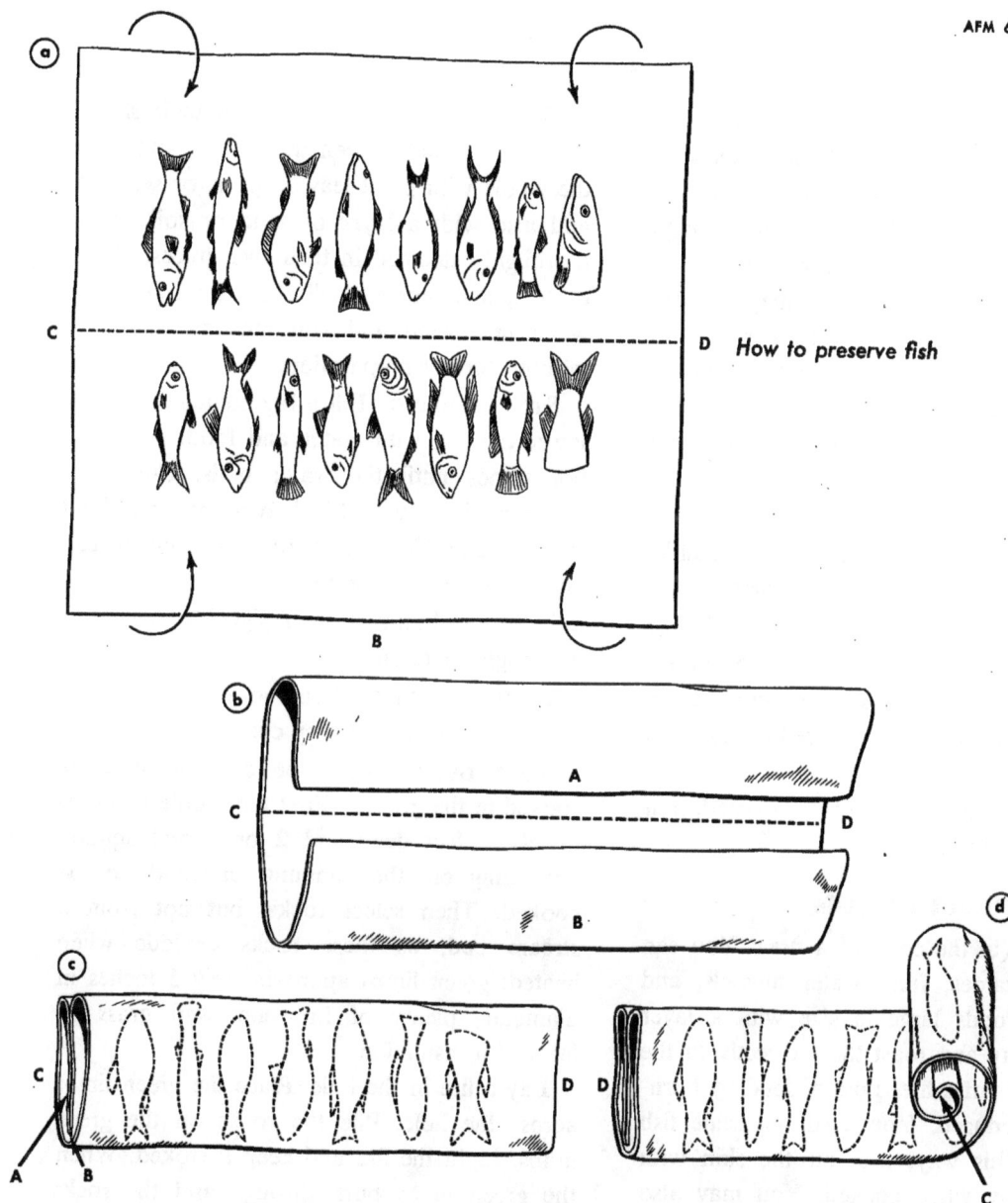

How to preserve fish

fabric until you reach the edge, D. Then, fold the roll thus formed in the center. You will have a rounded roll of protected fish. This roll should be securely, but not tightly tied and wrapped in a sleeping bag, parachute fabric, or clothing, as you would do with meat. This bundle can be placed inside your pack. During rest periods, or whenever the pack is removed, place it in the shade, if possible, to protect it from the direct rays of the sun. If the presence of predatory animals is suspected, suspend the fish from a pole or tree. Cover the package if rain threatens.

Fish may be dried in the same manner as described for smoking meat. To prepare fish for smoking, cut off heads and remove backbone. Then, spread them flat and skewer in that position. Thin willow branches with bark removed make good skewers.

Fish may also be dried in the sun. Hang them from branches or spread on hot rocks. When the meat has dried, splash them with sea water, if available, to salt the outside. Do not keep any sea food unless it is well dried or salted.

Cleaning Shell Food

Clams, oysters, mussels, crabs, and lobster left in clean salt water overnight will partially clean themselves and save you some work. Note warning about mussels on page 249.

COOKING. Cooking makes for a more enjoyable meal. All wild game, fresh water fish, clams, mussels, snails, and crawfish must be thoroughly cooked for safety. Mince tough mussels or large snails. Avoid eating raw or smoked fresh water fish, as they may be contaminated with parasites. Parrots, hawks, and crows can be tough, but they will soften up when stewed thoroughly. Most plant foods are made more digestible and palatable and yield more food value after heating.

Salt water shellfish may be eaten raw but are safest when cooked. Shark meat is edible, except in the Arctic, but it must first be cut into small pieces and soaked overnight or boiled in several changes of water to get rid of the ammonia flavor which accumulates in the flesh. Shark meat is not poisonous, just unpalatable.

Turtle eggs can be boiled or roasted, but the whites will not harden.

Cooking Without Utensils

ROASTING (in the coals of a fire). You can coat fish, potatoes, fresh water mussels, and many other foods large in size with a layer of mud or clay and roast them directly in the flames or coals of a fire. Loss of food by burning is thus reduced. You need not scale fish prepared in this way; peel off the skin with the baked clay when cooked. You may also wrap food in wet leaves or foil from rations.

STEAMING UNDER THE FIRE. Foods small in size, such as small bird eggs, fresh water snails, or any other shellfish, may be cooked in quantity in a pit beneath your fire. Fill a small, shallow pit with food, after lining it or wrapping the food in plant leaves, seaweed, cloth, or foil from rations. If nylon is used, do not allow it to scorch or melt. Cover the pit with a 1/4- to 1/2-inch layer of sand or soil, and build your fire directly over it. After cooking for about 1 hour, rake the fire away and recover the food.

STEAMING WITH HEATED STONES (clambake style). Heat a number of stones in a fire, then allow the fire to burn down to coals. Place such foods as fresh water mussels (in their shells) directly on and between the stones, and cover the whole with plant leaves, grass, or seaweed, and also with a layer of sand or soil. When thoroughly steamed in their own juices, clams, oysters, and mussels will show a gaping shell when uncovered and you may eat the food without further preparation.

STONE BOILING. Fill a big container or hollowed-out log with water and food. Add red-hot stones until the water boils. Cover for about an hour with big leaves, or until food is well done. Containers for steam boiling can also be made out of tree bark or by digging a hole and lining it with signal paneling or watertight materials.

BAMBOO JOINTS. Bamboo joints are good pots. Heat them until they char.

ROCK OVEN. Any type of food may be cooked in the ground. First dig a hole approximately 2 feet deep and 2 or 3 feet square, depending on the amount of food to be cooked. Then select rocks, but not from a stream bed, as these rocks explode when heated; green limbs approximately 3 inches in diameter; plenty of firewood; and grass or leaves for insulation.

Lay a fire in the hole. Place the green limbs across the hole. Pile the rocks on the green limbs. Light the fire and keep it stoked. When the green limbs burn through and the rocks fall into the hole, the oven is ready to use.

Remove the rocks and ashes. Clean any live fire from the hole. Line the bottom of the hole with hot rocks. Place a thin layer of dirt over the rocks. Place grass, moss or other insulating material on the dirt. Put in the food to be cooked, more insulating material, a thin layer of dirt, hot rocks and cover over with remaining earth.

Small pieces of meat (steak, chops, etc.) will cook in 1-1/2 to 2 hours. Large roasts take 5 to 6 hours.

PLANKING. Meat may be cooked by leaving it on a plank close to the fire. This method is wasteful as the meat loses most of its liquid content and *thorough* cooking is difficult.

ORIENTATION

Whether you plan to stay in one place or to travel, you will want to know where you are. If you are traveling, you need to know what direction to take. If you are staying, you want to know your location so that you can radio the information to your rescuers. Your position report doesn't have to be accurate to the mile to be helpful; any data you can give will reduce the area to be searched.

DIRECTION FINDING

Direction from Polaris

In the Northern Hemisphere one star, Polaris (the Pole Star), is never more than approximately 1° from the North Celestial Pole. In other words, the line from any observer in the Northern Hemisphere to the Pole Star is never more than one degree away from true north. You find the Pole Star by locating the Big Dipper or Cassiopeia, two groups of stars which are very close to the North Celestial Pole. The two stars on the outer edge of the Big Dipper are called pointers, as they point almost directly to Polaris. If the pointers are obscured by clouds, Polaris can be identified by its relationship to the constellation Cassiopeia. The illustration indicates the relation between the Big Dipper, Polaris and Cassiopeia.

Finding Due East and West by Equatorial Stars

Due to the altitude of Polaris above the horizon, it may sometimes be difficult to use it as a bearing. It may be more convenient to use a point directly on the horizon. In the Southern Hemisphere, of course, Polaris will not be visible, and an accurate bearing is difficult to obtain.

The celestial equator, which is merely a projection of the earth's equator onto the imaginary celestial sphere, always intersects the horizon line at the due east and west points of the compass. Therefore, any star on the celestial equator will rise due east and set due west (disallowing a small error due to atmospheric refraction). This holds true for all latitudes except those of the North and South Poles, where the celestial equator and the horizon will have a common plane. However, if you are at the North or South Poles you will probably know about it beforehand, so this technique can be assumed to be of universal applicability.

Certain difficulties arise in the practical use of this technique. Unless you are quite familiar with the installations, it may be difficult to spot a specific rising star as it first appears above the eastern horizon. Thus, it will probably be simpler to depend upon the identification of an equatorial star before it sets in the west.

Another problem is that caused by atmospheric extinction. As stars near the horizon they grow fainter in brightness, since the line of sight between the observer's eyes and the star passes through a constantly thickening slice of atmosphere. Therefore, faint stars will disappear from view before they actually set. However, a fairly accurate estimate of the

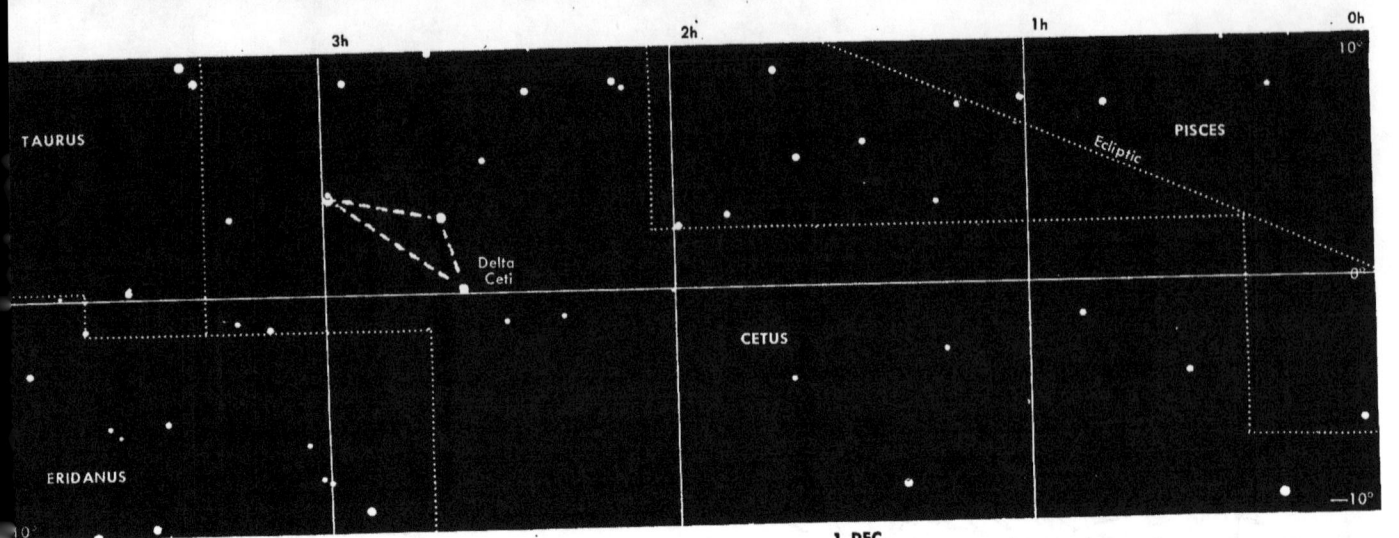

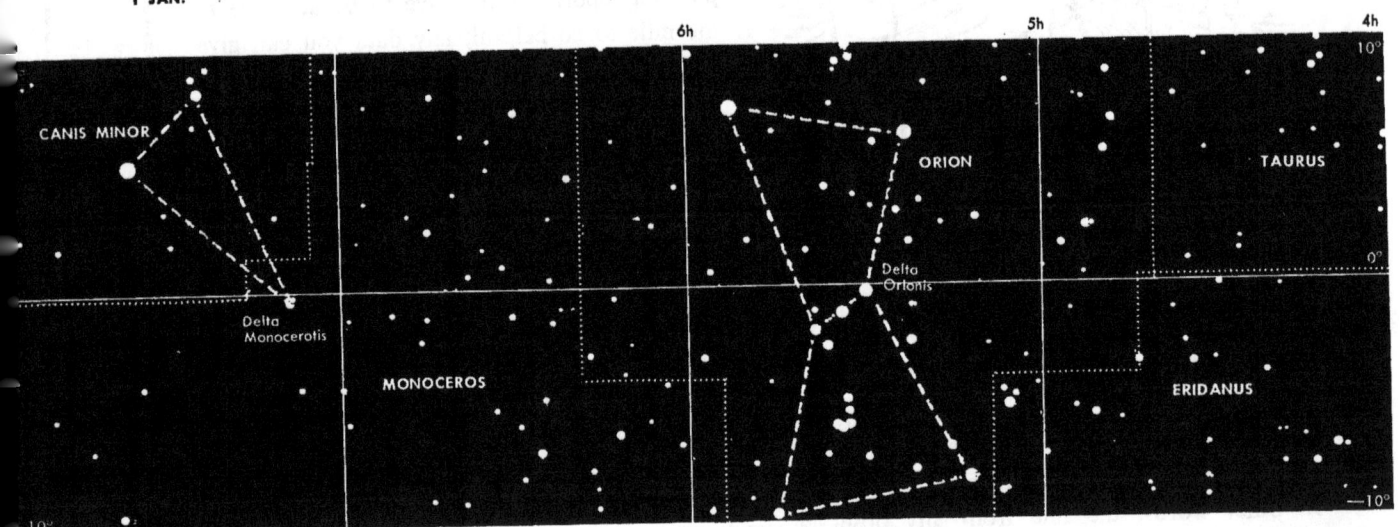

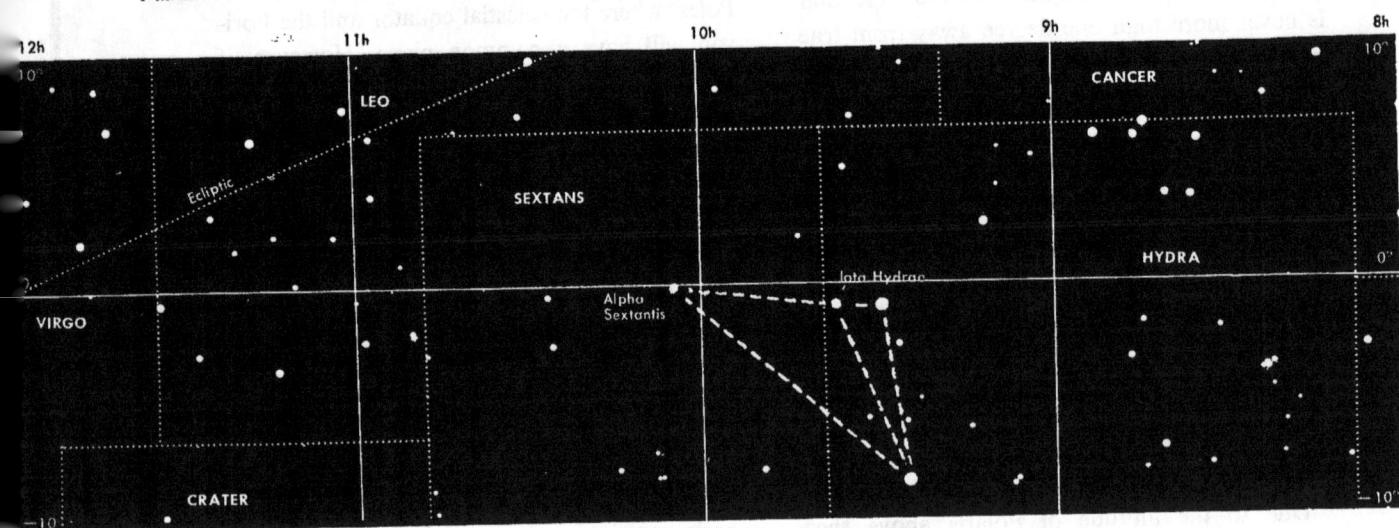

CHARTS OF EQUATORIAL STARS

The 6 star maps on these pages show only those star-groups which lie on the celestial equator. Each map covers a strip 20° wide (north and south) and 60° long. Most of the more conspicuous naked eye stars are shown, the brighter stars being indicated by larger dots. The fine dotted lines show the boundaries between the constellations, and the fine dashed line cutting diagonally through some of the charts is the ecliptic, or the apparent path of the sun and the planets. Configurations near the stars in question have been joined by rough dashed lines to aid in identification.

Below each chart will be found the months of the year. On the first of each month the stars shown above the month name will be on the celestial

100

16h **15h** **14h** **13h** **12**

10°

BOOTES

VIRGO

SERPENS

Zeta Virginis

0°   0

Gamma
Virginis

LIBRA

Ecliptic

−10°

1 JUL.   1 JUN.   Spica   −10

20h **19h** **18h** **17h** **16**

10°

Altair

HERCULES

SERPENS

Eta
Aquilae

0°

AQUILA   OPHIUCHUS

SCUTUM

−10°

1 SEP.   1 AUG.

24h **23h** **22h** **21h** **20**

10°

DELPHINUS

PEGASUS

PISCES

EQUULEUS

0°   0

Alpha
Aquarii

Theta
Aquilae

AQUARIUS

Ecliptic

AQUILA

AQUARIUS

−10°

1 NOV.   1 OCT.   −10

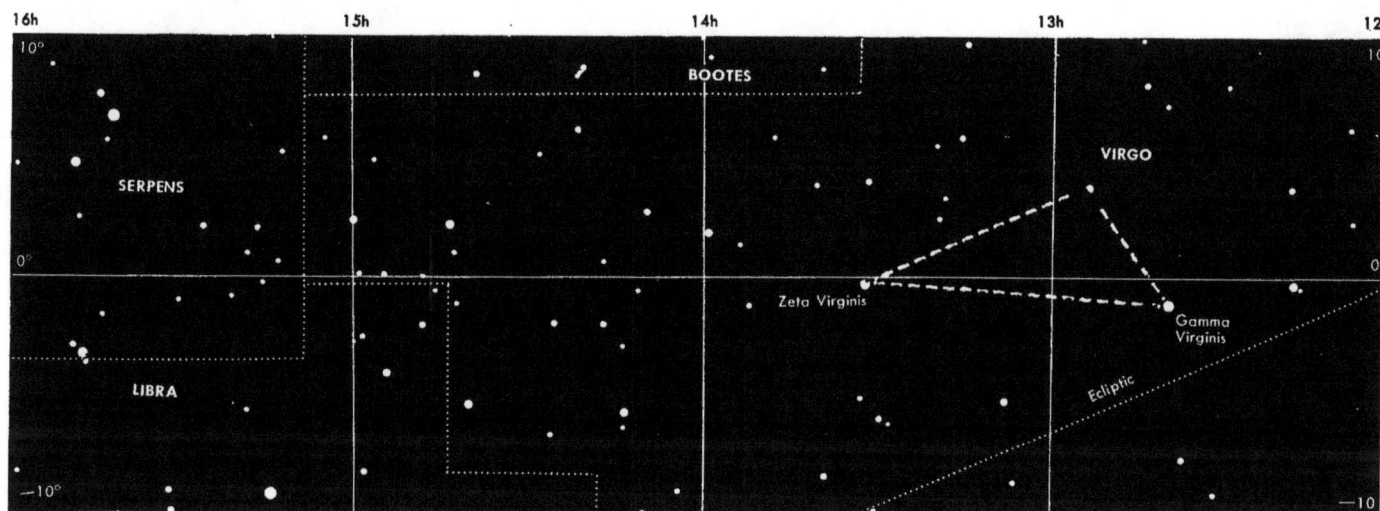

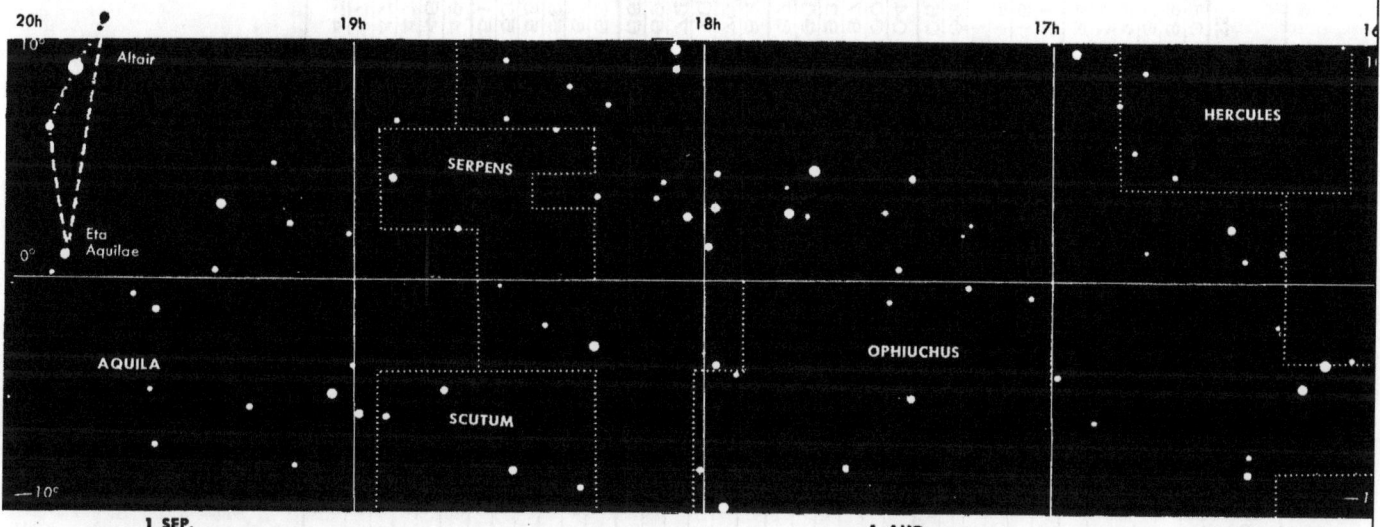

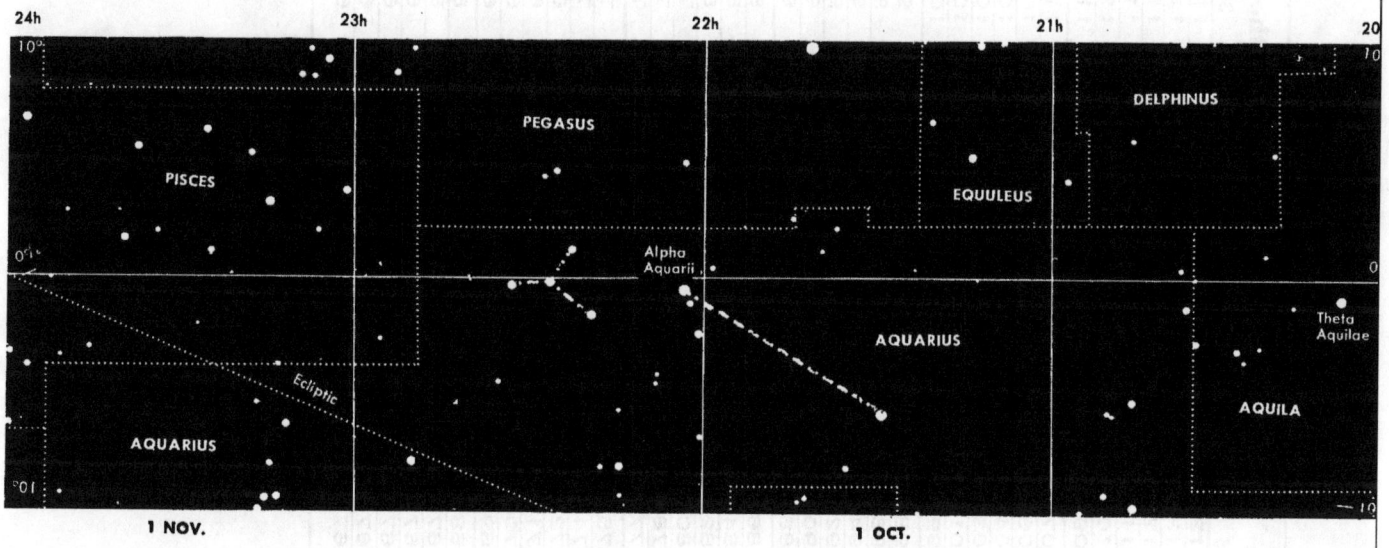

meridian (highest point of their path above the horizon) at 9 p.m. local time.

The celestial equator makes a 45° angle with the southern horizon at latitude 45° N. At 60° N. latitude it makes a 30° angle. In other words, degrees of latitude subtracted from 90° gives the angle formed by the celestial equator and the southern horizon.

The preceding information will enable the survivor to identify more easily the equatorial stars to be used in determining due east or west. When observing stars rising in the east, the charts should be slanted down and to the left; when observing stars setting in the west, they should be slanted down and to the right.

101

(SEE EXPLANATORY TEXT ON PAGE 104)

Azimuth of the rising and setting sun

LATITUDE	JANUARY						FEBRUARY						MARCH						APRIL						MAY						JUNE					
DATE	1	6	11	16	21	26	1	6	11	16	21	26	1	6	11	16	21	26	1	6	11	16	21	26	1	6	11	16	21	26	1	6	11	16	21	26
60	141	140	138	136	133	130	126	123	120	116	112	108	106	102	98	94	90	86	81	77	74	70	66	63	59	56	52	49	47	44	41	40	39	39	39	39
55	133	132	130	129	127	124	121	118	116	112	109	106	104	100	97	93	90	87	82	79	76	72	69	66	63	61	58	55	53	51	49	48	47	47	47	47
50	127	127	125	124	122	120	117	115	112	110	107	104	102	99	96	93	90	87	83	80	77	74	72	69	66	64	62	60	58	56	54	53	53	53	53	53
45	124	123	122	120	119	117	115	113	110	108	105	103	101	98	96	93	90	87	84	81	79	76	73	71	69	67	64	63	61	60	58	57	56	56	56	56
40	121	120	119	118	117	115	113	111	109	107	104	102	100	98	95	93	90	87	84	82	80	77	75	72	70	68	67	65	63	62	61	60	59	59	59	59
35	118	118	117	116	115	113	111	109	108	106	103	101	100	97	95	92	90	88	85	82	80	78	76	74	72	70	68	67	65	64	63	62	62	62	62	62
30	117	116	115	114	113	112	110	108	107	105	102	100	99	97	95	92	90	88	85	83	81	78	76	75	73	71	69	68	67	66	64	64	63	63	63	63
25	116	115	114	113	112	111	109	107	106	104	102	100	99	97	94	92	90	88	85	83	81	79	77	75	73	72	70	69	68	67	66	65	64	64	64	64
20	115	114	113	112	111	110	108	107	105	103	101	100	99	96	94	92	90	88	85	83	81	79	78	76	74	73	71	70	69	68	66	66	65	65	65	65
15	114	113	113	112	111	109	108	106	105	103	101	99	98	96	94	92	90	88	86	83	82	80	78	76	74	73	72	70	69	68	67	67	66	66	66	66
10	113	113	112	111	110	109	108	106	105	103	101	99	98	96	94	92	90	88	86	84	82	80	78	76	75	73	72	71	70	69	68	67	67	67	67	67
5	113	113	112	111	110	109	107	106	104	103	101	99	98	96	94	92	90	88	86	84	82	80	78	77	75	74	72	71	70	69	68	67	67	67	67	67
0	113	112	112	111	110	109	107	106	104	103	101	99	98	96	94	92	90	88	86	84	82	80	78	77	75	74	72	71	70	69	68	67	67	67	67	67

AFM 64-3 FEB 1956

Month	Date													
JULY	1	39	47	53	56	59	62	63	64	65	66	67	67	67
	6	40	48	53	57	60	62	64	65	66	66	67	67	67
	11	41	49	54	58	61	63	64	65	66	67	68	68	68
	16	43	50	55	59	62	64	65	66	67	68	68	68	69
	21	45	52	57	60	63	65	66	67	68	69	69	69	69
	26	48	54	59	62	64	66	67	68	69	70	70	70	70
AUGUST	1	51	57	61	64	66	68	69	70	71	71	72	72	72
	6	55	60	63	66	68	69	71	71	72	73	73	73	73
	11	58	63	66	68	70	71	72	73	74	74	74	74	75
	16	61	65	68	70	72	73	74	75	76	76	76	76	76
	21	65	68	71	72	74	75	76	76	77	77	77	78	78
	26	68	71	73	75	76	77	78	78	79	79	79	79	79
SEPTEMBER	1	73	75	77	78	79	80	80	81	81	81	82	82	82
	6	77	78	80	81	81	82	82	83	83	83	83	83	83
	11	81	82	83	83	84	84	85	85	85	85	85	85	85
	16	84	85	85	86	86	86	87	87	87	87	87	87	87
	21	88	88	88	89	89	89	89	89	89	89	89	89	89
	26	92	92	92	91	91	91	91	91	91	91	91	91	91
OCTOBER	1	96	95	95	94	94	94	93	93	93	93	93	93	93
	6	100	99	98	97	97	96	96	96	95	95	95	95	95
	11	104	102	101	100	99	99	98	98	97	97	97	97	97
	16	108	105	104	102	101	101	100	100	99	99	99	99	99
	21	112	109	107	105	104	103	102	102	101	101	101	101	101
	26	115	112	109	108	106	105	104	104	103	103	103	102	102
NOVEMBER	1	120	116	113	110	109	108	107	106	105	105	105	104	104
	6	123	119	115	113	111	110	109	108	107	107	106	106	106
	11	126	121	117	115	113	111	110	109	108	108	108	107	107
	16	130	124	120	117	115	113	112	111	110	109	109	109	109
	21	133	126	122	119	116	114	113	113	111	111	110	110	110
	26	135	128	124	120	118	116	114	114	112	112	111	111	111
DECEMBER	1	138	130	125	122	119	117	115	115	113	113	112	112	112
	6	140	132	126	123	120	118	116	116	114	113	113	113	113
	11	141	133	127	124	121	118	117	116	115	114	113	113	113
	16	141	133	127	124	121	118	117	116	115	114	113	113	113
	21	141	133	127	124	121	118	117	116	115	114	113	113	113
	26	141	133	127	124	121	118	117	116	115	114	113	113	113
	31	141	133	127	124	121	118	117	116	115	114	113	113	113

Table I

NOTE: When the sun is rising, the tabulated azimuth is reckoned from North to East. When the sun is setting, the tabulated azimuth is reckoned from North to West.

setting point of a star can be made some time before it actually sets. Also, the atmospheric conditions of the locality have a great effect on the obscuration of a star's light as it sets. Atmospheric haze, for example, will be much less of a problem on an arid desert than along a Temperate Zone coastal strip.

The accompanying charts show the brighter stars and some prominent star groups which lie along the celestial equator. There are few bright stars which are actually *on* the celestial equator. However, there are a number of stars which lie quite near it, so an approximation within a degree or so can be made. Also, a rough knowledge of the more conspicuous equatorial constellations will give the survivor a continuing checkpoint in maintaining his orientation.

Direction from the Sun at Sunrise and Sunset

You can find north by observing the sun when it rises or sets. Table I shows the true azimuth (true bearing) of the rising sun and the relative bearing of the setting sun for all the months in the year in the Northern and Southern Hemisphere (the table assumes a level horizon and will be inaccurate in mountainous terrain). On January 26 your position is 50°00′ N and 165°06′ W. In table I at that date and under 50° N latitude, you find the azimuth of the sun to be 120°. Therefore, north will be to your left 120° when you are facing the sun.

To find north from the setting sun, consider the same problem as above. Since the sun sets in the west, north must be to the right of the sun. Therefore, north will be 120° to your right when you face the sun.

The table does not list every day of the year nor does it list every degree of longitude. If you want accuracy to within 1 degree of azimuth, you may have to interpolate (split the difference) between the values given in the table. However, for all practical purposes, using the closest day and the closest degree of latitude listed in the table will give you an azimuth which will enable you to hold your course. For example: If you are at 32° north

latitude on the 13th of April, the azimuth of the rising sun is actually 79°22′; however, by entering the table with the closest day listed, 11 April, and the closest latitude, 30°, you get 81° as the azimuth of the rising sun. This value is accurate enough for field purposes.

Direction from the Southern Cross

In the Southern Hemisphere Polaris is not visible. There the Southern Cross is the most distinctive constellation. As you fly south, the Southern Cross appears shortly before Polaris drops from sight astern. An imaginary line through the long axis of the Southern Cross, or True Cross, points toward the South Pole. The True Cross should not be confused with a larger cross nearby known as the False Cross, which is less bright and more widely spaced. The False Cross has a star in the center, making five stars in all, while the True Cross has only four. Two of these are among the brightest stars in the heavens; they are the stars on the southern and eastern arms. Those on the northern and western arms are not as conspicuous, but are bright.

There is no conspicuous star above the South Pole to correspond to Polaris above the North Pole. In fact, the point where such a star would be, if one existed, lies in a region devoid of stars. This point is so dark in comparison with the rest of the sky that it is known as the Coal Sack.

The illustration above shows the True Cross and — to the west of it — the False Cross. Hold the page above your head for realism and note two very bright stars just to the east of the True Cross. With them and the True Cross as guides, you can locate the spot within the Coal Sack which is exactly above the South Pole.

First, extend an imaginary line along the long axis of the True Cross to the south. Join the two bright stars to the east of the Cross with an imaginary line. Bisect this line with one at right angles. The intersection of this line with the line through the Cross is approximately the point above the South Pole.

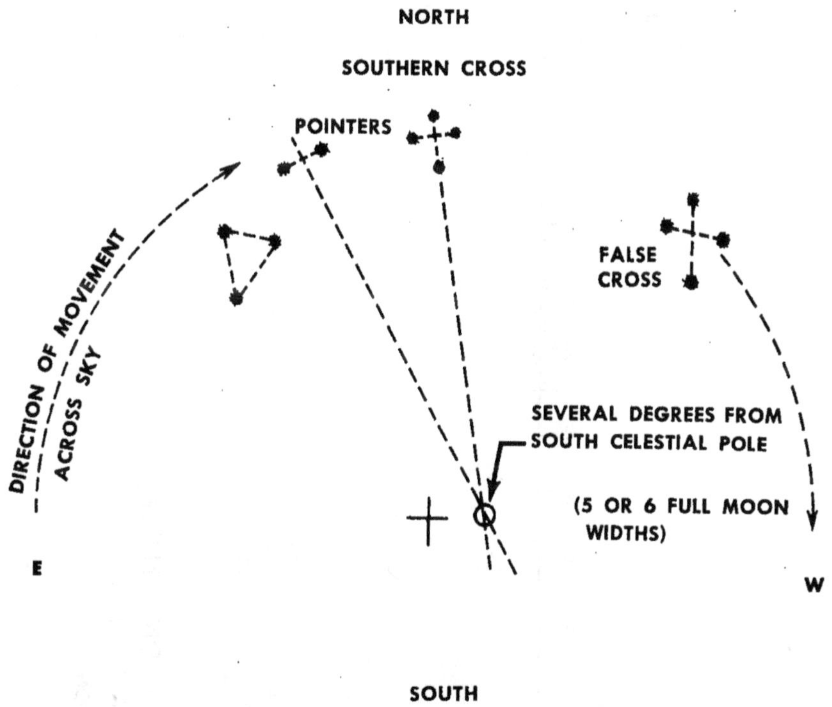

NORTH

SOUTHERN CROSS

POINTERS

FALSE
CROSS

DIRECTION OF MOVEMENT
ACROSS SKY

SEVERAL DEGREES FROM
SOUTH CELESTIAL POLE

(5 OR 6 FULL MOON
WIDTHS)

E

W

SOUTH

POSITION FINDING

Latitude by Length of Day

When you are in any latitude between 60°
N and 60° S, you can determine your exact
latitude within 30 nautical miles (1/2°), if you
know the length of the day within one minute.
This is true throughout the year except for
about 10 days before and 10 days after the
equinoxes — approximately 11-31 March and
13 September - 2 October. During these two
periods the day is approximately the same
length at all latitudes. To time sunrise and
sunset accurately, you must have a level
horizon.

Observations for Latitude

Find the length of the day from the instant
the top of the sun first appears above the ocean
horizon to the insant it disappears below the
horizon. This instant is often marked by a
green flash. Write down the times of sunrise

and sunset. Don't count on remembering them.
Note that only the length of day counts in the
determination of latitude; your watch may have
an unknown error and yet serve to determine
this factor. If you have only one water horizon,
as on a seacoast, find local noon by the stick
and shadow method given below. The length
of day will be twice the interval from sunrise
to noon or from noon to sunset.

Knowing the length of day, you can find the
latitude by using the following nomogram.

Longitude from Local Apparent Noon

To find longitude, you must know the correct time. You should know the rate at which
your watch gains or loses time. If you know
this rate and the time you last set the watch,
you can compute the correct time. Correct zone
time on your watch to Greenwich time; for
example, if your watch is on Eastern Standard
Time, add five hours to get Greenwich time.

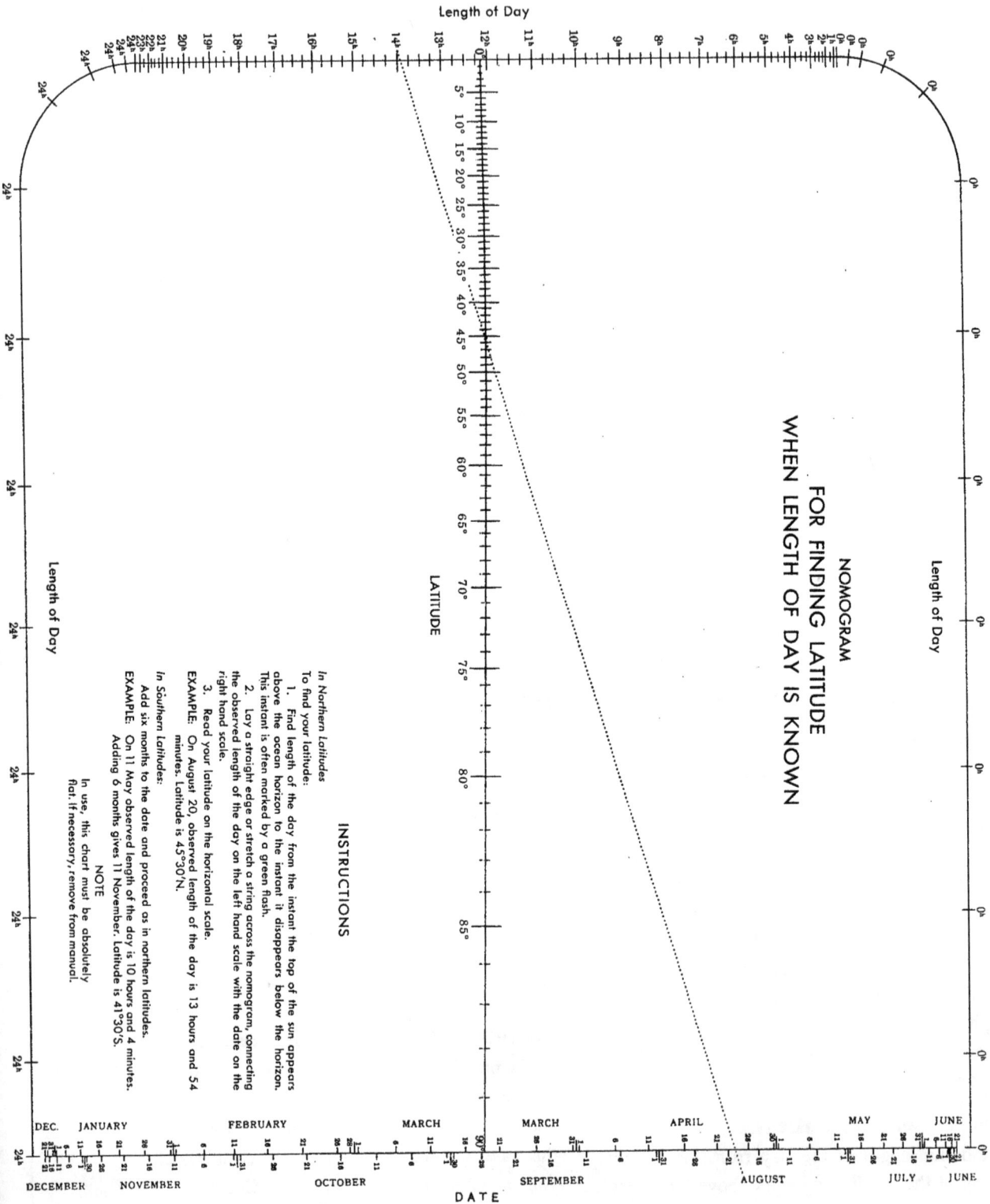

Length of Day

Length of Day

Length of Day

NOMOGRAM
FOR FINDING LATITUDE
WHEN LENGTH OF DAY IS KNOWN

LATITUDE

DATE

INSTRUCTIONS

In Northern Latitudes

To find your latitude:

1. Find length of the day from the instant the top of the sun appears above the ocean horizon to the instant it disappears below the horizon. This instant is often marked by a green flash.

2. Lay a straight edge or stretch a string across the nomogram, connecting the observed length of the day on the left hand scale with the date on the right hand scale.

3. Read your latitude on the horizontal scale.

EXAMPLE: On August 20, observed length of the day is 13 hours and 54 minutes. Latitude is 45°30'N.

In Southern Latitudes:

Add six months to the date and proceed as in northern latitudes.

EXAMPLE: On 11 May observed length of the day is 10 hours and 4 minutes. Adding 6 months gives 11 November. Latitude is 41°30'S.

NOTE

In use, this chart must be absolutely flat. If necessary, remove from manual.

DEC.   JANUARY   FEBRUARY   MARCH   MARCH   APRIL   MAY   JUNE

DECEMBER   NOVEMBER   OCTOBER   SEPTEMBER   AUGUST   JULY   JUNE

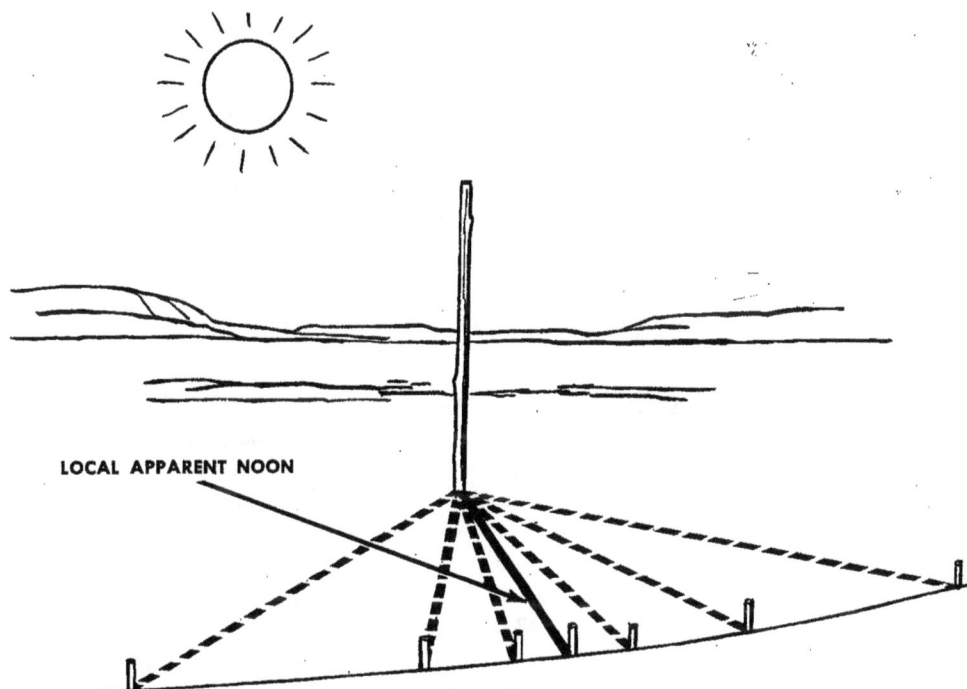

Stick-and-shadow method of determining local apparent noon

You can find longitude by timing the moment when a celestial body passes your meridian. The easiest body to use is the sun. Use one of the following methods.

a.   Put up a stick or rod as nearly vertical as possible, in a level place. Check the alinement of the stick by sighting along the line of a makeshift plumb bob. (To make a plumb bob, tie any heavy object to a string and let it hang free. The line of the string indicates the vertical.) Sometime before midday begin marking the position of the end of the stick's shadow. Note the time for each mark. Continue marking until the shadow definitely lengthens. The time of the shortest shadow is the time when the sun passed the local meridian or local apparent noon. You will probably have to estimate the position of the shortest shadow by finding a line midway between two shadows of equal length, one before noon and one after.

b.   If you get the times of sunrise and sunset accurately on a water horizon, local noon will be midway between these times.

c.   Erect two plumb bobs approximately 1 foot apart so that both strings line up on Po-

laris, much the same as a gun sight. Plumb bobs should be set up when Polaris is on the meridian and has no east-west correction. The next day, when the shadows of the two plumb bobs coincide, they will indicate local apparent noon.

Mark down the Greenwich time of local apparent noon. The next step is to correct this observed time of meridian passage for the equation of time — that is, the number of minutes the real sun is ahead of or behind the mean sun. (The mean sun was invented by astronomers to simplify the problems of measuring time. It rolls along the equator at a constant rate of 15° per hour. The real sun is not so considerate; it changes its angular rate of travel around the earth with the seasons.)

Table B gives the values in minutes of time to be added to or subtracted from mean (watch) time to get apparent (sun) time.

Now that you have the Greenwich time of local noon, you can find the difference of longitude between your position and Greenwich by converting the interval between 1200 Greenwich and your local noon from time to arc. Remember that 1 hour equals 15° of longitude, 4 minutes equal 1° of longitude, and 4 seconds equal 1′ of longitude.

Example: Your watch is on Eastern Standard Time. It normally loses 30 seconds a day. You haven't set it for 4 days. You time local noon at 15:08 on your watch on 4 February.

Watch correction is 4 x 30 seconds, or plus 2 minutes. Zone time correction is plus 5 hours. Greenwich time is 15:08 plus 2 minutes plus

5 hours or 20:10. The equation of time for 4 February is minus 14 minutes. Local noon is 20:10 minus 14 minutes or 19:56 Greenwich. Difference in time between Greenwich and your position is 19:56 minus 12:00 or 7:56. A time of 7:56 equals 119° of longitude.

Since your local noon is later than Greenwich noon, you are west of Greenwich. Your longitude then is 119° W.

Table II — Equation of time

Date	Eq. of Time*	Date	Eq. of Time*	Date	Eq. of Time*
Jan. 1	−3.5 min.	May 2	+3.0 min.	Oct. 1	+10.0 min.
2	−4.0	14	+3.8	4	+11.0
4	−5.0	May 28	+3.0	7	+12.0
7	−6.0			11	+13.0
9	−7.0	June 4	+2.0	15	+14.0
12	−8.0	9	+1.0	20	+15.0
14	−9.0	14	0.0	Oct. 27	+16.0
17	−10.0	19	−1.0		
20	−11.0	23	−2.0	Nov. 4	+16.4
24	−12.0	June 28	−3.0	11	+16.0
Jan. 28	−13.0			17	+15.0
		July 3	−4.0	22	+14.0
Feb. 4	−14.0	9	−5.0	25	+13.0
13	−14.3	18	−6.0	Nov. 28	+12.0
19	−14.0	July 27	−6.6		
Feb. 28	−13.0			Dec. 1	+11.0
		Aug. 4	−6.0	4	+10.0
Mar. 4	−12.0	12	−5.0	6	+9.0
8	−11.0	17	−4.0	9	+8.0
12	−10.0	22	−3.0	11	+7.0
16	−9.0	26	−2.0	13	+6.0
19	−8.0	Aug. 29	−1.0	15	+5.0
22	−7.0			17	+4.0
26	−6.0	Sep. 1	0.0	19	+3.0
Mar. 29	−5.0	5	+1.0	21	+2.0
		8	+2.0	23	+1.0
Apr. 1	−4.0	10	+3.0	25	0.0
5	−3.0	13	+4.0	27	−1.0
8	−2.0	16	+5.0	29	−2.0
12	−1.0	19	+6.0	Dec. 31	−3.0
16	0.0	22	+7.0		
20	+1.0	25	+8.0		
Apr. 25	+2.0	Sep. 28	+9.0		

*Add plus values to mean time and subtract minus values from mean time to get apparent time.

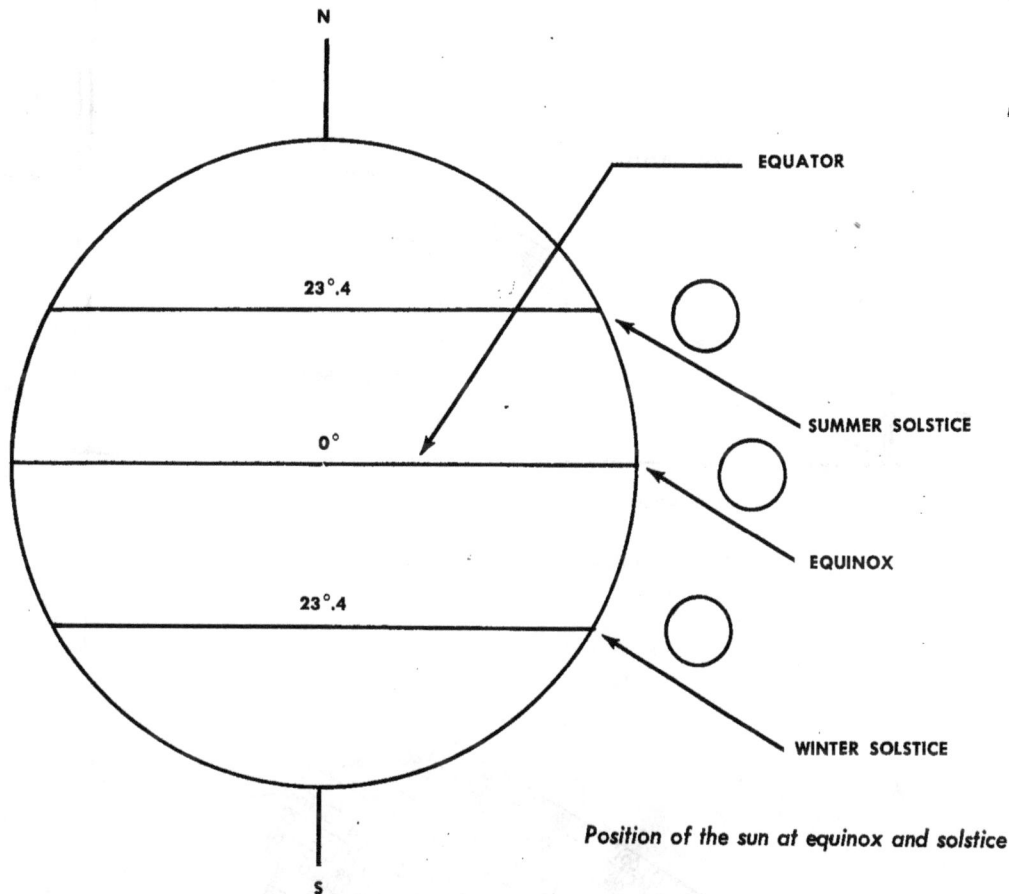

Position of the sun at equinox and solstice

Direction from the Sun at Noon

Determining local noon by the stick and shadow method will also give you direction. The line of the shortest shadow is also the line of the local meridian or north-south line. Whether the sun is north or south of you at midday will depend on your latitude. North of 23.4° N., the sun will always be due south of local noon; and the shadow will point north. South of 23.4° S., the sun will always be due north at local noon; and the shadow will point south. In the tropics the sun can be either north or south at noon, depending on the date, and your position.

Latitude by Noon Altitude of Sun

On any given day there is only one latitude on the earth where the sun will pass directly overhead or through the zenith at noon. In all latitudes north of this, the sun will pass to the south of the zenith; and in those south of it, the sun will pass to the north. For each 1° change of latitude, the zenith distance will also change by 1°.

Table III gives for each day of the year the latitude where the sun is in the zenith at noon.

If you have a Weems plotter or other protractor, you can use the maximum altitude of the sun to find latitude by measuring the angular distance of the sun from the zenith at noon. Find the time of local noon with the methods described earlier in this section. Stretch a string from the top of a stick to the point where the end of the noon shadow rested; place your plotter along the string and drop a plumb line from the center of the plotter. The intersection of the plumb line with the outer scale of the plotter shows the angular distance of the sun from your zenith.

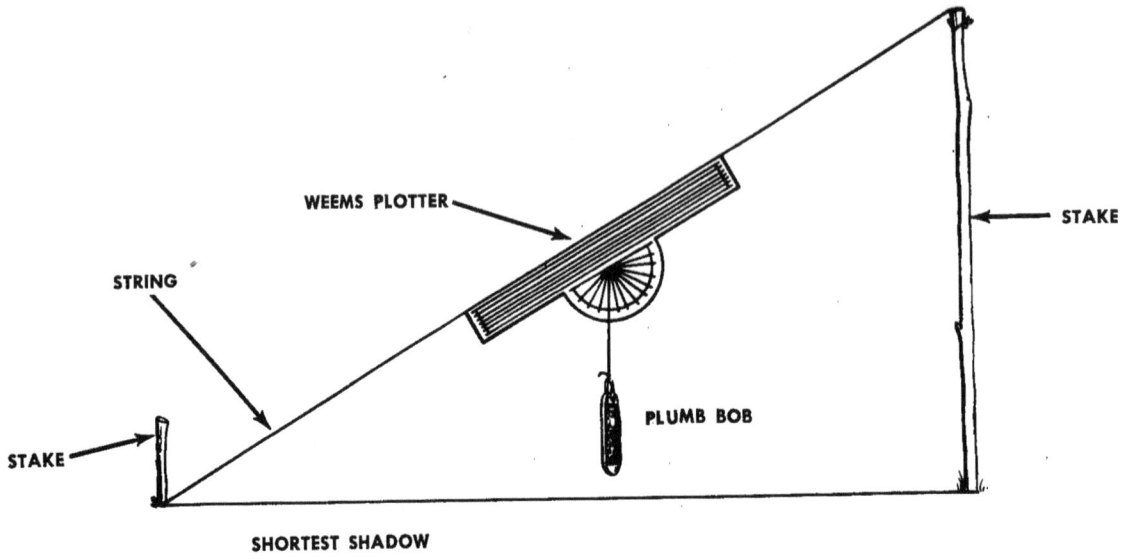

Angular distance of sun from zenith

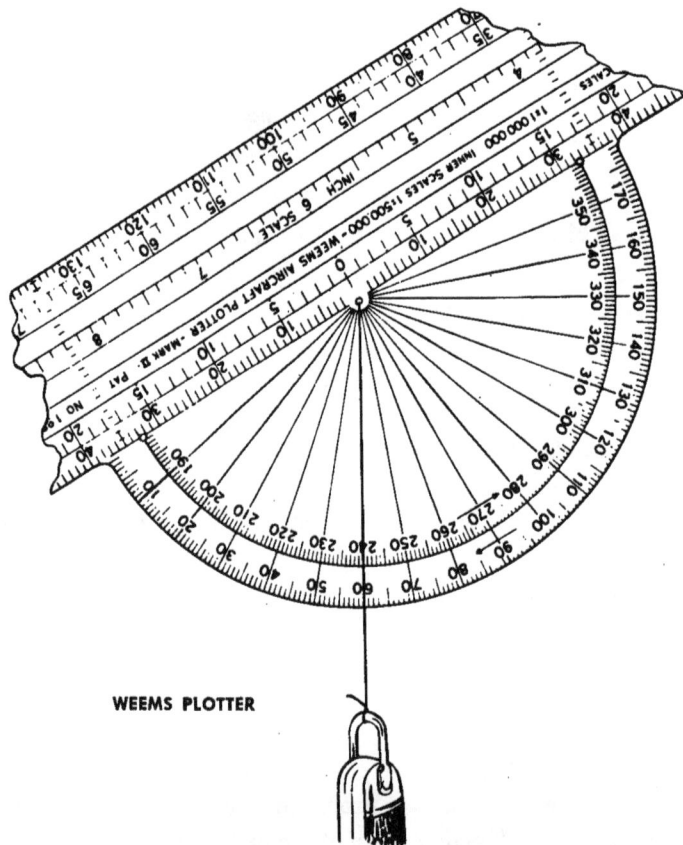

Finding zenith distance of the sun

Table III — Declination of the sun — In Degrees

Declination is tabulated to the nearest tenth of a degree rather than to the nearest minute of arc. If you want to use minutes in your calculations, remember that °.1 = 6'.

	Jan.	Feb.	Mar.	Apr.	May	June
1	S 23.1	S 17.5	S 7.7	N 4.4	N 15.0	N 22.0
2	23.0	17.2	7.3	4.8	15.3	22.1
3	22.9	16.9	6.9	5.2	15.6	22.3
4	22.9	16.6	6.6	5.6	15.9	22.4
5	22.8	16.3	6.2	5.9	16.2	22.5
6	S 22.7	S 16.0	S 5.8	N 6.3	N 16.4	N 22.6
7	22.5	15.7	5.4	6.7	16.7	22.7
8	22.4	15.4	5.0	7.1	17.0	22.8
9	22.3	15.1	4.6	7.4	17.3	22.9
10	22.2	14.8	4.2	7.8	17.5	23.0
11	S 22.0	S 14.5	S 3.8	N 8.2	N 17.8	N 23.1
12	21.9	14.1	3.5	8.6	18.0	23.1
13	21.7	13.8	3.1	8.9	18.3	23.2
14	21.5	13.5	2.7	9.3	18.5	23.2
15	21.4	13.1	2.3	9.6	18.8	23.3
16	S 21.2	S 12.8	S 1.9	N 10.0	N 19.0	N 23.3
17	21.0	12.4	1.5	10.4	19.2	23.4
18	20.8	12.1	1.1	10.7	19.5	23.4
19	20.6	11.7	0.7	11.1	19.7	23.4
20	20.4	11.4	0.3	11.4	19.9	23.4
21	S 20.2	S 11.0	N 0.1	N 11.7	N 20.1	N 23.4
22	20.0	10.7	0.5	12.1	20.3	23.4
23	19.8	10.3	0.9	12.4	20.5	23.4
24	19.5	9.9	1.3	12.7	20.7	23.4
25	19.3	9.6	1.7	13.1	20.9	23.4
26	S 19.0	S 9.2	N 2.1	N 13.4	N 21.1	N 23.4
27	18.8	8.8	2.5	13.7	21.2	23.3
28	18.5	8.5	2.9	14.0	21.4	23.3
29	18.3	S 8.1	3.2	14.4	21.6	23.3
30	18.0	...	3.6	14.7	21.7	23.2
31	S 17.7	...	N 4.0	...	N 21.9	...
	July	Aug.	Sept.	Oct.	Nov.	Dec.
1	N 23.1	N 18.1	N 8.4	S 3.1	S 14.3	S 21.8
2	23.1	17.9	8.1	3.4	14.6	21.9
3	23.0	17.6	7.7	3.8	15.0	22.1
4	22.9	17.3	7.3	4.2	15.3	22.2
5	22.8	17.1	7.0	4.6	15.6	22.3

	July	Aug.	Sept.	Oct.	Nov.	Dec.
6	N 22.7	N 16.8	N 6.6	S 5.0	S 15.9	S 22.5
7	22.6	16.5	6.2	5.4	16.2	22.6
8	22.5	16.3	5.8	5.7	16.5	22.7
9	22.4	16.0	5.5	6.1	16.8	22.8
10	22.3	15.7	5.1	6.5	17.1	22.9
11	N 22.2	N 15.4	N 4.7	S 6.9	S 17.3	S 23.0
12	22.0	15.1	4.3	7.3	17.6	23.1
13	21.9	14.8	3.9	7.6	17.9	23.1
14	21.7	14.5	3.6	8.0	18.1	23.2
15	21.6	14.2	3.2	8.4	18.4	23.3
16	N 21.4	N 13.9	N 2.8	S 8.8	S 18.7	S 23.3
17	21.3	13.5	2.4	9.1	18.9	23.3
18	21.1	13.2	2.0	9.5	19.1	23.4
19	20.9	12.9	1.6	9.9	19.4	23.4
20	20.7	12.6	1.2	10.2	19.6	23.4
21	N 20.5	N 12.2	N 0.8	S 10.6	S 19.8	S 23.4
22	20.4	11.9	0.5	10.9	20.1	23.4
23	20.2	11.6	N 0.1	11.3	20.3	23.4
24	20.0	11.2	S 0.3	11.6	20.5	23.4
25	19.7	10.9	0.7	12.0	20.7	23.4
26	N 19.5	N 10.5	S 1.1	S 12.3	S 20.9	S 23.4
27	19.3	10.2	1.5	12.7	21.1	23.3
28	19.1	9.8	1.9	13.0	21.3	23.3
29	18.8	9.5	2.3	13.3	21.4	23.3
30	18.6	9.1	S 2.7	13.7	S 21.6	23.2
31	N 18.4	N 8.8	...	S 14.0	...	S 23.1

Example: On 10 December the declination of the sun is 22°.9 S, so an observer who measures the zenith distance as 0° would know that he is at latitude 22°.9 S. If he measures a zenith distance of 5° with the sun south of this zenith, he is 5° north of 22°.9 S, or at latitude 17°.9 S; and if the sun is north, he is 5° south of 22°.9 S, or in latitude 27°.9 S.

Latitude from Polaris

You can find your latitude in the Northern Hemisphere north of 10° N. by measuring the angular altitude of Polaris above the horizon. Attach a thin string or thread to the center hole of your plotter and attach a small weight to the lower end of the string. Sight along the edge of the plotter at Polaris (next page), so that the string crosses the scale of the plotter in the 0°-90° quadrant. Subtract the reading of the point where the string crosses the scale from 90° to get the altitude of Polaris. To this reading apply the correction given below the illustration.

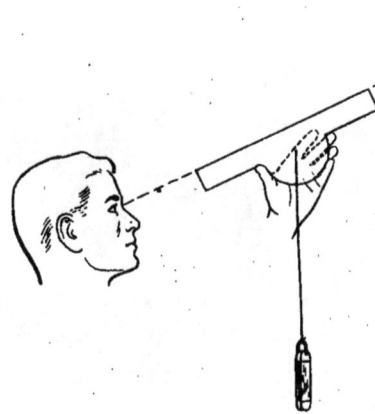

How to use a Weems plotter in sighting

1. After sighting, grasp string at outer edge of plotter and hold firmly against surface

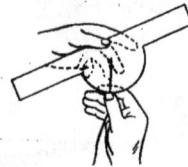

2. Holding string firmly against face of plotter, roll thumb under the edge of plotter and take reading.

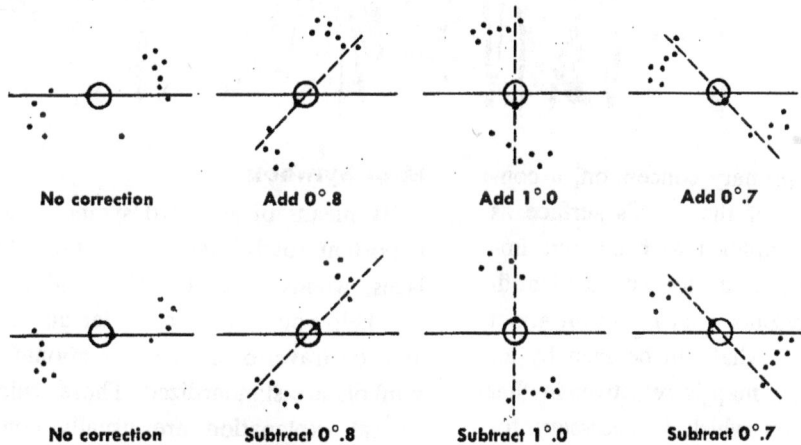

No correction   Add 0°.8   Add 1°.0   Add 0°.7

No correction   Subtract 0°.8   Subtract 1°.0   Subtract 0°.7

Correction for observed altitude of Polaris

The figures are drawn for angles of 0°, 45° and 90° between the vertical and the line through Cassiopeia and the Dipper. For intermediate positions the angle may be estimated and the correction taken from the following table. Subtract corrections of positions *above* Pole star, add those *below*.

Angle	Correction
0°	1°.0
10	1.0
20	0.9
30	0.9
40	0.8

Angle	Correction
50°	0°.6
60	0.5
70	0.3
80	0.2
90	0.0

Note that the correction changes very slowly near the time when the correction is greatest, and hence an error in estimation of the position has little effect at this time.

MAP READING

A map is, in its primary conception, a conventionalized picture of the earth's surface as seen from above, simplified to bring out important details and lettered for added identification. A map represents what is known about the earth rather than what can be seen by an observer. However, a map is selective, in that only that information which is necessary for the map's intended use is included on any one map. Maps also commonly include features which are not visible on the earth, such as parallels, meridians, and political boundaries.

Since it is impossible to accurately portray a round object, such as the earth, on a flat surface, all maps have some elements of distortion. Depending on the maps intended use, some sacrifice constant scale for accuracy in measurement of angles, while others sacrifice accurate measurement of angles for a constant scale. However, most of the maps used for ground navigation will be a compromise projection in which a slight amount of distortion is introduced into the elements which a map portrays, but in which a fairly true picture is given.

Map Symbols

By means of standard symbols, maps show important roads, side roads, trails, towns, villages, woods, streams, lakes and the features that help you recognize the terrain as you look at it or travel over it. Conventional signs and symbols are standardized. Those which require special explanation are usually contained in the legend included at the bottom of most maps. A great deal of information which is necessary for the proper interpretation of a map is usually printed on the borders of the map. *Always read the marginal information* before using a map. It may save you from making serious mistakes.

Contour Lines

Contour lines are the wiggly brown lines on a map and are drawn linking all points at a given height above sea level. You will note that these lines are broken at intervals and a figure inserted in the break, such as 6,500, 7,000, 7,500, or 8,000. These figures indicate the height of the contour line above mean sea level in feet. (Some foreign maps have the height indicated in meters, so be careful when using a map for the first time.) Always check the marginal information to find the contour interval. Some of the lines carry no identifying numbers, but since the contour interval is known, the height of any unnumbered line can be determined by its relation to the numbered lines. For example: the contour interval is 100 feet and an unnumbered line is two lines away from the 9,000-foot line and three lines from the 9,500-foot line, the elevation at any point on the unnumbered line is obviously 9,200 feet. The height of any point on a map can be determined by reference to adjacent contour lines. Elevations are further indicated on maps and charts by measured elevations for the peak or highest point of a mountain. The arrangement of the contour lines indicates the form of the land. The contour lines around a ridge point downhill, and those in a valley point upstream. The spacing of contours indicates the steepness of a slope. Contour lines close together indicate a steep slope, and contour lines which are far apart indicate a gentle slope. These are points for people who are traveling on foot to consider when planning a route.

Distance Scales

How far is it from where you are to where you want to go? Maps give this information by providing the user with a scale which he can use to measure distance on the map. These scales can be used to find the distances between any two points on the map. Lay any available straight edge, a folded piece of paper, a string, or the edge of a pencil on the map so that it joins the two points. Mark on the edge of the straight edge the position of the two points. Lay the marked straight edge on the graphic scale and read off the distance directly. The same technique can be used to measure distance along a crooked course such as a road or river by breaking the course up into short straight segments.

Longitude and Latitude

To describe a location in a city, the inter-section of two streets is commonly used. Knowing the name of only one street establishes the general area of the location, but the intersection of two streets constitutes an exact location. In the same fashion, in order to locate a point on a map or chart you must indicate the coordinates of this particular point, in degrees of longitude and latitude.

Latitude can be described as a division of the surface of the earth into north and south. An imaginary circle known as the Equator, drawn around the earth midway between the North and South Poles, serves as the starting point. The surface of the earth north of the Equator is divided into 90 equal divisions by circles drawn parallel to the Equator. Each circle is called a parallel of latitude and is numbered starting from 0° at the Equator to 90° at the North Pole. Any parallel of latitude north of the equator is known as north latitude. The earth's surface south of the Equator is divided in the same manner and is known as south latitude. Each degree is further subdivided into 60 divisions, called minutes. Using this system, you will find Offut AFB, Nebraska, is about 41° and 15′ north of the equator.

Longitude can be described as an east and west division of the earth's surface. Longitude is measured in degrees east and west of a base line which passes through Greenwich, England. This line is a circle which passes through both the North and South Poles and is called the prime meridian. Longitude is divided into 360 equal parts, or degrees. If you stand on the circle passing through Greenwich and face the North Pole, the lines on your left are numbered 1° W., 2° W., to 180° W., and the ones on your right are numbered 1° E., 2° E., etc., to 180° E. Longitudes 180° E. and 180° W. coincide. Again by using this system, you will find Offut AFB, Nebraska, to be about 95° and 56′ west of Greenwich.

All navigational maps and charts are laid out in latitude and longitude. The position of any point on the earth is described as so many degrees and minutes east or west of the prime meridian and so many degrees and minutes north or south of the Equator. The approximate location of Offut AFB, Nebraska, would thus be 41° and 15′ north latitude and 95° and 56′ west longitude.

How to Use a Map

How can the information on the map be used for ground navigation? This information can be used in several ways. First, you can locate your position on the ground by comparison of the map with the terrain. Second, you can determine the best route from one point to another by reference to the map. The map shows you how to avoid rough terrain, and will help you plan the easiest route. The contour lines add a third dimension to the flat map. Third, by marking your route on the map, you have a record of your journey. If you get off course, you can back track to the point where you made your mistake and start in again. Fourth, a man in a survival situation usually feels a lot better and approaches problems in a more confident manner if he knows exactly where he is. A map can give you that confident feeling.

USE OF THE MAGNETIC COMPASS

Direction is measured in degrees clockwise from north (360° or 0°) through 360°. The most common instrument for measuring direction is the *magnetic compass*. Since most survival kits contain some type of magnetic compass, it is imperative that you know something of its use. Compasses will generally be marked in degrees from 0° to 360°: east is 90°, south 180°, and west 270°. The easiest way to understand direction is to consider yourself to be at the center of a large compass. The 360 degrees of your compass dial are now 360 different paths or streets that you may use in following a map. The direction to a given point on the map is determined by measuring the angular distance clockwise from north to that point. This angular distance, expressed in degrees, is the direction of that point from you.

The term "north" is usually considered to mean the direction of the North Geographic Pole. The compass needle points directly to the North Geographic Pole is only a few places on the surface of the earth. The reason for this is that the North and South *Magnetic Poles* do not coincide with the North and South *Geographic Poles*. In addition, deposits of magnetic materials in various regions of the earth keep the compass from pointing to the North Magnetic Pole. A magnetic compass, therefore, points not toward the North Geographic Pole, nor exactly toward the North Magnetic Pole, but to the *magnetic north* for that particular area. The difference between true north and magnetic north is called "variation." Variation is represented on a map by lines joining points of equal variation and is expressed in degrees east and west of a base line where the variation is zero. If you are east of this line your compass will point west of true north, and if you are west of this line your compass will point east of true north. The variation of any point is indicated in your maps; for example, the variation at Offutt AFB is approximately 9° E. This means that your compass will point 9° east of true north. Therefore, if you were going to travel true north from Offutt AFB and maintain this direction with a magnetic compass, you would have to follow a heading of 351° on the compass. In other words, you would travel 9° left (west) of magnetic north.

ALASKAN BACK PACK

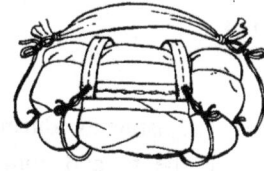

Tumpline attached to pack

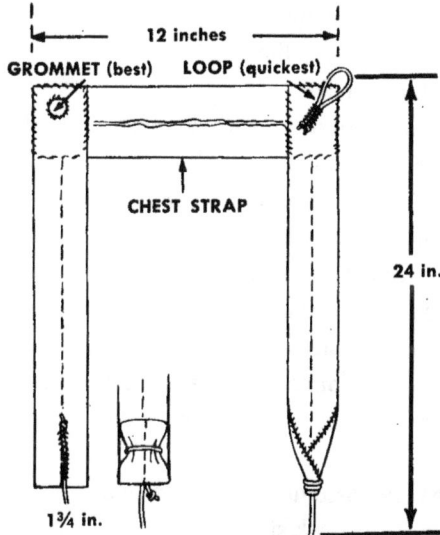

12 inches

GROMMET (best)   LOOP (quickest)

CHEST STRAP

24 in.

1¾ in.

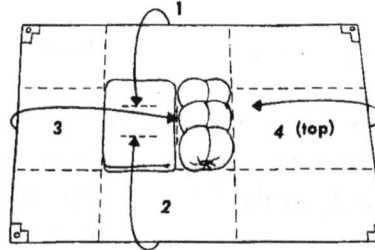

FOLDING PACK

HEADSTRAP

TUMPLINE

BACK PACK

Tumpline

Preparations

Before you start to travel, consider all the factors on pages 16 and 17. Lay careful plans and make a thorough estimate of the situation.

Backpacking

When no transportation is available and you must carry heavy loads for comparatively long distances, backpacking is essential.

The Alaskan packing method, which combines a fabric pack strap and a tumpline, is used with minor variations by primitive peoples throughout the world.

Although a heavy load is a burden, using a suitable harness and following certain approved loading and carrying techniques can eliminate unnecessary hardships and assist you in carrying the load with greater safety and comfort.

Carrying a burden initially develops mental irritation and fatigue, either of which can lower morale or cause hysteria. Experienced men know that when packing a heavy load it is advisable to keep the mind occupied with other thoughts. A survivor can divert his attention from a heavy load by surveying the landscape for the best travel routes and the safest means of passing undetected through hostile territory, or by searching for game or other sources of food.

117

Make slight adjustments during each rest stop to improve the fit and comfort of your pack.

Also, constantly regulate your pace to the weight of your pack and the nature of the terrain being crossed.

You can make this type of pack strap out of any soft, pliable, and strong material. Suitable materials usually available to a survivor include animal skins, canvas, and parachute-harness webbing. It can be made in the following manner:

1. Cut a strip approximately 12 inches long (outside measurement) and 3 inches wide for a cheststrap.

2. Use any soft material, such as an old sock or parachute cloth, for padding; however, take care to maintain an even surface in order to reduce or eliminate unnecessary body friction.

3. Sew loops or grommets into the lower outside corners of the cheststrap.

4. On the outer edges of the cheststrap, sew two shoulder straps about 2 inches wide and long enough to extend from the cheststrap over and beyond the shoulders. The shoulder straps need no padding if they are flat and smooth, but pad them if they irritate or cut into your shoulder.

5. At the end of the shoulder straps attach strings about 6 feet long. These strings may be made from rawhide or thin rope. You can also make excellent straps by braiding or twisting parachute shroud lines.

6. Encircle the pack with these strings and pass them under each arm before attaching them with a half hitch to the loops or grommets in the cheststrap. Tie the half hitch with a slip-loop so that you can quickly release the pack with a single pull.

ADVANTAGES OF THE ALASKAN PACKSTRAP. It is so small in bulk and so light in weight that you can carry it over one shoulder, tie it around your waist, or carry it in a pocket while hunting.

In an emergency you can quickly release it. The broad top of the pack bundle provides a firm, steady platform on which you can carry bulky items.

You can adjust this packstrap to efficiently pack items of a variety of shapes and sizes.

When properly assembled, the pack is soft and lies flat against your back.

When you use the packstrap with a tumpline, the two together distribute a pack's weight over your shoulders, neck and chest, thereby eliminating sore muscles and chafed areas.

DISADVANTAGES OF THE ALASKAN PACK-STRAP. Experience and ingenuity are necessary to use it with maximum efficiency.

The packstrap is not immediately available after an emergency landing but must be constructed.

The pack must be assembled and lashed before you can adjust the pack strap to it.

You must anticipate your needs for an entire day and keep outside the pack those articles you will need.

A novice cannot quickly remove or put on the pack when stopping to rest; however, it need not be taken off during the course of an entire day's travel.

Tumpline

A tumpline is the greatest single aid to backpacking, since it transfers part of the weight of a pack from your shoulders to your head and neck. Construction is as follows:

1. Attach a soft band, which rests on the upper forehead, to the pack by means of pieces of light line. You can make the band of any strong, soft material, such as pieces of animal skin with the hair still on them, tanned skin, and old sock, or parachute cloth. Make the band long enough to reach over your forehead and down to a point opposite each ear. A tumpline does not require sewing since the end knots keep any loose material along the edges in order.

2. Adjust the tumpline to fit your head by making loops at the ends. It is difficult to reach down and behind to make necessary adjustments at the bottom of your pack, but you can easily reach up to adjust the pack by means

of loops on either side of your forehead.

3. Make mainstrings from rawhide or parachute shroud lines. Tie them to the lower corners of the pack, bring them up to the loops at the ends of the tumpline, and tie them there with a slipknot.

You will learn from experience how to estimate proper adjustments before putting on your pack, but you can always make closer adjustments after the packstraps are adjusted.

How To Use A Tumpline

Have the tumpline just tight enough to transfer about half of the weight of the pack from your shoulders to your head. In other words, distribute and balance the weight of the pack as much as possible.

Occasionally a heavy pack can cut off the blood circulation of the shoulders and arms. In such cases a tumpline is of great value since, by slight adjustments, you can transfer most of the weight to your head and neck, thereby instantly loosening the shoulder straps and permitting circulation to return to numb arms.

For the first few days a tumpline may cause neck muscles to be slightly sore from the unusual strain placed on them; however, this discomfort soon disappears. With practice you can support heavy weights with only your neck and head.

Travel Hints

Wear shoes you can walk in comfortably or improvise footgear adequate for walking. Remember that you must depend on your feet to bring you out.

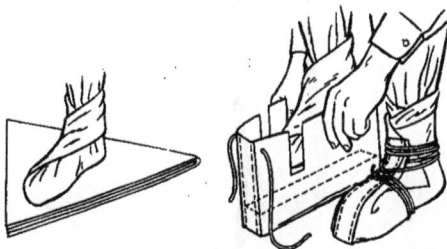

Improvised shoes

If you are in friendly territory, leave a note at the aircraft for rescuers, as well as a sign visible from the air. Describe your estimated destination and the route you intend to travel, and mark your trail.

If possible, remove aircraft magnetic compass (remove compensating magnets from compass before using).

If available, carry your antiexposure suit. It will be a good windbreak and protection from the elements. It will be invaluable in crossing streams and small bodies of water.

Always try to make camp early, well before darkness, so that you can get comfortable while there is still light. Unpack only what you need. Repack before going to sleep. For shelter, see page 16. For fire making, see page 17. Organize camp-work crews. Assign set tasks for each man; it will make your camping operations quicker and easier. Be methodical and neat around your camp. Sloppy camps usually indicate a sloppy plan and weak leadership.

Avoid swamps and wet mud flats. If you come down in one, step on roots or bunches of grass. Avoid "slick spots." In soft mud, lie flat and travel on your belly. Anti-exposure suits are invaluable in this type of terrain. If you have a life raft, you may be able to make your way out through meandering water channels.

Don't cross quicksand without testing it to see if it will bear your weight. Quicksand may have a firm crust and yet be almost fluid underneath, so try to puncture the crust when testing. Use a pole for a probe if you can find one. Wear a Mae West if you have one. If you do get caught in quicksand, fall on your back and stretch out your arms, so that your weight will be spread over the largest area possible. If you have companions, lie still until they throw a line or reach you with a pole. If you are alone, inflate your Mae West, try to get a pole, or other support under your hips and then pull your legs out of the sand; rest, then roll to firm ground. If you have to rest while getting to shore, lie on your back and spread out your arms.

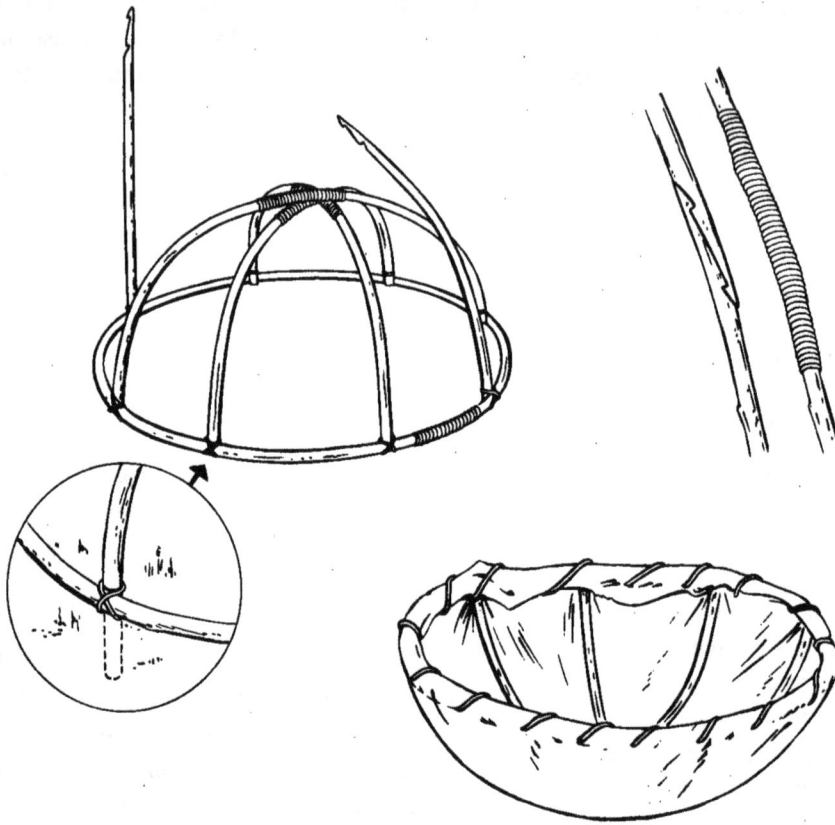

Construction of a bull boat

ANCHOR

Twist lines of fiber
to right, as shown.
Lay right hand line
over the left and
shift lines to
opposite hands.
Repeat until finished.

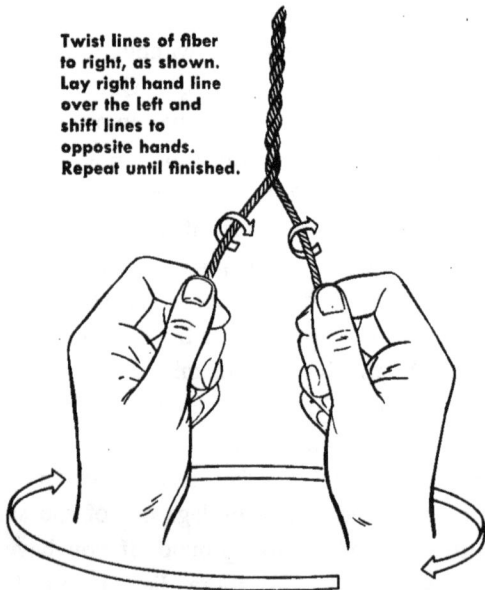

Methods of
adding new
material

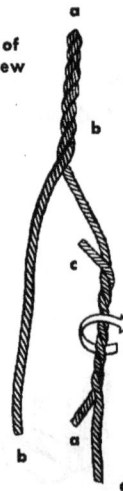

a

b

c

b   a   c

Making a rope

NORTH TEMPERATE ZONE LAND TRAVEL

Land travel techniques are based largely on experience, which in turn is acquired only through actual physical performance. However, experience can be replaced somewhat by the intelligent application of certain specialized practices that can be learned through instruction and observation. For example, travel routes may be established by observing the direction of a bird's flight, the actions of wild animals, the way a tree grows, or even the shape of a snowdrift. Bearings read from a compass or the sun or stars can improve on these observations and confirm original headings. All observations are influenced by the location and physical characteristics of the area where they are made and by the season of the year.

Successful primitive travel presupposes the ability of the individual to survive; however, never forget that you must depend on *regional* food supplies when traveling. *You must forage as you travel.*

Land travel requires knowledge beyond mere travel techniques. You should have at least a general idea of the location of your starting place and of your ultimate destination. You should know something about the country through which you will travel and the people in it. If the population is hostile, you must adapt your entire method of travel and mode of living to this one condition.

Wilderness travel requires continuous sightings. A novice views a landscape from the top of a hill with what he considers care and interest, and then says, "Let's go." The experienced man settles down comfortably and starts carefully surveying the surrounding countryside. A distinct blur may be mist or smoke; a faint, winding line on a far-off hill may be a manmade or an animal trail; a blur in the lowlands may be a herd of caribou or cattle. Plan your travel route for each day only after carefully reconnoitering the terrain. Carefully study distant landmarks for characteristics that

insure their recognition from other locations or angles. Careful and intelligent observation will train you to interpret correctly the things you see, whether they are distant landmarks or a broken twig at your feet.

Before leaving a place, study your back trail carefully. Know your route both forward and backward. After you have passed by, game may move out from cover to watch your movements. An error in route planning may make it necessary to backtrack in order to take a new course.

Topography

Mountain ranges frequently affect the climate of a region, and the climate in turn influences the vegetation, wild life and the character and number of people living in the region. For example, the ocean side of mountains has more fog, more rain and more snow than the inland side of a range. Forests may grow on the ocean side when the inland side is semi-arid. Therefore, a complete change in route-finding procedures and survival techniques may be necessary while crossing a mountain range.

Travel in mountainous country is simplified by conspicuous drainage landmarks, but it is complicated by the roughness of the terrain. A mountain traveler can readily determine the direction in which rivers or streams flow; however, he must reconnoiter to determine whether a river is safe for rafting, or if a snowfield or mountainside can be traversed safely. Mountain travel differs from travel through rolling or level country and certain cardinal rules govern climbing methods. A group descending into a valley, where descent becomes increasingly steep and walls progressively more perpendicular, may be obliged to climb up again in order to follow a ridge until an easier descent is possible. In such a situation, rappeling with a shroudline rope may save many weary miles of travel. In mountains a traveler must avoid possible avalanches of earth, rock and snow, as well as crevasses in ice fields.

Forests grow in humid areas. When forested areas are dense, river trails and ridges usually afford the easiest travel. In open forests, land travel is easy and offers a greater choice of direction of movement, but such forests may not offer sufficient cover or concealment. Isolated homes, villages, and towns may be found along rivers and these may require changes in travel methods. Where populations are unfriendly, it is often necessary to travel at night.

In certain parts of *northern prairies,* the direction in which streams flow can be determined only with difficulty. Countless lakes with poor drainage also can add to travel difficulties.

Finding Your Way by Natural Landmarks

Rain or fog may hide the sun, and at times you may have to orient a course by observing landmarks — such as vegetation, sand contours or snowdrifts — that are affected by prevailing winds. Travel under such conditions is difficult until streams, hills, or a seacoast running in a definite direction comes to your aid.

VEGETATION. Near a seacoast where prevailing winds blow inland from the ocean, thicket growth is dead or stunted on the windward side and slowly increases in height toward the lee side. Individual trees lean away from the prevailing wind and their branches are thicker and longer on the lee side.

SAND. Sand contours are affected by wind but less so than those of snow. Old sand drifts formed by strong winds are more firmly packed than recently formed drifts, and sand lies deeper on the leeward side.

SNOW. Learn the characteristics of drifts by studying snow surfaces after storms. You can tell the direction of the wind by the fact that a snowdrift is, generally, lower and narrower to windward and higher and wider to leeward before dropping off abruptly to a general level. When you travel at night and there is only diffused light which makes no shadows, or if it is so dark that you cannot see the drifts, stop and carefully feel the drifts with your feet or drop on all fours and examine them with your hands.

Glaciers

Many glaciers offer possible travel routes.

Their main contribution to emergency travel is that they serve as routes across mountain ranges. Glacier crossing demands special knowledge and techniques, such as the use of a lifeline and poles for locating crevasses. There are, however, numerous places in the north where mountain ranges can be negotiated on foot in a single day by following glaciers. Shelters designed for a minimum number of tentpoles and artificial heat are desirable.

Fuel As An Influence on Travel

The availability of fuel greatly influences the selection of travel routes. The timberline traveler must descend to spruce groves to camp overnight, and the seacoast traveler must watch for a good supply of driftwood. Along the southern coast of the Bering Sea, outcrops of coal are common. Many northern grasses are excellent not only for tinder and kindling but also as staple fuel. Green willow and alder generate hot fires and, when laid in the shape of a grill, help to start a coal fire. Green willow branches thrown on a fire at night form coals that last until morning.

A generous supply of wood makes a happy camp, but a fire that can be a survivor's best friend can also be his most dangerous enemy if it burns important equipment or irreplaceable clothing. *Never leave a fire without first taking precautions to put it out.*

Using Waterways

Rivers always offer the easiest and fastest avenues of communication through wilderness. In summer the use of rafts or boats insures speedy travel; in winter frozen, level river surfaces afford easy walking. Large lakes or connecting systems of smaller waterways also provide good travel avenues.

"Overflows," caused by *river* water flowing over ice, are extremely dangerous at low temperatures. Thin ice on lakes or streams is always dangerous. However, if you guard against these dangers, the level surfaces of water routes permit rapid traveling.

Route-Finding

The novice is prone to follow a compass line. The experienced man follows lines of least resistance, recognizing at a glance that a curved route may be shorter and easier, that an apparently innocuous stretch of forest may be filled with windfalls, or that a smooth, green meadow may contain a series of beaver ponds, which hamper travel or make it almost impossible.

Use game trails when they follow your projected course. Trails made by migrating caribou are frequently extensive and useful. On scree or rock slides, mountain sheep trails are helpful. Moose and bear trails are almost always unreliable, frequently leading into almost impenetrable thickets or swamps. Other routes offer varying prospects, such as the chance of securing game or of locating waterholes.

Route-finding through wild country requires great concentration, knowledge of wilderness "road signs," common sense, and judgment. Fortunately, trailwalking techniques develop progressively with experience and a clear mind registers observations and forms deductions almost subconsciously.

Calmness, self-confidence, constant watchfullness, courage, caution, and unlimited patience — all characteristics of the best types of outdoorsmen — develop with time.

Group Travel

In almost every group there is at least one individual who refuses to follow travel rules or lacks the patience and wisdom of a trained outdoorsman in selecting trails, locating game, or solving some of the countless other problems that arise during travel. He is the type of person who can, if allowed to, endanger an entire party. Some survival situations require great skill in order to avoid the slightest error in judgment. By breaking a survival rule, one man can destroy an opportunity for securing food or jeopardize the lives of others in the party.

Remember that the aircraft commander is in command. If he is not present, then the highest ranking individual is in charge. In any case, full use should be made of any survival experience or knowledge of *any* member of the group.

Mountain Walking

Mountain walking, depending on the general formation of the ground to be crossed, involves four different techniques. However, two fundamentals apply to all four techniques, and you must master *both* of these fundamentals in order to expend minimum energy and time.

You must keep the weight of your body DIRECTLY over your feet and you must place the soles of your shoes FLAT on the ground. You can accomplish both of these most easily by taking small steps and moving at a slow, steady pace.

Hard ground generally is firmly packed dirt that will not give way under the weight of a man's step.

When ascending hard ground, apply the two procedures mentioned previously and the following in addition:

a. Lock your knees briefly at the end of each step in order to rest your leg muscles.

b. Traverse steep slopes and, if necessary, climb in a zigzag direction and *not* straight up.

c. Turn at the end of each traverse by stepping off in the new direction with the uphill foot. This prevents crossing your feet and possibly losing your balance.

When traversing hard ground, you can place the full sole of your shoe down flat most easily by rolling your ankle away from the hill with each step.

For narrow stretches, you may use the herringbone step. Ascend straight up a slope with your toes pointed out and using all of the other principles already outlined.

Descending over hard ground is best accomplished by the following procedures:

a. Come straight down without traversing.

b. Keep your back straight and your knees bent so that they take up the shock of each step.

c. Keep your weight directly over your feet and place the full sole on the ground at each step.

d. Walk with a slight forward lean and with your feet slightly pigeon-toed.

In mountainous terrain, *grassy slopes* are usually made up of small hummocks of growth rather than a continuous field of grass. To ascend, step on the *upper side* of each hummock where the ground is more level than that on the lower side. Traverse with a slow, rhythmic, walking motion. Never run, because running on hard or uneven terrain can result in a sprained ankle. To *descend,* use the techniques mentioned for hard ground.

Scree slopes consist of small rocks and rock particles which have collected under cliffs. Scree varies in size from sand particles to pieces the size of your fist. Occasionally it is a mixture of various sizes, but normally each scree slope is made up of the same size particles.

To *ascend* scree is extremely difficult — avoid it when possible. All principles of ascending hard ground apply, but you must pack each step carefully so that your foot does not slide down when weight is placed on it. You can do this best by kicking in with the toe of the upper foot and the heel of the lower foot.

To *descend* scree, come down in a straight line. It is important to keep your feet in a slightly pigeon-toed position as well as to keep your back straight and your knees bent. Since there is a tendency to run down scree, take care not to attain too great a speed and thereby lose control. By leaning slightly forward, you can obtain greater control.

When a scree slope must be *traversed* and no gain or loss of altitude is desired, use the hop-skip method. This is a hopping motion in which the lower foot takes all the weight and the upper foot is used only for balance.

Talus slopes are similar in makeup to scree slopes, but the rocks are larger. To walk on talus, step on top of and on the uphill side of the rocks to keep them from tilting and rolling downhill. All other previously mentioned fundamentals apply.

General Precautions in Mountain Walking

It is of the utmost importance that you do *not* kick loose rocks so that they roll down hill. Falling rocks are extremely dangerous to men below, and they also make a great deal of noise. Carelessness by anyone in this respect can cause a well-planned mission to fail, since one rock no larger than a man's head can kill or severely injure several men, as well as ruin all security measures.

Step over rather than on top of obstacles such as rocks and fallen logs to help avoid fatigue.

Talus usually is easy to ascend and traverse while scree is a better avenue of descent.

Balance Climbing

Balance climbing is the type of movement used to travel on steep slopes. It combines the balanced movement of a tightrope walker and the unbalanced climbing of a man ascending a ladder. Body position is very important.

Climb with the body in balance — that is, with your weight poised over your feet or just ahead of them as you move. Your feet, not your hands, carry the weight except on the steepest cliffs — your hands are for balance. Your feet will not hold well when you lean in toward the rock.

With your body in balance, move with a slow, rhythmic motion. Use three points of support, such as two feet and one hand, whenever possible. Handholds that are waist- to shoulder-high are preferable. It is better to use small intermediate holds rather than stretching and changing to widely separated big holds. Avoid a spread-eagle position in which you stretch so far that you cannot let go.

In descending, face out when the going is easy, sideways when it is hard, and face in when it is extremely difficult. Use the lowest possible handholds.

You must relax, because tensed muscles tire

RIGHT

WRONG

Body position

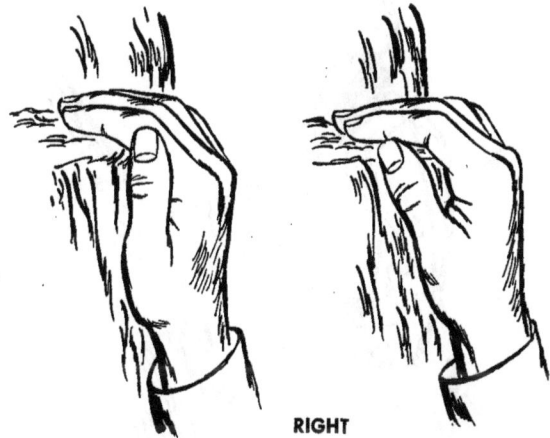

RIGHT

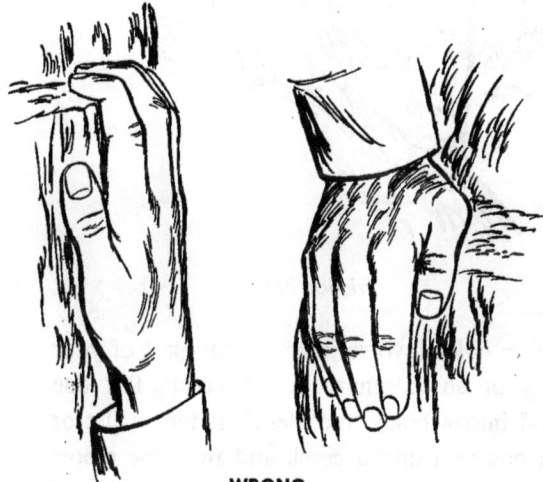

WRONG

Hand holds

quickly. When resting keep your arms low so that circulation is not impaired.

BASIC HOLDS. *Pull holds* are those with which you pull down; they are the easiest to use but also the most likely to break out.

Push holds are ones with which you push down; they help you to keep your arms low. They rarely break out, but they are more diffi-

cult to maintain in case of a slip. A push hold is often used to advantage in combination with a pull hold.

Friction holds depend solely on the friction of your hands or feet against a smooth surface. They are difficult to use because they give you a feeling of insecurity, which most climbers try to correct by leaning close to the rock, thereby increasing their insecurity. Friction holds often serve well as intermediate holds, some of which give needed support while you move over them but which would not support you were you to step on them.

You can combine and vary the above basic holds. The number of variations depends only upon the limit of your imagination. A few common combination holds are described below.

Pinch a protruding piece of rock firmly between your fingers and thumb.

Friction hold

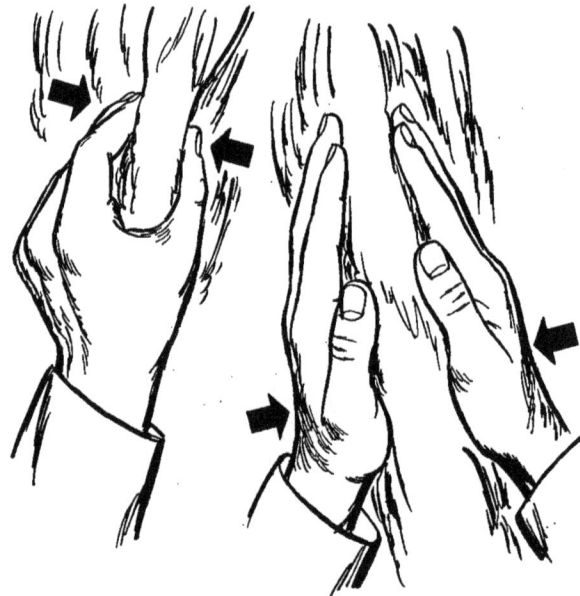

Pinch holds

Jam holds involve jamming any part of your body or an extremity into a crack. Put one hand into a crack and clench it into a fist or put one arm into a crack and twist the elbow against one side of the crack and the hand against the offset side.

Lean to one side of an offset crack with your hands pulling and your feet pushing against the offset side.

Jam holds

PULL OUT

PUSH IN

Lie-back

Inverted pull hold

Chimney climbing technique

The inverted pull or push hold is also called an under hold. It permits cross pressure between your hands and feet.

In chimney climbing, exert cross pressure between your back and feet, hands or knees.

The foothold is a common hold. The service shoe with rubber sole will hold on rock slabs that slope as much as 45°. On steep slopes, keep your body vertical and use small irregularities in the slope to aid foot friction.

Chimney climbing

Footholds

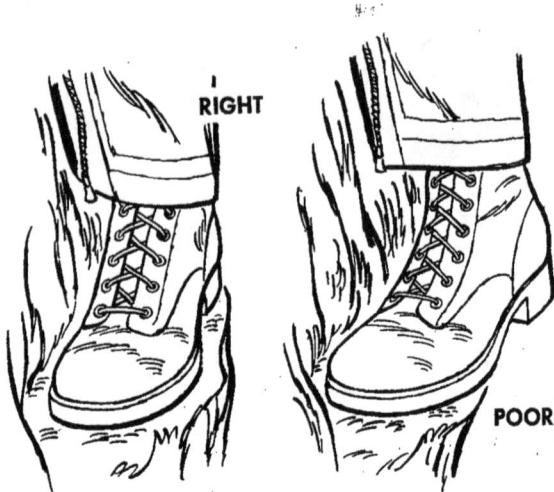

Footholds

USE OF HOLDS. A hold need not be large to be good nor must it be solid as long as the pressure you apply keeps it in place. Experienced climbers use holds so small that they are scarcely visible. You must roll your feet and hands over your holds and *not* try to skip or jump from one to another.

When traversing, however, it is often desirable to use either the hop step, in which you change feet, or a small hold with which you may move sideways more easily. This useful step involves a slight upward hop followed by precise footwork.

MARGIN OF SAFETY. Carefully test each and every hold before applying full pressure to it. Keep a margin of safety by never attempting to climb to the full limit of your ability. Carefully assess the climbing ability of yourself and all other members of your climbing party. Then, with equal care, study the terrain to be covered. Make every effort to plan climbs so that the *least* able climber in a group is never pushed to the fullest extent of his ability.

Roped Climbing

In group climbing, two or three men are tied into a 60- to 120-foot length of rope. *Belaying* provides the necessary safety factor that enables each man to climb. When any one man is climbing, he is belayed from above or below by another man to whom he is tied with a belay rope. Without belaying skill, using a rope is a hazard and not a help to group climbing.

WHEN BELAYING. Run the rope through your guiding hand (the hand on the rope running to the climber) and around your body to your braking hand, making certain that the rope will slide readily.

Make sure that the remainder of the rope is so laid out that it will run freely through your braking hand. See that the rope does not run over the sharp edge of a rock. Use the guiding hand to avoid letting too much slack develop in the rope as the climber moves. Gently tug the line running to the climber to sense his movements.

Avoid taking up slack suddenly, since this may throw the climber off balance. Brace well for the expected direction of a fall, so that the force of a fall, whenever possible, will pull you more firmly into position. Neither trust nor assume a belay position that has not been tested.

In case of a fall be able to perform the following movements automatically:

1. Relax your guiding hand.

2. Let the rope slide enough so that braking action is applied gradually by bringing your braking hand slowly across the chest.

3. Hold the belay position, even if this means letting the rope slide several feet.

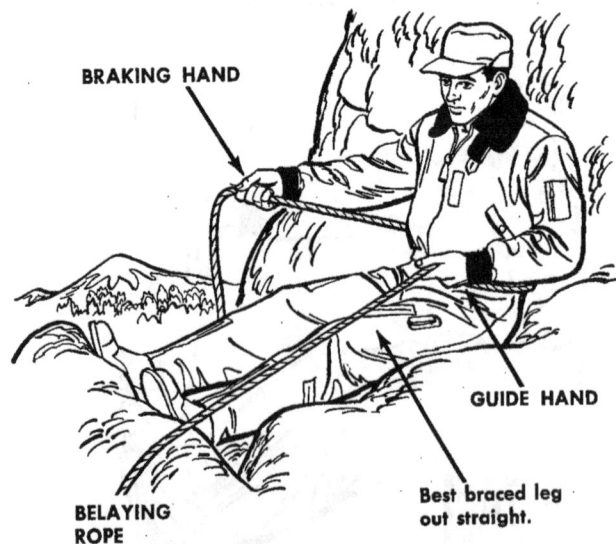

Sitting hip belay

THE SITTING BELAY. The belayer sits or leans against the rocks and attempts to get good triangular bracing between his two legs and his buttocks. Whenever possible, his legs should be straight. The rope should run around his hips in such a manner that a fall will maintain the belayer more firmly in position. This is facilitated by making certain that the rope always runs along the belayer's *best braced* leg to the climber.

After the belayer has found a belay position and has settled himself there, he calls "On belay," which is answered by the climber with "Up rope" (in order to have the belayer take up the slack).

When the slack has been taken up, the belayer calls "Test." The climber then calls "Testing" and puts his weight gradually on the rope. The climber must be careful not to jerk the rope suddenly, as this might pull the belayer out of position.

If the position is satisfactory, the belayer calls "Climb," and the climber calls "Climbing."

If the belayer finds his position unsatisfactory, he must call "Off belay," and the climber must release all tension at once. The belayer must then find another position and repeat the test procedure.

ROPED CLIMB (2-MAN PARTY).

1. One man, chosen as leader because of his ability and experience, always climbs first.

2. Both men tie in with a bowline or a bowline on a coil.

3. The second man takes a belay and starts the test procedure.

4. After finding that his position is satisfactory, he gives the order "Climb."

5. The leader then climbs to a suitable belay position. He should not take long leads, particularly where climbing is difficult. If there is no suitable belay position and he must take a long lead or if climbing is precarious, the leader should, whenever possible, lay the rope over rock nubbins. The belay man adapts his position to an upward pull of the rope.

6. The belayer should watch the slack and inform the climber, "20 feet," "15 feet," "10 feet," and "5 feet," by estimating the length of rope left at the belayer's position.

7. When the climber has reached a belay point, he establishes a firm belay position and follows test procedures. The No. 2 man climbs to his position, then the No. 1 man climbs again. Only when it is determined that both climbers are of equal ability is leapfrogging permissible.

8. The procedure is repeated until the objective is reached.

ROPED CLIMB (3-MAN PARTY).

1. In a 3-man party each man has a number: the leader is No. 1, the middle man No. 2, and the end man No. 3.

2. The signals are the same as for a 2-man party, except that the number of the man involved must be called out along with the signal. For example, the middle man may give the order "No. 1 climb," or "No. 3 climb."

3. The leader climbs from the starting point to the first belay position, brings up No. 2, and climbs to the second belay position. He provides what security he can while No. 2 brings up No. 3. No. 2 then follows No. 1 who climbs to the third belay position. When not climbing, No. 3 provides security as anchor man for No. 2 when he is belaying.

4. *No man climbs until ordered to do so, and only one man climbs at a time.*

Certain other *general rope signals*, in addition to the belay signals, are often useful. These signals are given orally.

a. "Up rope," is used when a climber discovers excess slack in his belay rope.

b. "Slack," is used when the belay rope is too tight to permit maneuvering.

c. "Tension," means the climber is in trouble and wants a tight rope.

d. "Falling," is used to warn the belay man if the climber believes he is about to fall.

e. When silence is necessary or when a high wind distorts oral signals, you can convey information by a prearranged system of jerks or gentle tugs on the rope.

SIMULTANEOUS MOVEMENT. When a slope becomes gentler for a stretch, all men can move at once. The No. 2 and No. 3 men carry the slack rope in neat coils which can be payed out or rolled up as the distance between the men varies. The rope must be kept off the ground but not taut.

RAPPELING. A climber with a rope can descend quickly by means of a rappel — sliding down a rope which has been doubled around such rappel (or holding) points as a tree or projecting rock.

In selecting a route, be sure that the rope reaches the bottom or an intermediate point from which additional rappels will reach the bottom. Test the rappel point carefully. Check to see that the rope will run freely around it when one end is pulled from below to retrieve the rope after the rappel has been completed.

To assume the body rappel position, face the anchor point and straddle the rope. Then pull the rope from behind and run it around either hip, diagonally across the chest, then back over the opposite shoulder. From there the rope runs to the braking hand, which is the hand on the same side as the hip that the rope crosses. (For example, from the right hip to the left shoulder to the right or braking hand.)

The climber should lead with the braking hand down and should face slightly sideways. He should keep the other hand on the rope above him as a guide and not as a brake.

He must lean out at a sharp angle to the rock. He should keep his legs well spread and relatively straight for lateral stability and his back straight to reduce unnecessary friction.

Turning up the collar prevents rope burns on the neck. Wear gloves and any other articles of clothing as padding for the shoulders and buttocks.

Glaciers and Glacial Travel

To cope with the problems that can arise in using glaciers as avenues of travel, it is important that you understand something of the

REAR VIEW

FRONT VIEW

Rappeling

TYPICAL GLACIAL TERRAIN

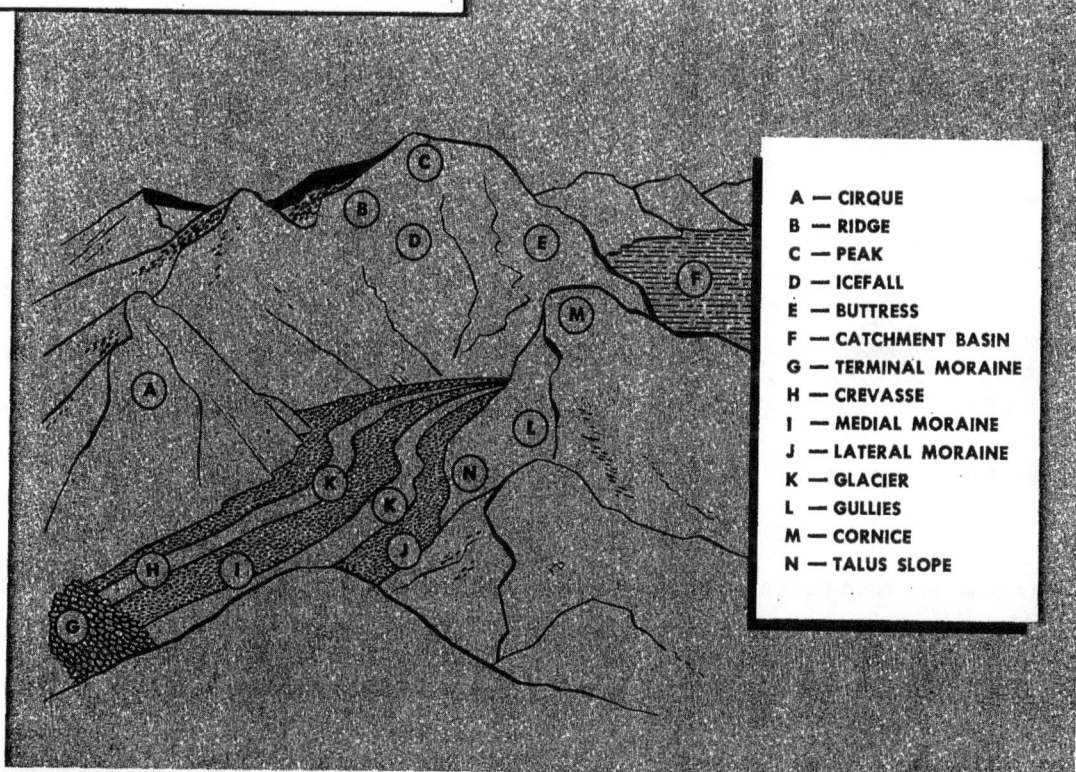

A — CIRQUE
B — RIDGE
C — PEAK
D — ICEFALL
E — BUTTRESS
F — CATCHMENT BASIN
G — TERMINAL MORAINE
H — CREVASSE
I — MEDIAL MORAINE
J — LATERAL MORAINE
K — GLACIER
L — GULLIES
M — CORNICE
N — TALUS SLOPE

nature and composition of glaciers. Also see page 183 for method of roping up for travel.

A valley glacier is essentially a river of ice. It flows at a rate of speed that depends largely on its mass and the slope of its bed.

A glacier consists of two parts:

a. The lower glacier, which has an ice surface that is devoid of snow during the summer.

b. The upper glacier, where the ice is covered, even in summer, with layers of accumulated snow that grade down into glacier ice.

To these two integral parts of a glacier may be added two others which, although not a part of the glacier proper, generally are adjacent to it and are of similar composition.

These adjacent features, the *ice* and *snow slopes,* are immobile, since they are anchored to underlying rock slopes. A large crevasse separates such slopes from the glacier proper and defines the boundary between moving and anchored ice.

Ice is plastic near the surface, but not sufficiently so to prevent cracking as the ice moves forward over irregularities in its bed. Fractures in a glacier surface, called crevasses, vary in width and depth from only a few inches to many feet. (Also see page 183.)

Crevasses form at right angles to the direction of greatest tension and, since within a limited area tension usually is in the same direction, crevasses in any given area tend to be roughly parallel to each other.

Generally crevasses develop across a slope. Therefore, when traveling up the middle of a glacier, you usually encounter only transverse crevasses (crossing at right angles to the main direction of the glacier).

Near the margins or edges of a glacier, the ice moves more slowly than it does in midstream. This speed differential causes the formation of crevasses which trend diagonally upstream away from the margins or sides.

GLACIAL FORMATIONS

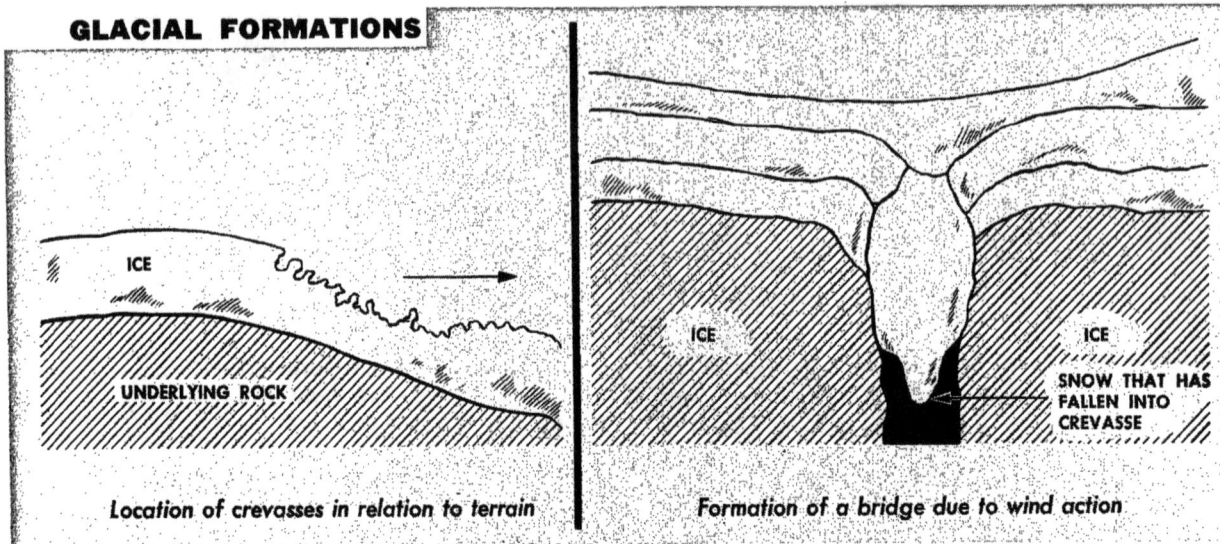

Location of crevasses in relation to terrain

Formation of a bridge due to wind action

While crevasses are almost certain to be encountered along the margins of a glacier and in areas where a steepening in gradient occurs, the gentlest slopes of a glacier also may contain crevasses.

An *icefall* forms where an abrupt steepening of slope occurs in the course of a glacier. Here stresses are set up in many directions. As a result, the icefall consists of a varied mass of ice blocks and troughs with no well-defined trend to the many crevasses.

GLACIAL SURFACE STREAMS AND MILLS. On those portions of a glacier where melting occurs, runoff water cuts deep channels in the ice surface and forms surface streams. Many such channels exceed 10 feet in depth and width. They usually have smooth sides and their banks are usually undercut. Many of these streams terminate at the margins of the glacier where in summer they contribute to the torrent that constantly flows between the ice and the lateral moraine. You must exercise the greatest caution in crossing a glacial surface stream, since the bed and undercut banks are usually of hard, smooth ice which offers no secure footing.

Other streams, however, disappear abruptly into crevasses or into round holes, called *glacial mills,* and then flow as subglacial streams. Glacial mills are cut into the ice by the churn-

ing action of water. They vary in diameter. Glacial mills differ from crevasses not only in shape but also in origin, since they do not develop as a result of moving ice. In places the depth of a glacial mill may equal the thickness of the glacier.

MORAINES. As a glacier moves forward, debris from the valley slopes on either side is deposited on its surface. Shrinkage of the glacier from subsequent melting causes this debris to be deposited along the receding margins of the glacier. Such ridges are called *lateral (side) moraines.*

Where two glaciers join and flow as a single river of ice, the debris on the adjoining lateral margins of the glaciers also unites and, flowing with the major ice-stream, forms a *medial (middle) moraine.* (By examining the lower part of a glacier, it often is possible to tell how many tributaries have joined to form the lower trunk of the glacier.)

Where the snout of the glacier has pushed forward as far as it can go — that is, to the point at which the rate of melting equals the speed of advance of the ice mass — a *terminal (end) moraine* is usually found. This moraine may be formed of debris pushed forward by the advancing snout or it may be formed by a combination of this and other processes.

Lateral and medial moraines may provide excellent avenues of travel. When the glacier is heavily crevassed, moraines may be the only practicable routes.

Ease of progress along moraines depends upon the stability of the debris that composes them. If the material consists of small rocks, pebbles and earth, the moraine usually is loose and unstable and the crest may break away at each footstep. If larger blocks compose the moraine, they have probably settled into a compact mass and progress may be easy.

In moraine travel, it is best either to proceed along their crest or, in the case of lateral moraines, to follow the trough which separates it from the mountainside. Since the slopes of moraines are usually unstable, there is great risk of spraining an ankle on them.

Medial moraines usually are less pronounced than lateral moraines, because a large part of their material is transported within the ice. Travel on them usually is easy but do not rely upon them as routes for long distances since they may disappear beneath the glacier's surface.

Only rarely is it necessary for a party traveling along or across moraines to be roped together.

Northern Rivers

Northern rivers are varied in type and present numerous problems to those who must cross or navigate them.

RIVER SOURCES. Wherever mountains and highlands exist in the Arctic regions, melting snows produce concentrations of water that pour downward in series of cataracts, falls and swift chutes. Their current is churned to foam and the roar drowns out the human voice. Such rivers cannot be successfully rafted in canoes, but *at times they must be crossed.*

GLACIAL RIVERS. Rivers flowing from icecaps and hanging, piedmont (lakelike), or serpentine (winding or valley) glaciers are all notoriously treacherous.

Northern glaciers may be vast in size, and the heat of the summer sun can release vast quantities of water from them.

Glacial ice is extremely unpredictable. From above an icefield may look innocent enough, but under its smooth surface there may be countless subglacial streams and water reservoirs. These reservoirs are either draining or are temporarily blocked or dammed. Mile-long lakes may lie under the upper snowfield, waiting only for a slight movement in the glacier to liberate them and to send their millions of gallons of water flooding into the valleys below.

Due to variations in the amounts of water released by the sun's heat, all glacial rivers fluctuate in water level. The peak of the flood water usually occurs in the afternoon as a result of the noonday heat of the sun on the ice. For some time after the peak has passed, rivers which drain glaciers may be unfordable or even unnavigable; however, by midnight or the following morning, the water may recede so that fording is both safe and easy.

When following a glacial river that is broken up into many shifting channels, choose routes next to the bank rather than taking a chance on getting caught between two dangerous channels.

FLOODING GLACIERS. Glaciers from which torrents of water descend are called flooding glaciers. There are two basic causes of such glaciers:

a. The violent release of water which the glacier carried on its surface as lakes, or

b. The violent release of large lakes which have been dammed up in tributary glaciers due to the blocking of the tributary valley by the main glacier. This release is caused by a crevasse or a break in the moving glacial dam coming opposite the lake, the water of which then roars down in an all-enveloping flood.

Flooding glaciers can be recognized from above by the floodswept character of the lower valleys — the influence of such glaciers is sometimes felt for many miles below. Prospectors have lost their lives while rafting otherwise safe rivers because a sudden flood entered by a side tributary and descended as a wall of white, rushing water.

FORDING STREAMS. Every man traveling on foot through wilderness must ford some streams. These may range from small, ankle-deep brooks that rush down from side valleys to large, snow- or ice-fed rivers. The latter are so swift that you can hear waterborne boulders on the bottom being crashed together by the current. If these streams are of glacial origin, allow them to decrease in strength during the night hours before attempting to ford them.

You must find a ford that is basically safe; this requires careful study. If there is a commanding hill beside the river, leave your pack in a safe spot, and climb the rise, Carefully examine the valley for:

a. Level stretches where the river breaks into a number of channels. Like an army, a river can best be defeated when it is separated into a number of parts.

b. Obstacles on the opposite bank which might hinder travel. Make certain that you end up on the side where travel is easier and safer.

c. A ledge of rocks which crosses the river and which often indicates the presence of rapids or canyons.

d. Any heavy timber growths, since they indicate where the channel is deepest.

When selecting a site for fording, remember the following:

a. Whenever possible, choose a course that leads across the current at about a 45° angle downstream.

b. Never attempt to ford a stream directly above, or even close to, a deep or rapid waterfall or a deep channel.

c. Always ford where you would be carried to a shallow bank or sandbar if you should lose your footing.

d. Avoid rocky places, since a fall can cause serious injury; however, an occasional rock that breaks the current may be of some assistance to you.

Depth is not necessarily a deterrent if you can keep your footing. Deep water may run more slowly and be safer than shallow water; you can always dry out your clothing later. There are places where it is easier to swim.

Before entering the water, plan exactly what you are going to do and how you are going to do it. Take all possible precautions, and if the stream appears to be treacherous take the following steps:

1. Remove your pants and underdrawers and lash them to the top of your pack. The water will then have less grip on your bare legs.

2. Keep your shoes and socks on to protect your feet and ankles from boulders and to give you firmer footing.

3. Tie important articles securely to the top of your pack. If you are forced to release your pack, you probably can eventually locate it; but, if single pieces of valuable equipment fall separately, you probably can never recover them.

4. Shift your pack well up on your shoulders; have the slipnooses in good operating condition in case it is necessary to drop your pack. Regardless of the type of pack you are carrying, make certain that you can quickly extricate yourself from it. Prepare yourself and your gear so that, if swept off your feet, you can quickly release your pack; then, unencumbered, you will be able to hold onto one end of the packstrap and, half-swimming and half-wading, fight your way to the far bank. Many competent swimmers have drowned because they could not get out of a heavy pack quickly enough.

A strong log, used as a pole, can greatly aid a lone man fording a swift stream. The log should be about 5 inches in diameter and about 7 or 8 feet long.

Use the log on your *upstream* side to break the current. Do *not* use it on your downstream side where the current tends to push you down on the log and to lift your feet from under you.

Keep the log grasped firmly on your upstream side and firmly plant your feet with each step. Lift the log a little ahead and downstream from its original position but still upstream from you.

Step below the log. Keep the log well slanted so that the force of the current keeps the log against your shoulder.

Several men entering a swift ford should follow the procedures already mentioned.

The log, or pole, is used differently when there is more than one man. The *heaviest* man forms the *downstream* anchor with the pole held *parallel* to the current. The *lightest* man is placed at the *upstream end* of the pole where he breaks the current; those below move in the eddy formed by his body.

If the current comes from the right, grasp the pole under the left armpit with the right hand extended for balance. If the current comes from the left, grasp the pole under the right armpit and extend the left hand for balance.

At times the upstream man may be temporarily swept from his feet, but the eddy formed by his body enables the man or men below him to move with comparative ease.

As in all fording, the route should quarter downstream. Currents too strong for one man to stand against usually can be crossed safely in this manner.

Experience can enable you to judge water and the swiftness of its flow with great accuracy, but there is always danger in fording. Take all possible precautions for your personal safety and that of your equipment.

Do not worry about having a heavy pack on your back, since nothing helps more in swift water than weight — *if* you can release it quickly. Indians used to shoulder heavy stones to help them to keep their footing in swift streams. The weight of your pack makes it inadvisable to complicate matters further with heavy stones, but remember that the weight of a pack is a help and not a hindrance.

Rafts and Rafting

Rafting rivers is one of the oldest known forms of travel and under survival conditions often the best and quickest mode of travel. You can make rafts of dry, dead, standing trees. Spruce, which is found near polar and subpolar rivers, make the best rafts.

BUILDING A RAFT. The greatest problem in raft construction is to make the craft strong enough to withstand the buffeting it may have to take from rocks and swift water. Even if 6- to 8-inch spikes are available, they are not satisfactory since they pull or twist out easily. Rope quickly wears out from frequent, rough contact with rocks and gravel.

Northern woodsmen have evolved a construction method that requires neither spikes nor rope, yet produces a raft that is superior

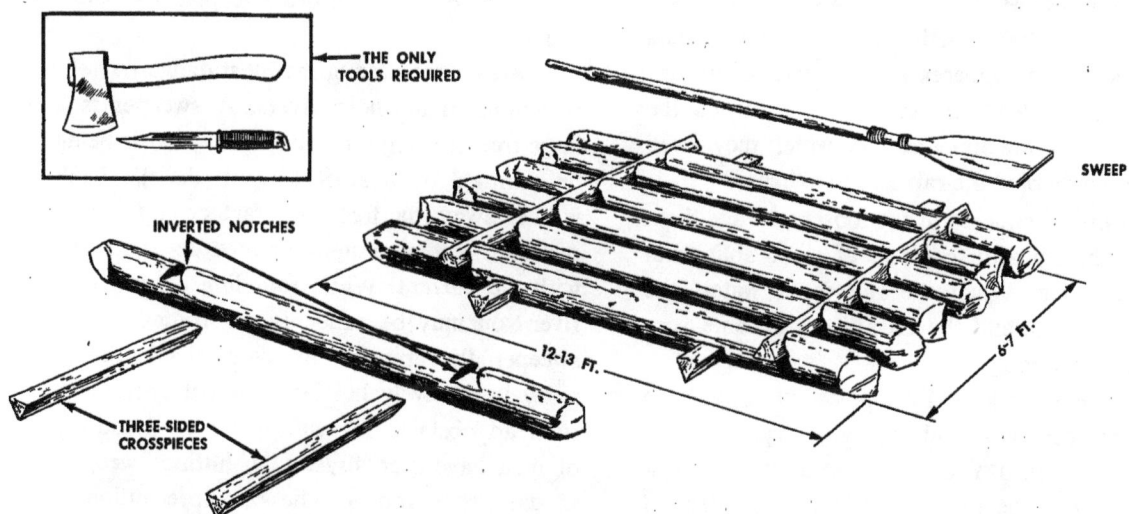

Wilderness raft

135

in strength. The only materials you need are logs, although rope is sometimes useful, and the only tools you need are an ax and a sheath knife.

A raft for 3 men should be about 12 or 13 feet long and 6 or 7 feet wide, depending on the size of the logs used. The logs should be 12 to 14 inches in diameter and so well matched in size that notches you make in them are level when crosspieces are driven into place.

Build the raft on two skid-logs placed so that they slope downward to the bank. Smooth the logs with an ax so that the raft logs lie evenly on hem. Cut two sets of slightly offset inverted notches, one in the top and bottom of both ends of each log. Make the notches broader at the base than at the outer edge of the log, as shown in the illustration. Use small poles with straight edges or a string pulled taut to mark the noches.

Drive through each of the four sets of notches a three-sided, wooden crosspiece about a foot longer than the total width of the raft.

Complete the notches on all logs at the top of the logs. Turn the logs over and drive a 3-sided crosspiece through on the underside of both sets of notches. Then complete the top set of notches, turn the raft over, and drive through the two additional sets of crosspieces.

You can lash together the overhanging ends of the two crosspieces at each end of the raft to give it added strength; however, when the crosspieces are immersed in water they swell and tightly bind the raft logs together.

If the crosspieces fit too loosely, wedge them with thin, boardlike pieces of wood split from a dead log. When the raft is in water, the wood swells, and the crosspieces become very tight and strong.

Make a deck of light poles on top of the raft to keep packs and other gear dry.

PROTECTING YOUR GEAR AND RIFLE WHEN HUNTING. The most important single item of equipment you have is your rifle, and few things sink faster. A raft is not foolproof and can turn over when it hits a rock. As a result, the beds of some northern streams are liberally spotted with rifles lost from rafts and canoes. Even when attached to rafts, rifles have gone to the bottom when the raft logs broke apart upon hitting obstructions. Tie your rifle to the raft, but lash it firmly to only *one log*. Thus, if the raft should be broken, you have a chance of recovering your rifle by going downstream and finding the one log to which your rifle is tied. You may have to swim to reach the log, but at least you have a chance to recover intact a valuable piece of equipment.

Protect packs and other gear by wrapping them in waterproof covering.

RAFTING. You can steer a raft by using sweeps and poles; in fairly shallow water a pole is more efficient, but when water is deep a sweep is preferable. Use poles and sweeps from both ends of the raft. The bow (front) man can see any obstructions ahead and the stern (rear) man can follow his directions in steering. Poles are also useful for pushing a raft in quiet water.

The most important rule in navigating an unknown stream is to cautiously study stretches that may be dangerous. Scout swift-water rapids or sharp bends where the current is strong and the view ahead is obstructed, by beaching the raft and carefully studying the questionable stretch in order to plan the safest route.

Sweepers are among the most dangerous obstructions in northern rivers. A sweeper is a large tree growing on a river bank that is being undermined by a swift current. As the bank washes away, the tree leans farther and farther out until it may actually bounce up and down with the current. While rounding a bend in a river you may be suddenly confronted with a sweeper that blocks the channel. A rafting party is relatively helpless when it encounters such an obstacle in swift water — hundreds of men have met disaster by hitting sweepers in dangerous rapids. The only precautionary measure is to land above a bend in order to study the river ahead.

Snags and sunken boulders make character-

istic disturbances on the surface of a current which you soon learn to recognize.

Navigating rivers in hostile territory is possible but difficult due to the necessity of traveling at night. Night navigation requires extremely close adherence to all normal precautionary measures The raft should be camouflaged during daylight hours.

While hard and fast rules are usually inadvisable, it is always wise to stay close to the *point* of a river bend. If the river bends to the left, keep close to the left bank; if it bends to the right, stay close to the right bank. Water is shallower along these points, and you frequently can jump out to ease your raft gently around the point. Attach a coil of rope or parachute shrouds to the stern of the raft to help you to control it.

EMERGENCY BOAT. An emergency boat can be made from a tarpaulin or light canvas cover stretched over a skilfully shaped framework of willows, adding a well-formed keel of green wood, such as slender pieces of spruce.

Attach gunwales (sides) of slender saplings to both ends and equalize the spreaders or thwarts as in a canoe. Tie ribs of strong willows to the keel, bend the ends of the ribs upward and tie them to the gunwales. Closely cover the inside of the frame with willows to form a deck upon which to stand.

Such a boat is easy to handle, buoyant, and lacks only strength to be suitable for long journeys. It is entirely satisfactory for ferrying a group across a broad, quiet stretch of river.

When such a boat has served its purpose, remove the canvas cover and take it along for constructing shelters or to make other boats.

CONTACT WITH NATIVES

Let the natives contact you. With few exceptions, natives are friendly. They know the country, its trails, waterways, available food and drink, and the way back to civilization. They can be your best help; it all depends on the way you handle them.

Deal with the recognized headman or chief to get what you want. Ask for help; don't demand it.

The important thing in approaching natives is to show friendliness, courtesy, and patience. Don't act scared. Don't threaten or display a weapon. Don't make sudden movements. Don't give a native cause to fear you; fear makes him hostile. Smile frequently.

Primitive people may be shy and unapproachable at first. They may run away when you enter a village or meet them. Approach a village slowly. Don't rush matters. Stop where you are — sit down and relax.

Call or clap your hands to attract the native's attention. Let him make the initial approach. It is best to wait until only one native is near, rather than a group. A native will be glad to help a survivor who appears to be in need. Don't be afraid to be an object of amusement to the natives. Be ready to entertain with songs, games, or any tricks of cards, coins, or string which you may know. Rock salt, twist tobacco, and silver (not paper) money should be used discreetly in trade. Don't overpay a native. It leads to later embarrassment and even danger. Display proper identification, such as a U.S. flag. You can go far with sign language or by acting out your needs or questions.

Once the ice is broken, go ahead and ask for what you need. Some one may understand a few words of English. If not, use sign language; natives are accustomed to it because they communicate a lot by signs themselves. State your business simply and frankly. Once you win confidence, later dealings are a matter of common sense.

Treat your new friends like human beings. Don't look down on them. Don't laugh at them or make fun of them. Don't bully or drive them. People who violate these "don'ts" get a spear in their bellies or get knifed in their sleep.

Don't pat children on the head when demonstrating your friendliness. Many natives consider the head to be the source of an individual's magic power and your actions may be considered to be highly dangerous to the child. If a native is sitting on the ground with his legs extended, do not step over his legs. A breach of this rule might indicate your extreme contempt for the man, and could lead to violence. Hospitality among some primitive people is such a strong cultural trait that they may seriously reduce their own supplies to make certain that you are well fed. Try to prevent them from starving themselves for your comfort.

If you make a promise, keep it.

Respect the local customs and manners even if they seem queer to you. Remember that to the natives you are the queer one. You are the stranger in their home.

Respect personal property. Always make some kind of payment for what you receive or take, but don't overpay.

Paper money is worthless in most places. Hard coin is good; in many places it has exchange value; in most places it has value as jewelry or trinkets. In isolated places, matches, tobacco, salt, razor blades, empty containers, or cloth may be worth more to the natives than any form of money.

Leave the native women alone at all times.

Respect privacy; don't go into a house unless you are invited. If you want to contact some one in a house, call or send a child in.

Certain areas may be taboo. They range from religious or sacred spots to diseased or danger areas. Certain animals must not be killed. Learn what the rules are and follow them.

If you have to live with natives for some time, do your share of entertaining them with tricks, games, songs, and dances. Be a good audience, too.

Don't take offense at pranks played on you; most primitive people are fond of practical jokes. If you're a victim join in the fun; be a good sport.

Try to pick up at least a few words of the local language. The natives will like you for it and will help you learn if you show an interest.

Don't ask questions that can be answered by "yes" or "no." If you ask: "Does this trail go to the river?" — the native feels that is what you want to know and he will probably say "yes" to make you happy. Ask the question this way: "Which is the shortest way to the river?" Or: "How do you get to the river?" Or: "Where does this trail go?"

Learn all you can from the natives about woodcraft and getting food and drink. The knowledge will help you if you have to travel out on your own.

Take the natives' advice on local hazards; they know their country. Find out from friendly natives where there are hostile tribes. Frequently natives insist that distant tribes are hostile. They generally can be trusted only in their opinion of immediate neighbors.

Natives suffer from diseases which you can catch. Build a separate shelter, if you can. The natives will probably help you build one. Avoid physical contact without seeming to do so. If you can do it without giving offense, prepare your own food and drink. If you're asked why you boil water, explain that it's your own personal custom; and they will respect it.

Whatever you do, leave a good impression. Other men in the same fix may come along later. Make it easier for them.

Always be friendly, firm, patient, and honest. Be generous but not lavish. Be moderate.

chapter **3**

LAND

SURVIVAL

... ARCTIC

In the Arctic, living off the land is a tough assignment, but it can be done. The first step is to analyze the dominant characteristics of the Arctic. From then on, with all the survival techniques and equipment available, the harsh implications of survival are lessened. After all, the Arctic is home to thousands of Eskimos, Norwegians, Finns, Lapps, Samoyeds, Yakuts, Chukchi, and to tens of thousands of Russians.

Aircraft have steadily lessened the remoteness of the Arctic since the 1920's. In this day of great circle routes, civilian and military craft alike fly over the Arctic.

After a general discussion of the Arctic environment, the chapter outlines specific techniques for overcoming the problems touched upon generally in the preceding chapter. The discussion covers in detail such topics as im-

mediate action, shelter and clothing, health and hazards, food, equipment, and travel.

Each person who uses the term has a different concept of the Arctic. Airmen may remember it as a paradise for hunting and fishing, or as a cold hell. An engineer may think of it as the region of permanently frozen ground, the permafrost zone. A physicist is reminded of intense magnetic disturbances and auroras. An astronomer visualizes the polar area as the region where the midnight sun is visible at least 1 day each year. A botanist pictures the lands north of the limits of tree growth.

However, most meteorologists and geographers think of the Arctic as "the region where the average temperature of the warmest month is less than 50° Fahrenheit." This condition is in general acceptance and is used as the basis for a definition of the Arctic.

AREAS COVERED IN THIS CHAPTER

For the purpose of this Manual and the problem of survival, "Arctic" areas covered will be loosely defined as any region having less than one person per square mile and in which the mean temperature of at least one month drops below 14° Fahrenheit.

A rough demarcation of the areas so defined is latitude 60° North. This part of the world includes the Arctic Ocean which is ice covered the year round. It includes the tundra, level or slightly rolling treeless wastes. It includes northern extensions of the forests of larch, spruce, and birch which cover the areas intervening between the "high latitudes" and our homeland of familiar trees and fields. The diversified areas have one thing in common — a cold climate.

ARCTIC ENVIRONMENT

Cold, isolation, and seasonal extremes of daylight and darkness are all dominant characteristics of Arctic environment. These conditions prevail far south into subarctic areas; in fact, temperatures there range lower than in the true Arctic. It is difficult to draw a hard and fast line between an outing in the northern woods and an Arctic survival experience.

Cold

Cold is a miserable condition unless you are prepared for it. Very low winter temperatures occur when a locality is far from the equator, far from an ocean, and in a lowland or valley bottom. The moderating influence of the Arctic Ocean, even through a film of ice, holds minimum temperatures at the North Pole to about −60° F. In contrast, inland areas of the subarctic often are much colder. Verkhoyansk, near the Arctic Circle in eastern Siberia, has recorded a low of −94° F.

To be hot in summer, again an Arctic locality must be far from the cooling effect of oceans. Temperatures rarely exceed 60° F. along Arctic coasts. Inland localities at similar latitudes occasionally warm to 100° F.

Animals

Although the number of animals is limited, they are quite vulnerable. Land animals leave tracks and may be snared at burrows or trapped in runs. Several species of seal breathe through blow holes in the ice which are found under small domes of crusted snow.

Isolation

The feeling of isolation is common to most Arctic localities away from the few established lines of communication. Chances of local help are extremely slim in Arctic regions.

During the survival period, life swings between fear and discomfort on one hand and self-assurance and capability on the other. Self-assurance is a matter of temperament, but it may be strengthened by experience and instruction. Capability results from intelligence, ingenuity, good training, and common sense.

Daylight and Darkness

Seasonal extremes of daylight and darkness result from the tilt of the earth's axis. Arctic nights are long, even continuous in winter; conversely, north of the Arctic Circle the sun is visible at midnight at least once a year.

Darkness presents a number of problems to the Arctic survivor. No heat is received directly from the sun in midwinter, thus the cold reaches extremes. Outside activities are curtailed of necessity, although the light from the moon, stars, and auroras, shining on a light ground surface, is of some help. Confinement to cramped quarters adds boredom to discomfort, and depression becomes the dominant mood as time drags on.

A few moonlight landings have been made on frozen bays, and airdrops have been provided camps marked by flares or fires. Fortunately, the period of complete darkness does not last long.

White-Out

A white-out may complicate a survival situation; more often it causes the accident which makes survival necessary. When the ground is snow-covered and the sky overcast, when light reflected by the snow has an intensity equivalent to that received from the sun, a white-out is the result. Everything seems hazy and looks milky. There is no horizon, no shadow, nothing to aid in judging distances. A man on the ground has to probe his way.

Radio Fadeout

Radio fadeouts in the Arctic are caused by solar explosions and sunspot activity. The accepted theory is that the sun emits electrified particles which produce heavy ionization on reaching the earth's atmosphere. This ionized blanket disrupts radio communications everywhere, but particularly in the polar regions. Long term fadeouts may last for several weeks. As these are caused by sunspot activity, they may be forecast.

Short-term fadeouts, caused by solar explosions similar to the detonation of atom bombs, may occur in the Arctic both during daylight and darkness. The atmospheric disturbance is manifest about 18 minutes after a solar explosion. The fadeout condition lasts from 15 minutes to several hours. It cannot be forecast. By blanketing radio reception, fadeouts are of obvious concern to survivors. Radios are unserviceable, and communication leading to rescue may be delayed.

Magnetic Variation

Magnetic variation is noticeable almost everywhere. A compass needle points to true north only from positions due south of the Magnetic Pole, or along the line of no variation on the far side of the North Pole from the Magnetic Pole. The peculiar condition in the Arctic is the enormous variation, up to 180° between the Magnetic and North Poles. A survivor who decides to travel between established points must know that areas of *local* magnetic attraction exist throughout the Arctic. Navigation based on magnetic compass readings will often be inaccurate.

MAJOR REQUIREMENTS FOR SURVIVAL

When the environmental characteristics of the Arctic are recognized, the major requirements for survival become evident. For example, temperatures range from cool to frigid. An inflight emergency may suddenly transfer an airman from a warm aircraft into a barren waste of snow. It is evident that *warm clothing* is essential to survival.

The same simple reasoning results in emphasizing the need for *shelter*. With a temperature of −5° F., and a breeze of 8 miles per hour, travel and life in temporary shelter become disagreeable. When it chills to −30° F., and the wind speed doubles, the face will freeze in 1 minute, and travel and life in a temporary shelter become dangerous.

Although the inland areas and the Arctic Ocean are among the calmest localities in the world, strong winds do sometimes sweep along the coasts and across the tundra. Winds of gale velocities may occur where a plateau descends abruptly to the ocean — as along the coasts of Greenland.

It can be seen that *food* is essential for survival in the Arctic. The colder the weather, the more rapidly heat is dissipated. The source of body heat is the food a person eats. Food is needed to compensate for the accelerated heat loss in cold climates.

IMMEDIATE ACTION

In winter, protection from cold is your immediate and constant problem. Keep dry, avoid snow blindness, check for frost bite.

To stay dry, keep snow out of your boots, gloves, and clothing; avoid open water. Overexertion causes perspiration, which will freeze inside your clothing, thus decreasing effective insulation and increasing the chances of freezing. Always remove outer clothing when working or moving; when you stop, throw your outer garments over your shoulders or replace them to avoid chilling. Have shelter at night, remove your underclothes and air them, or let them get cold and beat the frost out with a stick. *Keep hands and feet dry.*

Frostbite, one of the greatest problems of Arctic survival, is easier to prevent than to cure. If you don't have a companion to check your face for frostbite symptoms (and vice versa), the best method of prevention is always to be actively aware of any excessive cooling or chilling of the extremities or exposed parts of the body. Keep your hands warm, by exercise, if necessary, and use them as a means to check the cooling of other parts of your body.

Collect wood, gasoline, oil, grass roots, brush, or peat for fuel. Build a fire at a safe distance from the aircraft and get under shelter (see pages 16 and 146). Take steps to ration all fuel.

If the aircraft is flyable, drain oil; insulate wheels from ice with boughs or canvas; leave brakes off; remove battery and protect it from freezing.

If down in a glacier area, be on your guard against falling into crevasses when moving. Rope party together, preferably three men to a rope. As you walk, probe the snow in front of you with a pole or ice ax to detect crevasses covered by thin snow.

In summer, protect yourself against insects. Keep dry.

FIRST AID

Injured Personnel

Keep an injured man warm and dry. Put the patient in a sleeping bag, provide shelter, and build a fire. Warm food and liquids are desirable for conscious patients. Avoid alcohol. Improvise heat packs by heating rocks, sand, metal, or dirt, and wrapping it in fabric. Place packs at the small of the back, between thighs, under armpits, on stomach, on soles of feet, or as the patient requests. *Make sure not to burn the skin.*

Frostbite

Frostbite is the freezing of some part of the body. It is a constant hazard in subzero operations, especially when the wind is strong. As a rule, the first sensation of frostbite is numbness rather than pain. You can see the effect of frostbite (a grayish or yellow-white spot on the skin) before you can feel it.

Use the buddy system. Watch your buddy's face to see if any frozen spots show; and have him watch yours.

Get the frostbite casualty into a heated shelter, if possible.

Warm the frozen part rapidly. Frozen parts should be thawed in water until soft, even though the treatment is painful. This treatment is most effective when the water is exactly 105° F., but water either slightly cooler or warmer can be used. If warm water is not available, wrap the frozen part in blankets or clothing and apply improvised heat packs.

Use body heat to aid in thawing. Hold a bare, warm palm against frostbitten ears or parts of the face. Grasp a frostbitten wrist with a warm, bare hand. Hold frostbitten hands against the chest, under the armpits, or between the legs at the groin. Hold a frostbitten foot against a companion's stomach or between his thighs.

When frostbite is accompanied by breaks in the skin, apply sterile dressing. Do not use strong antiseptics such as tincture of iodine. Do no use powdered sulfa drugs in the wound.

Never forcibly remove frozen shoes and mittens. Place in lukewarm water until soft and then remove gently.

Never rub frostbite. You may tear frozen tissues and cause further tissue damage. Never apply snow or ice; that just increases the cold injury. For the same reason, never soak frozen limbs in kerosene or oil.

Do not try to thaw a frozen part by exercising. Exercise of frozen parts will increase tissue damage and is likely to break the skin. Do not stand or walk on frozen feet. You will only cause tissue damage.

Immersion Foot (Trench Foot)

Immersion foot is a cold injury resulting from prolonged exposure to moisture at temperatures just above freezing. In the early stages of immersion foot, your feet and toes are pale and feel cold, numb, and stiff. Walking becomes difficult. If you do not take preventive action at this stage, your feet will swell and become very painful. In extreme cases of immersion foot, your flesh dies, and amputation of the foot or of the leg may be necessary.

Because the early stages are not very painful, you must be constantly alert to prevent the development of immersion foot. To prevent this condition:

Keep your feet dry by wearing waterproof footgear and keeping your shelter dry.

Clean and dry your socks and shoes at every opportunity.

Dry your feet as soon as possible after getting them wet.

Warm them with your hands, apply foot powder, and put on dry socks.

When you must wear wet socks and shoes, exercise your feet continually by wiggling your toes and bending your ankles. When sleeping in a sitting position, warm your feet, put on dry socks, and elevate your legs as high as possible. Do not wear tight shoes.

Treat immersion foot by keeping the affected part dry and warm. If possible, keep the foot and leg in a horizontal position to increase circulation.

Severe Chilling

If you are totally immersed in cold water for even a few minutes, your body temperature will drop. Long exposures to severe dry cold on land can also lower your body temperature. The only remedy for this severe chilling is to warm the entire body. Warm by any means available. The preferred treatment is warming in a hot bath. Severe chilling may be accom-

panied by shock. Warm yourself from the inside out by drinking hot coffee, hot soup, or plain hot water. Build a circle of small fires and sit inside the circle. Exercise as much as possible without sweating.

Snow Blindness

Symptoms of snow blindness are burning, watering, or inflamed eyes, headaches, and poor vision.

Treat snow blindness by protecting the eyes from light and relieving the pain. Protect the eyes by staying in a dark shelter or by wearing a lightproof bandage. Relieve the pain by putting cold compresses on the eyes if there is no danger of freezing, and by taking aspirin. Use no eye drops or ointment. Most cases will recover within 18 hours without medical treatment. The first attack of snow blindness makes the victim more susceptible to later attacks. It can be avoided — wear goggles.

Carbon Monoxide Poisoning

Carbon monoxide poisoning can be caused by a fire burning in an unventilated shelter, or by incomplete combustion even in a ventilated shelter. Usually there are no symptoms; unconsciousness and death may occur without previous warning. Sometimes, however, there may be pressure at the temples, burning of the eyes, headache, pounding pulse, drowsiness, or nausea. Treat by getting into fresh air at once; keep warm and at rest. If necessary, apply artificial respiration. Give oxygen, if available.

SIGNALING

Keep snow and frost off aircraft surfaces to make a sharp contrast with the surroundings. Build your fire on a platform so it will not sink into snow. A standing spruce tree near timber line burns readily, even when green. Build a "bird nest" of quickly inflammable material in the branches to insure a quick start.

Tramp out signals in snow. Fill them in with

boughs, sod, moss, or fluorescent dye powder.

In brush country, cut conspicuous patterns in vegetation.

In tundra, dig trenches, turn sod upside down at side of trench to widen signal and cast a shadow.

A parachute tepee stands out in the forest or on the tundra in summer, especially at night with a fire inside.

NOTE: A sound does not carry well through snow. If your entire party is in a snow cave or igloo, you may not hear rescue aircraft. Keep someone on guard as spotter. Build the spotter a windbreak but don't roof it.

SHELTERS AND SHELTER LIVING

In the Summer

You will need shelter against rain and insects. Choose a camp site near water but on high, dry ground if possible. Stay away from thick woods as mosquitoes and flies will make your life miserable. A good camp site is a ridge top, cold lake shore, or a spot that gets a breeze.

If you stay with the aircraft, use it for shelter. Cover openings with netting or parachute cloth to keep insects out. Do your cooking outside to avoid carbon monoxide poisoning. Make your fire at a safe distance from the aircraft.

Make a simple outdoor shelter by hanging a tarpaulin or a parachute over the aircraft wing; anchor the ends to the ground by weighting them down with stones. A tent can be quickly improvised by placing a rope or pole between two trees or stakes and draping a parachute over it; make the corners fast with stones or pegs. However, a pole tepee or well-constructed lean-to is much more satisfactory.

A fine shelter for drizzly weather and protection against insects is a tepee made from your parachute. In it you can cook, eat, sleep, dress, and make signals — all without going outdoors. Use 6 panels of parachute for a 2 man shelter, 12 to 14 panels for a 3-man paratepee. Never use more than half the panels of the parachute. The method of construction is shown in the illustration. This shelter is worth building if you decide to say in one spot for some time.

Avoid sleeping on the bare ground. Provide some sort of insulation under yourself — soft boughs are good. Pick a bed site on level, well-drained ground free from rocks and roots. If you have to sleep on bare ground, dig depressions for your hips and shoulders and try out the site before you set up your shelter or spread your bedding.

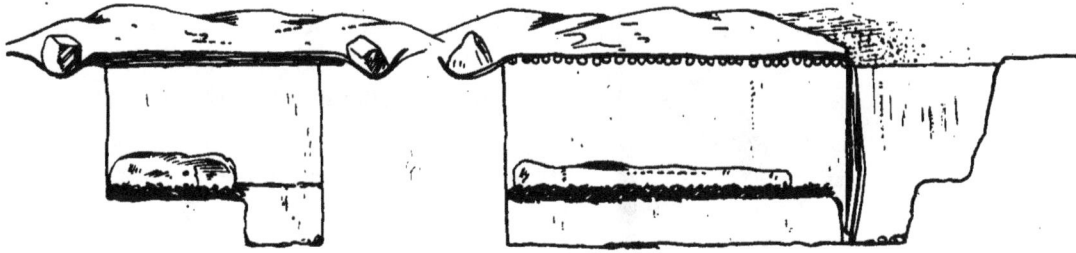
SNOW TRENCH

SNOWBLOCKS CUT FROM TRENCH

SNOW TRENCH

MAT OF INSULATING MATERIAL

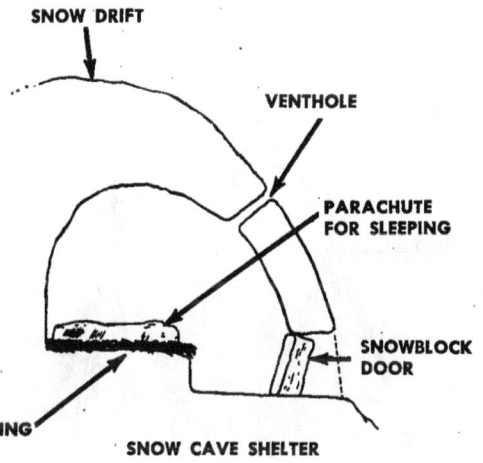
SNOW DRIFT

VENTHOLE

PARACHUTE FOR SLEEPING

SNOWBLOCK DOOR

SNOW CAVE SHELTER

TREE-PIT SHELTER

ONE-MAN SHELTER

Arctic shelters

SHROUDLINE LOOPS

WINGPOLES AND LOOPS

PEG IN GROUND

CHUTE SECTIONS ATTACHED

TIED

EXTRA POLES
LAID ON TRIPOD

COVERED WITH
CHUTE
CLOTH

FINISHED PARATEPEE

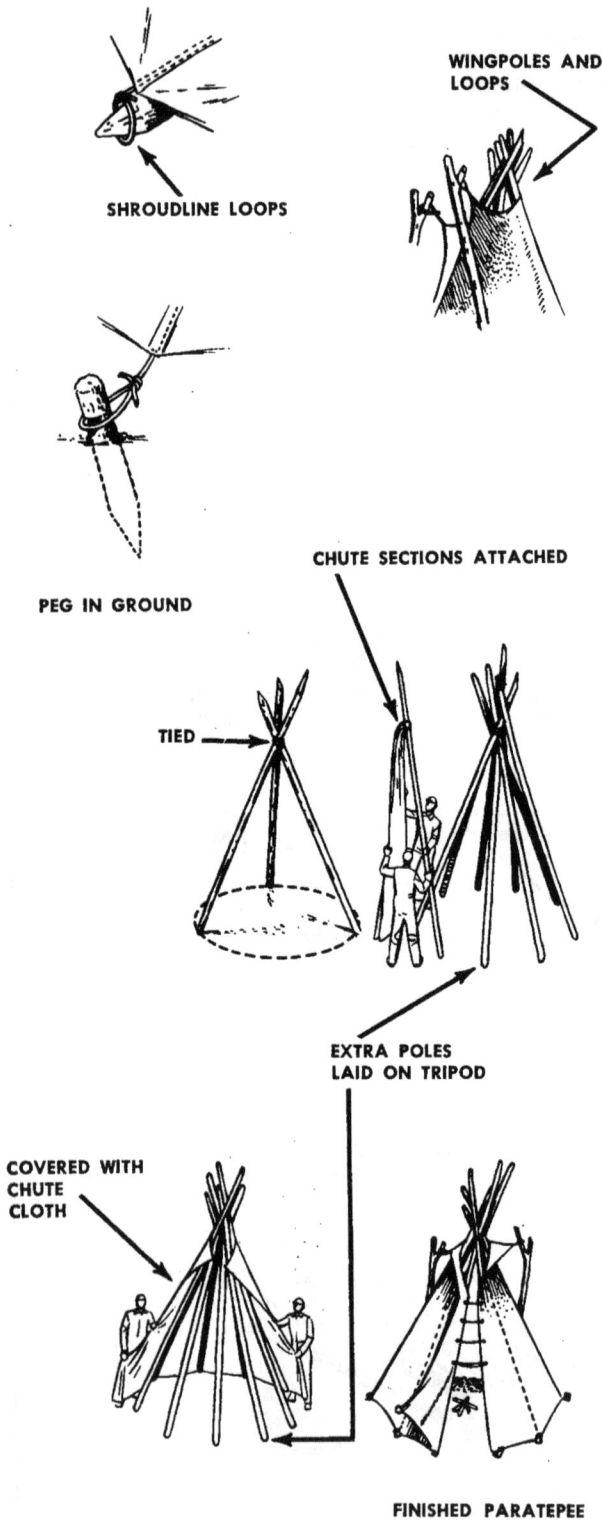

Construction of paratepee

In the Winter

You will need shelter against the cold. Don't live in the aircraft — it will be too cold. Try to improvise a better insulated shelter outdoors.

Camp in timber if possible, to be near fuel. If you can't find timber, choose a spot protected from wind and drifting snow. Don't camp at the bases of slopes or cliffs where snow may drift heavily or come down in avalanches.

Keep the front openings of all shelters crosswind. A windbreak of snow or ice blocks set close to the shelter is helpful.

In making shelters, remember that snow is a good insulator. Caves in the snow are usually rather satisfactory. However, keep your clothing dry when digging snow caves. Work slowly to avoid excessive sweating.

In timberless country, make a simple snow cave or burrow by digging into the side of a snowdrift and lining the hole with grass, brush, or tarpaulin. Snow caves must be ventilated. If the snow isn't deep enough to support a roof, dig a trench in a drift and roof it with snow blocks, tarpaulin, or other materials.

In wooded country make a tree-pit shelter if snow is deep enough. Enlarge the natural pit around a tree trunk and roof it with any available covering.

Look for cabins and shelter houses. They are likely to be located along bigger streams, at river junctions, along blazed trails in thick, tall timber leeward of hills.

Prevent carbon monoxide poisoning by providing good ventilation for closed shelters in which a fire is burning.

Don't sleep directly on the snow. Provide insulation under your sleeping bag or body. Lay a thick bough bed in shingle-fashion, or use seat cushions, tarpaulins, or even an inverted and inflated rubber life raft if available.

Keep your sleeping bag clean, dry, and fluffed up to give maximum warmth. To dry the bag, turn it inside out, beat out frost, and warm it before the fire — but don't burn it. Turn over *with* rather than *in* the sleeping bag.

Characteristics of Shelters

The only equipment needed to construct a snow shelter is a long knife or digging tool (see Axes and Knives, page 22). It takes 2 to 3 hours of hard work to dig a snow cave and twice as long or longer for the novice to build a snowhouse.

Since they cannot be heated many degrees above freezing, life in snow shelters is rather rugged. It takes several weeks to accustom yourself to the effects of living in such a cold atmosphere. You will require more food (especially fat) and hot drinks.

Regardless of how cold it may get outside, the temperature inside a small well-constructed snow cave probably will not be lower than $-10°$ F. (even when it is $-50°$ F. outside). A small 1-man snowhouse probably will not get colder than $-20°$ F. Body heat alone will raise the temperature of a snow cave $45°$ above that of the outside air. A burning candle will raise the temperature $4°$. Burning Sterno (small size, 2-5/8 oz.) will raise the cave temperature $28°$.

As you get out of your sleeping bag in the morning, the warm air released into the cave will raise the air temperature from $6°$ to $10°$. When it is $-50°$ outside, the temperature of a snow cave (with one man resting and a Sterno stove burning) will be about $32°$ F., while it will probably be $40°$ F. or above in a snowhouse (with one man resting and a one-burner gasoline stove burning).

While a tent can be erected or struck in a few minutes, its weight and bulk pose problems in traveling. A tent, however, may be more comfortable if adequate fuel is available for heating.

Tents are noisy in Arctic storms; it may be hard on the nerves to listen to a constant flapping. Tents may also be burned up, or damaged, or blown away by the wind.

Snow Caves

A snow cave can be dug with a shovel, a knife, or even a ration tin.

Dress lightly while digging as it is hard work; you can easily become overheated and dampen your clothing with perspiration.

First, dig a tunnel sloping upward, then level off and cut out an entry way. About 18 inches above the entry way, build the bed platform. To conserve heat this may be built just large enough to sleep, dress and undress while lying in the sleeping bag. If desired, the sleeping shelf may be walled in to conserve heat. In addition to the ventilation hole through the roof, there should be another at the door.

Take a shovel in with you at night in the event that you may need to dig yourself out. One storm may deposit a great quantity of snow, which may be very hard to remove without a cutting tool.

Always check ventilation holes before lighting a stove in a snow shelter. Carbon monoxide is a great danger.

Going In and Out

Keep entrances and exits to a minimum to conserve heat. Fuel is generally scarce in the Arctic. Therefore, it is important to keep the door closed as much as possible.

If someone must go out, plan to have him do as many necessary activities as possible, such as gather fuel, snow, or ice for the pot, empty the trash, etc. To expedite matters, the trash box may be kept just inside the door, and equipment may be stored in the entry way. Necessities which cannot be stored inside may be kept just outside the door.

Once the door is sealed for the night, you will make yourself very unpopular with your companions if you keep running back and forth. It can also be hard on *you*.

Toilet

It is standard practice in snow shelter living, to relieve yourself indoors whenever possible. This practice conserves body heat. If the snowdrift is sufficiently large to dig connecting snow caves, one may be used as a toilet room. If not, tin cans may be used for urinals, which

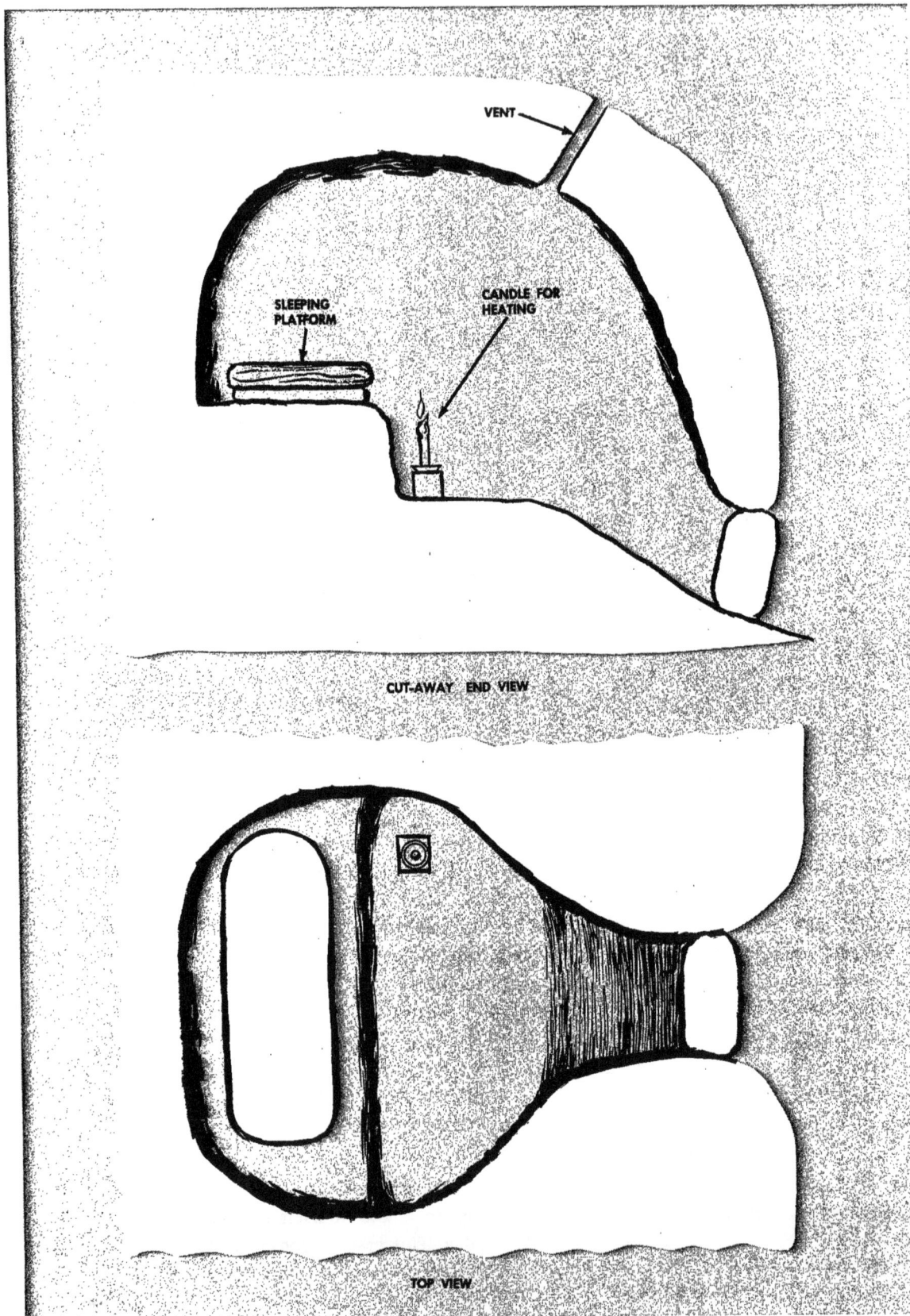

VENT

SLEEPING
PLATFORM

CANDLE FOR
HEATING

CUT-AWAY END VIEW

TOP VIEW

Snow cave

may be emptied in a remote corner opposite from the side from which snow is taken for cooking. Try to have your bowel movement just prior to leaving the shelter in the morning and remove the fecal matter with the trash.

Cooking Discipline

In the cramped quarters of any small emergency shelter, pots of food or drink can easily be kicked over accidentally. In a survival situation, this may seriously affect your chances of coming through safely. The cooking area, even if it is only a Sterno stove, should be located out of the way, possibly in a snow alcove.

It is generally safer to fill gasoline stoves outdoors or in a separate room in a snow shelter. A period of good weather should be chosen for this task. At this time, any needed maintenance work may be done. In so doing, there is less likelihood that the stove may burn out or clog up while you are using it.

Ice is better than snow for providing water, and compacted snow at the base of a drift is better than the powder snow on top.

Start with a little water in the pot to prevent burning. Otherwise the snow in the pot may absorb the water, the pot will burn on the bottom and the water will have a "burnt" taste.

The Snow-Brush is a Lifesaver

Once inside a warm shelter any snow remaining in the clothing will melt, and when the clothing is again taken outside, the water formed will turn to ice and reduce the insulation value. Brush your clothes before entering the shelter. In living conditions where drying clothing is difficult, it is easier to keep clothing from getting wet than to dry it out later.

If you cannot get all of the snow out of your outer clothing, take it off and store it in the entry way or on the floor far from any source of heat so that it will remain cold. If ice *should* form in clothing, it may be scraped off with a knife or beaten out with a stick.

Living in Your Sleeping Bag

With little between you and the ice, your sleeping bag can be pretty valuable. *Keep it dry.*

It will be more pleasant if you do most of your undressing and dressing in the sack. It's a good idea to have a hot snack or a hot drink just prior to getting in the sleeping bag. You will find it more comfortable to sleep in long woolen underwear (stored in the bag for that purpose) rather than in the clothes you wore during the day. Also put on dry bed socks. Outer clothing makes good mattress material. A parka held over the stove for a moment to trap some heat makes a good footbag. Shirt and inner trousers may be rolled up for a pillow. Socks and insoles should be separated, dried in the top of the shelter (when there is not a pot on the fire throwing off steam), then drying may be completed in the sleeping bag by stowing around the warmest section of the body, around the hips.

To keep frost (from your breath) from wetting the sleeping bag, improvise a frost cloth from a piece of clothing, a towel, or some parachute fabric. Wrap this around your head in such a way that the breath is exhaled through a sort of tunnel opening in the fabric, which goes to the outside of the bag. It is easier to dry a piece of fabric than the sleeping bag. If you should get cold during the night, exercise by fluttering your feet up and down. Fluff out the feathers in your bag by beating against the inside of it with your hands, try eating something, or make yourself a hot drink.

Don't forget your tin can urinal. One experience getting up to go outside at −50° F. will cure you.

In a snow cave, getting up is a slightly slower process than going to bed. Take your time! Begin dressing — *inside the bag.*

BEWARE OF DRIFTING SNOW

Discipline should be exercised so that "there is a place for everything and everything is in its place." A tent or snow cave can be buried so deep by drifting snow that you may have difficulty finding it, if it isn't marked with a long pole. Therefore, it is a sure thing you can't expect to leave small objects lying out on the snow and expect to find them again. A little organization should minimize the chances of losing equipment.

WARM STORAGE

In the Arctic in winter you have the problem of warm storage, not cold storage. A game carcass frozen rock-hard at −50° F. is extremely hard to cut unless you have a saw. The alternative is either to cut it into small pieces while it is warm or to insulate it from freezing. A caribou carcass may be kept from freezing for several days by placing the skinned carcass between an envelope of two skins which will seal quickly by freezing along the edges. Then bury this fur bundle in the snow during the night.

Thawed canned rations may be kept from freezing overnight by stowing in the foot of the sleeping bag.

REPAIR YOUR CLOTHING

Body heat will escape at an alarming rate from even the smallest openings under conditions of Arctic exposure, such as you face when walking over the Arctic sea ice with the air temperature at 40 or 50 below and a 10- or 15-mile wind blowing.

Be sharp. Carry a couple of strong needles (already threaded) in your cap visor. Repair your clothing before you bed down at night.

FIREARMS

During the winter, remove all lubricants and rust preventive compounds from your weapons. Strip them completely, and clean all parts. Use gasoline or lighter fluid, if available, or boiling water. Normal lubricants thicken in cold weather and slow down the action. In cold weather, weapons function best when absolutely dry.

A major problem is to keep snow and ice out of the working parts, sights, and barrel. Even a small amount of ice or snow may disable your weapon. Improvise muzzle and breech covers, and use them. Carry a small stick in your pocket to clean the sights and breech block.

Weapons sweat when they are brought from extreme cold into a heated shelter; and when they are taken out again into the cold, the film of condensation freezes. This ice may seriously affect their operations; so leave them outdoors or store them in unheated shelters.

If your shelter is not much warmer than the outside temperature, you may bring your weapon inside, but place it at or near floor level, here the temperature is lowest. When you take it into a heated shelter, wait until the weapon is warm before drying and cleaning. It may sweat for an hour.

If a part becomes frozen, do not force it abruptly. Warm it slightly, if possible, and move it gradually until unfrozen. If it cannot be warmed, try to remove all visible ice or snow and move it gradually until action is restored.

Before loading your weapon, always move the action back and forth a few times to insure that it is free.

If your weapon has a metal stock, pad it with tape or cloth, or pull a sock over it to protect your cheeks. If your hand becomes frozen to the metal parts, don't try to pull it away. Urinate on the skin where it is stuck to the metal.

AXES AND KNIVES

You can make yourself a wooden snow knife or saw if you can find a piece of wood 20 inches long and 3 inches in diameter. Split a plank, then shape a handle on one end, smooth down the other end, and you have a knife. Cut teeth in the edge and you have a snow saw. You can increase the efficiency of both items by wetting them once or twice to glaze the surface.

Use your tools carefully. Don't pry snow blocks roughly with a saw; the saw may snap. Frozen green wood is like a rock; chopping it with an ax is dangerous, for the ax may be chipped or it may strike a glancing blow that might injure someone.

CLOTHING

It is important to wear clothing properly to keep warm and dry.

Insulation combined with body heat is the secret of warmth. Insulation is largely determined by the amount of dead airspace inclosed by the garments. Your outer clothing should be windproof.

Minimize sweating — it's dangerous because it leads to freezing. When exerting yourself, cut down sweating by opening your clothes at the neck and wrists and loosening at the waist. If you're still warm, remove mittens and headgear, or take off a layer or two of outer clothing. When you stop work, put your clothes on again to prevent chilling.

Wear clothing loosely. Tight fits cut off circulation and increase danger of freezing. Keep ears covered with scarf.

Don't get your boots too tight by wearing too many socks.

If your boots are big enough, use dry grass or other material for added insulation around your feet. To maintain the insulation value you will have to dry the material and fluff it up when it becomes packed.

Felt boots, mukluk boots, or moccasins with the proper socks and insoles are best for dry cold weather. Shoepacs (rubber-bottomed, leather-topped boots) are best for wet weather. The thermo boot can be worn in any weather.

Improvise footgear by wrapping parachute cloth or other material lined with dry grass or kapok around your feet.

Keep your clothing as dry as possible. Brush snow from your clothes before you enter a shelter or go near a fire. Beat out frost before warming garments — dry them on a rack before the fire. Dry socks thoroughly. Don't get boots too near fire.

Wear one or two pairs of wool mittens inside a windproof shell. Try to do everything with mittens on. If you have to remove mitts, warm your hands inside your clothes — once they get cold you're in trouble.

Wear goggles or improvise a pair to prevent snow blindness (see page 154).

Keep your clothing as clean as possible. Replace buttons and repair holes promptly.

In strong wind or extreme cold, wrap yourself in your parachute and get into a shelter or behind a windbreak.

At night, arrange dry spare clothing loosely around your shoulders and hips — it will help keep you warm.

If you fall in water, roll in dry snow to blot up moisture. Roll, then brush off snow. Roll again, until all water is absorbed. Do not take off shoes until you are in shelter.

HEALTH AND HAZARDS

Freezing

You will freeze only if the air is carrying away more heat than your body can generate. If you prevent the air from reaching your skin by wearing proper clothing and keep your body in heat balance, you won't freeze. Your whole body must be kept warm to maintain circulation to your hands and feet. Excessive loss of heat from any part of your body restricts circulation, leaving your extremities with little heat. With no heat coming in, your hands and feet are liable to frostbite. *Stay dry.*

Snow Blindness

Snow blindness is caused by the exposure of the unprotected eye to glare on snow. *It can occur even on cloudy days.* You can prevent snow blindness by wearing dark glasses whenever you are exposed to the glare. *Prevention is the best cure.* Don't wait until your eyes hurt before you put your goggles on. A handy substitute for them is a piece of wood, leather, or other material, with narrow eye slits cut in it. This eyeshade is good in a blizzard because you can brush off the slits to keep them clean, while glasses may become frosted over. For treatment of snow blindness, see page 145.

Sunburn

You can get badly sunburned in northern regions, even on foggy or light overcast days. Cover up in bright sunlight. Use sunburn ointment or sea marker dye if you have it.

Carbon Monoxide Poisoning

Carbon monoxide poisoning is a great danger in the Arctic. It is colorless and odorless. Prevention of carbon monoxide poisoning is easy. Maintain good ventilation when a fire is burning. Never fall asleep without turning out a stove or lamp. Don't leave a shelter for long if a stove or lamp is burning and others are immobilized or asleep therein. Always make sure that the entrance is clear of snow and free from all obstacles which might prevent quick exit.

Carbon monoxide burns with a blue flame and is freely generated by a yellow flame. Therefore, when you see a yellow flame, check your ventilation. If you are cooking, lift your pot from the flame; if the flame turns blue, your stove is operating correctly. If possible, hang your cooking pot over the stove so that the bottom of the pot is approximately 3 inches from the top of the burner. Then the flame will stay blue as long as the stove is operating properly.

Flies

In northern regions the word "flies" has a special meaning. It refers to the insect pests that come after you in savage hordes — usually two or three kinds at once. They include mosquitoes, black flies, deerflies, and midges.

All of them bite; they do not sting. They do not carry disease in their bite. In the far north they come out during the day which may be 24 hours long; in southern regions, mosquitoes prefer the evening. Always on the lookout for a landing place, they swarm about their victim, centering their attack upon exposed skin or places where hair is thinnest. There they alight, probe, and bite away until a hand slaps them, a strong wind blows them away, or a chill rain disposes of them. Only with the end of summer does their onslaught stop.

Protective measures against these flies include headnets, which must stand out from the face so that they do not touch the skin; gloves; and clothing in several layers, for they do not often succeed in biting through two layers of cloth. Tuck your pants into the tops of your shoes or socks. Light-colored clothing will protet you better than dark. Make your bed flyproof, if your shelter is not. Be sure that your mosquito net is held away from your face and body. A net covering your whole sleeping bag is more satisfactory than one covering just your head.

A smudge fire properly made will furnish relief from flies during a meal or will drive them away from a tent. For a good smudge, clear away all debris and humus down to the mineral soil or permafrost, to prevent ground fire. Build up a brisk blaze of deadwood; let it burn until a bed of coals is formed. Meanwhile, gather a supply of additional fuel as well as a mass of green ferns, leaves, twigs, damp leaf mold, and rotten wood. Place new dry wood on the coals and let it burn brightly; then cover the whole fire with part of the green material. The dense smoke that now rises will banish black flies instantly and will repel most of the mosquitoes. The smoke will also irritate your eyes, so get down close to the ground. This smoke is the lesser of two evils.

Very useful is a bucket smudge built in a pail or pot — it can be moved easily in case the wind changes or can be taken inside your shelter. Put about 2 inches of noncombustible material into the pail before you start your fire.

Soaking in water is the easiest and best all-round treatment for fly bites.

Skin Care

A warm wet pack with no antiseptic added is one of the most effective methods of treating any skin irritation which might become infected. Use warm water and apply with cotton wicking or moistened and warmed moss.

The importance of removing accumulated body oils and perspiration from the surface of the skin is even greater under survival conditions than under normal ones. All such waste material acts as a conductor and drains your body's supply of heat. In addition, you will get such a boost in morale from a bath. The requirements for an Arctic bath are a rag at least a foot square (cotton or wool is best), a cooking pot half full of hot water, and some soap if you have it. (If you have no cloth, use wadded sphagnum moss.) Remove as many garments as you comfortably can and loosen the rest. Immerse the washrag, wringing it over the pot so as not to lose water, and start washing under your clothing. You must rinse the rag frequently.

Beards are particularly undesirable in the Arctic, for frost collects on them and cannot be readily removed. So if you can't shave, trim your beard as short as you can. A pair of small scissors would be a useful addition to your survival equipment.

If you come into contact with natives, watch to see if they scratch. If they do, they are probably infested with lice. Avoid bodily contact with them.

Tularemia

Tularemia is a disease of rodents, particularly of hares, rabbits, and squirrels. You can catch it from ticks or by handling infected animals, eating partially cooked and infected animals, and handling or drinking infected water. Avoid all rodents that are not active and healthy. Use gloves to skin rodents, and discard the hide.

Trichinosis

All Arctic game, large and small, may transmit trichinosis. Cook all meat thoroughly.

Animal Liver

Liver of polar bear and of the bearded seal has such a high concentration of vitamin A that it is toxic to man; never eat it.

WATER

In the winter, ice and snow provide water but fuel is needed to melt them. Never waste fuel in melting snow or ice when drinkable water from other sources is available. In the summer there is plenty of water in lakes, streams, and ponds. Surface water on the tundra may have a brownish color, but it is drinkable.

Whenever possible, melt ice for water rather than snow — you get more water for the volume with less heat and time. If you melt snow by heating, put in a little snow at a time and compress it — or the pot will burn. If water is available, put a little in the bottom of the pot and add snow gradually.

If the sun is shining, you can melt snow on a dark tarpaulin, signal panel, flat rock, or any surface that will absorb the sun's heat. Arrange the surface so that melt-water will drain into a hollow or container.

Use old sea ice for drinking water. It is bluish, has rounded corners when broken, and is free from salt. New sea ice is gray, milky, hard, and salty; don't drink it. Water in pools at the edges of ice floes is probably too salty to drink. Icebergs are good sources of fresh water and should be used if they can be approached safely.

If short on fuel, you can melt snow in your bare hands. It's best, however, to fill up on water at mealtime once you have melted ice or snow.

If fuel is plentiful, try to drink at least 2 quarts of hot beverage or water daily instead of cold water or snow.

ANIMAL FOOD

In no part of the Arctic are native animals and plants a reliable source of food. Your chances for survival are best along the coastlines of Asia, Alaska, the Aleutians, and Greenland, because seafood is more common there and gives you a dependable supply of food.

Depending on the time of year and the place, your chances for obtaining animal food will vary considerably. Arctic shores are normally scraped clean of all animals and plants by winter ice. Inland animals are migratory. Watch for tracks, trails, or dung.

Large Land Game

Caribou (reindeer) are migratory throughout northern Canada and Alaska. In northern Siberia they extend inland almost to 50° N. Some are found in West Greenland. All move close to the sea or into the high mountains in summer. In winter they feed on the tundra (open, treeless plains).

Musk oxen may be found in northern Greenland and on the islands of the Canadian archipelago.

Sheep descend to lower elevations and to valley feeding grounds in winter.

Wolves usually run in pairs or groups. Fox are solitary and are seen most frequently when mice and lemming are abundant.

Bears are dangerous, especially when wounded, startled, or with their young. They generally shun areas of human habitation.

Small Land Game

Tundra animals include rabbits, lemming, mice, ground squirrels, and fox. They may be trapped (see page 30) or shot, winter or summer, anywhere on the tundra. Most prefer some cover and can be found in shallow ravines, or in groves of short willows. Ground

Large arctic game

squirrels and marmots hibernate in winter. In summer, ground squirrels are abundant along sandy banks of large streams. Marmots live in the mountains, among rocks, usually near the edge of a meadow, or in deep soil — much like woodchucks. To find the burrow in rocky areas, look for a large patch of orange-colored lichen on rocks. This plant grows best on animal or bird dung; and the marmot always seeks relief in the same spot, not far from his well-hidden entrance.

Sea Ice Game

Sea ice game

In the winter and spring, sea mammals — seals, walrus, polar bears — are found on the frozen pack ice and on floes in open water. Seals with claws on their flippers can make breathing holes and live relatively close to land. Those that cannot make breathing holes must live on the edge of the pack ice. Most are in groups, but the bearded seal is often found alone.

Birds

Arctic birds

The breeding grounds of many birds are in the Arctic. In summer, ducks, geese, loons, and swans build their nests near ponds on the coastal plains or flats bordering lakes or rivers of the low tundra. A few ducks on a small pond usually indicate that setting birds may be found and flushed from the surrounding shores. Swans and loons normally nest on small grassy islands in the lakes. Geese crowd together near large rivers or lakes. Smaller wading birds customarily fly from pond to pond. Grouse and ptarmigan are common in the swampy forest regions of Siberia.

Sea birds may be found on cliffs or small islands off the coast. Their nesting areas can often be located by their flights to and from their feeding grounds. Jaeger gulls are common over the tundra, frequently resting on higher hillocks. These birds, as well as ravens and owls, are useful for food.

In winter, owls and ptarmigan are the only birds available. Ptarmigan are seen in pairs or flocks, feeding along grassy or willow-covered slopes.

Hunting Hints

Winter hunting is best in the early morning. In summer, with almost continuous light, animals have very irregular moving habits. On the open tundra, select a high hill and scan the horizon for game. Summer heat haze will distort distant objects, and low ridges or brush will look like animals. In mountain country, hunting is best in and near mountain passes. Maintain a watch from a high place. When traveling, always be ready to shoot any animal which you may accidentally flush.

LARGE LAND GAME. Caribou (reindeer) can be very curious, and if stalking is not feasible you may be able to attract them to you by waving a cloth and walking slowly toward them on all fours. If they are startled by your movements, try to approach them while they feed, stopping stock still when they raise their heads. Proceed cautiously, because reindeer are sharp-eyed and alert.

Wolves can also be brought close by a four-legged pose. You may expect moose in heavy brush; they may charge you.

Mountain sheep and mountain goats can sometimes be surprised on high ridges. They are hard to approach, for they have keen eyesight. Stalk them quietly, moving only when they are feeding.

Musk oxen leave broad cattlelike tracks and droppings. When alarmed, they will bunch together and remain in that position unless approached too closely; then one or more bulls may charge you. To kill, shoot in neck or shoulder.

Bears advertise their presence through great areas of torn-up sod where they have tried to dig up roots or ground squirrels. If you hunt bear, don't shoot unless you are sure to kill; fire at the base of the ear, the neck, or just behind the shoulder. Wounded bears are extremely dangerous and should not be followed into cover.

SMALL LAND GAME. Rabbits often run in circles, returning to the same place from which they were frightened. If you shoot, aim for the head or you will not have much meat left. If the animal is running, whistle, and it may stop long enough for a shot. Snares are more efficient. Ground squirrels and marmots will run right by you if you get between them and their holes; club or stone them. They may also be trapped or shot.

SEA ICE GAME. Successful ice hunting depends upon proper reconnaissance and patient stalking. Seals are hard to approach. To shoot or spear seal, you must approach slowly and patiently on your stomach, with arms and legs close to your body. Advance only when the animal's head indicates that it is sleeping. Keep downwind and avoid sudden moves. If you are hunting a bearded seal and it behaves as if it might move off, get up quickly and yell. The seal will be frightened enough to lie still and let you shoot or spear it. Always remember that where there are seal, there may be polar bears; and polar bears have been known to stalk and kill seal hunters.

The walrus and the bearded seal stay on floe ice. The seal is curious and can be attracted within gunshot. Walrus are indolent but at close quarters are extremely dangerous. You must usually approach them by boat. Both seal and walrus should be killed on the ice so that their carcasses may be recovered easily.

The polar bear is rarely found inland but is found in coastal areas. The female polar bear hibernates in coastal areas in winter. When it does come inland, it is attracted by the smell of food caches or animal carcasses. It is a tireless, clever hunter with good sight and extraordinary sense of smell. Treat it with caution.

BIRDS. To catch a nesting bird with a noose, attach cord or wire to a stick driven in the ground nearby and place it so that it will entangle the bird's foot. Where there are many birds, use long lines with many small nooses. If the birds are moulting, they may be run down and clubbed, speared, stoned, or shot with gun or slingshot.

Gulls and some other sea birds may be caught with a hook and line. Bait the hook and let it float on a piece of wood; or stake it out on a beach.

Ptarmigan are easy to approach, but hard to find, because they are protectively colored in their winter and summer plumages. They may be killed with stones, a slingshot, or a long club. They can also be netted or snared.

Skinning and Butchering

Skin all large game immediately, while the carcass is still warm. Roll the hide up before it freezes. Cut the meat into usable portions and pile them separately, so that after they are frozen they may be handled as individual pieces. In summer, store them in ground ice holes, carefully protected from animals. Leave the fat on all animals except seals. Remove all of the seal fat you can, for it will turn rancid and spoil the meat except in very cold weather. If you do not have time for skinning, at least remove the entrails, musk glands, and genitals.

Butcher smaller animals as soon as possible. Until you can skin them, carry them on a string or stick, away from your body. Slit the stomach, roll the skin backward as if you were removing a glove, and get rid of it.

Birds should be drawn soon after killing and should be protected from flies.

Cooking of Meat

As mentioned earlier in the chapter, cook all meat thoroughly. All Arctic game, large and small, may harbor trichinosis. *Never* eat polar bear meat unless it has been thoroughly cooked — preferably after it has been cut into small pieces and boiled. Polar bear meat is always contaminated with trichinosis. Don't eat the liver of the polar bear or of the bearded seal. It is dangerous to man because of its high concentration of vitamin A. Except marmots and porcupines, no small game is very fat; add available fat when cooking. Remember that rodents may have tularemia — handle carefully and cook thoroughly.

In selecting the meat to be cooked, remember that the best cuts are found on the head, brisket (breast or lower chest), backbone, and pelvis. The hams are likely to be tough and stringy.

SEAFOOD

Arctic and tom cod, sculpin, eelpout, and other fish may be caught in the ocean. The inland lakes and rivers of the surrounding coastal tundra generally have plenty of fish which are easy to catch during the warmer season.

In the North Pacific and in the North Atlantic extending slightly northward into the Arctic Sea, the coastal waters are rich in all seafoods. Varieties include all those mentioned on page 33 as well as one of the world's largest and meatiest crabs — the king crab of the Aleutian and Bering sea areas. In the spring when it comes close inshore to breed, this crab may be caught on fish lines set in deep water.

Ice fishing

Grayling, trout, Arctic char, and white fish are common to the lakes, ponds, and the Arctic coastal plain of North America and Asia. Many of the larger rivers have salmon and sturgeon.

Poisonous fish are rarer in the Arctic than in the tropics, but check the warnings on page 273. Some fish, such as sculpins, lay poisonous eggs, but eggs of the salmon, herring, or fresh water sturgeon are good eating. In Arctic or subarctic areas, the black mussel may be poisonous at any season. If mussels are the only available food, select only those in deep inlets far from the coast. Remove the dark intestinal gland before eating. Mussel poison is as dangerous as strychnine. Beware of Arctic shark meat, which is poisonous.

River snails or fresh water periwinkles are plentiful in the rivers, streams, and lakes of the northern coniferous forest. These snails may have pencil-point or globular shapes, 1 to 3 inches in length. Boil them in water and twist the meat out of the shell with a bent pin or wire.

Fishing Hints

Winter fishing is possible through a hole in the ice or in open leads. To keep the hole open, cover it with skins or brush, then heap loose snow over the cover.

Shallow lakes freeze to the bottom along the margins, and fish tend to congregate in deeper pools. Estimate the deepest part of the lake or pond before making a hole. Other good locations for ice fishing are at lake outlets or where tributaries flow into a pond or stream. Ice is thinnest over rapids or small falls, or at the edges of deep streams with banks holding drifting snow. Open water is often marked by "smoke," the mist formed by vaporizing water.

In warm weather look for shellfish in muddy waters by feeling the bottom with hands or feet. In deep water, jab a sharp-pointed stick into the slit between the two halves of the shell. When the shells close, pull the shellfish out of the water.

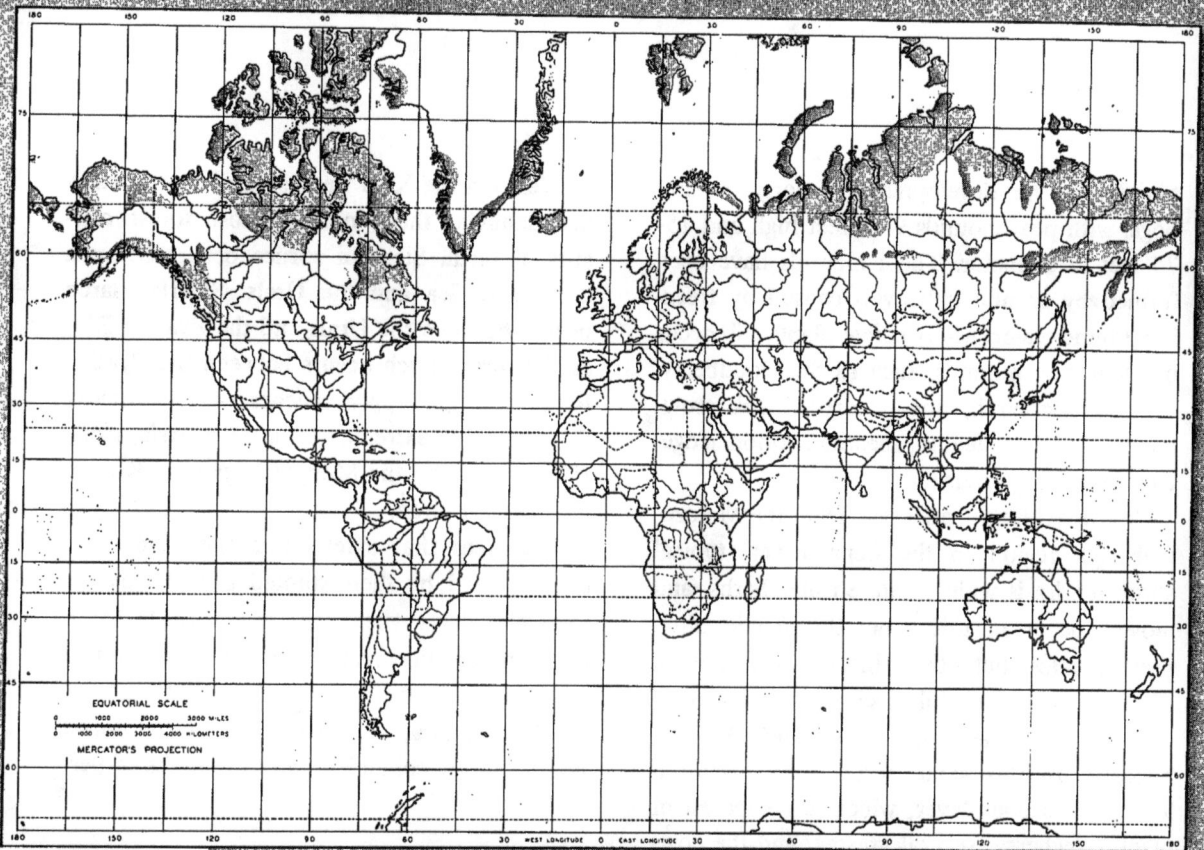

TUNDRA

EDIBLE PLANTS
OF THE TUNDRA

Even on the barren tundra, some food plants will be available. There is a greater variety and abundance of them during the short growing season than during the winter. Even during the winter, however, frozen yet edible fruits such as huckleberries and crowberries may be found. It may also be possible to dig roots and rootstocks from beneath the snow.

Some Characteristics of the Tundra

The plant life of the Arctic tundra regions is remarkably uniform. A species of food plants from Alaska, for instance, may also be found in northern Russia.

In its true form, the tundra is treeless. A few kinds of plants will cover very large areas, so that extensive stands of one variety of plant are common in the Arctic tundra. All tundra plants are small in stature as compared to the plants in the warmer climates of more southerly latitudes. The Arctic willow and birch, for

instance, spread along the ground in the tundra to form large mats. Stunted growth in all the woody plants is the rule, and although there are many evergreen plants, hardly any bulbous or tuberous plants occur. Lichens are numerous on the tundra, especially reindeer moss.

As mentioned before, the plant life of the tundra is remarkably uniform throughout its distribution — in Europe, Asia, and America. Some species are common to all three areas, but other species are more restricted in their distribution. The tundra also contains many species to be found also in the forest regions to the south.

Bogs. The tundra has often been classified as a place of a continuous bog, but this is far from the truth. Many bogs do occur. There are also many hilly and even mountainous areas with considerably drier soil. The moss, or sphagnum, bog is less common than the sedge bog. A characteristic feature of more southern

161

tundras is the development of large mound bogs, with peat mounds 9-15 feet high and 15-75 feet in diameter. These mounds have been formed by ground upheavals caused by freezing ground water. Many edible plants will occur on these bog mounds, such as the cloudberry, dwarf arctic birch, bog bilberry, black crowberry, crystal tea ledum, sheathed cotton sedge, cowberry, and others.

SHRUB TUNDRA. In Russia, from the Malozemelskaya region to the Lena River, typical shrub tundra is widespread. Shrubs, herbs, and mosses occur in this zone; the Arctic birch predominates, but other shrubs occur, several of which may be useful as supplementary food: the crystal tea ledum, willows, and the bog bilberry. In this same shrub zone occurs a lower herbaceous layer, which is composed of black crowberry, several grasses, and the cowberry. On the ground, mosses and lichens are present in abundance. The shrubs on the open tundra will reach a height of only 3-4 feet, but in valleys and along the rivers the same shrubs may reach the height of a man.

WOODED TUNDRA. The region immediately adjoining the treeless tundra is an extension of the coniferous forest areas to the south. These subarctic wooded areas include a variety of tree species. On the Kola Peninsula of northeastern Scandanavia, these northernmost forest consists of birth. Siberian spruce occurs between the White Sea and the Urals. Siberian larch occurs between the Urals and the Pyasina River. Dahurian larch occurs between the Pyasina River and the upper reaches of the Anadyr River. And in extreme northeastern Asia, along rivers are found the Mongolian poplar, Korean willow, and birch.

The trees that extend into the tundra are distinguished by their stunted growth (except in river valleys where they reach 18-24 feet), and sparse occurrence. Permanent ground frost, or permafrost, penetrates most parts of the true tundra, and the limits of the forest belt is closely coincident with the limits of permafrost.

Distribution of the Tundra

NORTH AMERICA. North and east of Hudson Bay north of Churchill. This area extends into Alaska north of the Brooks Range and along the Bering Sea to the Aleutian Islands.

GREENLAND. All ice-free land.

EUROPE. Lapland in northern Scandanavia and northern Russia.

ASIA. Siberia north of 70° latitude.

Wild raspberry (rubus chamaemorus)

© Vegetationsbilder

© Vegetationsbilder

Greenland

Lapland

© Vegetationsbilder

© Vegetationsbilder

Asia, Arctic tundra

Alaska

© Vegetationsbilder

Timberline, U.S.S.R.

Peat mound, U.S.S.R.

Willow (Salix reticulata)

© Vegetationsbilder

FLOWERING CATKINS

SHRUB 1-2 FT. TALL

EDIBLE SHOOTS

EDIBLE INNER BARK

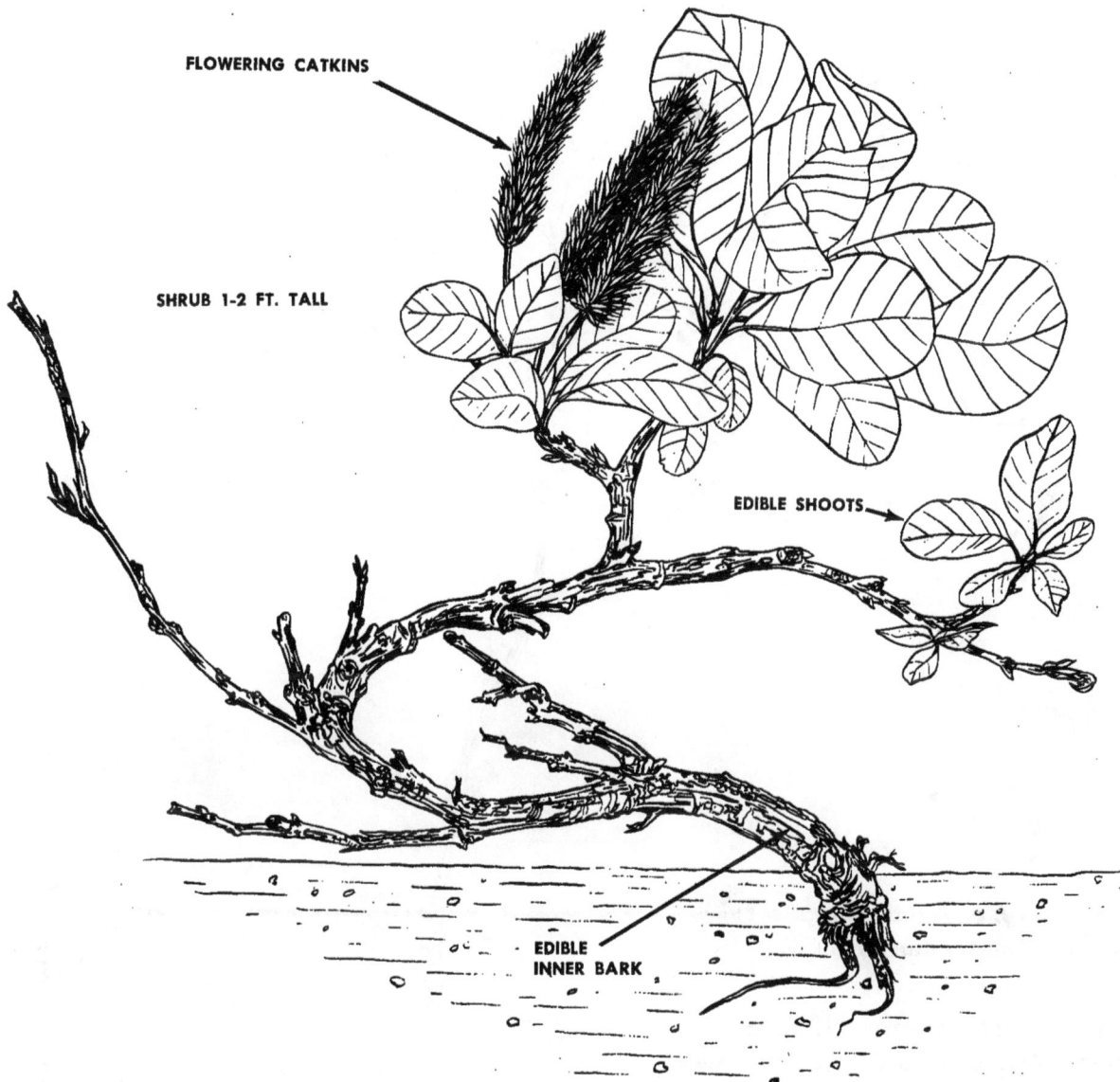

Arctic Willow (Salix)

WHERE FOUND. (Regions 11, 12.) The Arctic willow is common on all tundra areas in North America, Europe, and Asia.

APPEARANCE. The Arctic willow is a shrub which never exceeds more than 1 or 2 feet in height. It grows in clumps, which form dense mats on the tundra.

WHAT TO EAT. The succulent, tender young shoots of the Arctic willow can be collected in early spring. The outer bark of the new shoots is stripped off and the inner portion eaten raw.

The young underground shoots of any of the various kinds of Arctic willow can be peeled and eaten raw. Young willow leaves are one of the richest sources of vitamin C, containing 7-10 times more than an orange.

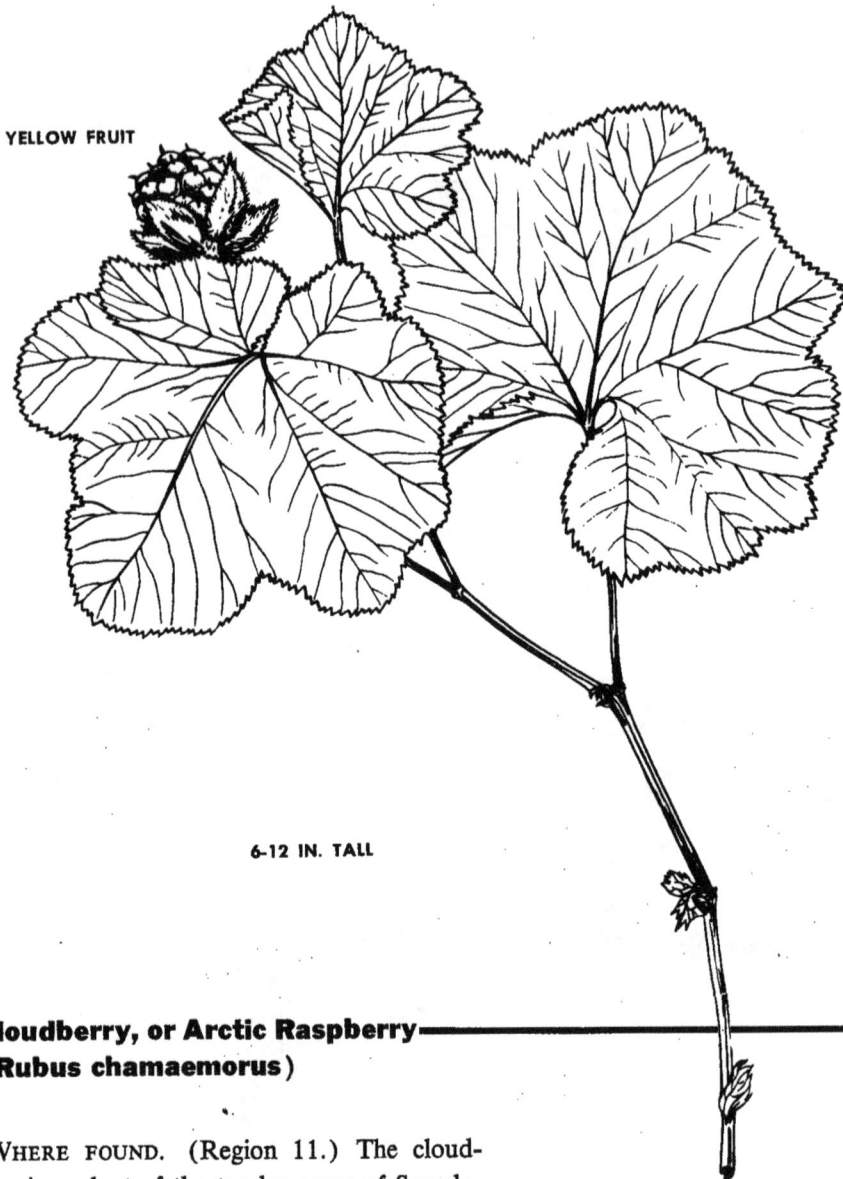

YELLOW FRUIT

6-12 IN. TALL

Cloudberry, or Arctic Raspberry
(Rubus chamaemorus)

WHERE FOUND. (Region 11.) The cloudberry is a plant of the tundra areas of Scandanavia, northern Asia, and North America. Anywhere north of 60° N. latitude, the cloudberry often covers many acres of ground. It is sometimes found in mountainous regions considerably farther south — often to 45° N. latitude.

APPEARANCE. The ripe cloudberry grows on an erect plant which seldom grows over a foot in height in the southern limit of its distribution and only a few inches tall on the Arctic tundra. The plants have a few undivided, rounded, scalloped leaves. The fruit is borne at the top of the plant, first pink, then amber, at last yellow and very juicy and soft.

WHAT TO EAT. The soft ripe fruit has a flavor strongly suggestive of poorly flavored baked apples. A taste must be developed for the cloudberry, but once acquired, large quantities can be consumed in season, usually late summer.

The cloudberry is only one of several kinds of wild berries related to the blackberry, raspberry, and dewberries, which the survivor can expect to find in northern regions.

EDIBLE BERRY

VARIETIES 3-5 FT. TALL.

TYPICAL
BLUEBERRY
PATCH

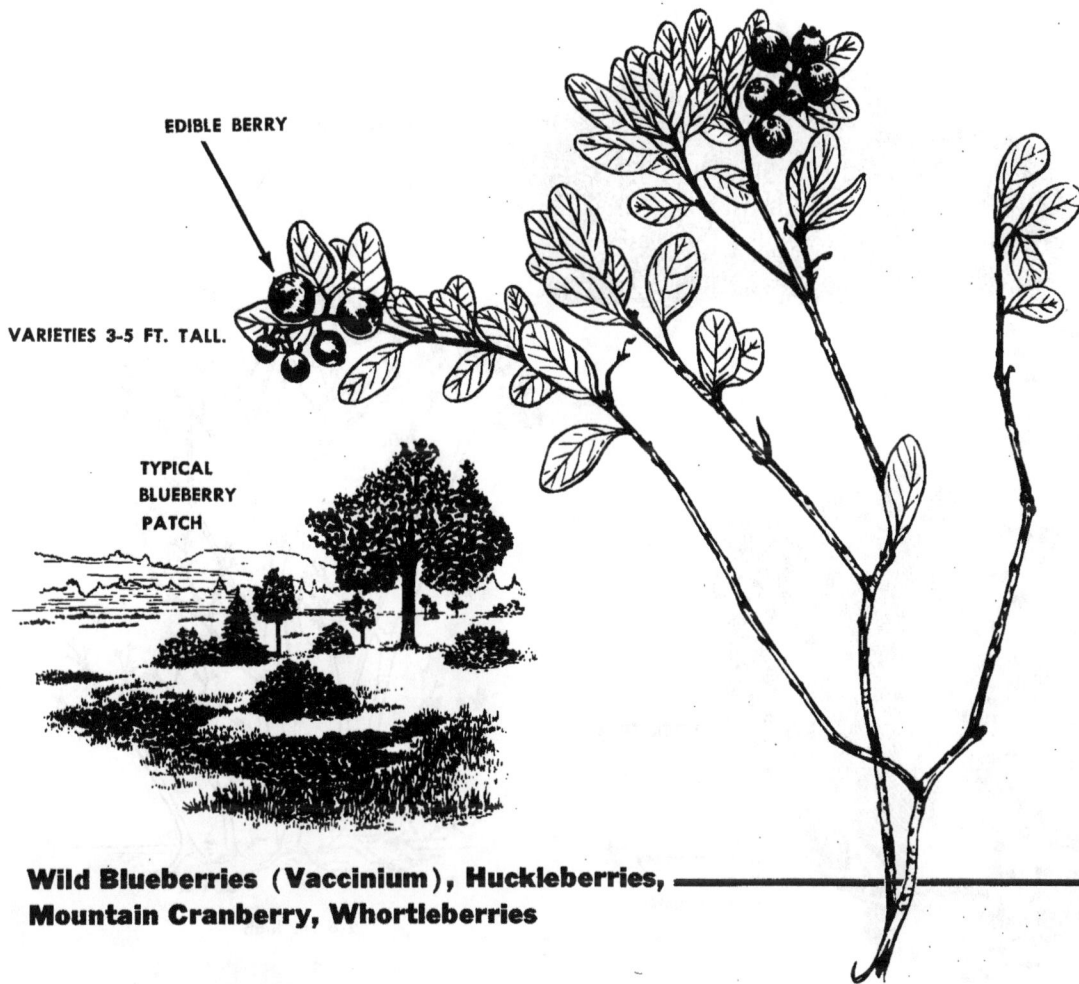

Wild Blueberries (Vaccinium), Huckleberries, Mountain Cranberry, Whortleberries

WHERE FOUND. (Region 11.) On the tundra in Europe, Asia and America in late summer, large patches of wild huckleberries abound with quantities of ripe fruit. In the areas farther south throughout the northern hemisphere, especially in forested areas, wild huckleberries and their relatives, the blueberries and whortleberries, are common. Usually these kinds of wild fruit occur in some abundance wherever they are found, whether it be on the tundra or in forested areas.

APPEARANCE. On the tundra, these wild berries grow on low bushes which are sometimes only a few inches tall. The varieties which grow farther south are produced on taller shrubs which may reach 6 feet in height. The ripe berries are blue, black, or red. These berries are sufficiently common to afford an abundance of fruit during late summer.

WHAT TO EAT. The ripe berries are eaten fresh from the bush or they may be cooked, which makes some kinds more palatable than if eaten fresh. Certain kinds may be dried and eaten like raisins during periods when little else is available.

Grows in
coral-like
clumps

REINDEER MOSS

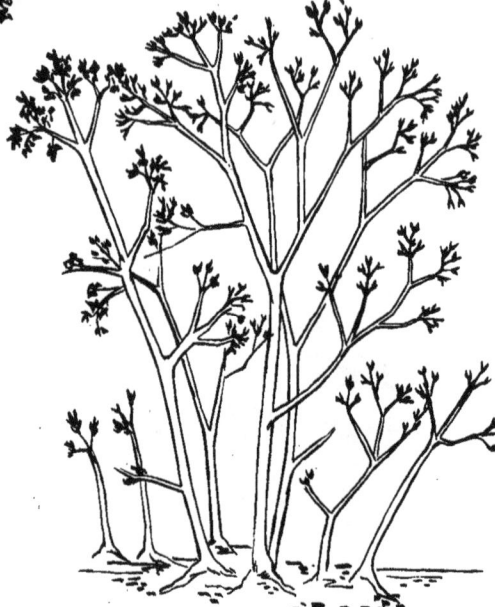

2-6 in. high

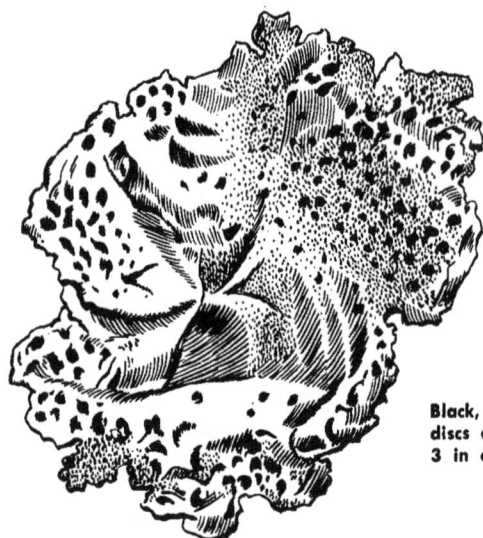

ROCK TRIPE

Black, leathery
discs about
3 in diameter

Lichens

Lichens are abundant and widespread in the far North and can be used as a source of emergency food. However, some of them contain a bitter acid which will cause irritation to the digestive tract.

If lichens are boiled, dried, and powdered, this acid is removed and the powder can then be used as flour or made into a thick soup.

REINDEER MOSS. (Cladonia rangiferina).

Where found — common in all tundra areas.

Appearance — gray-green and multi-branched.

What to eat — wash the whole plant. Boil or roast it.

ROCK TRIPE. (Umbilicaria sp.)

Where found — on certain rocks throughout the northern areas.

Appearance — grayish-black color, leathery and brittle when dry. When it is wet it takes on a dark green color.

What to eat — the whole plant. It will cause diarrhea unless it is dried before it is cooked. Boiling is best.

ICELAND MOSS. (Cetraria islandica).

Where found — on sandy soil.

Appearance — looks very much like an upright brown seaweed.

POISONOUS PLANTS IN THE ARCTIC (TUNDRA) AND SUBARCTIC

Plants which produce poisoning upon contact do not exist in these cold regions.

The following eight kinds of plants are poisonous only when eaten. They are internal poisons and are the only dangerous ones you are apt to encounter on the tundra and in the subarctic regions adjoining the tundra.

Baneberry (Actaea)

DESCRIPTION. Perennial from thick rootstock. Stems smooth or somewhat hairy, 2 to 3-1/2 feet high. Leaves large, divided into three leaflets. Leaflets thin, usually lobed and coarsetoothed. Flowers small, white, many in a spikelike cluster at the top of the stem, each flower with 4-10 small, white petals. The fruit is a round, multiseeded berry, red or white. Each berry is attached to the stem by a short, thick stalk, the white-berried plant having red stalks.

WHERE FOUND. Woods and thickets. This is a typical plant of the North Temperate Zone, especially from about latitude 40° N. to the Arctic and subarctic areas of Europe, Asia, and North America.

CONDITIONS OF POISONING. The berries of this plant are poisonous. As few as six berries can cause increased pulse, dizziness, burning in the stomach, and colicky pains. The rootstock is a violent purgative and emetic.

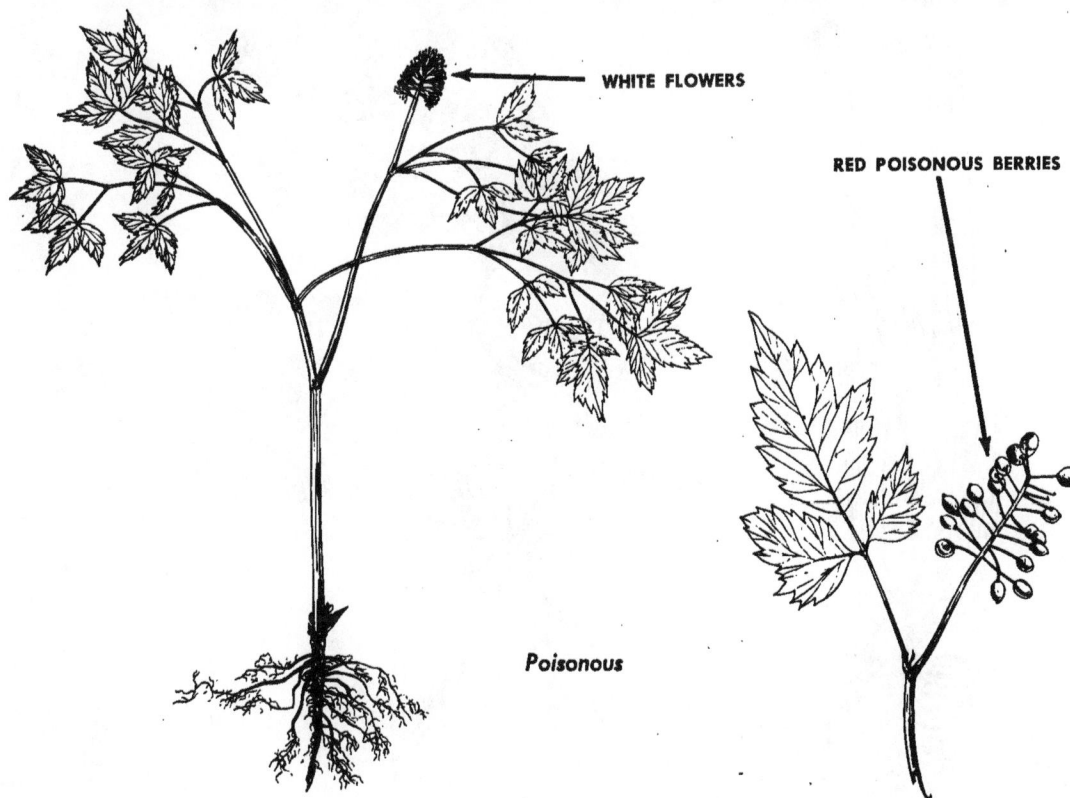

WHITE FLOWERS

RED POISONOUS BERRIES

Poisonous

Poison Waterhemlock (Cicuta)

DESCRIPTION. Perennial. Stems 3-1/2 to 7 feet high, stout, jointed, hollow between the joints, reddish. Leaves alternate, divided into narrow leaflets with toothed edges, and the leaf veins end at or near the tooth notches. Leafstalks sheath the stem. Rootstalk short, ringed on the outer surface and often, especially when young, has many fibrous rootlets; when older it has many spindle-shaped roots bunched at the base. When root and lower stem are split lengthwise, many cross-partitions or chambers can be easily noticed. Plant exudes drops of a yellow aromatic oil which gives it a characteristic odor. Flowers small and white, in umbrellalike clusters at the top of the stalk.

WHERE FOUND. Wet meadows, ditches, along streams, and around tundra lakes. This plant belongs to the parsley, carrot, and parsnip family, which contains many well-known edible plants, but it is better to avoid all members of this family as food in northern areas, since the related waterhemlock is fairly common in the North Temperate Zone.

CONDITIONS OF POISONING. A piece of waterhemlock root about the size of a walnut is said to be sufficient to kill a cow. This plant contains a sticky, resinlike substance called cicutoxin. It is most concentrated in the roots but is present in all parts of the plant. Symptoms are stomach pains, nausea, vomiting, weak and rapid pulse, and violent convulsions.

TREATMENT. In cases of hemlock plant poisoning, make the patient vomit, then give a cathartic. If vomiting is produced promptly, the victim is likely to recover.

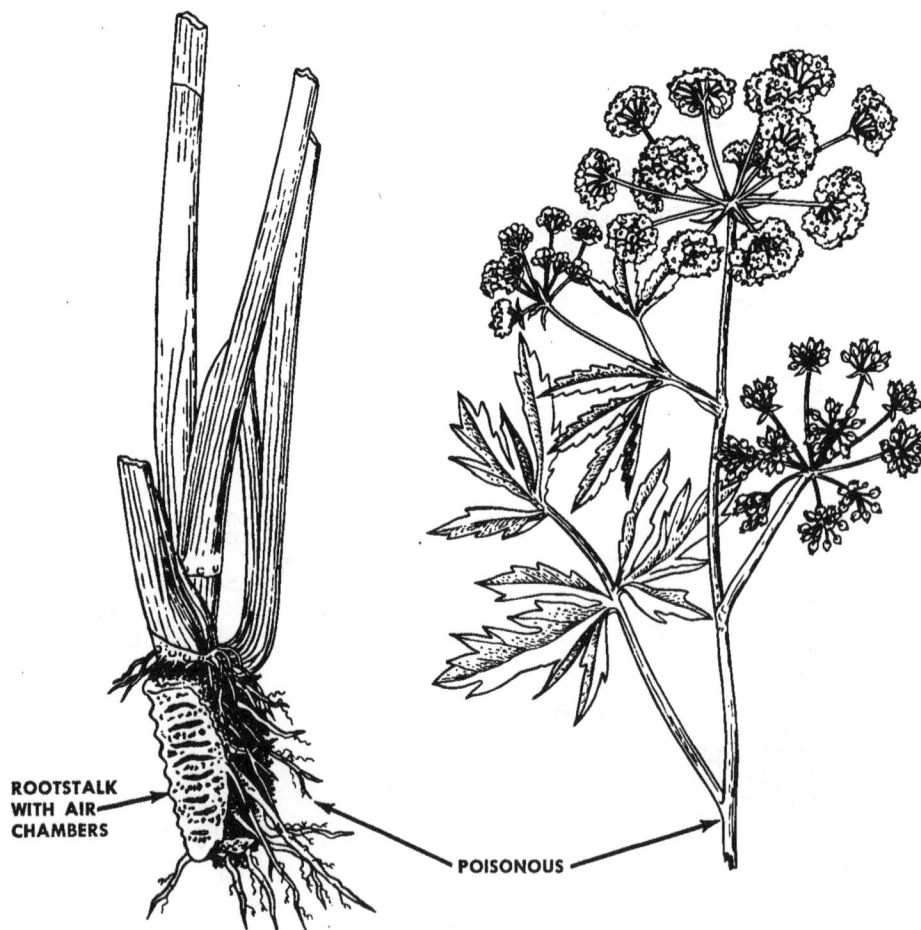

ROOTSTALK WITH AIR CHAMBERS

POISONOUS

Lupine (Lupinus)

DESCRIPTION. Perennial, with a long tap-root. Stems up to 3-1/2 feet high, clustered, branched, and smooth to densely hairy. Leaves alternate, basal leaves on short stalks, palmately (like a hand) divided with 6-8 leaflets. Flowers blue, often shaded pink or white, rarely pure white.

WHERE FOUND. Found only on the North American Continent. Only one kind occurs in the Arctic regions of Alaska.

CONDITIONS OF POISONING. Lupine contain alkaloids and are known to cause fatal poisoning in animals. It has been reported that when eaten in excess by humans it produces serious effects. It is thought that the excess woody fiber produces fatal inflammation of the stomach and intestines.

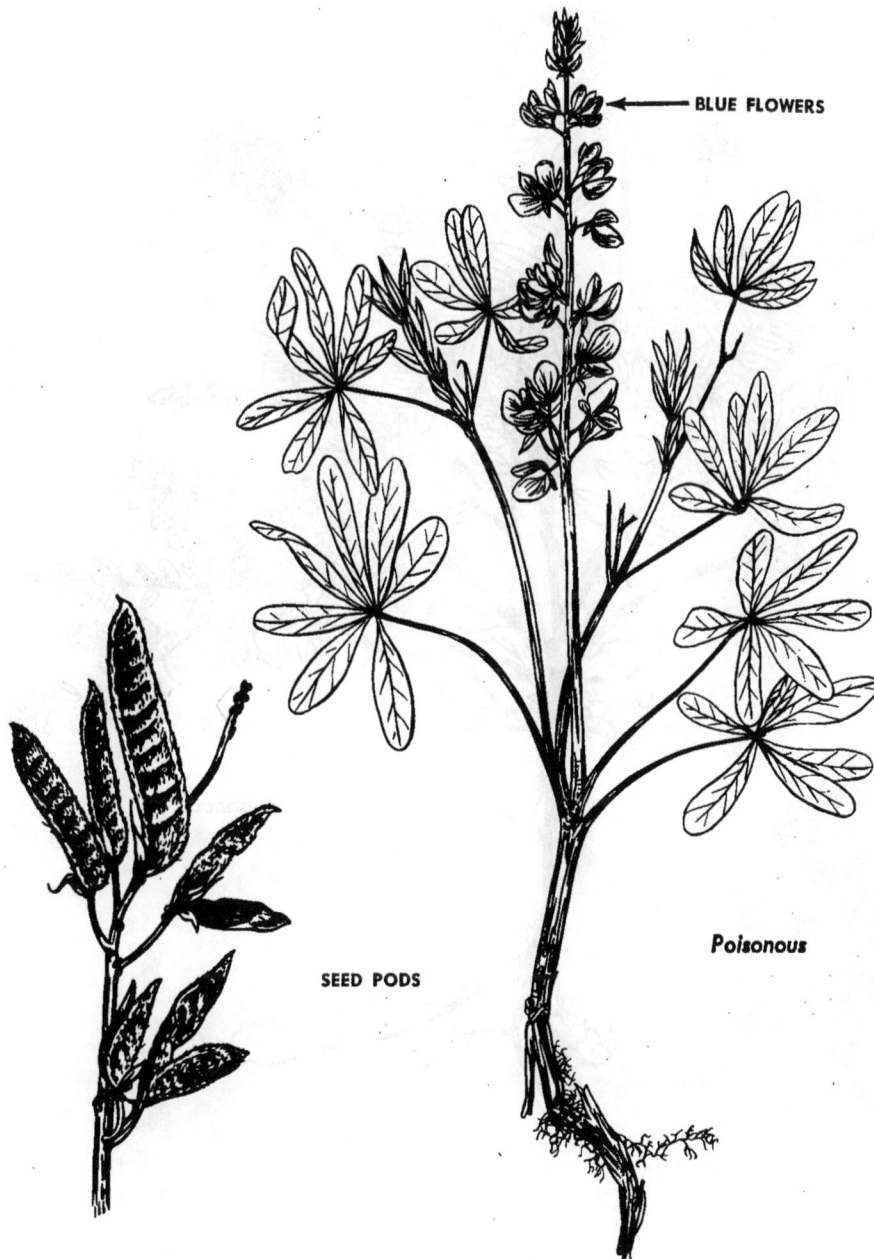

BLUE FLOWERS

SEED PODS

Poisonous

Vetch, Locoweed (Astragalus)

DESCRIPTION. Perennials. Stems erect or spreading. Leaves alternate, each with many leaflets, some smooth, some hairy. Flowers in spikelike clusters at top of stem. Individual flowers pealike in structure with five petals, white, yellow, or purplish.

WHERE FOUND. These plants occur rather abundantly in meadows, on hillsides, and on tundra throughout the North Temperate Zone.

CONDITIONS OF POISONING. Several species of locoweed have been reported as toxic. Avoid all kinds to be on the safe side.

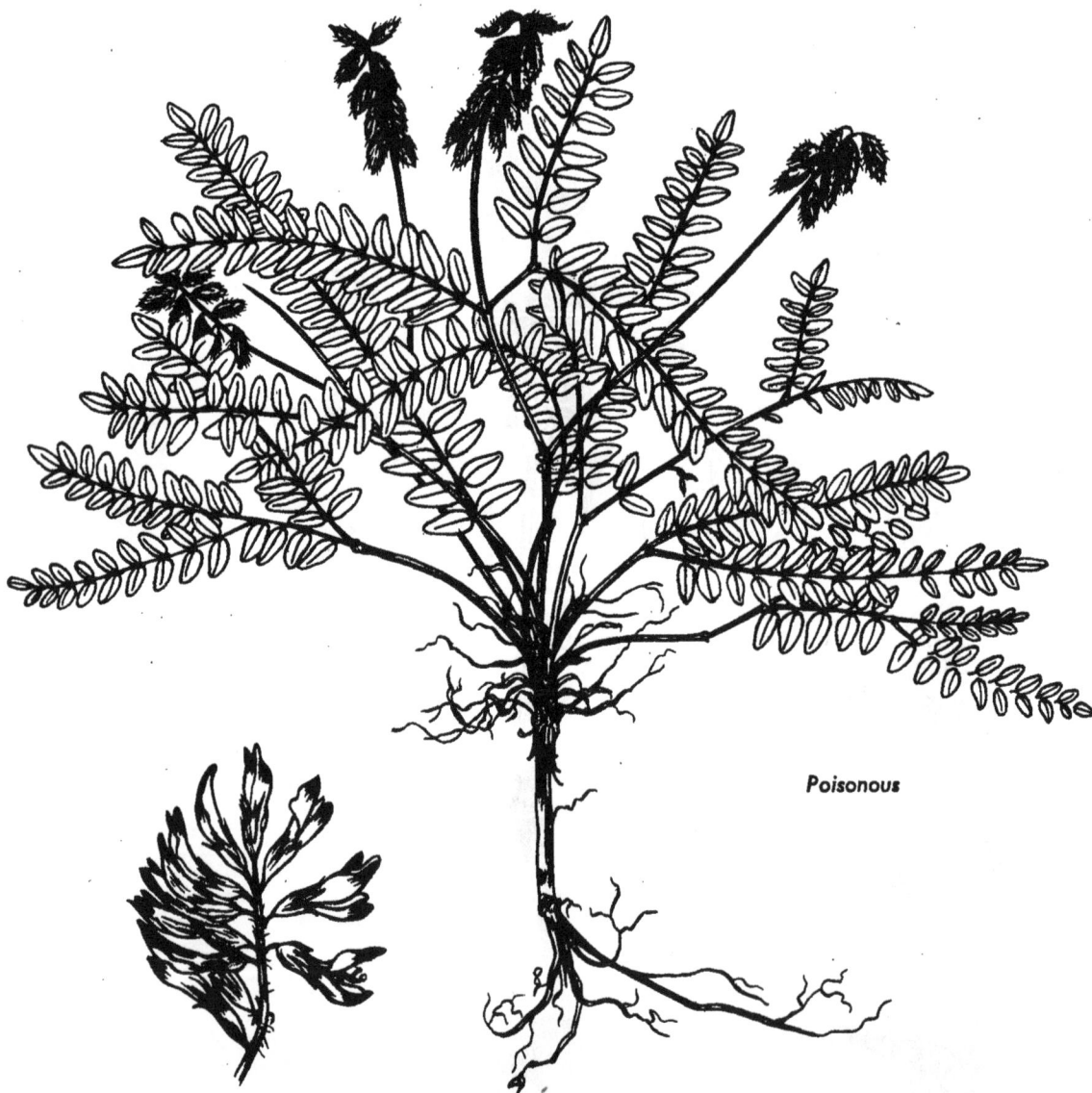

Poisonous

False Hellebore (Veratrum)

DESCRIPTION. Perennial. Stem stout, erect, 3-8 feet high, rising from a thick rootstalk. Leaves alternate, broadly round-oval with pointed tip, clasping the stem; blade smooth above, hairy beneath; veins parallel. Small flowers in large terminal spikelike clusters with drooping branches; three petals, often greenish, but sometimes white.

WHERE FOUND. Swamps and low grounds in Europe, Asia, and America from about 40° N. latitude. Occurs on the edge of the Arctic, although probably rare on the tundra.

CONDITIONS OF POISONING. Fatalities among humans from eating false hellebore are rare but are more common to sheep and other animals. Symptoms are salivation, vomiting, purging, abdominal pain, muscular weakness, general paralysis, tremors, spasms, and occasionally convulsions. Death results from asphyxia.

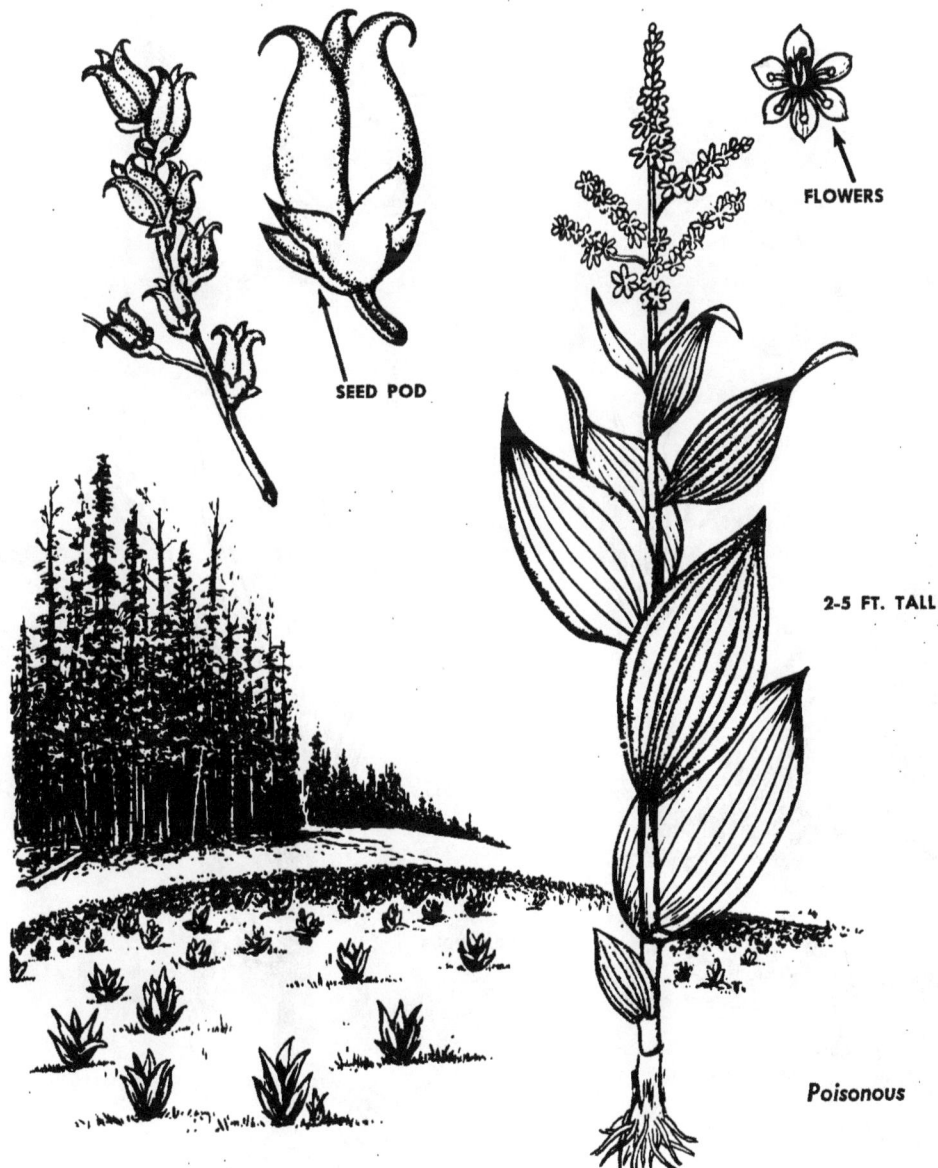

SEED POD

FLOWERS

2-5 FT. TALL

Poisonous

Death Camas (Zygadenus)

DESCRIPTION. Plant growing from a bulb. Stems 1 to 2 feet high, leafy, with linear leaves clasping the stem at the base. Flowers greenish-white in loose terminal clusters — contrasted with wild onion, which has flowers closely aggregated at the top of the stem; also no onion odor in death camas.

WHERE FOUND. The death camas occurs in meadows, and on edges of forests in parts of western subarctic North America and eastern Siberia; also occurs farther south to western United States.

CONDITIONS OF POISONING. The death camas contains the toxic alkaloid, zygadenine, in all parts of the plant from the bulb to the seed. Children have been known to be poisoned by eating the bulbs, probably mistaking them for onions.

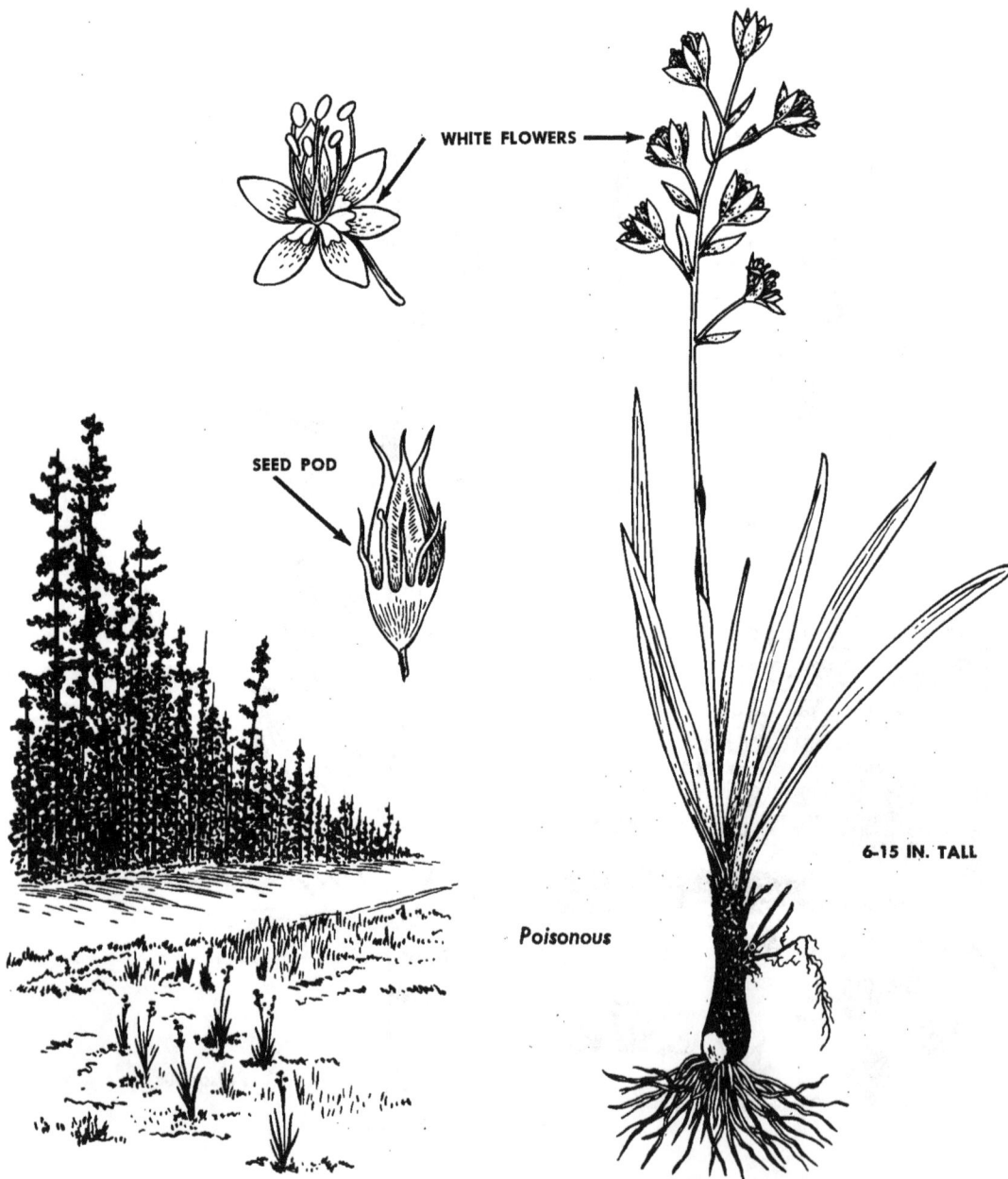

WHITE FLOWERS

SEED POD

6-15 IN. TALL

Poisonous

Buttercup (Ranunculus)

DESCRIPTION. Buttercups vary in size from a few inches to nearly 3 feet tall. Most kinds, especially those in Arctic regions, are diminutive in size, with divided or deeply notched leaves. All kinds have yellow flowers.

WHERE FOUND. Widely distributed through-out the North Temperate Zone and well into the tundra of Europe, Asia, and America.

CONDITIONS OF POISONING. If the leaves are eaten, severe inflammation of the intestinal tract may result.

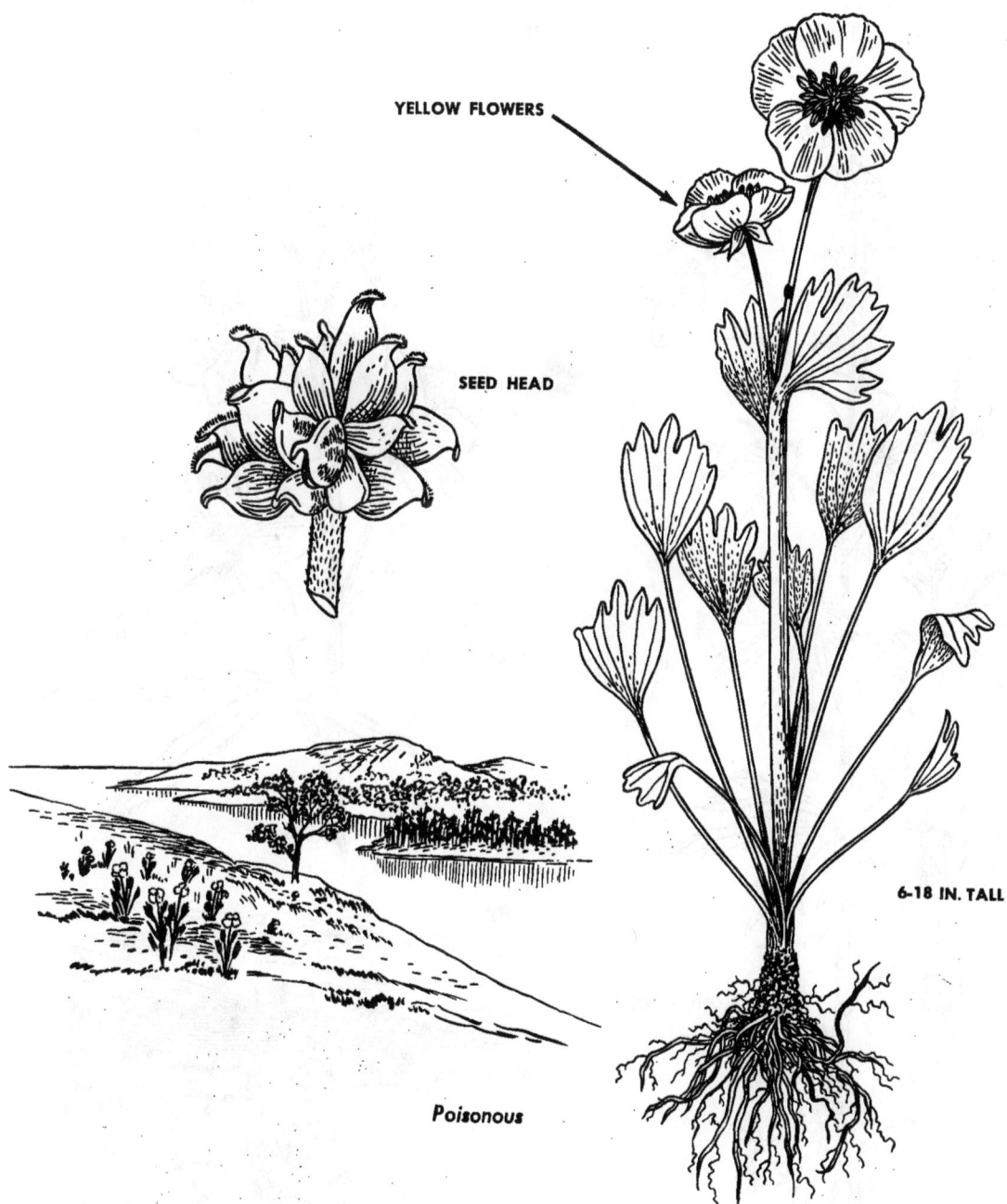

YELLOW FLOWERS

SEED HEAD

6-18 IN. TALL

Poisonous

Monkshood (Aconitum) and Larkspur (Delphinium)

DESCRIPTION. Monkshood is a perennial, 2-4 feet high. Leaves alternate, the upper clasping the stem, palmately veined, and lobed or divided; leaves and stems somewhat hairy or sticky. Flowers hooded or helmet-shaped, usually blue.

Larkspur is similar to monkshood, but the flowers are not hooded. Most kinds develop two spurs at the base of the flower.

WHERE FOUND. Monkshood and larkspur are distributed widely over the North Temperate and subarctic zones, especially in mountainous regions.

CONDITIONS OF POISONING. This plant, while poisonous at all times, seems to be most poisonous just before flowering. Symptoms are muscular weakness, irregular and labored breathing, weak pulse, bloating, belching, constant attempt at swallowing, and pupils contracted or dilated.

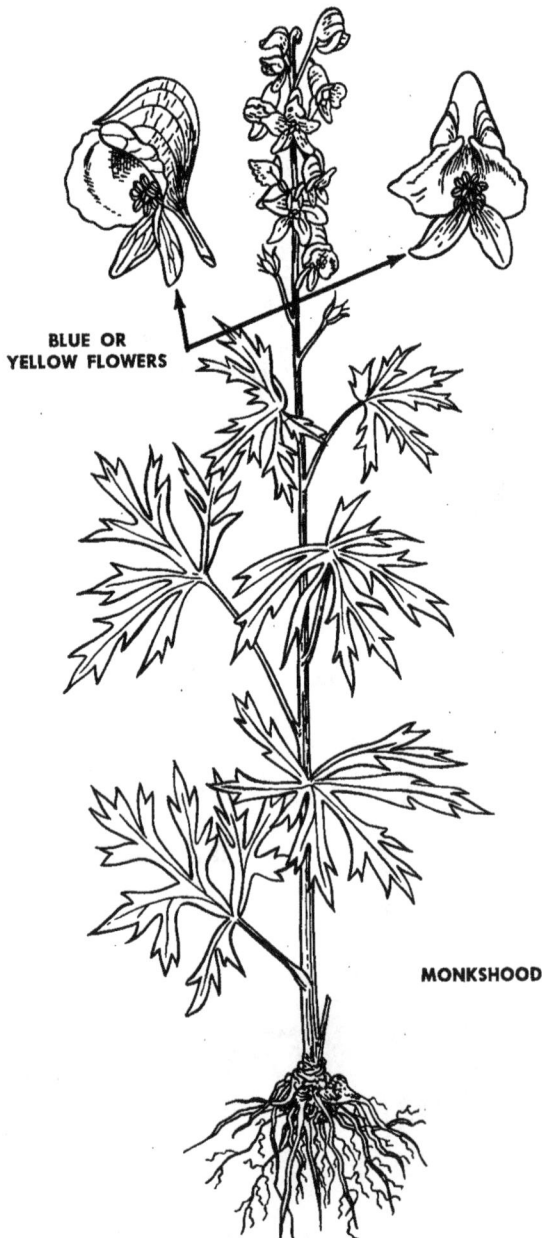

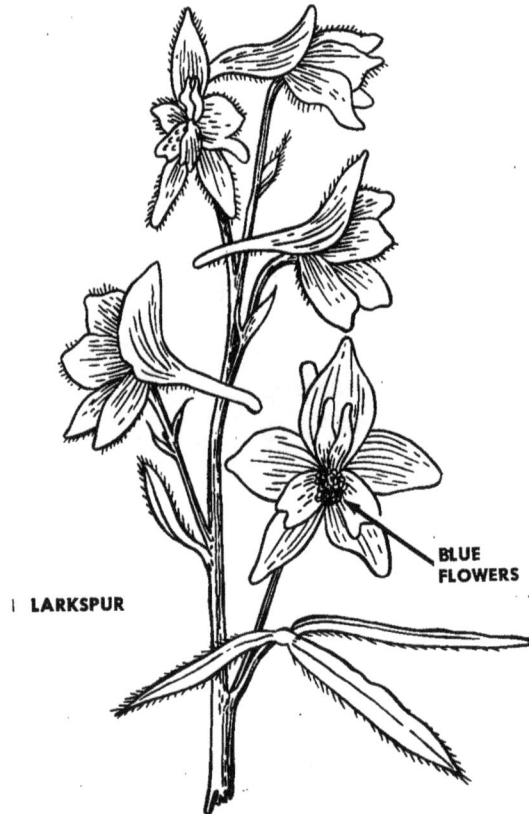

BLUE OR YELLOW FLOWERS

MONKSHOOD

LARKSPUR

BLUE FLOWERS

DECISION: TO STAY OR TO TRAVEL

NOTE: Do *not leave the aircraft* unless briefed to do so. (See page 88.)

• • •

Travel in the Arctic is extremely difficult and hazardous. The decision to travel should be reached only after careful consideration of the following requirements for *successful* travel.

    a.   Exact knowledge of your present location and of the objective of the journey.

    b.   Knowledge of orientation methods.

    c.   Unusual amount of physical stamina.

    d.   Suitable clothing.

    e.   Adequate food, fuel, and shelter, or the equipment for obtaining them.

These requirements are discussed in the paragraphs which follow.

Exact Knowledge of Present Location and Objective

You must, first of all, have exact knowledge of your location and must know exactly where your objective will be. Establishing a position within a 60-mile square by emergency navigation methods would be helpful to searching aircraft but not exact enough for locating a point of departure for travel on foot. An error of only a few miles in the calculation of travel distance can well be the deciding factor between success and failure.

Knowledge of Orientation Methods

The second requirement is adequate knowledge of orientation methods and means of confirming the course chosen. Natives use natural directional aids to guide them in their journeys. Strangers often wonder at the remarkable sense of direction possessed by comparatively primitive peoples. This wonder is caused by the fact that the stranger fails to recognize the natural aids which the native sees. This fact is as true in the Arctic as it is anywhere else.

Wherever snow falls in the Arctic, the wind whips it into drifts around some object which protrudes above the surface. The largest drifts will therefore be on the lee, or downwind side, of all protruding objects, such as rocks, ice hummocks, clumps of willow, or high banks of creeks. By determining the cardinal points of the compass and the direction of the drifts, you can use the angle at which you cross them as a check point in maintaining a straight course. Drastic changes in terrain features may alter wind direction and thus alter the drifts.

Cloud color is another method of orienting yourself. Clouds over open water will appear dark, while clouds over sea ice appear nearly white. In the early fall, before sea ice is formed, snow-covered land reflects light on low overcast to make it appear nearly white, while clouds over open water will appear dark. Viewed from the land in fall and spring, white sky is known as *ice blink*. During open winter this reflection is a sure indication of ice.

In the spring, the direction of land or water can often be determined by observing the type and flight of birds. Migrating water fowl, such as ducks and geese, fly toward land in the spring. Seagulls, sea parrots, and auks fly out to the sea ice in the morning and return to land at night, as does the long-tailed jaeger. The jaeger is known to the Eskimos as the *doctor bird* because of his white breast and neck and black plumage. This bird is easily recognized by his extremely long forked tail feathers and his raucous cry. He has the habit of diving on the Arctic tern in midair to make him disgorge his catch and then seizing it before it has dropped more than a few feet.

Unusual Physical Stamina

The third essential requirement for successful travel is an unusual amount of physical stamina and will to survive. In some cases in which the first and second requirements have been met, overestimation of physical prowess led to fatal results. In relation to this point, it is essential that the traveler realize the need for conserving energy. Survival is synonymous with "take your time." It is not wise to attempt to travel against strong headwinds or to attempt carrying heavy loads for long distances. If you should be caught in a blizzard, make a direction marker. Dig in and remain there until the storm passes. You should be prepared to see a tremendous change in the landscape, following the blizzard. Even with all the desirable equipment, such as snowshoes or skis, and with good weather conditions, Arctic travel is demanding on the physical resources of anyone. Without the necessary equipment and in poor weather, there are a few people who possess sufficient stamina to travel successfully.

Suitable Clothing

Suitable clothing is the fourth requirement for successful travel. If possible, carry clothing in sufficient quantity to give yourself a reasonable chance of remaining dry.

Adequate Food, Fuel, Shelter, or Equipment

The last requirements for successful travel are food, fuel, and shelter, or the equipment which will help you to obtain them from the surrounding environment. Travel consumes body heat at a high rate, and much more food will be necessary while traveling than while remaining relatively inactive in a camp. Therefore, if food supplies are limited and little game is present in the country to be crossed, *make certain* that travel is the only solution to the problem before starting out.

● ● ●

NOTE: It is undoubtedly true that the best policy is to remain with the aircraft in the event of an unexpected landing. Especially is this true when travel is considered in the light of the above-mentioned requirements. Since it is impossible to predict the circumstances which may surround a particular emergency, in the final analysis only the survivors can decide whether to travel or remain with the aircraft.

TRAVEL

If decision to travel has been reached after consideration of the requirements discussed in the previous section, make your preparations carefully and equip yourself as best you can. Don't travel in a blizzard or bitterly cold wind — make camp and save your strength until the wind lets up. Don't travel with poor visibility, even if the wind is not blowing.

Equipment

In winter, if you have them available, carry a sleeping bag, parka, mittens, snowshoes or skis, and mukluks. In summer don't forget mosquito netting and repellent, extra clothing (socks especially), and shoepacs. Wear goggles. Keep feet dry, summer and winter.

Traveling Aids

Improvise traveling aids. Make snowshoes from willow branches, aircraft inspection plates, small metal panels, seat bottoms, or metal tubing. Shroud lines and control cables can be used for webbing and harness. Sleds can be made from cabin doors, cowlings, or bomb bay doors. Ropes can be made from parachute lines (each line has about 450 pounds tensile strength).

Visibility

When the sky is overcast and the ground is covered with snow, the lack of contrast makes it difficult to judge the nature of the terrain. In these conditions, men have walked over cliffs before they saw them. Do not travel in these "white out" conditions.

In traveling, remember you are likely to misjudge distances to objects because of the clear Arctic air and lack of familiar scale such as trees and other landmarks. Underestimates of distance are more common than overestimates. Mirage is common in the Arctic.

Obstacles

Obstacles to summer travel are dense vegetation, rough terrain, insects, soft ground, swamps and lakes, and unfordable large rivers In winter the major obstacles are deep, soft snow, dangerous river ice, "overflows" (stretches of water covered only by a thin layer of ice or snow), severe weather, and a scarcity of native foods.

Selection of Objective

Head for a coast, major river, or known point of habitation. Most settlements are near the coast or near large junctions, lake outlets, points of land, and mouths of streams. Travel downstream — in summer use a raft, if possible. Rubber life rafts and antiexposure suits have been used successfully in Arctic rivers, but don't use them to travel through tide rips or in high winds. In winter the rivers generally make good highways, but look out for thin ice. Travel is sometimes easiest on ridges, particularly in summer when low land is wet. Beware of overhanging banks.

Time to Travel

In general, plan to travel during the period from early morning to early afternoon. Make camp early in the afternoon. Then you will have plenty of time to build a shelter (page 146) and a fire (page 17). Dry your clothes, and fix your evening meal, which should be hot and the biggest daily meal. Start again next morning as soon as it gets light.

On the other hand, when you are on glaciers, or on snow-covered terrain in the spring, travel from midnight to noon to avoid runoff streams. Surfaces are better for travel at night, and rest periods are more comfortable during the warmer day. On valley glaciers watch out for falling rocks early in the evening.

Timbered Terrain

The snow lies deep in the timbered areas, and travel is exceedingly difficult without snowshoes or skis. Progress is generally better when frozen rivers can be followed and the wind has packed the snow hard. However, winter river travel also has its dangers. These are discussed farther on in this section.

North of the timberline major vegetation thins gradually until it finally lies only along creeks and river beds. Here, travel along ridges is often preferable to following rivers unless they are large and fairly clear of snow. In summer, ridge travel is by far the best. The terrain is drier and the ground firmer under foot. Furthermore, if a breeze prevails, it is strongest on the ridges, blowing the mosquitoes down into the valleys and timber.

Rivers and Streams

A glance at any map of the Arctic will reveal that the majority of towns and settlements are located on rivers or on the coast. The reason is obvious. Waterways are the highways of the Arctic. In summer, boats are often the only transportation. In addition, food and fuel are usually available along the inland waterways. Vegetation, brush, and timber line the river banks; fish and bird life are in or on the waters. In short, the natural resources necessary to sustain life are to be found more readily along the rivers, either in winter or in summer.

Rivers which run comparatively straight follow such a course, because fast-flowing current cuts the straightest path through a terrain. The freezing of such rivers is a battle between the temperatures and the current of the river, a battle which never ceases throughout the winter. The current constantly cuts the ice away from below, while the outside temperature tries to maintain or increase the thickness of the covering ice. Snow is on the current's side in this battle, forming an insulation which tends to prevent the outside temperature from reaching the ice. Thus, all snowbanks, *especially those on cut banks,* are apt to lie on thin ice or no ice at all.

Where gravel bars exist in the bed of the river, overflow often occurs. Such bars freeze solidly and dam the river. The water then seeks an outlet, generally along the bank under a snowdrift or around a log or rock, about which the current is faster. In extremely cold weather these overflows "smoke" and can readily be mistaken by the uninitiated for the smoke of a habitation. Overflow often lies under deep snow on the surface of the ice and cannot be seen until a person sinks in it.

Because of these hazards, you should seek to travel the barest portions of the river and avoid all obstacles protruding through the ice. Keep to the inside of all curves and away from cut banks where the current is swiftest. As the river progresses to areas where the fall is slackened, the current is slower and the ice is thicker. However, overflow can also occur here, because the ice freezes deeper and blocks the shallower parts of the river bed. Very often after a freezeup the source of the stream or river dries up so rapidly that an air pocket is formed under the initial ice. This is particularly dangerous. Use an ice chisel to test the ice ahead of you.

One danger area still remains on any river anywhere in the Arctic. This is the junction of a creek or other river. Here the resulting whirlpool keeps the water open longer than anywhere else, except swift rapids. In bypassing all junctions of streams, cross well downstream from the mouth of the joining stream. Cross glacier-fed streams early in the morning when the water level is lowest.

When floating down a stream, watch out for "sweepers" — trees that lean nearly horizontally and may brush personnel or equipment off the raft.

Take special care when crossing thin ice. Distribute your weight by lying flat and crawling across. If traveling in a party, rope each man across. If one breaks through, pull him out and get him under shelter at once. Build a fire and dry his wet clothing.

Barren Land

Winter travel over barren lands is very demanding. Without snowshoes or skis progress can be difficult and slow. Gales, which are impossible to face, may sweep unchecked. There is no natural shelter except that provided by scattered high banks and willow thickets about lakes and along stream beds. Game is very scarce, and fires cannot long be maintained on the fuel generally found in the middle of winter. Most of the rivers follow ancient beds which wind and twist. Survivors who must travel fast cannot afford to follow these old streams which double and quadruple the distance to be covered.

Because of blowing snow, fog, and the lack of landmarks, a compass is a *must* for barren land travel. Even with a compass, one man has difficulty steering a straight course by himself, and variations in the higher latitudes are extreme. Two can do a little better, but three are best, to navigate when visibility is low. The three progress in single file, the last man carrying the compass. He must always keep the lead man in sight. Using the middle man as a reference point, he controls the course of the lead man by calling out corrections to him. *It is strongly recommended that any extended travel over barren land or sea ice be done in groups.*

The spring breakup, the summer, and the fall freeze present far greater travel difficulties than does the winter season. Travel must be accomplished on foot without the aid of skis or snowshoes. Equipment must be packed on the back. The masses of soggy vegetation on the tundra cause the traveler to slip and slide. Lake systems must either be crossed or circumnavigated. Use antiexposure suit, if available, in crossing lakes. Be careful in crossing sandbars and mud flats at the mouths and junctions of rivers, and lakes and lagoon outlets. Quicksands and equally dangerous bottomless muck may trap you. Mosquitoes rise in hordes. It is true that there is a much greater possibility of catching fish and shooting birds in summer than there is in winter, but the physical demands of summer travel are more exhausting than those of winter. Rain and fog prevail during breakup and freezeup. Thawing days are followed by freezing nights. The problem of keeping dry, even with rainproof equipment, is almost impossible to solve.

If a river flows in your desired direction, float down it rather than attempt to travel cross country. Time spent in constructing a raft will be quickly regained.

The months of July and August are about the best summer months for cross-country travel. Less rain falls during these months.

Mountainous Country

In mountainous country it is sometimes best to travel on ridges — the snow surface is probably firmer and you will have a better view of your route from above. Watch out for snow and ice overhanging steep slopes. Avalanches are a hazard on steep snow-covered slopes, especially on warm days and after heavy snowfalls.

Be especially careful on glaciers (p. 130). Watch out for crevasses (deep cracks in the ice) that may be covered by snow. Travel in groups of not fewer than 3 men, roped together at intervals of 30 to 40 feet. Probe before every step. Always cross a snow-bridged crevasse at right angles to its course.

Find the strongest part of the bridge by poking with a pole or ice ax. When crossing a bridged crevasse, distribute your weight by crawling or by wearing snowshoes or skis.

Crevasse Rescue

Rescue from a crevasse should be effected promptly.

The first requirement is to firmly anchor the rope by which the man is hanging. The second is to relieve the strain on the hanging man by dropping the other end of the rope or another anchored rope with a loop in the end for him to stand in. This not only facilitates the rescue but also eliminates the serious danger of suffocation from constriction by the rope. He can pass this rope through his chest loop as shown in the illustration. It will serve to prevent his falling backward in the ascent. The work will be greatly facilitated if an ice ax or other object can be placed under the ropes at the edge of the crevasse to prevent the rope cutting into the snow, while both ropes have a turn around another ice ax, pole, or solid object for a belay.

The victim now grasps the climbing rope firmly and brings his feet up as high as possi-

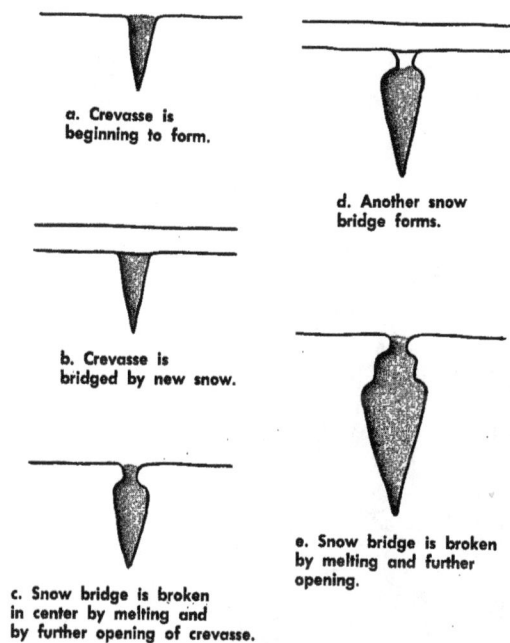

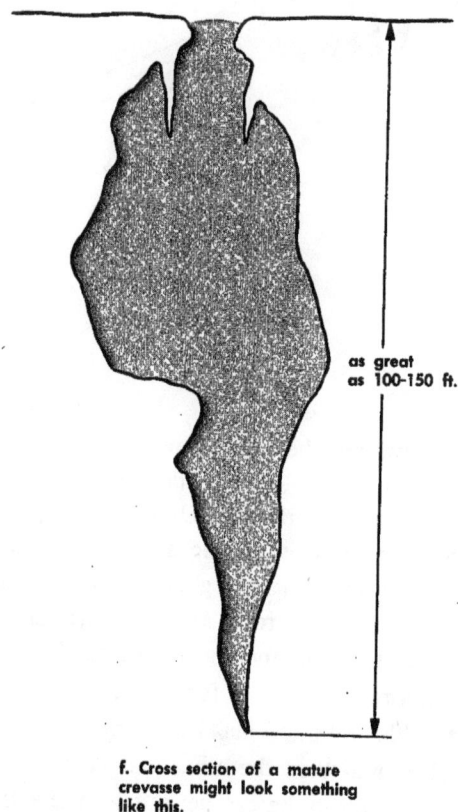

a. Crevasse is beginning to form.

b. Crevasse is bridged by new snow.

c. Snow bridge is broken in center by melting and by further opening of crevasse.

d. Another snow bridge forms.

e. Snow bridge is broken by melting and further opening.

as great as 100-150 ft.

f. Cross section of a mature crevasse might look something like this.

How a crevasse forms on a snow-covered glacier

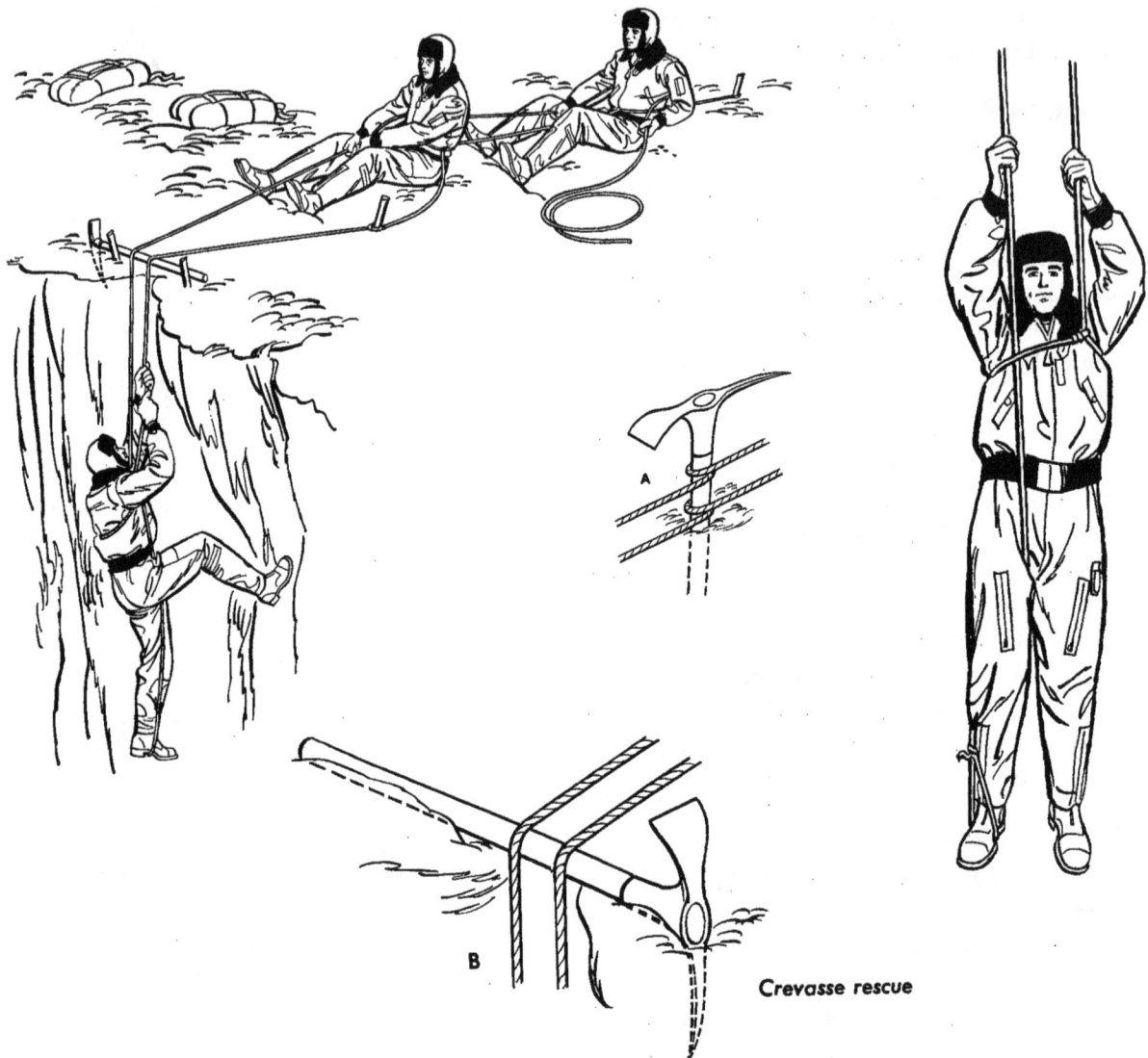

A

B

Crevasse rescue

ble, permitting the man above to take up the stirrup rope. He then stands up and repeats the process, ultimately reaching the lip, where some strong-arm work and a vigorous pull on the rope are necessary to get him over the edge.

If two ends of rope are available, an improvement on this method is to give the hanging man two loops, one for each foot as shown in the illustration. Then by alternately raising one foot and then the other and taking in the ropes at the top, he can get out with less exertion.

Certain precautions should be observed. The exact edge of the crevasse should be ascer-

tained; it may overhang and drop the rescuer into the void if approached too closely. An overhanging lip should be cut away if possible. Otherwise the rope will cut into it, and the man cannot easily be brought over the lip. If the edge is sharp ice, it should be rounded off so that the rope will not be cut. The handle of an ice-imbedded ax can be laid at the edge of the overhang to protect the rope.

The Prusik knot is a valuable means of saving yourself if you fall into a crevasse, and it is useful if you need to bring a man up a rock face. The knot will hold tightly when weight is is applied, but it will slide easily when un-weighted. The method of tying is shown in the illustration. Take a bight of line and turn it twice around the rope, then pull the loose ends of the line through the loop.

You can also use the Prusik knot for climb-ing a rope. Use three slings fashioned from lengths of line. Make two stirrups and a chest loop fastened by Prusik knots to the climbing rope, as shown in the illustration. There should be about 5 feet between the stirrup and the

knot in order to have the knot in front of the chest in an easy handling position. Then, by moving first one stirrup and then the other, it is possible to climb the rope. At the same time, by pushing up the chest loop, you are secured against loss of balance and can take a rest by leaning back at any time.

This is a valuable means of extrication from a crevasse or of rescuing someone from a diffi-cult rock face when strength fails or bad weath-er intervenes.

Crevasse rescue double-stirrup method

The Prusik knot

Use of Prusik knot to climb a rope

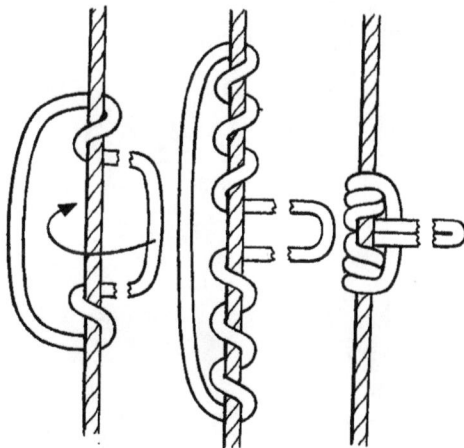

NATIVES

Natives are relatively few and all in North America and Greenland are friendly.

Eskimos live mostly along the coasts. Indians are found along streams and rivers in the interiors.

Prospectors, trappers, and hunters are sparsely scattered.

The natives have little enough to eat. Don't take advantage of their hospitality. Eat their food sparingly. Offer payment when you leave. Tobacco will be greatly appreciated.

Although population is scattered, caches are often found at old campsites, along river routes, and at portages. If you take anything from a cache make a note of its location so you can replace what you took.

4

LAND

SURVIVAL

...DESERT

All desert areas are characterized by scanty rainfall and the absence of trees. Usually there is no open water in deserts but some deserts do have true lakes. Permanent desert lakes with no outlets are salt lakes. Fresh water pools may last days or weeks in any desert after unusual rainstorms. However, don't count on them, for there may be 15 or 20 years between those rainstorms.

Extremes of temperature are as characteristic of deserts as lack of rain and great distances. Hot days and cool nights are usual. A daily minimum-maximum range of 45° F. in the Sahara and a 25° to 35° difference between night and day in the Gobi is the rule. The difference between summer and winter temperatures is also extreme in deserts. Because of these extremes it is often difficult to keep from freezing in some desert areas. However, summer daytime heat in any desert of the world will make your sweat glands work at capacity. You'll need drinking water to maintain that production.

There are more than 50 important named deserts in the world. They occupy nearly one-fifth of the earth's land surface, but only about 4% of the world's population lives there.

The term "desert" is applied to a variety of areas. There are salt deserts, rock deserts, and sand deserts. Some are barren gravel plains without a spear of grass, a bush, or cactus spine for a hundred miles. In other deserts there are grasses and thorny bushes where camels, goats, or even sheep can munch and nibble a subsistence diet.

In this study, references are most often cited from two deserts of climatic extremes, a north temperate desert and a near tropic desert. Other deserts fall in between these extremes. Check the latitude before you apply this information to a particular desert.

Anywhere you find them, deserts are places of extremes. They can be extremely dry, hot, cold, and often devoid of plants or trees or lakes or rivers. But most important in any desert, it is an extremely long time between drinks unless you carry your water with you.

SAHARA

The Sahara is the largest desert in the world, as well as the best known. It stretches across North Africa from the Atlantic Ocean to the Red Sea and from the Mediterranean and the Sahara Atlas Mountains in the north to the Niger River in tropical Africa. It consists of three million square miles of level plains and jagged mountains, rocky plateaus, and graceful sand dunes. There are thousands of square miles where there is not a spear of grass, not a bush or tree, not a sign of vegetation. But Sahara oases, — low spots in the desert where water can be reached for irrigation — are among the most densely populated areas in the world. Date groves and garden patches supporting 1,000 people per square mile are surrounded by barren plains devoid of life.

Only 10% of the Sahara is sandy. By far the greater part of the desert is flat gravel plain from which the sand has been blown away and piled up in the low places where the dunes are located. There are rocky mountains rising 11,000 feet above sea level, and there are a few depressions 50 to 100 feet below sea level.

The change from plain to mountain is abrupt in the Sahara. Mountains generally go straight up from the plain like jagged skyscrapers from a city street. Sharp-rising mountains on a level plain are especially noticeable in many desert landscapes, because there is no vegetation to modify that abruptness. The lack of trees or bushes makes even occasional foothills appear more abrupt than in temperate climates.

ARABIAN DESERT

Some geographers consider the Arabian Desert as a continuation of the Sahara. Half a million square miles in area, the Arabian Desert covers most of the Arabian Peninsula except for fertile fringes along the Mediterranean, the Red Sea, the Arabian Sea, and the valleys of the Tigris-Euphrates Rivers. Along much of the Arabian coastline the desert meets the sea.

There is more sand in the Arabian Desert than in the Sahara, and there are fewer date grove oases. These are on the east side of the desert at Gatif, Hofuf, and Medina. Also there is some rain in Arabia each year, in contrast to the decades in the Sahara that pass without a drop. Accordingly, Arabia has more widespread vegetation, but nomads find scanty pasture for their flocks of sheep and goats over large sections. They depend on wells for water. When unusual dry seasons threaten starvation to flocks, these nomads move toward the fertile fringes of the desert. Historically, the Arabian Desert has been a human reservoir from which people have pushed into more fertile regions. In drought years the border farmers still have to contend with nomad encroachment.

The Arabian Desert differs in one great respect from the Sahara. In Arabia there is oil. Aramco, or the Arabian-American Oil Company, has established modern communities on the edge of the desert. They have drilled many water wells over the area for use of the nomads and their flocks.

Oil is carried across the desert in great pipelines which are regularly patrolled by aircraft. Pumping stations are located at intervals. All these evidences of modern civilization have increased the well-being of the desert people and, as a result, your chances for a safe journey afoot. However, the desert of Arabia is rugged, and native Arabs still get lost and die from dehydration.

GOBI

As used here, "Gobi" means only that basin or saucer-like plateau north of China, and covering 125,000 square miles. The plateau includes Inner and Outer Mongolia.

On all sides of the Gobi, mountains form the rim of the basin. Many of them slope gently on the desert side but are abrupt and steep on the other side. The basin itself slopes so gently that much of it appears to be a level plain. There are rocks and buttes and numerous badlands, or deeply gullied areas, in the Gobi.

For a hundred miles or so around the rim of the Gobi, there is a band of grassland. In average years the Chinese find this to be productive farm land. Year by year they push the Mongol herdsman farther and farther toward the true Gobi. In drought years agriculture retreats.

As you move toward the center of the Gobi there is less and less rainfall; soil becomes thinner, and grass grows in scattered bunches. This is the home of the Mongol herdsman. His wealth is chiefly horses, but he also raises sheep, goats, camels, and a few cattle.

Beyond the rich grassland the Gobi floor is a mosaic of tiny pebbles, which often glisten in the sunlight. These pebbles were once mixed with the sand and soil of the area, but in the course of centuries the soil has been washed or blown away and the pebbles have been left behind as a loose pavement.

What rain there is in the Gobi drains toward the basin; almost none of it cuts through the mountain rim to the ocean. There are some distinct and well-channeled watercourses, but these are usually dry. Many of them are remnants of prehistoric drainage systems. In the east, numerous shallow salt lakes are scattered over the plain. They vary in size and number with the chances in rainfall of the area.

Sand dunes are found in the eastern and western Gobi, but these are not as pronounced a feature as they are in certain sections in Sahara. The Gobi is not a starkly barren waste like the great African desert. Everywhere there is some grass, although it is often scanty. Mongols live in scattered camps all over the plains instead of being concentrated in oases.

SOUTHWEST UNITED STATES

The flat plains with scanty vegetation and abruptly rising buttes of our Southwest are reminders of both the Gobi and the Sahara. But the spectacular rock-walled canyons found in the Southwest have few counterparts in the deserts of Africa or Asia. The gullied badlands of the Gobi resemble similar formations in both the Southwest and the Dakotas, but our desert rivers — the lower Colorado, lower Rio Grande and tributaries, such as the Gila and Pecos — have a more regular supply of water than is found in Old World deserts. The Nile and Niger are, in part, desert rivers but get their water from tropical Africa. They are desert immigrant rivers (like the Colorado, which collects the melting snows of the eastern Rockies) and gain sufficient volume to carry them through the desert country.

The scattered population of Navajo, Apache, and Papago Indians, who live in our southwestern desert regions, parallel the scattered population of Mongolia.

In general, our southwest deserts have more varied vegetation, greater variety of scenery, and more rugged landscape than either the Gobi or the Sahara. In all three areas it is often a long time between drinking water stops, and that spells "desert" in any man's language.

Death Valley, a part of the Mohave lying in southern California, holds second place as the hottest desert, with an official maximum temperature of 134° F. The Sahara in Tropoli has an official high of 134.4° F. to take first place. Actually, Death Valley probably has more water holes and more vegetation than exist in vast stretches of the Sahara. The evil reputation of the Valley appears to have been started by unwise travelers who were too terrified to make intelligent search for water and food. The dryness of Death Valley atmosphere is unquestioned, but it lacks the vast barren plains stretching from horizon to horizon in the Sahara. The sand dunes of Death Valley and nearby deserts make excellent movie stand-ins for Sahara dunes, but geographically they occupy far less territory than their African counterparts.

Compared to the Sahara, the desert country of southwestern United States sometimes looks like a luxuriant garden. There are many kinds of cactus plants in the American desert, but these are not found in either the Sahara or Gobi (unless imported from America).

After a good spring rain — not every year, by any means, but sometimes — there are more than 140 different kinds of plants which blossom in the American desert. Many of these are "quickies," whose seeds can withstand long months and even years of drought. White primroses, lavender verbenas, orange poppies, and yellow desert sunflowers are just a few of the colorful flowers which carpet the desert floor after a hard spring rain.

In contrast to the "quickies," which blossom only after desert rains, are the cactus plants. These store up moisture in their stems or trunks, and their blossomtime is not so dependent on uncertain rains.

Although the cactus plants are not found in either the Gobi or the Sahara, both of these larger deserts do show a few of the quick-flowering plants after a hard rain. The displays of flower colors in these Old World deserts, however, are very poor shows compared to the variety and brilliance of the American desert.

IMMEDIATE ACTION

Water will be your biggest problem if you are down in the desert. Get into the shade as soon as possible; keep your head and the back of your neck covered. Wait until nightfall to travel. If you have crashed or bailed out, reserve any decisions or activity until possible effects of shock have passed.

FIRST AID

Exposure to desert sun can be dangerous.

It can cause three types of heat collapse: heat cramps, heat exhaustion, and heat stroke.

Heat Cramps

The first warning of heat exhaustion usually is cramps in leg or belly muscles. Keep the patient resting; give him salt dissolved in water, but only if there is plenty of water to drink.

Heat Exhaustion

Patient is first flushed, then pale; sweats heavily. His skin is moist and cool; he may become delirious or unconscious. Treat him by placing him in the shade, flat on his back. *Give him salt dissolved in water* — two tablets to a canteen. Since he is cold, keep him wrapped up and give him warm drinks, if available.

Heat Stroke

Heat stroke may come on suddenly. The face is red, skin hot and dry. All sweating stops. The head aches severely; pulse is fast and strong. Unconsciousness may result. Treat the patient by cooling him off. Loosen his clothing; lay him down flat, but off the ground, *in the shade.* Cool him by saturating clothes with water and by fanning. Do not give stimulants.

NOTE: People whose bodies have become acclimatized to working in high temperatures will find their normal salt needs are satisfied at mealtime by food salted to their taste. During acclimatization a man's heart action, circulation, sweat glands, and all body functions become adjusted to function in the heat. This is the period of natural adjustment to the conservation of body salt.

Sunblindness

Symptoms of sunblindness are burning, watering, or inflamed eyes, headaches, and poor vision.

Treat sunblindness by protecting the eyes from light and relieving the pain. Place the patient in a dark shelter or wear a lightproof bandage. Relieve the pain by putting cold compresses on the eyes. Give the patient APC's. Use no eye drops or ointment. If patient has complete rest, he will probably recover within 18 hours. When travel is necessary before 18 hours, patient will have to be led. Remember: the first attack of sunblindness makes the victim more susceptible to others.

SIGNALING

You can make a good improvised flare from a tin can filled with sand soaked with gasoline. Light it with care. Add oil and pieces of rubber to make dense smoke for daytime signal. Burn gasoline or use other bright flame at night.

Dig trenches to form signals, or line up rocks to throw shadow.

If you can find brush in the area, gather it into piles and have it ready to light when a search aircraft is heard or sighted.

Smoke fires and smoke grenades are best for use in daytime. Flares and bright flames are hard to see.

The mirror is a very good desert signal. Practice using it. Use brightly polished metal as a substitute.

DECISION TO STAY WITH THE AIRCRAFT OR TO LEAVE

The best advice generally is to stay with the aircraft. You'll last much longer without water if you stay near the aircraft, in the shade, rather than exhausting yourself by trying to walk out.

Travel only if you are sure that you can walk easily to assistance, and if you are absolutely certain that you have enough water (see desert water supply table on page 197), or if there is reasonable doubt that rescue is possible.

SHELTER

You will need shelter mostly from sun and heat.

Natural Shelter

Natural shelter is limited to the shade of cliffs or the lee side of hills. In some desert mountains you can find good cavelike protec-

DOUBLE LAYER OF PARACHUTE CLOTH DRAPED FROM WING

COLD WEATHER SHELTER

SHADE SHELTER

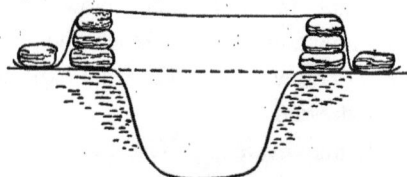

SHADE TRENCH

Desert shelters using parachute cloth

tion under the tumbled blocks of rocks broken from cliff sides. Occasionally you may find a twisted, stunted bush or tree over which you can spread your parachute for shade. But out on the open plain you must carry your shelter, like your food and water, with you.

NOTE: If you camp or travel in a desert canyon or dry river bed, be prepared for a quick exit. Cloudbursts, although rare, do cause sudden and violent floods which sweep along a dry valley in a wall of roaring water.

Aircraft

If you stay with the aircraft, don't use the inside of it for shelter in the daytime — it will be too hot. Get under the shade of a wing, if you have no other shelter. You can make a good shade shelter easily by tying a spread-out parachute as an awning to the wing, leaving the lower edge at least 2 feet clear of the ground for air circulation. Use sections of aircraft tubing for tent poles and pegs. Make sure that the aircraft is securely moored and the wing solidly guyed to prevent movement in a storm.

Parachute

If the aircraft is not available, make a shelter of your parachute, as shown in the illustration. The layers of cloth separated by an airspace of several inches make a cooler shelter than a single thickness. The parachute can also be placed across a trench dug in the sand.

Sahara

During Sahara winter (October to May) the absence of shelter is not serious. It gets cold at night, but not much below freezing, while daytime temperatures reach the 80's and low 90's. You will not suffer from exposure if properly dressed.

It may even rain. Use the inside of the aircraft then for protection against cold and rain, but do your cooking outside to prevent carbon monoxide poisoning.

The summer months bring hot days, and shelter from the midday sun is advisable. Na-

tives on desert journeys carry tents either of skins or of woven wool cloth. They also carry their tent poles and stakes. These tents are about 4 feet high in the center, sloping to about 18 inches above the ground. During the heat of the day these tents have good circulation of air and offer cool places to rest. When it begins to get too cool in late afternoon or evening, matting is unrolled around the inside edges of the tents to stop the breeze and make the tents warm. Some nomad groups raise and lower the edges of the tents as the temperature rises and falls.

In Sahara oases, dwellings are thick-walled, flat-roofed adobe structures. These are often whitewashed and painted blue around the windows and doors. Blue reduces glare and seems to keep away some of the flies.

Gobi

The Mongols of the Gobi have semipermanent dwellings called *yurts*. These are circular with a willow or bamboo frame (purchased from China) over which is lashed a thick sheet of felt. The conical roof is also of felt with an open smoke hole like an American Indian tepee

Mongol lamaseries are adobe structures built by Chinese laborers and decorated with red and gold. Many lamas, however, erect felt yurts in temple courtyards for their sleeping quarters. The felt yurt, like the adobe house, is well insulated against both the summer heat and the winter cold. The latter is a serious hazard in the Gobi, where January and February temperatures are regularly down to 15° or 20° below zero, Fahrenheit.

For light travel, especially in summer, the Mongols use a light cotton cloth tent. This is blue outside and white inside. It is an A-shaped tent, also sloping to the ground at both front and back. Like the circular yurt, it offers minimum wind resistance. Tent poles and pegs are carried with the cloth, as no supports are available in the desert. During hot middays of July and August the edges of the tent are propped up to allow free circulation of air.

When strong winds blow, extra ropes over the ridge pole and sides are staked down to keep the tent from ballooning off across the desert.

FIRE-MAKING

In some deserts fuel is extremely rare. Wherever you find plant growth, use all twigs, leaves, stems, and underground roots for burning.

Sahara

Cooking fires are not large in the Sahara. Rarely is a fire needed to warm the adobe houses of oases. In the houses of wealthy natives, where floors are covered with rugs, fires are built in various types of braziers. In ordinary houses and in caravan and nomad camps, fire is built on the ground.

Stems of palm leaves and similar wood serve as fuel in and near oases. Out on the open desert dry roots or bits of dead vegetation are carefully hoarded to boil tea or cook a meal. Dried camel dung is the standard fuel where woody fibers are lacking.

Gobi

In the Gobi, dried heifer dung is the preferred fuel. Heifer dung has a symmetrical shape, in contrast to the broad irregular pattern of cow dung. It burns with a hot blue flame, in contrast to the smoky yellow flame of cow dung, sheep droppings, etc. Bricks of handpressed dung are used to build winter corrals, and as the cold becomes severe the top layers of the corral walls are used as fuel for cooking and for heating the yurts. *Argol* is the Mongol word for all kinds of dung. The natives have large argol baskets and argol forks which are used in collecting animal droppings for winter fuel supply.

CLOTHING

In hot deserts you need your clothing for protection against sunburn, heat, sand, and insects, so don't discard any of it. Keep your head and body covered during the day — you'll last longer on less water. Wear long pants and blouse them over the tops of your

T-SHIRT USED AS FACE PROTECTION AGAINST SAND

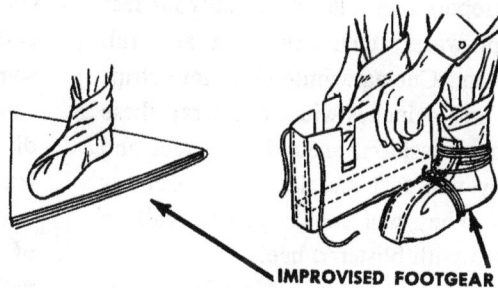

IMPROVISED FOOTGEAR

FACECLOTH

NECKCLOTH

Desert clothing

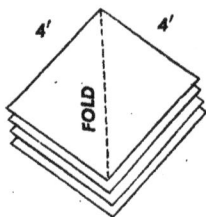

4 PIECES OF
CHUTE CLOTH

MAKING ARAB-TYPE HEADDRESS

Making Arab-type headdress

boots. Roll down your shirtsleeves, but keep them loose and flapping to stay cooler.

Wear a cloth neckpiece to cover the back of your neck from the sun. Your T-shirt makes an excellent neck drape, with the extra material used as padding under your cap. If you have no hat, make a headpiece like that worn by the Arabs, as shown in the illustration. You can adapt your pilot chute for use as a parasol; don't be too proud to use one. During duststorms, wear a covering for your mouth and nose; parachute cloth will do.

If you have lost your shoes or if they wear out, make sandals as shown in the drawing. Those hardy desert soldiers, the French Foreign Legionnaires, follow the practice of wearing "Russian socks" on their long desert hikes. These are prepared as follows: Wash your feet in lukewarm water; then dry them and rub grease on them. Cut parachute cloth into strips 2 feet long and 4 inches wide, and wrap these strips, bandage fashion, around your feet and ankles. They will feel and look like ordinary white socks. They will enable you to walk in comfort, even with blistered heels.

Deserts are not always hot. Heat is a desert characteristic in summer daytime — from May to October in the Sahara; during July and August in the Gobi. During the rest of the year, you'll need winter clothing in the Sahara, Arctic winter clothing in the Gobi.

HEALTH AND HAZARDS

Deserts are quite healthy places, since dry air is not favorable to bacteria. Wounds usually heal rapidly in the desert, even without treatment. Except in some oases of the Sahara, malaria does not exist. The social diseases, however, are prevalent in both Gobi and Sahara. They are much more common in Mongolia than in Africa. Until you lose your sense of sight and your sense of smell, you will probably not become contaminated.

Summertime dysentery can be avoided by watching your diet and not eating or drinking uncooked native food. In the fall and early winter, typhoid and paratyphoid are present, but your inoculation shots will give you normal protection from these.

Crowded living quarters in family yurts or in adobe lamaseries and inadequate diet during winter and early spring are probably responsible for the appearance of tuberculosis and the seasonal occurrence of scurvy among some natives. The Mongols believe that scurvy can be cured by drinking lots of milk. Proper diet, of course, is your protection against contracting either scurvy or tuberculosis.

Any American who follows his natural habits of cleanliness and his normal ideas of diet will find the deserts of the world quite free from disease, probably safer in that respect than the crowded cities of the United States or Europe.

Mosquitoes

Ordinarily mosquitoes do not travel far from their breeding place. They breed in quiet or stagnant water such as rain pools, swamps, water pockets in plants, old tin cans, or similar places. Since their usual life span is 15 to 20 days, under some conditions even a couple of months, their presence does not mean that you are near a supply of water. In 1942 sentries in the Libyan Sahara saw "a cloud of vapour coming from the north which looked like a duststorm by moonlight." The "cloud" was a swarm of mosquitoes, and the nearest breeding places were 18 to 28 miles to the northeast. A strong wind carried the insects into the desert. Possibly they could have traveled even farther.

All mosquitoes are unwelcome company, but only some species of the anopheles carry malaria. You can usually distinguish the anopheles from other mosquitoes by the way they settle on your skin or other surface. The anopheles settles with the proboscis and long axis of the body in one straight line at an angle of 45° with its "landing field." The culicine mosquitoes, which in general do not carry disease, land with the abdomen parallel to or inclined toward the surface upon which it rests. Cold weather slows them up.

Singing mosquitoes are not anopheles. The singres do not generally carry disease.

Malaria, yellow fever, dengue, filariasis (elephantiasis) and other ills are mosquito-borne.

Unless the female anopheles has bitten a patient with malaria or other mosquito-carried disease before she bites you, no harm is done. She is only a vector, not an originator. If a strong silent mosquito drills you at a 45° angle play safe and reach for the antimalaria pill.

Flies

Flies are sometimes found so far out in the desert that you wonder how they got there. In Egypt and Libya they are *bad*. They buzz and pry about any exposed part of your body without letup. They settle on your lips, the corners of your eyes, your ears. There is no rest from flies unless you cover your face and every part of your body when you are in a fly-infested desert.

Since WW II, many areas have been treated against flies. If garbage is covered, and if kitchens, food-handling areas, and sleeping quarters are screened, relief from flies is possible. If you travel in the desert, they will probably be hitchhiking on your back, but in time you can get rid of them until you reach another inhabited area.

Other Insects

Other insects are less numerous. In some regions you might shake a scorpion out of your shoes in the morning. On the other hand you can spend months in the desert without seeing one.

Snakes

Snakes are not numerous in desert areas. Some individuals manage to see snakes where others, just as sober, see none at all. An American scientific expedition in the Gobi of Mongolia once camped on the private property of a nest of vipers. Every man in the outfit was killing snakes for an hour or two, but other years the same group saw almost no live snakes. Cold weather keeps them sluggish, and you probably will not see one in wintertime even in southern deserts.

Sandstorms

Sandstorms are not a serious hazard unless you make them so. If you try to travel when visibility is zero, you can get lost in a hurry. That is true on a black desert night when sentries can't find their post or can miss a white tent at 50 feet. It is true in severe sand or duststorms.

If wind and dust impede your progress or shut out visibility, *stop traveling*. Mark the direction you are traveling with a deep scratched arrow on the ground, a row of stones, or other markers. Then lie down and sleep out the storm with your back to the wind. You may get some comfort by covering your face with cloth.

Don't worry about being buried by a sandstorm. Desert romance stories have got to make the storms "good," but no man was ever buried alive by a desert sandstorm. Even in the sand dune areas it takes years for the sand to cover a dead camel. You won't have to sleep out a storm more than a few days at worst. Remember sandstorms are not blizzards. Your real danger is getting lost by traveling in zero visibility.

Sunglare

The color of the ground varies a great deal in different deserts. In areas where there is light sand, as much as 80% of the light which falls on it is reflected back. That is getting near the amount of reflection from snow.

Snow blindness (photophthalmia) is due to the reflection of short wavelength ultraviolet light. Since there is a higher percentage of ultraviolet light in equatorial regions, there is probably a damaging concentration of these light rays at eye level from the reflected light in some desert regions.

Solar retinitis produced by the short infrared and visible light rays can also occur in deserts. You won't be bothered by this, however, unless you look at the sun or are scanning the sky in the area immediately adjacent to the sun.

In other words, sunglasses of some sort are good for you. Even though the glare does not seem painful to you the very high light intensities of the desert will cause a decrease in your night vision.

Improvised glasses

Regular flying sunglasses in large frames are the easy and satisfactory solution to the problem of sunglare. Lenses should be preferably neutral density lenses of 12-16% transmission. They should be large enough to prevent side light from striking the eye. Such glasses will be some protection against dust, but by no means complete protection.

If you do not have flying sunglasses the next best help is to make slit goggles as shown in the illustration. Another method is to shade the eyes from above with a hat or a turban which has cloth down the sides of your face. Smear charcoal or dirt on the bridge of your nose and below your eyes, to cut down glare.

WATER REQUIREMENTS

In the desert your life depends on your water supply. The following table shows how long you can survive on specific amounts of water at various temperatures.

The normal temperature of your body is 98.6° F. Any variation reduces your efficiency. An increase of 6° to 8° for any extended period is fatal. Your body gets rid of excess heat by evaporating water on the skin surface. You can see how effective the system is if you fill a desert water bag and a canteen with water and hang both in the sun. When the water in the canteen is 110° F., the water in the sweating desert bag will be only 70°. Evaporation of sweat on the desert bag keeps it 40° cooler.

When you sweat, however, your body loses water, and you must replace the loss by drinking water. Otherwise you will pay for the loss in reduced efficiency and perhaps death. A man who has lost 2-1/2% of his body weight by sweating (about 1-1/2 quarts) loses 25% of his efficiency. Also, if he is working in temperatures of 110° F., his normal ability will be cut another 25%. These statistics mean that if your body is short 1-1/2 quarts of water and the air around you is 110° F., you can do only about half as much work as you normally do; you can walk only half as far as you could in normal temperatures with plenty of water.

In hot deserts you need a minimum of a gallon of water a day. If you walk in the cool desert night, you can get about 20 miles for that daily gallon. If you do your walking in daytime heat, you'll be lucky to get 10 miles

NO WALKING AT ALL . . .

Max. daily in shade temperature (°F)	Available water per man, U. S. quarts					
	0	1	2	4	10	20
120	2	2	2	2.5	3	4.5
110	3	3	3.5	4	5	7
100	5	5.5	6	7	9.5	13.5
90	7	8	9	10.5	15	23
80	9	10	11	13	19	29
70	10	11	12	14	20.5	32
60	10	11	12	14	21	32
50	10	11	12	14.5	21	32

WALKING AT NIGHT UNTIL EXHAUSTED AND RESTING THEREAFTER

Max. daily in shade temperature (°F)	Available water per man, U. S. quarts					
	0	1	2	4	10	20
120	1	2	2	2.5	3	
110	2	2	2.5	3	3.5	
100	3	3.5	3.5	4.5	5.5	
90	5	5.5	5.5	6.5	8	
80	7	7.5	8	9.5	11.5	
70	7.5	8	9	10.5	13.5	
60	8	8.5	9	11	14	
50	8	8.5	9	11	14	

Reprinted from Physiology of Man, Adolph and Associates, Interscience Publisher, New York; 1947.

to the gallon. Whether you sit out your desert survival or walk home, you'll need water — at least 3 to 4 quarts a day.

The only way to conserve your water is to ration your sweat. Drink water as you need it, but keep heat out of your body by keeping your clothes on. Clothing helps ration sweat by not letting it evaporate so fast that you get only part of its cooling effect. You may feel more comfortable in the desert without a shirt or pants, because your sweat evaporates fast. But then you need more sweat — and sunburn is a painful trouble. Desert sun will burn you even if you have a good coat of tan, so wear a hat, use a neckcloth, and keep your clothes on. Light-colored clothing turns away the heat of the sun better than dark clothes. Clothing also keeps out the hot desert air. Keep in the shade as much as possible during the day. Desert natives have tents open on all sides to allow free circulation of air during the day-time. Sit up a few inches off the ground, if possible do not lie right on it. The temperature can be 30° cooler a foot above the ground, and that difference can save you a lot of sweat.

Slow motion is better than speed in hot deserts. Slow and steady does it. If you must move about in the heat, you'll last longer on less water if you take it easy. Remember the Arab — he is not surviving in the desert; he lives there and likes it. He isn't lazy — he's just living in slow motion, the way the desert *makes* him live. Don't fight the desert — you won't win.

Here is how you feel if you are not getting enough water:

SIGNS AND SYMPTOMS OF DEHYDRATION IN MAN AT VARIOUS DEFICITS OF BODY WATER

1%-5% of body weight	6%-10% of body weight	11%-20% of body weight
Thirst	Dizziness	Delirium
Vague discomfort	Headache	Spasticity
Economy of movement	Dyspnea (labored breathing)	Swollen tongue
Anorexia (no appetite)	Tingling in limbs	Inability to swallow
Flushed skin	Decreased blood volume	Deafness
Impatience	Increased blood concentration	Dim vision
Sleepiness	Absence of salivation	Shriveled skin
Increased pulse rate	Cyanosis (body blue)	Painful micturition
Increased rectal temp.	Indistinct speech	Numb skin
Nausea	Inability to walk	Anuria (defective micturition or none)

SOURCES OF DESERT WATER

Although it is not wise to depend on finding natural water in an unfamiliar area, there are a number of sources from which water may be obtained.

Wells

In all deserts, wells are the sources of most water. Hand-dug wells have furnished water to irrigate Sahara oases for many centuries, and there are almost as many ways of hauling the water to the surface as there are wells. Hand-dug wells, like the oases themselves, are located in low places of the desert. Basins, dry river valleys, and hollows in the dunes are typical locations. The best of these, of course, are ancient river beds.

In the western Sahara the natives have dug elaborate tunnels for irrigation. Starting at the edge of a basin or in the bed of an old river, they dig a ditch toward the desert, keeping the bottom of the ditch on a gentle slope away from the basin. As the ditch extends out into the desert it soon becomes too deep to be maintained as an open trench. The workmen extend it as a tunnel as far as they can see without artificial light. Leapfrogging ahead along the same line, they set down a well and tunnel back and forward. Then another jump is made to another well. These chains of wells, connected by a tunnel in the moist sand, extend for miles into the desert. Water collects in the underground channel and flows to the basin, where it irrigates the gardens. A similar system has been discovered in the central Asian desert nearly ten thousand miles from the tunnels in Sahara. Although they are still being used and are being extended in modern times, the origins of these tunnels are still hidden to historians.

The Gobi is itself a great basin with only internal drainage, so that water falling on its mountain edges, if not evaporated, replenishes the ground water supply. Wells dug in valley bottoms or other low places of the Gobi tap that water supply at a depth of 10 to 15 feet. Natives dip the water with a skin bag on the end of a stick to which a rope is attached, or use a bucket on a hand rope. Elaborate pulleys, well sweeps, or pumps so common in the Sahara are not necessary at shallow Gobi wells.

In northern Mongolia, wells are less numerous than in the south, because there are more springs. All roads lead to water, however. You'll know you are going in the right direction when your trail joins another. The "arrow" formed by two connecting trails points toward the water.

Desert wells are generally located along trails. In rocky deserts and on some gravel plains, however, it is not always easy to find the well. This is particularly true if it does not have any super structure or is in a protected valley.

In desert and near-desert regions, wells are gathering places for native peoples as well as stopping places for caravans. Permanent camps or habitations may be some distance away from the well, sometimes as much as 2 or 3 miles away. Passing caravans may camp within a few yards or a few hundred yards from a well. Camp fire ashes, animal droppings, and generally disturbed surface will tell you that others have camped there. Such indications will also tell you that a well is not far off. Paths leading from the camping area should lead you to the well.

On some flat plains, wells which are not often used are covered against sandstorms. Even though there is no sand in the immediate area, sandstorms would in time fill up such wells. In sand dune areas this is even more likely. Desert people have learned to cover such wells a little below the top. Sand drifts in, but the well is protected. You can dig out the cover and reach water easily in such wells but be careful not to dump the sand into the cavity. There may be only a shallow pool of water in the well bottom.

You sometimes hear stories about poisoned wells. Many of these are based on bad-tasting water which is not necessarily poisonous. Actually the danger of poison from water in the Sahara can only be cited as a curiosity, for there are just two wells in this class. One is at Tini-Hara in Esh-Shish Erg. It is so strong of chlorine that it will burn clothing. In the same Erg, General Laperine found another well so strong of saltpeter that it caused vomiting. Occasionally in the Gobi a traveler will encounter a well so strongly alkali that he will prefer to go the 6 or 8 miles to a fresher water supply.

Rivers

Great desert rivers like the Nile, the Tigris, and the Euphrates have been used to irrigate the desert for centuries. Shorter streams on the desert edges are also diverted into irrigation ditches to water the feet of palm trees. At other points, where mountain streams lose themselves in desert sands, the natives plant their trees and crops right over the lost rivers so that roots can reach the water without difficulty.

Lakes

There are shallow lakes in most deserts, and many of them are undrained. These have been without outlets for many thousands of years so that evaporation has concentrated the amount of salt in the water and has made them distinctly salt water lakes. Some of the salt water tastes like table salt. In other areas it may contain magnesium or alkali. If not too strong, such waters are drinkable even though they may have a laxative effect.

Natural Pools and Cisterns

In the Sahara deep hollows on rocky plains act as cisterns and collect surface water from the rare torrential rains. These tanks may be dry for 10 or 15 years, then suddenly be deep enough for a good swimming hole. The water in them is fresh and drinkable and may take several weeks or months to dry up. Unfortunately there is no way for the casual traveler or stranger to the area to know of the existence of such water holes, and there is no rule to guide one to them. They are natural drainage basins like any depression on a plain or plateau. If you know there has been a rain recently in your area, then keep an eye out for hollows or any protected cavity which would naturally collect surface drainage.

Many desert water holes are not true wells but are natural tanks or cisterns. These may be located behind rocks, in gullies or side canyons and under cliff edges. Often the ground surface near them is solid rock or hard-packed soil on which paths do not show up. In such cases you may have to search for the water point. In the Libyan Sahara, doughnut-shaped mounds of camel dung often surround the wells. Unless you recognize the small mound ring you could easily miss the well.

Water from Plants

The thirsty traveler in tropical jungles will find many plants containing suitable drinking water. In the Gobi and Sahara, plants are not a source of water supply. American deserts are slightly better favored. The large barrel cactus does contain considerable moisture which can be squeezed out of the pulp if you have the energy to cut through the tough, outer spine-studded rind. Botanists argue both that the juice *can* and *cannot* be used to quench thirst.

Three men did drink it and found the taste bitter. "Reminded me of the taste when I take an aspirin tablet without a drink of water to wash it down," said one. The taste disappeared in about half an hour. A barrel cactus 3-1/2 feet high contained moisture from top to bottom and "about a quart of liquid could be obtained by crude methods of crushing the pulp and squeezing out the milky juice." (This is an exception, like dandelions, to the rule that milky or colored sap-bearing plants should not be eaten.) Working with a scout knife, one of the men took 40 minutes to get to the moisture-bearing pulp of this kind of plant. Less time was required when a machete was available. So far the evidence for getting your water supply out of desert plants indicates that you had better find a well or other source.

Digging for Water

When you are away from trails or far from wells, you may still find water. Along the seashore or on sandy beaches or desert lakes your best chance is to dig a hole in the first depression behind the first sand dune. Rainwater from local showers collects here. Stop digging when you hit wet sand. Water will seep out of the sand into the hole. This first water is fresh or nearly fresh. It is drinkable. If you dig deeper, you may strike salt water.

Damp surface sand anywhere marks a good place to scoop out such a shallow well, from which you can collect water into your canteen or other receptacle. Among sand dunes away from surface water the lowest point between the dunes is where rain water will collect. Dig down 3 to 6 feet. If sand gets damp, keep digging until you hit water. If you dig in the dune itself, you may strike a foot or so of damp sand with dry sand below. When that happens, you had better look for a lower spot to dig your well.

In a sand dune belt, water will most likely be found beneath the original valley floor at the edge of the dunes rather than in the easy digging middle.

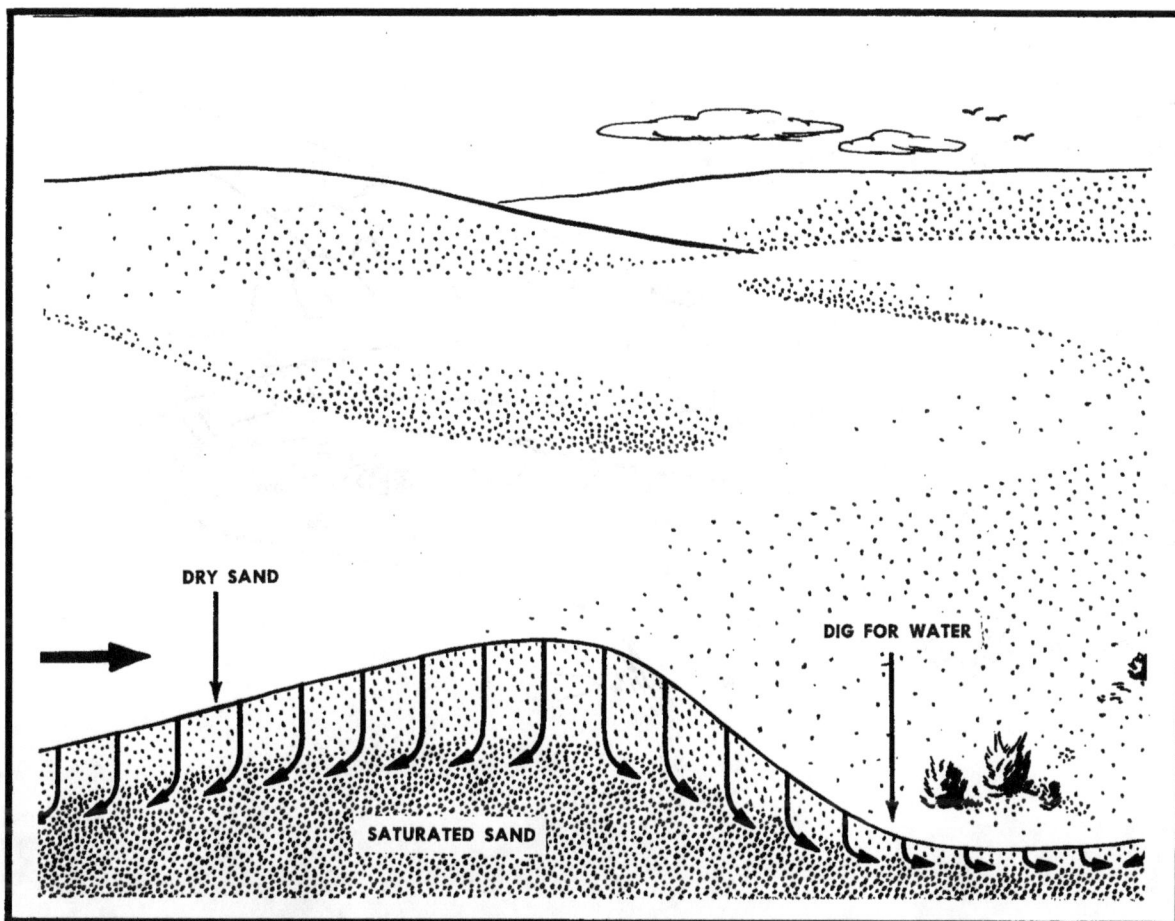

DRY SAND

DIG FOR WATER

SATURATED SAND

Sand dunes

Dry stream beds often have water just below the surface. It accumulates and sinks at the lowest point on the outside of a bend in the stream channel as the stream dries up. You may catch a drink if you dig on such outside bends.

In mud flats during winter you may find wet mud at the lowest point. Wring mud out in a piece of cloth to get water — but don't drink if the water is too salty or soapy tasting.

Condensed Moisture

In the Arabian Desert near the Persian Gulf and the Red Sea and in the Libyan Sahara near the Mediterranean Sea there is considerable moisture in the air. This moisture will condense on cool objects. Often condensed moisture or dew will be heavy enough to drip from metal awnings or roofs on cool mornings. In Arabia this morning dew and even fog extends inland several miles. Occasionally fog occurs as much as 200 miles from the Persian Gulf.

In the Negev desert of Israel, ancient piles of stone are found in regular lines. In some of them old stumps of grape vines have been discovered. Some achaeologists believe that the ancients heaped stones around the grape vine base so that dew would collect and water the vines.

If you find dew on the metal wings of your crashed aircraft, you may collect the drip in a container or you might get more water by wiping it off the cool metal with a handkerchief or soft cloth and wringing it out into a container.

Cool stones, collected from below the hot surface of the desert, if placed on a waterproof tarp may cause enough dew to collect for a

BEND

DIG

CONCAVE BANK

DIG

Dry river bed

SPRING OR
SEEPAGE

WATER CREEPS
ALONG CRACKS
IN ROCKS

Desert mountains of crystalline rock

refreshing drink. Exposed metal surfaces like aircraft wings or tin cans are best dew condensers. They should be clean of dust or grease to get the best flavored water.

Soon after sunrise in the desert the dew evaporates. If you expect a good drink, you will have to collect the dewdrops very soon after sunup.

Tips on Locating Sources of Water

Desert natives often know of lingering surface pools in dry stream beds or other low places. They cover them in various ways to protect them from excessive evaporation. If you look under likely brush heaps or in sheltered nooks you may locate such pools in semi-arid brush country.

Birds all need water. Some of them fly considerable distances at sunset and dawn to reach waterholes. If you hear their chirping in the early morning or evening, you may locate their private drinking fountain. In true desert areas flocks of birds will circle over waterholes.

The presence of vegetation does not always mean that surface water is available. Many plants have an extensive shallow root system. This enables them to make maximum use of water from rare desert rains. Other plants have long taproots which go down several feet to reach a permanent supply of ground water. In the American desert, mesquite is an outstanding example. Where it grows, you can reach water if you dig — but you may have to dig down 30 to 60 feet. The roots of this plant are known to grow to those depths to reach ground water.

Places which are visibly damp, where animals have scratched or where flies hover are more reliable places to dig for water, because they indicate that surface water was there recently.

ANIMAL FOOD

In most deserts, animals are scarce. Their presence depends upon water and vegetation, and true deserts offer little of either. However, few animals have been able to adjust their body processes to desert conditions, the best known of these being the camel and the gazelle. Apparently the desert antelope, or gazelle, can get enough moisture from its food, for no records indicate that these creatures drink water at any time.

Camels have adapted to an *irregular* supply of water rather than to its absence. They make up for periods of enforced drought — 8 to 10 days — by drinking copiously when they are watered. Camel men say that their charges drink about as much water in the course of a year as other beasts of equal size (about 6 gallons a day). Their advantage is that they carry storage tanks.

Some small rodents (rabbits, prairie dogs, rats), snakes, and lizards have learned to live in deserts. They keep in the shade or burrow into the ground, protecting themselves from the direct sun and heated air as well as from the hot desert surface.

Hunting

Look for animals at waterholes, in grassy canyons, low-lying areas, dry riverbeds — where there is a greater chance of moisture — or under rocks and in bushes. Animals are most commonly seen at dusk or early morning. The smaller animals are your best and most reliable sources of food. You may catch rodents by finding their burrows and snaring them with loop snare, trap, or deadfall when they come out at dusk or dawn. Look for land snails on rocks and bushes.

Try kissing the back of your hand to make squalling sounds; you may attract birds. Sand grouse, ducks, bustards, pelicans, and even gulls have been seen over some desert lakes. Trap them in baited deadfalls or use a hook or gorge.

When hunting an animal on the desert, remember that distances are fooling. Make certain the animal is actually within range before you fire. You'll probably get just one shot.

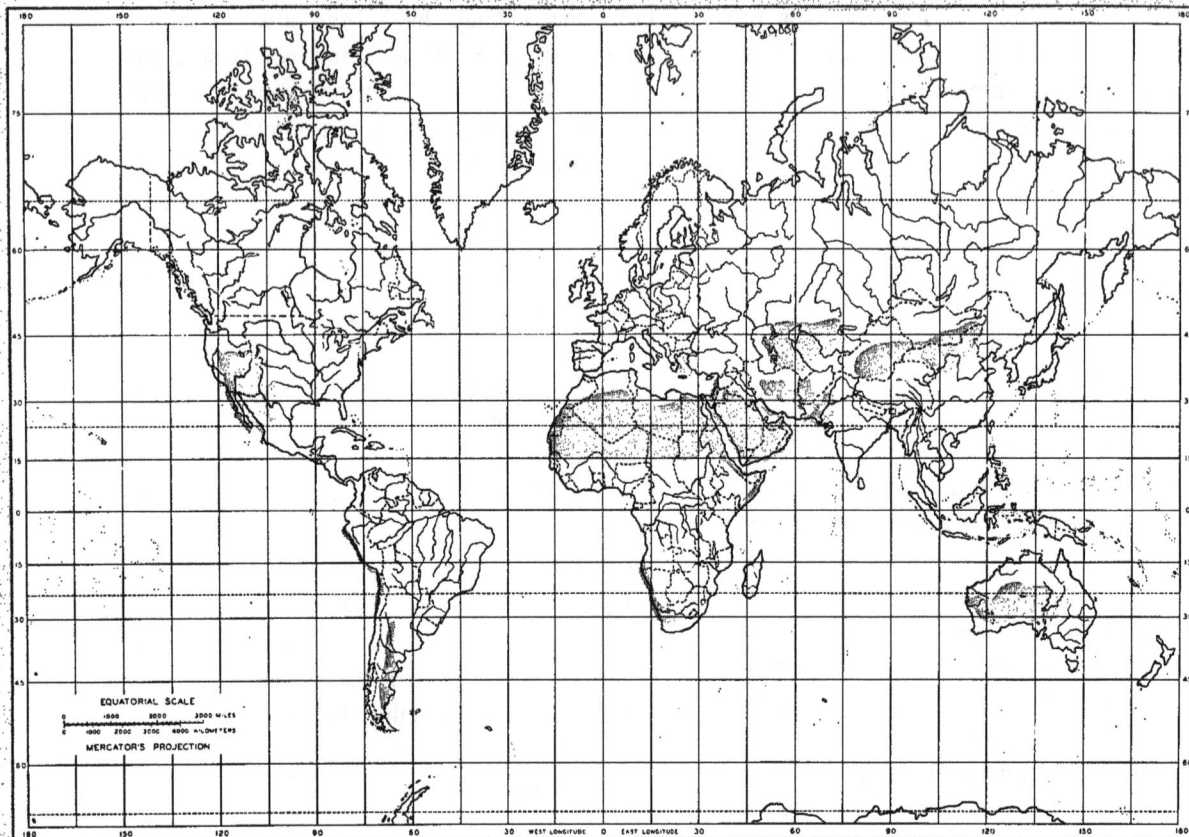

DESERT SCRUB AND WASTE

EDIBLE DESERT PLANTS

The plants that grow in deserts are fairly well restricted to particular desert areas. For example, American desert plants are almost wholly different from African desert plants. Possibly one reason for this is that unbroken stretches of desert scrub and waste are usually never so widespread as the other vegetation regions, such as the tropical rain forest, prairie, steppe, or tundra. The northern conif-

erous forests of America, Europe and Asia are similar, not only in aspect, but also as to the kinds of plants. The general aspects of all hot deserts are much alike, but the similarity ends there. For instance, native cacti occur only in American deserts, and not in Asia and Africa.

Typical examples of edible desert plants are described and illustrated on the following pages.

CUT OFF TOP, MASH PULP, SUCK WATER THROUGH GRASS STRAW.

INTERIOR OF BARREL CACTUS — WATERY PULP

Using the barrel cactus for drinking water

North Mexican desert

© Vegetationsbilder

Russian Turkestan

Southwest Africa

© Vegetationsbilder

Egyptian desert

Date palms on the Sahara

© Vegetationsbilder

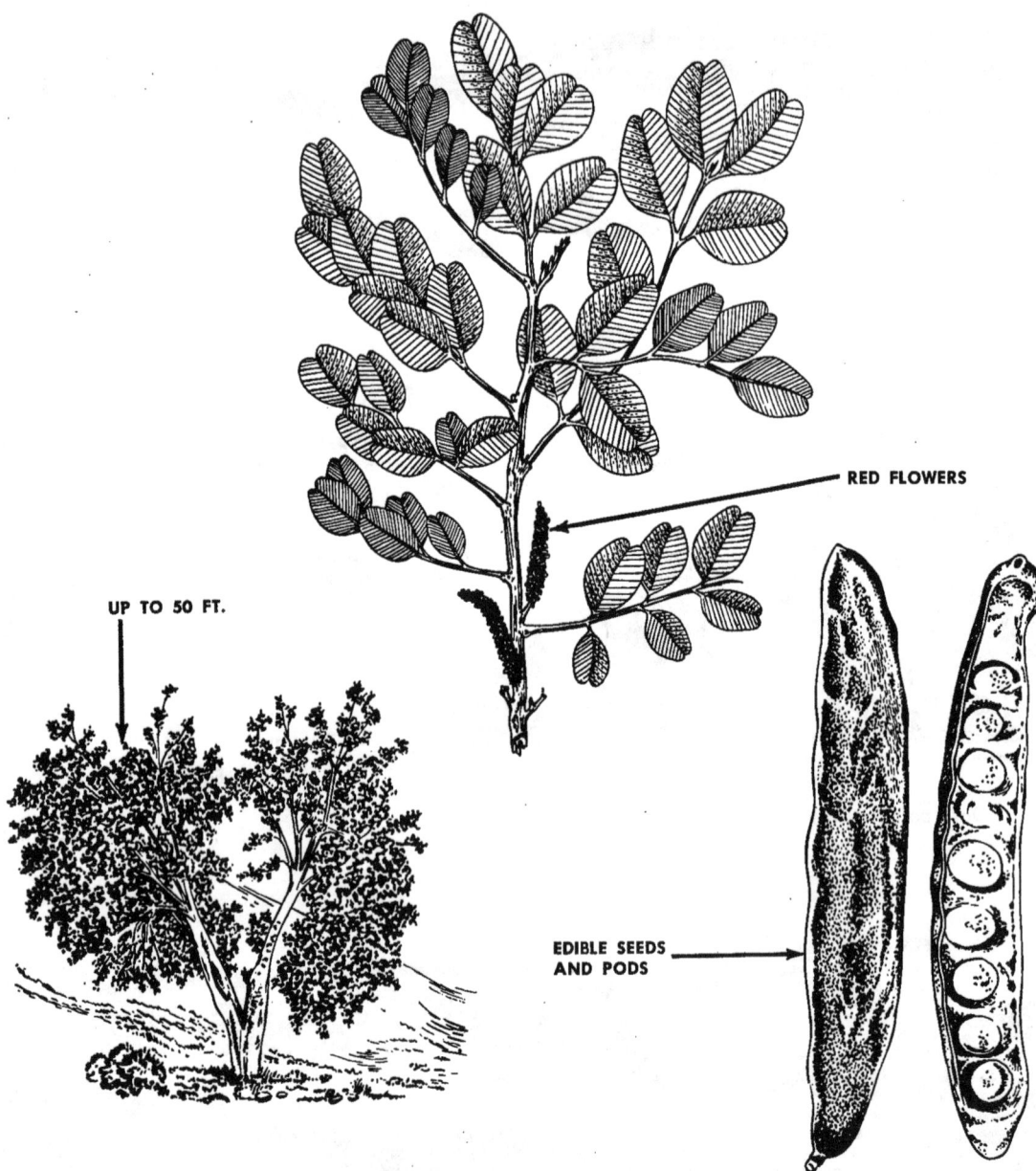

RED FLOWERS

UP TO 50 FT.

EDIBLE SEEDS
AND PODS

St. John's Bread (Ceratonia siliqua)

WHERE FOUND. (Regions 3, 10.) The St. John's bread occurs in arid wastelands bordering the Mediterranean Sea on the fringes of the Sahara, across Arabia, Iran, and into India.

APPEARANCE. This is an evergreen tree that reaches a height of 40-50 feet. The leaves are leathery and glistening, with 2-3 pairs of leaflets. The flowers are small and red.

WHAT TO EAT. The pods, full of sweet, nutritious pulp, are edible when young. The mature pods produce a number of seeds which may be pulverized and then cooked as porridge. The seeds of the St. Johns bread are among the most nutritious of the wild desert plants in the Middle East. They are ordinarily used for stock food, but there is no reason that humans couldn't eat them in times of scarcity.

PURPLE NUTS

SHRUB
OR TREE

EDIBLE NUT

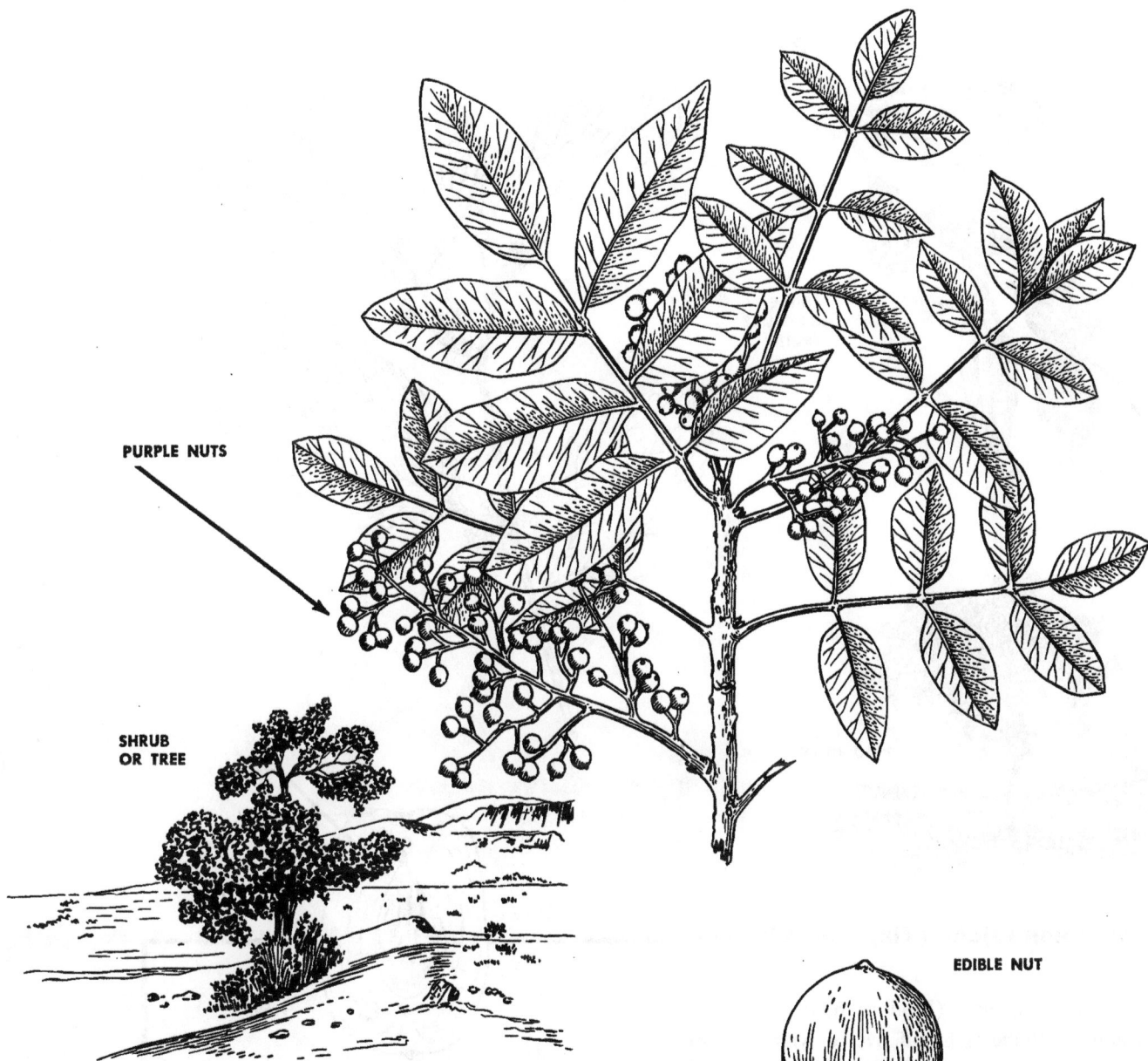

Wild Pistachio Nut (Pistacia)

WHERE FOUND. (Regions 3, 5, 10.) About seven kinds of wild pistachio nut occur in desert or semidesert areas surrounding the Mediterranean Sea to Asia Minor and Afghanistan.

APPEARANCE. Some kinds of pistachio trees are evergreen, while others (deciduous) lose their leaves during the dry season. The leaves alternate on the stem and have either 3 large leaves or a number of leaflets. The fruits or nuts are usually hard and dry at maturity.

WHAT TO EAT. The oily nut kernels are eaten, usually after being parched over coals.

EDIBLE
DATE-LIKE
FRUIT

UP TO 40 FT.

SEED

EDIBLE
FLESH

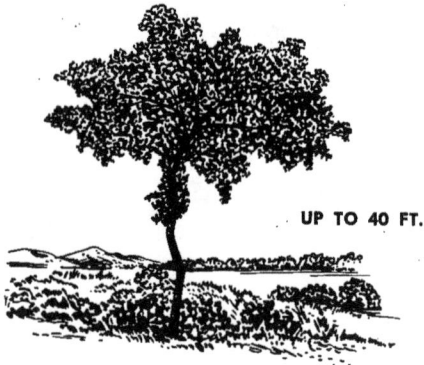

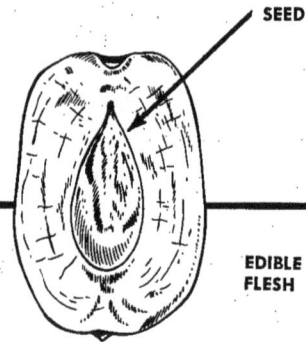

Common Jujube (Zizyphus jujuba)

WHERE FOUND. (Regions 6, 7, 10.) The common jujube is found over a wide area in the tropical and subtropical parts of the Old World. In Africa it is found mainly bordering the Mediterranean, and in Asia it is especially common in the drier parts of India and China. The jujube also occurs throughout the East Indies. It does occur bordering desert areas, thus its inclusion at this point.

APPEARANCE. The common jujube is either a deciduous tree growing to a height of 40 feet or only a large shrub, depending upon where it grows and how much water is available for growth. The branches are usually spiny. The fruit is oblong to ovoid, 1-1/4 inches or less in diameter and acid in flavor.

WHAT TO EAT. The edible fruits are reddish-brown, smooth and sweet, but with rather dry pulp around a comparatively large stone. The pulp, crushed in water, gives a refreshing beverage. If time permits, the ripe fruit may be sun-dried like dates.

RED, YELLOW OR
ORANGE FLOWERS

SEED POD

EDIBLE BULB

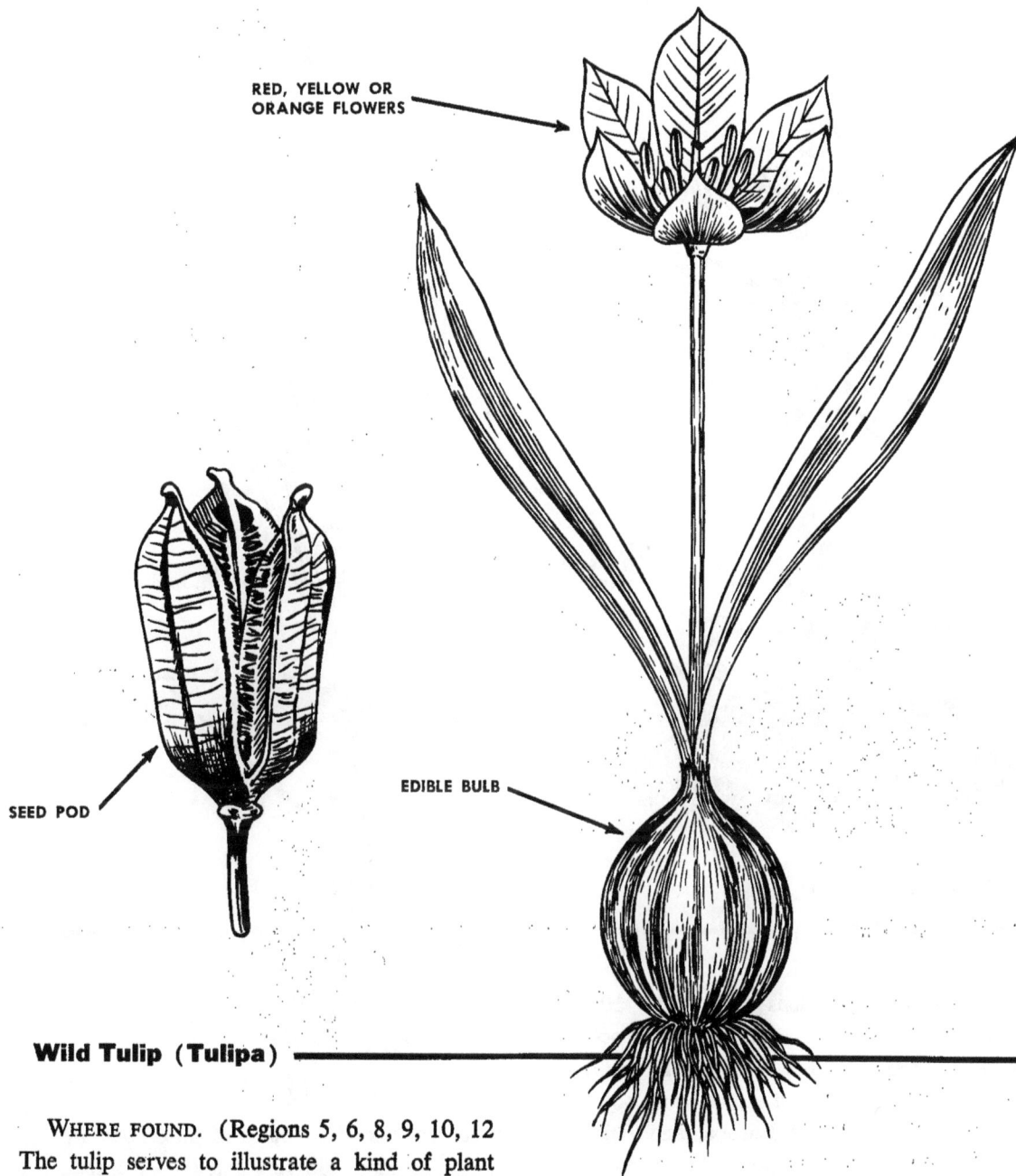

Wild Tulip (Tulipa)

WHERE FOUND. (Regions 5, 6, 8, 9, 10, 12
The tulip serves to illustrate a kind of plant
with relatively large edible bulbs. Wild tulips
are common from the Mediterranean region,
through Asia Minor to central Asia. Tulips
flower for a short time only in the spring, although the plant may be identified by the seed
pod which can be found most of the year.

APPEARANCE. The wild tulip resembles the
cultivated forms seen in gardens, except the
wild ones are smaller. The flowers on the wild
sorts are red, yellow, and orange.

WHAT TO EAT. The relatively large fleshy
bulbs are full of starch and would serve as a
good substitute for potatoes. They should be
cooked.

BROAD-LEAVED
VARIETY

GRASS-LIKE
VARIETY

EDIBLE BULB

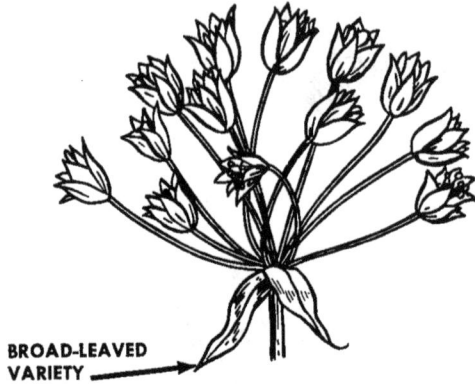

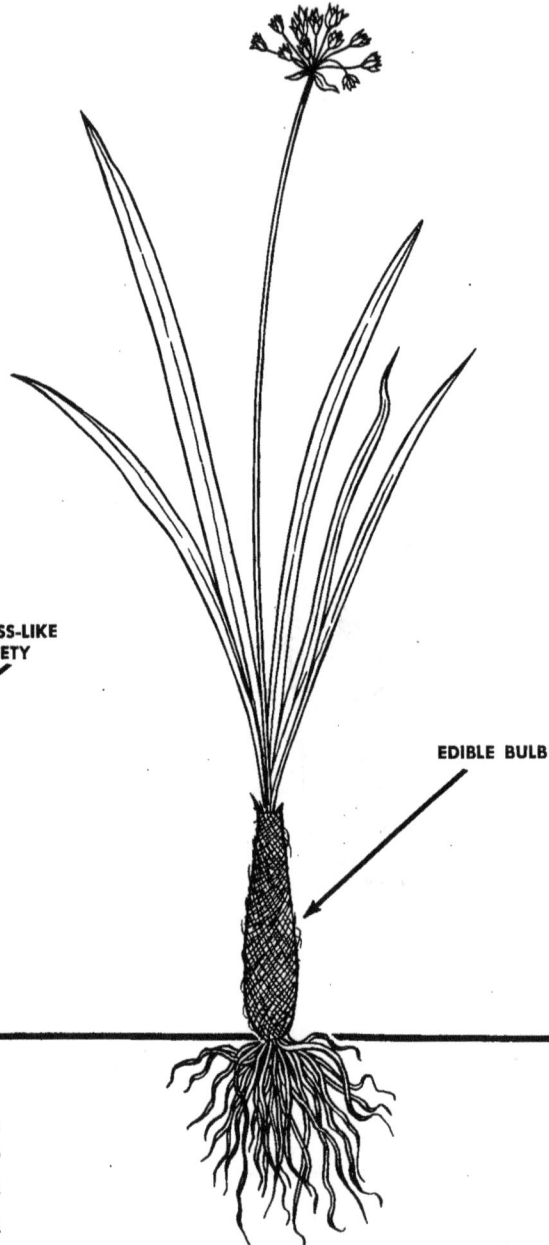

Wild Onion (Allium)

WHERE FOUND. (Regions 5, 6, 8, 9, 10, 12.) Wild relatives of the common onion occur widely throughout the North Temperate Zone. Many occur in North America in both moist and arid regions. In Europe, and Asia wild onions are very common over a wide range of habitats: moist areas, deserts, and mountain tops. Wild onions are especially common in Central Asia.

APPEARANCE. The onion plant grows from a bulb, which may be buried 3-10 inches below the ground. On most kinds of onions, the leaves are usually somewhat grasslike, although there is a whole group of wild onions with leaves that are several inches wide. Onion flowers are white, blue, and shades of red.

WHAT TO EAT. The bulbs of all onions are edible. Some kinds are very small — 1/2 inch in diameter — whereas some of the larger kinds may be 5 inches in diameter. The foliage and bulbs of all onions emit a characteristic oniony odor and taste. This is a good test to distinguish them from other kinds of bulbous plants.

Wild onions are never poisonous.

YELLOW FLOWERS

1-8 FT.

EDIBLE PULP

3-4 IN.

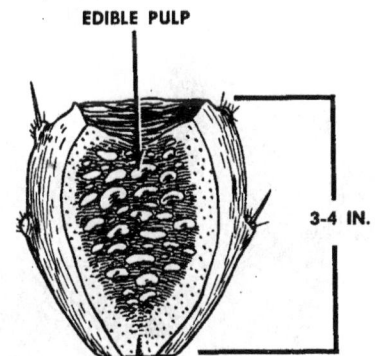

Prickly Pear (Opuntia)

EDIBLE FRUIT

WHERE FOUND. (Regions 3, 10.) The prickly pear and all other kinds of cacti are native only to America, but they have been taken to many desert areas in the Old World and also in Australia. The prickly pear is native to the American Southwest, Mexico, and South America. In the Old World it is now found along the shores of the Mediterranean into Asia Minor and India.

APPEARANCE. Do not mistake the prickly pear for other kinds of thick, fleshy cactuslike plants, especially those in Africa. The spurges of Africa sometimes look like cacti but all spurges contain a milky juice which is poisonous. The prickly pear never exudes milky juice.

The prickly pear has a thickened stem — sometimes an inch in diameter which is full of water. The outside is covered with clusters of very sharp spines spaced at intervals. The prickly pear has bright yellow or reddish flowers.

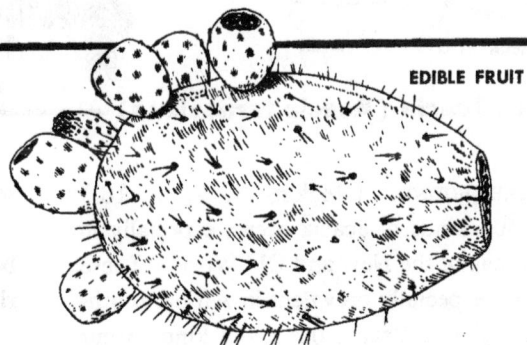

WHAT TO EAT. The egg-shaped fruit borne at the top of the cactus pad is edible. Merely slice off the top of the fruit, peel back the outer layer to get rid of the spines, and then eat the inner contents, seeds and all. They are mildly sweet and very juicy. The prickly pear pads also may be eaten by cutting away the spines and slicing the pad lengthwise into strips like string beans. They may be eaten raw or boiled.

The prickly pear is not poisonous.

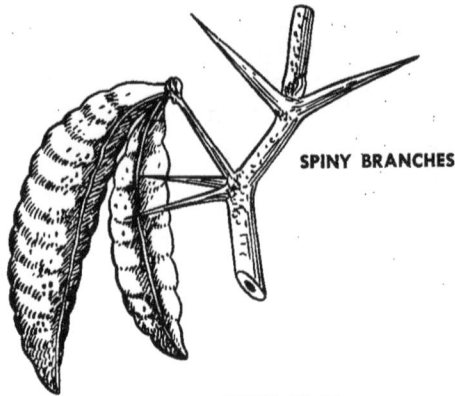

SPINY BRANCHES

SHRUB 10 FT. TALL

FLOWERS WHITE AND FRAGRANT

CHECK ROOTS FOR WATER

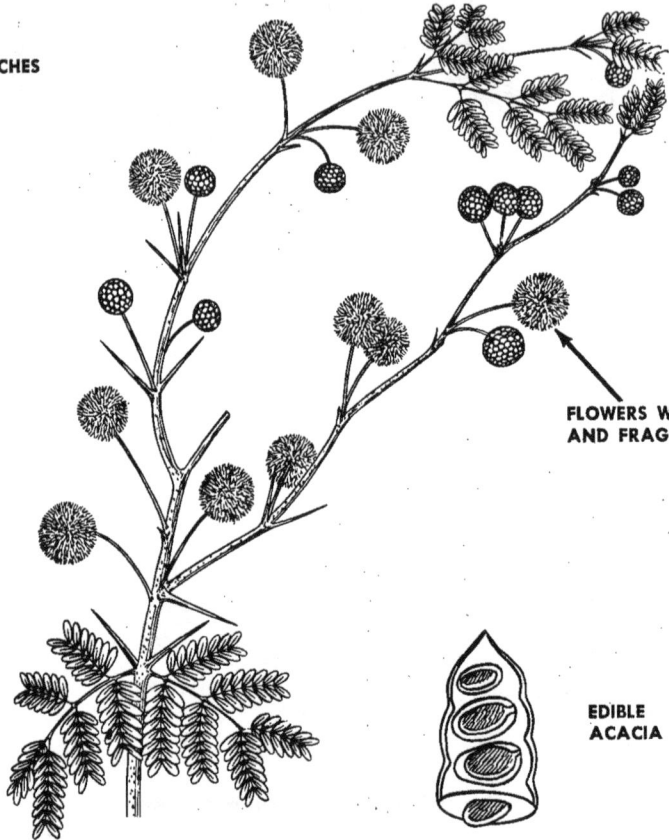

EDIBLE ACACIA BEAN

Sweet Acacia (Acacia farnesiana)

WHERE FOUND. (Regions 3, 7, 9, 10.) About 500 kinds of acacia occur, especially in desert areas of the New and Old Worlds. These plants are especially prevalent in Africa, southern Asia and Australia, but many kinds occur in the warmer and drier parts of America. The sweet acacia illustrated here is found over a wide area in the drier parts of the Old World and may be considered a typical example of this kind of plant.

APPEARANCE. The sweet acacia is a spiny, much branched shrub up to 10 feet tall. Other kinds, however, often reach the proportions of trees. The flowers usually are white, greenish or yellow in dense ball-shaped clusters. The acacias belong to the bean family.

WHAT TO EAT. Most acacias are desert plants and for this reason will be dormant over much of the year, except during rainy seasons. However, acacia beans can be found still hanging on the trees at all seasons. These beans, when pulverized and cooked as porridge, are a highly sustaining food.

Some acacias produce a kind of gum on the bark of the tree, such as gum arabic which comes from *Acacia arabica*. This gum is highly nutritious and may be eaten like candy.

The roots of the acacia will also yield water. Locate the root 4 or 5 feet from the tree trunk, pry it out of the ground, cut it into 2- or 3-foot lengths, and peel off the bark. Drain each section into a container or suck out the water. Trees growing in hollows between ridges will have the most water, and roots 1 to 2 inches thick are ideal in size. Water can be carried in these roots for some distance by plugging one end with soil.

EDIBLE FLOWERS

CROSS-SECTION THROUGH FLOWERS

EDIBLE WATERFILLED SHOOTS

EDIBLE GROUND SEED

CROSS-SECTION OF GOURD

GOURD VINE 15 FT. LONG

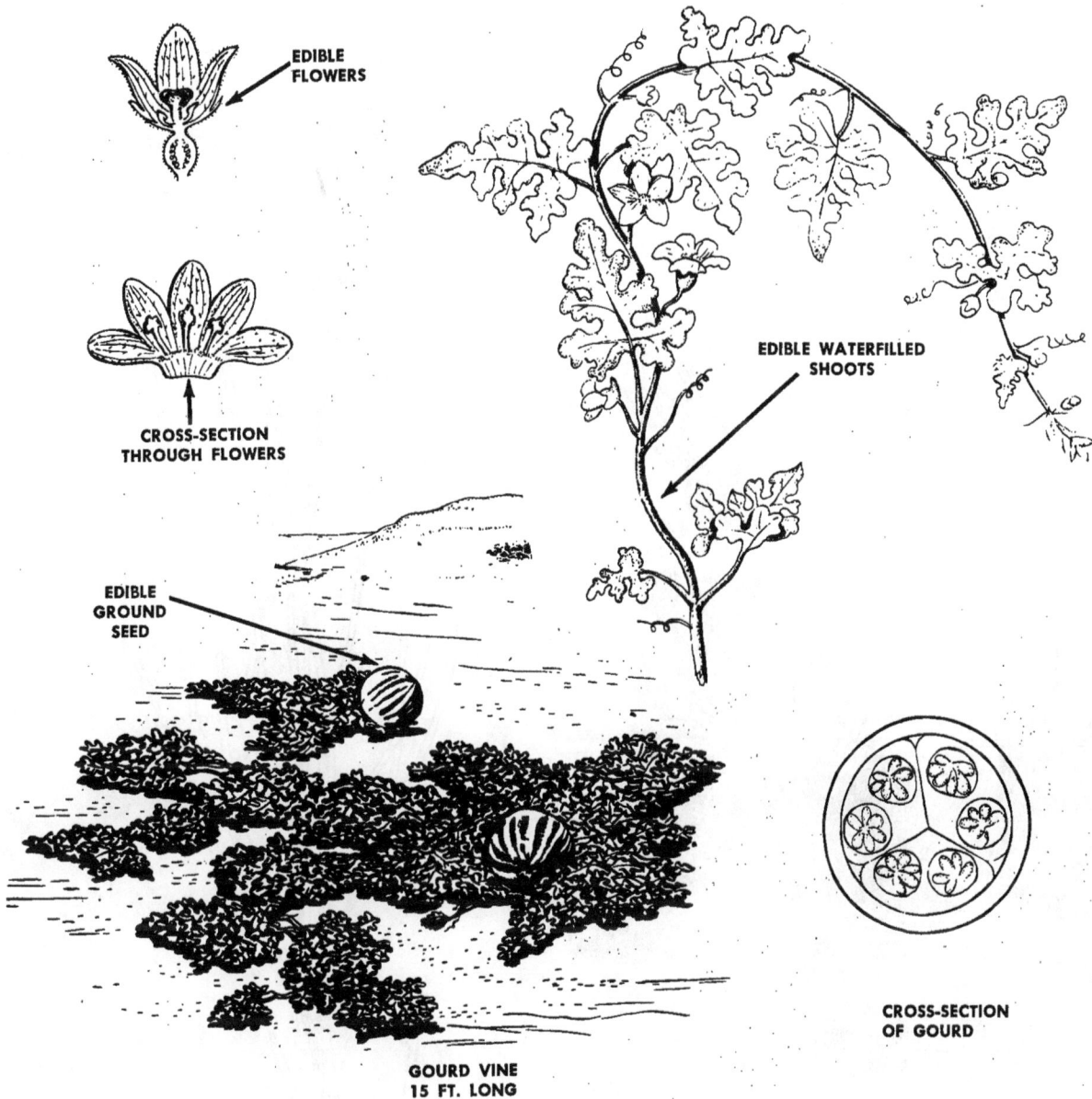

Wild Desert Gourd — Colocynth (Citrullus colocynthis)

WHERE FOUND. (Region 10.) This creeping plant grows abundantly in the Sahara, in Arabia, on the southeastern coast of India, and in some of the islands of the Aegean Sea.

APPEARANCE. The wild desert gourd is a member of the watermelon family. It produces a ground-trailing vine 8-10 feet long. The perfectly round gourds are as large as an orange and yellow when ripe. The wild desert gourd will grow in the hottest localities.

WHAT TO EAT. The seed inside the ripe gourd are edible after they have been com-

pletely separated from the very bitter pulp. The seeds are roasted or boiled first. The kernels are rich in oil.

CAUTION

The pulp inside the gourd is a violent purgative. Some seeds are reported to be poisonous. Use the edibility test.

The flowers are edible. Also, the succulent stem-tips are full of water and may be chewed.

SEED POD

SMALL YELLOW
FLOWERS

YOUNG
PLANT

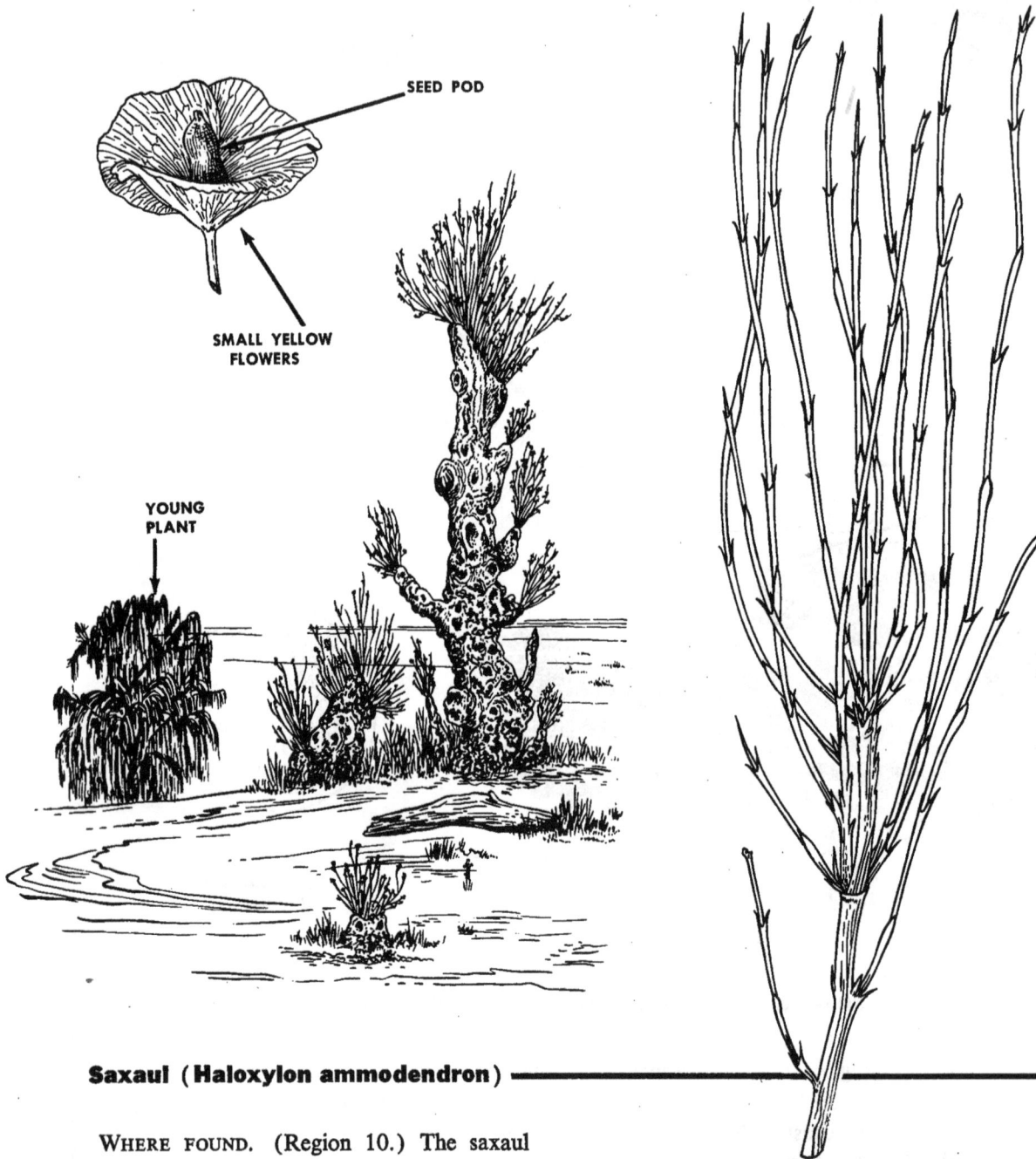

Saxaul (Haloxylon ammodendron)

WHERE FOUND. (Region 10.) The saxaul occurs on the arid salt deserts of Central Asia, particularly in the region of Turkestan and east of the Caspian Sea.

APPEARANCE. The saxaul is found either as a small tree or as a large shrub with heavy, coarse wood and spongy, water-soaked bark. The branches of the young trees are vivid green and pendulous. The flowers are small and yellow.

WHAT TO EAT. The thick bark acts as a water storage organ. By pressing quantities of the bark, drinking water may be obtained. This plant is an important source of water in the arid regions in which it grows.

USE LEAVES FOR GREENS

**CLOSE-UP
OF LEAF**

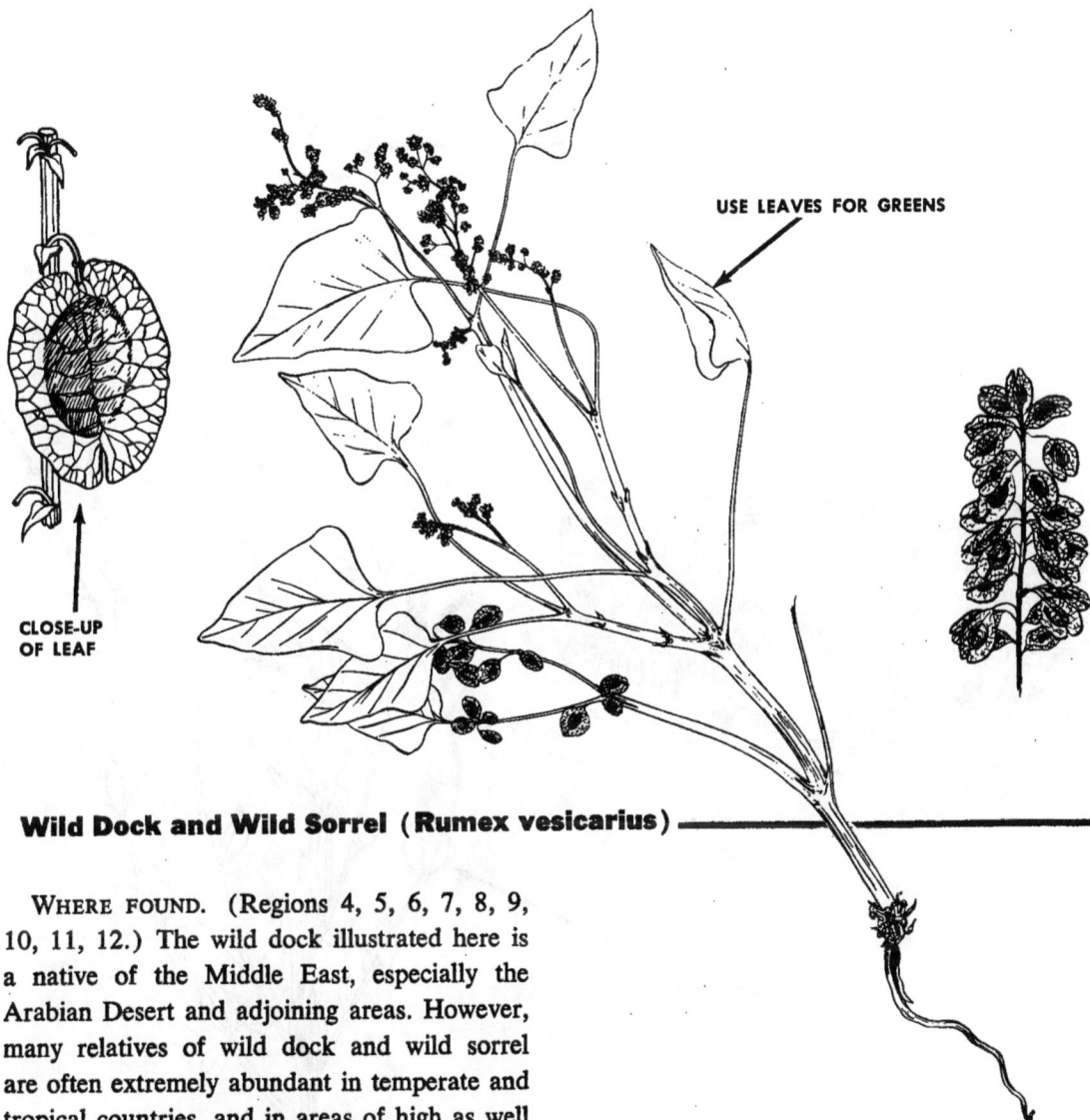

Wild Dock and Wild Sorrel (Rumex vesicarius)

WHERE FOUND. (Regions 4, 5, 6, 7, 8, 9, 10, 11, 12.) The wild dock illustrated here is a native of the Middle East, especially the Arabian Desert and adjoining areas. However, many relatives of wild dock and wild sorrel are often extremely abundant in temperate and tropical countries, and in areas of high as well as low rainfall. Many kinds are found as weeds in fields, along roadsides, and in waste places, and for this reason they make a most useful addition to the list of survival plants.

APPEARANCE. *Wild dock* is a stout plant with most of its leaves at the base of its stem, which is commonly 6-12 inches long. The plants usually develop from a strong, fleshy, carrotlike taproot. The flowers are usually very small, growing in green to purplish plumelike clusters.

Wild sorrel is similar to the docks but smaller. Many of the basal leaves are arrow-shaped but smaller than those of the docks and containing a sour juice.

WHAT TO EAT. The plant shown here is a desert type of sorrel which occurs from the Mediterranean eastward into Arabia. Because of the tender nature of the foliage, both the sorrels and docks are useful plants, especially in the desert areas. Their succulent leaves, which may be eaten fresh or else slightly cooked. In order to take away the strong taste, the water should be changed once or twice during cooking. This latter tip is a useful hint in the preparation of many kinds of wild greens.

FLOWERS

SALT MARSH HABITAT

EDIBLE GRAY LEAVES

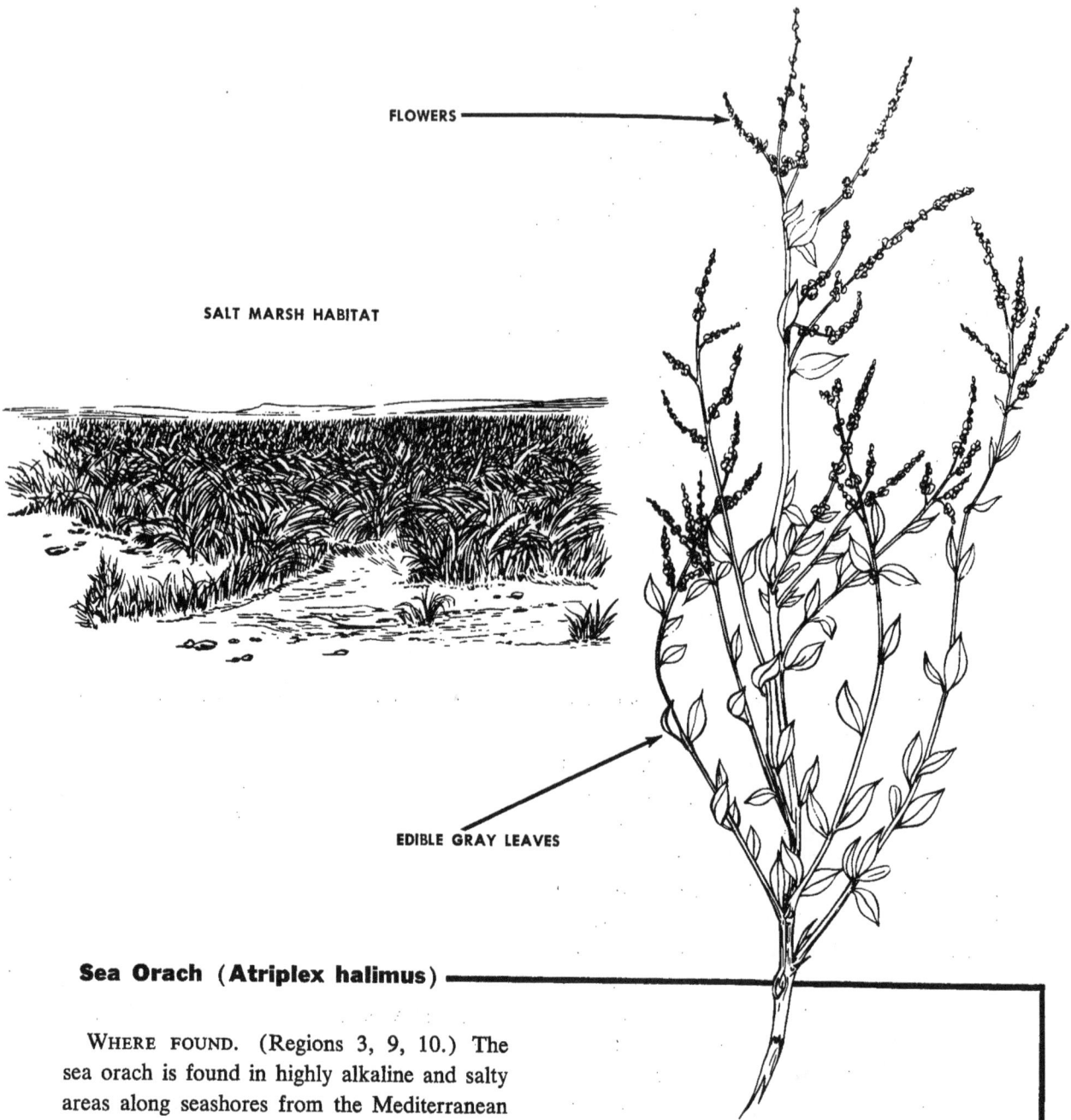

Sea Orach (Atriplex halimus)

WHERE FOUND. (Regions 3, 9, 10.) The sea orach is found in highly alkaline and salty areas along seashores from the Mediterranean countries to inland areas in North Africa and eastward to Asia Minor and central Siberia.

APPEARANCE. The sea orach is an herbaceous plant, sparingly branched and with small, gray-colored leaves up to an inch long. Sea orach resembles lambs quarters, which is a common weed in most gardens in the United States. The flowers of the sea orach are produced in narrow, densely compacted spikes at the tips of the branches.

WHAT TO EAT. The sea orach has the healthy reputation in the areas where it grows of being one of the few native plants that affords sustenance to man in times of want. For this reason, the survivor should become acquainted with the sea orach.

FLOWERING BRANCH

**TREE OR SHRUB —
TO 20 FT.**

YOUNG FRUIT

EDIBLE FRUIT

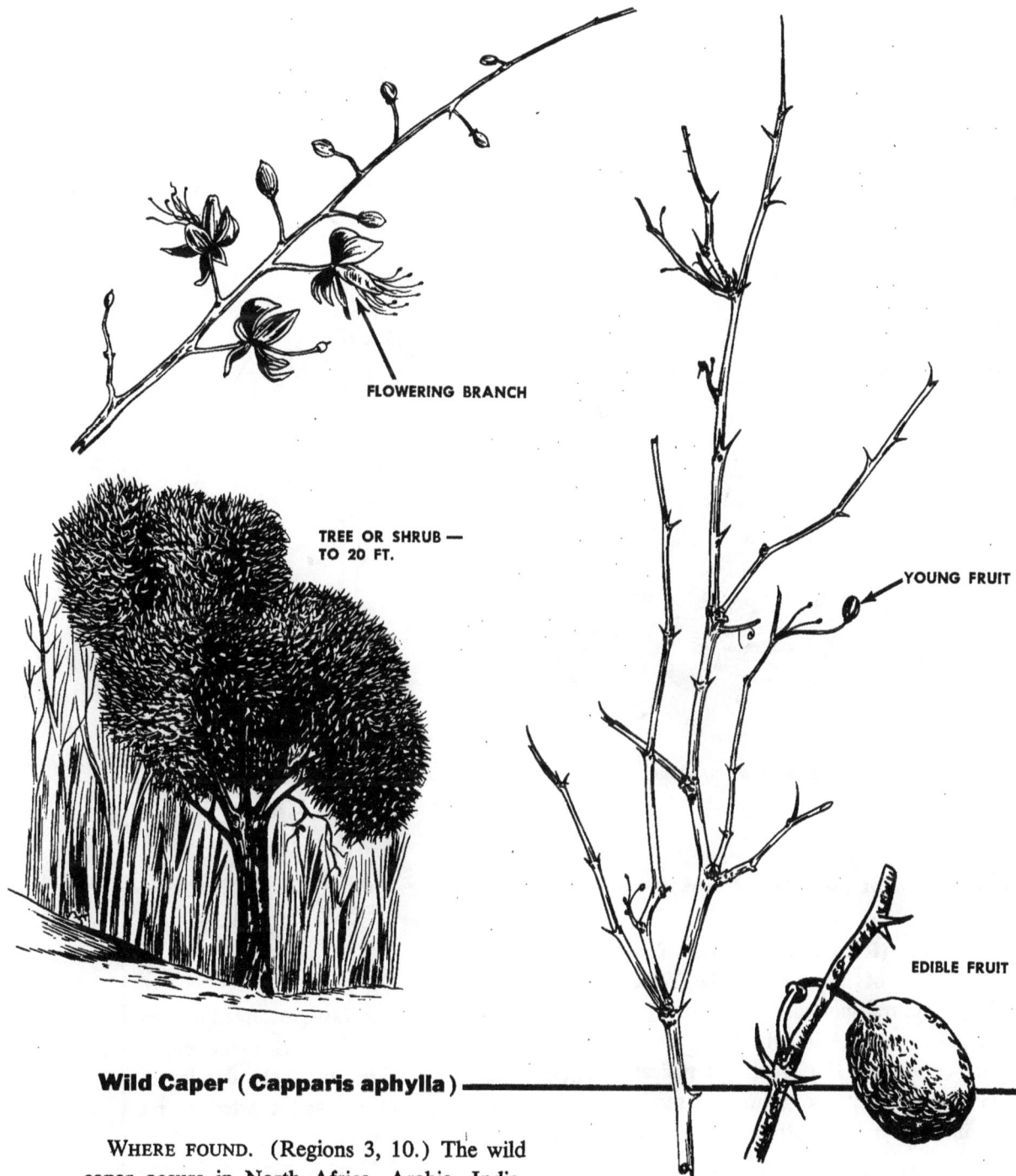

Wild Caper (Capparis aphylla)

WHERE FOUND. (Regions 3, 10.) The wild caper occurs in North Africa, Arabia, India, and Indonesia.

APPEARANCE. The wild caper is found either as a spiny shrub or a small tree not more than 20 feet tall. The plant is leafless with spine-covered branches. The flowers and fruit are found near the tips of these spiny branches.

WHAT TO EAT. Both the unripe and ripe fruit of the caper, while somewhat bitter, are a welcome food source in the desert areas of the Middle East. The young flower buds may also be eaten right off the bush.

EDIBLE SHOOT

YELLOW FLOWERS

CUT ENDS FOR
WATER

3-15 FT. IN DIAMETER

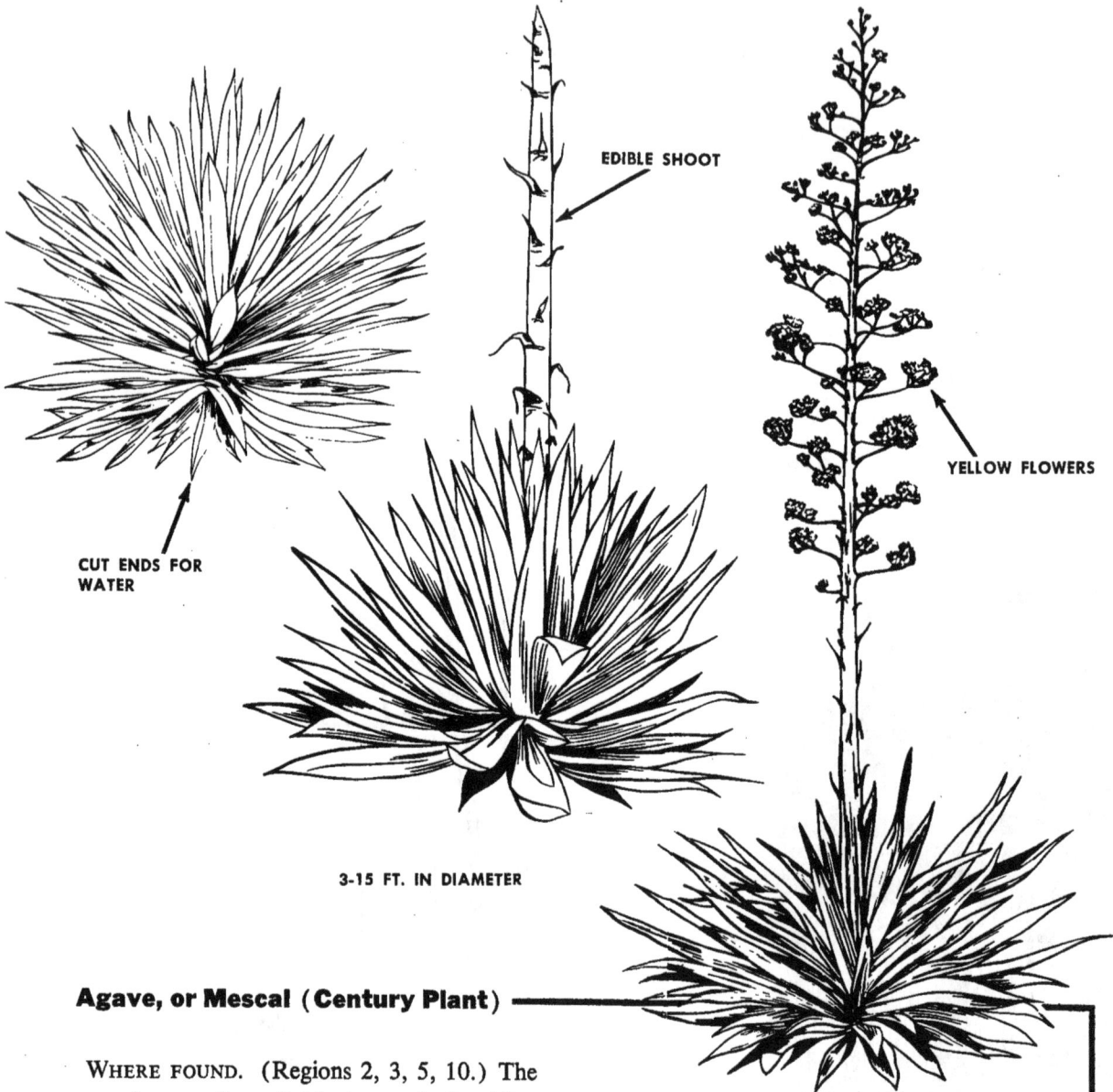

Agave, or Mescal (Century Plant)

WHERE FOUND. (Regions 2, 3, 5, 10.) The agave is a native of Mexico and the West Indies, but it was transported a long time ago to Europe, Africa, and Asia, where it is used largely for hemp fiber. The agave is a typical desert plant, although it also grows in a semi-wild state in moist parts of tropical areas in Asia.

APPEARANCE. The agave, when fully grown, is an imposing plant because of its size. The thick, tough leaves with stout, sharp tips are borne in an enormous rosette. The flowering stalk in the center of the plant rises very rapidly like a candle to produce the enormous flowering head. After flowering the plant dies.

WHAT TO EAT. The fast-growing flowering shoot of the agave is the part to be eaten. Before the flowers are noticeably developed, these shoots are cut off and roasted in pit ovens (see description on p. 93). The roasted shoots consist of fibrous, molasses-colored layers, sweet and delicious to the taste and nutritious. It has been found that pieces dried in the sun will keep for years. The cut ends of agave leaves can supply drinking water.

SEED PODS

FLOWER

POD

ABAL ON ARABIAN DESERT

EDIBLE FLOWERS

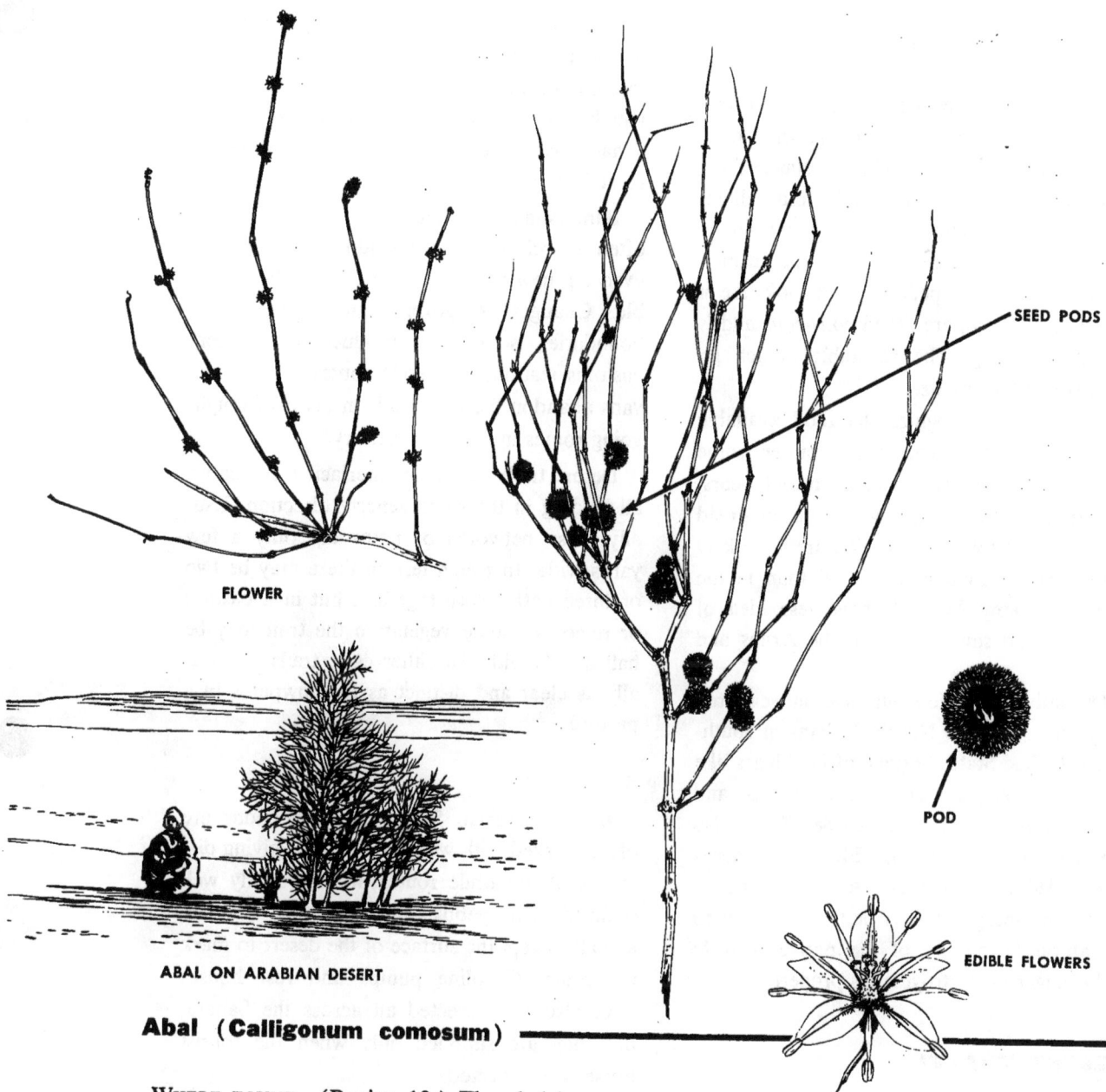

Abal (Calligonum comosum)

WHERE FOUND. (Region 10.) The abal inhabits much of the North African desert. It may also be found on the desert sands of Arabia and as far eastward as the Rajputana desert of Western India.

APPEARANCE. The abal is one of the few shrubby plants that exists in the sandy deserts. This plant grows to about 4 feet high, and its branches look like wisps from a broom. The stiff, green branches produce an abundance of ball-like flowers in the early spring months (March, April).

WHAT TO EAT. The general appearance of the abal plant would not indicate its usefulness to the survivor, but during the time this plant is in flower in the spring, the fresh flowers can be eaten. This plant is common in the areas it is found. An analysis of the food value of this plant has shown it to be high in sugar and nitrogenous components.

FOOD FROM NATIVES

Once natives have been contacted in any desert, food and water are available. In normal times desert people are hospitable. Native food in the Sahara is both palatable and edible. The meat offered may be goat or mutton or chicken; in rare cases it may be camel. Steamed wheat flour pellets which look like a great platter of rice, are called *cous-cous* and is really good eating. The vegetables which go with it you will recognize.

You will also recognize the food available in the Gobi. Natives eat cheese, butter, some rice, and drink buttered tea. In recent years, under Russian tutelage, they have been urged to eat bread and vegetables. You are less likely to enjoy native food in the Gobi than in the Sahara, as many Mongols have less idea of cleanliness and sanitation than the Arabs and the Berbers.

The natives of Mongolia live in scattered family units, like the Navajo Indians in southwestern United States, instead of in villages like agricultural people. They raise sheep and goats, horses, camels, and cattle. They also keep large, unfriendly dogs. Flocks and herds are guarded and are taken to water twice a day. In an emergency it is better to appeal to the natural hospitality of the native than to risk his anger by destroying his property.

DESERT TRAVEL

The great deserts of the Old World have been crossed and recrossed for hundreds and thousands of years. These crossings follow definite routes along marked trails from oases to wells and wells to waterholes or other oases. In the course of centuries some routes have been abandoned when easier routes were discovered.

In some areas governments have provided for keeping wells open or digging new wells, but most desert travelers are public-spirited enough to fix a well that needs repairs. Their generosity doesn't extend to leaving a rope for the next traveler. Unless you are agile enough to go down and up a chimney like Santa Claus, you had better carry a 100-foot rope in the Sahara. A 30-foot rope will reach water in most Gobi wells.

Bandits and smugglers, especially in Asia, often search out old abandoned routes and even dig new wells to make difficult trails usable. Changes in governments and political boundaries sometimes produce confiscatory customs stations on desert routes. Then caravans abandon the easy trails in favor of tough-going routes in friendly territory.

Desert trails resemble interlacing cowpaths, all leading in the same general direction. Usually these networks of paths are only a few yards wide. In rough terrain there may be two or three paths close together, but in a pasture or region of some vegetation the trail may be half a mile wide. In either case, trails are usually as clear and distinct as the cowpaths in a pasture.

Sahara

In the Algerian Sahara, trail junctions are often marked with wooden signposts giving distances. Automobile routes are frequently well outlined with pebbles, for the trail markers actually swept the surface of the desert to mark the route. Gasoline pumps and rest houses have also been erected all across the Sahara, but they are supplied only when the tourist busses are expected.

Automobile routes in the Sahara do not always follow the camel routes. Frequently the auto trails traverse more barren country where waterholes are great distances apart, while camel routes generally strike water every 20 to 40 miles. In the extremely dry Tanezroufts and in Tripoli there are waterless stretches of over 100 miles, but these are rare.

In dune areas wind soon obliterates camel tracks, but the trail can be followed by watching the accumulation of camel droppings in hollows just below the dune crests. On the open plain, automobile tracks remain visible for years after a car has passed.

Gobi

Caravan trails in Mongolia are well marked with 6- to 10-feet high piles of stone placed like lighthouses on prominent buttes and mesa edges. They are called obos and serve the double purpose of sign posts to travelers and religious monuments. Some have small openings in the stone structure where once a year the Mongol lamas place food for the spirits who inhabit the area. This is done at the time of a religious feast when the obo is decorated with silk prayer cloths. Desert winds soon whip the silk to shreds, but some bits of cloth will cling to the strings on the monument until the next ceremony and will waft lama prayers aloft to desert gods.

Transportation

Transportation in both the Gobi and the Sahara has been by camel caravan for centuries. Where distances between wells or watering places are not more than 1 day's march in the Sahara, the horse and little donkey are considered more speedy than the camel. Those animals must be watered twice a day, however, which forces them to give way on long dry marches to the slower, more cantankerous camel, which can travel 8 to 10 days without a drink.

Cumbersome two-wheeled ox carts covered with matting to protect the freight from rain and snow lurch over many Gobi trails from June to snowfall (late August or September). Plodding oxen and heavy wheels cut deep into Gobi grasslands when rain soaks the trail. Then the route may be 1/2 or 3/4 mile wide, and motor cars swing wide from the trail to avoid the ruts.

Natives of the deserts have little idea of distances. Once in the Sahara an American asked a sheik how far it was to the next oasis.

"Seventy-five kilometers," said the Arab.

"But we have an automobile," said the American, thinking perhaps that the camel route would be too rough and the car would have to detour.

"Oh, with an automobile it is only 25 kilometers," replied the sheik. Time and distance are thoroughly mixed in the native concept. To the sheik kilometers are not a standard of measurable distance. They are just a way of expressing how long it takes to travel from here to there. Don't take a native's statement of distance too seriously, but if he tells you how many days it will take you to walk to the next well, he will state the time with accuracy.

Caravans travel at night in summer if visibility is adequate. They also travel in the early morning or late afternoon. In hot weather they almost never travel after 10 a.m., and before 5 or 6 p.m. There is more daytime travel in winter. Traveling at night, a large caravan may pass close by without your seeing it. If your ears are keen, however, you will hear the creak of boxes on camel saddles or the swish and whispered rustle of rubbing bales and bags.

Walking is not at all difficult in deserts. Caravan men walk as much as they ride and frequently wear only light sandals. Trails avoid the difficult terrain like loose sand or broken rocky areas.

Travel Route

If you cannot follow a trail in the Sahara or Arabian Desert your best bet is to head for the coast, providing you know where it is and the distance is within range of your strength and water supply. Once you reach the coast you can conserve your sweat by soaking your clothes in the sea.

Valleys, ancient stream beds or dry water courses lead to inland basins in desert areas. In Libyan Sahara such valleys start within a few hundred yards of the sea and run inland. Great, through-going rivers like the Nile, Tigris and Euphrates, the Rio Grande and Colorado, which carry water all year, do reach the sea. Even some short valleys join the ocean, but you had better have a map to guide you in following stream beds or valleys in the desert.

Maps of desert regions are often inaccurate.

Try to check the accuracy of maps you carry in the desert before you have to use them.

NATIVES

People who inhabit the great deserts are conservative and pretty well adjusted. In general, they have come to terms with nature's elements. They have learned to endure extreme heat in summer and cold in winter. They expect long periods of dryness, and know how to conserve water. They get along with little food, but know how to enjoy a banquet on occasions. They know the limits of the land which can be grazed or used by their family and their tribe. They know who are their friends and who are their enemies. They understand what to expect from both and how to act toward each of them. They know the rules. They believe in those rules and they act in accordance with that belief.

When an American like you steps into the land of desert people, that adjustment is thrown off balance. The picture is out of focus. The desert native does not know where you fit into his scheme of things. You make confusion in his world. He or she has no idea what to do about you.

What he or she does will depend on several things, but above all else it will probably depend on *you*. If his group has any contact with trouser-legged individuals like you, he'll treat you according to the pattern his people have decided upon. Chances are that the native will give you the same treatment as he received from the outsiders who were there before you. If the previous contacts were friendly, you will probably be treated well. In any case, put your best foot forward.

Arabs are exchangers of gifts. Gifts represent friendship. If you learn what simple presents you can give in your particular section of Sahara or Arabia you can get more cooperation than money can buy.

For example, one traveler gave a Swiss jackknife to a Tuareg noble in the Sahara. It cost 50 cents in the States. Later he received courtesies out of proportion to the demands of hospitality. Finally the noble explained. "When you first came here you gave me a knife that closes. All my life I have wanted a knife that closes. You are my friend. Anything I have is yours."

The Bedouins you are likely to meet on the Sahara and Arabian deserts have a really hard life. They have little food and few clothes in a rugged climate. Cash is hard to come by, and it is usuable in many ways.

He will do a great many things for money, but money will not tempt him to sacrifice his concept of honor. He sticks rigidly to his code.

    a.   Duty toward God.

    b.   Protection of his tent neighbor.

    c.   Attention to the laws of hospitality.

    d.   Duty to a traveler under his "safe conduct."

    e.   Attention to the laws of personal protection and sanctuary.

    f.   Duty to himself; to raid when he can and to keep what he has captured.

According to this code, raiding is no sin but a virtue; payment, you might say, for the 5 good deeds above. Killing an enemy is a greater virtue. To steal an enemy's cattle isn't robbery; it is something to be proud of. The enemy will do the same if given a chance.

Some Americans and other foreigners have gone among the desert people as friends. They have lived among them as equals. Those who have treated the desert people as decently and honestly as they would treat their friends at home all agree that desert people are hospitable, dignified, and friendly.

Experienced desert travelers have found that an honest effort to understand the desert people pays off. A sincere respect for their customs, no matter how different from yours they may be, will result in satisfactory relationships all around. This applied even in the exceptional regions where groups or individuals may be hostile or trigger happy.

Remember when you enter the land of desert people, you are the foreigner in their homeland. It is up to you to act in accordance with their customs. When you are the foreigner, act with the decency you'd expect of a foreigner in the United States.

Desert Law

Among desert people if you give your word you must keep it. In Saudi Arabia the courts see that you keep your oral agreements. For example, if you say you will pay a certain price for a rug and later see another which you like better, you can't back out of your first oral deal, even though you have not paid anything down or taken delivery.

The people of Saudi Arabia can't understand our custom of signing a written agreement and having witnesses sign. They give their word and keep their promises.

Desert people are not fist fighters. They don't lay violent hands on each other in anger or in horseplay, as youthful Americans sometimes do. To inflict physical injury on an Arab, for example, is a very serious offense. You may find yourself legally obliged to support the injured and his family.

Saudi Arabian law prohibits a person from striking another by hand or by tongue or from treating him with scorn or contempt.

There are many very interesting angles to the customs of desert people, and in well-organized Saudi Arabia many of those old custom are written into law.

Here are a few of the most important don'ts. In general they apply to the deserts everywhere.

a. Don't bawl out an offender in front of other people.

b. Don't draw sand pictures or maps with your foot. Stoop down and draw with right hand.

c. Don't swear at a native.

d. Don't expose the soles of your feet to others. Sit tailor fashion or on your heels.

e. Don't ask about a man's wife.

f. Don't throw a coin at a man's feet, that is insulting.

g. Gambling is forbidden.

h. Don't be impatient when dealing with desert people.

i. Don't forget to act friendly.

Greeting Customs

Greeting customs differ in different desert regions and even vary sometimes between tribes of the same region. For instance, some natives in the Gobi stick out their tongue as a friendly gesture of greeting. This greeting is more characteristic of Tibet than Mongolia. Others in Mongolia extend the right hand as a fist but with the thumb up. In the Algerian Sahara a lone traveler may advance to meet you with his right hand raised like the traditional American Indian pose when saying "How." Others extend the right hand to touch yours, almost like a simple handshake. There is no firm grip and shake but just a touch of the right palms. Then each man puts the back of his hand to his lips.

These are just a few of the greeting customs of desert people. This manual is not large enough to give the customs of all groups. Its purpose is to give you general ideas of what customs to look for. With this background you should catch on quickly to the local social customs in any desert area. Learn the customs for your region. When a man shakes his fist at you, he may be saying, "Hello, friend."

Approaching an Encampment

In some parts of the Gobi you should only approach a yurt or a tent from the east. That will be the front, where the only door is located. If you happen to come from some other direction, you should circle the yurt at a reasonable distance. Give the Mongols a chance to see you before you get close to their dwelling.

In Mongolia dogs will probably warn of your approach. Then you'll need a club or some stones to keep them at bay while you shout to the inhabitants, "Call off the dogs!" Learn the proper words in the native language of the

desert you are traveling. Women, girls, or anyone else around will come out and quiet the animals.

You enter the yurt through the left side of the door. You leave your whip or club outside. There are rules regarding what part of the yurt is reserved for each member of the family and for guests. Your good nature and friendliness, however, will get you by until you know the rules.

In Arabia the guest must also approach the tent from the front. Front will be to the lee of the wind. If the wind changes, the back will be raised and become the front. Stop some distance away to give the people time to ready themselves. During summer heat, all sides of the tent will be raised, so you had better observe the people from a distance to be sure which is front.

On the edge of the Sahara in Algeria it is customary to call out on approaching a tent. This is particularly true if there are no men around. In that region, do not enter the tent unless invited.

Hospitality

Don't surprise people in the desert if you expect their help or hospitality. Their reaction to surprise may be a disappearing act. It may also be a hostile reception, especially if you are in bandit country.

In some sections of the Arabian Desert and in some parts of the Sahara a guest will be welcomed with a bowl of milk. In Arabia it will probably be buttermilk. In the Algerian Sahara, travelers have usually been offered sheep or goats milk and a tray of dates. In the Gobi it was a piece of stone-hard cheese. In parts of the Arabian Desert, when the man of the tent is away, his wife will welcome a passing group. If she has reason to believe that the approaching group is led by the sheik or other important personage, she hangs out her best dress as a banner on a pole by the tent.

Set phrases of welcome and greeting are repeated and answered in all regions. Learn those used in your region. Even if you pronounce the phrases badly, your effort will be appreciated. It may even cause some merriment among your hosts, and that always increases friendliness.

The followers of Islam in North Africa, Arabia and the deserts of Central Asia consider hospitality an important duty. The traveler in those regions accepts that hospitality naturally. However, gentlemanly instincts are highly developed even among the poorer desert men. They approach a tent "modestly and with becoming diffidence" and call out a friendly greeting like "salaam alaikum" (peace be upon you). A guest would never dream of offering payment for his accommodations, and such an offer would not be accepted. Neither would the guest think of imposing on the hospitality of a neighbor if he could make it to his own tent.

Three days is the limit for a stay in a host's tent. A longer stay is not only bad manners, but it permits the host to urge you to continue on your journey.

The rule of hospitality is so rigid that it could easily cause the ruin of a poor man if his tent were located on a main trail. Those who are poor often hide their camp in a hollow or behind a hill away from traveled routes. They dare not refuse hospitality, even to a stranger, although feeding him may force them to go without. Their best bet is to keep their camp hard to find. Your best bet is to look for a side trail leading off behind a hill. It may lead to hospitality.

Religion

Religion among desert people ranges from fanatical adherence to rigid forms through dignified sincerity to the most casual lip service.

In the Gobi (until recently) two-thirds of the male Mongol population were lamas or priests of Lamaism. Most westerners consider Lamaism a decadent form of Buddhism. Certainly it has absorbed a great many local spirits, and the common people were imposed upon by the lamas through serious superstitions which they kept alive. The largest collections of permanent buildings in Mongolia were the lamasaries. Since the region has been controlled by the Russians, the number of lamas has been greatly reduced. It is thought that they now include only 3 percent of the male population. Probably the average Mongol should be considered more superstitious than religious. The Russians have reduced the power of the lama, but it is doubtful if they have eliminated superstition.

Among the Arabs of Arabia and the Sahara many of the tribes are really sincere. They truly believe in one God. They do not need anyone to intercede for them, but each man prays direct to God. This he does with dignity, secure in the knowledge that before God he stands on an equal footing with every other man.

The true believer in the Moslem religion knows that there is no God but Allah, and Mohammed was his Prophet.

He says his prayers five times each day. He gives alms to the poor and needy. During the month of Ramadhan he does not eat, drink, or have sexual intercourse between sunrise and

sunset, but he can and does indulge during the night.

If his means permit, he will make the journey to Mecca at least once in his lifetime. This is becoming easier to do now that airlines in the Near East can fly the pilgrims to Jidda.

The believer in Islam prefers to be called a Moslem. Remember that, while he knows that Mohammed was the Prophet of Allah, the Moslem does not worship Mohammed. It is, therefore, not correct to call him a Mohammedan.

A Moslem can and does worship wherever he is. When prayer time comes, he will stop whatever he is doing, face Mecca, and go through the seven positions of prayer while he repeats set phrases or sections from the Koran. That applies out in the desert or in the lobby of an office building in the city.

In cities and in oases, there are mosques where Moslems go to pray and to meditate. In the courtyard or somewhere near the entrance will be a place for the believer to wash his hands and feet before entering the religious sanctuary. He always removes his shoes or sandals before entering the mosque. You will show the same courtesy and remove your shoes. In tourist cities extra sandals are sometimes provided for non-Moslems who are visiting the holy places. Put these on over your shoes. In the desert you may not be allowed inside the mosque at all, but don't defile the holy place with your shoes if you are allowed to enter. The offense is serious in some places and may start a riot against you.

Many desert people are superstitious about photographs. They rationalize their fear by saying that the Koran forbids pictures. There is no such ban on pictures in the Moslem religious book, but it will do you no good to try to argue the matter. In Damascus individuals have been urged by guides in a mosque to take all the pictures they want. In the same city, however, other natives objected violently to any photographs, even out on the street.

You will have to learn the temper of the desert people you encounter and follow their taboos. Respect their prejudices. Don't ridicule or make fun of desert people. All of them are proud people. They are following customs that have proved satisfactory to them for thousands of years.

Women

Among desert people, women have a varied status. Except among the very wealthy families, all desert women do their share of work about the camp. In Mongolia there is no double standard of morals. Among the Arabs most tribes do not allow their women to show their faces to any men except the closest members of the family. In contrast to this strict seclusion, the women of tribes just north of Yemen on the Arabian Peninsula expose more of their persons than would be tolerated in other parts of Arabia. They have greater freedom and freer intercourse with men than in the stricter districts of Arabia proper.

Most Arabs and the Berber peoples of Arabia or the Sahara tolerate no nonsense between their women and men to whom they are not married. Violation of the code brings swift, sure punishment, sometimes including the death of the woman.

In contrast the Tuaregs of Sahara pride themselves on the complete absence of jealousy. The women go unveiled before all men while the men never show their faces even in all male gatherings. Their Ahal gatherings include young married and unmarried men and women. They play the imzad (single-stringed violin) and sing during the early part of the evening. Then they go back to their tents, milk the camels, and eat supper. After supper the second session of the Ahal continues far into the night as a petting party. Although a

man will show no sign of annoyance when a fellow Tuareg steals his woman, there is no assurance that his tolerance will extend to you.

As far as desert women are concerned, there are three factors which should hold you in check; swift, sure trouble from most tribes for violations of the code; the certainty of VD where the women are given liberty; and your sense of sight and smell.

Cleanliness

Cleanliness among desert people varies as much as the observance of religion. If you compare a poor shepherd with an American businessman, the desert shepherd is definitely dirty. However, some wealthy Arabs wear spotlessly white garments and bathe as regularly as you do. The Moslem religion prescribes that one must wash before prayers. You will see men doing so in the entrances to mosques. The good Moslem prays five times a day, so in the desert, where water is scarce, he may go through the motions of washing with sand. Religion also prescribes that both men and women must have a complete bath after sexual intercourse, even though only a small bowl of water is available. Nevertheless, many of the desert people you meet will certainly seem very dirty. Unless you have lucky contacts, you are not likely to meet many of the wealthy class who can afford the luxuries of regular baths and clean clothes.

In the deserts of Mongolia, where people wipe their fingers on their garments, you can smell the rancid mutton fat almost as far as you can see the man. Even there, cleanliness varies with individuals.

Toilet habits also vary among desert people. Their voluminous flowing robes permit them to squat and relieve themselves wherever nature calls. In oases and towns of Sahara or Arabia there are pit latrines. In some desert camps each individual will dig a small hole and cover his feces.

Eating

If you are invited to eat with desert people watch their etiquette, and follow your host's lead. The Mongols of the Gobi carry their own food bowl and chopsticks. In Arabia and the Sahara a central dish heaped high is placed in front of the diners. Each serves himself from the section directly in front of him, using his right hand and making an excavation in the mound of food before him. Each mouthful is a small bite-sized ball formed with the fingers and plopped into the mouth. In some regions on the north edge of the Sahara spoons may be provided. If meat is served, it is torn off with the right hand.

Your host may or may not appear while you are served in Arab desert regions. His women certainly will not eat until after you have been served, and you probably will not even see them. They will watch you through tiny openings in tent curtains, and will hear your conversation.

In some tribes of Arabia all diners must stop eating when one guest indicates he has finished. That means you gobble your food or leave the banquet still hungry. Among many tribes it is most courteous to belch loudly after a meal. That shows your appreciation of good cooking and bountiful food. To break wind, however, is a very serious breach of manners under any circumstances or in any Arab company.

Cooking in desert regions is all done over open fires. In Africa and Arabia you will probably find the food palatable. In some cases wood ashes will flavor the roast, sand and ashes may cling to the bread. The cooked food will be safer to eat.

You may not be enthusiastic about the tea of Mongolian deserts. Often it is thickened with flour, and butter is added.

Dates are good in Arabia and Africa. They vary from soft, delicious, honey delicacies to hard, dry fodder resembling peanut shucks. All are nourishing, however.

Eat the dates with your right hand and watch your companions. In some Sahara regions it is insultingly bad form to throw the date stones over your shoulder. Remove the stone from your mouth with your right hand and place it on the edge of the serving tray. Date pits are collected and crushed between rocks for camel food. Don't waste them.

When you sit in the company of desert people, sit cross-legged, tailor fashion, or on your heels, depending on how the people of the region sit. Generally, it is bad form, even insulting, to show the soles of your feet when sitting in company. Your joints may creak and tire in proper position, but you will get used to it if you keep trying and live long enough.

chapter **5**

LAND

SURVIVAL

...TROPICS

Some people think of the Tropics as an enormous and forbidding jungle through which every step taken must be hacked out, and where every inch of the way is crawling with danger. Actually, much of the Tropics is not jungle. What jungle there is must be traveled with some labor and difficulty, it is true, but with little danger from anything bigger or more terrifying than malaria-carrying mosquitoes. Your tropical area may be jungle, mangrove or other swamps, open grassy plains, or semi-arid brushland. It may contain deserts or cold mountainous districts. So, you may find useful information for survival in all parts of this manual.

IMMEDIATE ACTION

Take shelter from tropical rain, sun, and insects. Malaria- carrying mosquitoes and other insect pests are the immediate dangers, so protect yourself against bites. Don't leave the

crash area without carefully blazing or marking your route. Use your compass. Know what direction you are taking.

In the Tropics, even the smallest scratch can quickly become dangerously infected. Promptly disinfect any wound.

Sending up smoke signals from a jungle is difficult — the trees disperse the smoke so much that it cannot be recognized as a signal. Set up your fires and other signals in natural clearings and along edges of streams.

Small radio transmitters do not operate effectively under wet jungle foliage; find a clearing.

DECISION TO STAY OR LEAVE

If you come down in dense jungle where your aircraft and signals can't possibly be seen from the air, you will probably do wisely to travel out. You can find shelter, food, and water along the way. Streams are plentiful in most places; they are often good routes to habitation.

With the proper equipment, care, and commone sense, you should be able to travel successfully. See page 345 for further instructions.

SHELTER

Try to pick a campsite on a knoll or high spot, in an open place well back from swamps. You'll be bothered less by mosquitoes, the ground will be drier, and there will be more chance of a breeze. Leaves or grass on the ground will make a more comfortable camp. A thick bamboo clump or matted canopy of vines for cover will reflect the smoke from your campfire and discourage insects. It will also keep the extremely heavy dew of early morning off your bed.

Don't, however, build a shelter under dead trees or trees with dead limbs. They may fall and wreck your camp or hurt someone. Don't sleep or build a shelter under a coconut tree — a falling coconut can disable you.

In the wet jungle forest you will need shelter from dampness. If you stay with the aircraft, use it for shelter. Try to make it mosquito-proof by covering openings with netting or parachute cloth.

The easiest improvised shelter is made by draping a parachute or tarpaulin over a rope or vine stretched between two trees. Keep one end of the canopy higher than the other. Discourage insects by having few openings and

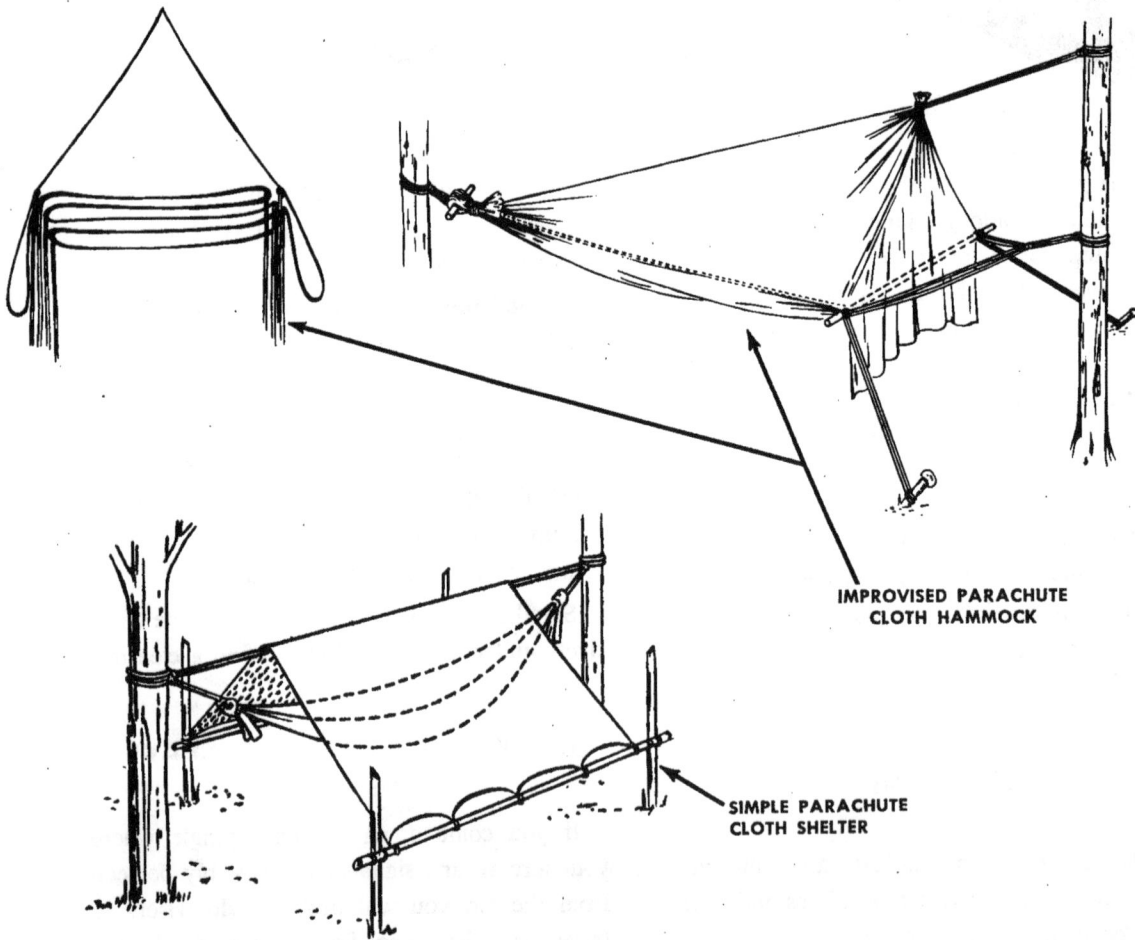

IMPROVISED PARACHUTE
CLOTH HAMMOCK

SIMPLE PARACHUTE
CLOTH SHELTER

Tropic shelters

by burning a smudge.

A good rain shelter can be made by covering an A-type framework with a good thickness of palm or other broad leaves, pieces of bark, or mats of grass. Lay the thatch shingle-fashion, with the tips of leaves pointing downward, starting from the bottom and working up, to shed the rain.

Dig a small drainage ditch just inside the eaves of your shelter and leading downhill — it will help keep the floor dry.

Don't sleep on the ground. Contact with the ground is chilling. Make a hammock from your parachute. It will keep you off the ground and will discourage ants, spiders, leeches, scorpions, and other pests. You can make a fair bed by covering a pile of brush with layers of palm fronds or other broad leaves. A better bed can

be made by building a frame of poles and covering the top with long, spineless palm leaves to a depth of 4 or 5 layers; cut the corner poles long enough to support a mosquito net or parachute fabric cover.

Nights will be cold in the mountain areas. Get out of the wind. Make your fire a few feet from a cliff or against a rock pile. Build your shelter so that you get reflected heat. Arrange the reflector so that the fire doesn't blow back at you.

Cutting away a great deal of the underbrush around your permanent campsite is a good idea; you will let out more of your firelight, which will keep prowling animals away.

Don't camp too near a stream or pond, especially during the rainy season. Don't camp on game trails or near waterholes.

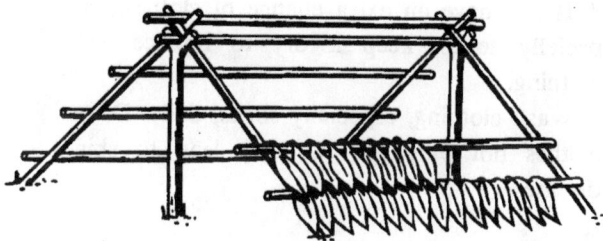

CONSTRUCTION OF THATCH SHELTER

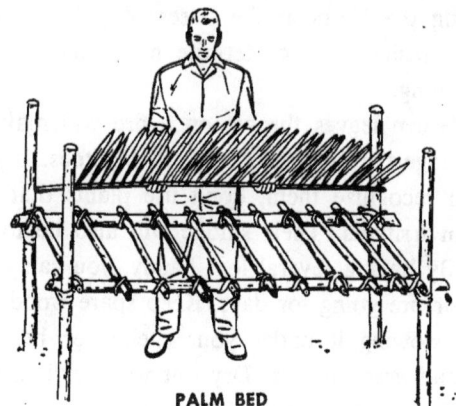

PALM BED

More tropic shelters

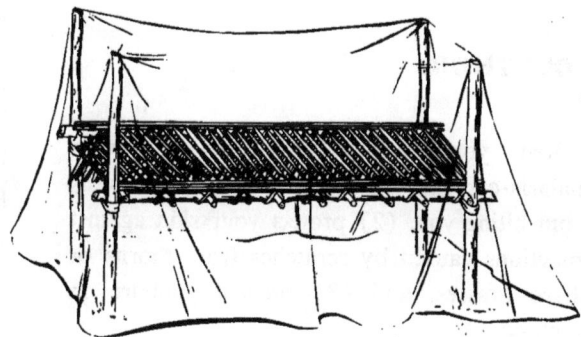

FIRE-MAKING

Wood is usually plentiful in the Tropics. During the rainy season, the fire problem may be more complicated by the difficulty of finding dry fuel, but many of the larger trees — whether dead or alive — have hollow trunks. Cut strips of the dry inner lining for kindling. When the fire is good and high, you can add wet *deadwood*. Even if the outside is wet, you can burn the heart of deadwood. You may also find dry wood hanging in the network of vines or lying on bushes.

A few pieces of green wood mixed in are good for cooking. When they dry out, they give more heat than seasoned wood.

A partly decayed log is the best bank for your campfire; it will smoulder all through the night.

Don't use bamboo for fuel; it burns too quickly, emits dangerous fumes, and may explode.

In palm country you can get good tinder by using the fibers at the bases of palm leaves. The insides of dry termite nests make good kindling.

Green leaves thrown on a fire will make a smudge that will discourage mosquitoes. If you can recognize them, don't use plants that are skin irritants. Their smoke will also be toxic.

By having several logs handy, you can keep your fire going for days. Keep spare wood dry by stowing it under your shelter or beneath broad green leaves. Dry out wet kindling and fuel near your fire for future use.

CLOTHING

Keep your body covered to (1) prevent malaria-carrying mosquitoes and other pests from biting you, (2) protect your skin against infections caused by scratches from thorns or sharp grasses, and (3) prevent sunburn in open country.

Wear long pants and shirts with the sleeves rolled down. Tuck your pants in the tops of your socks and tie them securely, or improvise puttees of canvas or parachute cloth to keep out ticks and leeches.

Loosely worn clothes will keep you cooler.

Wear a mosquito headnet or tie an undershirt or T-shirt around your head. Wear it especially at dawn and dusk.

In open country or in high grass country, wear a neckcloth or improvised head covering for protection from sunburn and dust. (See illustration.) Move carefully through high grass; some sharp-edged grasses can cut your clothing to shreds.

If you lose your shoes or if they wear out, you can improvise a practical pair of sandals by using the rubber sidewall or an aircraft tire or a piece of bark for the soles, with parachute cloth or canvas for the uppers.

Dry your clothing before nightfall to avoid discomfort from cold.

If you have an extra change of clothes, especially socks, keep it dry to replace wet clothing.

Wash clothing, especially socks, daily. Dirty clothes not only rot but may lead to skin diseases.

HEALTH AND HAZARDS

Most stories about the animals, snakes, spiders, and nameless terrors of the jungle are not based on fact. You are safer from sudden death in the jungle than in most big cities. You might never see a poisonous snake or a large animal. What may bother you most are the howls, screams, and crashing sounds made by noisy monkeys, birds, night insects, and falling trees. The real dangers of the Tropics are the insects, many of which pass on diseases or parasites.

Malaria

Malaria may be your worst enemy. It is transmitted by mosquitoes, which are normally encountered from late afternoon until early morning. They may also bite in the shade during the day. Guard against bites by camping away from swamps, on high land. Sleep under mosquito netting if you have it; otherwise smear mud on your face as a protection against insects, especially when sleeping. Wear full clothing, especially at night; tuck your pants into the tops of your socks or shoes. Wear moquito headnet and gloves if available. Rub mosquito repellent on your hands and all exposed skin. Take antimalaria tablets, if available, according to directions as long as the supply lasts; even if you are bitten by infected mosquitoes, you won't get sick for a month.

Ticks

Ticks may be numerous, especially in grassy places; you may get dozens of them on your body. Strip to the skin once a day or oftener and inspect *all* parts of your body for ticks, leeches, bed bugs, and other pests. If there are several men in your group, examine each other. Brush ticks off clothing; flick them off the skin. If they get attached, cover them with a drop of iodine — they will let go. Heating them will also make them let go, but don't burn your skin. Touch up the bite with antiseptic. Be careful when removing a tick — the head may stay in and start infection.

Fleas

Fleas are common in dry, dusty buildings. The females will burrow under your toenails or into your skin to lay their eggs. Remove them with a sterilized knife; keep the cut clean. In India and southern China, bubonic plague is a constant threat. Rat fleas carry this disease, and discovery of dead rats usually means a plague epidemic in the rat population, which may be a prelude to an outbreak among human beings. Fleas may also transmit typhus fever and in many parts of the Tropics — especially Malaya and Indonesia — rats also carry parasites which cause jaundice and other fevers. Keep your food in ratproof storage, containers, or rodentproof caches.

Typhus Fever

In many tropical and temperate parts of the Far East, from Ceylon to Assam and Burma, and from New Guinea to Japan, a type of typhus fever is carried by tiny red mites. These mites resemble the chiggers of southern and southwestern United States. They live in the soil and, burrowed a few inches into the ground, are common in tall grass, cutover jungle, or stream banks. When you lie or sit on the ground, the mites emerge from the soil, crawl through your clothes, and bite. Usually you don't know that you have been bitten, for the bite is painless and does not itch. Mite typhus is a serious disease; prevent it by not getting bitten. Clear your camping ground and burn it off, leep above the ground, and treat your clothing with insect repellent.

Other Insect Pests

Leeches are most common in wet underbrush and during the wet season. You may pick them up from plants, the ground or water. They will get through your shoe eyelets or over your shoe tops. Flick them off with your knife or touch them with a pinch of salt.

Spiders, scorpions, and centipedes are often abundant, and some are large. Shake out your shoes, socks, and clothing; and inspect your bed morning and evening — especially for scorpions. A few spiders have poisonous bites, which may be as painful as a wasp sting. Black widow spiders are dangerous. The large spiders called tarantulas rarely bite, but if you touch them, the short, hard hairs which cover them may come off and irritate the skin. This is also true of some moth wings.

Centipedes will sting if you touch them, and their sting is like that of a wasp. Avoid all types of many-legged insects.

Scorpions are real pests, for they like to hide in clothing, bedding, or shoes, and they strike without being touched. They have poison glands in the large claws and tail; their sting can make you sick.

Stings of all these insects cause swelling and pain. Use cold compresses, mud, or coconut meat applied locally.

Chiggers, wasps, and wild bees are pests and may be serious. Chiggers, mites, and fleas bore under the skin and cause painful sores; but a drop of oil, resin, or pitch kills them.

Treat ant, wasp, and bee stings with cold compresses. Don't camp near an ant hill or an ant trail. Use caution in climbing trees, for many types of biting ants live in branches and foliage of tropical trees. Mangrove swamps have hanging plants attached to the branches of the mangroves which are almost always inhabited by biting ants.

Never walk barefoot — your shoes guard against crawling mites, ticks, cuts, and subsequent bacterial infection. When you are accidentally dunked or forced to wade in fresh waters suspected of being infested with fluke parasites, observe the following precautions: wring out your clothes, drain and dry your shoes, and rub your body dry of all droplets. Apply insect repellent over exposed areas.

In the jungles of southeastern Asia you may encounter thousands of white ants, which will eat your clothing if you leave it on the ground. Cut green grass and spread it down before you place your bed or clothing; then the white ants will not bother you.

Crocodiles

The marine crocodile of the Indo-Australian region is very dangerous. It is abundant along the seashores, in coral reef areas as well as in salt water estuaries and in bays. Either crocodiles or alligators may be expected in any tropical waters. They prefer to lie on banks or float like logs with just their eyes above the water. Exercise the greatest caution in fording deep streams, in bathing, and whenever you have occasion to be in or near the water, especially where crocodiles or alligators are evident. Do not attract them to you by thrashing in the water. Avoid them at all times.

Food Poisoning from Contaminated Fish

Food poisoning will result from eating contaminated or decomposed fish. All freshly caught fish are very susceptible to spoilage, and fresh water fish often contain human parasites.

Dangerous Fish

Dangerous fish are discussed in the next section.

DANGEROUS FISH

When crossing a muddy stream, slide your feet instead of stepping freely, in order to avoid stepping on spiny fish. Don't wade barefooted over reefs.

Watch out for poisonous, venomous, and ferocious fish.

Poisonous Fish

Many species of reef fish have flesh containing toxic substances. These substances are found in some species of fish at all times, and in other species during certain periods of the year. Fish poisoning may occur during any season. The toxins are found in all parts of the fish, especially in the liver, intestines, and eggs. An ounce of liver or flesh of the puffer fish will kill a man in 20 minutes.

The toxins produce a numbness of the lips, tongue, tips of fingers and toes. They also

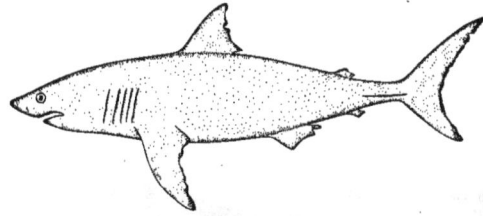
GREAT WHITE SHARK

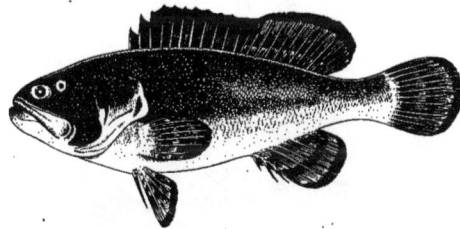
SEA BASS

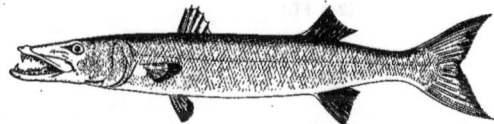
BARRACUDA

MORAY EEL

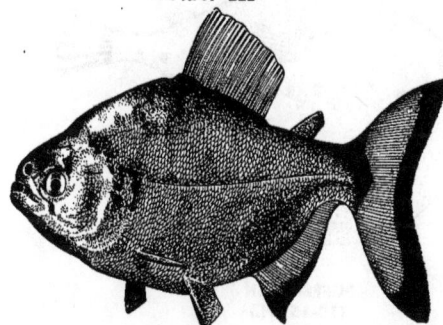
PIRANHA

Ferocious fish

237

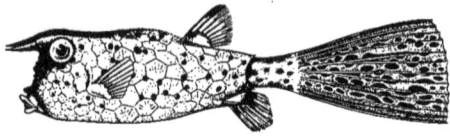

COWFISH
(6-12 IN.)

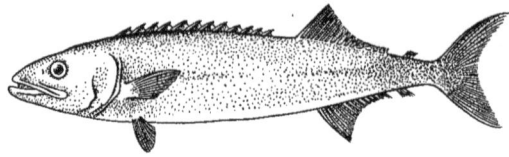

OILFISH
(3-5 FT.)

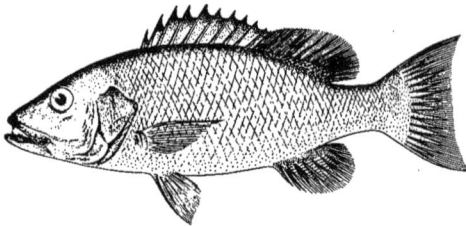

RED SNAPPER FISH
(2-3 FT.)

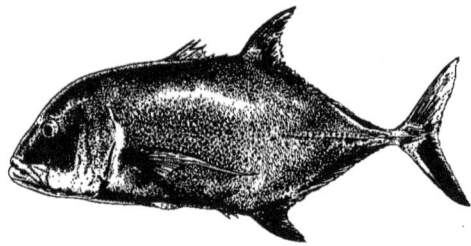

JACKFISH
(ABOUT 2 FT.)

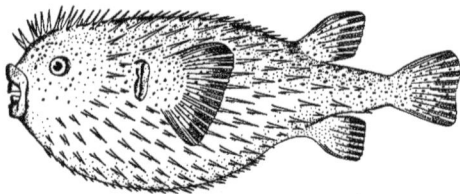

PORCUPINE FISH
(ABOUT 1 FT.)

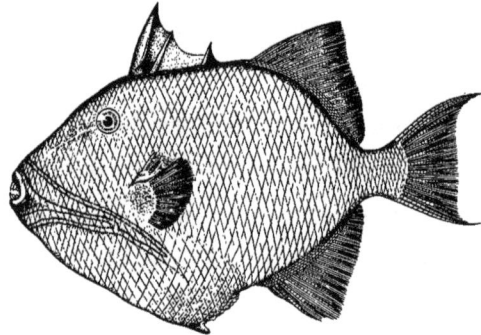

TRIGGER FISH
(1-2 FT.)

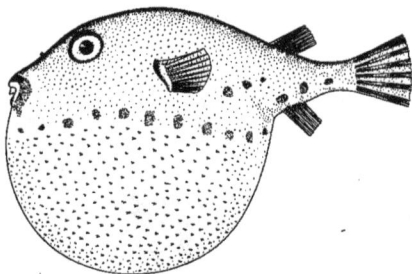

PUFFER FISH
(10-15 IN.)

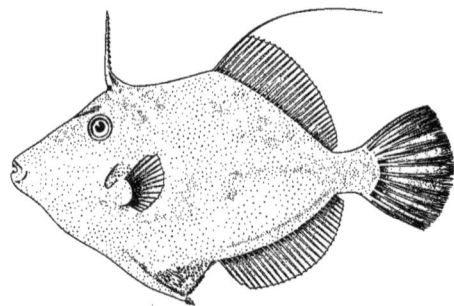

THORNFISH
(ABOUT 1 FT.)

Fish with poisonous flesh

produce severe itching, and a reversal of temperature sensations, which makes hot objects feel cold, and cold feel hot. These sensations are accompanied by nausea, vomiting, dizziness, loss of speech, and a paralysis which in its final stage will result in death.

Fish toxins are water-soluble, so that even broth from a chowder containing parts of a poisonous fish will be harmful. Fish toxins cannot be destroyed by heat, and no amount of cooking will destroy the poison. Nor is freshness any guarantee of safety, since fish toxins are not the result of food spoilage. You cannot detect a poisonous fish from a nonpoisonous one by appearance, even if you know it by sight. The best example of this is the red snapper, a well-known table delicacy in many parts of the world, but which in the Tropics accounts for many fatal cases of fish poisoning.

There are no reliable rules for testing the edibility of questionable fish. Various methods, such as the discoloration of a silver coin in contact with cooking fish, black discoloration at the base of fish teeth, unusually dull appearance of fish eyes, variations in color, or the tests that are normally used to detect spoiled fish, are valueless. Standard edibility rules are useless, since the toxins are tasteless and the flesh usually appears palatable. Birds are least susceptible to the poison, so fish should not be accepted just because birds are seen eating questionable fish. The cat and pig are least affected, while dogs and rats are most susceptible to fish poisons. Even in these animals, reactions to the poison may not be noted for 24 hours. In general, the severity of illness from eating the poisonous flesh of fish is dependent upon the amount eaten. This will be more severe if the liver, intestines, or eggs are eaten. An attack of fish poisoning does not give the victim any immunity. Antidotes are not known. Induced vomiting and bowel movements should be attempted. Aside from this, only the symptoms can be alleviated, and these only to a degree.

Poisonous fish are widely distributed in the warm waters of the Tropics and are especially numerous in the shallow waters of the Caribbean, and Central and South Pacific. In the Central Pacific around the Phoenix, Canton, Sidney, Midway, Fanning, Line, and Johnston islands, it has been estimated that there are some 300 species of poisonous reef fishes. Fish poisoning may occur at any time of the year and is more dangerous during the breeding period. Detailed information on the number and distribution of poisonous species was not available when this manual was prepared, but the information in the paragraphs which follow will help you to avoid poisonous fish.

CHARACTERISTICS OF POISONOUS FISH. There are no simple rules to tell desirable fish from undesirable ones. The worst offenders are illustrated on p. 238. These have the following characteristics:

1. Almost all live in the shallow waters of lagoons or reefs.

2. Many have round or boxlike bodies with hard shell-like skins which are covered with bony plates or spines. They have small parrot-like mouths, small gill openings, and the belly fins are small or absent. Their names suggest their shape: puffer fish, file fish, globe fish, trigger fish, trunk fish, trumpet fish, moon fish, butterfly fish.

Some fish which are usually considered edible, such as red snapper and barracuda, are poisonous when taken from atolls and reefs.

Survivors stranded on inhabited islands may follow the advice of the local natives. But, natives are not infallible guides to the edibility of fish in their home waters. In many cases the development of poison in a previously edible species has been so sudden and unpredictable that local inhabitants eat them and fall ill. However, natives are aware of the most common offenders and should provide some information of the safer fishing grounds.

GENERAL PRECAUTIONS. Survivors without benefit of local information should observe the following precautions:

1. Don't fish in lagoons. These are normally shallow, sandy, or broken coral bottoms with few fish species; all are undesirable as food.

2. Don't fish on the leeward or protected side of an island. This area of shallow water consists of patches of living corals interspersed with open spaces and may extend seaward for some distance. Numbers and varieties of fish are usually very abundant; all are undesirable as food.

3. Don't eat fish caught in any area where the water is unnaturally discolored. It is believed that most fish become poisonous after feeding on microscopic marine algae or small animals whose presence can be noted by eye only when they occur in sufficient mass to change the color of the water. This condition best exists in warm, shallow, protected sides of an island.

4. Do all your fishing on the seaward or windward side, or in deep passages leading from the open sea to the lagoon. The reefs of live coral drop off sharply into deep water and form a dividing line between the suspected fish of shallows and the desirable deep water species. Strong swells and wind will keep the waters free of toxic foods that may affect fish, and the deep water will permit ocean fish to approach close to the island. Even in this area, morays, snappers, barracuda, parrot fish, rockfish, sea bass, and other reef fish may be caught; all suspected reef fish should be discarded, whether caught on the ocean or reef side. Survivors on life rafts on the open ocean are safe from fish poisoning. But, if you are on a reef, don't try to reach open ocean on a life raft. You may not get back.

Fish and Shellfish with Venomous Spines

Venomous fish produce their injurious effects only by means of spines, stingers, or "teeth" which inject irritating toxins into the hands or feet of the unwary. Some fish, as the surgeonfish, may be armed with venomous spines and have poisonous flesh as well. Typical members of the venomous group are shown in the illustration.

Coral reefs are no place for bare feet. Coral, dead or alive, can cut them to ribbons. Seemingly harmless sponges and sea urchins can slip fine needles of lime or silica into your skin, and they will break off and fester. Don't dig them out; use lime juice or citrus fruit juice, if available, to dissolve them. The almost invisible stonefish will not move from your path. It has 13 poisonous spines that will cause you agony or death. Treat as for snakebite (see 344).

Don't probe with your hands into dark holes; use a stick. Don't step freely over muddy or sandy bottoms of rivers and seashores; slide your feet along the bottom. In this way you will avoid stepping on stingrays or other sharp-spined animals. If you step on a stingray, you push its body down, giving it leverage to throw its tail up and stab you with its stinging spine. A stingray's broken-off spine can be removed only by cutting it out.

Cone shell and long, slender, pointed terebra snails have poison teeth and can bite. Cone snails have smooth, colorful mottled shells with elongate, narrow openings. They live under rocks, in crevices of coral reefs, and along rocky shores of protected bays. They are shy and are most active at night. They have a long mouth and a snout or proboscis which is used to jab or inject their teeth. These teeth are actually tiny hypodermic needles, with a tiny poison gland on the back end of each. This action is swift, producing acute pain, swelling, paralysis, blindness, and possible death in 4 hours. Avoid handling all cone snails.

Handle the big conches with caution. These snails have razor-sharp trapdoors, which they may suddenly jab out, puncturing your skin in their effort to get away. Don't use your hands to gather large abalones and clams. Pry them loose with bars or wedges; they will hold you if they clamp down on your fingers.

Ferocious Fish

In crossing deeper portions of a reef, check the reed edge shadows for sharks, barracudas, and moray eels. Morays are angry, vicious, and aggressive when disturbed. They hide in dark holes among the reefs. In northeastern South America, the rivers are infested with piranha fish, which, though small, attack in schools and can devour a 300-lb. hog in a few minutes.

In salt water estuaries, bays, or lagoons, man-eating sharks may come in very close to shore. Many sharks have attacked in shallow

water on bathing beaches in the tropic seas. Barracudas have also made such attacks. Usually sharks 4 feet long and shorter are timid. Beware, however, of all larger ones, including hammerheads. They are potentially dangerous. Not all sharks show fins above the water. See section on sharks later in this chapter.

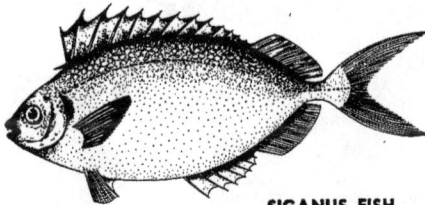

SIGANUS FISH
(4-6 IN.)

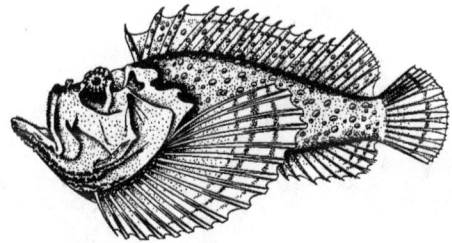

ZEBRA FISH
(10-30 IN.)

STURGEON FISH
(8-10 IN.)

TOAD FISH
(ABOUT 1 FT.)

STONE FISH
(ABOUT 15 IN.)

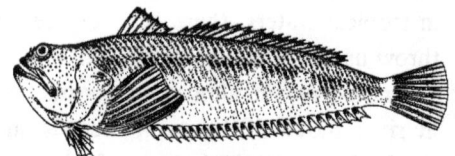

WEEVER FISH
(ABOUT 1 FT.)

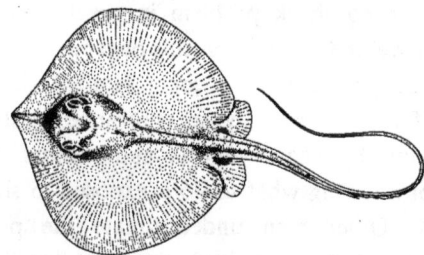

TEREBRA SHELL

CONE

STINGRAY (TOP VIEW)

Venomous shells

Venomous fish

SHARKS

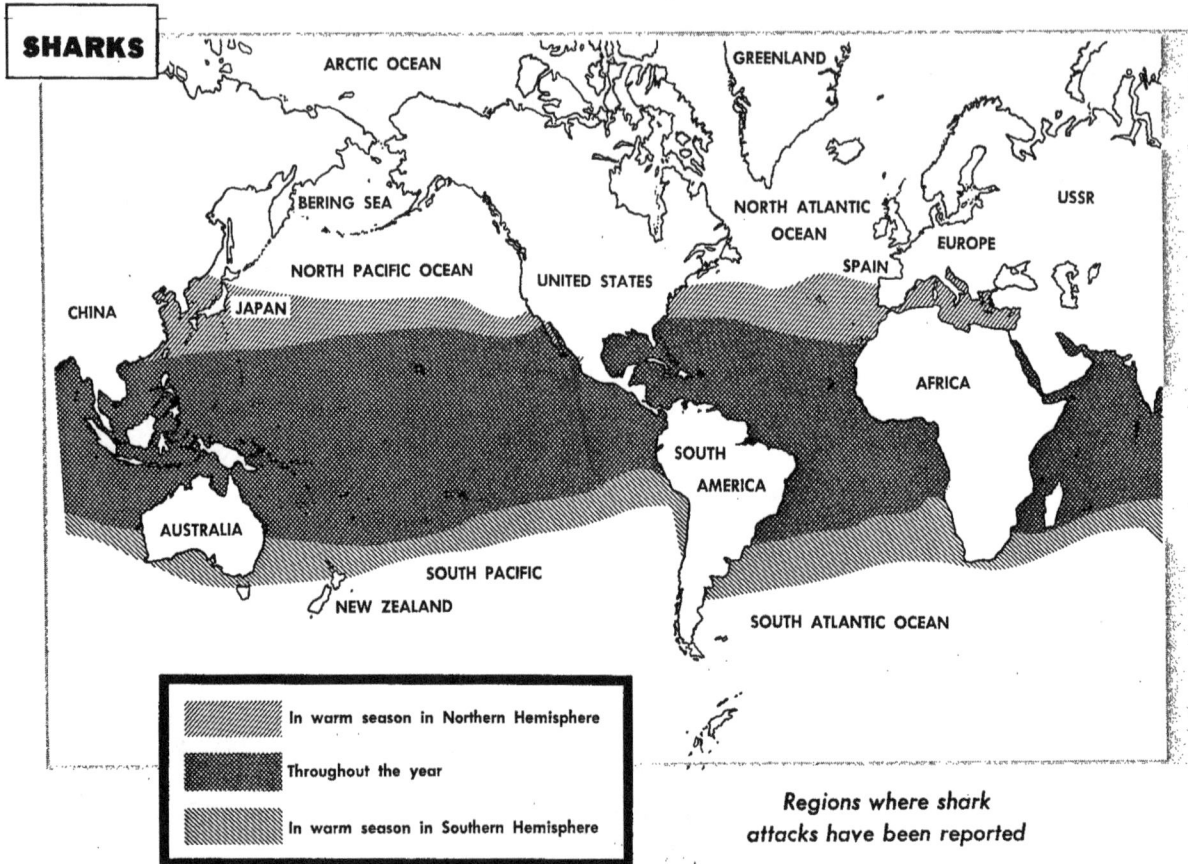

In warm season in Northern Hemisphere

Throughout the year

In warm season in Southern Hemisphere

Regions where shark attacks have been reported

Plenty of fiction but very little fact has been circulated on the subject of sharks and shark attack. With an ever-increasing number of men in the United States Armed Forces operating in tropical waters, there is a very real need to throw useful light on the subject.

Sharks live in almost all oceans, seas, and in river mouths. However, records show that sharks have attacked men only in water with temperatures ranging from 65° F. upward. There is no shark problem in great areas of colder water (see map on this page).

Some people have a great fear of sharks. This fear is caused by an ignorance of shark behavior, by vague reports and rumors, and by not knowing what to do if exposed to shark attack. Other men underestimate the possibility and hazard of shark attack. All military personnel should know the facts about sharks.

The truth is that the chances of being attacked by a shark are very small. Even in warm oceans where attacks are possible, the risk can be reduced by knowing what to do and how to do it and by the use of shark repellent (effective only on small sharks).

Kinds of Sharks

There are hundreds of different kinds of sharks distributed throughout the world, but only a few are really dangerous. Of these, four types account for most human casualties. They are the *white, tiger, hammerhead,* and *blue* sharks. *Ground, gray nurse,* and *mako* sharks also have been known to attack people occasionally. These sharks are illustrated on page 243.

Sharks vary greatly in size, but there is no close relationship between the size of a full-grown shark and the risk of attack. Full-grown sharks of the dangerous kinds may vary in length from 8 to 16 feet. Even the smaller sharks may be dangerous and should be

MAKO   7-9 FT.

TIGER   10-12 FT.

HAMMERHEAD   9-11 FT.

WHITE   10-15 FT.

GREY NURSE   8-10 FT.

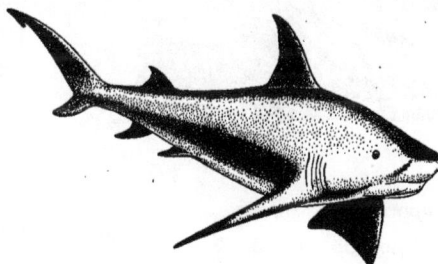

GROUND   7-8 FT.

BLUE   8-10 FT.

THRESHER   10-12 FT.

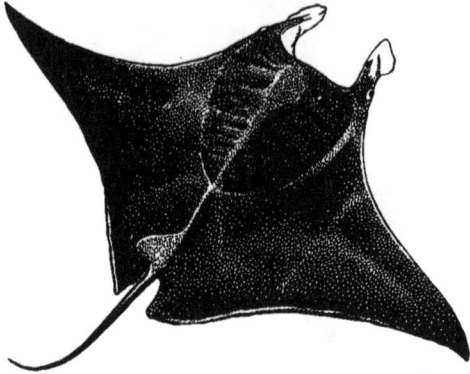

GIANT RAY OR MANTA

SHARK

*Comparison of jumping
form of porpoise and shark*

PORPOISE

*Animals sometimes
mistaken for sharks*

avoided, especially when they are found in schools. Basking and whale sharks, which are the largest known, may get to be 45 feet in length, but they are entirely harmless because their teeth are very small. The whale shark should not be confused with the smaller *whaling* shark which is found in Australian waters.

Animals Sometimes Mistaken for Sharks

PORPOISES. Porpoises are large ocean mammals which are often seen in tropical waters. A school of porpoises gracefully breaking the surface, blowing and grunting, may look alarming. Actually it should be a reassuring sight, because porpoises and sharks are enemie. Where there are porpoises, sharks are not likely to be found nearby. Porpoises are harmless to man.

RAYS. Giant rays or mantas, which also occur in tropical waters, may be mistaken for sharks. A swimming ray curls up the tip of its fins, and when seen from water level, the fins somewhat resemble the fin on the backs of two sharks swimming side by side. Closer observation will show that the animal is a ray and not two sharks; if both the fins disappear together periodically, it is a ray. In deep water all rays are harmless to swimmers; however, some are dangerous if stepped on in shallow water.

Shark Habits

Some sharks live and feed at considerable depths, and much of the time most of them feed on the ocean bottom. Hungry sharks sometimes will follow fish up to the surface and into shallow waters along the shore. When a shark explores such water, it is likely to be dangerous.

Sharks seem to feed most actively during the night and particularly at dusk and dawn. After dark, they show an increased tendency to move toward the surface and into shore waters.

A shark's natural food generally consists of a wide variety of relatively small marine animals such as fish, squids, crabs, and shellfish. A shark seeks food which is fairly easy to get and especially goes after stragglers from schools of fish and after prey which has been wounded or is helpless. It will follow a ship and eat garbage thrown overboard.

Man's strange appearance probably alarms a shark. There is evidence also that a group of clothed men when bunched together in the water will be safer than a single individual.

The evidence is that a shark first locates food by smelling it. Such things as garbage, body wastes, and blood probably stimulate him to explore for food. A shark is attracted by weak fluttery movements and is repelled by strong, regular movements and certain loud, strange noises. A feeding shark, especially when feeding in a school, will use sight to locate and catch food.

Fishermen have observed that a shark will swim under and around schools of fish. The schools are indicated by many fine surface ripples, by fish breaking the surface, and by flights of feeding ocean birds. When a gamefish is hooked, it is often attacked vigorously by a shark. Wherever fish are being caught, sharks are likely to be found.

While a shark will investigate any large floating object, it will not attack a man unless it is hungry. Often the shark will swim away after investigating. At other times it may approach and circle the object once or twice, or it may swim close and nudge the object with its snout.

When swimming, a shark cannot stop suddenly or turn quickly in a tight circle. A good swimmer can avoid a single large shark by evasive action.

A shark rarely jumps out of the water to take food; however, it may grasp its prey near the surface. For this reason, men on rafts are relatively safe unless they dangle their hands, arms, feet, or legs in the water.

Sharks in schools sometimes jump clear of the water and fall back with a plash. Such actions possibly involve play or courtship; they do not mean that the sharks are feeding, hungry, or vicious. There is no need to be alarmed by jumping sharks.

PROTECTIVE MEASURES AGAINST SHARKS

In the Water

Keep a sharp lookout for sharks.

Keep your clothing and shoes on.

If sharks have been noticed, be especially careful of the methods in which you eliminate body wastes.

Urinate in short spurts and allow it to dissipate between spurts. Fecal matter should be passed in as small a quantity as possible into the hand and thrown as far away as possible.

Vomiting, when it cannot be prevented by swallowing the regurgitation, should be done into the hand and thrown away as above.

If in a group threatened or attacked by a shark, bunch together and form a tight circle Face outward so you can see an approaching shark. If the sea is rough, tie yourselves together. Ward off attack by kicking or stiff-arming the shark.

Stay as quiet as possible. Float to save energy. If necessary to swim, use strong regular strokes; don't make frantic irregular movements.

When swimming alone stay away from schools of fish.

If a single shark threatens at close range:

1. Use strong regular swimming movements; try feinting toward the shark — it may be scared away.

2. Don't swim away directly in the shark's path; face the shark and swim quickly to one side; outmaneuver it.

3. Kick or stiff-arm a shark to push it away, or grasp a side fin and swim with shark until you can veer away from it.

4. Make loud sounds by slapping the surface of the water with cupped hands; use regular slaps. Or, put your head under water and shout; skin divers report that this will scare away most sharks.

5. Use a knife at close quarters in a showdown.

On a Raft

Don't fish from raft when sharks are nearby. Abandon any hooked fish if a shark approaches. Don't clean fish into the water when sharks are sighted.

Don't throw waste overboard if sharks are around.

If a shark threatens to attack or to damage the raft, discourage it by jabbing snout or gills with oar. Be careful not to break the oar, and don't take roundhouse swings that may upset you.

Fire a pistol above a shark — it will frighten him away.

Check for sharks around and under the raft before going into the water or in landing.

First Aid For Shark Victims

The first and most important measure is to stop bleeding quickly. Help the victim into a raft or ashore as soon as possible. Stop bleeding and treat for shock.

If in the water in a group, form a circle around the victim and stop bleeding by using a tourniquet improvised from an article of clothing. (See p. 9.)

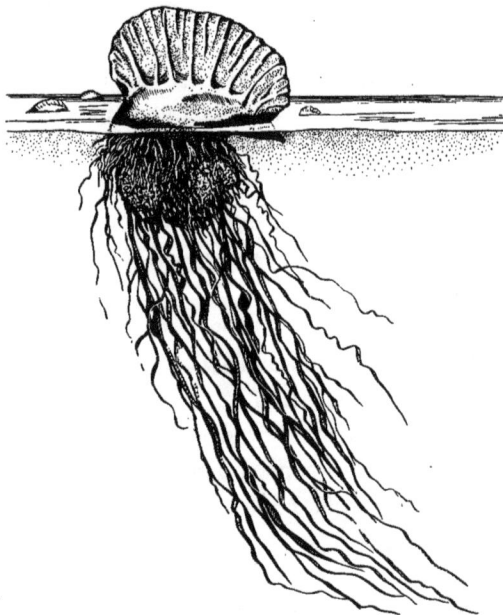

Portuguese man-of-war

PORTUGUESE MAN-OF-WAR

In warm salt water watch out for the Portuguese man-of-war. These jellyfish-like creatures have stinging tentacles which may be as much as 50 feet long. The sting is extremely painful and may even disable a swimmer who tangles with a man-of-war in the water. On the surface of the sea the man-of-war appears like a blue bladder, 4-5 inches long, with a wrinkled top, and a mass of long streamers underneath. They are especially common in the Gulf Stream.

WATER

You can get nearly clear water from muddy streams or lakes by digging a hole in sandy soil 1 to 6 feet from the bank. Allow water to seep in, and then wait for the mud to settle.

Water from tropical streams, pools, springs, and swamps is safe to drink only *after it has been purified*. Some water may be discolored or turbid. It may be partially cleared by filtering through an improvised filter such as parachute cloth.

You can get water from some plants, and it can be used without further treatment. Coconuts contain refreshing water — the green, unripe coconuts about the size of a grapefruit are best. (See illustration on p. 261.) Vines are often good sources. Choose a good-sized vine and cut off a 3- to 6-foot length. Make first cut at the top. Sharpen one end and hold a container or your mouth to the sharpened end. The water will be fresh and pure. Never drink from a vine that has milky sap. Bamboo stems sometimes have water in the hollow joints. Shake the stems of old, yellowish bamboo — if you hear a gurgling, cut a notch at the base of each joint and catch the water in a container. (See illustration on p. 276).

In the American Tropics, the branches of large trees often support air plants (relatives of the pineapple) whose overlapping, thickly growing leaves may hold a considerable amount of rainwater. Strain the water through cloth to eliminate most of the dirt and water insects. In climbing one of these trees, you may also find small frogs or snakes.

Collect rainwater by digging a hole and lining it with a tarpaulin or a piece of canvas. Catch water from dripping trees by wrapping a clean cloth around a sloping tree, and arrange one end of the cloth to drip into a container.

Animal trails often lead to water. Follow them, but take care not to get lost.

ANIMAL FOOD

Land Animals

Paths and roads are the normal passageways along which animals travel through tropical forests. Look on the ground for hedgehogs, porcupines, anteaters, mice, wild pigs, deer, and wild cattle; in the trees for bats, squirrels, rats, and monkeys. Dangerous beasts — tiger, rhinoceros, elephant — are rarely seen and best left alone. In the Old World Tropics, fruit bats or flying foxes are good sources of meat.

If you want to shoot game in the jungle, you'll have a better chance of getting it if you make it come to you. Stalking animals without making any noise will be difficult and you will probably frighten them away. Animals will often come if you just sit on a log and don't make any noise. Find a comfortable place and stay there quietly for 5 to 10 minutes. Animals and birds can be "called" by experts, but this is a form of woodsmanship not easily taught in a manual. If you can deliver an authentic birdcall, you won't have to read about it here. If you can't, you can't learn the technique by reading about it.

Sea Food

Review the discussion of dangerous fish earlier in this chapter.

Rocks, along beaches or extending out into deeper water as reefs, provide a fruitful source of survival food.

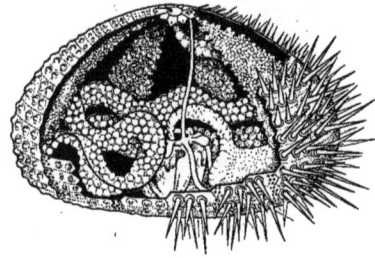

SEA URCHIN

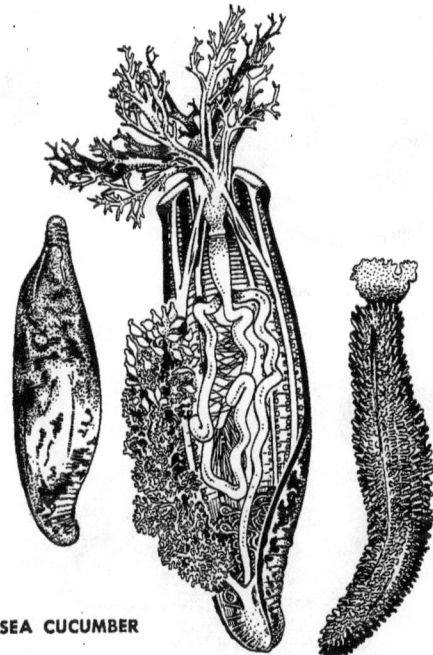

SEA CUCUMBER

OCTOPUS

Invertebrates

SNAIL

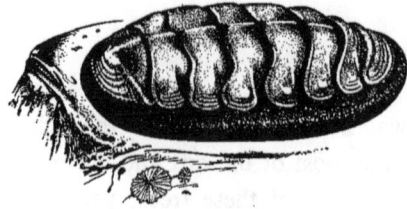

CHITON

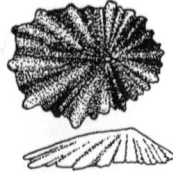

RAZOR CLAM

LIMPETS

PERIWINKLES

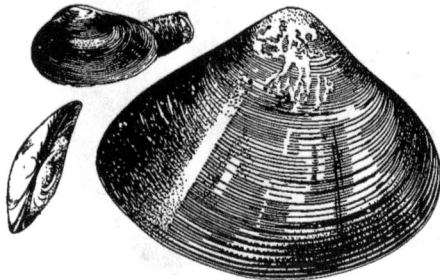

CLAMS

OYSTERS

MUSSELS

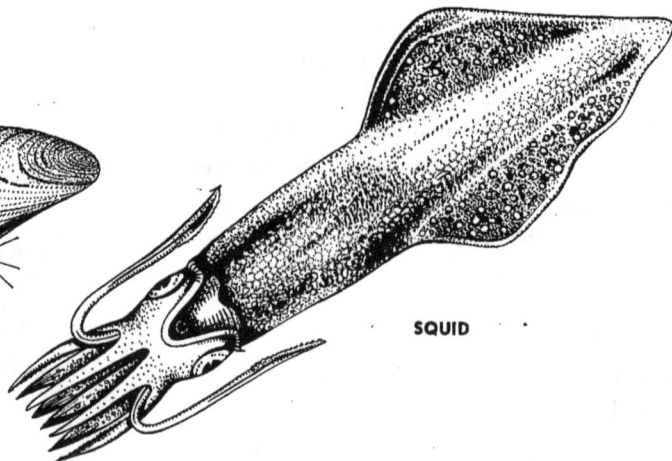

SQUID

Invertebrates

Rocks often bear clinging shellfish. Be sure that all the shellfish you take are healthy. Do not select them from colonies where some are dead or dying, or where shellfish are not covered with water at least 5% of the time.

Fish, crabs, lobsters, crayfish, sea urchins, and small octopi can be poked out of holes, crevices, or rock pools. Be ready to spear them before they move off into deep water. If they are in deeper water, tease them shoreward with a baited hook, piece of string, or stick. You will find flower-like sea anemones in pools and crevices. They shrink closed when you touch them. Detach them with a knife. Wash well to remove slime and dirt in and outside of animal; boil or simmer.

A small heap of empty oyster shells near a hole may indicate an octopus. Drop a baited hook into the hole and wait until the octopus has entirely surrounded the hook and line; then lift it quickly. To kill, piece it with your fish spear. Octopi are not scavengers like sharks, but hunters, fond of spiny lobster and other crablike fish. At night they come into shallow water and can then be easily seen and speared.

Snails and limpets cling to rocks and seaweed from the low-water mark up. Large snails called chitons adhere tightly to rocks just above the surf line. Mussels usually form dense colonies in rock pools, on logs, or at the base of boulders. Mussels are poisonous in tropical zones during the summer, especially when seas are highly phosphorescent or reddish.

Sluggish sea cucumbers and conchs (large snails) live in deep water. The sea cucumber can and does shoot out his stomach when excited. Don't eat that; boil the animal and eat the skin and the five strips of muscle inside the body.

The safest fish to eat are those from the open sea or deep water beyond the reef. Silvery fishes, river eels, butterfly fishes, and flounders from bays and rivers are good to eat. Remember that fish caught in the Tropics spoil quickly.

Land crabs are common on tropical islands and are often found in coconut groves. Use an open coconut for bait.

Cooking Hints

Broiling is the quickest way of preparing fish. A rock broiler may be made by placing a layer of small stones on top of hot hardwood coals, and laying the fish on the top. It is not necessary to scale the fish to cook by this method, and small fish need not be cleaned. Cooked in this manner, fish have a moist and delicious flavor. Crabs and lobsters may also be placed on the stones and broiled. Breadfruit is frequently cooked in this manner.

The earth oven is used by some South Pacific islanders, and it is particularly well suited to their foods. Make a shallow excavation about 2-1/2 feet wide by 8 or 12 inches deep in soft soil or sand. Build a fire of hardwood and let it burn until a heavy bed of coals has accumulated. Lay over this a grate of hardwood sticks and pile on a large number of small rocks. By the time the grate has burned through, the rocks should be quite hot. Remove the larger coals and burning brands and spread the stones smoothly over the bottom and along the sides of the pit. Spread a thin layer of breadfruit leaves on the hot stones. Wrap the fish, or whatever else is to be cooked, in more leaves and place it in the oven. Sprouted coconuts, lobsters, large clams, and crabs may be put in without wrapping. Cover with a final layer of leaves and loose sand so that the oven is covered. The size of the oven and cooking time vary with the type of food.

FISHING HINTS

Hook and Line Fishing

Hook and line fishing on a rocky coast requires considerable care to keep the line from becoming entangled or cut on sharp edges. Most shallow water fish are nibblers. Unless your bait is well placed and hooked and the barb of the hook offset by bending (see illustration), you will lose it without gaining a fish. Use hermit crabs, snails, or the tough muscle of shellfish. Take the cracked shells and any other animal remains and drop it into the area you wish to fish. This will bring the fish to your area and give you a somewhat better selection.

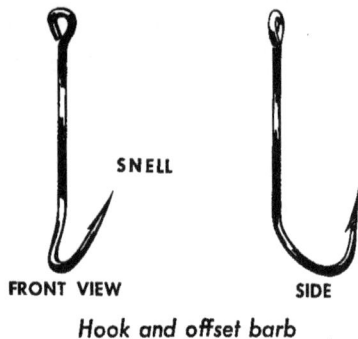

SNELL

FRONT VIEW   SIDE

Hook and offset barb

If hook-and-line fishing doesn't work out, try chop fishing.

Chop Fishing

Chop fishing is effective at night during low tide. This method requires a torch and a machete. The fish are attracted by the light of the torch and then may be stunned by slashing at them with the back of the machete blade. You should get enough fish for several days by this method. Be careful while swinging the machete. In a situation such as this, fish may also be speared.

Spear Fishing

Spear fishing will produce good catches, provided you have goggles, spears, and lung attachments. But it takes a good swimmer to go after fish with a minimum of homemade equipment, and the danger of cuts from coral, venomous fish, and ferocious fish is hardly justified under survival conditions. You will also find that fish can be wary and hard to corner.

Fishing in Tides, Rips, Currents, and Surf

Tides are difficult to predict without good tide tables. The survivor should take careful note of tides in his locality, for his schedule of living and traveling will be affected by the daily change of tides. Normal low tide is the best time for lobster fishing and hunting shellfish on the reefs.

The islands of the Pacific have fairly regular diurnal tides with an approximate range of 2-1/2 feet. Normal ebb and flow may be interrupted by periods of prolonged high and low tides caused by the presence of storms in the general vicinity. Low tide is best for gathering shellfish and other forms of reef life. Small fish, and at night, lobsters and sharks, are particularly active during the first few hours of the incoming tide. Dangerous rip tides are not noticeable where tidal inlets are wide. During any change of tide, a great volume of water passes through atoll inlets, and a swimmer should not attempt to swim or raft across the deeper channels until the tide reaches a lull at peak or ebb. Don't get caught far out on a reef by incoming tides, since these may sweep over a reef with a current that makes walking difficult and swimming dangerous.

Surf is not dangerous unless the survivor is in a weakened condition or unless storms have built the wave action above the normal 8-foot height. Waves do not break until they are almost on the reef, and they move shoreward in a definite cycle. The swimmer should take advantage of the lull between series of large waves to get through the surf. It is important to head *into* the waves. If a large wave is ready to break in front of you in shallow water, dive, grab hold of a rock and hang on until the crest of the wave is passed. Let the declining force of the wave carry you shoreward.

Practically all shorelines of atoll islands are rimmed by coral reefs, backed by sandy beaches in sheltered spots and outcrops of coral limestone in exposed areas. Reefs of windward shores are usually reduced to flat, waveswept shelves. On the sea side of islands there is more of a tendency for barrier formation to take place, creating shallow lagoons which are very productive to sea life. Deep inlets cut the reefs at the mouths of island streams. Many of these streams appear insignificant, but they discharge enough fresh water, especially in rainy seasons, to stop the formation of coral growth in reef inlets. As a consequence, many of these inlets are abrupt submarine canyons, and dangerous rip tides may form at change of tide. Surf may be dangerous on the windward side. Steady northeast trades or storm winds pile up breakers 7 to 15 feet high. Surf is usually highest near the peak of the incoming tide. Surf is less dangerous in coves and there is a good chance that inlets through the reef will be found in such places.

Poisoning Fish

The extreme lows of moon tides (those with the lowest ebb occurring at daybreak) are best for poisoning fish. Fish are most active on the incoming tide.

To prepare fish poison, crush the ripe, fallen seeds of barringtonia and allow them to stand overnight. Seashells burned in a fire can also be used. Place these in coarse sacks or nets and drag through the water of the tide pools. The poison stupefies the fish, and they can be caught as they rise to the surface. However, many will hide out in crevices and must be pulled out by hand.

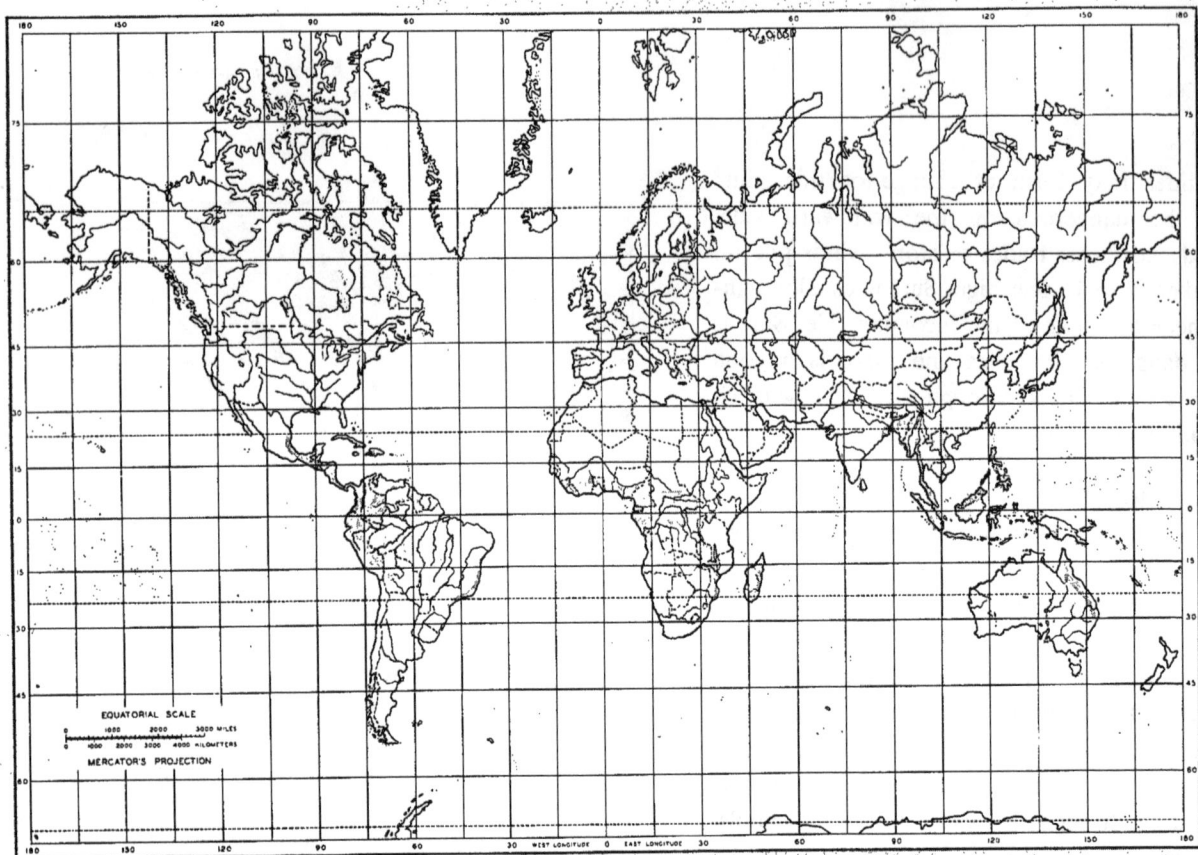

TROPICAL RAIN FOREST

EDIBLE PLANTS OF TROPICAL AREAS

Plant foods of the Tropics will be found in four general vegetation areas — the tropical rain forests, the tropical semievergreen seasonal forests, the scrub and thorn forests, and the savanna. These areas are discussed in the sections which follow.

> *Portions of this introductory material on the tropical rain forest are based on pages 2-12 of *The Tropical Rain Forest*, P. W. Richards, 1952. Permission granted by the publishers, Cambridge University Press, New York.

The jungle in America, Asia, and Africa is more correctly called tropical rain forest. The tropical rain forest forms a belt around the entire globe, bisected somewhat equally by the equator, so that more rain forest lies in the Northern Hemisphere than in the Southern Hemisphere. Actually, the tropical rain forest belt, as shown on the map, is not a continuous one, even in any of the various regions in which it occurs. Usually it is broken by moun-

tain ranges, plateaus, and even by small semidesert areas, according to the irregular pattern of climate which regulates the actual distribution of rain forest.

Some of the leading characteristics of the tropical rain forest common to these areas in America, Asia, and in Africa, are as follows:

a. Vegetation consists of five stories.

b. High rainfall (100 inches or more) distributed more or less equally throughout the year.

c. Areas of occurrence lie between 20° N. and 20° S. latitude.

d. Evergreen trees predominate, many of large girth (10 feet in diameter) with thick leathery leaves.

e. Vines (lianas) and air plants (epiphytes) are abundant.

f. Herbs, grasses, and bushes rare in understory.

g. Uniformity in aspect wherever rain forest is well developed.

h. Tree bark thin, green, smooth and usually lacking fissures.

252

The overwhelming majority of plants that grow in the forest of the rainy tropics are woody and of the dimensions of trees. The vines and air plants that grow on the trunks and branches of trees are woody. Grasses and herbs, which are common in the temperate woods of the United States, are rare in the tropical rain forest. Trees form the principal elements of the vegetation in the rain forest. The undergrowth consists of woody plants — seedling and sapling trees, shrubs, and young woody climbers. All of the plants grow very large. The bamboos, which are really giant grasses, (see illustration p. 276), grow to giant proportions, 40-80 feet high in some cases. Bamboo thickets in parts of some rain forests are impenetrable.

The variety of trees and other plants in the rain forest is great. There are wide variations in size. It is rare, indeed, to find in the rain forest stands of trees which consist of but one or a few kinds, such as exist in the coniferous forest belt of America and Europe. The plants that produce edible parts in the jungle are often scattered, and searching to find several of the same kind will be a part of the survivor's activities.

Jungle trees are never as large, however, as the giant redwoods of California nor as tall as the eucalyptus of Australia. The average height of the taller trees in the rain forest is rarely more than 150-180 feet. Occasionally, venerable giants of the tropical rain forest attain 300 feet in height, but this is extremely rare. Trees more than 10 feet in diameter are also rare in the jungle, but scattered ones of this size may occur. The trunks are, as a rule, straight and slender and do not branch until

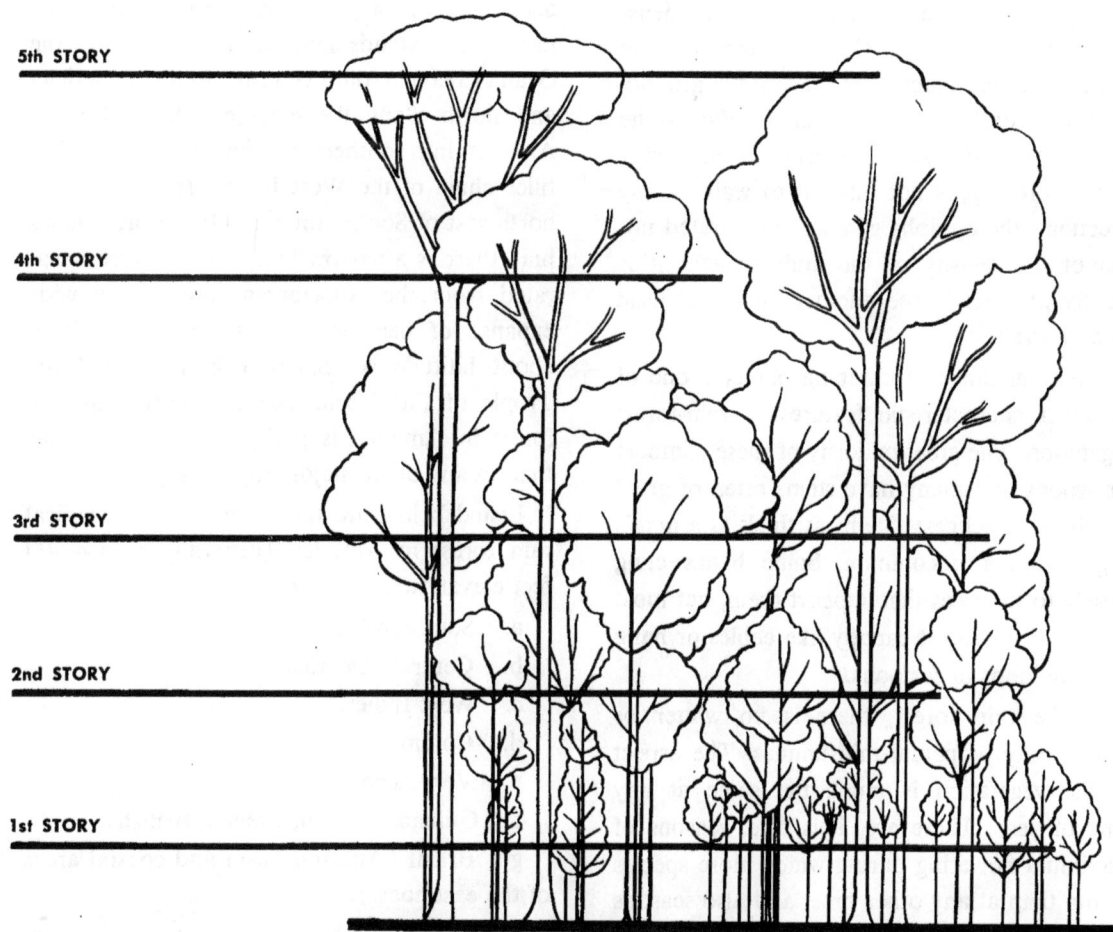

Five stories of tropical rain forest vegetation

near the top. The base of many trees is provided with plank buttresses, flangelike outgrowths which are common in all tropical forests. The bark of tropical trees generally is thin and smooth and rarely has deep fissures.

The greatest majority of mature tropical trees have large, leathery, dark-green leaves which resemble laurel leaves in size, shape, and texture. The foliage is so uniform that the casual observer might easily be excused for supposing that the forest was predominantly composed of species of laurel. The general aspect is monotonous, and large and strikingly colored flowers are uncommon. Most of the trees and shrubs have inconspicuous, often greenish or whitish, flowers.

The undergrowth of the rain forest consists of shrubs, herbaceous plants, and vast numbers of sapling and seedling trees. Travel books often give a misleading impression of the density of tropical forests. On river banks or in clearings, where much light reaches the ground, there is a dense growth which is often quite impenetrable. But in the interior of old undisturbed forest, it is not difficult to walk in any direction. Photographs give an exaggerated notion of the density of the undergrowth; it is usually possible to see another person at least 60 feet away.

The abundance of climbing plants is one of the most characteristic features of rain-forest vegetation. The great majority of these climbers are woody and many have stems often of great length and thickness. Stems as thick as a man's thigh are not uncommon. Some lianas cling closely to the trees that support them, but most ascend to the forest canopy like cables or hang down in loops or festoons.

In the rain forest, there is no winter or spring, only perpetual midsummer. The aspect of the vegetation is much the same at any time of year. There are, it is true, seasons of maximum flowering during which more species bloom than at any other time, and also seasons of maximum production of young leaves. But, for the most part, plant growth and reproduction are continuous and some flowers can be found at any time.

The marginal area of a tropical rain forest, clearings, and areas around abandoned dwellings abound in edible plants. However, in the center of the virgin rain forest, foraging for food will not be easy; at least, the kinds of food plants easily obtained will not be abundant. The lofty trees will be so tall that fruits and nuts will generally be out of reach.

Distribution of Tropical Rain Forest in America

The largest continuous mass of rain forest is found in the New World, in the basin of the Amazon River. This extends west to the lower slopes of the Andes and east to the Atlantic coast of the continent; it is broken only by relatively small areas of savanna and deciduous forest. This great South American rain forest extends south into the region of the Gran Chaco (south-central South America) and north along the eastern side of Central America into southern Mexico and into the Antilles chain of the West Indies. In the extreme northwest of South America (Ecuador, Colombia) there is a narrow belt of rain forest, separated from the Amazonian forest by a wide expanse of deciduous forest, extending from about latitude 6° S. to a little beyond the Tropic of Capricorn. The distribution of rain forest in America is perhaps less well known than in any other major tropical region.

Listed below are the main areas of tropical rain forest in America (generally below 500 feet elevation).

a.   Southern Mexico.

b.   Central America.

c.   West Indies.

d.   Colombia.

e.   Venezuela.

f.   Guianas (Dutch, French, British).

g.   Brazil (Amazon basin and coastal areas of the east coast).

h.   Ecuador.

i.   Peru (eastern slopes of Andes).

© Vegetationsbilder

Rain forest in Southern Mexico

Rain forest in Costa Rica

© Vegetationsbilder

Distribution of Tropical Rain Forest in Africa

In Africa, the largest area of rain forest lies in the Congo basin and extends westward into French Equatorial Africa and the Cameroons.

As a narrow strip the forest continues still farther west, parallel to the coast of the Gulf of Guinea, through Nigeria and the Gold Coast to Liberia and French Guinea. Southward from the Congo basin the forest extends toward Rhodesia.

Tropical rain forest, East Africa

© Vegetationsbilder

© Vegetationsbilder

Togo rain forest, West Africa

Tropical rain forest, Central Africa

© Vegetationsbilder

Distribution of Indo-Malayan Rain Forest of Southeastern Asia, Indonesia, New Guinea, and Australia

In the eastern Tropics, the rain forest extends from Ceylon and western India to Thailand, Indochina, and the Philippines, as well as through the Malay Archipelago to New Guinea. The largest continuous areas are in New Guinea, the Malay Peninsula, and the adjoining islands of Sumatra and Borneo, where the Indo-Malayan rain forest reaches its greatest luxuriance and floral wealth.

In India the area of rain forest is not large, but it is found locally in the western and eastern Ghats (coastal ranges) and, more extensively, in the lower part of the eastern Himalaya, th Khasia hills and Assam.

In Burma, Siam, and Indochina, the rain forest is developed only locally, the principal vegetation being the monsoon forest. The monsoon forest is a tropical type which is partly leafless at certain seasons (see p. 268).

In the eastern Sunda Islands from western Java to New Guinea the seasonal drought (due to the dry east monsoon from Australia) is too severe for the development of rain forest, except in locally favorable situations.

In Australia the tropical rain forest of Indo-Malaya is continued south as a narrow strip along the eastern coast of Queensland. Rain forest also extends into the islands of the western Pacific (Solomons, New Hebrides, Fiji, Samoa, etc.)

●　　●　　●

Food Plants

Some of the food plants in the rain forest are also found in other regions. The following plants in this category are described on the pages indicated.

Bael fruit (p. 307).
Cashew nut (p. 295).
Sweet sop (p. 279).
Bignay (p. 304).
Sugar palm (p. 292).
Breadfruit (p. 296).
Jew's ear fungus (p. 48).
Bamboo (p. 276).
Ceylon spinach (p. 300).
Rattan palm (p. 303).
Canna lily (p. 281).
Papaya (p. 275).
Fishtail plum (p. 293).
Water fern (p. 271).
Taro (p. 313).
Ti plant (p. 290).
Buri palm (p. 294).
Nut grass (p. 312).
Tropical yam (p. 277).
Roseapple (p. 306).
Ferns (p. 83).
Wild fig (p. 284).
Rice (p. 285).
Pearl millet (p. 286).
Italian millet (p. 287).
Wild gourd (p. 308).
Mango (p. 282).
Manioc (p. 309).
Horse-radish tree (p. 289).
Mulberry (p. 64).
Bananas and plantains (p. 274).
Lotus lily (p. 310).
Water lily (p. 270).
Yam bean (p. 291).
Screw pine (p. 298).
Pokeweed (p. 269).
Purslane (p. 311).
Goa bean (p. 301).
Oak (p. 69).
Sugarcane (p. 280).
Sterculia (p. 283).
East Indian arrowroot (p. 287).
Tamarind (p. 305).
Indian or tropical almond (p. 288).
Trapa nut, water chestnut (p. 65).
Cattail (p. 58).
Wild grape (p. 63).

●　　●　　●

Those food plants found only in the rain forest are described in the paragraphs which follow.

© Vegetationsbilder

Tropical rain forest in Queensland

Tropical rain forest in Samoa

© Vegetationsbilder

Tropical forest in Malaya

© Vegetationsbilder

Coconut (Cocos nucifera)

WHERE FOUND. (Region 1.) The coconut palm is widely cultivated although it grows spontaneously throughout much of the moist Tropics, especially on the east coast of Africa, tropical America, Asia, and the South Pacific islands. It grows mainly near the seashore, but sometimes the coconut palm will grow for some distance inland. It does not abound along desert coasts, which applies mainly to the west coast of continental areas.

APPEARANCE. The coconut palm is usually unbranched and towering in mature specimens to 90 feet high. The trunk is columnar, straight or bowed outward from the base. The flowers are produced at the top in large whitish plumes. The nuts are produced in large clusters which hang downward among the leaves.

WHAT TO EAT.

Cabbage. Coconut cabbage can be eaten cooked or raw. This is the snow-white heart at the top of the tree. The cooked cabbage can be mixed with other wild vegetables.

Nuts. The various stages in the development of the nut and their uses are:

a. Very young —— small, no use.

b. Young — larger size with edible husk at stalk end.

c. Drinking stage — flesh soft (this stage produces much food).

d. Flesh — fluid stage.

e. Flesh — fluid not used for drinking.

f. Flesh — fluid all absorbed.

g. Mature nut, brown husk, thick hard flesh — for grating.

h. Sprouting nut — spongy material fills cavity. Eaten raw or cooked.

The two most useful stages are the drinking stage and the mature stage.

260

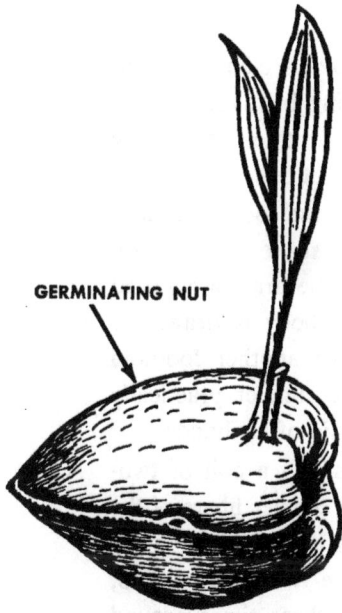

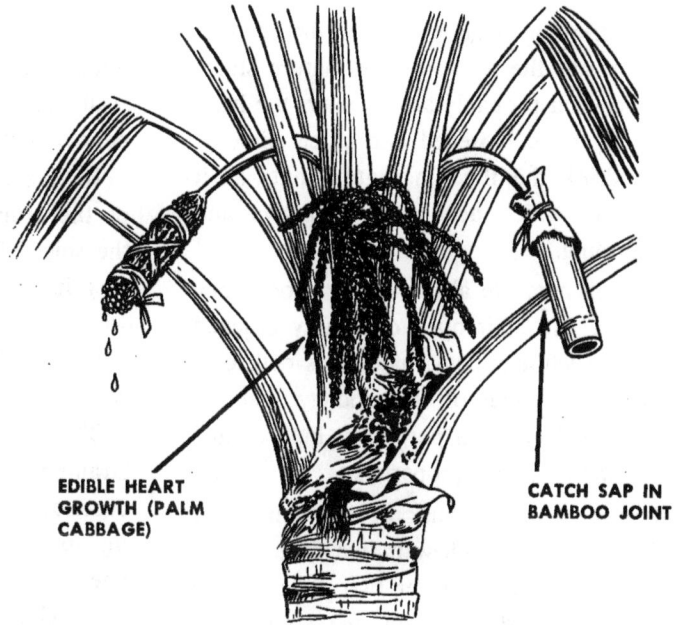

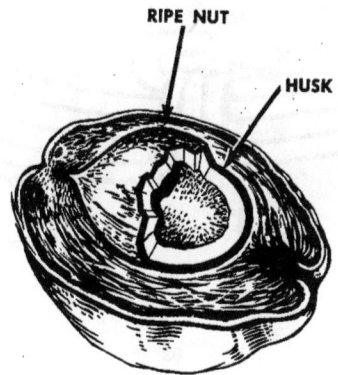

GERMINATING NUT

EDIBLE HEART
GROWTH (PALM
CABBAGE)

CATCH SAP IN
BAMBOO JOINT

RIPE NUT

HUSK

Coconut

In the drinking stage, split open the coconut and scoop out the meat. In the mature stage, with which you probably are familiar, the hard nut meat can be loosened and eaten directly. Do not drink the fluid in mature nuts as it contains oil which acts as a purgative and causes griping.

Sprouting nuts are also used for food. They are husked and split open or simply cracked in two. The white spongy material is delicious. However, too much of this spongy material eaten raw will act as a purgative, but cooking removes the purgative properties.

All or part of the husk of the young nut may be sweet; if so, chew it like cane. Drink the milk from the nut. Over two pints of cool fluid may be produced from one young nut, especially in the jelly stage when the flesh is soft. A ripe nut will gurgle when shaken near your ear. Do not drink from very young or too old nuts.

Fallen nuts germinate where they lie. In these, both milk and meat are used up, but the cavity is filled with a spongy mass, called the bread. Eat this raw or toasted in a shell over the fire. It tastes good and is very sustaining. Eat the sprouts like celery.

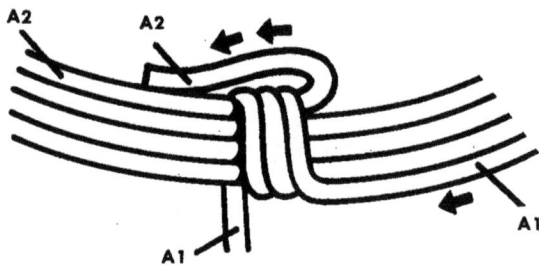

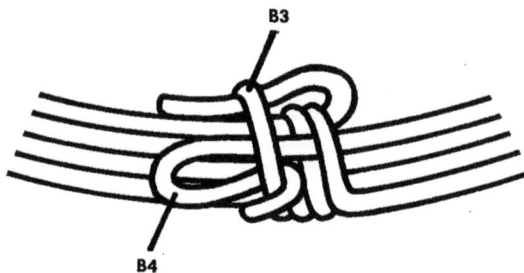

Coconut climbing loop

COCONUT CLIMBING LOOP. A climbing loop, often referred to as climbing bandage, is generally used to scale coconut trees, but many people climb the trees without one.

In tree climbing without the loop, the sides of the trunk are gripped, so to speak, with the soles of the bare feet, the arms are raised to grip the trunk, and the body is drawn up with the knees bent to take another foothold higher up. In this way, the climber practically walks up the tree with the aid of his hands.

The climbing loop is usually a coil of two-strand cord made from the coarser fibers of the coconut husk. Following is a method for making such a loop: Where the two ends overlap, one end (A1) is wrapped three times around the coil including the doubled-back end, and second end is doubled back over the turns, the wrapping end takes another turn (B3) around the coil including the double-back end, and finished with an overhand knot (B4) on itself with a loop.

Loops may also be made of cords of wild hibiscus bark or breadfruit bark fiber (in the southwest Pacific) or any other suitable tough fiber. The loop should be of such size that when the feet are in, it will encircle slightly less than half the circumference of the palm trunk near the base.

In using the loop, pass the coil around both feet keeping them apart to hold the loop taut. Grasp the tree trunk with upstretched hands, draw your body upward with bent knees, and press the taut loop against the tree trunk. Coconut palms have rough rings made by the leaves in successive years, and the coil holds against the rough bark. With a firm hold for your feet, straighten the knees and grasp the trunk higher up with your hands. Repeat these movements until the top is reached.

Take the coconuts by the free end and then twist to break the stalk. Hold the nut by the same end, and then twist it on release. The twist gives the nut a spin, causing it to land on its pointed end, which prevents it from splitting and wasting the drinking fluid. For mature nuts, the spin is not necessary.

When there is a bunch of drinking nuts attached to the one main stalk, the whole bunch may be brought down together. If you intend to do this, carry a rope made of the same material as the climbing loop, and tie one end around the stalk. Lower the bunch after severing the stalk with a knife. If you have no knife, tie the rope to the bunch and let someone on the ground pull the bunch loose. To husk the nuts, a husking stick is required.

HUSKING STICK. The husking stick should be made of a hard wood. Cut off a piece about 3-1/2 feet long from a branch about 1-1/2 to 2 inches in diameter. Trim lower end to a rounded point for sticking into the ground, but cut the upper end on a long slant from one side so that the point will penetrate more readily between the husk fibers. Drive the stick into the ground, and slant it slightly away from you.

Hold the coconut horizontally by the two ends and drive it down on the husking point so that the stick penetrates the husk on the far side of the nut. (Experience teaches the amount of husk to penetrate without striking the nut.) Then force the coconut downward and lever it toward yourself so as to pry off a portion of the husk. Turn the nut until all of the outer segments, of which there are three, are removed. A knob of husk which usually remains attached to the shell can be knocked off by jabbing it against the husking point, except on drinking nuts.

Another method of removing the husk segments is to penetrate the husk with the stick on the near side of the nut. The segments can be pried off by outward pressure, or away from the body. Either way is equally effective.

COCONUT OIL. Coconut oil is a good preventive for sunburn as well as an aid in keeping off chiggers and other insects. It can be used also for cooking. Coconut oil can be rendered by exposing the meat of the coconut to the sun or to the heat over a slow fire. The oil will run more quickly if the meat is pounded or grated (with a jagged shell or piece of coral) before placing it in the sun or over the fire.

Another method for extracting the oil is to boil the coconut meat in a container of water (section of bamboo will do). When the mixture cools, the oil will rise to the top.

The natives of Oceania have discovered that coconut oil is a good preventive of salt water sores and bloating. Before going fishing on the reef, they smear their legs and feet with this oil, which keep their skin in good condition even though they stand in salt water for many hours.

Husking coconuts

REDDISH
EDIBLE FRUIT
1 IN. IN DIAMETER

FRUITING
BRANCH

15-45 FT. TALL

FRUIT IN SECTION

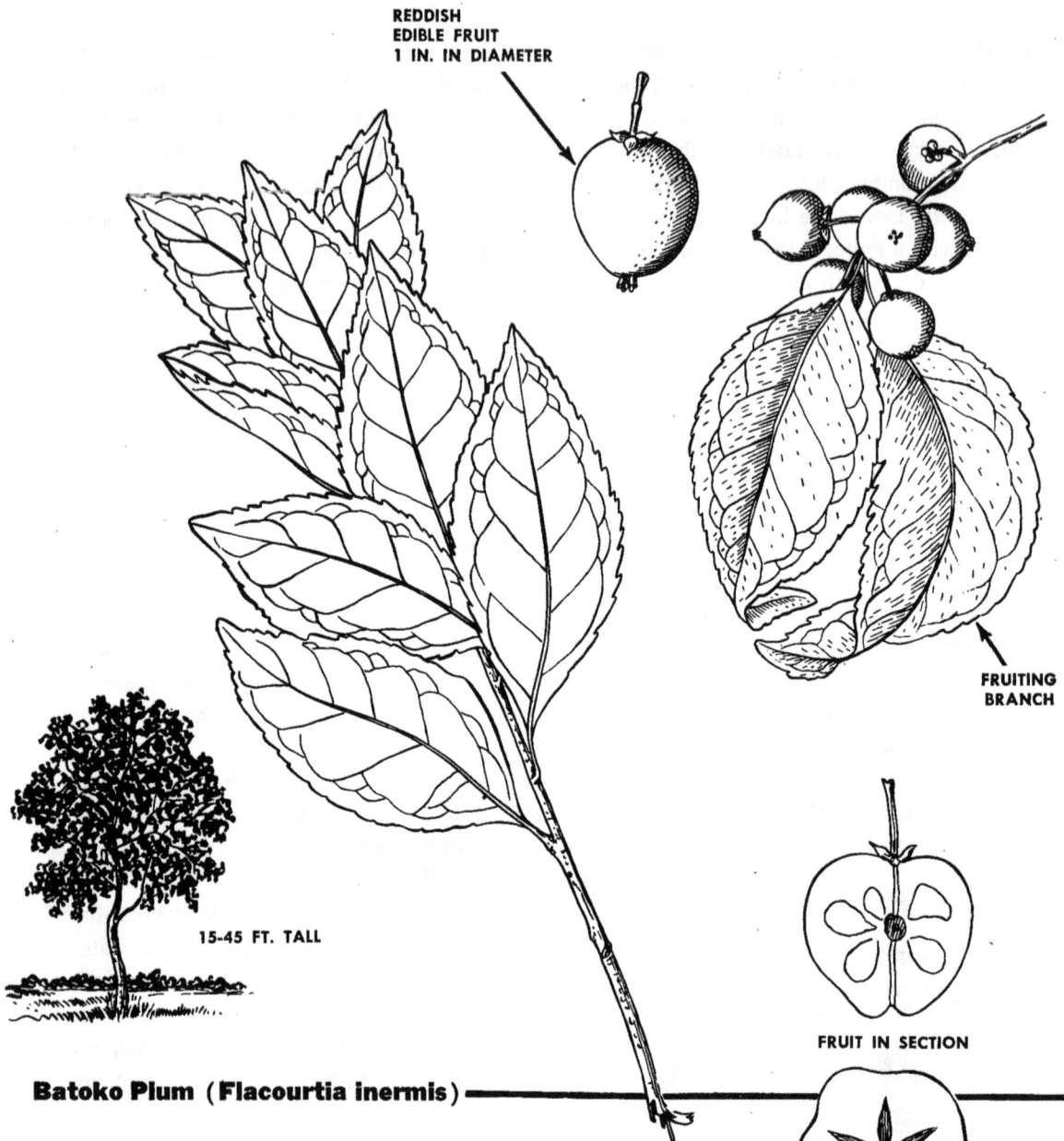

Batoko Plum (Flacourtia inermis)

WHERE FOUND. The batoko plum illustrated here is a representative example of one kind of batoko plum (about 15-20 kinds are known). This group of fruit trees is widely distributed in Africa and Asia, mostly in clearings and the edges of forests in the rainy tropical areas. The kind here shown is native of Indonesia, where it is widely cultivated and has escaped in a semiwild state.

APPEARANCE. The batoko plum is a rather low, spineless tree, 15-45 feet tall. The fruit resembles a small apple, 2-4 inches in diameter and dark red when ripe, and can be either very sour or sweet. There are many varieties.

WHAT TO EAT. The fruit may be eaten raw or cooked. All kinds are eaten by native peoples in the regions where they grow.

SMOOTH-STEMMED SAGO
(30 FT.)

SPINY-STEMMED
SAGO

EDIBLE NUTS

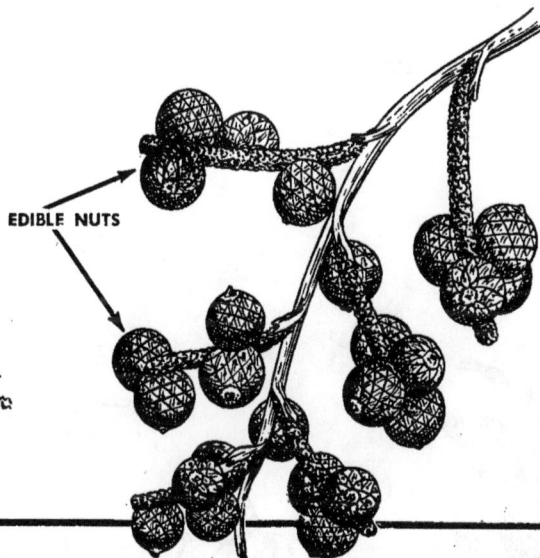

Sago Palm (Metroxylon sagu)

WHERE FOUND. (Region 1.) The sago palm flourishes in damp lowlands in the Malay Peninsula, New Guinea, Indonesia, the Philippines, and adjacent islands. It occurs mainly in shore swamps, along streams, lakes, and rivers.

APPEARANCE. These palms are low trees, rarely over 30 feet in height, with a stout spiny trunk. The outer rind is about 2 inches thick and hard as bamboo. The rind incloses a spongy inner pith containing a high proportion of starch.

WHAT TO EAT. These palms, when available, will be of great use to the survivor. One trunk, cut just previous to flowering time, will yield

600 pounds of sago, enough for a man for 1 year. Sago has an especially high starch content.

Obtain sago starch from *nonflowering* sago palms.

To extract the edible sago, cut away the bark lengthwise from one-half the trunk, and pound the soft, whitish inner parts as fine as possible. Knead this in water and strain through a coarse cloth. The coarse clothlike fiber at the base of the palm leaves may be used for this. The escaping water will carry the edible starch into a container which may be a wooden trough hewn from the empty sago palm trunk. The fine, white sago will soon settle out. Pour off the water after one or two more washings. The sago is now ready for use. Knead the remaining water from the sago and roll the material into balls and dry over a fire or else in the sun. After this it may be wrapped in palm leaves and kept indefinitely.

Sago meal is nutritious and easy to digest. The natives have two methods of cooking it: as a gruel and as pancakes. Sago gruel is made by adding boiling water to a lump of flour and stirring it in a pot over the fire until the whole is a uniform, thick consistency. The natives then dip out spoonfuls of the gruel onto leaves and allow it to cool. When cool, it is a gelatinous cake which may be eaten at once or kept for several days. Natives usually carry these cakes with them when they go on trips.

In New Guinea, small quantities of meal are roasted in stick form after being wrapped in young nipa palm leaves (see p. 267). Sago may also be fried, in which case it is palatable and very filling. Another method of preparing sago is to powder it finely, then pour boiling water over it. It turns to jelly and, with the addition of sweetening, makes an acceptable pudding.

The core of the upper part of the trunk does not yield sago, but it may be roasted in lumps over an open fire.

Two pounds a day of sago is the equivalent of a pound and a half of rice, or seven pounds of yams or taro.

Young sago nuts are edible.

The growing shoots or palm cabbage may also be eaten.

Extracting sago from split trunk

LEAVES 20 FT. LONG

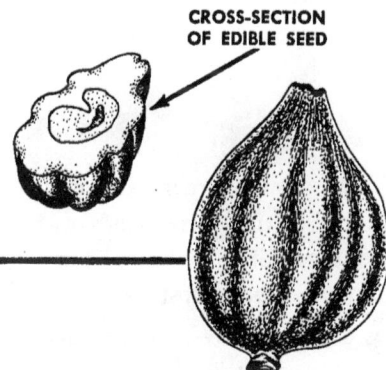

SEED HEAD

SEVER STALK —
COLLECT SWEET
SAP HERE

CROSS-SECTION
OF EDIBLE SEED

Nipa Palm (Nipa fruticans)

WHERE FOUND. (Region 1.) The nipa palm occurs only along tidal streams and bordering mangrove swamps within the influence of brackish or salt water from India, Malaya, to the Philippines and Australia. In favorable habitats it sometimes covers hundreds of acres.

APPEARANCE. The 20-foot leaves of the nipa palm rise from the mud in which the plant grows, and the stem or trunk is a creeping woody extension which grows along the surface of the mud. The base of each leaf is considerably swollen. The erect stalk, which produces the flowering head rises among the palm leaves. The fruiting head which is produced becomes a foot in diameter and is dark brown.

WHAT TO EAT. To obtain sweet sap for drinking purposes, find a curved stalk carrying the young fruiting head. Bruise the stalk with a wooden club. Above the part bruised, cut through the stalk and attach a bamboo joint or similar vessel to catch the juice which runs out the cut end.

The seeds and cabbage of this palm are also edible.

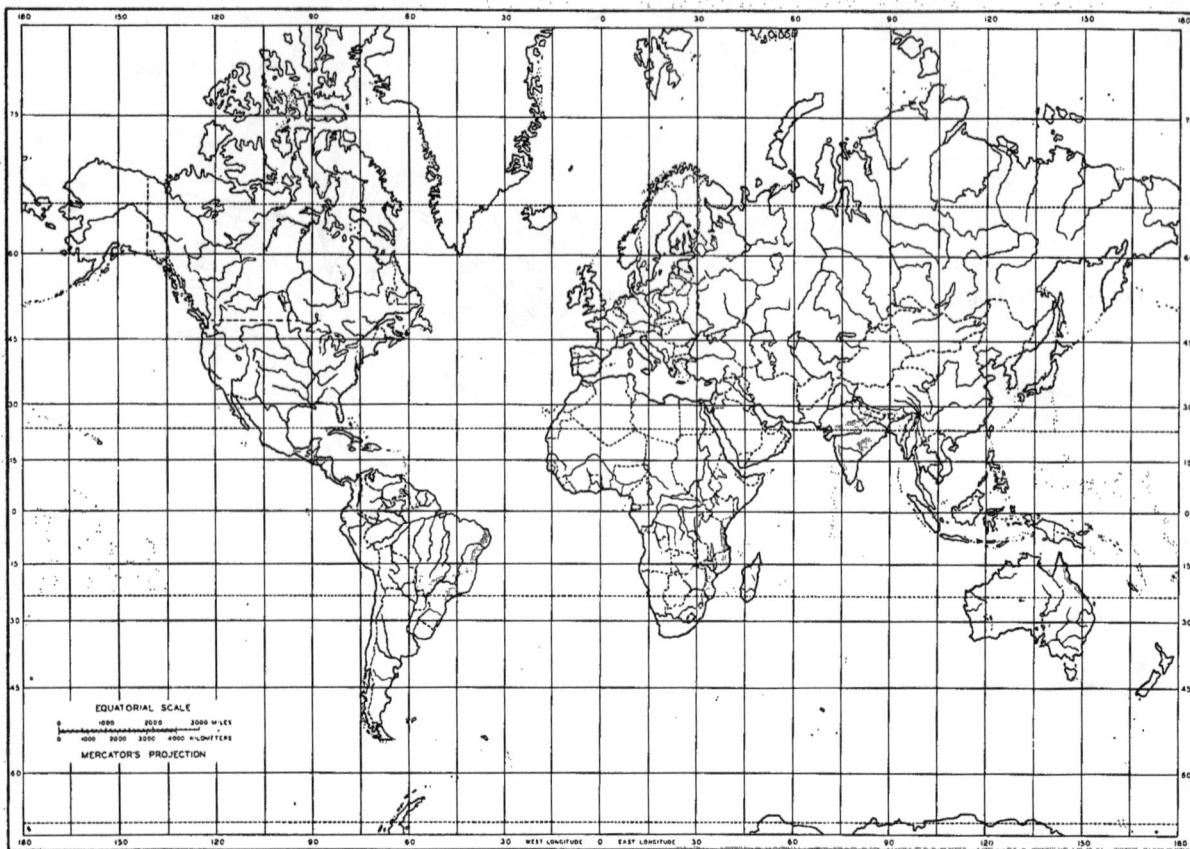

SEMIEVERGREEN SEASONAL FOREST

In character, the semievergreen seasonal forest in America and Africa corresponds essentially to the monsoon forest of Asia. Characteristics of the semievergreen forest are:

a.   Two stories of tree strata — upper story 60-80 feet high, lower story 20-45 feet high (tree strata five-storied in tropical rain forest).

b.   Large trees rare, average diameter about 2 feet.

c.   Seasonal drought causes leaf fall; more in dry than wet years.

The peculiar distribution of the rainy season and the dry season which occurs in the countries bordering the Bay of Bengal in southeastern Asia brings on the monsoon climate. The monsoons of India, Burma, Siam, and Indochina are of two types. The *dry monsoon* occurs from November to April, when the dry northern winds from central Asia bring long periods of clear weather with only intermittent rain. The *wet monsoon* occurs from May to October, when the southern winds from the Bay of Bengal bring rain usually in torrents that last for days and often weeks at a time. During the dry season, most leaves drop completely off, giving the landscape a wintry appearance, but as soon as the monsoon rains begin the foliage reappears immediately.

• • •

Areas of the world having tropical semievergreen and monsoon forests are as follows:

a.   *America.* Portions of Colombia, Venezuela and Amazon basin.

b.   *Africa.* Portions of southeast coastal Kenya, Tanganyika, and Mozambique.

c.   *Asia.* Northeastern India, much of Burma, Siam, Indochina, Java, and parts of other Indonesian Islands.

POISONOUS ROOTS

TO 12 FT. TALL

COOK YOUNG LEAVES
(NON-POISONOUS)

PURPLE-BLACK
RIPE BERRIES
(NON-POISONOUS)

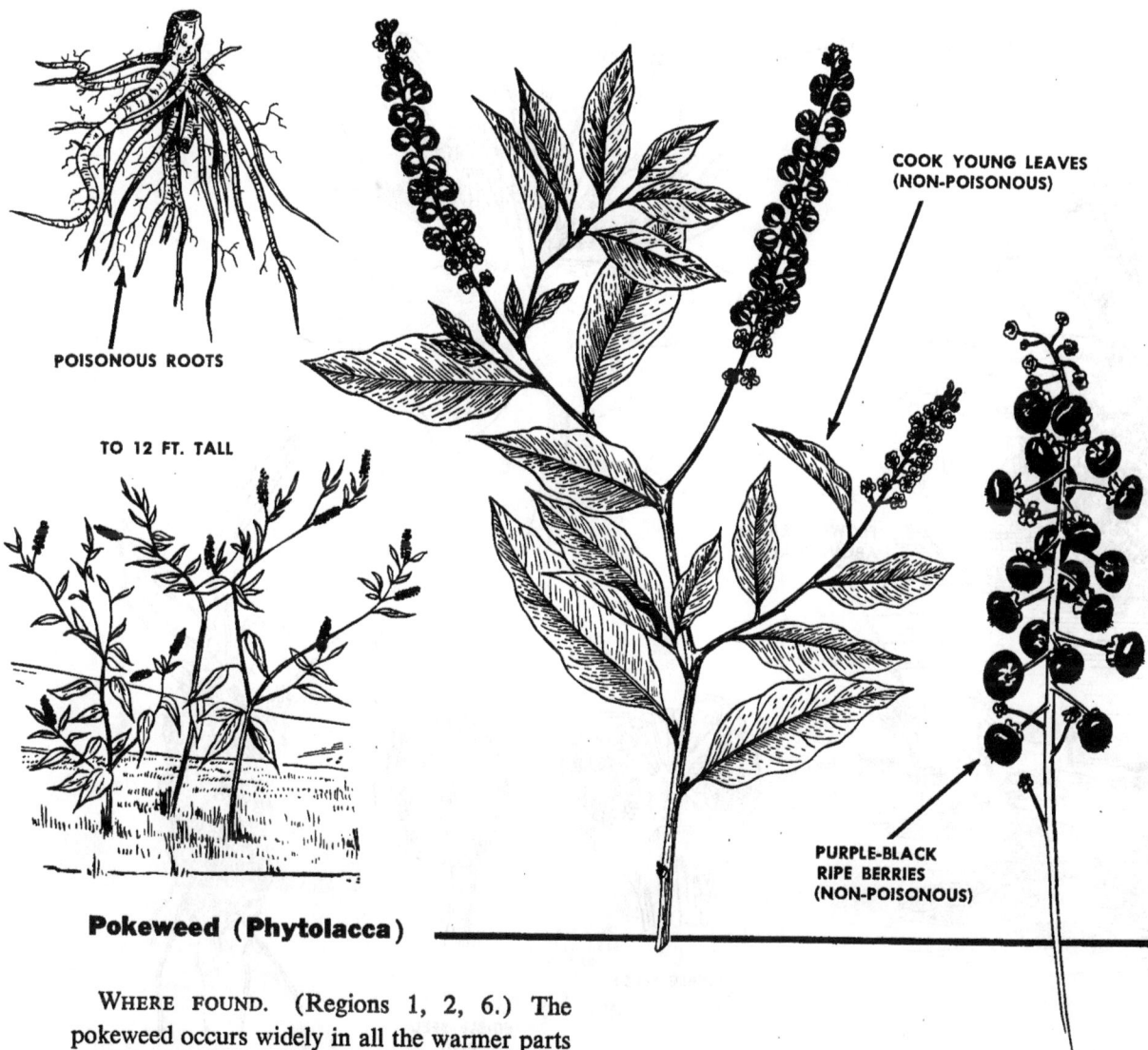

Pokeweed (Phytolacca)

WHERE FOUND. (Regions 1, 2, 6.) The pokeweed occurs widely in all the warmer parts of the tropical and temperate zones. The pokeweed which is common in the eastern United States is common also in Asia, Africa, Australia, and Micronesia. It is most often found on dumps, along roadsides, ditches, fencerows, hedges and vineyards. It is also found in ravines, bottomland, woods, and along river banks but almost never in deep forest.

APPEARANCE. The pokeweed is a large, coarse, perennial herb up to 13 feet high. The whole plant, especially while young, is tender and quite succulent. The branches are green, magenta, or purple. The leaves are 4-12 inches long. The flowering and fruiting spikes usually droop, and the flowers are followed by deep reddish purple berries.

WHAT TO EAT. The tender young shoots and leaves of poke can be eaten as a cooked vegetable.

The juicy berries are bitter and may be toxic when raw, but they are palatable when cooked.

CAUTION

The roots are poisonous at all times.

VARICOLORED PETALS

FLOWERS RAISED
ABOVE WATER

EDIBLE ROOTSTALK

EDIBLE SEEDS

EDIBLE SEED
POD

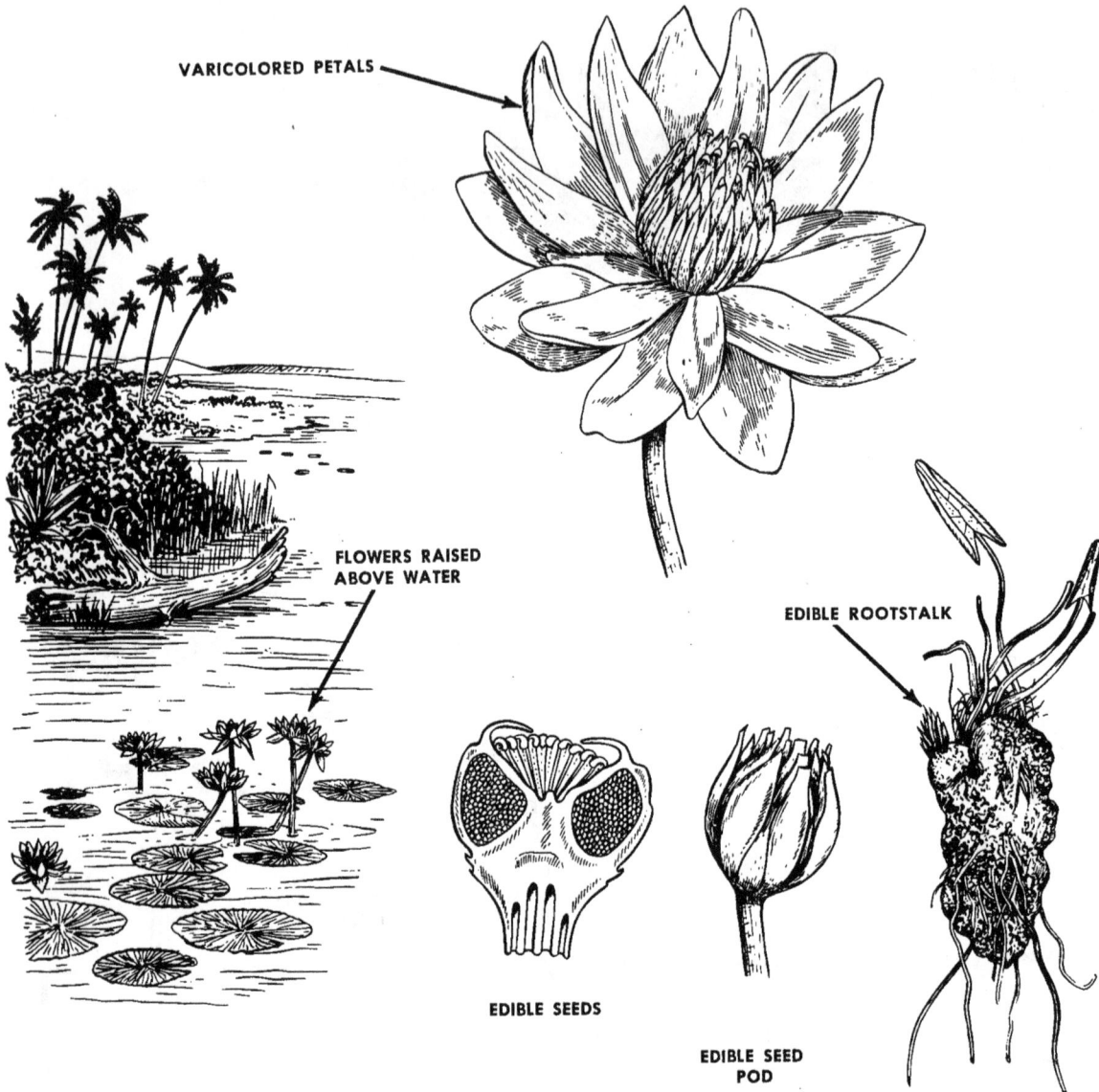

Water Lily (Nymphaea)

WHERE FOUND. (Regions 1, 2, 3, 4.) Tropical water lilies grow in lakes, rivers, and streams in tropical Africa, India, and South America.

APPEARANCE. Tropical water lilies have heart-shaped floating leaves, 6-15 inches in diameter, and red, white, blue, or yellow flowers which are elevated above the water surface. Large, edible, potatolike tubers are produced in the mud by the growing plant.

WHAT TO EAT. The edible rootstalks or tubers may be difficult to obtain because of deep water in the rainy season, but roots are starchy and full of nourishing food. They may be eaten either raw or boiled. Only one wild South African water lily is suspected of having poisonous properties; all others are perfectly safe.

The stems may be cooked in a stew, and the young seed pods may be sliced and eaten as a vegetable. The seeds are bitter, but they are very nourishing; they may be parched and rubbed between stones to produce flour. The water lily is considered an important food article by native peoples in many parts of the world.

EDIBLE FIDDLEHEADS

TREE FERN
(10-50 FT. TALL)

BRACKEN

BRACKEN
(1-6 FT.)

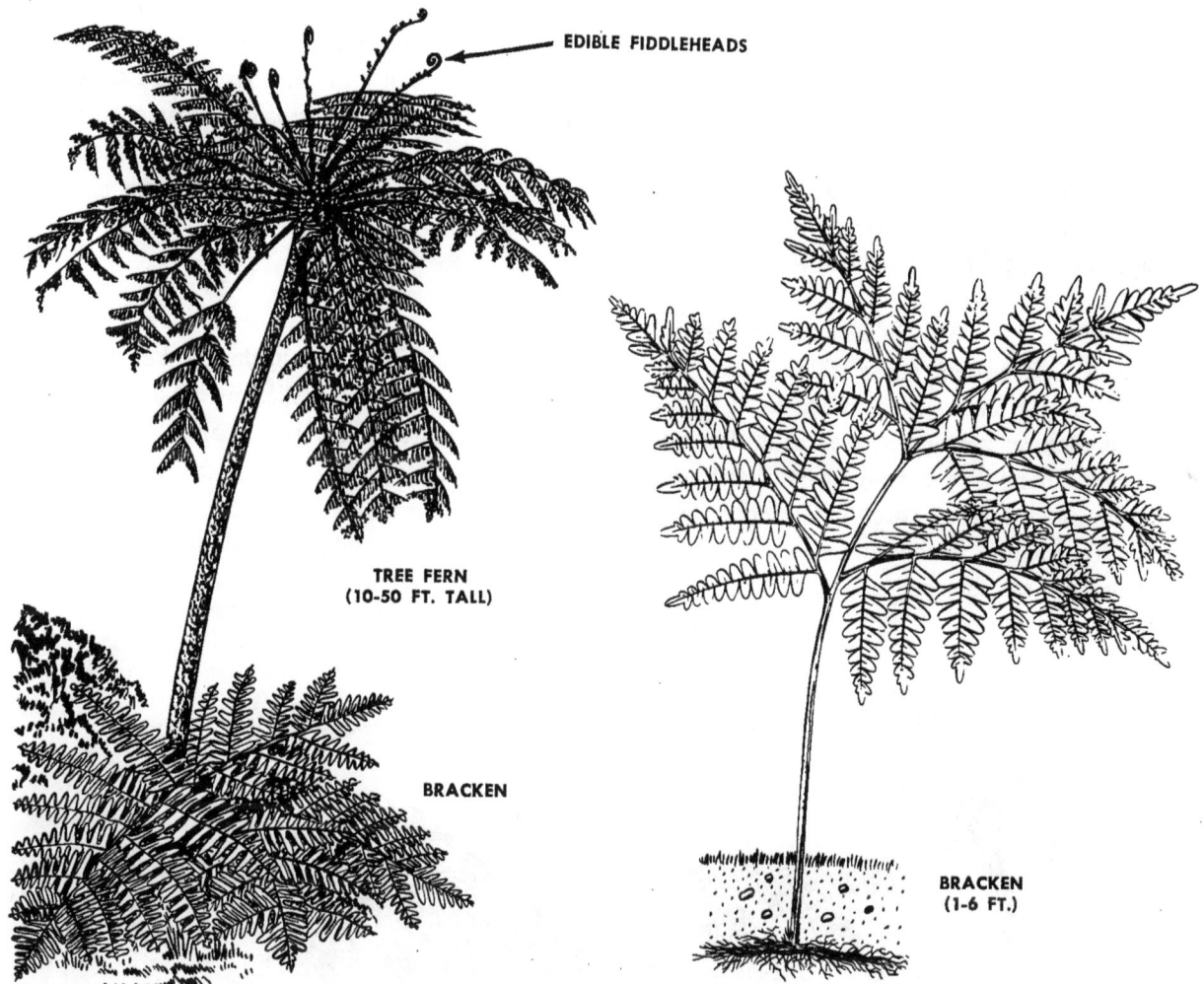

Edible Ferns (Tree fern, bracken, polypody)

WHERE FOUND. (Regions 1, 2, 6, 7, 12.) In the moist regions of all countries, especially in forested regions, gullies, along streams, and on the edge of woods, ferns are very abundant. Ferns are common throughout the tropical parts of Africa, Asia, Australia and America (both North and South).

APPEARANCE. Fern plants might easily be mistaken for flowering plants, especially with the relatives of the wild parsnip, the water hemlock (see illustration p. 172), and the wild carrot. However, with a little care and observation, the survivor can easily distinguish ferns from all other kinds of green plants. In ferns, the underneath surface of the leaves is usually covered with masses of brown dots, which themselves are covered with yellow, brown, or black dust. These dots are actually filled with spores (spores are produced in ferns instead of seeds), and the presence of these spore structures easily distinguishes ferns from plants with flowers.

The *pasture brake,* or bracken, is one of the most widely distributed ferns. It occurs in every continent in open dry woods, recently burned clearings and pastures, from the subarctic to the Tropics. It is a coarse fern with solitary or scattered young stalks often 1/2-inch thick at the base, nearly cylindrical and covered with rusty felt; the uncoiling frond (fiddlehead) is distinctly 3-forked, usually with a purplish spot at the angles which secretes a sweetish juice; old fronds conspicuously 3-forked; rootstock extensively creeping and branching, blackish and almost woody, about 1/4 inch thick.

WHAT TO EAT. This information applies to all ferns. Select young stalks (fiddleheads) not more than 6-8 inches high. Break them off as low as they remain tender, then draw through the closed hand to remove the wool. Wash and boil in salted water or steam until tender (usually 30 minutes to an hour). If available, season with salt and pepper and add an edible oil, e.g., coconut oil.

The raw stalks have a very sticky juice. The juice is somewhat altered in cooking, but the boiled vegetable retains some of the sticky quality. Because of this, the pasture brake is not attractive to some tastes, but most people who have tried it properly prepared have found it palatable. As a survival food it should not be overlooked.

CAUTION

No one who is not certain that he knows a true fern from other delicately cut leaves should venture to eat the smaller kinds of ferns. Many plants, such as the notorious poison hemlock (see illustration p. 172) which is deadly poison, have delicately cut leaves which look something like ferns.

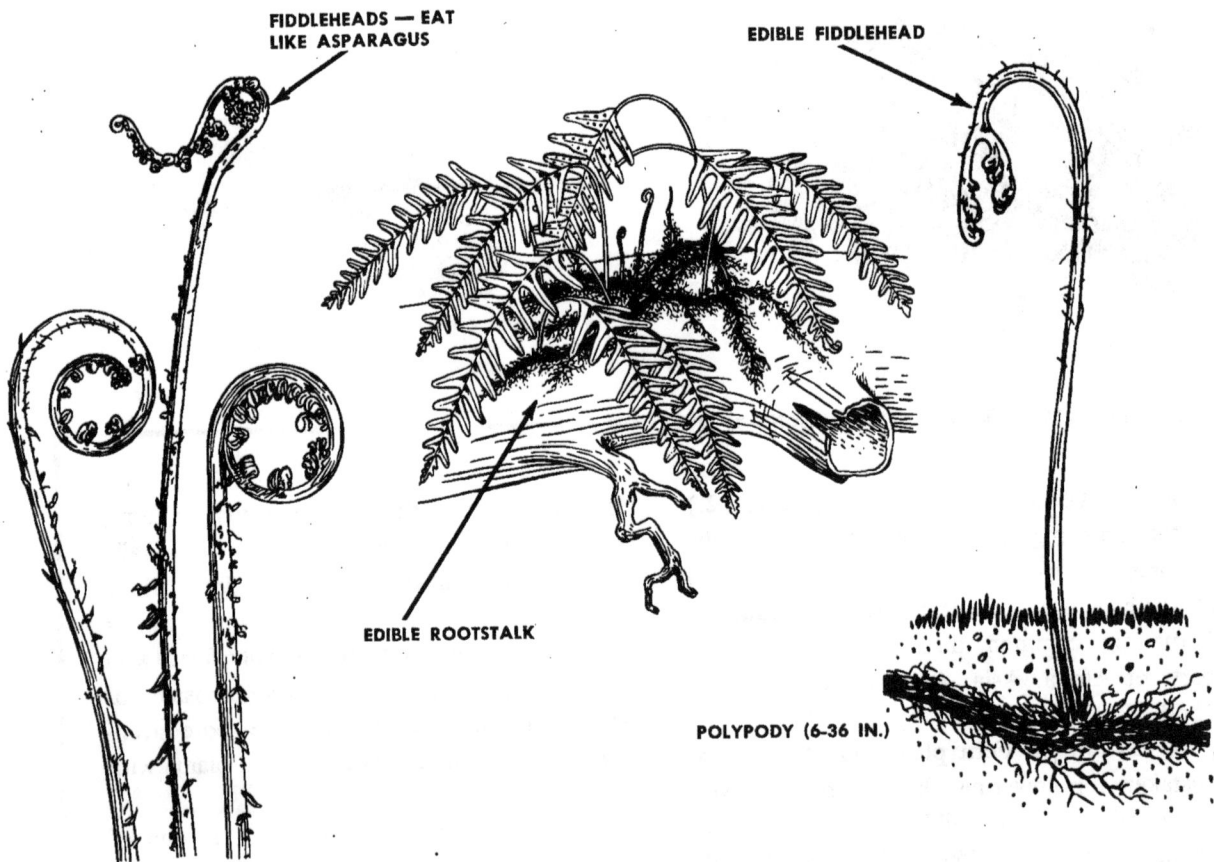

FIDDLEHEADS — EAT LIKE ASPARAGUS

EDIBLE FIDDLEHEAD

EDIBLE ROOTSTALK

POLYPODY (6-36 IN.)

Edible ferns

MATURE PLANT
(2-3 FT. TALL)

EDIBLE YOUNG
FLOATING LEAVES

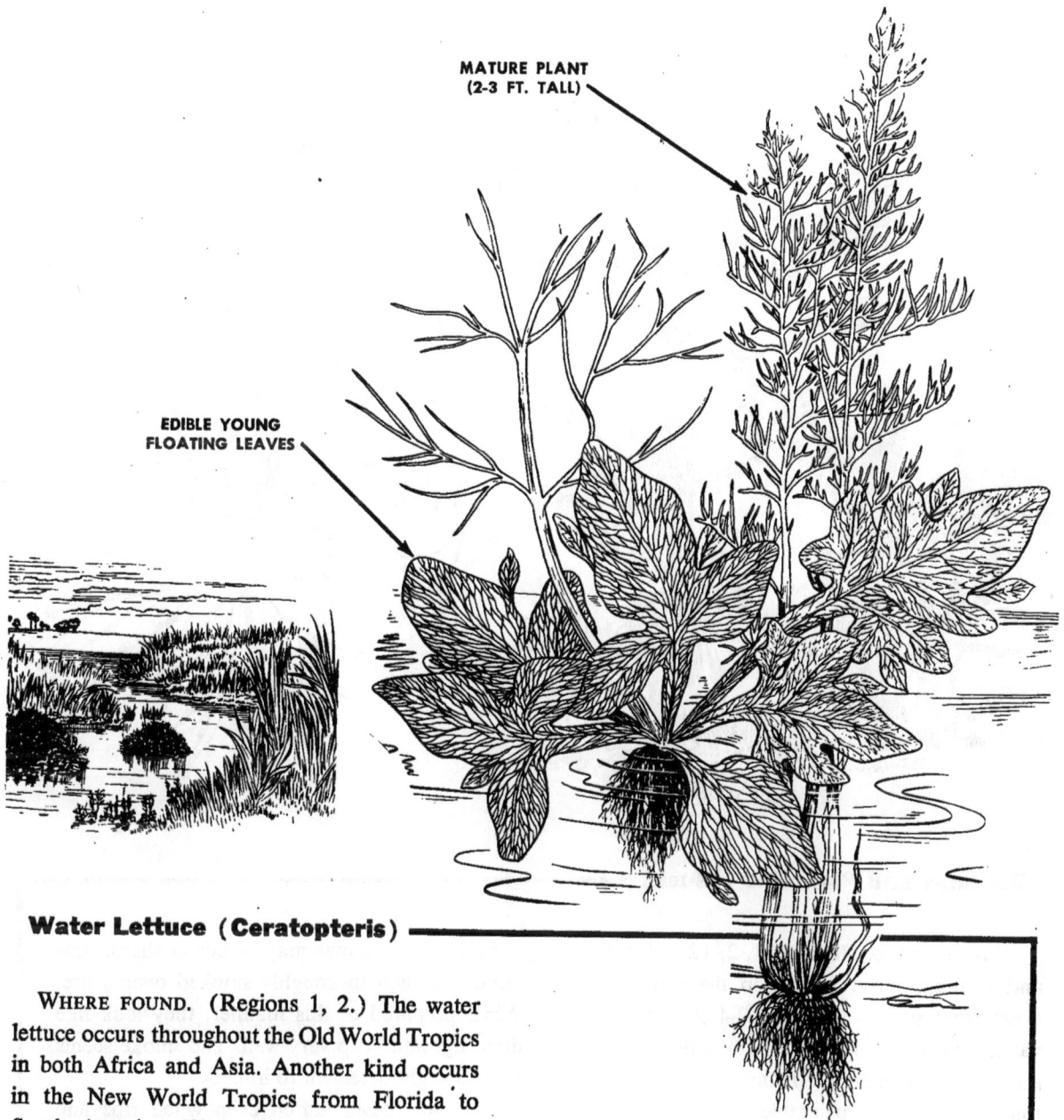

Water Lettuce (Ceratopteris)

WHERE FOUND. (Regions 1, 2.) The water lettuce occurs throughout the Old World Tropics in both Africa and Asia. Another kind occurs in the New World Tropics from Florida to South America. Water lettuce grows only in very wet places, and often as floating water plants. They should be looked for in still lakes, ponds, and the backwaters of rivers.

APPEARANCE. The leaves of the water lettuce are much like lettuce and are very tender and succulent in texture. One of the easiest ways of distinguishing water lettuce is by its little plantlets which grow from the margins of the leaves. These little plantlets grow in the shape of a rosette, and they often cover large areas in the regions they are found.

USES. The fresh leaves are eaten like lettuce. Be careful not to dip the leaves in the contaminated water in which they are growing. Eat only the leaves that are well out of the water.

EDIBLE FLOWER

15-20 FT. TALL

RIPE FRUIT HARD —
MUST BE COOKED

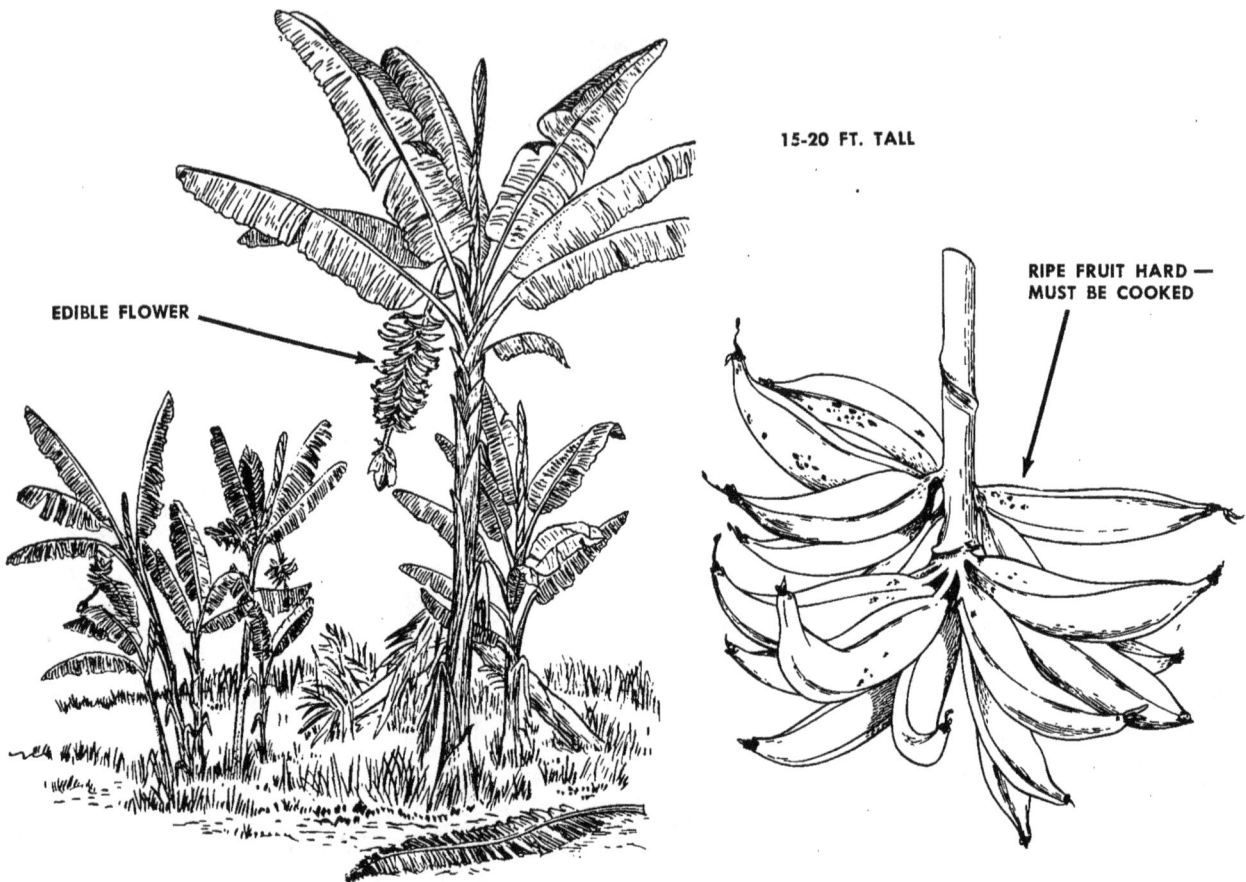

Bananas and Plantains (Musa)

WHERE FOUND. (Regions 1, 2, 12.) Bananas and plantains grow mostly in the rain forest areas from sea level to 3,000-4,000 feet elevation. In the jungles of Asia wild bananas are common, although many wild forms are tough and not very palatable.

APPEARANCE. The banana and plantain look essentially alike. The banana is a soft, sweet fruit that is eaten fresh, but the plantain has a hard fruit which must be cooked. The banana plant is not a tree, although it looks like one. The large, undivided leaves overlap each other at the base, thus producing a kind of trunk, which is soft and easily broken.

WHAT TO EAT. In areas where bananas grow, they should be utilized for food as much as possible. They are extremely nourishing, and a diet of them alone would sustain life.

Fully ripe bananas may be cut in slices, sun-dried and then thoroughly smoked over a fire. When prepared in this manner, they look like dried figs and keep very well. The smoke seems to be a slight deterrent to insects.

Plantains never soften even when ripe and must be roasted or boiled. When roasted, plantains become very dry and mealy. Large coarse plantains are dried when green and later boiled as a vegetable when needed. The dried fruit may also be made into a meal. This meal is about the color and consistency of graham flour and makes very tasty porridge, but it is not good for making bread. It can, however, be formed into round flat cakes, fried and eaten with sugar.

274

COOK FOR
GREENS

TENDERIZE MEAT
WITH MILKY JUICE
OF YOUNG FRUIT

6-20 FT. TALL

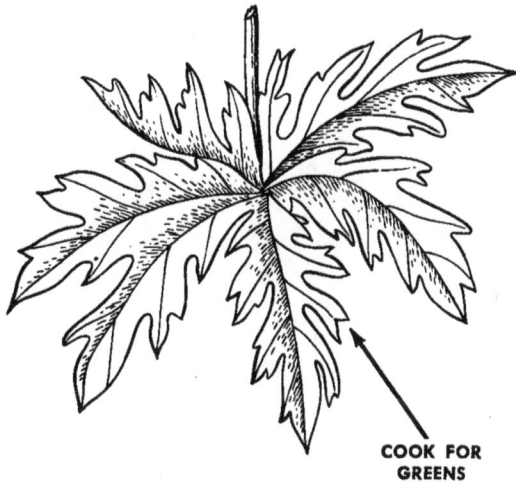

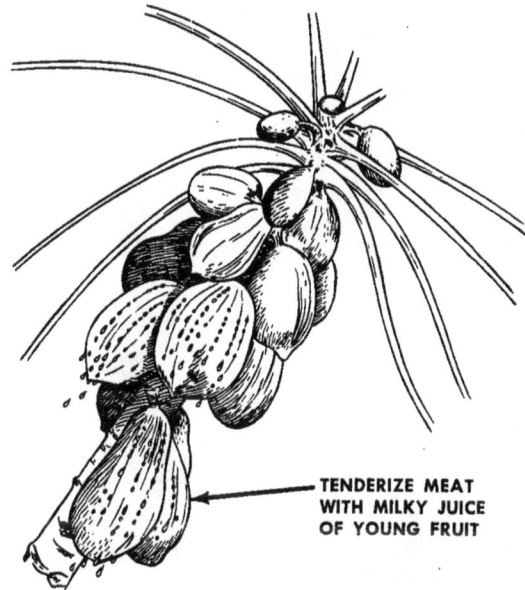

YELLOW OR GREENISH
RIPE FRUIT

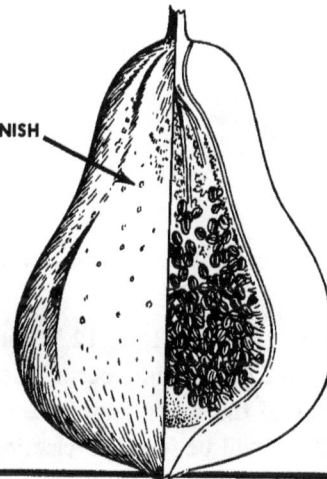

Papaya (Carica papaya)

WHERE FOUND. (Regions 1, 2, 12.) The papaya grows in all tropical countries (especially in the moister areas), around clearings and former habitations, and also in open sunny places in uninhabited jungle areas.

APPEARANCE. The papaya is a small tree, 6-20 feet tall, with a soft hollow trunk. Don't try to climb the papaya because it will break under your weight. When cut, the entire plant exudes a milky juice. The trunk is rough and the leaves are crowded at the apex of the trunk. The fruit is borne directly from the trunk among and below the leaves. It is shaped like a squash and is yellow or greenish when mature.

WHAT TO EAT. The ripe fruit is high in vitamin C. Eat raw (pepsin-flavored) or cook like squash. The fruit is green before ripening. When ripe, it turns yellow or remains greenish with a squashlike appearance. Green fruit may be placed in the sun, where it will ripen in a very short time. Be careful not to get the milky sap from the unripe fruit into your eyes — it will cause intense pain and temporary, sometimes even permanent, blindness.

The young papaya leaves, flowers and stems may be cooked carefully, changing the water as for all edible plants with milky juices.

To make tough meat tender, rub it with the milky juice of the unripe papaya.

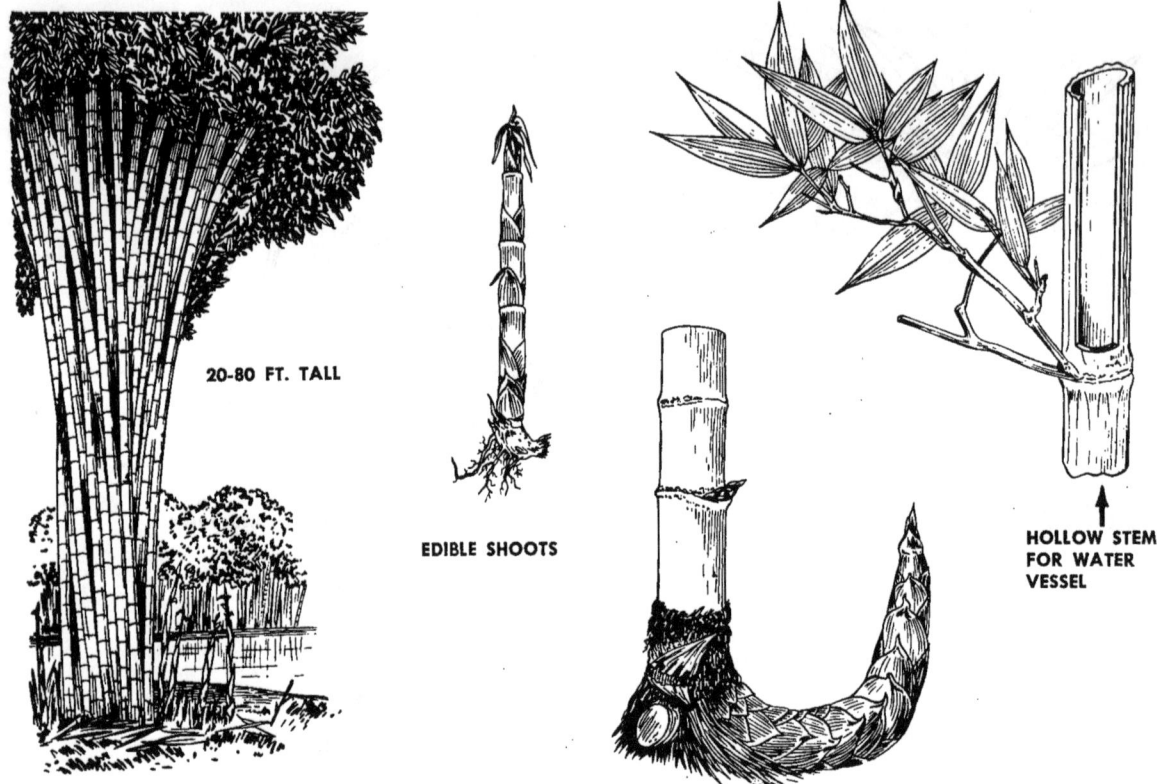

20-80 FT. TALL

EDIBLE SHOOTS

HOLLOW STEM
FOR WATER
VESSEL

Bamboo (various sorts)

WHERE FOUND. (Regions 1, 2, 12.) These giant members of the grass family occur chiefly in the moist areas of the warm temperate and tropical zones. They will be found in clearings, around abandoned gardens, in the forest, and along rivers and streams. Bamboo thickets form one of the densest kinds of jungle growth. Bamboos abound in the warm, moist parts of Asia, Indonesia, and Africa. The American Tropics support fewer kinds of bamboo than the eastern Tropics.

APPEARANCE. Nearly everyone is acquainted with bamboo in some form or other. Fishing poles are the commonest use for bamboo in the United States. Bamboo canes resemble corn plants and sugarcane. The stems of the bamboo become very hard and woody when they mature. The young shoots, on the other hand, are very tender and succulent. Bamboo varies in size from a few inches to nearly 100 feet, with canes of the largest kinds growing to nearly a foot in diameter.

WHAT TO EAT. The young shoots of bamboo are edible and appear in quantity during and immediately following rains. They grow very rapidly, some kinds as much as 15 inches a day. Cut these young shoots in the same way as asparagus, and eat the soft tip ends. Freshly cut bamboo shoots are bitter and must be boiled before eating. A second change of water may even be necessary. In fact, some kinds of bamboo shoots may have to be buried in mud for 3 or 4 days to remove the bitterness. Bamboo shoots may be salted, either raw or boiled, and eaten as a pickle; they have as much food value as fresh asparagus.

Bamboo shoots are wrapped in protective sheaths which are tough and coated with tawny or red hairs. If eaten, these hairs cause much irritation to the throat. Remove these outer sheaths carefully before eating bamboo shoots.

The seed grain of the flowering bamboo may be eaten. Pulverize, add a little water, and press into cakes or boil as you would rice.

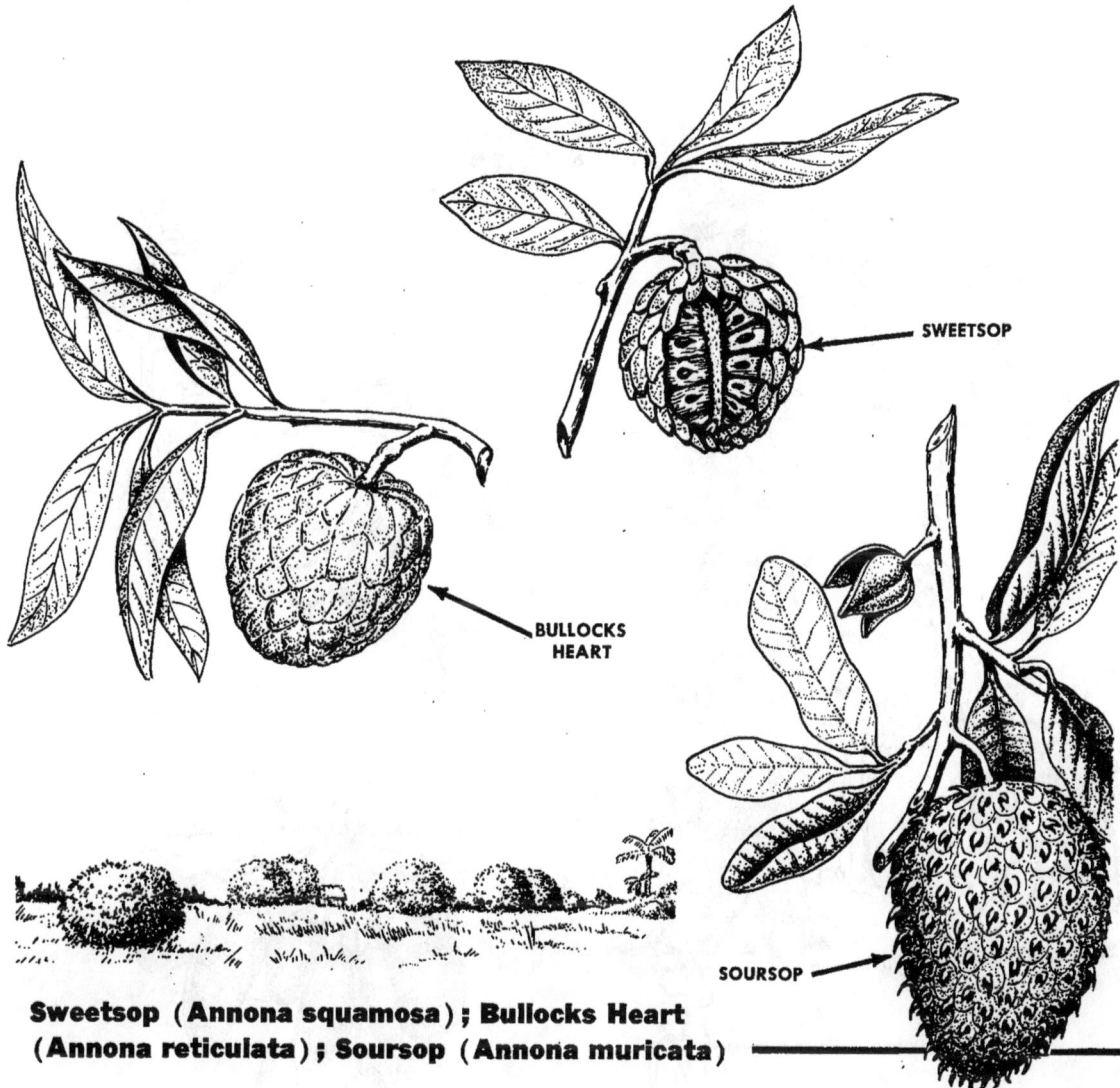

Sweetsop (Annona squamosa); Bullocks Heart (Annona reticulata); Soursop (Annona muricata)

WHERE FOUND. (Regions 1, 2.) These delicious small fruits came originally from the American Tropics, but already several centuries ago all three kinds listed above had been transported to the Tropics of the Old World, where they are now firmly established, both in cultivation and in a semiwild state. They should be looked for in abandoned gardens and near settlements. They are not forest plants.

APPEARANCE. These fruit trees are comparatively small, about 15-25 feet tall.

The *sweetsop* has leaves to 6 inches long, which are shed during the dry season. The flowers are greenish yellow and up to 1 inch long. The fruit is heart-shaped or conical, yellowish green and covered with a whitish bloom, up to 3 inches across, and of a warty appearance.

The *bullocks heart* has leaves up to 8 inches long, evergreen or half evergreen. The flowers are yellowish, 1 inch long. The fruit is heart-shaped or oval, reddish or brown, up to 5 inches across and smooth.

The *soursop* has leaves up to 5 inches long. The flowers are yellow, 1 inch or more long. The fruit is ovoid to 8 inches long, dark green and covered with short fleshy spines.

WHAT TO EAT. The fruit of the *annona* is white, soft and melting, and contains black beanlike seeds. It is a dessert fruit of great delicacy, with a mildly acid flavor somewhat suggestive of the pineapple.

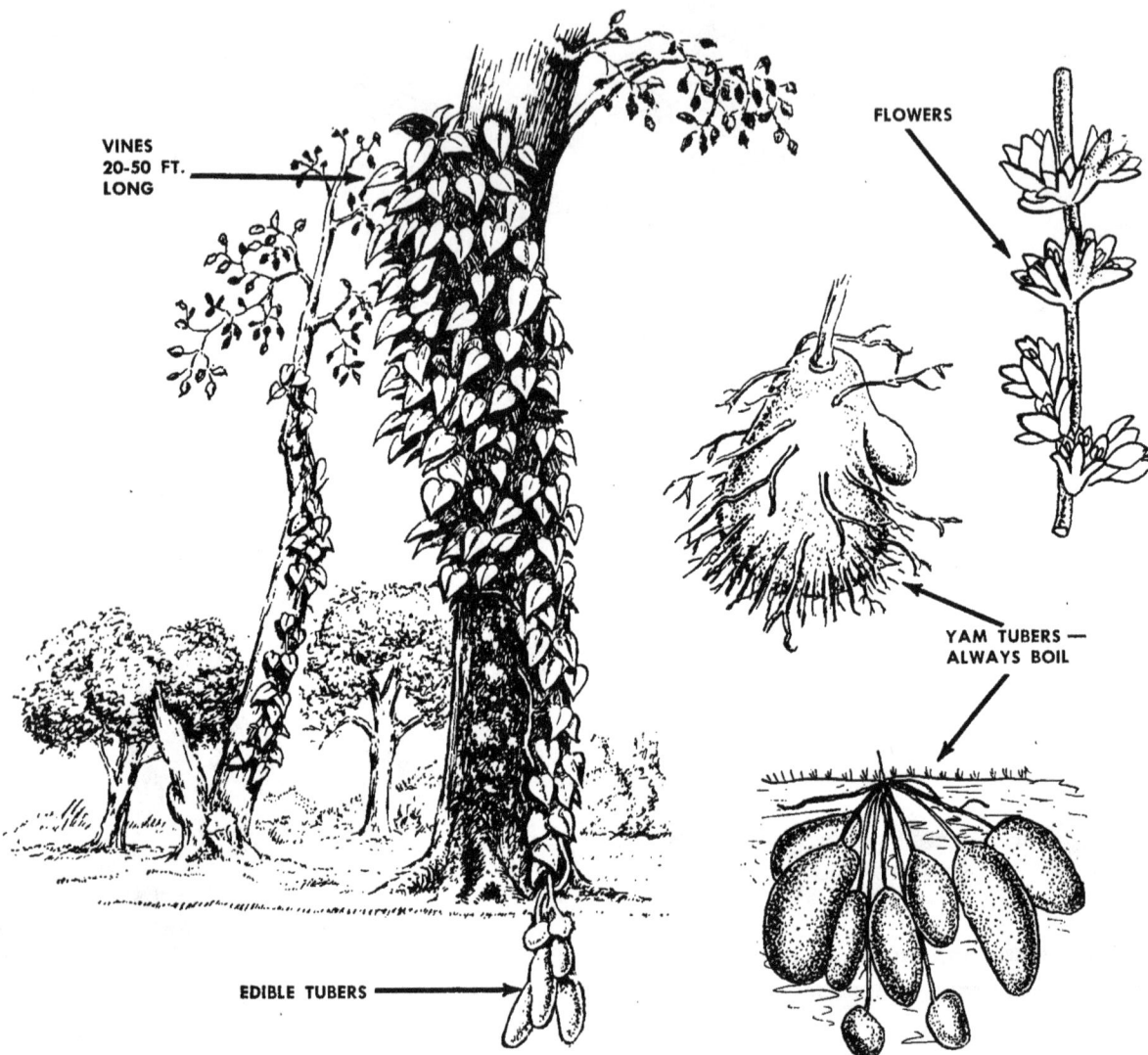

VINES 20-50 FT. LONG

FLOWERS

YAM TUBERS — ALWAYS BOIL

EDIBLE TUBERS

Tropical Yam (Dioscorea)

WHERE FOUND. (Regions 1, 2, 3, 6, 12.) About 700 kinds of yams grow in the tropical and subtropical areas of the world. They occur in all parts of the moist, rainy tropics — both the tropical rain forest and the monsoon forest areas. A few kinds occur in warm temperate areas as well, but desert varieties are rare. Do not confuse the tropical yam with the sweet potato, or yam, as it is sometimes called in American markets — these are not true yams. Tropical yams occur in abandoned gardens of the natives, in clearings in the jungle areas, and in forested areas that are not too dense.

APPEARANCE. The vine of the tropical yam produces a thickened tuber, which varies considerably as to size and shape according to the various kinds.

Yam vines may be divided into two rather distinct groupings: those with undivided heart-shaped leaves, and those with divided leaves, usually 5-parted. The flowers are small, greenish, and inconspicuous.

WHAT TO EAT. All kinds must be cooked prior to eating, because of the irritant properties of the raw tuber.

INCONSPICUOUS FLOWERS

AIR POTATO

3-ANGLED
SEED POD

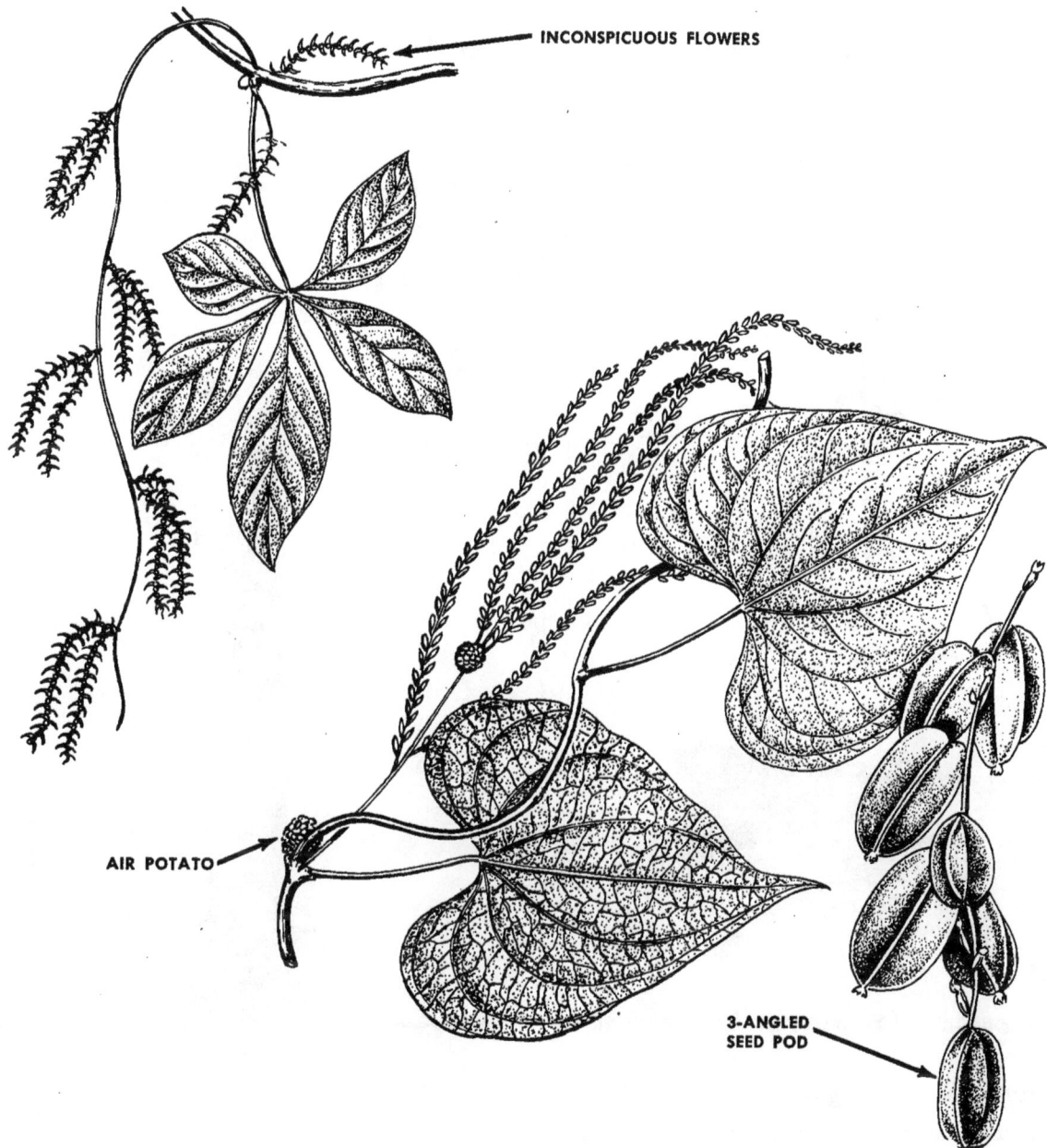

To prepare yams, first cut them into thin slices. All kinds may be eaten safely after being covered with wood ashes and soaked in streams or salt water for 3-4 days. The yams may be cooked after this initial treatment by boiling or baking in an earth oven (see p. 249). The native method of preparing yams is to dig a pit, put in large rocks, and build a fire. When the rocks are hot, the yams are placed in the pit on green leaves, and the hole is then covered with palms or other large leaves. Earth may also be mounded over the leaves. In a half hour or so, the yams are considered well done.

The *air potato* comes from a certain kind of tropical yam, the *dioscorea bulbifera*. The air potato is a small potatolike offset produced at the stem base of the yam leaves. These air potatoes are full of starch and are, for all practical purposes, like tubers that are produced under ground. To eat the air potato, prepare it in the usual way for tropical yams.

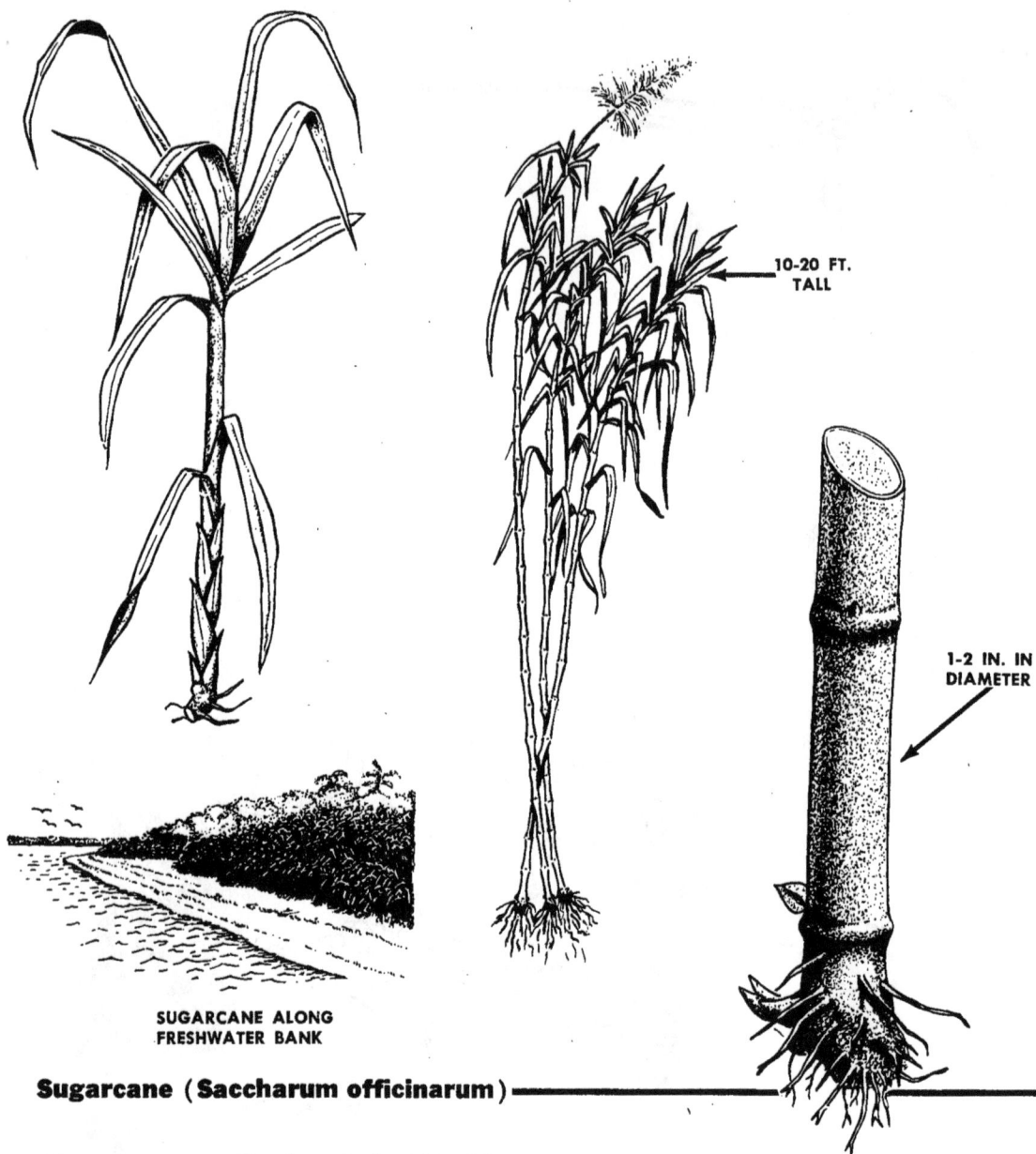

10-20 FT.
TALL

1-2 IN. IN
DIAMETER

SUGARCANE ALONG
FRESHWATER BANK

Sugarcane (Saccharum officinarum)

WHERE FOUND. (Regions 1, 2, 12.) The cultivated sugarcane plant has been widely planted in the Tropics. Wild relatives produce an inferior grade of sugar, but both forms will be found. Sugarcane also grows semiwild in many regions, especially in parts of southeastern Asia, on the neighboring islands of the Indes, in Africa, and in America.

APPEARANCE. Both the cultivated and wild relatives of sugarcane are large, coarse grasses, not too unlike ordinary corn in appearance. Sugarcane produces a large tassel of flowers at the summit of the plant. The stems are yellow, green, or reddish.

WHAT TO EAT. As survival food, the sugarcane and its wild relatives are valuable for the sweet juice which may be chewed out of the ripe cane. The outer layer of the stem may be peeled off and the inside pith chewed for the refreshing and nourishing sweet sap. This sweetness is characteristic of many kinds of grasses, especially the young growing parts.

RED FLOWERS

STARCHY
ROOTSTALK

EDIBLE
STARCHY ROOTS

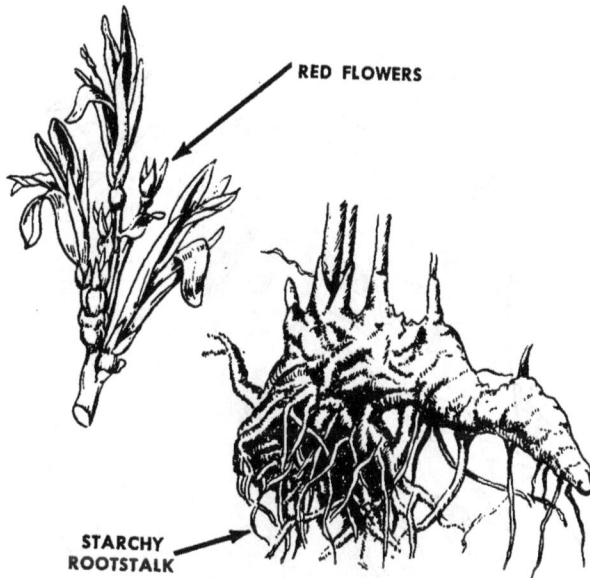

Canna Lily (Canna indica)

WHERE FOUND. (Regions 1, 2, 12.) As a wild plant, the canna lily is found in all tropical countries, especially in moist places along streams, springs, ditches, and the margins of woods. The canna will be easily recognized, because it is so commonly cultivated in flower gardens in the United States.

APPEARANCE. The canna is a coarse perennial herb, 3-10 feet tall. The plant grows from a large, thick underground rootstalk which is edible. The large leaves resemble the banana but are not so large. The flowers in wild forms of canna are usually small, relatively inconspicuous and usually red.

WHAT TO EAT. The large and much branched rootstalks are full of edible starch. The younger parts may be finely chopped and then boiled or pulverized into a sort of meal. Mix in the young shoots of palm cabbage for flavoring.

RIPE FRUIT
SMOOTH, DEEP
YELLOW

40-100 FT. TALL

EDIBLE
PEACH-LIKE
FLESH

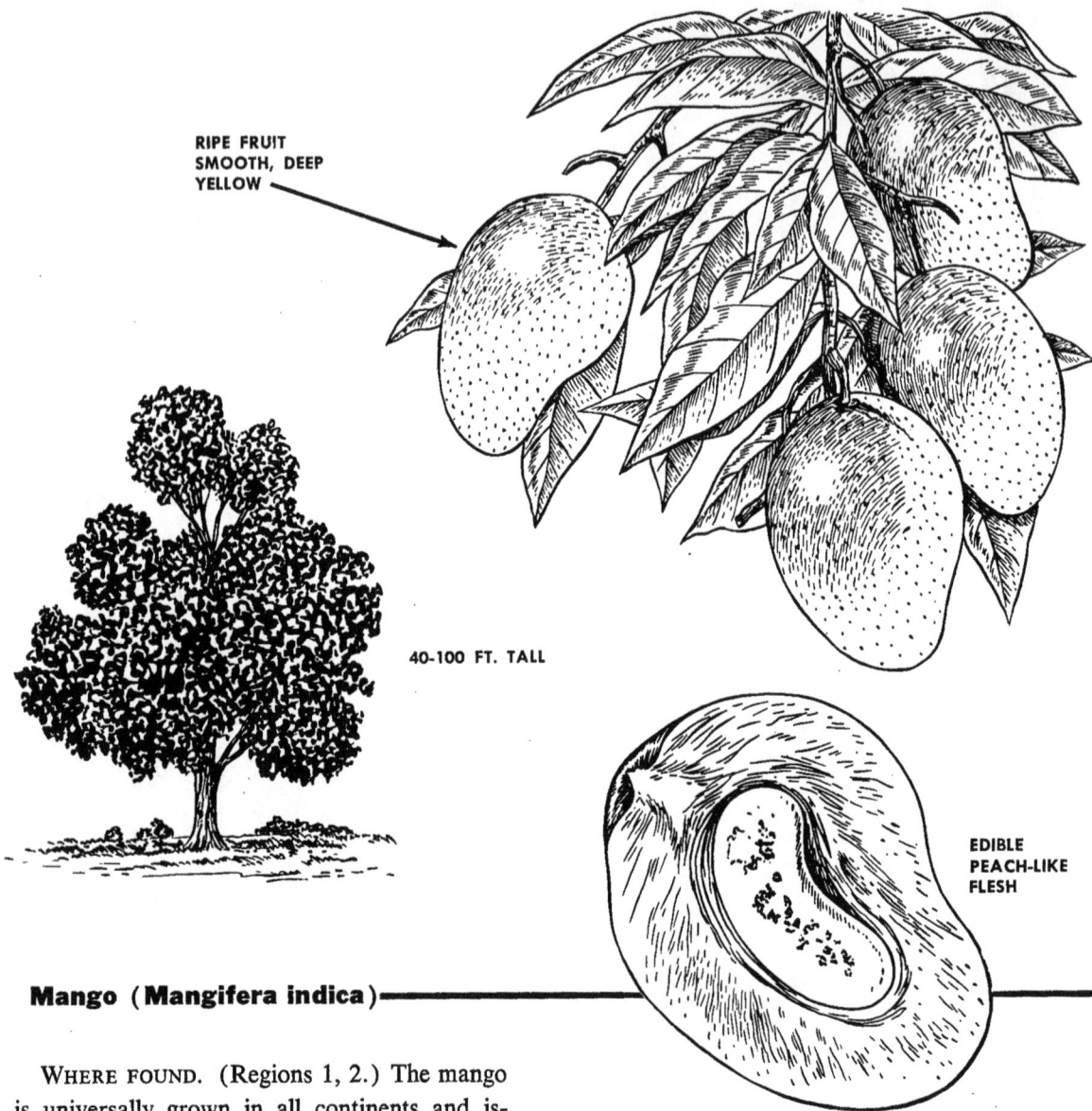

Mango (Mangifera indica)

WHERE FOUND. (Regions 1, 2.) The mango is universally grown in all continents and islands throughout the Tropics, especially in the nondesert parts. In addition to the common mango shown here, other kinds exist in southeastern Asia. The common mango will be found near human habitation, and it persists for many years in abandoned gardens in tropical areas.

APPEARANCE. The mango is an evergreen tree, nearly 100 feet tall when mature. The leaves are stiff and lance-shaped to 16 inches long. The fruit is usually somewhat heart-shaped, commonly 3-5 inches long, smooth, mostly yellow and reddish when ripe, and containing one very large flat stone or seed.

WHAT TO EAT. The ripe fruit blends the consistency of a firm plum with rather stringy peachlike texture. Many varieties are known. Some varieties are more palatable than others. The worst taste like turpentine, and the best have a delightful flavor. In rare cases an individual may be allergic to mango fruit or leaves, and in such cases a skin rash may develop.

SEED POD (RED)

FLOWERS RED
OR PURPLISH

TO 100 FT.
TALL

EDIBLE BLACK SEEDS

SEED POD

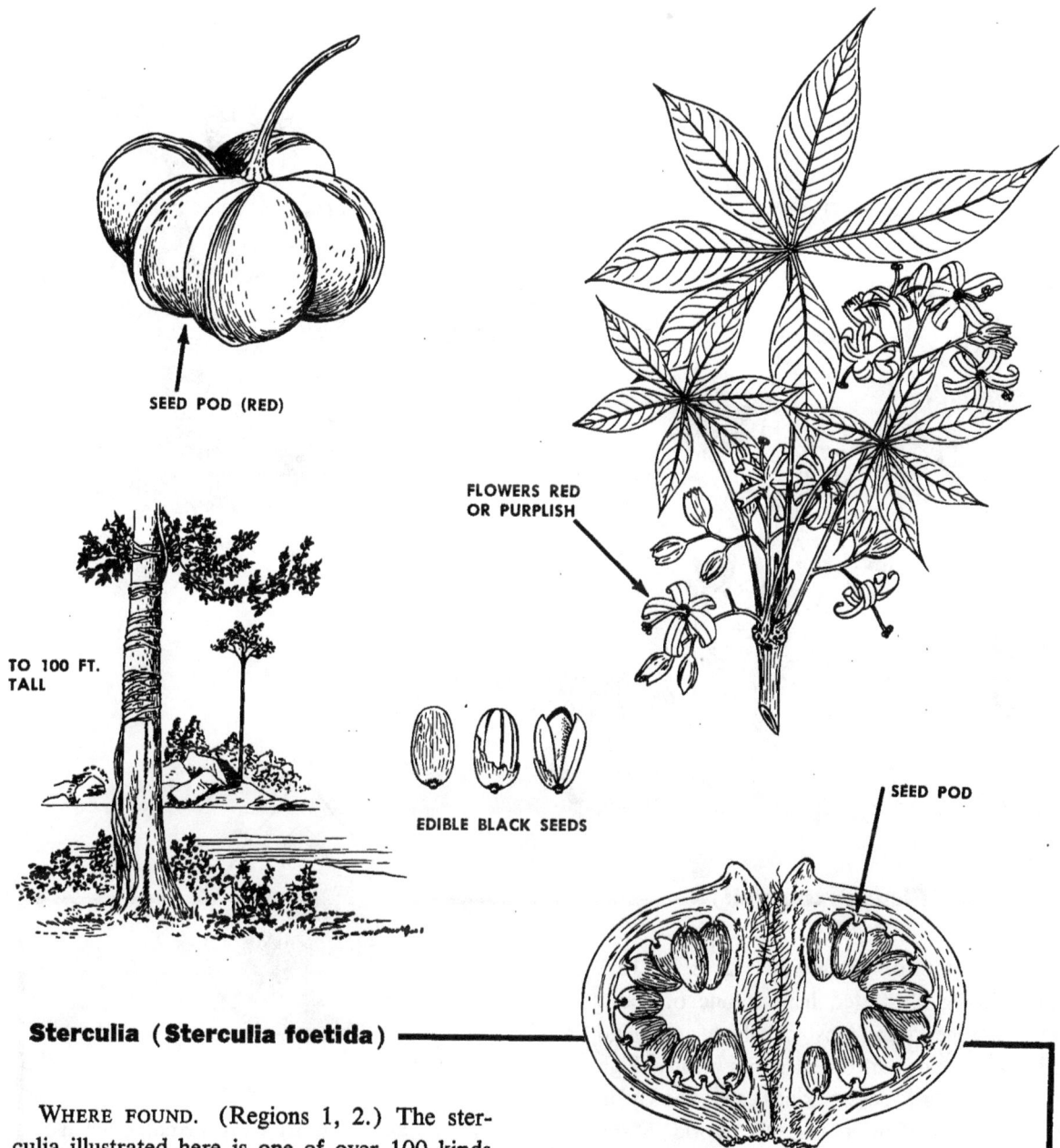

Sterculia (Sterculia foetida)

WHERE FOUND. (Regions 1, 2.) The sterculia illustrated here is one of over 100 kinds distributed through all warm or tropical climates. The one illustrated is widespread in southern Asia and Indonesia; it occurs also in Africa and tropical Australia. These are mainly trees of the forest.

APPEARANCE. Sterculias are tall trees, rising in some instances to 100 feet. The leaves are either undivided or palmately lobed. The fruit in all sterculias is similar in aspect to the one shown here.

WHAT TO EAT. The large red pods produce a number of edible seeds. The seeds in all kinds are edible and have a pleasant taste like cocoa. They can be eaten like nuts, either raw or roasted. Avoid eating large quantities, for they have a purgative action.

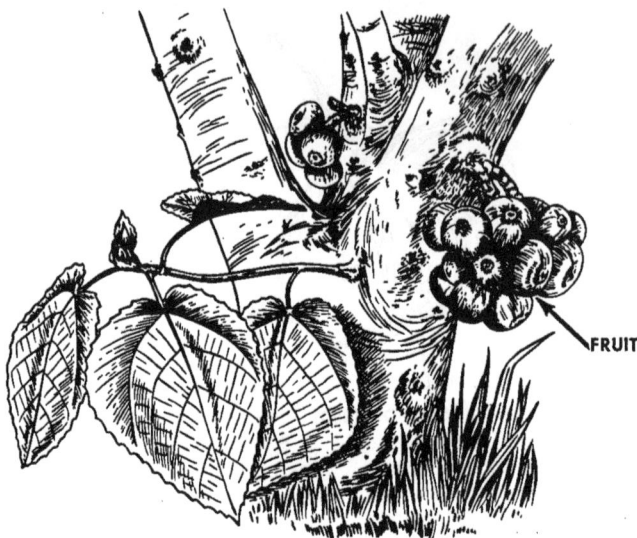

FRUIT

20-100 FT. TALL

PROP ROOTS

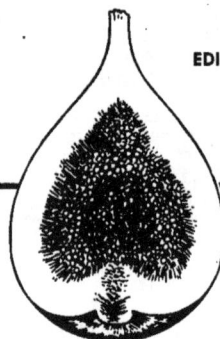

EDIBLE FRUIT

Wild Fig (Ficus roxburghii)

WHERE FOUND. (Regions 1, 2, 3, 4, 12.) The wild fig illustrated here is one of about 800 different kinds, most of which are found in tropical and subtropical zones with a high rainfall. A few desert kinds are known in America as well as in the Old World. Many sorts are cultivated. Fig trees can be found in abandoned gardens, along roadways and trails, and in fields.

APPEARANCE. The fig fruit grows out directly from the branches of the fig tree. The leaves of most kinds are large, evergreen, and leathery. An easy way to distinguish a fig tree is by the long aerial roots which grow out from the trunk and branches and descend to the ground where they take root. These prop roots often give the fig tree a grotesque appearance.

WHAT TO EAT. The fruit can be eaten when ripe. Most kinds resemble a top or a pear somewhat squashed in shape. Ripe figs will vary greatly as to palatability — many kinds are hard, woody, covered with irritating hairs, and worthless as survival food. The edible varieties are delectable, soft when ripe, almost hairless, and green, red, or black in color.

RICE GRAINS

3 FT. TALL

RICE GRAIN
INSIDE HUSK

GROUND LEVEL

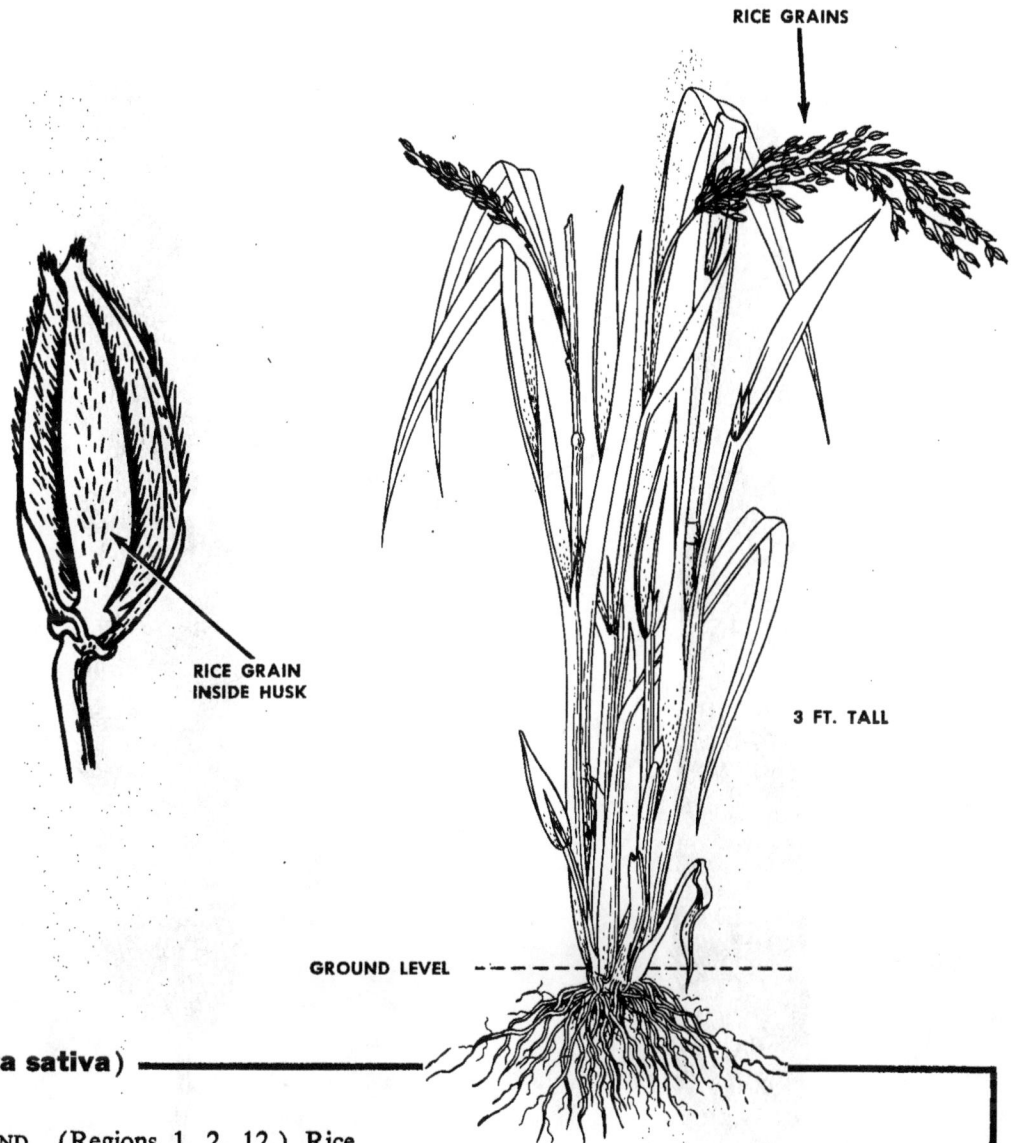

Rice (Oryza sativa)

WHERE FOUND. (Regions 1, 2, 12.) Rice is widely grown in tropical and warm temperate countries throughout the world. Rice is not often found in the wild state, although in parts of southeastern Asia it is possible to find abandoned fields where rice has persisted in a semi-wild condition. Truly wild rice does occur, however, in both Asia and Africa. Rice grows always in wet places.

APPEARANCE. The rice plant is a coarse grass which grows to a height of 3-4 feet. The leaf blades are rough and quite hard and from 1/2-2 inches wide. The rice grains are inclosed in a hairy, straw-colored covering out of which the mature rice grains shatter when ripe.

WHAT TO EAT. Native rice can be roasted and beaten to a fine flour together with native honey and often a small quantity of palm oil. It can then be carried as a powder or as a cake wrapped in large green leaves to preserve it. Properly dried, it will keep for a long time.

Rice may also be prepared in the ordinary way by boiling in water.

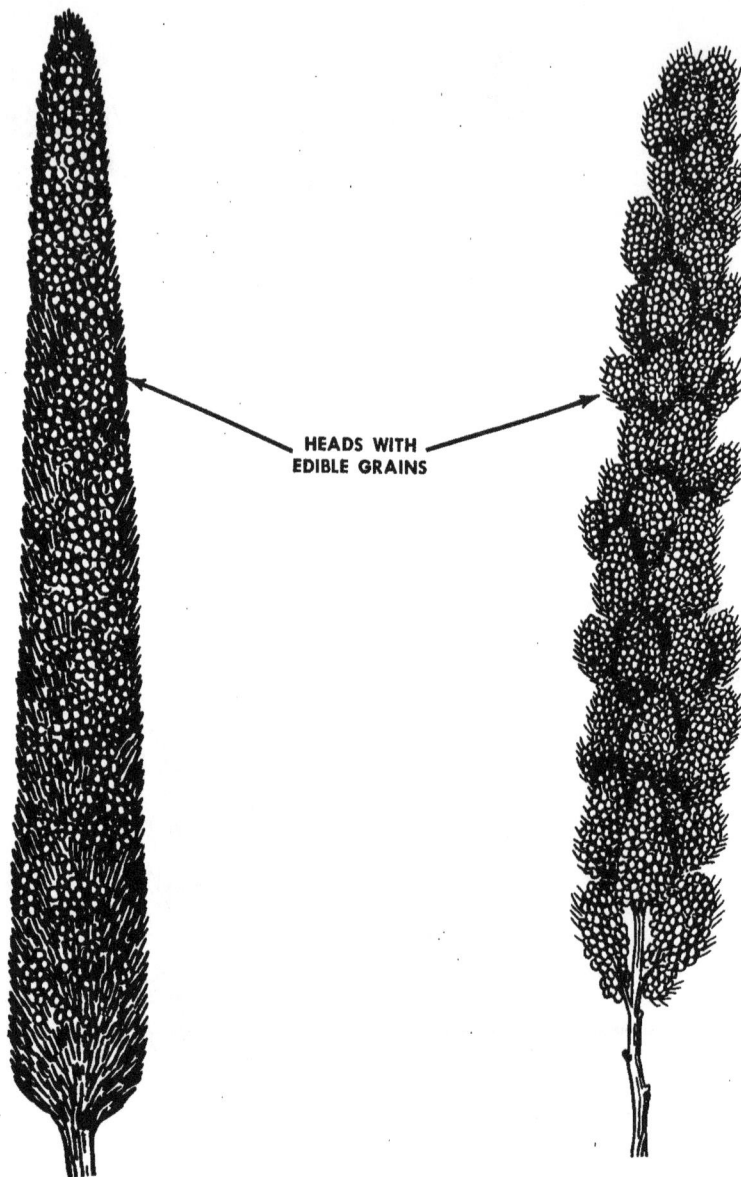

HEADS WITH
EDIBLE GRAINS

Pearl Millet (Pennisetum glaucum) ———— **Italian Millet (Setaria italica)**

WHERE FOUND. (Regions 1, 2, 12.) Pearl millet may be found around abandoned dwellings and in clearings in the tropical areas of southeastern Asia and Africa.

APPEARANCE. This is a coarse grass several feet tall. The heads are from 3-6 inches long and compact. The edible grains in the head are the size of a mustard seed.

WHAT TO EAT. Pearl millet grain can be pulverized and cooked as porridge, pressed into cakes, or used to thicken soup.

WHERE FOUND. (Regions 1, 2, 12.) The Italian millet is widely grown in Asia and Africa, especially where the cultivation of rice is not possible.

APPEARANCE. The Italian millet is a coarse grass over 2 feet tall. The millet grains are produced in a fairly loose, whiskery head.

WHAT TO EAT. The small yellowish grains are produced in abundance in the head. The grains, if pulverized and eaten as a porridge, are very high in food value.

GREENISH FLOWERS

3 FT. TALL

EDIBLE TUBERS

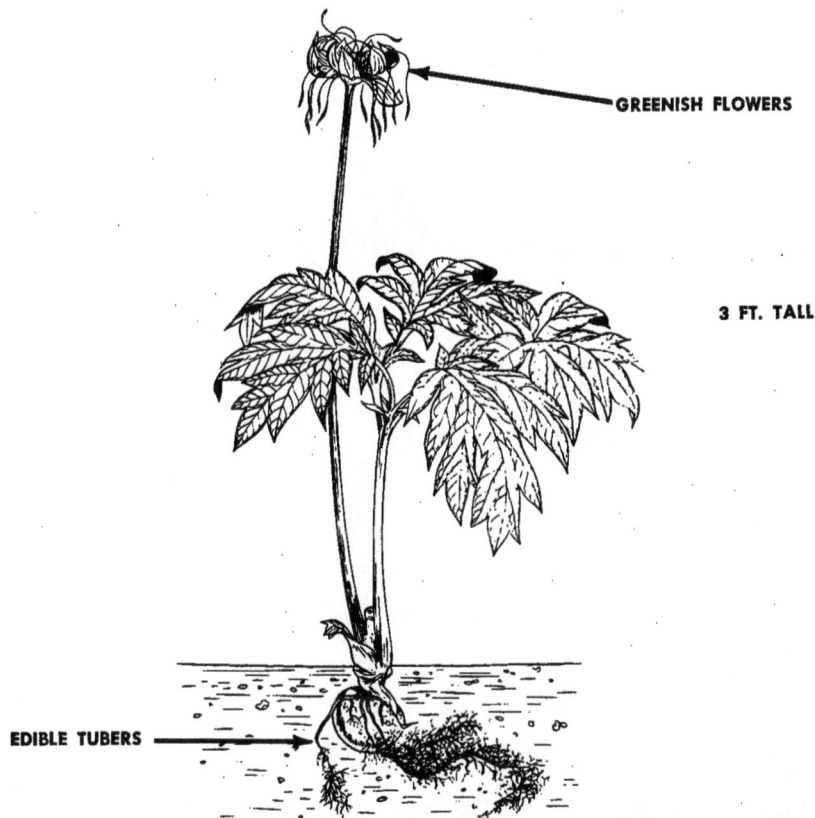

East Indian Arrowroot (Tacca pinnatifida)

WHERE FOUND. (Regions 1, 2.) The arrowroot is found as a wild plant in parts of tropical Africa, tropical Asia and the islands of the southwestern Pacific. In the wild state this plant is found in forested areas with a high rainfall. It is a typical rain forest plant. The arrowroot has been cultivated by man, and for this reason it is quite possible to find these plants in abandoned fields and gardens and in wet places along roadsides.

APPEARANCE. The arrowroot is a large, coarse herb. The stems are about an inch in diameter and often 3 feet tall. The leaves are from 3 - 3-1/2 feet in diameter and divided into three parts, which are again divided. The flowers are green and purplish. The edible underground tubers are sometimes nearly a foot across.

WHAT TO EAT. The arrowroot has underground tubers which sometimes weigh up to 2 pounds. These are very bitter when raw, but when boiled or roasted, they become sweet and quite palatable for food. The starch content has been found to be as much as 22%, and for this reason they should be made use of by the survivor whenever required.

To prepare flour from the fresh tubers, first peel the fresh tubers. Then rasp them to a fine pulp directly into a container of water. Rough stones or pieces of coral may be used for the rasping. The water becomes milky and after the grating process is finished let the contents stand until the water again becomes clear. Pour off the water and save the white starch on the bottom. Repeat this washing process several times until all trace of bitterness disappears from the starch. After thorough washing, dry the white arrowroot in the sun.

The dried arrowroot flour can be used to make bread or pancakes.

FLOWERING BRANCH

TO 100 FT. TALL

EDIBLE NUT

SEED POD

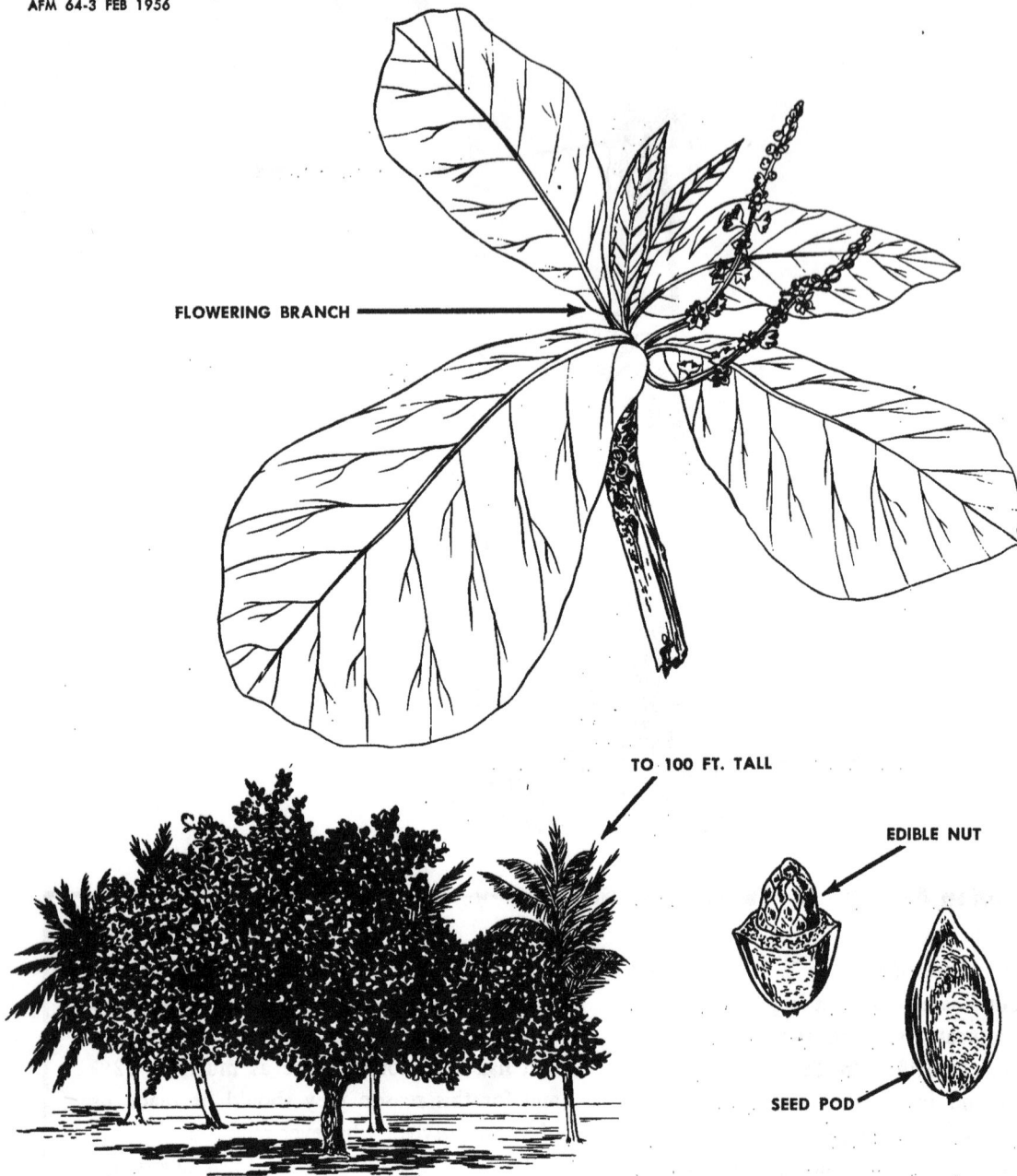

Indian or Tropical Almond (Terminala catappa)

WHERE FOUND. (Regions 1, 2.) The Indian almond is native to tropical southeastern Asia, northern Australia, and Polynesia. However, it is now widely dispersed in all tropical countries around the globe. In its native habitat, the Indian almond is found only upon sandy seacoasts. It is now so widely dispersed that it has become semiwild in many tropical areas and should be looked for in abandoned fields, gardens, and along roadsides.

APPEARANCE. The Indian almond is a tall tree, growing to 100 feet in height. The edible seeds or kernels are surrounded by a spongy, husklike covering from 1 to 3 inches long. These fruits are produced at the tips of the branches. The leaves of the Indian almond are clustered at the ends of the young branches.

WHAT TO EAT. The kernels of the fruit are of a fine almondlike consistency and flavor.

EDIBLE YOUNG
LEAVES

FLOWER

FLOWERS

30 FT. HIGH

SEED POD
INTERIOR

EDIBLE
SEED
POD

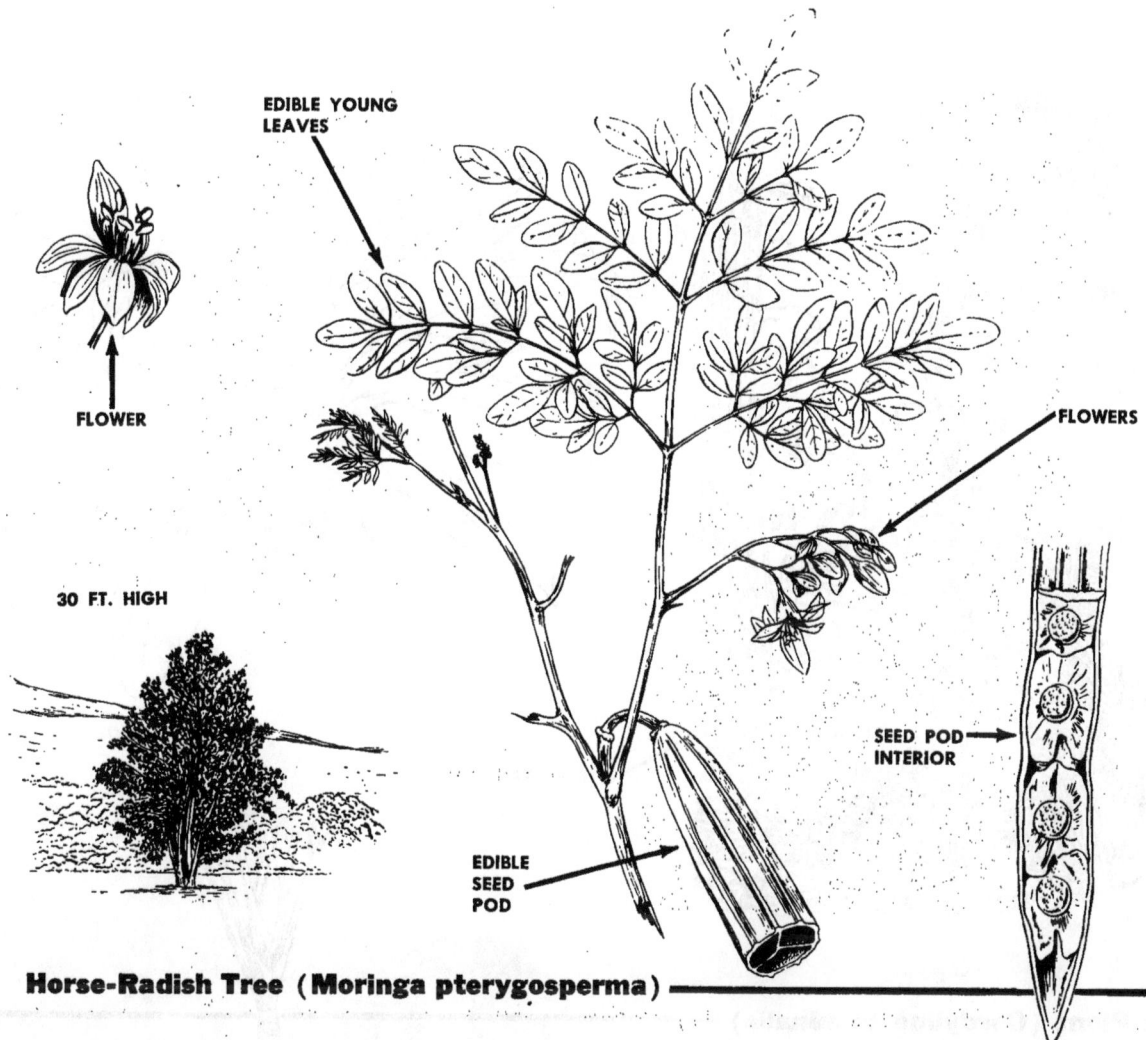

Horse-Radish Tree (Moringa pterygosperma)

WHERE FOUND. (Regions 1, 2.) The horse-radish tree is a tropical plant, native to India, but it is now widespread in many other tropical countries throughout southeastern Asia, Africa, and America. The horse-radish tree may be found in a wide variety of places, from old abandoned fields and gardens to the edge of forest areas. The tree is especially common in Asia. It has pungent roots similar to the horse-radish plant.

APPEARANCE. The horse-radish tree is not a towering forest giant but a rather low tree from 15-45 feet in height. The leaves have a fernlike appearance. At the ends of the branches are produced the flowers and the long pendulous fruits, which are similar in appearance to a giant bean. The pods are triangular in cross section with strong ribs and are from 10-25 inches long.

WHAT TO EAT. The leaves can be eaten either old or young, fresh or cooked, depending upon their state of hardness.

The fruit can be used as a vegetable wherever the plant grows. Cut the long, young seed pod into short lengths and cook in the fashion of string beans, or fry in oil, if such is available. Oil can be obtained from the young fruits of palms by boiling them and then skimming the oil off the surface of the water.

The young seed pods can be chewed when fresh, in which case the inner pulpy part and soft seeds are eaten.

The flowers may be eaten as an ingredient in a salad.

The roots may be ground as a substitute for seasoning in the same manner as the true horse-radish.

6-15 FT. TALL

Ti Plant (Cordyline terminalis)

WHERE FOUND. (Regions 1, 2.) The ti plant grows on the shores of many islands in the southwest Pacific. And it is cultivated over wide areas in tropical Asia where it is used for food. In many areas it has escaped from cultivation and may be found in a semiwild state. The ti plant will also be found in forested areas, as it is a shade-loving plant. This is a typical jungle species.

APPEARANCE. The ti plant may become a fairly tall shrub from 6-15 feet tall. The large, rather coarse, shiny, leathery leaves are arranged in a crowded fashion at the tips of the thick, rather succulent stems. The leaves are usually green or sometimes reddish. The flowers are borne at the apex of the plant in large plumelike clusters which are usually drooping. The ripe berries are red.

EDIBLE ROOTSTALK

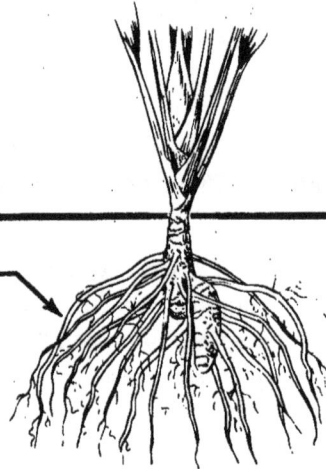

WHAT TO EAT. The large fleshy rootstalk is the principal edible part. It is full of starch, and for best results, the root ought to be oven-baked in the manner described for taro (see page 313). In the East Indies, the natives eat the young unopened leaves cooked with rice.

BLUISH OR
PURPLISH FLOWERS

TWINING STEM

SEED POD
(OPEN)

YAM
BEAN
PLANT

SOIL
LEVEL

STARCHY EDIBLE
TUBERS

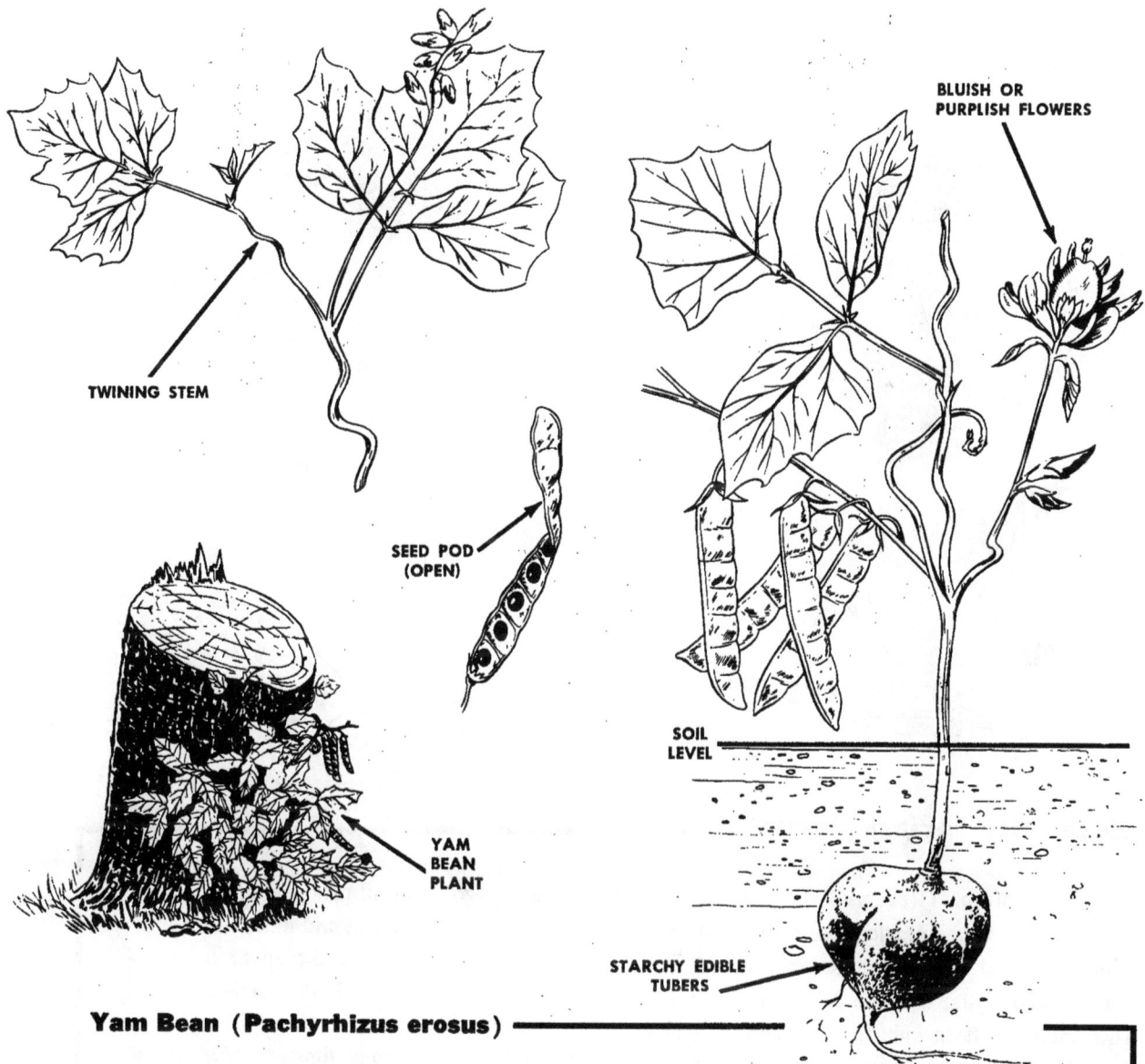

Yam Bean (Pachyrhizus erosus)

WHERE FOUND. (Regions 1, 2.) The yam bean is native of the American Tropics, but it was carried by man a long time ago to Asia and the Pacific islands. Now it is commonly cultivated in these places, and it may also be found growing wild in forested areas. It is found in the wet areas of the tropical regions.

APPEARANCE. The yam bean is a climbing plant, with 3-lobed leaves and a turniplike root. This plant belongs to the bean family. The flowers are pealike in shape and bluish or purplish. The plants are often so rampant that they cover the vegetation upon which they are growing.

WHAT TO EAT. As the tubers come from the ground they are about the size of a turnip and to the taste they are crisp, sweet, juicy, and of a nutty flavor. They are nourishing and at the same time quench the thirst. They may be eaten raw or else boiled plain.

To make flour, slice the raw tubers and let them dry in the sun, then grind up the dry tubers. This flour is high in starch and may be used to thicken soup.

The raw seeds are *poisonous,* but the cooked seeds and pods are perfectly safe.

FLOWER STALK
(SAP)

15-20 FT. TALL
60 FT. AT MATURITY

EDIBLE
PALM NUT

CROSS-SECTION
OF PALM NUT

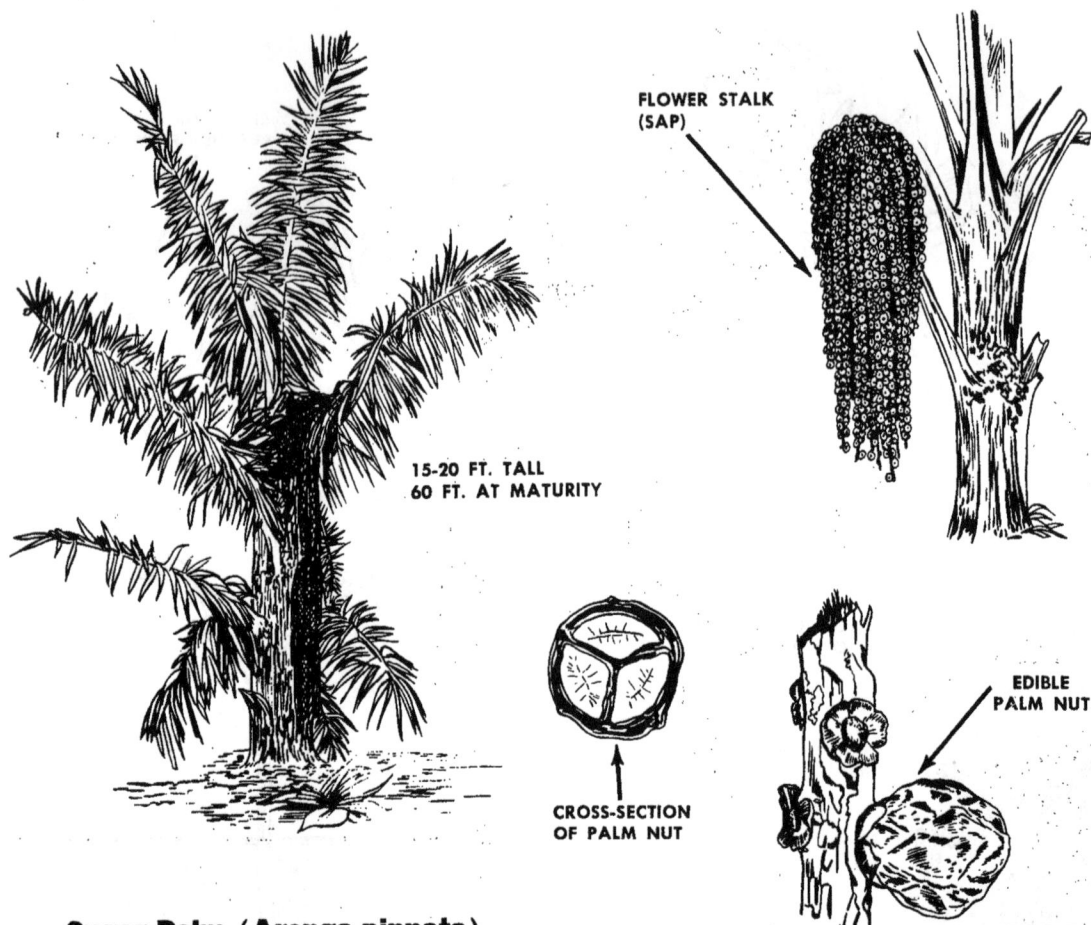

Sugar Palm (Arenga pinnata)

WHERE FOUND. (Regions 1, 2.) The sugar palm is native to the jungle areas of the eastern Himalayas and the region southeastward to Malaya, Indonesia, and the Phillipine Islands. This palm has been cultivated around villages throughout this entire area. Abandoned gardens and jungle areas are the places where the survivor should look for the sugar palm.

APPEARANCE. The sugar palm is so named because of the large quantities of sugar which can be extracted from the boiled-down sap. It is a rather large palm, 40-60 feet tall when mature. The leaves are sometimes 25 feet long, with 100 or more pairs of narrow leaflets which are whitish beneath. The fruit, or palm nuts, are borne on pendulous stalks that grow along the upper portion of the trunk.

WHAT TO EAT. The sugar palm is of considerable utility, and the survivor should keep in mind that the sugar palm, buri palm, fishtail palm, and sago palm all produce edible starch, sap, sugar, palm cabbage, and nuts.

The method of tapping the sugar palm described here may be used for obtaining sugar from the other palms covered in this manual. (This process is of only limited value to the survivor because of the long period of time required for producing results.)

To tap the sugar palm, select a flowering stalk and beat with a stick or wooden mallet for a short period each day. Repeat the beating over a period of two or three weeks the object being to produce wound tissue and stimulate the flow of sap to the injured part. Then cut off the stalk at the base of the flowering portion, and catch the exuding sap in a hollow joint of bamboo. Remove a thin slice from the wounded end of the stalk once or twice each day during the period of sap flow. This maintains the steady flow of sap.

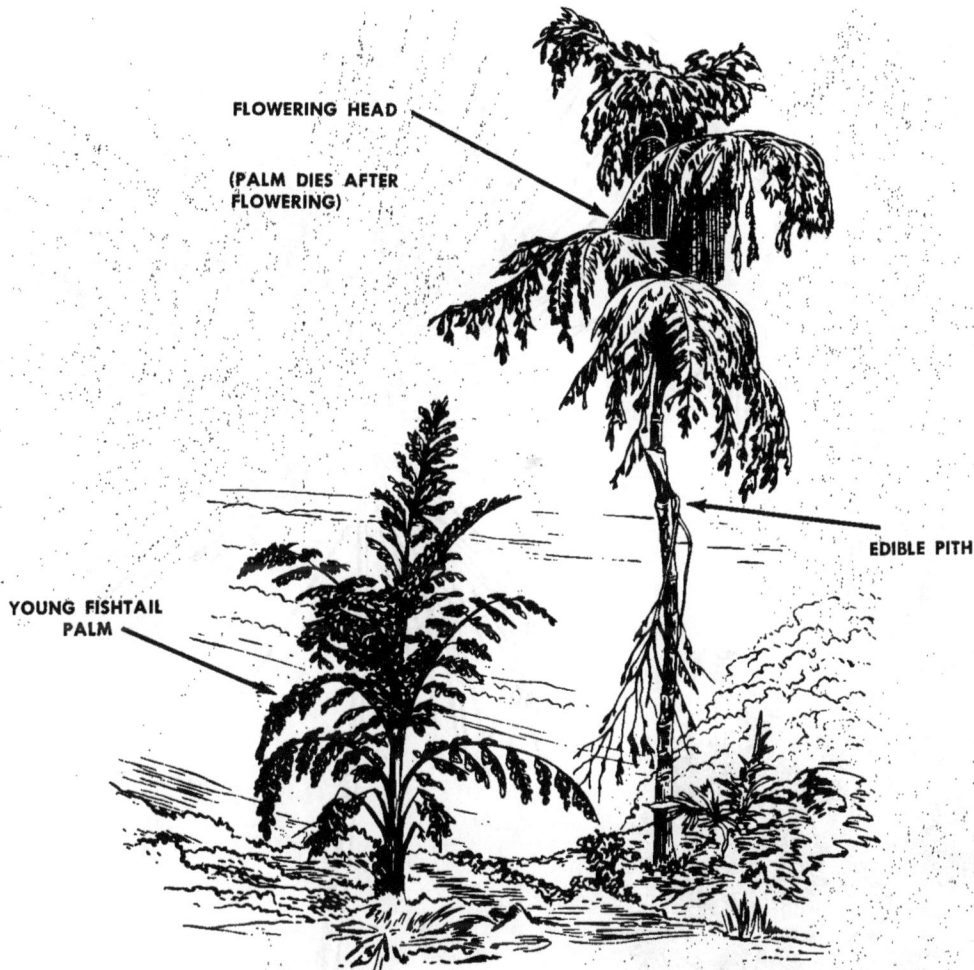

FLOWERING HEAD

(PALM DIES AFTER FLOWERING)

EDIBLE PITH

YOUNG FISHTAIL PALM

Fishtail Palm (Caryota urens)

WHERE FOUND. (Regions 1, 2.) The fishtail palm is native to the Tropics of India, Assam, and Burma. Several kinds also exist in other parts of southeastern Asia and the Philippines. These are palms of the open hill country and jungle areas, and are found in areas where the true sago palm does not occur.

APPEARANCE. The fishtail palms are large trees, at least 60 feet tall. The leaves of the fishtail palm are unlike those of any other palm. The leaflets are inequilateral and toothed on the upper margins. All other palms have either fan-shaped or featherlike leaves. The massive flowering shoot of the fishtail palm is borne at the top of the tree and hangs downward.

WHAT TO EAT. The uses of the fishtail palm are very similar to those of the sago palm. The chief food sought from the fishtail palm is the starch which is stored in the trunk in large quantities. This product may be utilized in the same way as the starch from the sago.

Toddy, or the juice from the fishtail palm, can be obtained from the expanding flowering shoot. (See description of sugar palm for method of obtaining toddy.) Fresh toddy is very nourishing but should be drunk shortly after it is obtained from the palm flower shoot. Boil down the toddy, and a rich sugar syrup will be obtained.

Fishtail palm starch, after being prepared, may be boiled into a thick, nourishing gruel.

The palm cabbage may also be eaten.

DRINKABLE
SAP

60 FT. TALL

EDIBLE
STARCH
IN TRUNK

LEAF

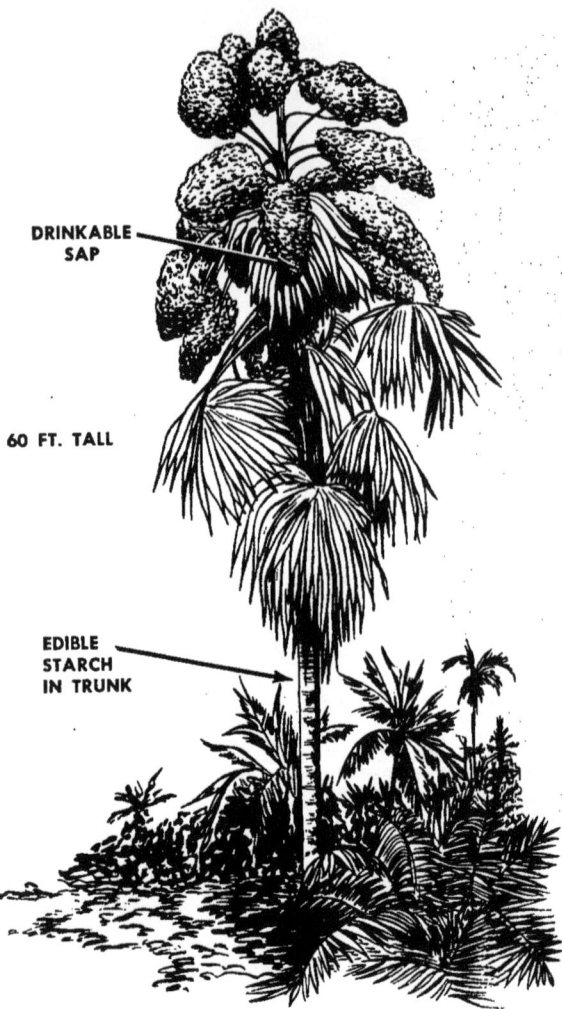

Buri Palm (Corypha elata)

WHERE FOUND. (Regions 1, 2.) There are several kinds of palms closely related to the true buri palm, but all types are native to tropical southeastern Asia, Malaya, and Indonesia. The buri palm itself occurs in jungle areas from eastern India to the Philippine Islands.

APPEARANCE. The buri palm is one of the stateliest of palm trees, frequently reaching 60 feet in height. The large fan-shaped leaves of this palm often are over 9 feet in length with the outer part split into about 100 narrow segments. The stalks of the leaf are often 6-9 feet long, and their margins are edged with very hard black teeth.

WHAT TO EAT. The buri palm has large quantities of starch in the trunk. The method of extraction is the same as that for the sago palm described on p. 265.

A sweet drink can be obtained from the sap of the severed flower stalk. (See method of extraction for sugar palm, p. 292).

Palm cabbage can be obtained by severing the growing shoot of the tree.

The kernels of the young nuts are edible.

BRIGHT YELLOW OR
RED PLUM-LIKE
FRUIT

CASHEW NUT

FRUITING BRANCH

EDIBLE NUT

40 FT. TALL

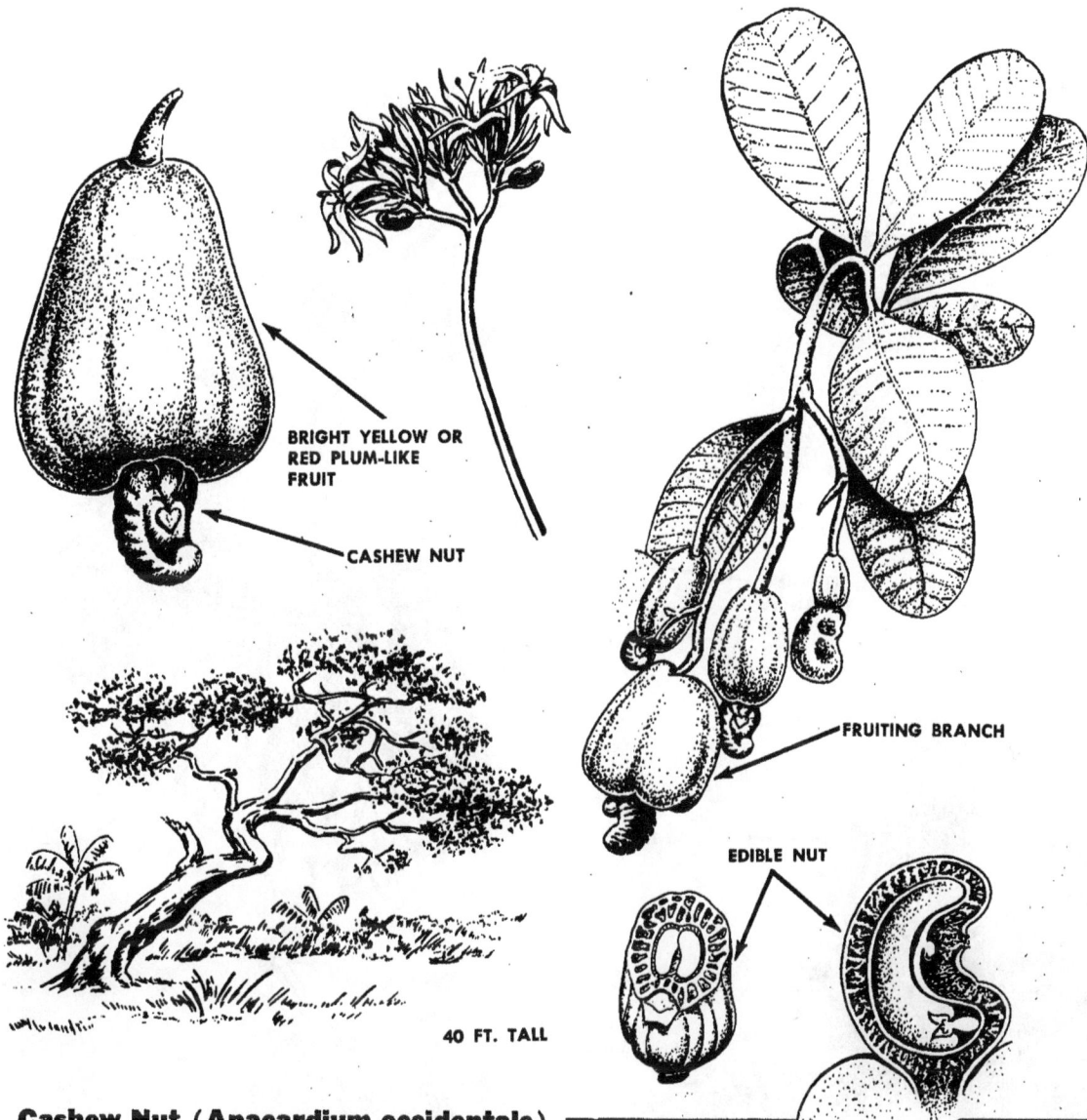

Cashew Nut (Anacardium occidentale)

WHERE FOUND. (Regions 1, 2, 3.) The cashew is native to the West Indies and northern South America, but it has been spread by transplantation to all tropical climates. In the Old World it has escaped from cultivation and appears to be wild at least in parts of Africa and India.

APPEARANCE. The cashew is a spreading evergreen tree growing to a height of 40 feet, with leaves to 8 inches long and 4 inches wide; the flowers are yellowish-pink. The fruit is very easily recognized by its peculiar structure.

WHAT TO EAT. The fruit is thick and pear-shaped, pulpy and red or yellow when ripe. This bears at its tip a hard green kidney-shaped nut, smooth, shiny, and green or brown according to its stage of maturity. The nut incloses one seed. It is edible when roasted.

CAUTION

The green hull surrounding the nut contains a resinous irritant poison that will blister lips and tongue like poison ivy. This poison is destroyed by heat when the nuts are roasted. The pear-shaped fruit is juicy, sweet-acid, and astringent; however, this fleshy fruit is quite safe and is considered delicious by most people who eat it.

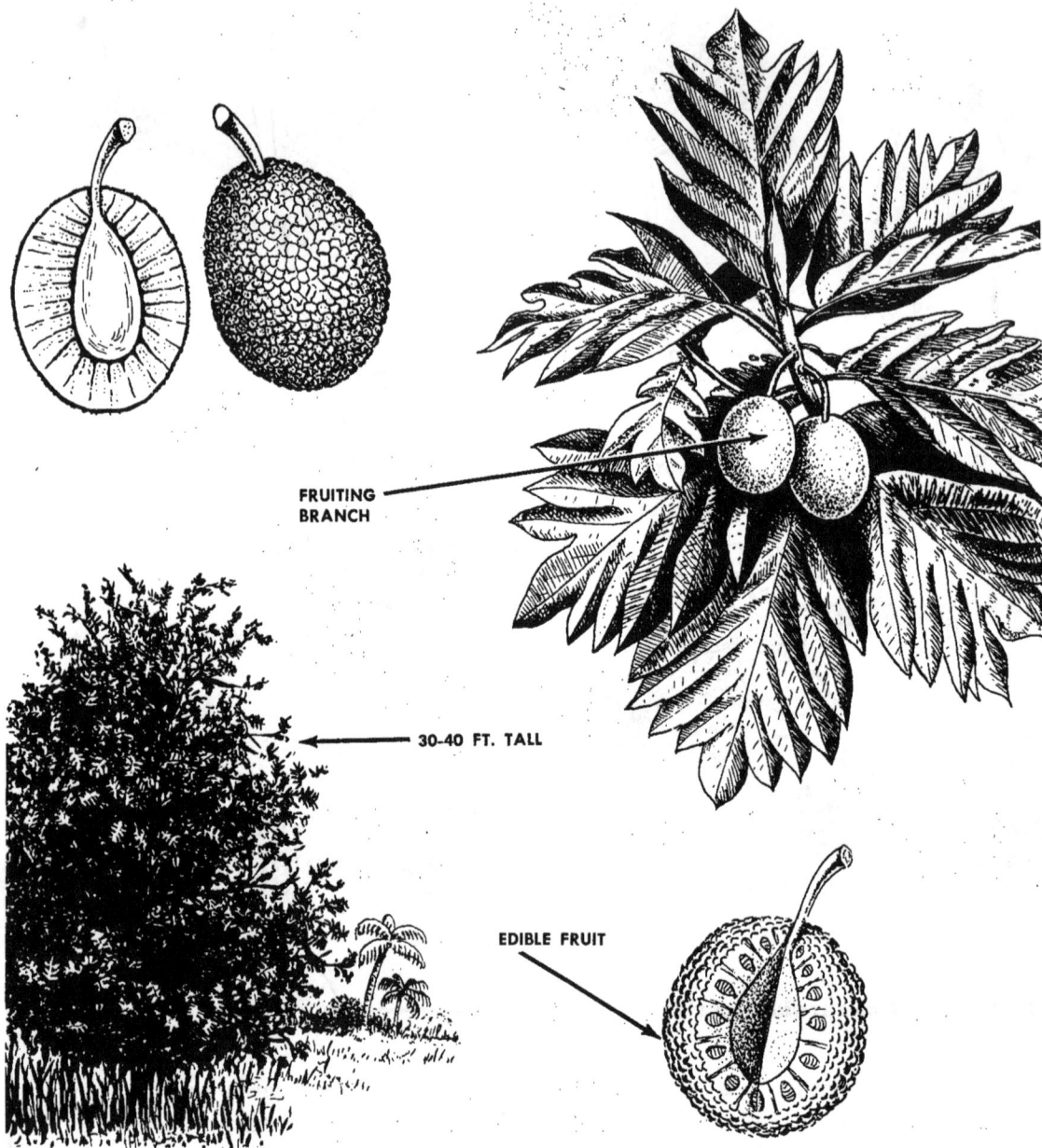

FRUITING
BRANCH

30-40 FT. TALL

EDIBLE FRUIT

Breadfruit (Artocarpus incisa)

WHERE FOUND. (Regions 1, 2.) The breadfruit grows in most tropical countries, but it is especially common throughout the southwest Pacific, Indonesia, New Guinea, and tropical Asia and America. It is less common in Africa.

APPEARANCE. The breadfruit is a tree 30-40 feet tall with a sticky, milky juice which exudes from fresh wounds. The leaves are 1-3 feet long, leathery, and the upper part has 3-9 lobes. The trees are frequently found near human habitation.

WHAT TO EAT. Ripe breadfruits can be eaten raw. They should be scraped lightly with a shell to remove the skin. Then pick off the lumps of flesh with your fingers, separating the seeds, and discarding the hard outer covering.

When a sufficient quantity has been prepared in this manner, squeeze the flesh into a container to form a mash. Some water may be mixed with this mash. The mashed breadfruit has a greenish color caused by the inner layer of skin, which is not removed by the light scraping. It is now ready for eating in coconut shells. This preparation is surprisingly delicious and is considered quite as delectable as any good fruit salad.

Whole breadfruit can be cooked also. After light scraping and removal of the stalk, breadfruit may be grilled on embers of an open fire, or on heated coral spread out without any subsequent cover.

There are four other methods of cooking breadfruit in the mature, or firm stage. The first method consists of packing pieces of breadfruit, grated to a creamy consistency, into a *green* coconut shell and cooking it. Remove the stalk end of the green nut by cracking around the shell. Remove the flesh around the upper edge of the main shell, as it is likely to come off in lumps and spoil the consistency. Pour out all but a small amount of fluid. Then place the grated breadfruit and coconut meat into the shell. Some of the fluid may be poured back until it rises to within a short distance of the rim. Replace the top part of the shell as a cover. The coconut shell container then acts as a natural casserole when placed in the oven.

A second method of cooking is with coconut cream in a *mature* nut casserole. For this preparation, cook the sliced breadfruit in an uncovered mature coconut shell with coconut cream added. Coconut cream can be prepared by grating ripe coconut with a jagged shell or piece of coral, placing the gratings in a porous cloth, and then squeezing out the juice (cream).

The third method is to cook the breadfruit with coconut cream in a wrapping of breadfruit and banana leaves as a receptacle on a green coconut-leaf platter. To construct this platter, arrange whole breadfruit leaves first with their stalks down, then sections of breadfruit leaves, and finally sections of banana leaf for the inner layer. Place pieces of breadfruit or taro in the leaf receptacle, leaving enough leaf to fold over the food. Pour in freshly prepared coconut cream until it is seen rising toward the upper level of the food. Fold the tips of the leaves over from the sides and the ends. Tie the package with a green coconut leaf. The usual way of tying is to twist the two ends together and shove the twist under the band formed by the leaf. When the tie is unfastened and the coconut-leaf receptacle removed, the opened-out leaves serve as a dish from which to eat.

A fourth way of preparation is cooking the breadfruit in a leaf wrapping, pounding it and then mixing it with grated meat of mature coconuts. Cut the breadfruit or taro into small pieces, wrap it in leaves, and cook in an oven. Then pound it in a bowl and grind it with a wooden mallet until soft. All lumps should be eliminated. Then add grated mature coconut flesh and mix thoroughly before eating.

Breadfruit in a *soft ripe* condition can also be cooked. The breadfruit can be thinly peeled or left as it is. Pat the fruit with the hands to loosen the core. Grip the stalk with your teeth and gently pull the fruit away to withdraw the core, which can be discarded. Wrap the fruit in three breadfruit leaves with the tips downward. Fold the tips upward on opposite ends, reaching to just beyond the middle of the breadfruit. Tie the middle of the bundle transversely with a strip of pandanus leaf (p. 299) or hibiscus fiber. Fold the talk ends of the leaves which project above the fruit downward to clear the opening made by the removal of the core. Pour coconut cream through the opening to fill the cavity. Pinch a lump of ripe breadfruit off the side and plug it into the opening as a stopper. Straighten out the stalk ends and tie with another strip of pandanus or hibiscus to seal the package, which is now ready for the oven. (See p. 249 for construction of oven.) After about 2 hours, the food is ready to be removed from the oven. *This method for breadfruit is adaptable for other kinds of tropical fruits.*

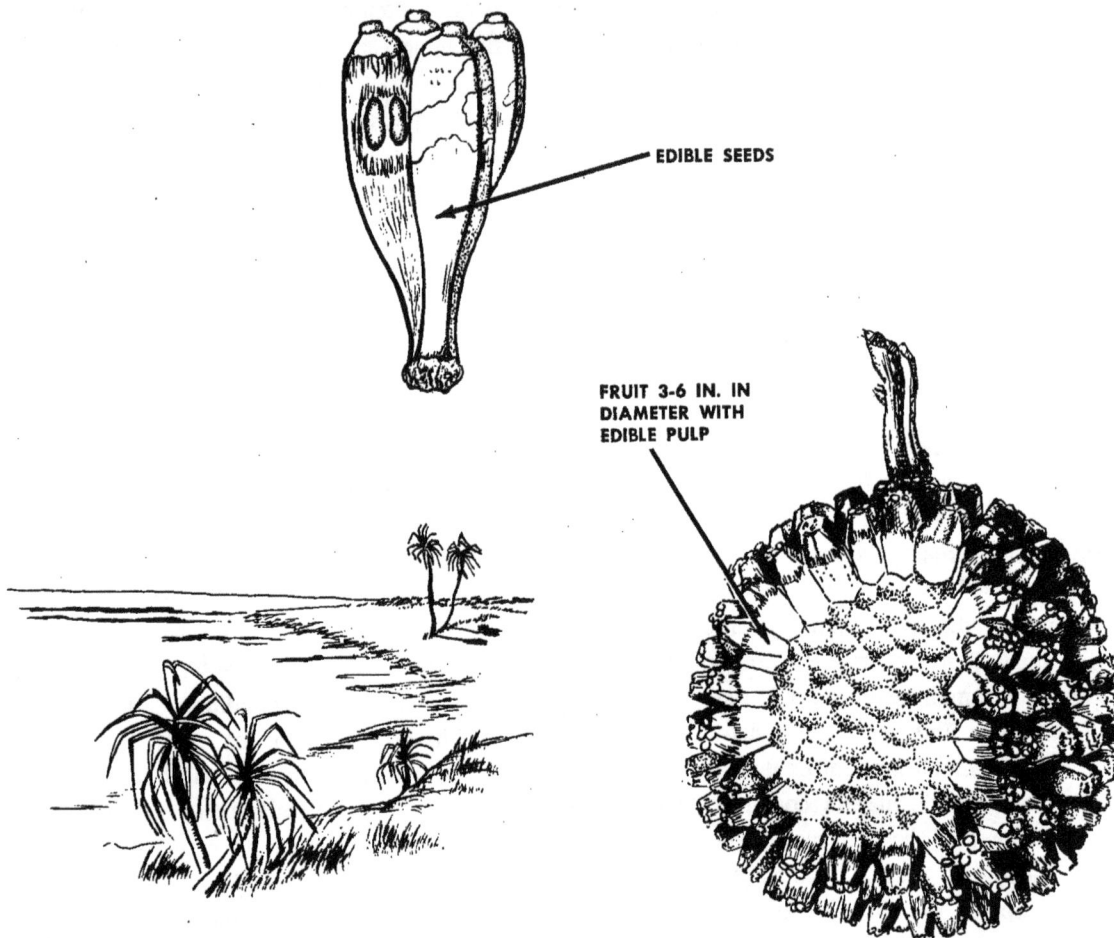

EDIBLE SEEDS

FRUIT 3-6 IN. IN DIAMETER WITH EDIBLE PULP

Screw Pine (Pandanus)

WHERE FOUND. (Regions 1, 2.) The screw pine grows predominantly along the seashore, although certain kinds occur inland for some distance, from Madagascar to southern Asia and the islands of the southwestern Pacific. About 180 kinds occur throughout this area.

APPEARANCE. The screw pine is a curious plant on stilts, or prop roots, which support the plant above ground so that it appears to be suspended more or less in midair. These plants are either shrubby or treelike, 10-30 feet tall, with stiff leaves having sawlike edges. The fruits are large roughened balls like a pineapple but without the tuft of leaves at the end.

WHAT TO EAT. Bump the ripe fruit on the ground to separate the fruit segments, which are held together by the hard outer covering. Chew the inner fleshy part.

Fruit which is not fully ripe should be cooked in an earth oven. Before cooking, wrap the whole fruit in banana leaves, breadfruit leaves, or any other suitable thick leathery leaves. After cooking for about 2 hours in the earth oven, the fruit segments can be chewed like ripe fruit.

Screw pine flour is made by a long process which takes 2-3 days, but it is worth doing if the time is available. Cut off the inner fleshy

10-30 FT. TALL

AERIAL PROP
ROOTS

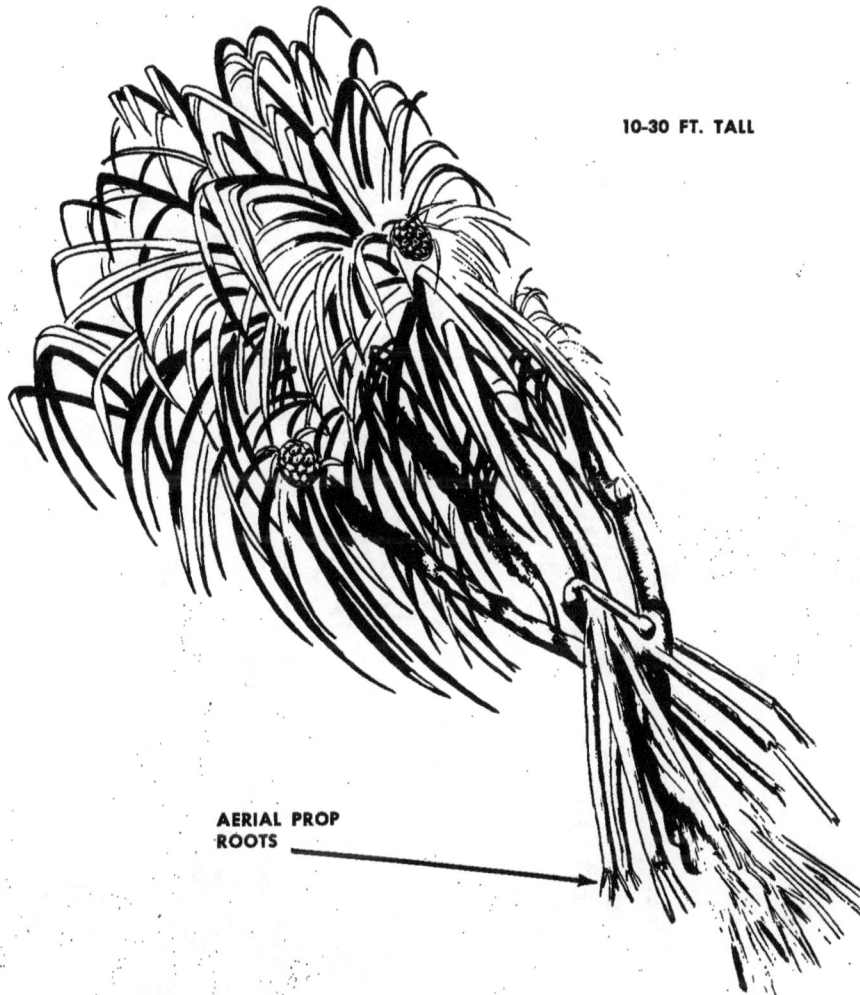

parts of the fruit segments of very ripe fruit, wrap in a coconut leaf container, cover in the earth oven, and cook for about 2 hours. Then place the cooked fruit into a coconut shell or other large container. Pound the fruit with a wooden mallet until a smooth paste is formed. Place handfuls of this substance on banana leaves or similar material and smooth with the hands into a flat, round pancake about 14 inches in diameter. Place the cakes, with a banana or breadfruit leaf under each one, in a round, coconut-leaf basket. Then cook them on a grill, which may be manufactured from the woody midrib of the coconut palm. After the pancakes have been hardened on both sides from

successive burnings, remove them from the grill.

Place the cakes in the sun for further drying. After they have hardened in the sun, again place them on the grill in pairs, one above the other. Turn them until they are well hardened over a slow fire. Then place the cakes into a container and break, grind, and pound them into flour. The flour can be kept and used when desired. For eating, it can be mixed with water and cooked to form a kind of porridge.

The very young leaves at the growing tip of the plant may be eaten raw or cooked. The young growing root-tips may also be eaten.

LEAVES GREEN,
RED OR PURPLISH

INCONSPICUOUS FLOWERS

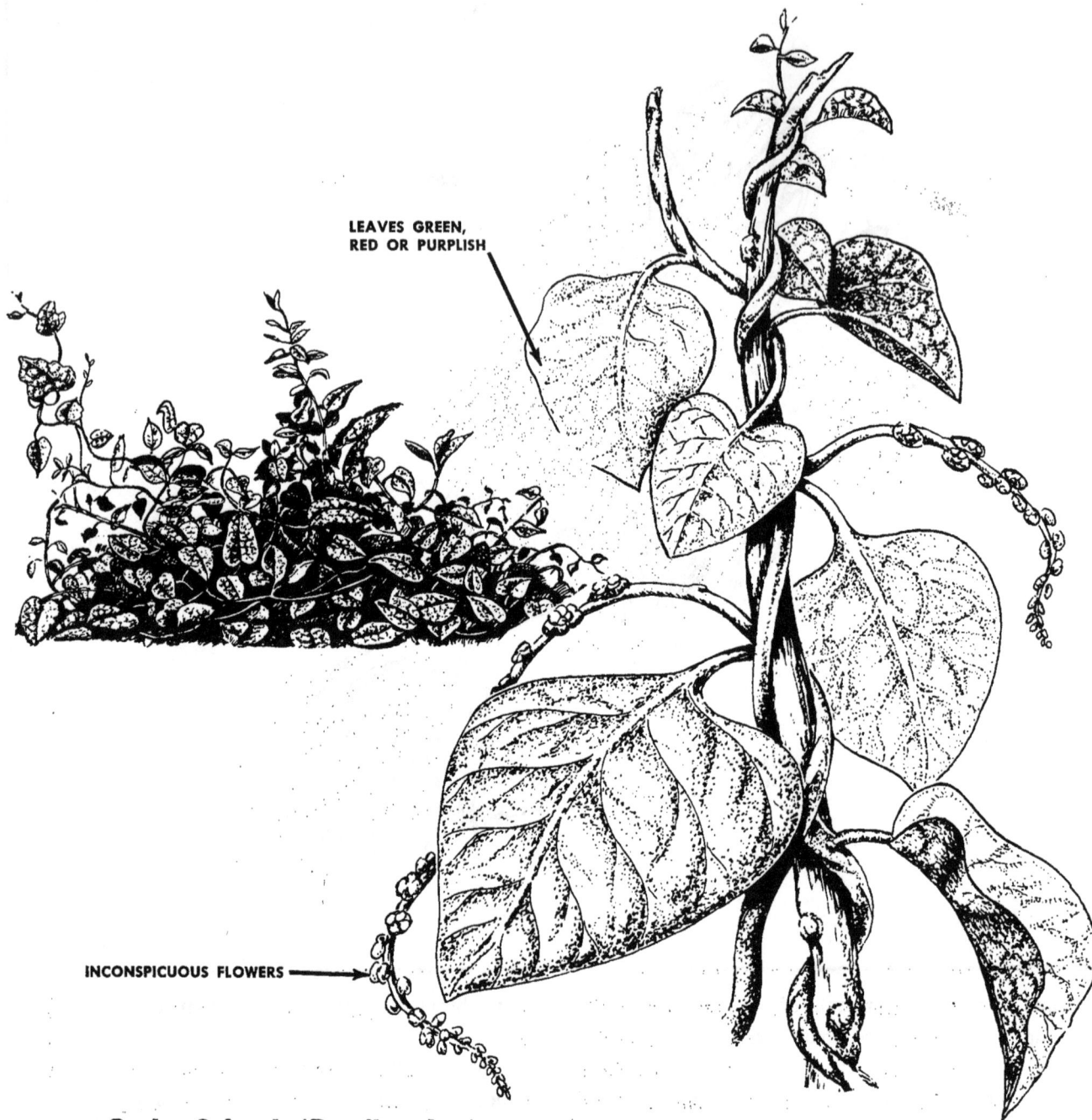

Ceylon Spinach (Basella rubra)

WHERE FOUND. (Regions 1, 2.) Ceylon spinach occurs throughout the Old World Tropics in both Africa and Asia. This fleshy, entwining vine grows in hedges, along trails, and near old abandoned habitations. It does not occur in the forest.

APPEARANCE. The twining stems and the leaves may be green, red, or purplish. The small flowers are pink, and the fruits are black or dark purple.

WHAT TO EAT. The whole plant may be eaten raw or cooked like spinach.

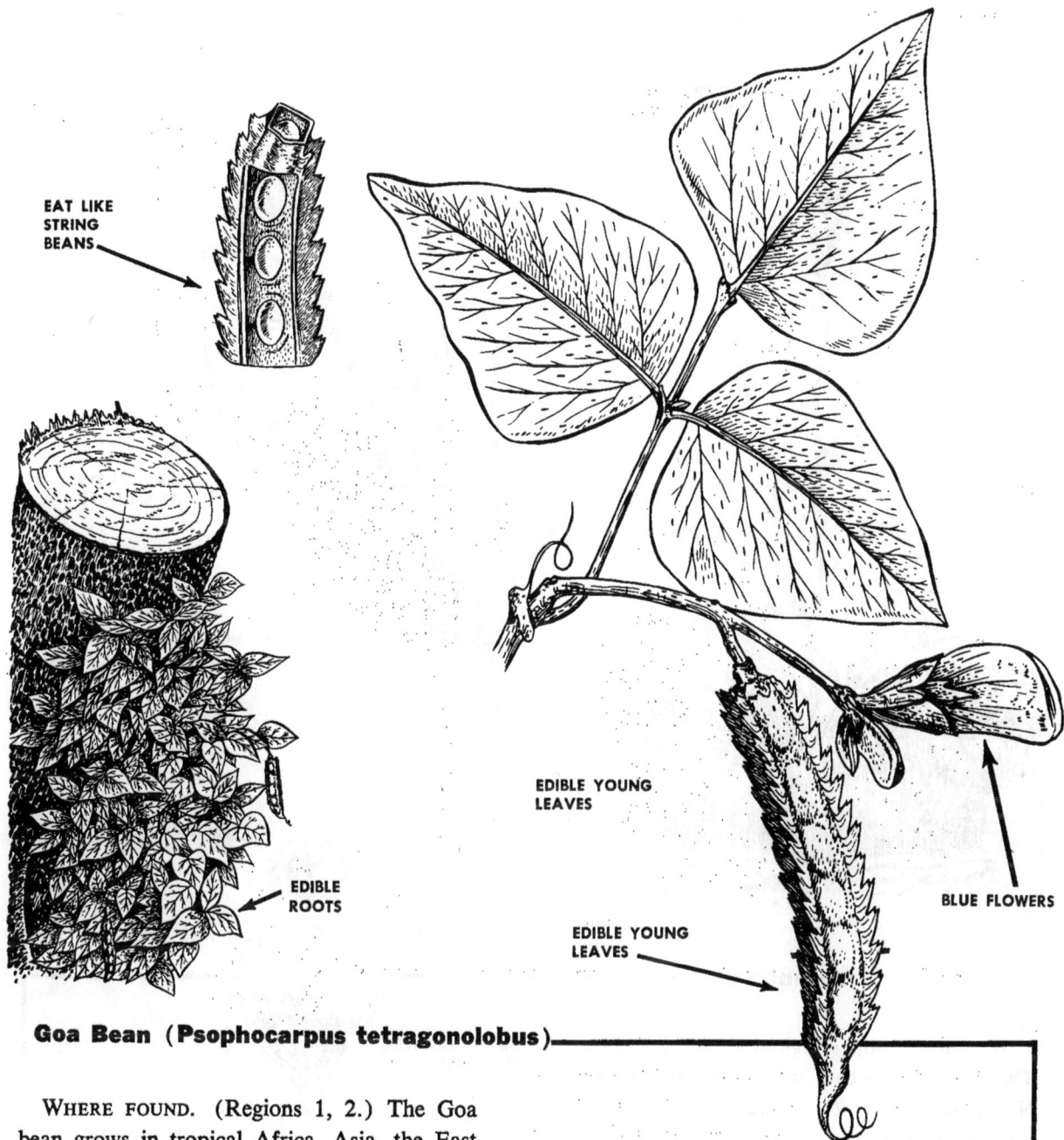

EAT LIKE
STRING
BEANS

EDIBLE YOUNG
LEAVES

BLUE FLOWERS

EDIBLE
ROOTS

EDIBLE YOUNG
LEAVES

Goa Bean (Psophocarpus tetragonolobus)

WHERE FOUND. (Regions 1, 2.) The Goa bean grows in tropical Africa, Asia, the East Indies, the Philippines, and Formosa. This member of the bean (legume) family serves to illustrate a kind of edible bean common in the Tropics of the Old World. Wild edible beans of this sort occur most frequently in clearings and around abandoned garden sites. They are rarer in forested areas.

APPEARANCE. The Goa bean is a climbing plant which may be expected to cover small shrubs and trees with a bean 9 inches long, leaves 6 inches long, and bright blue flowers. The mature pods are 4-angled, with jagged wings on the pods.

WHAT TO EAT. The young pods may be eaten like string beans. The mature seeds are considered a valuable source of protein after parching or roasting over hot coals. The seeds may also be germinated (as can many kinds of beans) in damp moss and the resultant sprouts eaten.

The thickened roots may be eaten raw. They are slightly sweet, with the firmness of an apple. The young leaves can be eaten as a vegetable, raw or steamed.

REDDISH
SEED HEAD

3-5 FT.
TALL

LEAVES USED
AS SPINACH

SEED HEAD

EDIBLE SEED

FIELD WEED

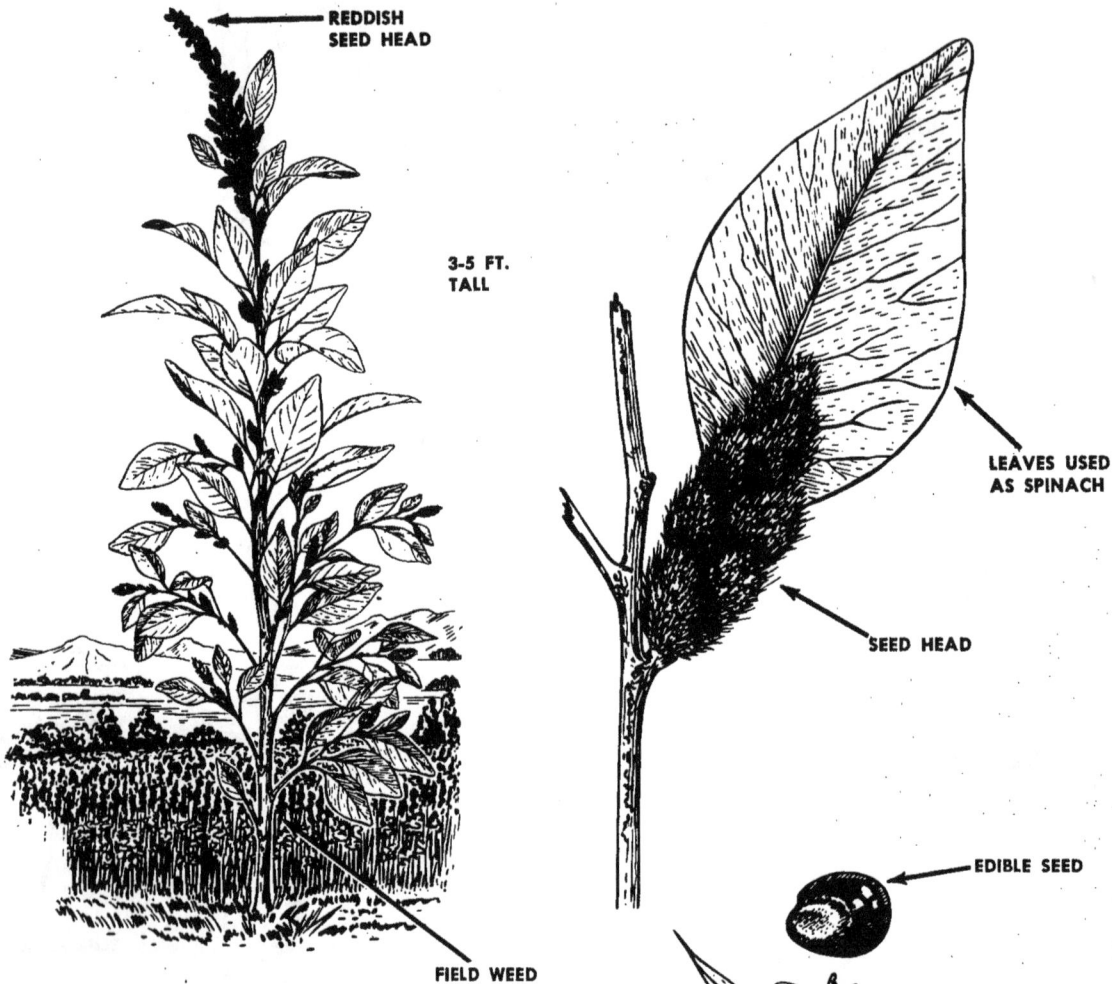

Amaranth (Amaranthus)

SINGLE FLOWER
WITH SEED

WHERE FOUND. (Regions 2, 4, 6, 9, 12.) The amaranth occurs widely throughout the North Temperate Zone and the Tropics of America and Asia but is rare in Africa. It is usually a weed found in abandoned fields or along roads and trails where it has been spread largely by grazing animals. The amaranth is not to be looked for in dense forested areas. In both tropical America and Asia the amaranth is a cultivated crop plant. It is a common garden weed in most parts of the United States.

APPEARANCE. The amaranth grows quickly after a warm rainy season. The plant is usually coarse in appearance and 3-5 feet tall. The flowers are minute and occur in a dense, plumy head. The seeds shatter away from the flowering head at maturity and are easily picked up.

WHAT TO EAT. The black, shiny seeds may be beaten out and then pulverized with stones. The flour produced by this method may be used as an additive in soup, or it can be cooked as porridge of high food content.

The young, tender leaves of the amaranth may be used for spinach.

EDIBLE PALM CABBAGE

SINGLE LEAF

100-200 FT. TALL

CUT STEM FOR WATER

SWOLLEN STEMS EDIBLE

EDIBLE FRUITS

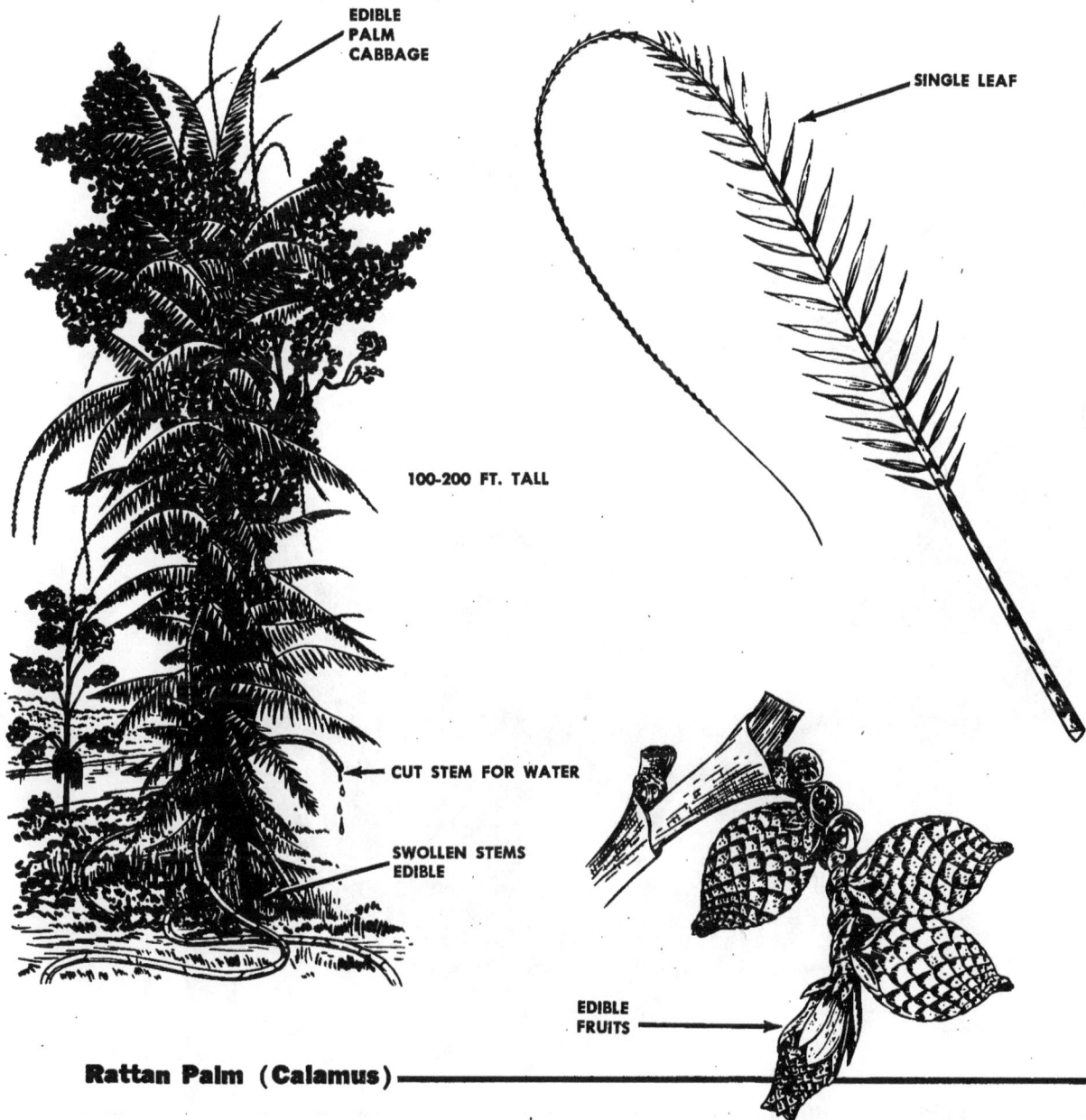

Rattan Palm (Calamus)

WHERE FOUND. (Regions 1, 2.) The rattan palm occurs from tropical Africa through tropical Asia to the East Indies and Australia. These are all climbing palms and are easy to recognize. They occur chiefly in the rain forest.

APPEARANCE. The rattan palm is a stout, robust climber with hooks on the midrib of the leaves which enable the plant to remain attached to trees on which it grows. Sometimes mature stems grow to a height of 300 feet.

WHAT TO EAT. In a few kinds of rattan palm the slightly swollen basal part, just above the surface of the ground, contains a considerable amount of starch, which may be roasted and eaten. In some kinds, the seeds are surrounded by a gelatinous pulp, either sweet or sour, which may be sucked out. The palm cabbage of some kinds of also edible.

SOURCE OF WATER. By severing the long stems it is possible to obtain large quantities of drinking water. The procedure is outlined on page 246. This palm is especially valuable in regions where drinking water is scarce.

GREEN MALE
FLOWERS

TO 30 FT. HIGH

EDIBLE FRUIT,
DARK RED TO
BLACK

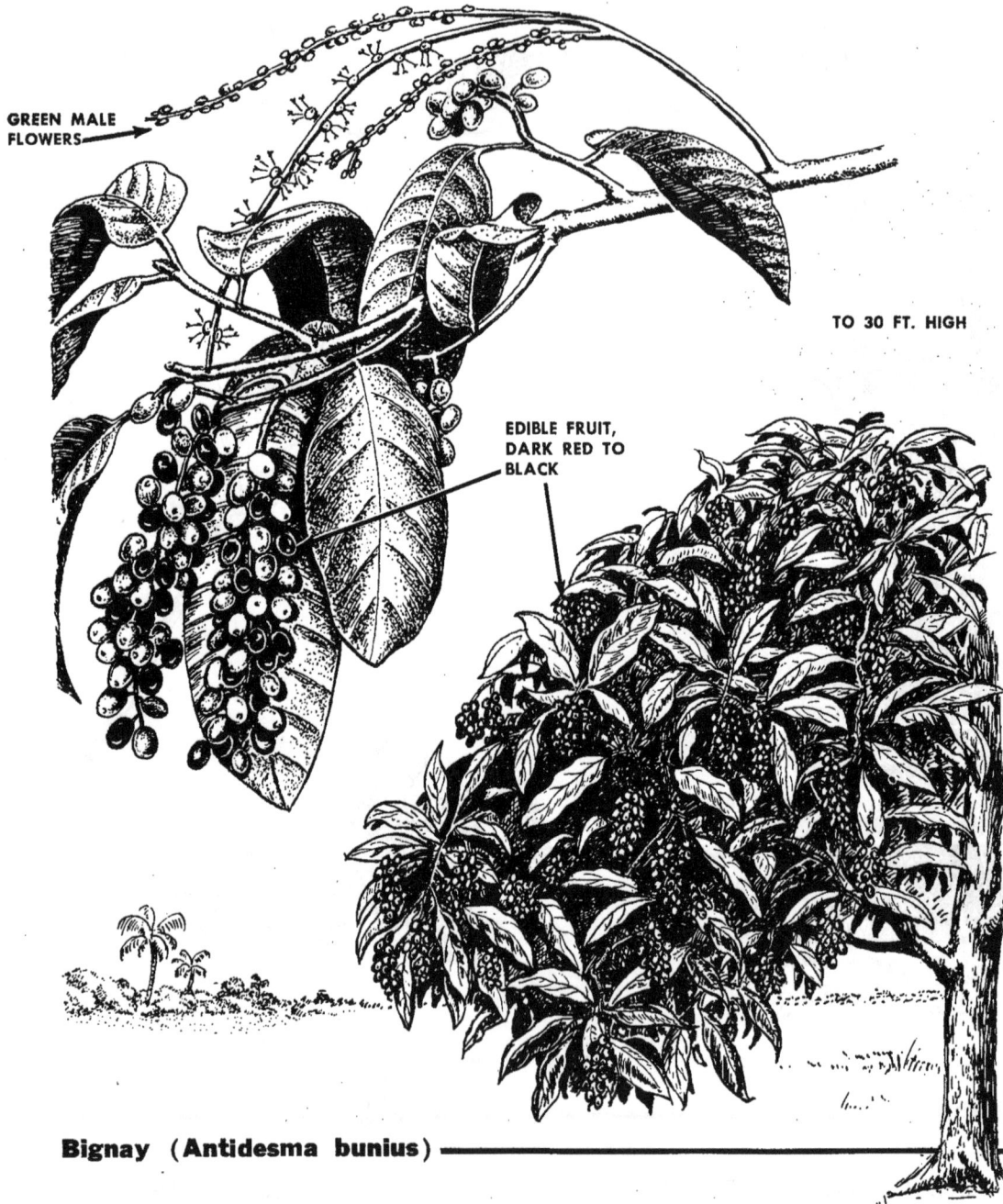

Bignay (Antidesma bunius)

WHERE FOUND. (Regions 1, 2.) The bignay occurs wild from the Himalayas to Ceylon and eastward through Indonesia to northern Australia. This shrub or tree is frequently cultivated elsewhere in tropical climates and about 70 known varieties exist. They are found in open places and in secondary forests.

APPEARANCE. These are shrubs to small trees, 12-40 feet tall, with leaves 6 inches long, shiny and pointed at the tip. The flowers are small and green.

WHAT TO EAT. The fleshy, currantlike fruit is about 1/2 inch in diameter. The fruit is dark red to black in color, acid, and with a single seed. It can be eaten raw.

EDIBLE FLOWERS

TO 8 FT. HIGH

CINNAMON-
BROWN POD

EDIBLE SEEDS
AND PULP

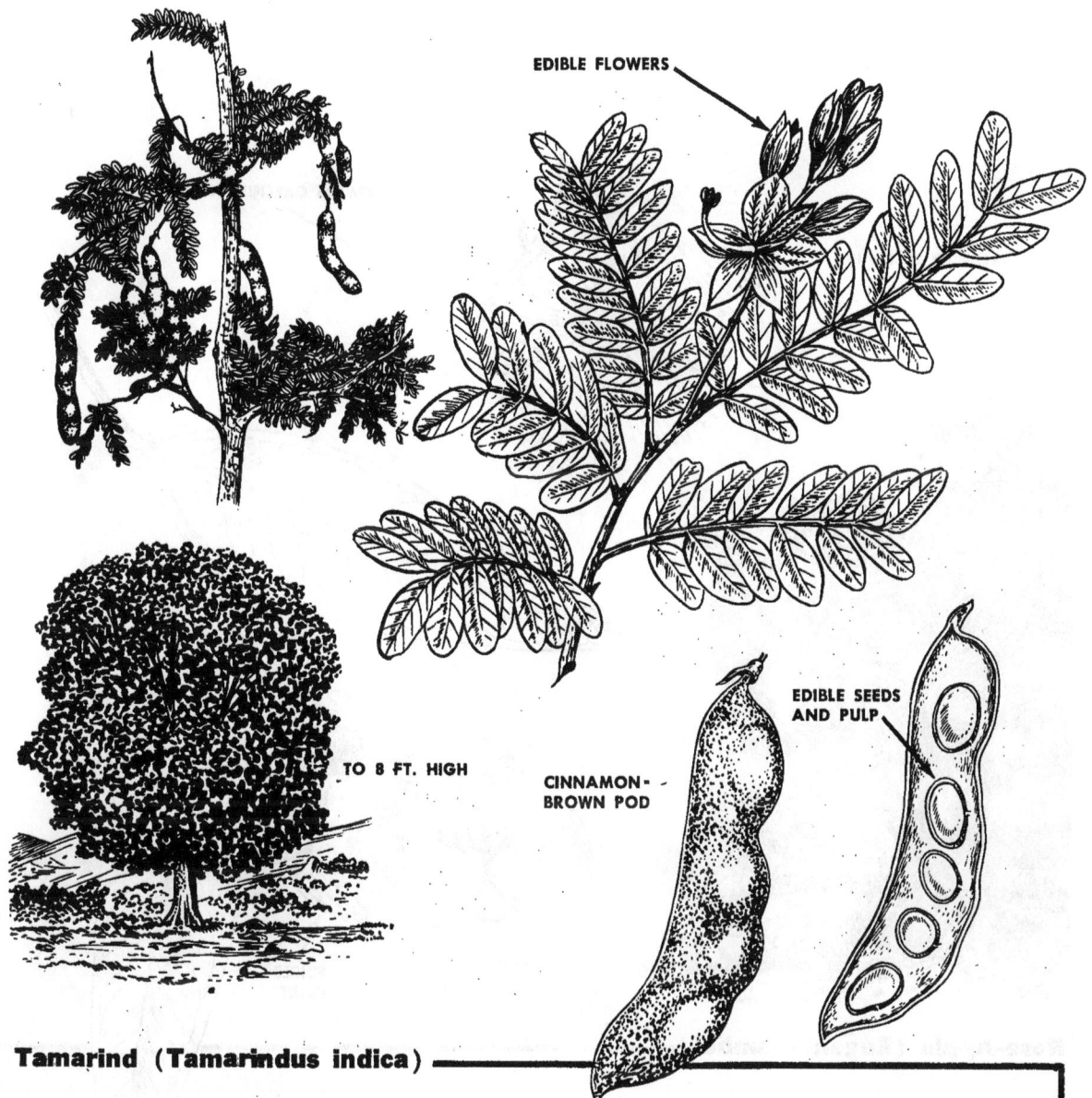

Tamarind (Tamarindus indica)

WHERE FOUND. (Regions 1, 2, 3, 4.) The tamarind grows in the drier parts of tropical Africa, Asia, and the Philippines. It is thought to be a native of Africa, but in India the tamarind has been cultivated for so long it has the appearance of a native tree. It also occurs in the American Tropics, the West Indies, Central America, and tropical South America.

APPEARANCE. The tamarind is a large, densely branched tree, up to 80 feet tall. The leaves are divided like a feather (pinnate) with 10-15 pairs of leaflets.

WHAT TO EAT. The pulp surrounding the seeds is rich in vitamin C, and is an important survival food. A pleasantly acid drink can be made by a cold mixture of the pulp with sugar or honey and water, left to mature for several days. The pulp itself can be sucked to relieve thirst.

The young, unripe fruits or seed pods may be cooked with meat, and the young leaves may be used in soup.

The seeds can be eaten after being roasted above a fire or in ashes. Another method is to remove the seed coat and soak the seeds in salt water and grated coconut for 24 hours. Then cook the seeds; the seeds are eaten cooked.

Tamarind bark can be peeled and chewed.

TREES TO 30 FT. HIGH

FLOWERS GREENISH WHITE

EDIBLE
FRUIT

GREENISH
OR YELLOW

EDIBLE FRUIT
2 IN. IN DIAMETER

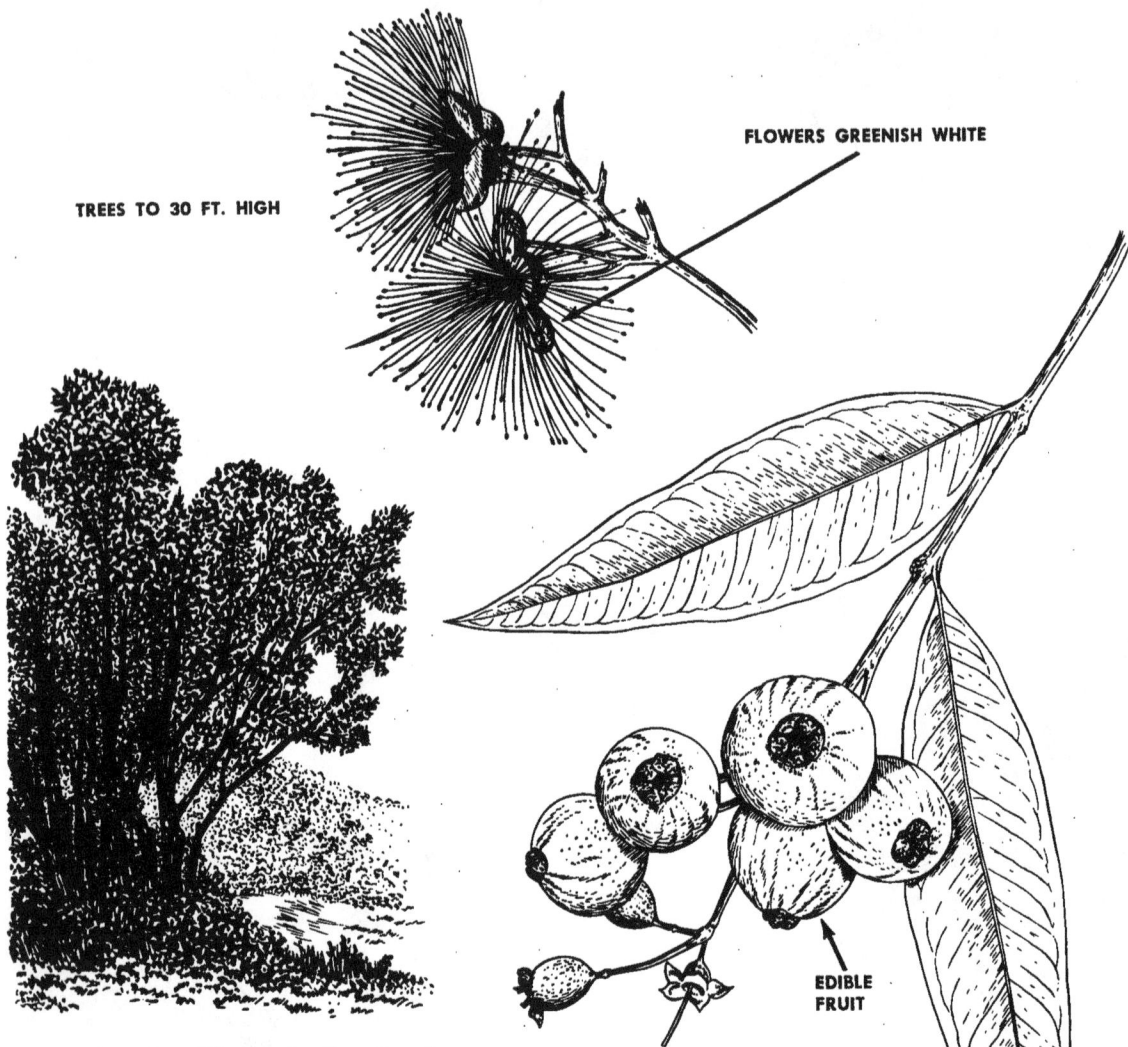

Rose-Apple (Eugenia jambos)

WHERE FOUND. (Regions 1, 2.) The rose-apple is a native of the Indo-Malayan region. It has been widely planted in most other tropical countries, where it is also found in the semiwild state. It usually occurs in thickets, waste places, and secondary forests.

APPEARANCE. The rose-apple is a small tree, 10-30 feet tall, with tapering leaves up to 8 inches long. The flowers are greenish-white and up to 3 inches across. The fruit is 2 inches in diameter, greenish or yellow. The relatives of the rose-apple (all of the myrtle family and the eucalyptus) are very numerous especially in the Old World Tropics. Most related forms look enough like the rose-apple that they can be easily distinguished.

WHAT TO EAT. The pear-shaped, rose-scented, greenish-white fruits can be eaten fresh or cooked with sugar, honey, or palm sap.

GREENISH WHITE
FLOWERS

8-15 FT. TALL

GRAY OR YELLOWISH
EDIBLE FRUIT, 2-4 IN.
IN DIAMETER

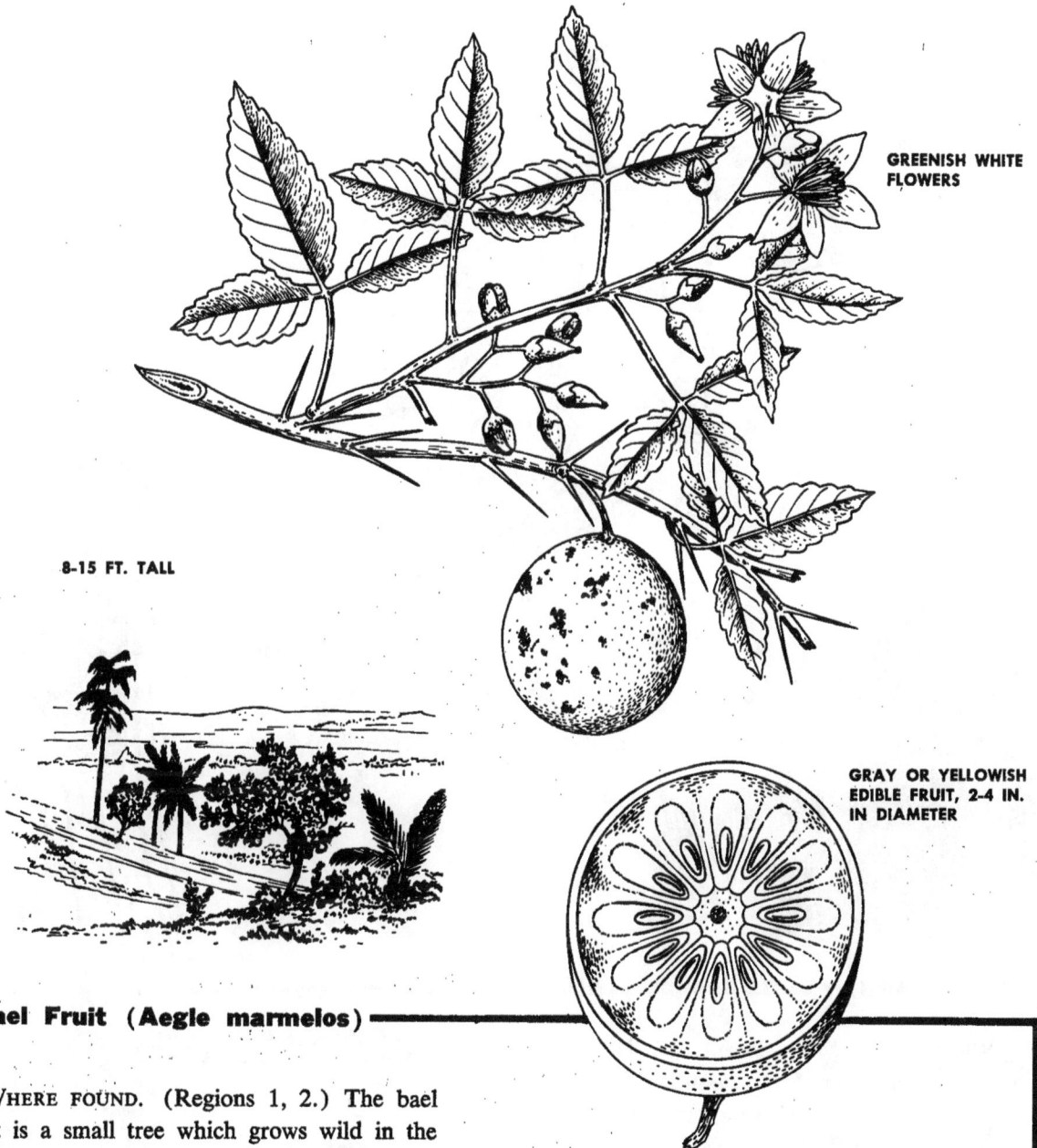

Bael Fruit (Aegle marmelos)

WHERE FOUND. (Regions 1, 2.) The bael fruit is a small tree which grows wild in the region of India bordering the Himalaya mountains, in central and southern India, and in Burma. It is a type of citrus tree. Asia is the home of the orange, lemon, grapefruit, and many of their wild relatives will be found in this region. The bael fruit is an example of citrus fruit which is generally unknown in America.

APPEARANCE. The tree is 8-15 feet tall with a dense and spiny growth. The fruit is 2-4 inches in diameter, gray or yellowish, and full of seeds.

WHAT TO EAT. The fruit is at its best when just turning ripe. The ripe fruit, diluted with water and mixed with a small quantity of tamarind and sweetening, makes a delicious and cooling drink. The fruit, if eaten fresh, is sour but refreshing, and like other citrus fruits is rich in vitamin C. The fruit ripens in December.

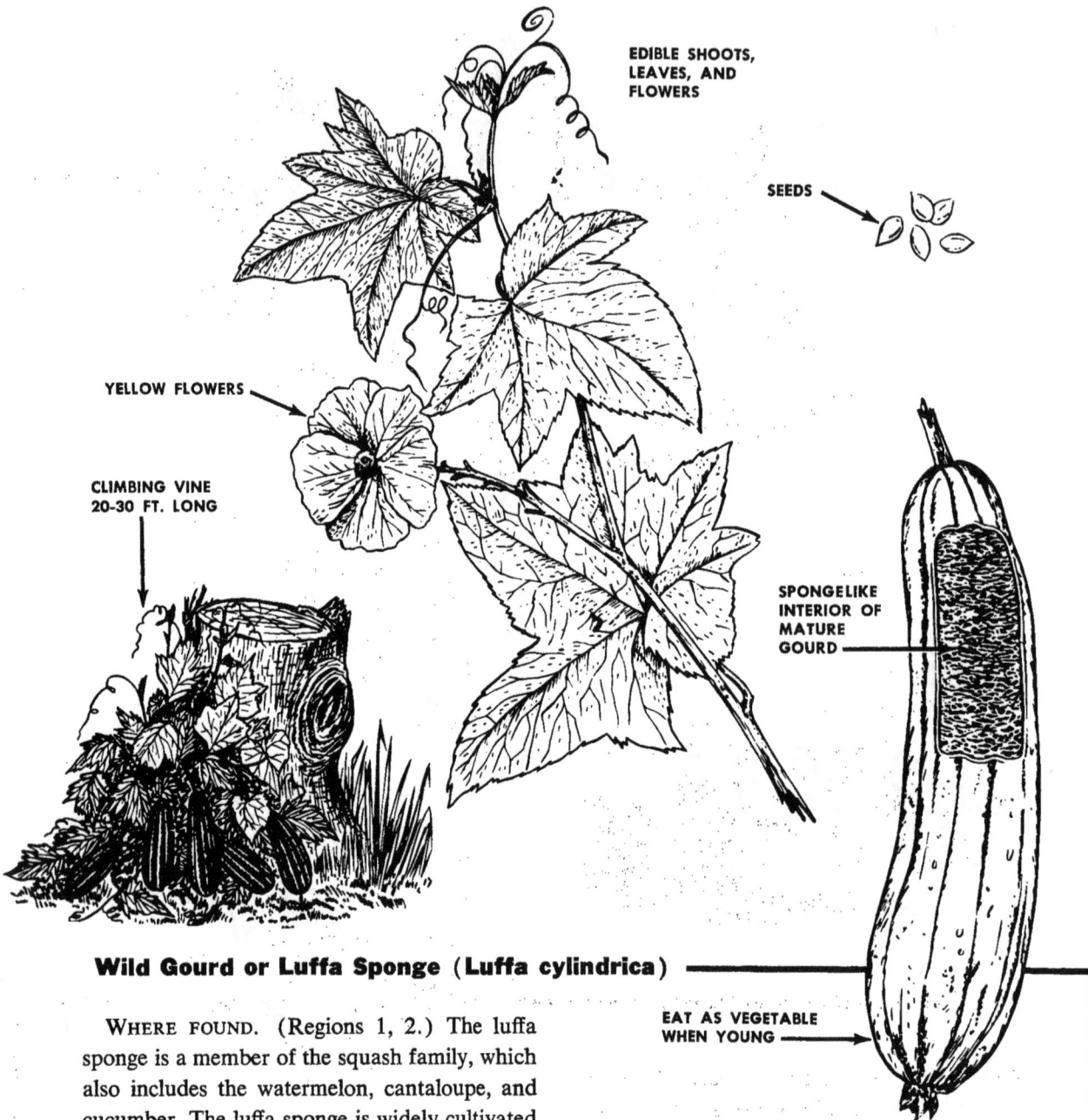

EDIBLE SHOOTS, LEAVES, AND FLOWERS

SEEDS

YELLOW FLOWERS

CLIMBING VINE 20-30 FT. LONG

SPONGELIKE INTERIOR OF MATURE GOURD

EAT AS VEGETABLE WHEN YOUNG

Wild Gourd or Luffa Sponge (Luffa cylindrica)

WHERE FOUND. (Regions 1, 2.) The luffa sponge is a member of the squash family, which also includes the watermelon, cantaloupe, and cucumber. The luffa sponge is widely cultivated throughout the tropical zone, and it may be expected to occur in a semiwild state in old clearings and abandoned gardens.

APPEARANCE. The luffa sponge has been selected as a widely distributed and fairly typical example of a wild squash. Actually, there are several dozen kinds of wild squashes in tropical regions. Like most squashes, the luffa is a vine with leaves 3-8 inches across and with 5-7 lobes. Some squashes have leaves twice this size. Luffa fruits are oblong or cylindrical, smooth, and many-seeded.

WHAT TO EAT. The young green (half ripe) fruits may be boiled and eaten as a vegetable. The addition of coconut milk, if available, will improve this dish.

After ripening, the luffa sponge develops a spongelike texture in the interior of the fruit, which is not edible.

The tender shoots, flowers, and young leaves may be eaten after cooking. The mature seeds may be slightly roasted and eaten like peanuts.

FLOWERS INCONSPICUOUS

SHRUBS TO
9 FT. HIGH

EDIBLE ROOTSTALK

BOIL OR ROAST
BEFORE EATING

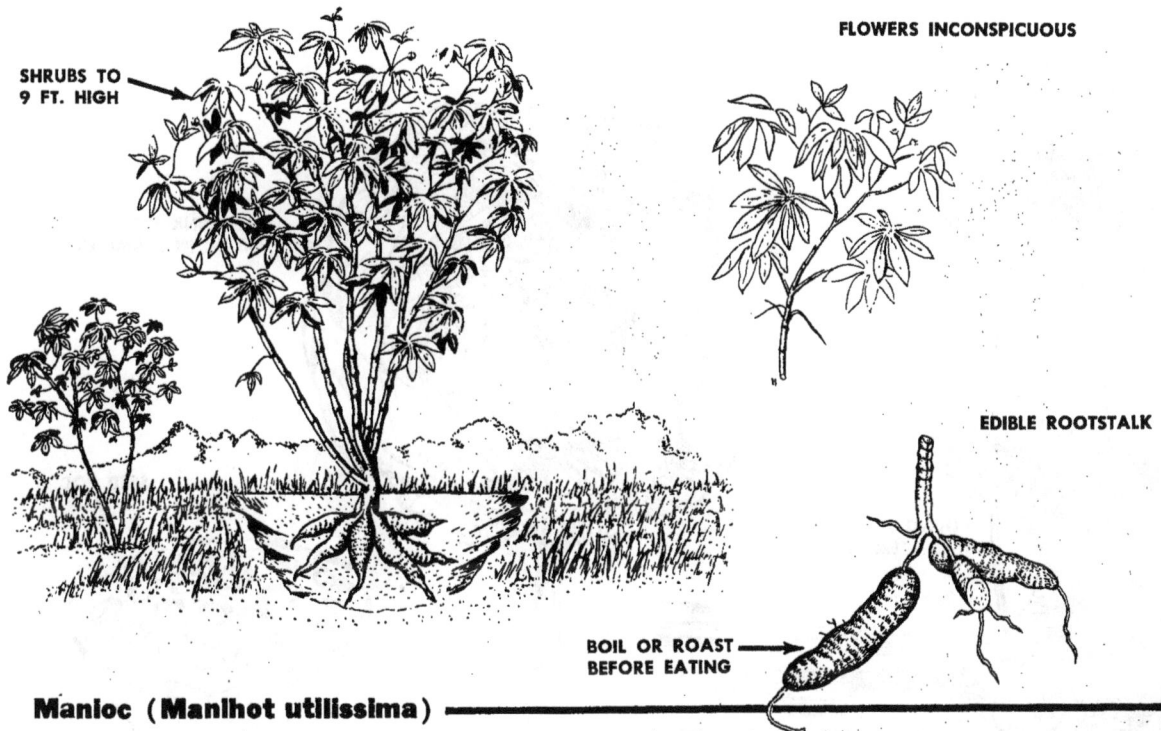

Manioc (Manihot utilissima)

WHERE FOUND. (Regions 1, 2, 3.) Manioc is widespread in all tropical climates, especially in the moister districts. Although cultivated extensively in most parts, it will be found in abandoned gardens and growing wild over wide areas.

APPEARANCE. Manioc is a perennial shrubby plant, 3-9 feet tall, with jointed stems, and deep green fingerlike leaves. The large fleshy rootstalks are full of starch and are the part eaten.

WHAT TO EAT. Manioc is known by many names, including manioca, mandioc, manihot, cassava, casabi, yuca, and rumu. It is high in food value. Commercial tapioca and a sauce which forms the basis of Worcestershire sauce are derived from this plant.

Two kinds of manioc are known, bitter and sweet. Both kinds are edible, but the bitter variety is poisonous if eaten uncooked.

The *bitter manioc* is the common variety in many areas. Its poisonous properties are due to minute quantities of hydrocyanic acid. To test for bitterness just nibble on a piece of the rootstalk, and if it tastes bitter, prepare it in the following manner. First grind the fresh manioc root into a pulp, then cook it for at least 1 hour. The poisonous properties will have been driven off completely, leaving the manioc quite safe and edible. The wet pulp can then be flattened into cakes and baked as a kind of bread.

Another method is to cook the roots in large pieces, for at least 1 hour, after which they can be grated and peeled. Press this pulp and knead it with a little water in order to remove the milky white juice. Steam it and then pound it into a plastic mass. Roll the paste into small balls and flatten into thin cakes by means of a bamboo or wooden roller. Dry the cakes in the sun. These can be eaten baked or roasted with salt or sugar added, if available.

One of the great advantages of manioc is its keeping qualities. Both manioc flour and manioc cakes keep almost indefinitely if they can be protected from insects and dampness. Manioc flour seems immune to weevils or moulds if packed in baskets lined with banana leaves.

The roots of the *sweet manioc* are not bitter and may be eaten raw, roasted as a vegetable, made into flour, or boiled in dumplings. Roasted manioc has an agreeable flavor faintly resembling chestnuts.

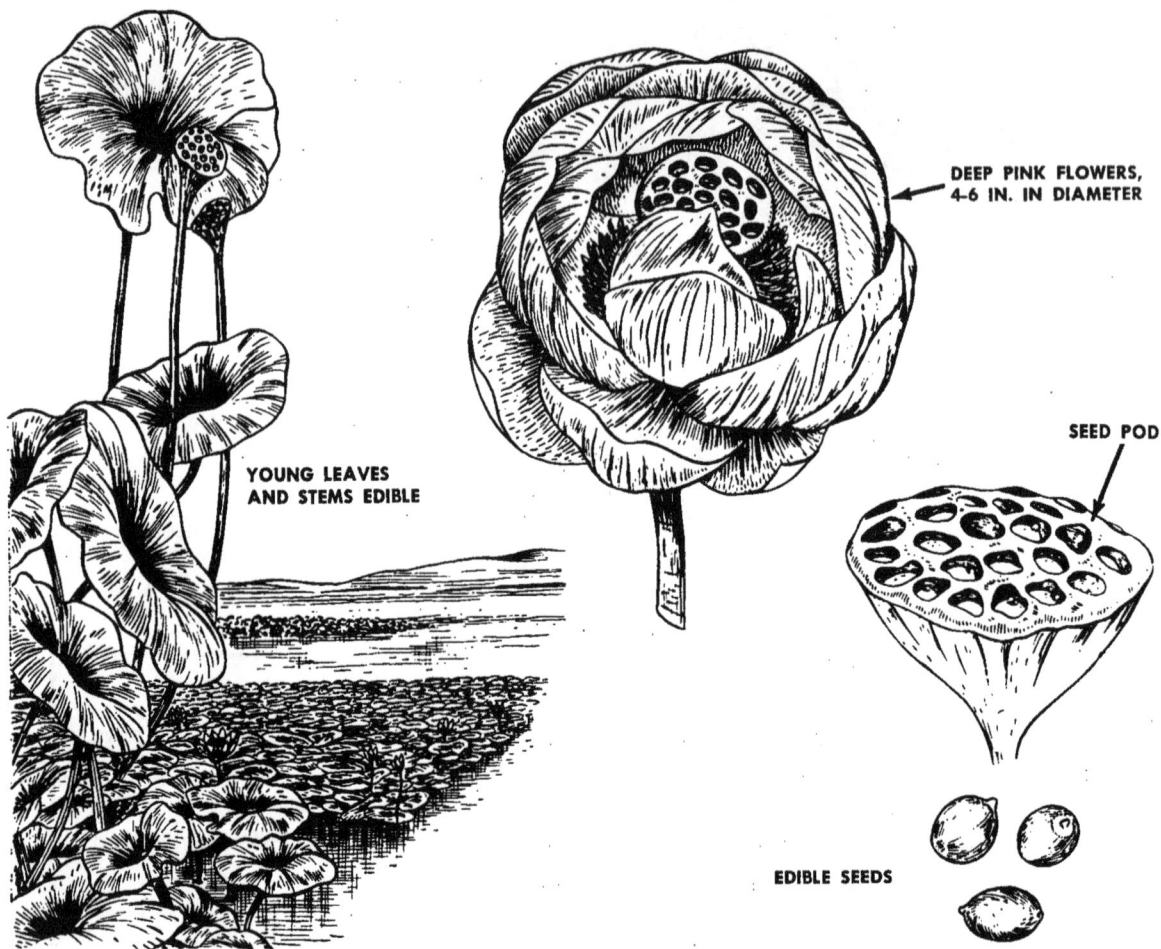

DEEP PINK FLOWERS, 4-6 IN. IN DIAMETER

YOUNG LEAVES AND STEMS EDIBLE

SEED POD

EDIBLE SEEDS

Lotus Lily (Nelumbium)

WHERE FOUND. (Regions 1, 2, 6.) Lotus lilies are aquatic plants of fresh water lakes, ponds, and slow streams wherever they occur in the Old and the New World. The lotus lily in the Old World occurs from the Nile basin through Asia to China and Japan and southward to India and the Himalayan region. It occurs also in the Philippines, Indonesia and northern Australia.

In the New World, the lotus lily is confined to the eastern United States.

APPEARANCE. The leaves are shield-shaped, usually standing 5-6 feet above the surface of the water. The leaves are 1-3 feet across. The flowers are 4-10 inches in diameter, pink in the Old World species, white or yellow in the American species. The large flat-topped seed pods contain numerous seeds.

WHAT TO EAT. The seeds are edible when ripe. To prepare them, remove the very bitter, but nonpoisonous embryo (the tiny growing point within the seed), and then boil or roast them. The seeds may be eaten raw when slightly unripe (less bitter).

The rootstalks often become 50 feet long, with tuberous enlargements which become filled with starch in the fall. These tubers may be boiled and eaten like potatoes.

The young stems and young leaves can be eaten after cooking. But the rough outer layer of the young stems should be removed beforehand.

The young tender seed pods are considered a delicacy by people in Indonesia, especially as a salad.

3-6 IN. TALL

GROWS AS SPREADING COLONY

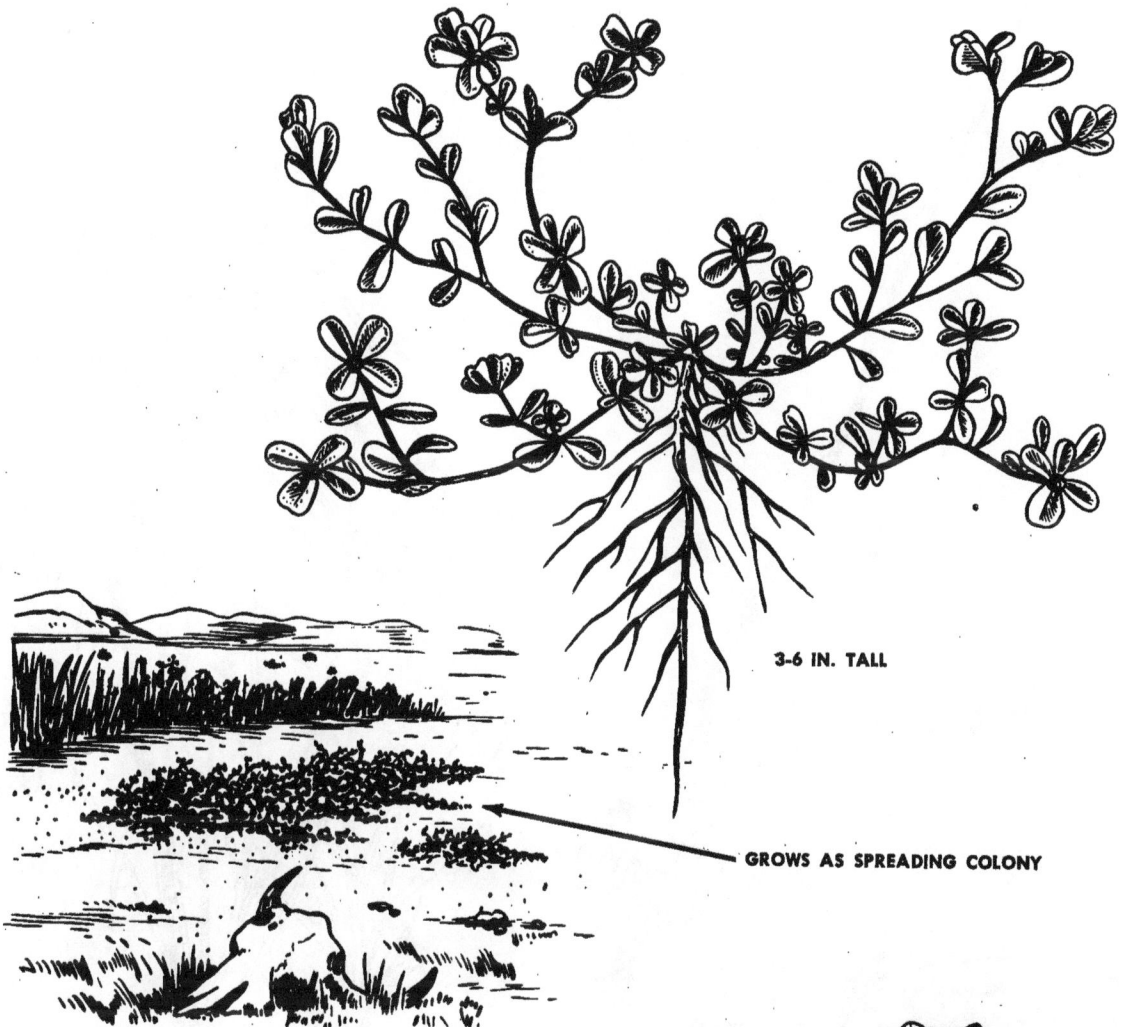

Purslane (Portulaca oleracea)

SMALL YELLOW
FLOWERS

WHERE FOUND. (Regions 1, 2, 4, 6, 10.)
The purslane is extremely common as a weed
in many parts of the United States and throughout the Tropics and Temperate Zones. It is
found in abandoned fields, along roadsides and
trails, and on beaches. Wherever it occurs, large
quantities may be found.

APPEARANCE. The purslane is a rather
small, nondescript-looking plant which might
easily be overlooked. The whole plant has a
reddish hue, and the stems are quite fleshy. Its
flowers are small and yellow. The plant grows
no more than 3 to 6 inches high, but it has
the habit of spreading along the ground for a
foot or so.

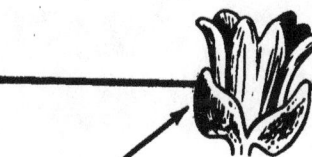

WHAT TO EAT. All parts of the plant, except the roots, may be eaten raw as a salad or
cooked like spinach.

**EDIBLE TUBER
½-1 IN. IN DIAMETER**

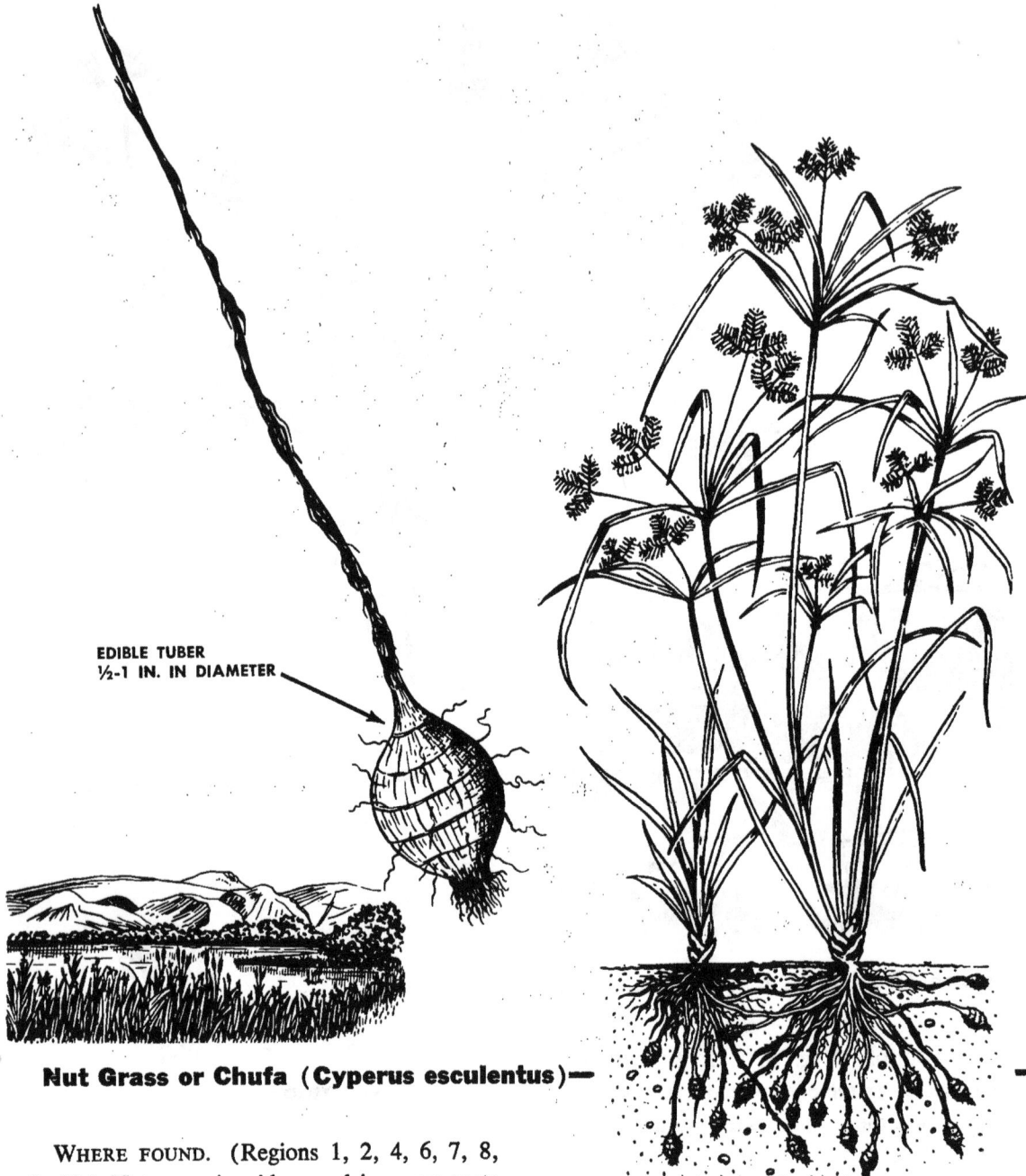

Nut Grass or Chufa (Cyperus esculentus)—

WHERE FOUND. (Regions 1, 2, 4, 6, 7, 8, 9, 12.) Nut grass is widespread in many parts of the world and may be looked for in any moist sandy place, along the margins of streams, ponds, and in ditches. It occurs as frequently in tropical as in temperate climates but is not found in Arctic regions.

APPEARANCE. The nut grass has a grasslike appearance but differs from true grasses by having a 3-angled stem and thick underground tubers, which grow to a diameter of 1/2-1 inch.

WHAT TO EAT. The underground nutlike tubers contain starch. They are slightly sweetish and nutty, although the tough, dry rind is not easily chewed. They can be boiled, peeled, and ground into a palatable and wholesome flour, which may be brewed as a coffee substitute.

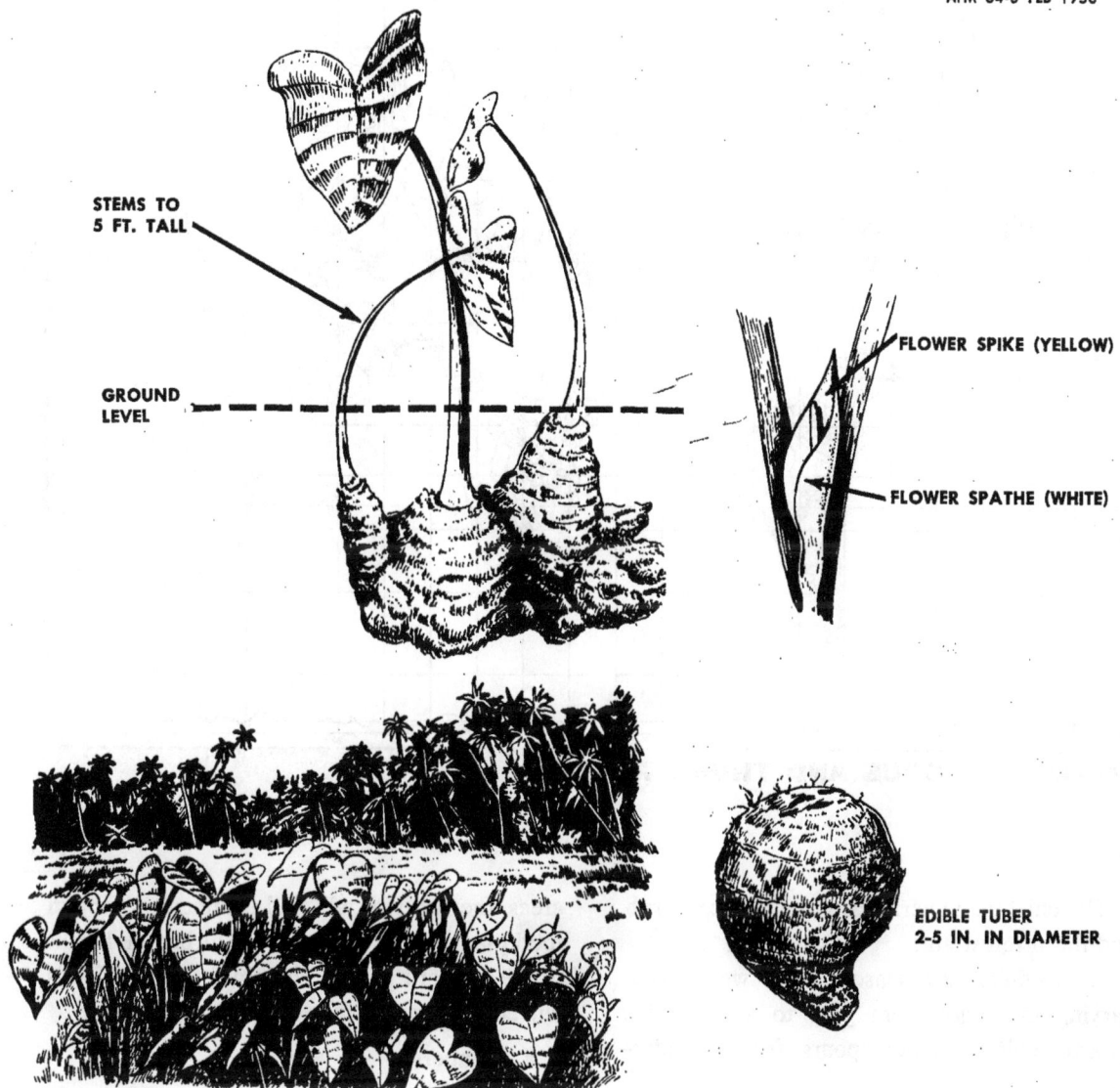

STEMS TO
5 FT. TALL

GROUND
LEVEL

FLOWER SPIKE (YELLOW)

FLOWER SPATHE (WHITE)

EDIBLE TUBER
2-5 IN. IN DIAMETER

Taro (Colocasia esculentum)

WHERE FOUND. (Regions 1, 2.) The taro grows in nearly all the tropical countries. It is a plant of moist, forested regions, but it may also be looked for near abandoned villages, along streams, and in ditches.

APPEARANCE. The taro plant has the appearance of a calla lily plant, with leaves to 2 feet long and stems to 5 feet high. The flower is pale yellow and may be up to 15 inches long.

WHAT TO EAT. The tubers, only slightly below ground level, can be cooked and eaten like potatoes.

CAUTION

The tubers must be boiled to destroy the minute crystals which are very irritating.

The young leaves can be eaten like spinach, but they should always be boiled for the reason mentioned above.

NOTE: The taro belongs to a large plant family called the *araceae*. Many varieties of *araceae* occur throughout the moist Tropics in both America and the Old World, and many of these develop underground tubers. However, all kinds must first be cooked before eating because of the minute irritating crystals contained therein. The foliage of most varieties strikingly resembles the taro.

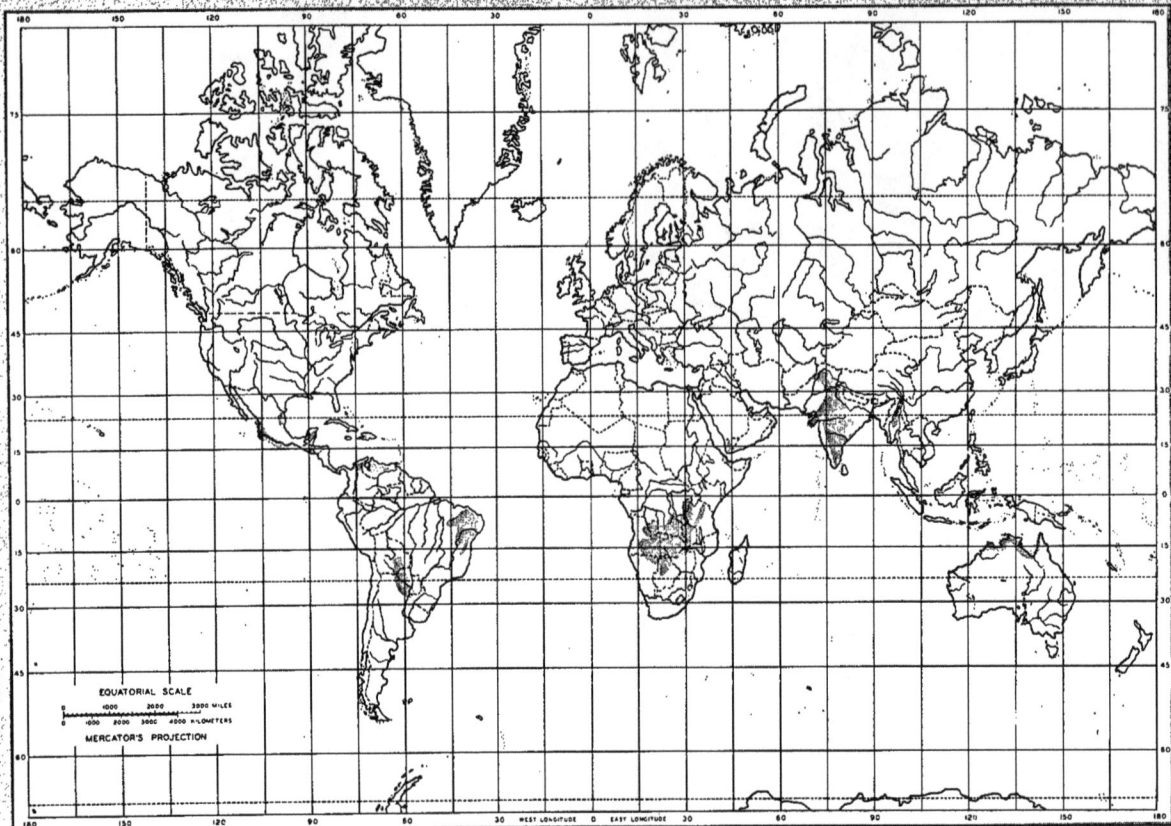

TROPICAL SCRUB AND THORN FOREST

The chief characteristics of the tropical scrub and thorn forest are:

a. Definite dry season, with wet season varying in length from year to year. Rains appear mainly as downpours from thunderstorms.

b. Trees leafless during dry season, average height 20-30 feet with tangled undergrowth in places.

c. Ground bare except for a few tufted plants in bunches; grasses not common.

d. Plants with thorns predominate.

e. Fires occur at intervals.

The principal areas of tropical scrub and thorn forest are:

a. America — West coast of Mexico, Yucatan, Venezuela, and Brazil.

b. Africa — Coastal northwest Africa and south-central Africa — Angola, Rhodesia, Tanganyika, Nyasaland.

c. Asia — Turkestan, and India.

Plant Foods

Within the tropical scrub and thorn forest areas, the survivor will find it difficult to obtain food plants in the dry season. During the height of the drought period, the chief kinds of foods will come from the following plant parts:

a. Tubers.
b. Rootstalks.
c. Bulbs.
d. Corms.
e. Pith.
f. Gums and resins.
g. Nuts.
h. Seeds and grains.

During the rainy season in the tropical scrub and thorn forest, plant food will be considerably more abundant than in the dry season. At this time the survivor should look for the following edible plants, which are discussed on the pages indicated.

Sweet acacia (p. 214).
Baobab (p. 321).
Mescal (p. 220).
Cashew nut (p. 295).
Sea orach (p. 218).

314

Wild capers (p. 219).
St. Johns bread (p. 208).
Wild chicory (p. 61).
Tropical yam (p. 277).
Wild fig (p. 284).
Juniper (p. 78).

Manioc (p. 309).
Water lily (p. 270).
Prickly pear (p. 213).
Pistachio nut (p. 209).
Almond (p. 68).
Tamarind (p. 305).

© Vegetationsbilder

Baobab tree of Africa in its habitat

East African scrub forest

AFM 64-3 FEB 1956

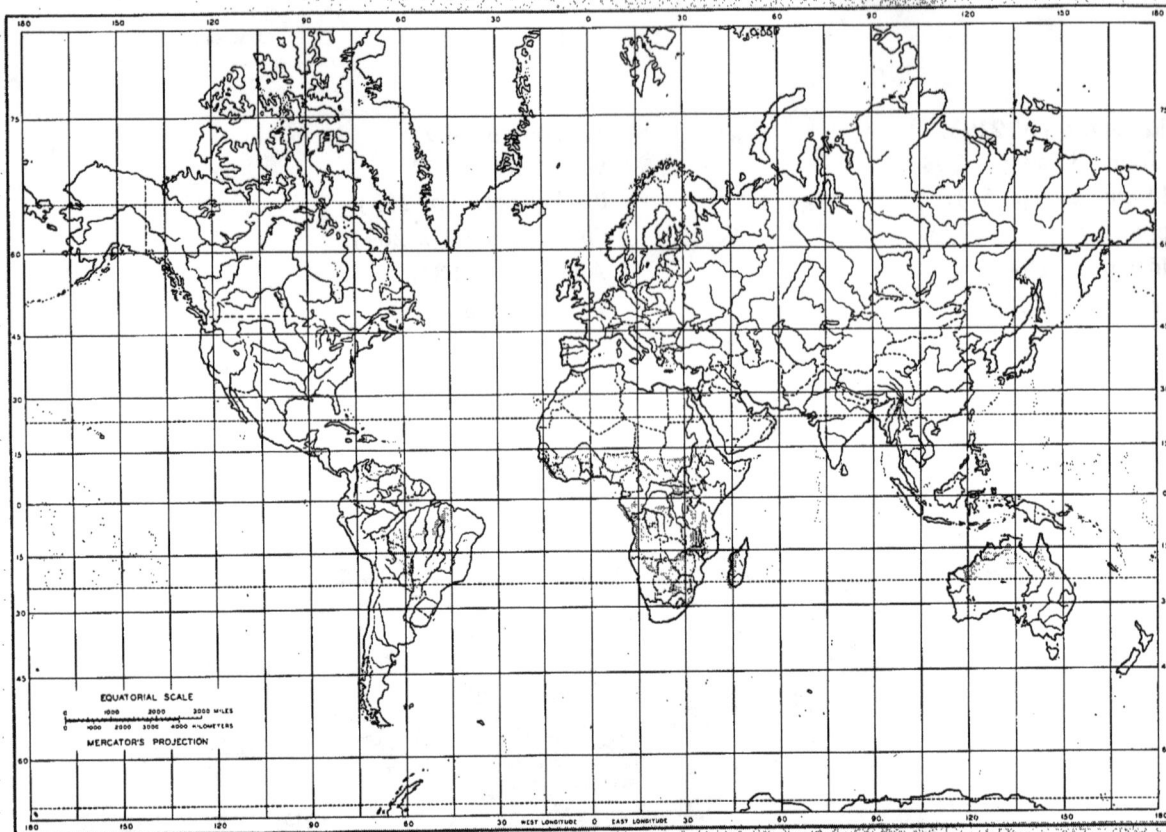

SAVANNA

Some general characteristics of the savanna are listed below.

a. Savannas lie wholly within the tropical zone in South America and Africa.

b. The savanna looks like a broad grassy meadow with trees spaced at wide intervals. The grasses of the tropical savanna often exceed the height of a man. However, none of the savanna grasses are sod-forming in the manner of lawn grasses but are bunch grasses with a definite space between each grass plant.

c. The soil in the savanna is frequently red.

d. The scattered trees usually appear stunted and gnarled like apple trees. Palms also occur on savannas.

Savannas occur in the following areas:

a. South America — Parts of Venezuela, Brazil, and the Guianas.

b. Africa — Southern Sahara (north-central French Equatorial Africa and southern Sudan), northern Gold Coast, most of Nigeria, northeastern Belgian Congo, northern Uganda, western Kenya, part of Nyasaland, part of

Tanganyika, southern Rhodesia, Portuguese East Africa, and western Madagascar.

Savanna of South America

The great expanse of savanna in eastern South America occurs in Venezuela, the Guianas, and northeastern Brazil. In Venezuela the savannas are called "llanos" and in Brazil "campos." For the most part, the vegetation is of the bunch-grass type. A long dry season alternates with a rainy season. In these areas both high and short grasses are present. Bright colored flowers appear between the grass bunches during the rainy season. The grains from the numerous grasses are useful as survival food, as well as the underground parts of the many seasonal plants that appear with and following the rains.

Savanna in Africa

The *high grass tropical savanna* of Africa is dominated by very tall, coarse grasses which grow from 5-15 feet high. Unless the natives burn the grass during the dry season, the sa-

Brazilian Catinga

© Vegetationsbilder

vanna becomes almost impenetrable. This type of savanna occurs in a broad belt surrounding the tropical rain forest and extends from Senegambia in west Africa eastward beyond the Nile River. From the Nile it extends southward over most of Uganda and westward to French Equatorial Africa.

The *tropical bunch grass savanna* comprises the greatest part of the African savannas consisting of grasses about 3 feet tall.

Food Plants

The food plants found on the savanna are also found in other vegetation areas. The fol-lowing plants in this category are described on the pages indicated.

Amaranth (p. 302).

Wild chicory (p. 61).

Nut grass (p. 312).

Wild fig (p. 284).

Water lily (p. 270).

Purslane (p. 311).

Tamarind (p. 305).

The African savanna possesses both dwarf trees and large, even gigantic ones. The most renowned of these giants of the African savanna is the monkeybread, or baobab, which is described on p. 321.

317

© Vegetationsbilder

Southwest African savanna-steppe

Abyssinia

© Vegetationsbilder

© Vegetationsbilder

Southwest Uganda

East African savanna

© Vegetationsbilder

© Vegetationsbilder

Gold Coast

Congo savanna

© Vegetationsbilder

WHITE FLOWERS 6 IN. IN DIAMETER

TO 60 FT. TALL

EDIBLE FRUIT
1 FT. LONG —
ROAST SEEDS

Baobab (Adansonia digitata)

WHERE FOUND. (Regions 3, 4, 7, 9.) The baobab is found throughout tropical Africa, from about 16° N. to 22° S. Although common, it is usually isolated into groups in open bush country.

APPEARANCE. No other tree in tropical Africa can readily be confused with the baobab. It is easily distinguished from all other large trees by the enormous girth and swollen appearance of the trunk in comparison with the relatively low stature of the tree. A mature tree 60 feet high may have a trunk 30 feet in diameter. The flowers are large and white, about 3 inches across, and hang loosely from the tree. The mature fruit is filled with a mealy pulp and numerous seeds.

WHAT TO EAT. The pulp and seeds of the fruit are edible. The young leaves can be used as a soup vegetable. The tender root of the young baobab tree is also edible.

POISONOUS SNAKES

Almost everyone is afraid of snakes. Even the harmless kinds are regarded with loathing and often with terror. Fear of snakes is caused partly by our unfamiliarity with them but mostly as the result of misinformation.

No one expects you to like snakes. But there is no need for you to fear snakes once you know something about them, their habits, how to identify the dangerous kinds, the simple precautions to take to prevent snakebite, and the first aid measures to use in the very rare emergency of being bitten.

Actually, the chances of being bitten by a poisonous snake are very small. The danger of death from snakebite is considerably less than the possibility of being killed in a jeep wreck or getting shot by accident.

You can dismiss as exaggerations most of the popular literature you've read and the stories you've heard about snakes. Don't believe all the hair-raising tales about the number, size, and ferocity of the local snakes in your area. Natives know all the poisonous kinds, but in addition, they will tell you that many harmless species are deadly. For example, in the United States, the common puff adder is considered almost universally to be dangerous. This is nonsense; the American puff adder is nonpoisonous and will hardly ever bite. The African variety, however, is quite venomous.

Statistics on the number of people bitten by poisonous snakes are unreliable. This is especially true in the wilder areas where dangerous snakes are numerous. Furthermore, the fatalities are almost always among people who go about barefoot and get bitten on the feet or ankles. For a man wearing shoes and trousers and living in a camp, the danger of being bitten by a poisonous snake is small compared to the hazards of malaria, cholera, dysentery, or other diseases. Mosquitoes are a thousand times more dangerous than snakes.

Men living in camps and barracks, even where snakes are relatively plentiful, may seldom see one. Men working or fighting in the jungle may see them occasionally. Those engaged in clearing ground, cutting grass or jungle, or digging up soil may see a good many snakes.

There are many reasons why snakes are but a minor hazard. First of all most snakes are harmless and not numerous. It depends mainly on the maturity of the snake. Usually, only a grown one is really dangerous to a man. The bite of the less mature snake is not so likely to be fatal.

However, there are small snakes that are a maximum of about 5 feet and are very poisonous even from the time of birth. A few are listed below:

Snake	Average Size (ft.)	Location
Asiatic cobra	5	India
Asp-Egyptian cobra	3-1/2	Egypt and South Africa
Tic pologna	4	India
Puff adder (African variety)	3-1/2	Morocco and Arabia
Mamba	5	West, Central South Africa
Tiger snake	4	Australia
Sand viper	2	North Africa
Gaboon viper	3-4	Tropical Africa
Urutu	4	Brazil
Coral	1-2	United States, Southwest Pacific

Nearly all snakes avoid man if possbile. It is reported that the king cobra of southeast Asia, the bushmaster of the tropical rattlesnake of South America, and the mamba of Africa sometimes aggressively attack man, but even these snakes do so only occasionally. Most snakes get out of the way (some of them do it slowly) and seldom are seen.

The distance at which a snake may bite has often been exaggerated. This striking distance seldom is more than half the snake's length; in the large snakes, about a third of the length; and in some snakes, even less. However, some of the small vipers have been known to strike from a distance equal to their full length. In a full coil, some snakes have been known to strike from a distance equal to two-thirds their length. The distance a cobra can strike is easy to judge since the part raised is never bent into deceptive S-curves but merely is jabbed forward and downward; commonly the distance is almost 1 foot; in a 12-foot king cobra the striking distance may be as much as 3 feet. Generally, you must be at least within a long step of even a large snake before he can bite you. A normally alert person should be able to see the snake before he gets within striking range. Most bites occur when a snake is stepped on by accident.

All these facts do not mean that no one is going to be bitten or that poisonous snakes are harmless creatures which will make fine pets. *It is stupid and highly dangerous for an inexperienced person to pick up a snake unless he is positive the snake is harmless.*

No one need fear snakes who knows these facts about them. You can minimize the possibility of being bitten by keeping your eyes open, by keeping your hands off *all* snakes, by learning how to identify the dangerous kinds in your own local area, by following the simple precautions for avoiding snakes, and by knowing what to do in the very rare event you are bitten.

Identification of Kinds of Poisonous Snakes

It is not easy to identify a poisonous snake. There is *no single* characteristic which distinguishes a poisonous snake from a harmless one except the presence of poison fangs and glands. You can determine the presence of these parts without danger only in dead specimens, and even then the fangs may be hard to find.

The notion that all poisonous snakes have lance-shaped or triangular heads or some other warning feature is wrong and dangerous. While it is true that many dangerous snakes do have a lance-shaped head, many do not.

The only sure way to identify dangerous snakes is to learn to know and recognize the poisonous kinds on sight in the particular area in which you happen to be based. The illustrations on the following pages describe the important kinds found in your area. In any given locality you are not likely to see more than one or two kinds, and you can learn to identify them further by studying dead specimens. The ability to distinguish a poisonous snake from a harmless one will minimize the danger of snakebite and help to eliminate fear.

Although they are not poisonous, it is worth knowing some facts about pythons, boas, anacondas, and other constrictors. Some of these are large snakes which may grow to 25 feet in length. In spite of the many hair-raising tales concerning these reptiles, they are timid and rarely, if ever, attack man. Boas are found in the American Tropics, pythons in the Tropics of Africa and Asia. They sometimes attack small children but will not deliberately tackle anything that is too big to swallow. A man is too big for even the largest python. If caught or cornered, these snakes may fight back by wrapping their coils around the attacker. If left alone, they are not dangerous.

THE POISONOUS SNAKES OF SOUTHEASTERN ASIA
IDENTIFICATION AND HABITS
THE COBRA FAMILY

COBRAS

Description

The typical combat attitude of the raised head and spread hood is the easiest characteristic by which the cobras can be identified. The most common species is the Indian cobra (shown), which may grow as long as 6 feet. The "spectacle" mark on the hood is typical of this species; the mark may consist of only one spot or of two without the bridge. Cobras usually (but not always) form a hood when angered. The king cobras are the largest of all poisonous snakes; they average 10 to 12 feet long; some may reach 18 feet. For the proportion of the snake, the hood formed by the king cobra is narrower than that of other cobras.

Habits

Cobras are the most common poisonous snakes in much of the region; they are particularly numerous in India where natives do not destroy them because of religious beliefs. Cobras are found most frequently in rocky places or in old buildings where they feed on rats. The most common species are not particularly vicious. However, king cobras may attack deliberately, especially if guarding eggs. Cobras are slow snakes; they always raise the head to strike. They can be killed with a stout stick swung in a plane parallel with the ground, aimed at the head or raised part.

KRAITS

Description

Most kraits are brightly banded in black and white or black and yellow. They have a ridged backbone on which there is a row of enlarged scales. The head is small and not much larger than the neck. Kraits average 4 to 5 feet long but may reach six.

Habits

The common krait of India moves around mostly at night. It lives in open country rather than in thick jungle brush, and is often found near inhabited places and on trails at night. The banded krait (shown) prefers thick jungle. All kraits are very poisonous. However, they are inoffensive snakes who will not bite unless stepped on. Unlike the cobra, kraits do not raise the head to strike, nor do they strike in a loop like a viper — they simply flip the head to one side or the other and bite. Fatalities result mainly from stepping on these snakes at night with bare feet. Shoes should be worn at all times.

CORAL SNAKES

Description

Usually have bright red or pink bellies and brightly colored bands on the back. There are 3 or 4 kinds of coral snakes in this region, generally averaging under 2 ft.; one species may grow 4 ft. long.

Habits

Coral snakes are inoffensive; they stay hidden and are not inclined to bite unless disturbed. They bite in the same manner as kraits. Coral snakes seldom are seen and are the cause of very few fatalities.

POSITIVE IDENTIFICATION OF COBRA FAMILY

(Cobras, Kraits and Coral Snakes)

These snakes can be identified positively by examining the scales of a dead specimen. If the third scale on the upper lip touches *both* the nostril scale and the eye, the snake is a cobra or coral and is poisonous.

If there is also a row of enlarged scales down the ridged back, the snake is a krait.

INDIAN COBRA

KRAIT

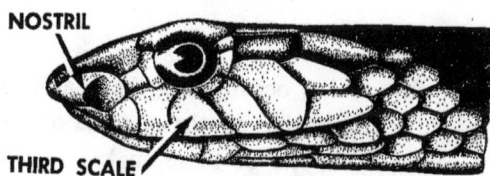

NOSTRIL

THIRD SCALE

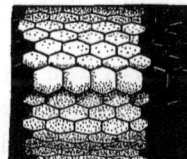

Positive identification of cobra family (cobras, kraits and coral snakes)

THE POISONOUS SNAKES OF SOUTHEASTERN ASIA

IDENTIFICATION AND HABITS

VIPERS

Description

Vipers usually have heads which are much wider than the neck. The most common and most dangerous species is Russell's viper (shown). It is a thick snake which grows up to 5 feet long. There are conspicuous markings on the back, consisting of three rows of spots formed by black rings bordered with white and with reddish or brown centers.

The saw-scaled viper is another dangerous species. These are small snakes, about 2 feet long, generally light in color with dark quadrangles. The side scales are rough and somewhat sawtoothed. When disturbed, these snakes writhe vigorously and make a hissing noise.

Habits

Russell's viper prefers open, sunny spots, but can be found almost anywhere, except in thick jungle. It is not particularly vicious and will not strike unless it is considerably irritated. The saw-scaled viper, though small, is vicious and bites readily; snakes only a foot long have been known to kill. It prefers desert or dry areas and is not found in thick jungle.

PIT VIPERS

Description

Pit vipers in this region either may be slender or thick-bodied. Usually, they have heads which are much wider than the necks. These snakes commonly are brown with dark blotches; some kinds are green. These snakes take their name from the deep pit located between the eye and the nostril.

Habits

India has about a dozen species of these snakes. The pit vipers occur in all types of terrain and may be found in the trees or on the ground. The tree snakes are slender; the ground snakes are thicker and heavy-bodied. Only the larger ones are dangerous. One of the pit vipers of China is a *moccasin* similar to those found in North America; it occurs in the rocky areas of the remote mountains of South China; it attains a length of 4½ feet but is not vicious unless irritated. A small pit viper, about 1½ feet long, is found often on the plains of Eastern China; it is too small to prove dangerous to a man wearing shoes.

POSITIVE IDENTIFICATION OF VIPERS

Vipers and pit vipers have two long and distinctive fangs; none of the other teeth are comparable in size. Fangs may be covered with a curtain of flesh or folded back into the mouth.

SEA SNAKES

Description

These snakes have a flattened oarlike tail and are distinguished from eels by the fact that the snakes have scales and the eels do not. Sea snakes vary widely in color and shape; they average in length from 4 to 5 feet, but sometimes reach a length of 8 to 10 feet.

Habits

Sea snakes occur along the coasts, but also are found at the mouths of some of the larger rivers. The bite of these snakes is dangerous but rare. Sea snakes sometimes may be seen in large numbers but they seldom will bite unless they are handled. They are not known deliberately to attack a man in the water.

RUSSELL'S VIPER

PIT VIPER

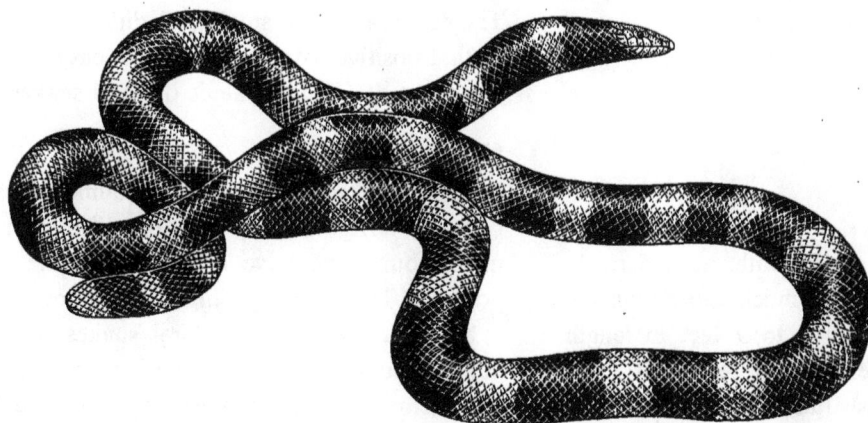

SEA SNAKE

THE POISONOUS SNAKES OF CENTRAL AND SOUTH AMERICA

IDENTIFICATION AND HABITS

THE PIT VIPER FAMILY

RATTLESNAKES

Description

Of the five kinds of rattlesnakes in this area, only the tropical rattlesnake (shown) is widely distributed. This snake and its close relatives are large snakes, averaging about 5 feet long. The characteristic tropical rattlesnake has a pair of dark stripes extending along the neck, with geometrical body markings. The Mexican rattlesnake is similarly marked but without the dark stripes. A smaller rattlesnake, found on Aruba Island, has a pale gray back and a white belly. The rattle on the tip of the tail is sufficient identification for all the rattlesnakes.

Habits

The tropical rattlesnake is a vicious reptile. It is large and aggressive and its venom is highly poisonous. This snake may strike with very little warning rattle and before coiling. If teased it may advance toward the tormentor. It is found only in dry, hilly country, not in thick forests. The tropical rattlesnake is also known as the "cascabel" in Mexico and Central America and as the "cascavel" in Brazil.

BUSHMASTERS

Description

This is a large snake with a moderately slender body and a head much wider than the neck. It averages from 7 to 9 feet in length but may grow longer than 11 feet. It is light-brown with a pinkish hue and has a series of dark blotches which are wide on the back and narrow down the sides. The scales are extremely rough and raised like the teeth of a rasp.

Habits

The bushmaster is found mostly in forests at low altitudes. It prefers dry ground and often hides in animal burrows. When lying on the forest floor its camouflage is hard to see. The snake may either remain motionless until touched or it may attempt to escape when cornered. It may strike viciously; sometimes it may even edge towards an intruder. The tail is vibrated when the snake is irritated and if it rattles among dry leaves, the snake may be mistaken for a rattlesnake. The bushmaster is a savage and dangerous snake, but it seldom is seen. The best precaution is to wear boots and to keep bare hands out of holes and brush close to the ground.

CORAL SNAKES

Description

These snakes are brightly colored in combinations of red, black, yellow or white, with bands of color running completely around the body. Coral snakes average about 2 feet in length but may attain a maximum of 4 feet. The fangs are very small and difficult to find so that positive identification is not easy. There are about 40 different kinds of coral snakes.

Habits

These snakes can be found in almost every type of terrain. However, they live mostly underground and have a lazy and gentle disposition. The venom is highly poisonous and a bite can cause death. Coral snakes do not coil and strike in the manner of the pit vipers; they remain flat on the ground and bite by twisting the head to one side if they are picked up or stepped on. Coral snakes are not dangerous except to a barefoot man.

TROPICAL RATTLESNAKE

BUSHMASTER

CORAL SNAKE

THE POISONOUS SNAKES OF CENTRAL AND SOUTH AMERICA

IDENTIFICATION AND HABITS

THE PIT VIPER FAMILY

FER-DE-LANCE GROUP

Description

There are several closely related species in this group. The fer-de-lance and about six of its relatives are gray to brown or reddish in color, with dark geometrical blotches which generally are narrow on the back and broad at the sides. It is a moderately thick snake with a head which is much wider than the neck. The fer-de-lance averages about 3 to 4 feet long but may grow as large as 8 or 9 feet. Some members of the group are smaller and display almost any color, including green or yellow; some have thick bodies. The fer-de-lance is also known as the "barba amarilla".

Habits

This group of snakes is widespread throughout Central America and South America. The large kinds are ground snakes; some of the small kinds, known as palm vipers, live in trees, especially at the base of the leaves of a palm tree. The larger snakes are dangerous. They may be common in certain areas and are found often in cane fields or around dwellings where they come to catch rats. This snake loops its body before striking.

SEA SNAKES

Description

This snake is found only in salt water and occurs on the Pacific Coast from the Gulf of California to Ecuador. It is sometimes very abundant in the Gulf of Panama. It is not found in the Atlantic Ocean. The sea snake of this area has a brown to black back and a yellow belly. The tail is flattened like an oar. The sea snake can be distinguished from an eel by the fact that the snake has scales and the eel does not. Sea snakes may average from 2 to 3 feet long.

Habits

The sea snake is found in salt or brackish water near the coast. Its bite is dangerous but very rare. Occasionally one may be caught in a fishing net; it should be carefully discarded. The snake has not been known to attack a man swimming and there is little cause for fearing it. Even where it is abundant there is no need to worry.

POSITIVE IDENTIFICATION FOR THE PIT VIPER FAMILY

The rattlesnake, the bushmaster and the fer-de-lance group are all related to pit vipers. All have two long fangs in the upper jaw and have no other teeth of comparable size. The two long fangs may be covered with a curtain of flesh or they may be folded back in the mouth. Another characteristic of these snakes is the presence of a deep pit between the eye and the nostril.

FER-DE-LANCE GROUP

SEA SNAKE

NOSTRIL

PIT

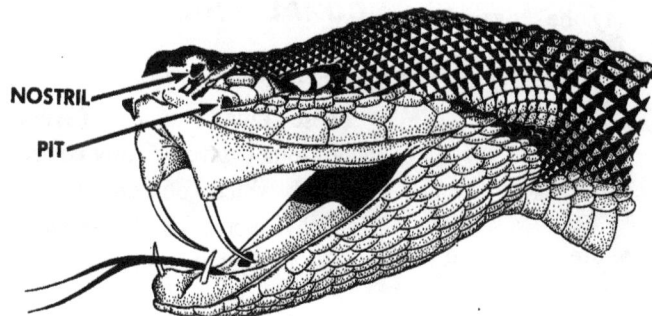

Positive identification for the pit viper family

THE POISONOUS SNAKES OF EUROPE, AFRICA, AND NEAR EAST

IDENTIFICATION AND HABITS

EUROPEAN VIPERS

Description

These snakes have a short thick body and a wide head which is much broader than the neck. Usually there is a zig-zag stripe down the back; colors may be gray, olive-brown, reddish or yellowish. The European viper averages from 2 to 3 feet in length. There are 8 species on the European continent; these snakes sometimes are known also as adders or asps.

Habits

Vipers generally are found in the wilder areas, particularly in rocky places, such as in the Pyrenees, the Appenines and in the Balkan mountains, where they may be found up to 5,000 feet. They occur as far north as 67° in Scandinavia and across Siberia. Sunlit slopes, moors and heaths, grain fields and trash piles are favorite prowling places. Some of the European vipers are aggressive and savage, causing occasional deaths.

POSITIVE IDENTIFICATION OF VIPERS

Vipers have two long and distinctive fangs in the upper jaw; none of the other teeth are comparable in size. Fangs may be covered with a curtain of flesh or folded back in the mouth.

AFRICAN VIPERS

Description

The vipers of North Africa are similar to those of Europe, except for the puff adder (shown). This is a large brownish or sand-colored snake with striking markings, a heavy body and a very short tail. This snake grows to a length of 5 feet. Central Africa and South Africa have several additional kinds of vipers.

Among the largest are the rhinoceros viper and the Gaboon viper. The rhinoceros viper, found in West Africa, has horns on its nose, a very wide head and a thick body covered with colored marks down the back; it reaches a maximum length of 4 feet. The Gaboon viper has one horn on the nose, a wide head and thick body with oblong markings on the back, and triangular colored spots on the sides; it has been known to reach a length of 6 feet. There are a number of other African vipers, most of them small; with the exception of one kind, they have a wide head and thick body.

Habits

The puff adder prefers open forests or grasslands near streams. The rhinoceros viper is found in or near streams. The Gaboon viper lives in heavy forests. The bite of any of these snakes is extremely dangerous, but they are not aggressive and not inclined to bite. The smaller vipers, found in sandy country, open brush, grassland or light forest are likely to be aggressive and dangerous in spite of their small size. One of the smaller kinds buries itself in the sand and may strike at a passing man; its presence is disclosed by a characteristic coiling pattern in the sand.

CORAL SNAKES

Description

These small snakes (average under 24 inches long) have brightly colored bands across the back which generally do not extend across the belly. Some of the smaller kinds have a reddish or bright orange stripe along the back.

Habits

Coral snakes are secretive and inoffensive; they seldom are seen. These snakes hardly can be regarded as dangerous; they bite only if stepped on or picked up.

EUROPEAN VIPER

AFRICAN VIPER

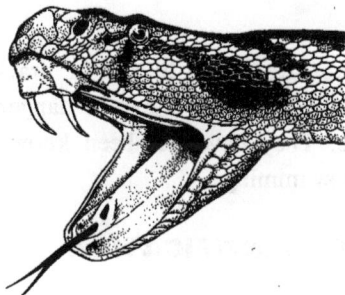

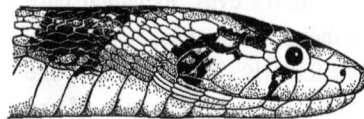

CORAL SNAKE

*Positive identification
of vipers*

THE POISONOUS SNAKES OF EUROPE, AFRICA, AND NEAR EAST
IDENTIFICATION AND HABITS

COBRAS

Description

There are several varieties of cobras in Africa and the Near East. The characteristic combat attitude is the simplest means of identification. In this posture, the forepart of the body is raised vertically and the head tilted sharply forward. Usually the neck is flattened out to form a hood; however, some kinds do not have a hood and others do not spread the hood unless they are extremely angry. The cobras of this area may be black, brown, gray or yellowish, and with or without markings. Cobras often are 6 to 7 feet long; one kind — the water cobra — may attain 8 feet.

Habits

The cobras of Africa and the Near East can be found almost anywhere. One kind lives in or near water; another may climb trees. Some of the cobras in this area are reported to be aggressive and savage. The fairly common Egyptian cobra (shown) of North Africa and adjacent regions, is found often around rocky places and ruins. The distance the cobra can strike in a forward direction is equal to the distance the head is raised above the ground. However, some cobras can spit venom a distance of 10 to 12 feet; this venom is harmless unless it gets into a man's eyes, in which case it may cause blindness if not washed out immediately. It is particularly dangerous to poke around in holes and rock piles because of the likelihood of encountering a spitting cobra.

MAMBAS

Description

These snakes are very slender and have small heads. They generally have a green or dark uniform color, without conspicuous spots or markings. The scales are smooth, symmetrical and large. Mambas attain lengths up to 12 feet. An 8-foot mamba is about half the thickness of an ordinary broomstick. It is difficult to identify mambas positively; the fangs in an 8-foot snake are only about ½-inch long, the thickness of a pin, and almost covered with flesh.

Habits

Mambas occur over all of Africa, except in the extreme northern portions. The South African mamba ranges from Tanganyika to West Africa south of the Congo and southward to Natal; it has two color phases — one black and one green. The green mamba (shown) is found in West Africa, from the Senegal to the Niger. Mambas live in trees or on the ground and have been known to enter houses in search of rats. They are very quick snakes. They may attack deliberately during their breeding season, but at other times they are timid and glide away. The bite of the mamba is very dangerous.

SEA SNAKES

Description

These snakes are found only in salt water. They occur on the east coast of Africa and in the Persian Gulf. Sea snakes of this area have a brown to black back with a yellow belly.

Habits

These snakes are found in salt or brackish water on seacoasts. Their bites are dangerous but very rare. They have not been known to attack a man swimming.

POSITIVE IDENTIFICATION

The cobras and near relatives can be identified positively by examining the scales on the head of a dead specimen. If the third scale on the upper lip touches both the nostril scale and the eye, the snake is a cobra and poisonous.

EGYPTIAN COBRA

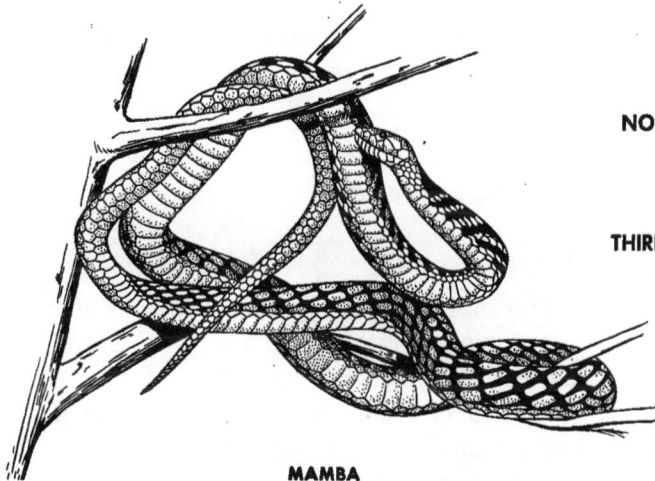

MAMBA

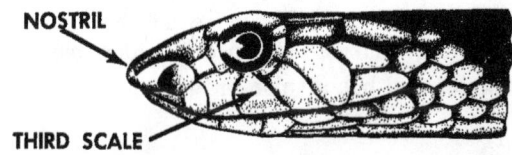

NOSTRIL

THIRD SCALE

Positive

SEA SNAKE

THE POISONOUS SNAKES OF AUSTRALIA, NEW GUINEA, AND PACIFIC ISLANDS

IDENTIFICATION AND HABITS

ALL THESE SNAKES, EXCEPT THE SEA SNAKE,
BELONG TO THE COBRA FAMILY

DEATH ADDERS

Description

This snake has a short, thick, clumsy body with a head much wider than the neck, and a short thin tail. It seldom grows more than 2 feet long. It may be gray, brown, pink or brick-red, depending on the sandstone of the region in which it lives and into which its camouflage blends skilfully. There are bands of darker color across the body, particularly in the young snakes. The death adder has rough scales and has a spine on the tail.

Habits

This snake is found in sandy localities over most of Australia except Victoria, and in southern New Guinea and the Moluccas. Because the death adder resembles the ground it lives on, it is likely to be stepped on. While the snake is not quick to strike, it can be dangerous if irritated or stepped on. The venom of this snake is highly poisonous.

TIGER SNAKES

Description

The tiger snake has dark bands on a tawny background of green, gray, orange or brown; sometimes the bands are indistinct. It has a stout body with a rather wide head. It averages about 4 to 5 feet long when full-grown, but may reach 6 feet. The tiger snake spreads its neck when angry.

Habits

This snake lives in dry country, ranging extensively throughout Australia and Tasmania. It is a savage and dangerous reptile which causes more deaths in Australia than all the other snakes combined which are found there. Tiger snakes are quick to bite, spreading the neck and lunging with a flashing stroke that is so vigorous it may sometimes move the body forward, so that the snake seems to be making a short jump.

COPPERHEADS

Description

This snake has a moderately thick body and may attain a length up to 6 feet. It usually has a reddish or dark-brown color but may be bright red or black; the head usually has a coppery tone, especially in the young. There are about two dozen other closely related species in Australia, but some of these are no more than 15 inches long and have weak venom.

Habits

The copperhead is found in the southerly portions of Australia. It frequents swamps and feeds on lizards and frogs. When angry, the snake rears its head a few inches from the ground, with the neck arched slightly, somewhat in the manner of a cobra. Normally, the copperhead is not aggressive unless irritated or stepped on.

DEATH ADDER

TIGER SNAKE

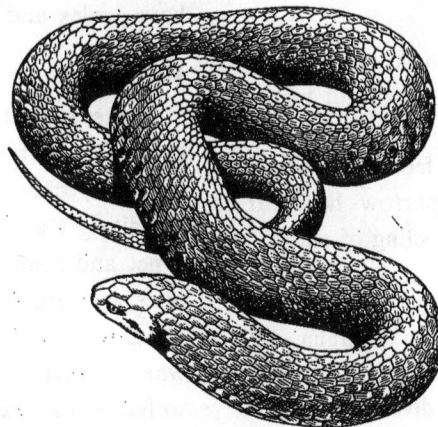

COPPERHEAD

THE POISONOUS SNAKES OF AUSTRALIA, NEW GUINEA, AND PACIFIC ISLANDS

IDENTIFICATION AND HABITS

*ALL THESE SNAKES, EXCEPT THE SEA SNAKE,
BELONG TO THE COBRA FAMILY*

BROWN SNAKES

Description

This is a slender snake, with a small narrow head, which usually attains a length of 4 to 5 feet. The eyes are large. The color is light yellow to brown or gray above and white beneath; the young are pale brown and have a pretty ringed pattern. There are about a dozen relatives of this snake, some of which are called whip snakes. In spite of the small size of the head, the venom of this snake is highly poisonous.

Habits

The brown snake is widely distributed all over Australia and is found also in New Guinea. It is not an aggressive snake unless it is disturbed. It strikes from a looped position.

BLACK SNAKES

Description

The black snake is blue-black on top and brilliant scarlet underneath, edged with black. The scales are symmetrical and satiny-smooth. This snake averages 6 to 7 feet long, has a slender body and a small narrow head. It spreads the neck at the least feeling of alarm.

Habits

This snake occurs throughout Australia, except in the north and Tasmania. It prefers marshy places or streams; it dives and swims well and can stay under the water for long periods of time. Because it lies still on the bottoms of streams, it may be dangerous to bathers. The black snake will not attack unless stepped on or cornered. When angry it raises its head a few inches from the ground on a slanting plane and strikes from that position. While the black snake bites more people in Australia than any other snake, its venom is relatively weak and very few victims die of the bite.

SEA SNAKES

Description

There are many species of sea snakes and they vary greatly in color and shape. They occur in salt water along the coasts throughout the Pacific. They have a tail which is flattened like an oar. The sea snakes can be distinguished from eels by the fact that the snakes have scales and the eels do not.

Habits

These snakes usually are found in salt or brackish water near the coast, but sometimes they may crawl up on land. Fishermen occasionally get a bite from a sea snake caught in a net and such a bite is dangerous. However, bites are rare. These snakes are not known to attack a man swimming. Even in those areas where they may be abundant there is no need to fear sea snakes.

BROWN SNAKE

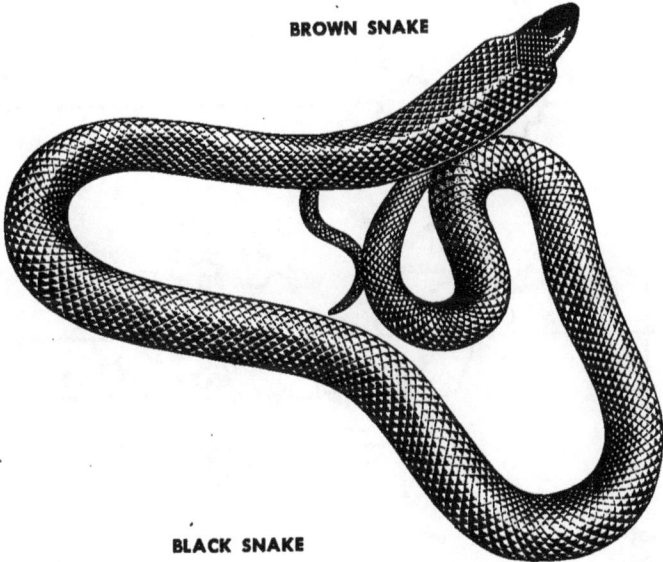

BLACK SNAKE

SEA SNAKE

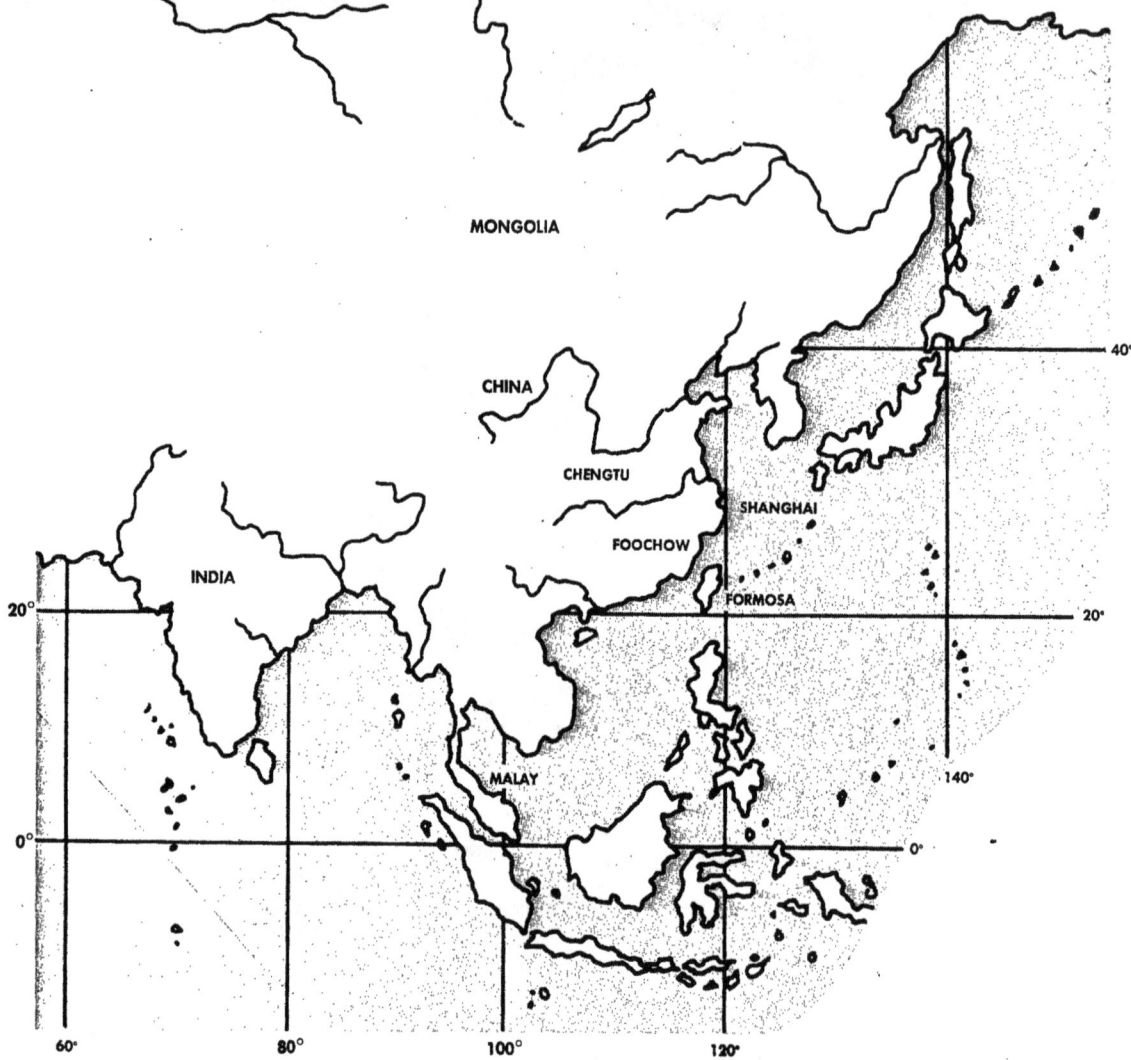

DISTRIBUTION OF POISONOUS SNAKES OF SOUTHEASTERN ASIA

Cobras

Found throughout the area as far north as Foochow in China.

Kraits, Coral Snakes and Vipers

Found throughout the area south of a line drawn from Shanghai to Chengtu. Only one viper, Russell's viper, occurs in the East Indies, the Malay Peninsula and Formosa.

Pit Vipers

Found throughout the area. These are the only poisonous snakes in China found north of the Shanghai-Chengtu line.

Sea Snakes

Found along all coasts as far north as Foochow; rare in Chinese coastal waters.

DISTRIBUTION OF POISONOUS SNAKES OF CENTRAL AND SOUTH AMERICA

Rattlesnakes

Found from Southern Mexico down to about 32° S. latitude. Occur in dry hilly country but not in tropical rain forests. Have not been found in Panama or in the Amazon Basin.

Bushmasters

Found at low altitudes on both coasts of eastern Costa Rica south to the coast of Brazil, along the state of Bahia, and on Trinidad.

Fer-de-Lance Group

Found in Martinique, St. Lucia, Trinidad, Southern Mexico and all of Central America and South America with the exception of all of Chile and the Andean highlands above 10,000 feet.

Coral Snakes

Found in all of Mexico, Central America, South America and Trinidad, down to and including the territory of Rio Negro in Argentina.

Sea Snakes

Found in the waters of the Pacific Coast from the Gulf of California to Ecuador.

There are no poisonous snakes in all of the Caribbean Islands, except Martinique, St. Lucia and Trinidad. Chile and the Andean highlands above 10,000 feet have no poisonous snakes.

DISTRIBUTION OF POISONOUS SNAKES OF EUROPE, AFRICA, AND THE NEAR EAST

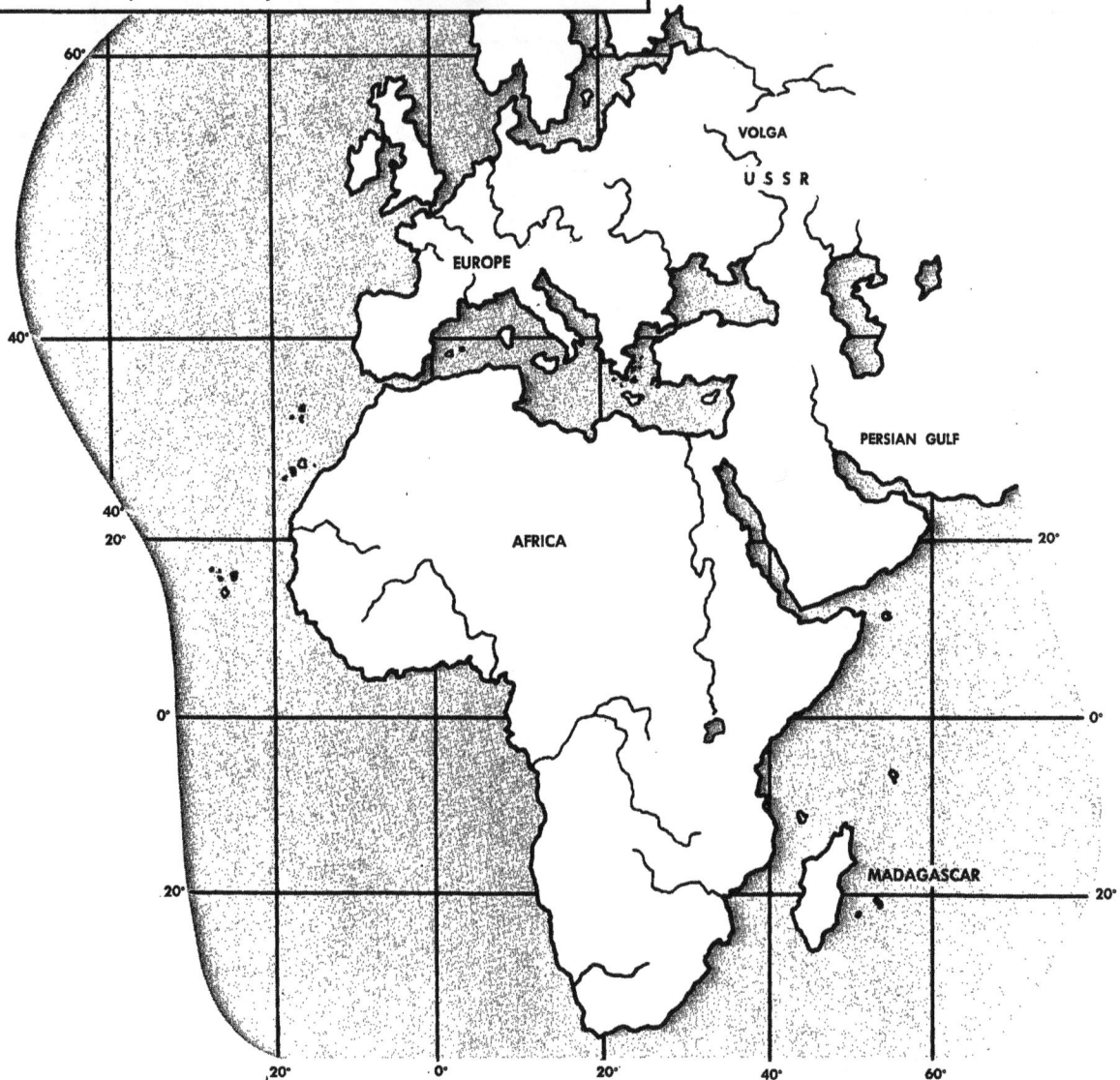

Europe, West of the Volga

Vipers are the only poisonous snakes found. There are no snakes in Ireland.

Near East and Africa (North of 20° North)

Cobras and vipers are found in this area.

Africa (South of 20° North)

Cobras, vipers, mambas and coral snakes are found in this area. There are sea snakes on the east coast of Africa and in the Persian Gulf. There are no poisonous snakes on Madagascar.

DISTRIBUTION OF POISONOUS SNAKES OF AUSTRALIA, NEW GUINEA, AND THE PACIFIC ISLANDS

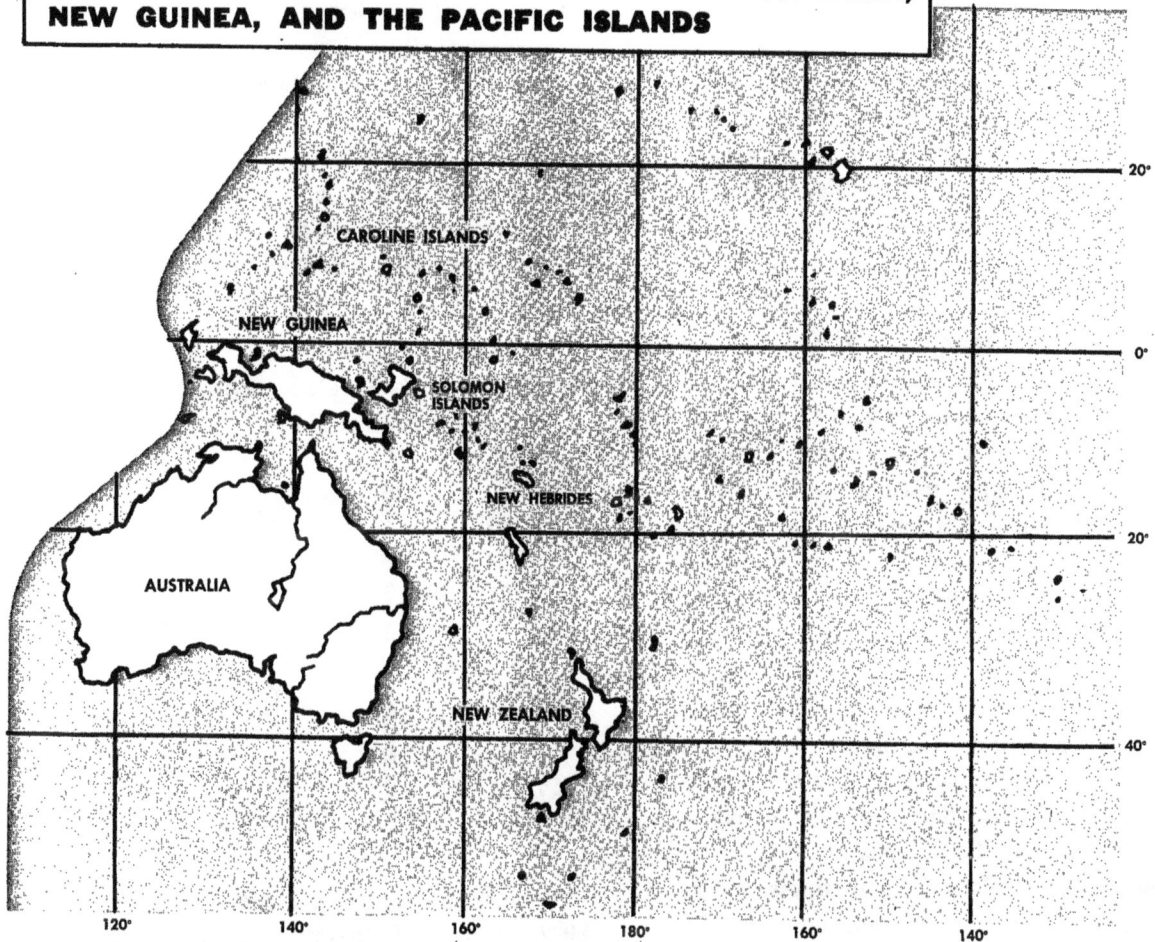

Australia, New Guinea, New Hebrides, The Carolines, The Solomons and Adjacent Islands

Nearly all the snakes in this area are poisonous. The most dangerous snakes are the tiger snake, the brown snake, the black snake, the copperhead, the death adder and the taipan. Of these, only the death adder and brown snake occur in New Guinea.

Islands East of New Zealand, New Hebrides and The Carolines

There are no poisonous land snakes. The sea snake is the only poisonous snake in this area. In Australia, several snakes have names which are the same or similar to those of snakes in the United States. However, they are not the same snakes and do not resemble the U. S. snakes of the same names.

FIRST AID FOR SNAKEBITE

The first problem in treating snakebites is to determine whether it has been caused by a poisonous snake. Many harmless snakes will bite in self-defense. The only reliable way to tell whether the snakebite is poisonous is to identify the snake. However, the wound itself may give some clues.

One good indication of the bite of a poisonous snake is the intense pain which results almost immediately. A severe bite from a harmless snake will hurt no more than a wound made with any sharp instrument. The bite of a viper will cause immediate swelling. A cobra bite may have no local symptoms except for an intense burning pain in the area of the wound.

The appearance of the wound gives additional clues. Vipers do not really "bite." They stab with their fangs. The wound usually consists of two small punctures, generally half an inch or more apart. Sometimes there may be only one puncture if the snake partially misses or has one fang missing. Coral snakes, cobras, mambas, and kraits often hang on and chew; the result may be one, two, or more puncture marks. Harmless snakes usually have several teeth so that a bite may consist of several punctures formed in a semicircle. However, it is not always easy to distinguish for certain between the bites of a harmless and a poisonous snake.

Emergency Treatment of Snakebites

What you do in the first minute after being bitten by a poisonous snake will determine the effectiveness of the treatment. Unless you have a snakebite kit on your person or within easy reach, you should not waste time and energy in going after one. The venom circulates quickly, and any exercise will quicken the circulation. All personnel who expect to be flying over snake-infested areas, whether or not they expect to have a snakebite kit with them, should carry several sterile razor blades. They

are convenient to carry and are always useful for a number of purposes.

In a survival situation you cannot be certain that you will have a snakebite kit handy, but you can be fairly certain that you won't have a medical officer to treat you. Therefore, you will have to act quickly and wisely. In such a case, undertake the following first aid measures immediately; speed is essential!

●   ●   ●

Follow this procedure if you are bitten:

1. Daub the knife blade and fang marks with antiseptic from first-aid kit.

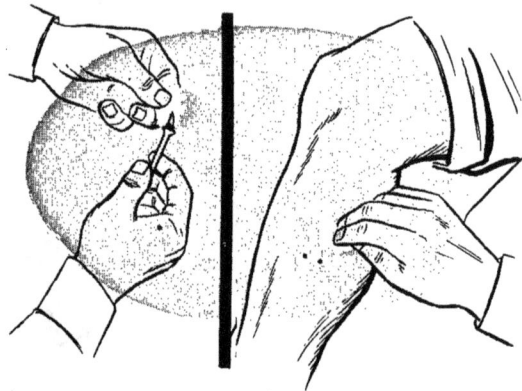

2. Make a number of crosscuts through each fang mark. In fleshy tissue make each cut about 1/2 inch long and 1/4 inch deep; in thin tissue over bones make shallow cuts parallel to bone. Be careful not to cut large blood vessels, tendons, or nerves. Some snakes will sink their fangs much deeper than 1/4 of an inch. In such a case, make the cuts as deep as the fangs penetrated.

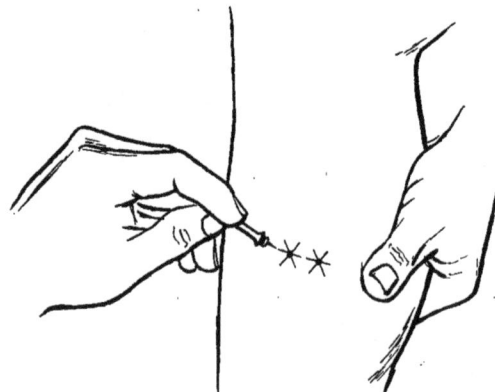

3.   Tie a handkerchief, belt, tape, or cord around the limb 1-1/2 inches above the fang marks. Don't tie it so tightly as to cut off the blood circulation; it is not a tourniquet but merely keeps the lymph from spreading into the surrounding tissues. Blood flow should *not* be stopped. If tied too tightly or left on too long, the lymph constrictor can cause gangrene. Every 10 minutes remove for 1 minute. Then apply again slightly higher, so as the swelling extends, the tape remains 1-1/2 inches above the swelling. Redness, swelling, and throbbing, which are relieved when the tape is loosened, indicate that it has been too tight. Don't be alarmed if the bite is located in a spot where the constricting band cannot be applied. Suction is more important.

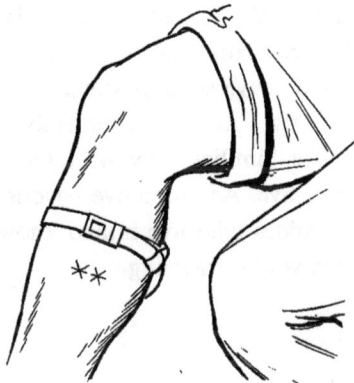

4.   Apply suction cup over bite. If a suction cup is not available, suck by mouth over a piece of rubber tissue; if no tissue is available, it is safe to suck the poison into the mouth if there are no open sores in mouth. Spit the poison out immediately.

Don't get excited. Mortality from snakebite, properly treated, is less than 1%. It is only 10 to 15% without any treatment — hence the fame of such useless remedies as kerosene, gunpowder, potassium permanganate, freshly killed chickens, whisky, etc.

Avoid doing anything which increases the circulation. Don't take alcohol, or start running back to camp. Sit right where you are, follow instructions calmly, and carry out the first part of this treatment. Don't do more harm to yourself than the bite would have done if you hadn't treated it, particularly if you are not sure you have been bitten by a poisonous snake. Don't overdo the use of the knife, and don't tie the lymph constrictor too tight or leave it on too long.

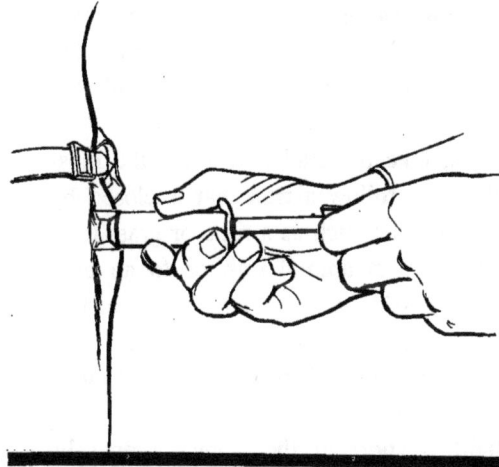

TRAVEL

The most useful aids to travel in the Tropics are a *machete,* to help cut your way, find food, make a raft; a *compass,* for maintaining direction; a *first aid kit* to keep you going in the face of fever and the risk of infection; *stout shoes,* which will save your feet and enable you to walk, and a *hammock.*

Travel only in daylight. Avoid obstacles such as thickets and swamps. Don't try to crash through thick jungle; push vegetation aside or use your machete. Part the brush to pass through, cut your way as a last resort. Don't climb over logs if you can walk around them. You will not only avoid injuries such as a sprained or broken ankle, bruises, and scratches but also save your strength as well.

Find a trail and follow it. Go downhill until you find a stream — then follow the stream. In some dense jungles, however, you will find that you must travel on ridges where thin vegetation makes cross-country travel possible. Your best chance of finding villages and people is along trails and streams and on coasts.

345

A good place to pick up a trail is where two streams meet; here you will often find a crossing of trails which follow the adjoining ridges. There is almost always a trail crossing a low pass over a range of hills. Trails are also found at rapids. On all trails, keep your eyes open for signs of natives.

At clearings or openings in the jungle, you may not be able to see the trail. Cross the clearings and work along the edges until you pick up the track again among the trees.

At forks, take the trail that looks the most traveled. Don't follow a trail that is closed by an obvious barrier such as a rope or grass-mat; it may lead to an animal trap or to an area forbidden to strangers. Watch for disturbed places on animal trails — they may indicate a pitfall or trap. Don't sleep on a game trail at night — the traffic may be heavy.

Twilight is short in the tropics (generally less than 30 minutes), and darkness sets in early. Make camp and get under mosquito netting before sunset. Stay there until after dawn. Pick a good camp site (see page 231); make shelter (page 232) and fire (page 234). Get plenty of sleep and rest.

Raft down streams whenever possible. Bamboo will make a good raft, but it may be hard to find. To cut large bamboo, hack around stem below joint and then break. Soft, light wood, such as balsa, is easy to work and makes the best raft material.

If you are traveling on a river, land and make camp before dusk. Avoid the hazard of rising water resulting from violent rainstorms by pitching your camp on high ground well above the high water mark (shown by mud line on trees). Moor your craft with a long line so that it will not be upset or pulled under as the water rises.

NATIVES

Natives and habitation are found mostly along the coasts or along streams and trails.

If you take food from native gardens when no one is around, leave some payment.

If you use natives as guides, remember that most natives are familiar only with the local area where they live. As you move beyond this area, get new guides who live in and know the region in which you're traveling.

chapter 6

SURVIVAL

ON . . .

SEA ICE

Much of the material on Arctic survival also applies to sea ice survival. Read the chapter on Arctic survival.

IMMEDIATE ACTION

Your action after landing should follow as closely as possible the checklist given below.

1. Take care of the injured.

2. Check your clothing to make sure that it provides maximum possible protection against cold and wet.

3. Establish temporary shelter immediately — and if possible build a fire inside the shelter.

4. Try to establish radio contact with rescuers.

5. Make a survey of surrounding area to determine the safest camp site, considering the availability of food and water and the proximity to crashed aircraft if it is remaining on the surface.

6. Build a camp. (Do not use the interior of aircraft as shelter unless it is absolutely necessary.)

7. Try to find and mark a safe landing area for use of rescue planes.

Do not get separated from your party. There is always a danger of floes moving apart. In very broken ice, rope party together. Always have ropes handy. Parachute shroud lines are excellent for this purpose.

The preceding instructions for immediate action will not always be valid. Records of sea ice landings by aircraft indicate that the locating of a suitable landing area took from 1 to 4 hours, and under many conditions, such as fire in the aircraft, fuel shortage, or structural damage, extensive searching would be impossible. Therefore, many situations might arise in which a controlled bailout would be advisable. This will, of course, alter ground activities, and eliminate the use of the aircraft and its equipment, supplies, and materials.

DECISION TO STAY OR TO TRAVEL

Unless you know that you are within walking distance of land, stay at the scene of the crash or as close to it as ice conditions will permit. If you are on ice which is breaking up, you will have to travel to the nearest stable ice or to land before you make your camp.

SHELTER

All information in the discussion of Arctic shelters in chapter 3 is appropriate, except certain shelters requiring materials not available on ice floes. The only materials available for shelter building on sea ice are snow, ice, parts of the aircraft, aircraft equipment, parachutes, and possibly a raft.

Construct your shelter on solid ice floes as far away as possible from open water or from cracks which may open into water leads.

Raft Shelter

If you have a 20-man raft aboard the aircraft, it will make an excellent shelter with the canopy erected. Be sure to anchor the raft securely.

Snow Block and Parachute Shelter

A snow block and parachute shelter is shown in the illustration on the next page. Level off a circular space 10 feet in diameter. Build a circular wall of snow blocks at least 4 feet high. In the center of this circle, build a pillar of snow blocks higher than the snowblock walls. Stretch one or more parachute canopies

Twenty-man raft used as a shelter on sea ice

over the wall and pillar, and drape excess material over the outside wall for extra insulation. Snow suitable for cutting into blocks will not be found on open ice but usually forms in the lee of pressure ridges or ice hummocks. Often the packed snow will be so shallow that the snow blocks will have to be cut horizontally.

Dig snow from a trench around the outside border of the snow wall. Tuck excess parachute material into this trench and anchor it tightly by replacing the snow. Or place another row of blocks on top of the material on the wall.

Cut an opening for the door 90° from prevailing wind, and screen it with a tunnel or L-shaped entrance of snow blocks.

Snowhouse

Snowhouse construction is difficult but not impossible. If time permits, try to construct a shelter of this type, for it offers the best protection possible. For aid in constructing it, follow the diagrams closely.

Ice Shelter

If snow is not available, it may be possible to make a shelter of thin ice slabs. Make it as small as convenient, so that less area will have to be heated. Use the lee side of a pressure ridge that seems old and solid. You can make this shelter with your hands alone, if necessary.

Shelter Living

Remember that all shelters with inside fires should be well ventilated.

Overturned, inflated life rafts make excellent mattresses. However, under certain conditions, condensation or body heat can cause a pool of water to form between the sleeping bag and the waterproof raft. Put a folded parachute or other padding between the bag and whatever surface it is resting on.

Arrange your equipment inside the shelter so that you can pack it in a hurry. *Any ice floe may break up at any time of the year. Leads may form at any time.* Be ready to move your camp at a moment's notice.

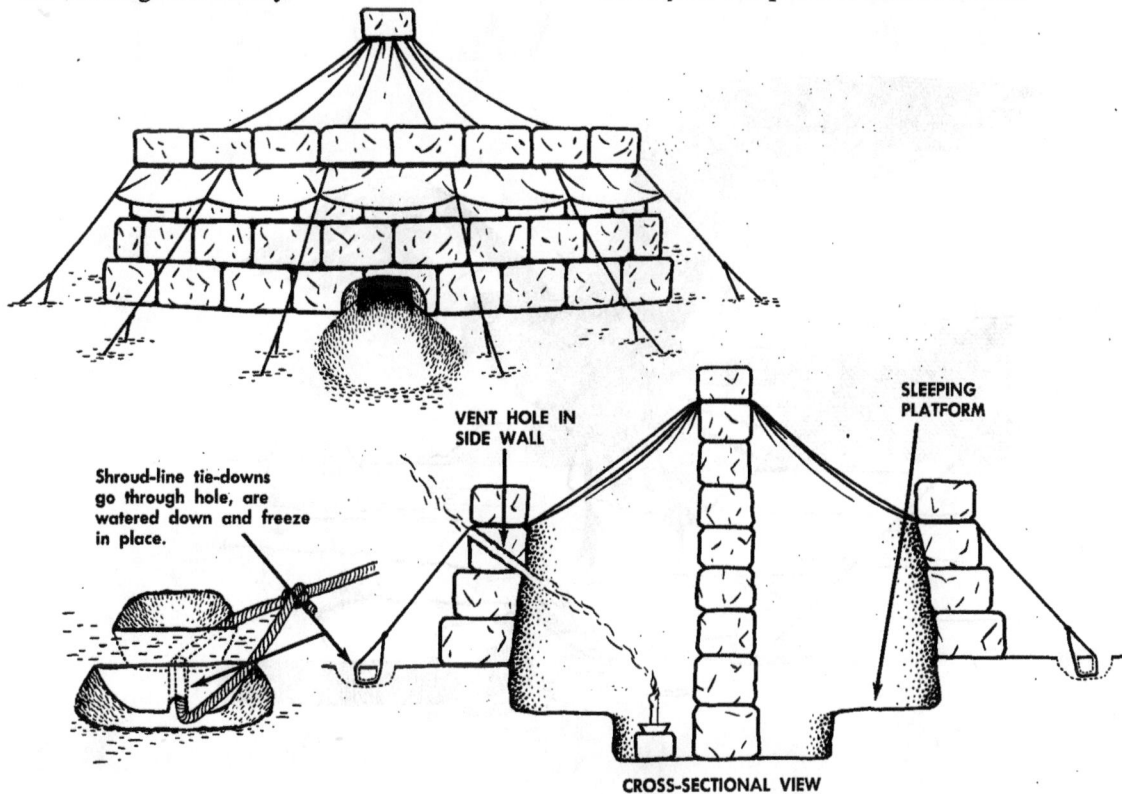

Shroud-line tie-downs go through hole, are watered down and freeze in place.

VENT HOLE IN SIDE WALL

SLEEPING PLATFORM

CROSS-SECTIONAL VIEW

Para-snow house

FIRE-MAKING

Combustible material is limited to aircraft contents and animal fats.

To use aircraft oil and gasoline, you will need a metal, bone, or hide container. Oil can be burned in it with a wick cut from a parachute harness or other material. To burn gasoline, soak your parachute harness or other material in it and burn the material.

You can burn animal fats in a metal container by using a wick to ignite the fat and adding more fat as old fuel is consumed.

Seal blubber will make a satisfactory fire without a container, if gasoline or heat tablets are available to provide an initial hot flame. Light the tablets on the raw side of the blubber, with the hairy side on the ice. It should ignite quickly if four tablets are burned at once. A square foot of blubber will burn for several hours. Large blubber fires need no shelter; in fact, the stronger the wind, the better the fire.

Tinder of any description burned with the heat tablets will help, but once the blubber catches fire, save your heat tablets. Eskimos light a small piece of blubber and use it to kindle increasingly larger pieces.) The smoke from a blubber fire is dirty black and heavy but not nauseating. The flame is very bright and can be seen for several miles. The smoke will penetrate your clothes and blacken your skin. Burned blubber cinders are edible.

FOOD AND WATER

Your only available foods on polar ice are game and foods from the sea. Game animals include seals, polar bears, and occasional foxes. Birds may be found in the summertime. They can be caught with baited fish hooks, as shown in the illustration.

Catching birds with a fish hook

Seals

Seals will be your main source of food. They are to be found wherever there is open water in the ice.

Seals come up to breathe in patches of open water, keeping their heads above the surface for perhaps 30 seconds. They do not come on the ice until May and June and then only occasionally. They show head, neck, and shoulders. A head or neck shot will usually kill them. Whether they sink when shot depends on the amount of blubber. In winter they do not usually sink when shot.

In the summertime, seals that are shot in the water may sink, so seals basking on the ice are better targets and easier to recover. Approach basking seals from behind natural cover, if you can, or use a shield fastened from clean parachute material.

During February and March, the male seal has a disagreeable odor, which does not, however, greatly affect the taste of the meat and does not make it poisonous. Almost all of the seal can be used. You can make moccasins from the skin, use the blubber for fuel, and eat the flesh. Frozen seal meat, especially frozen liver, is palatable and easily swallowed. Cook it thoroughly if you can, for seals may have trichinosis.

You can recover a seal from the water with an improvised "manak," or grapple hook attached to a throwing weight. A weight made of material which floats is ideal but not absolutely essential. A shroud line attached to the weight is a satisfactory pull line. If you can't reach the seal with a grapple, move to the ice where it will eventually drift.

Seal hunting in any season requires a good deal of patience, so don't be discouraged.

Where there is no open water, seals make breathing holes in the ice. These breathing holes are usually under the snow, near upended blocks of ice. Any small opening in the ice, with open water beneath, is a possible breathing hole. If you have or can improvise a 3-pronged hook, you may be able to catch a seal at a breathing hole with only the labor of setting the hook and pulling out the seal.

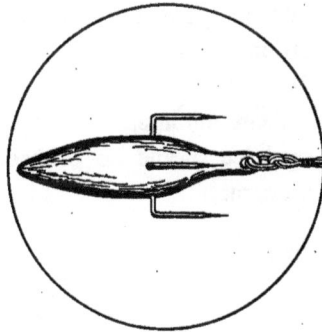

MANAK

Seal-hunting shield

To the 3-pronged hook attach a wire, section of control cable, or a heavy line 2 or 3 feet long. At the other end of the wire, put a stout piece of wood or a metal bar to serve as a toggle. To set the hook, enlarge the breathing hole enough to drop the hook through into the water. Then let the hook drop through the hole so that the hook hangs about 6 inches below the undersurface of the ice, with the toggle across the top of the hole acting as an anchor. Then cover the hole with snow and erect a marker near it so that you can find it again. If the seal uses that particular hole, he will almost be sure to hook himself, since breathing holes are usually only a little larger than the seal's body.

Check your hooks once or twice a day. Any movement of the toggle or disturbance of the snow and ice in the hole means a seal on the hook. If you catch a seal, you will probably have to enlarge the hole to get his body through.

Polar Bears

Avoid polar bears, if at all possible. Polar bears are very curious and are dangerous especially if wounded or if the female's cub is molested. If two or more bears are sighted simultaneously, always shoot the largest, thereby eliminating the latter danger. Don't chase polar bears; their natural curiosity will bring them within range of your weapon. They may also be shot in the water without sinking. Recover them as you would seals.

Soaking the bear meat in sea water for 24 to 48 hours will tenderize it and make it more palatable.

Always cook bear meat until well done. Almost all bears have trichinosis. Do not eat polar bear liver. Its high vitamin A content makes it dangerous to man.

Water

Old sea ice has lost most of its salt and can be used as a source of drinking water. The best test for finding out whether ice is fresh or salty is to melt and taste it. With experience, however, you can recognize the old ice, since it is generally rough and different in texture from the recently frozen ice. Old sea ice is usually blue in color, and salty ice is usually white.

Snow which has not been soaked by salt spray is also a source of drinking water. After a thaw, there may be free fresh water between the ice and the snow cover. In summer, the melting of the old ice forms fresh water pools on top of the floes.

TRAVEL

The decision to move across sea ice must be made as a last resort unless land has been sighted. In both winter and summer, snow conceals thin ice and often hides cracks and crevices in the ice.

Travel conditions on sea ice vary greatly from place to place and from season to season. The smoothest ice is that frozen in protected fjords or bays; and the roughest, the pressure ridges found anywhere in the pack. Beware of the pressure ridges between the fast ice frozen to shore and the moving pack.

Usually, solid sea ice, 4 to 6 inches thick, can be traversed, but for the inexperienced traveler, 10 inches is a safer minimum. On the other hand, fresh water ice is solider, and 6 inches is a safe minimum for travel across it. Snow-covered ice should be probed to determine its strength.

Navigation

The problems of navigation are almost identical with those on the barren lands, but with one very great exception: the polar ice pack is in constant motion because of current and wind. As a rule the sea ice is faster moving during the summer months, when the ice is loose, than during the winter months when the ice is more firmly cemented. Therefore, determination of direction may be particularly difficult. Landmarks in the form of high pressure ridges and hummocks are usable only over short distances, since it may be that they are located on other floes which are changing position. Add to this the fact that the magnetic compass is very unreliable in high latitudes, and the necessity for constant directional checks on the sun and stars becomes obvious.

Maintaining a straight course over sea ice is very difficult due to the lack of landmarks, blowing snow, and fog. Even with a compass one man has difficulty keeping to a desired course. Two can do better, but 3 or more men are best. One man always stands still while the other two move in single file ahead of him. The last man carries the compass and lines up the other two on course. Then the rear man moves up and the process is repeated. If possible, build snow cairns or leave flags to mark your back trail and use as reference points for back sighting.

Winter

Those who know the Arctic well are rather closely in agreement that they would prefer to be down on winter sea ice rather than on barren land. Their reason is that food, in the form of seals, foxes, and polar bears, is more likely to be obtainable.

Travel over the ice in winter should be accomplished by the whole party at the same time, since there is generally nothing to be gained by anyone who remains behind. Splitting of the party will almost always lead to increased hardships for all concerned.

In winter there is generally very little open water, and that is between the edges of the floes. In summer there is water on top of the floes, between them, and in large openings surrounded by floes. When crossing from one floe to another, jump from a point a couple of feet in from the edge of the ice, not from the edge itself. When the ice is closely packed, you can walk as though it were solid — using, of course, common sense. You can easily tell if the touching or overlapping edges are solid enough to walk on.

When large, heavy floes are touching each other, the ice between the floes is usually ground and powdered and can bear no weight, but moving with the powdered ice will be larger chunks that can hold you up. The powdered ice may be as much as 20 feet wide, but if you will move against the ice, you will usually find a place to cross, especially when moving ice touches fast ice frozen solidly to shore.

When crossing pressure ridges, be careful to step only on solid ice. Bridges of snow can form between peaks of ice and these bridges are not always solid.

Summer

All that has been said about winter travel applies also to summer travel.

Spring

Springtime melting can make an ice surface very rough. Salty sea ice also becomes soft and honeycombed in spring, even though the air temperature remains below freezing. It is advisable to avoid areas of ice covered with melt water, because the surface beneath is likely to be pitted and rough. It is true, however, that melt water standing on ice is an indication of the soundness of that ice. As thawing progresses, the water disappears into the ice, indicating that it is honeycombed and therefore weak and unreliable. After the melt water runs off, the ice surface is dry, white, soft, and slippery.

Sometimes in spring, water on the ice refreezes on the surface, leaving a layer of slush beneath. This bad condition is to be expected following a cold snap during breakup.

It is a good idea to wear an antiexposure suit when traveling over broken or slushy ice. It will keep you dry and warm even if you fall into the water. Move slowly to avoid perspiring.

High Latitudes

In the very high latitudes, ice is comparatively solid in winter. Wherever the ice joins open water, however, the edges are always broken and subject to fairly rapid movement. As the sun returns, the ice recedes, and there is open water along the entire Arctic coast. Along the north coast, ice lies offshore, and with strong north or west winds floes are often driven ashore. Riding one of these floes is definitely a last resort procedure, since there is no guarantee that the wind will continue until the floe grounds. The ice is honeycombed with holes and covered with lakes and water-soaked snow. There is practically no dry surface anywhere, even at the Pole. Fogs abound, and misting rain is frequent.

Icebergs

All icebergs frozen in the ice are liable to have open water around them. This is due to the force exerted by the current on the greater mass of the berg below the surface. Icebergs driven by the currents have been known to crash through ice over several feet in thickness. Towering icebergs are always a danger in open water. The area below the surface melts faster than that in the air. When the berg's equilibrium is upset, it topples over. When this happens, the adjoining area is no place to be. The resulting tidal waves throw the surrounding small ice pieces in all directions. Therefore, stay away from pinnacled bergs. Seek out low, flat-topped bergs for shelter at sea.

Floating Ice

During winter and spring, floating ice is usually solid enough to hold up a tremendous weight; but in fall, until December, you must be careful of it, as large patches may not be strong enough to hold up a man. If you have no ice spear, knife, or other means of testing the ice, see if you can drive your heel through it. If you can't, the ice is probably safe to cross.

chapter 7

SURVIVAL

AT . . .

SEA

Four-fifths of the earth's surface is covered by open water. Although accounts of survival incidents are often pessimistic, successful survival is very possible.

Modern equipment for survival was designed to give all aircrewmen the means to remain alive until rescue can be effected.

The basic rules for ground survival and the areas of discussion in preceding chapters are still the major concern of survivors.

In general, shelter yourself from the elements, keep as dry as possible, keep trying for food, signal for help, observe strict water discipline, and *do not despair*. (See air rescue procedure, appendix I, p. 369.)

IMMEDIATE ACTION

Checklist

Stay upwind and clear of the aircraft (out of gasoline-covered waters) but in the vicinity until the aircraft sinks.

Search for missing men.

Salvage floating equipment. Stow and secure all useful items by lashing them to the raft. Check rafts for inflation, leaks, and points of possible chafing. Bail out your raft. Be careful not to snag it with shoes or sharp objects. Put out the sea anchor.

In cold oceans, put on your antiexposure suit, if available. Rig a windbreak, spray shield, and canopy. If you are with others, huddle together. Exercise regularly.

Check the physical condition of all aboard. Give first aid if necessary (see page 12). Take seasickness pills if available. Wash gasoline from yourself.

If there is more than one raft, connect rafts with at least 25 feet of line. Connect rafts *only* at life line around outer periphery of raft. Unless the sea is very rough, shorten the line if you hear or see an aircraft. Two or more rafts tied close together are easier to spot than scattered rafts.

Get the emergency radio into operation. Directions are on the equipment. Use emergency transceiver only when aircraft are likely to be in the area. Prepare other signaling devices for instant use.

Keep compasses, watches, sextant, matches, and lighters dry. Place them in waterproof containers.

In warm oceans, rig sun shade and canopy. Keep your skin covered. Use sunburn cream and chapstick. Keep your sleeves rolled down and your socks pinned up or pulled up over trousers. Wear a hat and sunglasses.

Make a calm estimate of your situation and plan your course of action carefully.

Ration water and food. Assign duties to each person. Use canopy or paulins for catching and storing rainwater.

Keep a log. Record the navigator's last fix, time of ditching, names and physical condition of personnel, ration schedule, winds, weather, direction of swells, times of sunrise and sunset, and other navigation data. Inventory all equipment.

Keep calm. Save water and food by saving energy. Start fishing as soon as possible. Don't shout unnecessarily. Don't move around unnecessarily. Keep your sense of humor active; use it often. Remember that rescue at sea is a cooperative project. Search aircraft contacts are limited by the visibility of survivors. Increase your visibility by using all possible signaling devices. Keep your mirrors handy. Use your radio whenever you can. Use your signal panel and dye marker when you think an aircraft can see them.

Personnel

As soon as the rafts are assembled and tied, make a careful check of the physical condition of personnel. Give first aid to the injured.

Make a thorough search for missing men. Carefully patrol the entire area near the crash, especially in the direction toward which waves are moving. Look very carefully — some of the missing men may be unconscious and floating low in the water. If men are in the water and sharks are in the vicinity, use shark repellent.

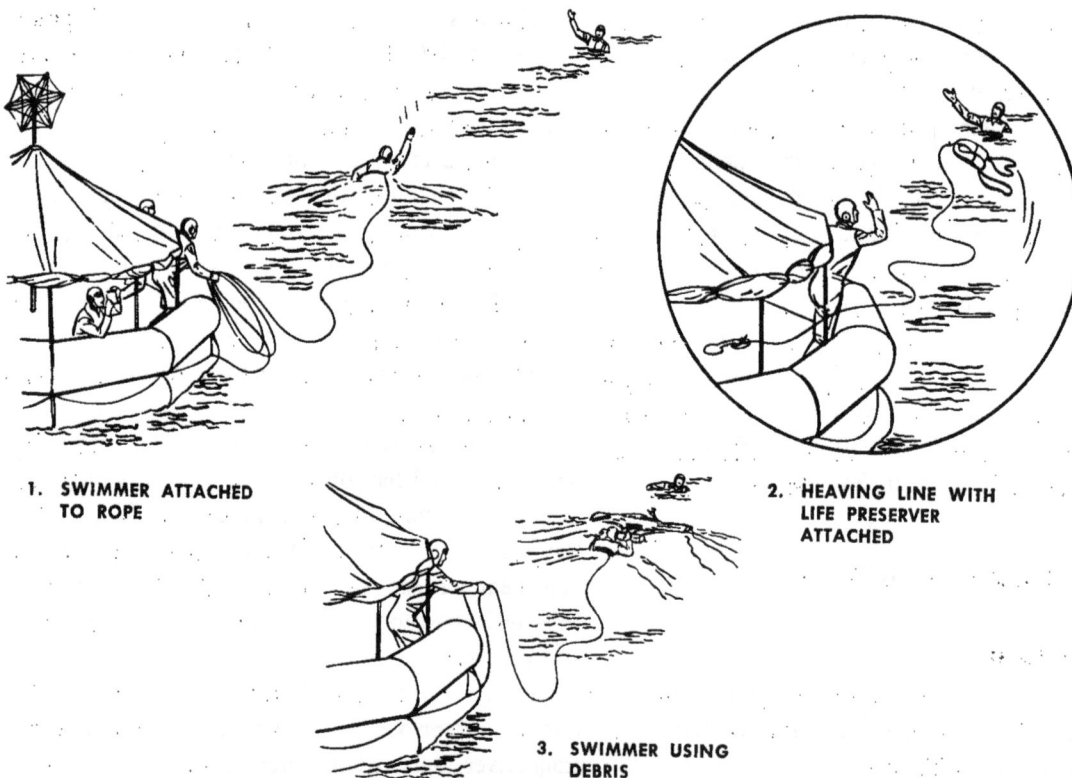

1. SWIMMER ATTACHED TO ROPE

2. HEAVING LINE WITH LIFE PRESERVER ATTACHED

3. SWIMMER USING DEBRIS

Rescue from water

Equipment

Inspect all debris that comes from the aircraft. Salvage all rations, canteens, thermos jugs and other containers, parachutes, seat cushions, extra clothing, and maps. Don't overlook the tube containing the kite and balloons for emergency radio. Beware of sharp metal objects.

Secure equipment by lashing it to raft and storing it in raft pockets and kit containers where provided. Keep these closed when not in use. Keep dry such items as flashlights, signal guns, and flares.

Protection Against Exposure

IN COLD OCEANS. You must stay dry and keep warm. If you are wet, get down behind windshield. Remove, wring out, and replace outer garments or get into dry clothing, if possible. Dry your hat, socks, and gloves. (See shock in first aid section.)

If you are dry, share clothes with those who are wet. Give them the most sheltered positions on the raft. Let them warm their hands and feet against your body.

Put on any extra clothing available. If no antiexposure suits are provided, drape extra clothing around your shoulders and over your head. Keep your clothes loose and comfortable. Try to keep the floor of the raft dry. For insulation, cover the floor with canvas or cloth.

Huddle with the others on the floor of the raft. Spread extra tarpaulin, sail, or parachute over the group. If you are on a 20-man raft, lower canopy sides. Take mild exercise to restore circulation. Repeatedly bend and open fingers and toes. Exercise shoulders and buttock muscles. Warm hands under armpits. Periodically, raise your feet slightly and hold them up for a minute or two. Move your face muscles frequently to detect frostbite. Shivering is normal — it's the body's way of quickly generating heat. However, persistent shivering may lead to uncontrollable muscle spasms. Avoid this by exercising your muscles.

Give extra rations to men suffering from exposure to cold.

IN WARM OCEANS. Protection against the sun and securing drinking water will be the most important problems. Exposure to the sun increases thirst, wasting precious water and reducing the body's water content. The sun also causes serious burns. Improvise and get under a sunshade. If you are on a 20-man raft, erect the canopy and furl the sides. Use the paulin, light side up, to attract attention — blue side up for camouflage in unfriendly waters. In rigging your sunshade (see illustration), leave space for ventilation. In a 1-man raft, use the spray shield for a sunshade.

Keep your body well covered. Don't throw any clothes away. Roll down your sleeves. Pull up your socks. Close your collar. Wear a hat or improvised headgear. Use a piece of cloth as a shield for the back of your neck. Wear sunglasses or improvise eye cover from cloth. (See illustrations, page 193.) Use a chapstick and the sunburn preventive.

Care of Raft

Be sure that your raft is properly inflated. If main buoyance chambers are not firm, top off with pump or mouth inflation tube. See that valve is open before pumping (to open, turn to the left). Inflate cross seats where provided unless there are injured men who must lie down. Don't overinflate. Air chambers should be well rounded but not drum tight. Regularly check inflation. Hot air expands, so on hot days release some air. Add air when the weather cools.

Always throw out the sea anchor or improvise a drag from the raft case, bailing bucket, or roll of clothing. A sea anchor will help you stay close to your ditching site, and your searchers' problem will be easier. Wrap the sea anchor rope with cloth so that it will not chafe the raft. It will also help to keep the raft headed into the wind and waves.

Be careful not to snag the raft. In good weather, take off your shoes; tie them to the raft. Don't let fishhooks, knives, ration tins, and other sharp objects cut. Keep them off the bottom.

In stormy weather, rig the spray and wind-

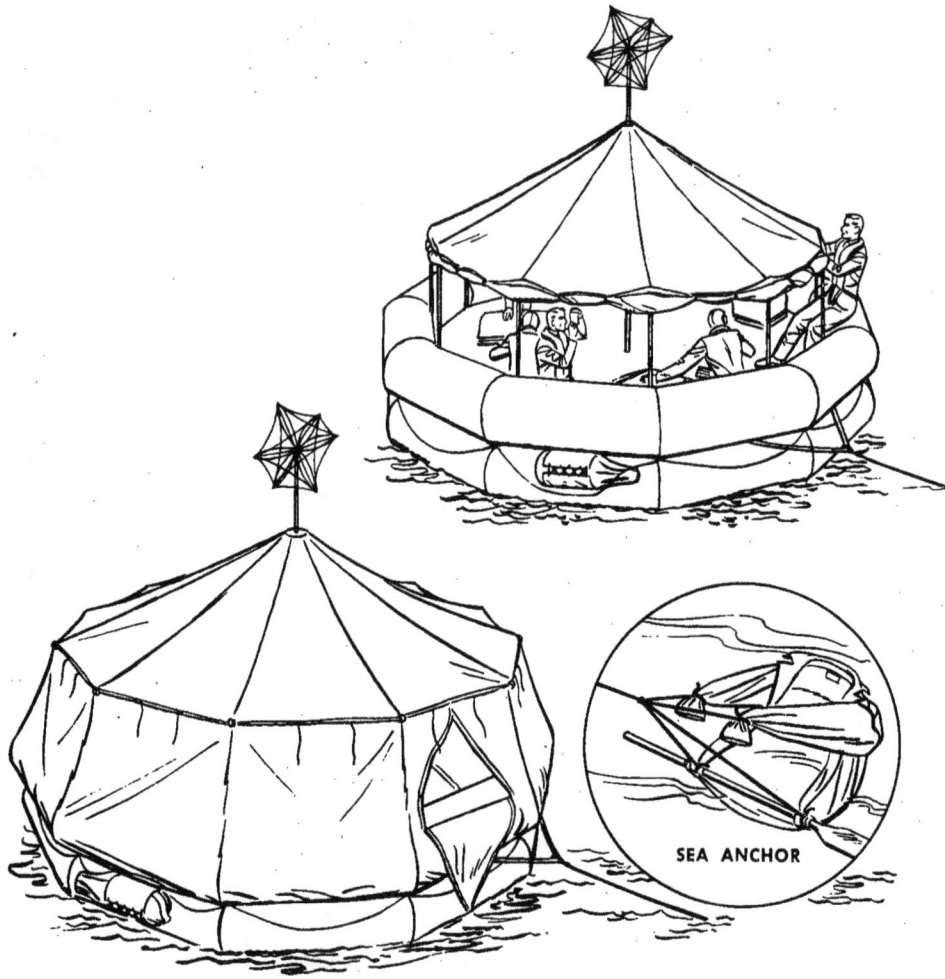

SEA ANCHOR

20-MAN RAFT

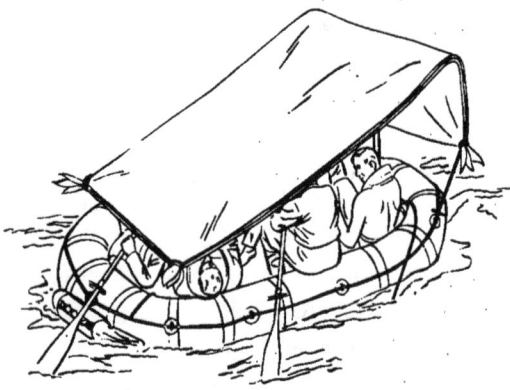

6-MAN LIFE RAFT
WITH SUN SHIELD

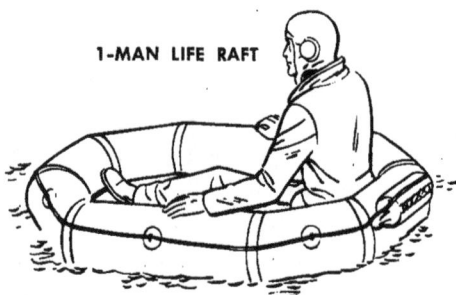

1-MAN LIFE RAFT

Types of rafts

shield at once. In a 20-man raft, keep the canopy erected at all times. Keep your raft as dry as possible. Keep it properly balanced. All men should stay seated, the heaviest men in the center.

Leaks are most likely to occur at valves, seams, and underwater surfaces. They can be repaired with the repair plugs provided. Most multiplace rafts have buoyancy tubes separated into two chambers. If one chamber is damaged, keep the other fully inflated.

Measures to Avoid Detection

If you are down in unfriendly waters, take special security measures to avoid detection. It is generally best not to travel in the daytime. Throw out the sea anchor and wait for nightfall before paddling or hoisting sail. Keep low in the raft; stay covered, with blue side of camouflage cloth up.

Use the radio as briefed.

Don't use signaling devices to attract attention of passing ships or aircraft until they have been identified as friendly or neutral.

If you are detected, destroy log book, radio, navigating equipment, maps, signaling equipment, and firearms. If enemy starts strafing, be prepared to jump overboard and submerge.

SIGNALING

Emergency Radio

Transmit your radio distress signals at frequent intervals or otherwise follow briefing instructions. Send signals as indicated in instructions packaged with transmitter. Send steadily when using hand-energized transmitters. Exercise discretion in using battery-operated transceivers.

If you have a corner reflector or other radar signaling device, set it up and leave it up except during storms. Handle it carefully.

Mirror

Practice signaling with the mirror in the raft kit. As a substitute, use an ordinary pocket mirror or any bright piece of metal. Punch a hole in the center of the metal piece for sighting. On hazy days, aircraft can see the flash of the mirror before survivors can see aircraft, so flash the mirror in the direction of an aircraft when you hear it, even when you cannot see it. When the aircraft is sighted, keep signaling. Some raft paddles and oars are coated with material which will reflect the beam of a searchlight at night.

Pyrotechnics

Use smoke signals in the daytime, and fire signals at night. Keep signal flares dry; don't waste them. *Be very careful of fire hazard when using flares.* Keep the flares dry at all times.

Sea Marker

Use sea marker during daytime *only in friendly areas.* Except in very rough sea, these spots of dye remain conspicuous for about 3 hours. Conserve by rewrapping when not in use. Use the marker only when aircraft is heard or sighted.

Lights

At night, use flashlights, recognition light, or blinker signal light of the radio. Any light can be seen from the air over water for several miles.

Whistle

At night or in fog, use the whistle from the emergency kit to attract surface vessels or people on shore, or to locate another raft if it becomes separated.

FIRST AID

Read the first aid and health sections on pages 9 and 24 of this manual. In addition, you may have to treat the following conditions.

Seasickness

Do not eat or drink if you are seasick. If you are not vomiting but feel nauseated, lie down. If you experience some relief, try the seasickness remedy and remain supine. The pills may make you drowsy, so secure all equipment before dozing.

Salt Water Sores

Do not open or squeeze salt water sores; use antiseptic. Keep sores dry.

Immersion Foot

Immersion foot is caused by exposure to cold, immersion in water, cramped quarters, and restricted circulation. You will notice tingling, numbness, redness, and swelling. Blotchy red areas and blisters eventually appear. Keep your feet warm and dry; maintain circulation by exercising toes and feet; loosen footgear. Elevate feet and legs for 30-minute periods several times a day. If you are suffering from immersion foot, stay off your feet after landing. If you cannot dry your socks, at least wring them out occasionally.

Sore Eyes

Glare from sky and water may cause your eyes to become bloodshot, inflamed, and painful. Wear regular sunglasses or improvise an eye cover from cloth or bandage. If your eyes hurt, bandage them lightly.

Constipation

Lack of bowel movement is normal on rafts. Don't be disturbed about it. *Don't* take laxatives even if available. Exercise as much as possible.

Difficulty in Urinating

If there is a shortage of drinking water, or if you are sweating a lot, you may have some difficulty in urinating. The dark color of urine and difficulty in passing it are normal — don't get worried.

Mental Disturbances

Fear is normal among men in dangerous situations. Admit your feeling to yourself but carry on in spite of it. Remember that other men have had the same fear, yet have come through similar experiences. Fatigue and exhaustion resulting from severe hardships often lead to mental disturbances, which may take the form of extreme nervousness, excessive and violent activity, or depression. The best prevention is to get as much sleep and rest as possible. When not resting, keep busy with routine raft duties. Seeing mirages is not a sign of mental unbalance. Cheerfulness is a tonic and will spread to others.

Cracked and Parched Lips and Skin

Use chapstick or any oil or salve on cracked and parched lips and skin.

Frostbite

Frostbite may occur when wet skin is exposed to wind during winter in northern oceans. Your face, ears, hands, and feet are most susceptible. Try to keep them dry and covered. If your shoes are tight, take them off and wrap your feet in dry cloth. (See page 144 for treatment.)

Sunburn

Keep your head and skin covered to avoid sunburn. Stay in the shade. Use cream or chapstick from kit. Remember that reflection from water causes sunburn, too. Protect your neck with an improvised shield.

WATER

Water is your most important need. With it alone you can live for 10 days or longer, depending on your will to live.

Short Water Rations

When your water supply is limited and cannot be replaced by chemical or mechanical means but only by chance rain, use it efficiently. Keep your body well shaded from overhead sun and from reflection off the sea surface. Allow ventilation of air. Dampen your clothes with sea water during the hottest part of the day. Do not exert yourself. Relax and sleep when possible. Fix your daily water ration after considering the amount of water you have, the output of sun stills and desalting kit, the number and physical condition of your party.

If you have no water, don't eat. If your water ration is 2 quarts or more a day, you may eat any part of your ration or any additional food that you may catch, such as birds, fish, shrimp, crabs, etc. The motion of a raft and the excitement may cause nausea; and if you eat when nauseated, you may lose your food immediately. So rest and relax as much as you can, and take only water.

To cut down loss of water from sweating, soak your clothes in the sea and wring them out before putting them on again. Don't overdo this during hot days when no canopy or sun shield is available. Be careful not to get the bottom of the raft wet.

Watch the clouds and be ready for any chance shower; keep paulin handy for catching water. If your paulin is encrusted with dried salt, wash it in sea water. Normally, a small amount of sea water mixed with rain will hardly be noticeable and will not give you any bad physiological reaction. In rough seas you cannot get uncontaminated fresh water.

At night, secure your paulin as for a sunshade and turn up its edges to collect dew. Rain water does not always satisfy; it lacks minerals and is tasteless. Mix it with a bit of sea water, or dissolve hard candy or coffee or tea solubles in it to give it taste. When it rains, drink as much as you can hold.

Sun Stills

When sun stills are available, read instructions and set them up immediately. Use as many stills as possible, depending on the number of men in your raft and the amount of sunlight available. Secure sun still to raft with stout line.

De-Salting Kits

When de-salting kits are available in addition to sun stills, use them only for immediate water needs or during long periods of overcast when sun stills cannot be used. In any event, retain de-salting kits and emergency water stores for such periods when you cannot use sun stills or catch rain water.

Don't drink urine or sea water.

In Arctic waters, use old sea ice for water. This ice is bluish, has rounded corners, and splinters easily. It is nearly free from salt. New ice is gray, milky, hard, and salty. Water from icebergs is fresh, but icebergs are dangerous to approach and should be used as a source of water only in emergencies.

See discussion of water on page 25.

FISH AND FISHING

Most fish in the open sea are edible. Jellyfishes are messy and can sting. If your fishing kit is lost, improvise hooks from insignia pins, pencil clips, shoe nails, pocketknives, fish spines, bird bones, and pieces of wood. Make hooks small and use as light a line as possible. You can get cord from shoelaces, parachute shroud lines, or thread from clothes. First catch small fish that usually will gather underneath the shadow of your raft or that you may shake out of clumps of seaweed. Use them for bait, with heavier hooks and lines. Fish will generally be attracted to the shadow of your raft. Use dip net to scoop up fish, crabs, and shrimp. If the net is lost, make one from mosquito headnet, parachute cloth, or clothing fastened to a section of oar. In using either the dip net or an improvised net, hold it under water and scoop upward. A fish snare can also be used, as shown in the illustration.

Shine flashlight on water at night or use a mirror to reflect moonlight onto the water. The light will attract fish. At night some fish, especially flying fish, may land in your raft. Do not be alarmed by any fish that sails in; use it for food. Rig your rubber sheeting in such a way that it will reflect moonlight. Natives use this trick to get leaping or flying fish.

When fishing, don't make lines fast to the raft or person. Fish or bright objects dangling in water alongside of raft may attract large dangerous fish. Be careful. Large fish should be handled without capsizing or damaging raft. Land fish with net or harpoon. Avoid spiny fish and those with bony, irregular teeth. Kill fish with a blow on the head before you bring them into the raft. Don't molest large fish or sharks.

Clean and cut all fish immediately and eat them before they spoil. To preserve any fish left over, cut them into thin strips and dry thoroughly in the sun. Don't eat eggs or liver. Don't eat fish with unpleasant odor, pale and slimy gills, sunken eyes, flabby skin, or flesh that stays dented when pressed. (See Poisonous Fish, p. 239.) All guts of fish and birds can be used for bait. Sea turtles are good for bait, too. Kill them by shooting them in the head; or snag them with a hook and then kill with blows on the head. Avoid their beaks and claws. The liver and fat are edible. The muscle is tough but can be chewed for a while, then thrown away.

BIRDS

All birds are potential food. They can be caught on baited hooks, triangular pieces of shiny metal with a noose, or a baited toggle of metal or wood. (See illustration of toggle on page 350.) Many birds will be attracted to the raft as a possible perching place. Sit still in the raft, and they may settle on the raft or even on your head or shoulder. Grab them as soon as they have folded their wings. But don't grab until you are sure you can reach the bird.

SHARKS

Avoid attracting or annoying sharks. Most of them are scavengers, continuously on the move for food. If they don't get it from you, they will lose interest and swim on. Your chances of being attacked by sharks are very small. Even in warm oceans where attacks are possible, you can reduce the risk by knowing what to do and how to do it. For detailed discussion on sharks, see page 242.

SURVIVAL SWIMMING

When entering the water from the aircraft or in your parachute, discharge only one of your CO_2 cartridges. One cartridge will keep you afloat, but two will hamper your activity.

A man who knows how to relax in the water is in very little danger of drowning, especially in salt water where the body is of lower density than the water. Trapping air in your clothes will help to buoy you up in the water and give you a rest. If you are in the water for long periods, you will have to rest from treading water. If you are an experienced swimmer and able to float on your back, do so if the sea conditions permit. Always float on your back if possible. If you can't float on your back or if the sea is too rough, practice the following technique:

Resting erect in the water, inhale. Put your head face down in the water and stroke with your arms. Then rest in this face-down position until you feel the need to breathe again. Raise your head, exhale, support yourself by kicking arms and legs, inhale, and then repeat the cycle.

SEAMANSHIP

Put out your sea anchor immediately. Do not attempt to navigate your raft unless within sight of shore or in unfriendly waters. Remember that the majority of successful rescues are made within 7 days of ditching. You can't go very far on a raft in 7 days.

Watches and Lookouts

Assign watches; they should not exceed 2 hours. All men should serve except those who are badly injured or completely exhausted. Keep at least one lookout posted at all times. He should watch for signs of land, passing vessels or aircraft, wreckage, seaweed, schools of fish, birds, and signs of chafing or leaking of raft. He should be tied to the raft with at least a 10-foot line.

Traveling

Whether you like it or not, your raft will move. The course it will take is the result of both wind and ocean current, modified by the use of oars or paddles, tiller, sea anchor, and sails.

USING OCEAN CURRENTS. When ocean currents are moving toward your destination, but the winds are unfavorable, put out a sea anchor. Huddle low in the raft to offer as little wind resistance as possible. In the open ocean, currents seldom move more than 6 to 8 miles a day.

USING THE WIND. Rafts are not equipped with keels, so they can't be sailed into the wind, even if you are an experienced sailor. However, anyone can sail a raft downwind, and multiplace (except 20-man) rafts can be successfully sailed 10° off from the direction of the wind. Don't try to sail your raft unless you know that land is near.

When the wind is blowing directly toward your destination, inflate the raft fully, sit high, take in the sea anchor, rig a sail, and use an oar as a rudder, as shown in the illustration.

In a multiplace (except 20-man) raft, rig a square sail in the bow, using oars with their extensions as mast and crossbar. If the regular sail is not available, substitute the waterproof tarpaulin or one or two thicknesses of parachute cloth. If the raft has no regular mast socket and step, erect the mast by tying it securely to the front cross seat; provide braces. Whether or not a socket is provided, pad the bottom of the mast to prevent it from chafing or punching a hole through the floor. The heel part of a shoe with the toe wedged under the seat makes a good improvised mast step.

Don't secure the corners of the *lower edge* of the sail. Hold the lines attached to the corners in your hands so that a sudden storm or gust of wind will not rip the sail, break the mast, or capsize the raft.

Raftsmanship

Take every precaution to prevent your raft from turning over. In rough weather, keep the sea anchor out from the bow. Sit low in the raft, with the passengers' weight distributed to hold the weather side down. Don't sit on the sides or stand up. Never make sudden movements without warning the other men. Don't tie a fishline to yourself or the raft; a large fish may capsize the raft.

In rough seas tie stern of first raft to bow of second and rig sea anchor to stern of second raft. Use approximately a 25-foot line between rafts; adjust the length of the line to suit the sea. Keep the sea anchor line long. Adjust its length so that when the raft is at the crest of a wave, the sea anchor will stay in a trough. In very rough weather, keep a spare sea anchor rigged and ready for instant use in case the one that is out breaks loose.

Raft with sail rigged

Correct method for righting raft

Lacking a keel and influenced by the currents and wind, the raft will sail to one side of an island. If the island is friendly, stow the sail and paddle in. If the island is in unfriendly hands, it is best to avoid it, at least until darkness.

When the sea anchor is not in use, tie it to the raft and stow it so that it will hold immediately if the raft capsizes.

To right multiplace (except 20-man) rafts, toss the righting rope over the bottom, move around to the other side, place one foot on flotation tube, and pull on the righting rope. This is shown in the illustration. If you have no righting rope or if you can't improvise one from the sea anchor line, a belt, or a shirt, slide up on the bottom, reach across, grab the lifeline on the far side, and then slide back into

the water, pulling the raft back and over. Most rafts are equipped with righting handles on the bottom. Twenty-man rafts are identical on both sides and therefore require no righting.

If several men are in the water, one man should hold down the far side of the multiplace (4-6 man) raft while the rest climb in singly from the other side. Grasp the seat to haul yourself in, or use the boarding ladder provided on the newest types of raft. Without help, the best place to board the raft is over the end. If the wind is blowing, board the raft with the wind at your back. The 20-man raft is provided with a deflated boarding station, which is hand-inflated after occupants are aboard.

To board the 1-man raft, climb in from the narrow end; slide up as nearly horizontal as possible.

Making a Landfall

The lookout should watch carefully for signs of land.

A fixed cumulus cloud in a clear sky or in a sky where all other clouds are moving often hovers over or slightly downwind from an island.

In the Tropics, a greenish tint in the sky is often caused by the reflection of sunlight from the shallow lagoons or shelves of coral reefs.

In the Arctic, ice fields or snow-covered land are often indicated by light-colored reflections on clouds, quite different from the darkish gray caused by open water.

Deep water is dark green or dark blue. Lighter color indicates shallow water, which may mean land is near.

In fog, mist, rain, or at night when drifting past a nearby shore, you may sometimes detect land by characteristic odors and sounds. The musty odor of mangrove swamps and mud flats, and the smell of burning wood will carry a long way. The roar of surf is heard long before the surf is seen. Continued cries of sea birds from one direction indicate their roosting place on nearby land.

Usually more birds are found near land than over the open sea. The direction from which flocks fly at dawn and to which they fly at dusk may indicate the direction of land. During the day, birds are searching for food and the direction of flight has no significance.

In the Tropics, mirages may be seen, especially during the middle of the day. Be careful not to mistake a mirage for nearby land. A mirage will disappear or change its appearance and elevation if viewed from slightly different heights.

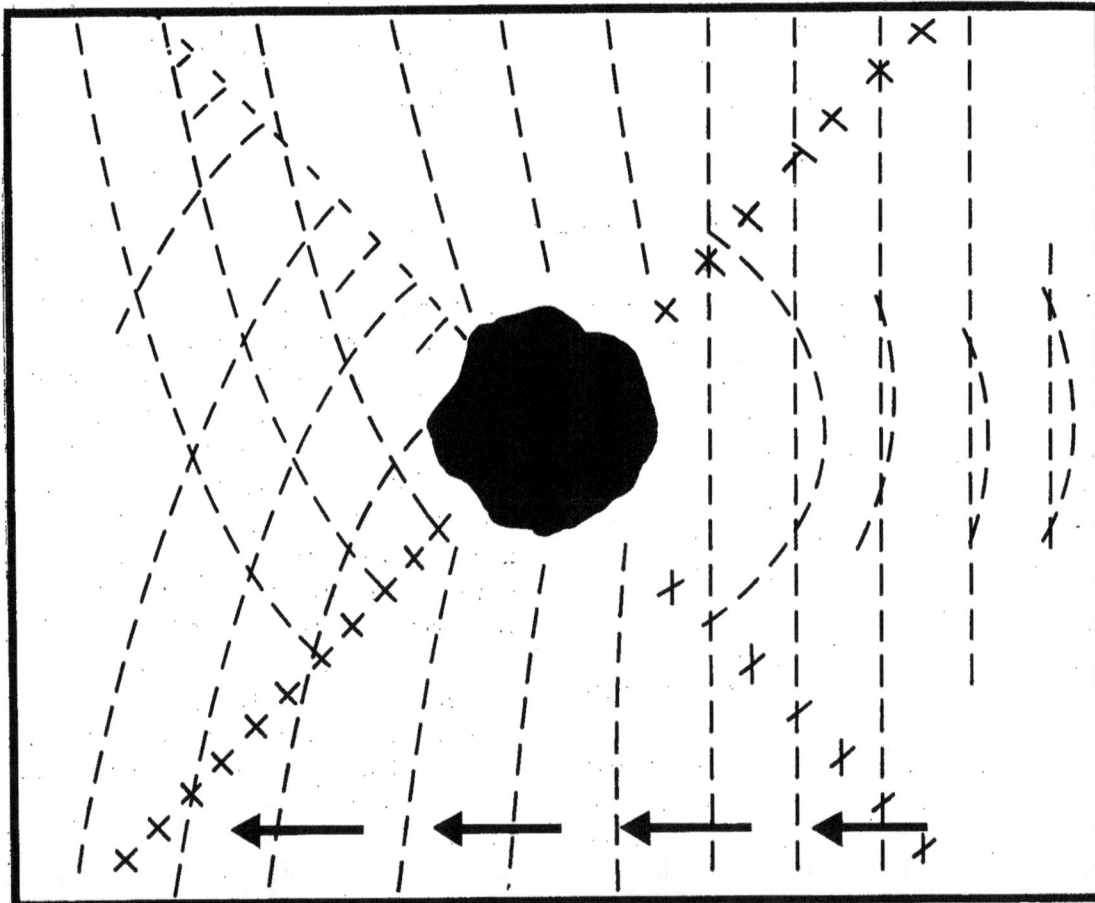

Diagram of wave patterns about an island

Wave Forms

You may be able to detect land by the pattern of the waves, which are refracted as they approach land. The drawing on p. 366 shows the form the waves assume. As you note this pattern, turn parallel to the slightly turbulent area marked "X" on the illustration and follow its direction. This should bring you to land.

Getting Ashore

SWIMMING ASHORE. Wear your shoes and at least one thickness of clothing if you plan to swim ashore. In unknown waters use the side or breast stroke to conserve strength.

If surf is moderate, ride in on the back of a small wave by swimming forward with it. Shallow dive to end your ride just before the wave breaks.

In a high surf, swim shoreward in the trough between waves. When the seaward wave approaches, face it and submerge. After it passes, work shoreward in the next trough.

If you are caught in the undertow of a large wave, push off the bottom or swim to the surface and proceed shoreward as above.

If you must land on a rocky shore, look for a place where the waves rush up onto the rocks. Avoid places where the waves explode with a high white spray. Swim slowly in making your approach — you will need your strength to hold on to the rocks.

After selecting your landing point, advance behind a large wave into the breakers. Face shoreward and take a sitting position with your feet in front, 2 or 3 feet lower than your head, so that your feet will absorb shocks when you land or strike submerged boulders or reefs.

If you don't reach shore behind the wave you have picked, swim with hands only. As the next wave approaches, take sitting position with feet forward. Repeat procedure until you land.

Water is quieter in the lee of a heavy growth of seaweed. Take advantage of such growth. Don't swim through the seaweed; crawl over the top by grasping the vegetation with overhand movements.

Cross a rocky reef just as you would land on a rocky shore. Keep your feet close together and your knees slightly bent in a relaxed sitting posture to cushion blows against coral.

RAFTING ASHORE. The 1-man raft can be used in most cases with no danger. Going ashore in a strong surf is dangerous. Take your time. Select your landing point carefully. Try not to land when the sun is low and straight in front of you. Try to land on the lee side of an island or of a point of land. Keep your eyes open for gaps in the surf line, and head for them. Avoid coral reefs and rocky cliffs. Coral reefs don't occur near the mouths of fresh water streams. Avoid rip currents or strong tidal currents which may carry you far out to sea. Either signal shore for help or sail around and look for a sloping beach where the surf is gentle.

If you have to go through surf to reach shore, take down the raft mast. Keep your clothes and shoes on to avoid severe cuts. Adjust and inflate your life vest. Trail the sea anchor over the stern with as much line as you have. Use the oars or paddles and constantly adjust the sea anchor to keep a strain on the anchor line. It will keep your raft pointed toward shore and prevent the sea from throwing the stern around and capsizing you. Use the oars or paddles to help ride in on the seaward side of a large wave.

Surf may be irregular and velocity may vary, so your procedure must be modified as conditions demand. A good method of getting through surf is to have half the men sit on one side of the raft, half on the other, facing each other. When a heavy sea bears down, half should row (pull) toward the sea until the crest passes; then the other half should row (pull) toward the shore until the next sea comes along.

Against strong wind and heavy surf, the raft must have all possible speed to pass rapidly through the oncoming crest in order to avoid being turned broadside or thrown end over end. If possible, avoid meeting a large wave at the moment it breaks.

In medium surf with no wind or offshore wind, keep raft from passing over a wave so rapidly that it drops suddenly after topping the crest.

If the raft turns over in the surf, try to grab hold.

As the raft nears the beach, ride in on the crest of a large wave. Paddle or row hard and ride in onto the beach as far as you can. Don't jump out of the raft until it has grounded. Then get out quickly and beach it.

If you have a choice, don't land at night.

If you have reason to believe that the shore is inhabited, lay away from the beach, signal, and wait for the inhabitants to come out and bring you in.

LANDING ON SEA ICE. Land only on large, stable floes. Avoid icebergs, which may capsize, and small floes, or those obviously disintegrating. Use oars and hands to keep raft from rubbing on ice edge. Take raft out of the water and store well back from ice edge. Keep raft inflated and ready for use. Any flow may break up.

See discussion of travel on page 352.

INDEX

www.ingramcontent.com/pod-product-compliance
Lightning Source LLC
Chambersburg PA
CBHW050618110426
42813CB00010B/2604